CORPORATE
FINANCE

T0342026

Pearson

At Pearson, we have a simple mission: to help people make more of their lives through learning.

We combine innovative learning technology with trusted content and educational expertise to provide engaging and effective learning experiences that serve people wherever and whenever they are learning.

From classroom to boardroom, our curriculum materials, digital learning tools and testing programmes help to educate millions of people worldwide – more than any other private enterprise.

Every day our work helps learning flourish, and wherever learning flourishes, so do people.

To learn more, please visit us at **www.pearson.com/uk**

CORPORATE
FINANCE

PRINCIPLES AND PRACTICE

Eighth edition

Denzil Watson and
Antony Head

Sheffield Hallam University

PEARSON

Harlow, England • London • New York • Boston • San Francisco • Toronto • Sydney • Dubai • Singapore • Hong Kong
Tokyo • Seoul • Taipei • New Delhi • Cape Town • São Paulo • Mexico City • Madrid • Amsterdam • Munich • Paris • Milan

PEARSON EDUCATION LIMITED
KAO Two
KAO Park
Harlow CM17 9SR
United Kingdom
Tel: +44 (0)1279 623623

First published under the Financial Times Pitman Publishing Imprint 1998 (print)
Second edition published under the Financial Times Prentice Hall Imprint 2001 (print)
Third edition published 2004 (print)
Fourth edition published 2007 (print)
Fifth edition published 2010 (print)
Sixth edition published 2013 (print and electronic)
Seventh edition published 2016 (print and electronic)
Eighth edition published 2019 (print and electronic)

© Pearson Education Limited 2001, 2010 (print)
© Pearson Education Limited 2013, 2016, 2019 (print and electronic)

The rights of Denzil Watson and Antony Head to be identified as authors of this work have been asserted by them in accordance with the Copyright, Designs and Patents Act 1988.

The print publication is protected by copyright. Prior to any prohibited reproduction, storage in a retrieval system, distribution or transmission in any form or by any means, electronic, mechanical, recording or otherwise, permission should be obtained from the publisher or, where applicable, a licence permitting restricted copying in the United Kingdom should be obtained from the Copyright Licensing Agency Ltd, Barnard's Inn, 86 Fetter Lane, London EC4A 1EN.

The ePublication is protected by copyright and must not be copied, reproduced, transferred, distributed, leased, licensed or publicly performed or used in any way except as specifically permitted in writing by the publishers, as allowed under the terms and conditions under which it was purchased, or as strictly permitted by applicable copyright law. Any unauthorised distribution or use of this text may be a direct infringement of the authors' and the publisher's rights and those responsible may be liable in law accordingly.

All trademarks used herein are the property of their respective owners. The use of any trademark in this text does not vest in the author or publisher any trademark ownership rights in such trademarks, nor does the use of such trademarks imply any affiliation with or endorsement of this book by such owners.

Contains public sector information licensed under the Open Government Licence (OGL) v3.0. http://www.nationalarchives.gov.uk/doc/open-government-licence/version/3/.

Contains Parliamentary information licensed under the Open Parliament Licence (OPL) v3.0. http://www.parliament.uk/site-information/copyright/open-parliament-licence/.

Pearson Education is not responsible for the content of third-party internet sites.

The Financial Times. With a worldwide network of highly respected journalists, *The Financial Times* provides global business news, insightful opinion and expert analysis of business, finance and politics. With over 500 journalists reporting from 50 countries worldwide, our in-depth coverage of international news is objectively reported and analysed from an independent, global perspective. To find out more, visit www.ft.com/pearsonoffer.

ISBN: 978-1-292-24431-0 (print)
      978-1-292-24433-4 (PDF)
      978-1-292-24434-1 (ePub)

British Library Cataloguing-in-Publication Data
A catalogue record for the print edition is available from the British Library

Library of Congress Cataloging-in-Publication Data
Names: Watson, Denzil, author. | Head, Antony, 1953- author.
Title: Corporate finance : principles and practice / Denzil Watson and Antony
   Head, Sheffield Hallam University.
Description: Eighth edition. | Harlow, England ; New York : Pearson, 2019.
Identifiers: LCCN 2018060711| ISBN 9781292244310 (print) | ISBN 9781292244334
   (pdf) | ISBN 9781292244341 (epub)
Subjects: LCSH: Corporations—Finance.
Classification: LCC HG4026 .W373 2019 | DDC 658.15—dc23
LC record available at https://lccn.loc.gov/2018060711

10 9 8 7 6 5 4 3 2 1
23 22 21 20 19

Front cover image © Denzil Watson

Print edition typeset in 9.25/13.5pt Stone Humanist ITC Pro by Pearson CSC
Printed in Slovakia by Neografia

NOTE THAT ANY PAGE CROSS REFERENCES REFER TO THE PRINT EDITION

ABOUT THE AUTHORS

Denzil Watson is a Principal Lecturer in Finance in the Sheffield Business School at Sheffield Hallam University (*http://www.shu.ac.uk*). Denzil has been teaching finance since he joined Hallam in 1991, having completed his BA(Hons) in Economics and MA(Hons) in Money, Banking and Finance at Sheffield University in the 1980s. He has taught financial management, corporate finance, risk management, microeconomics and financial markets for 28 years over a range of undergraduate, postgraduate and distance learning modules.

Photo: Andy Brown

Finance is by no means Denzil's only passion. He is a committed traveller, having now visited over 50 countries including ones as diverse as Peru, Syria, Uzbekistan, Vietnam, Laos and travelled along the Chinese Silk Road. Travel photography is also high up on his list as evidenced by the covers of this book and its previous editions. He is a keen Urbexer and, along with his co-author, a long-suffering Derby County fan.

His other great love is music. He can be found fronting Sheffield post-New Wave indie group RepoMen (http://repomen.bandcamp.com), alt-rockers Batman's Treaty or listening to the likes of Joy Division, The Stranglers, The Perfect Disaster, Spear of Destiny, Dubioza Kolektiv, That Petrol Emotion, Sleaford Mods, British Sea Power, Dead Kennedys, The Clash and Cabbage. His inspirations include his mother Doreen, his sadly departed father Hugh, Kevin Hector, Ian Curtis, Michael Palin, Joe Strummer and John Peel. Denzil lives with his wife Dora and their two children, Leonardo and Angelina.

Antony Head is an Associate Lecturer in the Sheffield Business School at Sheffield Hallam University, having formerly been a Principal Lecturer in Financial Management there and Leader of the Financial Accounting and Management Accounting Subject Group. Tony joined Hallam after various jobs, which included spells as a chemical engineer and health-food shop proprietor. His higher education began in Sheffield, where he took an honours degree in Chemical Engineering and Fuel Technology at Sheffield University in the early 1970s.

Since then Tony has completed an MBA and a PGCFHE and can be found teaching financial management, corporate finance and risk management as required on undergraduate, postgraduate and professional modules at Sheffield Hallam University.

Photo: Denzil Watson

Tony, like Denzil, has many interests outside of academia. As well as being a dedicated Derby County fan he is studying for a classics degree with the Open University. His musical tastes are wide and varied, including Bob Dylan, Miles Davis, King Crimson, David Sylvian, Gustav Mahler and Philip Glass. Tony lives with his wife Sandra and has a daughter Rosemary, a son Aidan, a step-daughter Louise, step-sons Michael and Robert, and six grandchildren: Joshua, Isaac, Elizabeth, Amelia, Magnus and Arlo, with a seventh grandchild on the way.

CONTENTS

6 An overview of investment appraisal methods   168

7 Investment appraisal: applications and risk   199

Lecturer Resources

For password-protected online resources tailored to support the use of this textbook in teaching, please visit **www.pearsoned.co.uk/watsonhead**

ON THE WEBSITE

PREFACE

Introduction

Corporate finance is concerned with the financing and investment decisions made by the management of companies in pursuit of corporate goals. As a subject, corporate finance has a theoretical base which has evolved over many years and which continues to evolve as we write. It has a practical side too, concerned with the study of how companies actually make financing and investment decisions, and theory and practice can sometimes appear to be at odds with each other.

The fundamental problem facing financial managers is how to secure the greatest possible return in exchange for accepting the smallest amount of risk. This necessarily requires that financial managers have available to them (and are able to use) a range of appropriate tools and techniques. These will help them to value the decision options open to them and to assess the risk of those options. The value of an option depends on the extent to which it contributes towards the achievement of corporate goals. In corporate finance, the fundamental goal is usually taken to be to increase the wealth of shareholders.

The aim of this book

The aim of this book is to provide an introduction to the core concepts and key topic areas of corporate finance in an approachable, 'user-friendly' style. Many texts on corporate finance adopt a theory-based or mathematical approach that is not appropriate for those coming to the subject for the first time. This book covers the core concepts and key topic areas without burdening the reader with what we see as unnecessary detail or too heavy a dose of theory.

Flexible course design

Many undergraduate courses are now delivered on a modular or unit basis over one teaching semester of 12 weeks' duration. In order to meet the constraints imposed by such courses, this book has been designed to support self-study and directed learning. There is a choice of integrated topics for the end of the course.

Each chapter offers:

■ a comprehensive list of key points to check understanding and aid revision;

■ self-test questions, with answers at the end of the book, to check comprehension of concepts and computational techniques;

■ questions for review, with answers available in the accompanying downloadable Instructor's Manual, to aid in deepening understanding of particular topic areas;

- questions for discussion, with answers available in the accompanying downloadable Instructor's Manual;
- comprehensive references to guide the reader to key texts and articles;
- suggestions for further reading to guide readers who wish to study further.

A comprehensive glossary is included at the end of the text to assist the reader in grasping any unfamiliar terms that may be encountered in the study of corporate finance.

New for the eighth edition

The vignettes have been reviewed and updated to reflect the changing economic environment in which corporate finance exists. Relevant changes in regulations and taxation, such as the UK tax treatment of dividends, have been considered and incorporated where appropriate.

Target readership

This book has been written primarily for students taking a course in corporate finance in their second or final year of undergraduate study on accounting, business studies and finance-related degree programmes. It will also be suitable for students on professional and postgraduate business and finance courses where corporate finance or financial management are taught at introductory level.

ACKNOWLEDGEMENTS

Authors' acknowledgements

We are as always grateful to our reviewers for helpful comments and suggestions. We are also grateful to the undergraduate and postgraduate students of Sheffield Business School at Sheffield Hallam University who have taken our courses, and who continue to help us in developing our approach to the teaching and learning of the subject. We are particularly grateful to Carole Drummond and Richard Townrow of Pearson Education for their support and encouragement. We also extend our gratitude to our many colleagues at Sheffield Hallam University.

Publisher's acknowledgements

Photo credits:

(key: b-bottom; c-centre; l-left; r-right; t-top)
v(t) Andy Brown v(b) Denzil Watson
All chapter opener images © **Denzil Watson**

Text credits:

8 The Financial Times Limited: Foroohar, R. (2018) 'The backlash against shareholder value', *Financial Times*, 4 March © The Financial Times Ltd. **18 Crown copyright:** National Statistics. © Crown copyright 2017. Reproduced by permission of the Office for National Statistics, licensed under the Open Government Licence v.3.0. **18 The Financial Reporting Council Limited:** UK Financial Reporting Council **21 Organisation for Economic Co-operation and Development:** Risk Management & Corporate Governance By Richard Anderson & Associates **18 The Financial Times Limited:** 'Investors falling short as active owners', *Financial Times*, 11/09/2011 (Ruth Sullivan) **23 The Financial Times Limited:** Marriage, M. (2017) 'UK corporate governance code changes to hit dozens of chairmen', *Financial Times*, 11 December. © The Financial Times Limited 2018. All rights reserved. **24 The Financial Times Limited:** Belger, T. (2018) 'UK to force companies to justify pay gap between CEOs and staff', *Financial Times*, 10 June. © The Financial Times Limited 2018. All rights reserved. **27 The Financial Times Limited:** Owen, G. (2011) 'A very British split at the top', *Financial Times*, 14 March. © The Financial Times Limited 2011. All Rights Reserved. **29 Spencer Stuart:** Spencer Stuart 2010 Board Index. **40 The Financial Times Limited:** Bounds, A. (2018) 'Aim investors should hold their nerve despite volatility', *Financial Times*, 18 February. © The Financial Times Limited 2018. All Rights Reserved. **41 Pearson Education:** Megginson, W.L. (1997) *Corporate Finance Theory*, Reading, MA: Addison-Wesley. **45 The Financial Times Limited:** Authers, J. (2018) 'Indices don't just measure markets — they drive performance', *Financial Times*, 23 June. © The Financial Times Limited 2018. All Rights Reserved. **53 The Financial Times Limited:** Alexandra Scaggs (2018) 'Financial reporting relativism is running deeper and deeper', *Financial Times* 4 May. © The Financial Times Limited 2018. All Rights Reserved. **65 Penguin Random House:** Smith, T. (1996) *Accounting for Growth: Stripping the Camouflage from Company Accounts*, 2nd edn, London: Century Business. **81 The Financial Times Limited:** Binham, C. (2018) 'Banks "reluctant to lend" to small businesses, MPs told', *Financial Times*, 30 March. © The Financial Times Limited 2018. All Rights Reserved. **90 The Financial Times Limited:** Hodgson, C. and Milne, R. (2018) 'H&M profits dive in "tough" first half of the year', *Financial Times*, 28 June. © The Financial Times Limited 2018. All Rights Reserved. **96 The Financial Times Limited:** Gordon, S. (2018) 'Large UK companies accused of "supply chain bullying"', *Financial Times*, 29 May. © The Financial Times Limited 2018. All Rights Reserved. **97 The Financial Times Limited:** Ralph, O. (2018) 'Longer customer payment terms spark corporate fears', *Financial Times*, 3 May. © The Financial Times Limited 2018. All Rights Reserved. **110 The Financial Times Limited:** Ram, A. and Waters, R. (2018) 'European tech IPOs begin to rival US successes', *Financial Times*, 14 June. © The Financial Times Limited 2018. All Rights Reserved. **119 The Financial Times Limited:** Martin, K., Rovnick, N. and Eley, J. (2018) 'Mothercare to close more stores as it seeks to raise £32.5m', *Financial Times*, 9 July. © The Financial Times Limited 2018. All Rights Reserved **121 The Financial Times Limited:** Lewis, L. and Inagaki, K. (2018) 'Nintendo faces calls to split stock to aid governance', *Financial Times*, 19 February. © The Financial Times Limited 2018. All Rights Reserved. **124 The Financial Times Limited:** Hume, N. (2018) 'Glencore launches $1bn share buyback', *Financial Times*, 5 July. © The Financial Times Limited 2018. All Rights Reserved **127 The Financial Times Limited:** Ralph, O. and Martin, K. (2018) 'Aviva drops plan to cancel preference shares', *Financial Times*, 23 March. © The Financial Times Limited 2018. All Rights Reserved. **138 The Financial Times Limited:** Daneshkhu, S. and Espinoza, J. (2018) 'House of Fraser on hunt for financing', *Financial Times*, 25 March. © The Financial Times Limited 2018. All Rights Reserved **139 The Financial Times Limited:** Atkins, R. (2015) 'Petrobras century bond makes more sense than first appears', *Financial Times*, 4 June. © The Financial Times Limited 2015. All Rights Reserved **141 The Financial Times Limited:** Scaggs, A. (2018) 'AT&T downgraded after Time Warner deal closes', *Financial Times*, 15 June. © The Financial Times Limited 2018. All Rights Reserved. **144 The Financial Times Limited:** Smith, R. (2018) 'Barclays and Pimco to securitise £5.3bn of UK mortgages', *Financial Times*, 27 April. © The Financial Times Limited 2018. All Rights Reserved **148 The Financial Times Limited:** Scaggs, A. (2018) 'Convertible bonds surge highlights late stage of credit cycle', *Financial Times*, 8 June. © The Financial Times Limited 2018. All Rights Reserved. **186 The Financial Times Limited:** Pozen, R. and Hamacher, T. (2012) 'A realistic discount rate for pensions', *Financial Times*, 19 August.© The Financial Times Limited 2018. All Rights Reserved. **188 The Financial Times Limited:** Sun Yu (2018) 'China's war on debt hits heart of private enterprise glut', *Financial Times*, 5 July. © The Financial Times Limited 2018. All Rights Reserved. **201 The Financial Times Limited:** Lex (2015) 'RBS: never mind the price', *Financial Times*', 11 June. © The Financial Times Limited 2015. All Rights Reserved. **203 The Financial Times Limited:**

Pickard, J., Houlder, V. and Marriage, M. (2017) 'Tax experts call for "rethink" of UK corporation tax in Budget', *Financial Times*, 12 July. © The Financial Times Limited 2017. All Rights Reserved. **241 The Financial Times Limited:** Somerset Webb, M. (2014) 'Messy portfolios and the "be busy" syndrome, *Financial Times*, 9 May. © The Financial Times Limited 2014. All Rights Reserved. **251 The Financial Times Limited:** Stevenson, D. (2009) 'Diversification made easy', *Financial Times*, 21 August. © The Financial Times Limited 2009. All Rights Reserved. **252 John Wiley & Sons, Inc:** Sharpe, W. (1964) 'Capital asset prices: a theory of market equilibrium under conditions of risk', *Journal of Finance*, vol. 19, pp. 768–83. **253 John Wiley & Sons, Inc:** Sharpe, W. (1964) 'Capital asset prices: a theory of market equilibrium under conditions of risk', *Journal of Finance*, vol. 19, pp. 768–83. **256 London Business School:** London Business School, Risk Measurement Service, vol. 40, no. 4, April–June 2018. **258 The Financial Times Limited:** Tett, G. (2011) 'Get used to a world without a "risk-free" rate', *Financial Times*, 1 September. © The Financial Times Limited 2011. All Rights Reserved. **261 The Financial Times Limited:** Johnson, S. (2011) 'Developed world returns set to weaken', *Financial Times*, 13 February. © The Financial Times Limited 2011. All Rights Reserved. **291 The Financial Times Limited:** Kavanagh, M. (2014) 'Water operators hit by Ofwat's demands', *Financial Times*, 27 January. © The Financial Times Limited 2014. All Rights Reserved. **293 Emerald Publishing Limited:** Stanley, T. (1990) 'Cost of capital in capital budgeting for foreign direct investment', *Managerial Finance*, vol. 16, no. 2, pp. 13–16. **296 Bureau van Dijk Electronic Publishing:** FAME, published by Bureau van Dijk Electronic Publishing. **297 The Financial Times Limited:** Morarjee, R. (2009) 'Companies address the call for more equity', *Financial Times*, 25 March. © The Financial Times Limited 2009. All Rights Reserved. **305 American Economic Association:** Miller, M. and Modigliani, F. (1958) 'The cost of capital, corporation finance and the theory of investment', *American Economic Review*, vol. 48, pp. 261–96. **327 The Financial Times Limited:** Campbell, P. (2018) 'AA shares tumble nearly 30% after dividend cut', *Financial Times*, 21 February. © The Financial Times Limited 2018. All Rights Reserved. **333 The Financial Times Limited:** Beioley, K. (2018) 'UK dividends look unsustainable, investors warned', *Financial Times*, 13 April. © The Financial Times Limited 2018. All Rights Reserved. **335 J Sainsbury plc:** J Sainsbury plc annual reports. Reproduced by kind permission of Sainsbury's Supermarkets Ltd. **337 The Financial Times Limited:** Cornish, C. (2018) 'UK share buybacks accelerate as market lags behind', *Financial Times*, 16 March 2018. © The Financial Times Limited 2018. All Rights Reserved. **339 The Financial Times Limited:** Smith, A. (2011) 'Companies face difficult calls on returning cash', *Financial Times*, 17 March. © The Financial Times Limited 2011. All rights reserved. **341 The Financial Times Limited:** Warwick-Ching, L. (2013) 'Do shareholder perks add up for investors'? *Financial Times*, 22 November. © The Financial Times Limited 2013. All Rights Reserved. **360 Crown copyright:** Business Monitor and Financial Statistics, National Statistics. © Crown Copyright 2018. **361 The Financial Times Limited:** Fontanella-Khan, J. and Massoudi, A. (2018) 'Global dealmaking reaches $2.5tn as US megadeals lift volumes', *Financial Times*, 28 June. **372 The Financial Times Limited:** Whipp, L. (2015) 'Altria clouds SABMiller deal prospects', *Financial Times*, 30 September. © The Financial Times Limited 2015. All Rights Reserved.

377 The Financial Time Limited: Pfeifer, S. (2018) 'Competition watchdog refers SSE and Npower merger for full probe', *Financial Times*, 8 May. © The Financial Times Limited 2018. All Rights Reserved. **379 The Financial Times Limited:** Massoudi, A. (2015) 'Mylan readies its poison pill defences', *Financial Times*, 22 April. © The Financial Times Limited 2015. All Rights Reserved. **381 The Financial Times Limited:** Gordon, S. (2018) 'Golden parachutes leave unhappy investors behind', *Financial Times*, 8 February. © The Financial Times Limited 2018. All Rights Reserved. **383 Elsevier:** Comment, R. and Jarrell, G. (1995) 'Corporate focus and stock returns', *Journal of Financial Economics*, vol. 37, pp. 67–87. **385 The Financial Times Limited:** Eley, J. (2018) 'Whitbread bows to investor pressure to spin off Costa', *Financial Times*, 25 April. © The Financial Times Limited 2018. All Rights Reserved. **387 The Financial Times Limited:** Arnold, M. and Marriage, M. (2015) 'Management to buy Barclays private equity arm after stalled sale', *Financial Times*, 23 June. **390 The Financial Times Limited:** Espinoza, J. (2017) Private equity funds find strength in numbers', *Financial Times*, 28 November. © The Financial Times Limited 2018. All Rights Reserved. **392 Simon & Schuster:** Grubb, M. and Lamb, R. (2000) *Capitalize on Merger Chaos*, New York: Free Press. **406 Crown copyright:** Bank of England. © Crown Copyright 2017. **409 Crown copyright:** Bank of England. © Crown Copyright 2018. **407 The Financial Times Limited:** Joe Rennison (2018) 'Alternatives to Libor begin to make an impact', *Financial Times*, 01 Oct. © The Financial Times Limited 2018. All Rights Reserved. **409 The Financial Times Limited:** Wildau, G. (2018) 'Trade dispute teeters on verge of currency war as Trump weighs in', *Financial Times*, 23 July. © The Financial Times Limited 2018. All Rights Reserved. **427 The Financial Times Limited:** Stafford, P. (2017) 'Clearing houses see record volume as new rules boost activity', *Financial Times*, 5 April. © The Financial Times Limited 2018. All Rights Reserved **433 The Financial Times Limited:** Mackenzie, M., Bullock, N. and Demos, T. (2012) 'JPMorgan loss exposes derivatives dangers', *Financial Times*, 15 May. © The Financial Times Limited 2012. All Rights Reserved. **437 Warren E. Buffett:** Warren Buffett **438 The Financial Times Limited:** McCrum, D. (2011) 'Hedging exchange rate risk: a tempting option', *Financial Times*, 1 April. © The Financial Times Limited 2011. All Rights Reserved. **440 The Financial Times Limited:** Gray, Alistair (2017) 'MetLife to review hedging strategy after $2.1bn loss', *Financial Times*, 2 February. © The Financial Times Limited 2018. All Rights Reserved. **441 Emerald Publishing Limited:** Goddard, S. (1990) 'Political risk in international capital budgeting', *Managerial Finance*, vol. 16, no. 2, pp. 7–12.

1 THE FINANCE FUNCTION

Learning objectives

After studying this chapter, you should have achieved the following learning objectives:

- an understanding of the time value of money and the relationship between risk and return;
- an appreciation of the three key decision areas of the financial manager;
- an understanding of the reasons why shareholder wealth maximisation is the primary financial objective of a company, rather than other objectives a company may consider;
- an understanding of why the substitute objective of maximising a company's share price is preferred to the objective of shareholder wealth maximisation;
- an understanding of how agency theory can be used to analyse the relationship between shareholders and managers, and of ways in which agency problems may be overcome;
- an appreciation of the role of institutional investors in overcoming agency problems;
- an appreciation of how developments in corporate governance have helped to address the agency problem.

■ ■ ■ INTRODUCTION

Corporate finance is concerned with the efficient and effective management of the finances of an organisation to achieve the objectives of that organisation. This involves planning and controlling the *provision* of resources (where funds are raised from), the *allocation* of resources (where funds are deployed to) and finally the *control* of resources (whether funds are being used effectively or not). The fundamental aim of financial managers is the *optimal allocation* of the scarce resources available to the company – the scarcest resource being money.

The discipline of corporate finance is frequently associated with that of accounting. However, while financial managers do need to have a firm understanding of management accounting (in order to make decisions) and a good understanding of financial accounting (in order to be aware of how financial decisions and their results are presented to the outside world), corporate finance and accounting are fundamentally different in nature. Corporate finance is inherently forward-looking and based on cash flows; this differentiates it from financial accounting, which is historic in nature and focuses on profit rather than cash. Corporate finance is concerned with raising funds and providing a return to investors; this differentiates it from management accounting, which is primarily concerned with providing information to assist managers in making decisions within the company. However, although there are differences between these disciplines, there is no doubt that corporate finance borrows extensively from both. While in the following chapters we consider in detail the many and varied problems and tasks faced by financial managers, the common theme that links these chapters is the need for financial managers to be able to *value alternative courses of action* available to them. This allows them to make a decision as to which is the best choice in financial terms. Therefore before we look at the specific roles and goals of financial managers, we introduce two key concepts that are central to financial decision-making.

1.1 TWO KEY CONCEPTS IN CORPORATE FINANCE

Two key concepts in corporate finance that help managers to value alternative courses of action are the **time value of money** and the relationship between risk and return. Since these two concepts are referred to frequently in the following chapters, it is vital that you have a clear understanding of them.

1.1.1 The time value of money

The *time value of money* is perhaps the single most important concept in corporate finance and is relevant to both companies and investors. In a wider context it is relevant to anyone expecting to pay or receive money over a period of time. The time value of money is particularly important to companies since the financing, investment and dividend decisions made by companies result in substantial cash flows over a variety of periods of time. Simply stated, the time value of money refers to the fact that the value of money changes over time.

Imagine as a student you can take a £4,000 student grant either today or in one year's time. Faced with this choice, you will (hopefully!) prefer to take the grant today. The question to ask yourself is *why* do you prefer the £4,000 grant today? There are three major factors at work here:

■ *Time*: if you have the money now, you can spend it now. It is human nature to want things now rather than to wait for them. Alternatively, if you do not wish to spend your money now, you will still prefer to take it now, since you can then invest it so that in one year's time you will have £4,000 plus any investment income you have earned.
■ *Inflation*: £4,000 spent now will buy more goods and services than £4,000 spent in one year's time because inflation reduces the purchasing power of your money over time. Unless, of course, we are in a deflationary period, when the reverse will be true, but this is rare.
■ *Risk*: if you take £4,000 now you definitely have the money in your possession. The alternative of the *promise* of £4,000 in a year's time carries the risk that the payment may be less than £4,000 or may not be paid at all.

Different applications of the time value of money are considered in Section 1.1.3.

1.1.2 The relationship between risk and return

This concept states that an investor or a company takes on more risk only if a higher return is offered in compensation. *Return* refers to the financial rewards resulting from making an investment. The nature of the return depends on the form of the investment. A company that invests in **non-current assets** and business operations expects returns in the form of *profit*, whether measured on a before-interest, before-tax or an after-tax basis, and in the form of *cash flows*. An investor who buys **ordinary shares** expects returns in the form of *dividend payments* and **capital gains** (share price increases). An investor who buys **corporate bonds** expects regular returns in the form of *interest payments*. The meaning of risk is more complex than the meaning of return. An investor or a company expects or anticipates a specific return when making an investment. *Risk* refers to the possibility that the actual return may be different from the expected return. If the actual return is greater than the expected return, this is usually a welcome occurrence. Investors, companies and financial managers are more likely to be concerned with the possibility that the actual return is *less* than the expected return. A *risky investment* is therefore one where there is a significant possibility of its actual return being different from its expected return. As the possibility of actual return being different from expected return increases, investors and companies demand a higher expected return.

The relationship between risk and return is explored in several chapters in this text. In 'Investment appraisal: applications and risk' (Chapter 7) we will see that a company can allow for the risk of a project by requiring a higher or lower rate of return according to the level of risk expected. In 'Portfolio theory and the capital asset pricing model' (Chapter 8) we examine how an individual's attitude to the trade-off between risk and return shapes their utility curves; we also consider the capital asset pricing model, which expresses the relationship between risk and return in a convenient linear form. In 'The cost of capital and capital structure' (Chapter 9) we calculate the costs of different sources of finance and find that the higher the risk attached to a source of finance, the higher the return required by the investor.

1.1.3 Compounding and discounting

Compounding is the way to determine the *future value* of a sum of money invested now, for example in a bank account, where interest is left in the account after it has been paid. Because interest received is left in the account, interest is earned on interest in future years. The future value depends on the rate of interest paid, the initial sum invested and the number of years for which the sum is invested:

$$FV = C_0(1 + i)^n$$

where: FV = future value
C_0 = sum deposited now
i = annual interest rate
n = number of years for which the sum is invested

For example, £20 deposited for five years at an annual interest rate of 6 per cent will have a future value of:

$$FV = £20 \times (1.06)^5 = £26.77$$

In corporate finance, we can take account of the time value of money through the technique of discounting, which is the opposite of compounding. While *compounding* takes us *forward* from the current value of an investment to its future value, *discounting* takes us *backward* from the future value of a cash flow to its **present value**. Cash flows occurring at different points in time cannot be compared directly because they have different time values; discounting allows us to compare these cash flows by comparing their present values.

Consider an investor who has the choice between receiving £1,000 now and £1,200 in one year's time. The investor can compare the two options by changing the future value of £1,200 into a present value and comparing this present value with the offer of £1,000 now (note that the £1,000 offered now is already in present value terms). The present value can be found by applying an appropriate **discount rate**, one which reflects the three factors discussed earlier: time, inflation and risk. If the best investment available to the investor offers an annual interest rate of 10 per cent, we can use this as the discount rate. Reversing the compounding illustrated above, the present value can be found from the future value by using the following formula:

$$PV = \frac{FV}{(1 + i)^n}$$

where: PV = present value
FV = future value
i = discount rate
n = number of years until the cash flow occurs

Inserting the values given above:

$$PV = 1{,}200/(1.1)^1 = £1{,}091$$

Alternatively, we can convert our present value of £1,000 into a future value:

$$FV = £1{,}000 \times (1.1)^1 = £1{,}100$$

Whether we compare present values (£1,000 is less than £1,091) or future values (£1,100 is less than £1,200), it is clear that £1,200 in one year's time is worth more to the investor than £1,000 now.

Discounting calculations are aided by using *present value tables*, which can be found at the back of this text. The first table, of present value factors, can be used to discount *single point* cash flows. For example, what is the present value of a single payment of £100 to be received in five years' time at a discount rate of 12 per cent? The table of present value factors gives the present value factor for five years (row) at 12 per cent (column) as 0.567. If we multiply this by £100 we find a present value of £56.70.

The next table, of cumulative present value factors, enables us to find the present value of an **annuity**. An annuity is a regular payment of a fixed amount of money over a finite period. For example, if we receive £100 at the end of each of the next five years, what is the present value of this series of cash flows if our required rate of return is 7 per cent? The table gives the cumulative present value factor (annuity factor) for five years (row) at a discount rate of 7 per cent (column) as 4.100. If we multiply this by £100 we find a present value of £410.

The present value of a **perpetuity**, the regular payment of a fixed amount of money over an infinite period of time, is equal to the regular payment divided by the discount rate. The present value of a perpetuity of £100 at a discount rate of 10 per cent is £1,000 (i.e. £100/0.1).

Discounted cash flow (DCF) techniques allow us to tackle more complicated scenarios than the simple examples we have just considered. Later in the chapter we discuss the vital link existing between shareholder wealth and *net present value* (NPV), the specific application of DCF techniques to investment appraisal decisions. NPV and its sister DCF technique internal rate of return are introduced in 'An overview of investment appraisal methods' (Chapter 6). The application of NPV to more complex investment decisions is comprehensively dealt with in Chapter 7. In 'Long-term finance: debt finance, hybrid finance and leasing' (Chapter 5), DCF analysis is applied to valuing a variety of debt-related securities.

1.2 THE ROLE OF THE FINANCIAL MANAGER

While everyone manages their own finances to some extent, financial managers of companies are responsible for a much larger operation when they manage corporate funds. They are responsible for a company's *investment decisions*, advising on the allocation of funds in terms of the total amount of assets, the composition of non-current and current assets, and the consequent risk profile of the choices. They are also responsible for *raising funds*, choosing from a wide variety of financial institutions and markets, with each source of finance having different features of cost, availability, maturity and risk. The place where supply of finance meets demand for finance is called the financial market: this consists of

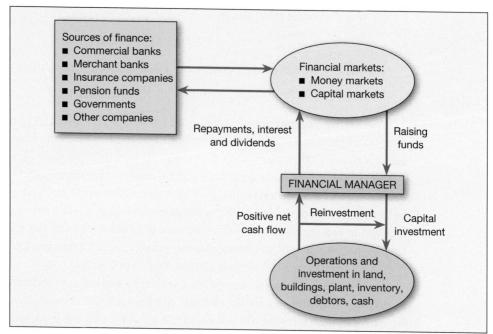

Figure 1.1 The central role of the financial manager in a company's financing, investment and dividend decisions

the short-term money markets and the longer-term capital markets. A major source of finance for a company is internal rather than external, i.e. using part of the cash or earnings generated by its business activities. The managers of the company, however, must strike a balance between the amount of earnings they retain and the amount they pay out to shareholders as a dividend.

We can see, therefore, that a financial manager's decisions can be divided into three general areas: investment decisions, financing decisions and dividend decisions. Figure 1.1 illustrates the position of the financial manager as a person central to these decisions and their associated cash flows.

While it is convenient for discussion purposes to split a financial manager's decisions into three decision areas, it is important to recognise the high level of interdependence that exists between them. Hence a financial manager making a decision in one of these three areas should always take into account the effect of that decision on the other two areas. Figure 1.2 gives examples of possible knock-on effects in the other two areas of taking a decision in one of the three areas.

Who makes corporate finance decisions in practice? In most companies there will be no one individual solely responsible for corporate financial management. The more strategic dimensions of the three decision areas tend to be considered at board level, with an important contribution coming from the *finance director,* who oversees the finance function. Any financial decisions taken at this level will be after extensive consultation with accountants, tax experts and lawyers. The daily cash and treasury management duties of the company and its liaison with financial institutions such as banks will be undertaken by the *corporate*

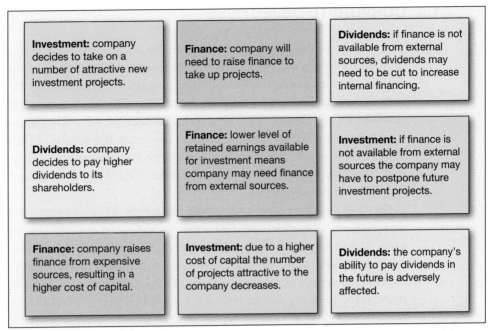

Figure 1.2 The interrelationship between financing, dividend and investment decisions

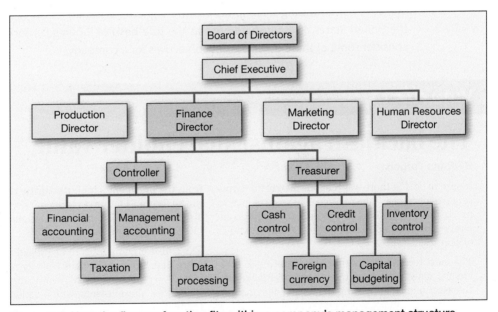

Figure 1.3 How the finance function fits within a company's management structure

treasurer. It is common for both finance director and corporate treasurer to have an accounting background. An important responsibility for the corporate treasurer is hedging **interest rate risk** and **exchange rate risk**. Figure 1.3 illustrates the various functions within the finance department of a large company.

1.3 CORPORATE OBJECTIVES

What should be the primary financial objective of corporate finance and, therefore, the main objective of financial managers? The answer is that the objective should be to make decisions that maximise the value of the company for its owners. As the owners of the company are its *shareholders,* the primary financial objective of corporate finance is usually stated to be the maximisation of shareholder wealth. Since shareholders receive their wealth through *dividends* and *capital gains* (increases in the value of their shares), shareholder wealth will be maximised by maximising the value of dividends and capital gains that shareholders receive over time. How financial managers go about achieving this objective is considered in Section 1.3.1.

Owing to the rather vague and complicated nature of the concept of shareholder wealth maximisation, other objectives are commonly suggested as possible substitutes or surrogates. Alternative objectives to shareholder wealth maximisation also arise because of the existence of other groups with an interest in the company (**stakeholders**). These groups, such as employees, customers, creditors and the local community, will have different views on what the company should aim for. It is important to stress that while companies must consider the views of stakeholders other than shareholders, and while companies may adopt one or several substitute objectives over shorter periods, from a corporate finance perspective such objectives should be pursued only in support of the overriding long-term objective of maximising shareholder wealth. Vignette 1.1 analyses the recent backlash in the United States of using share price as the sole basis of judging corporations. We now consider some of these other possible objectives for a company.

Vignette 1.1

The backlash against shareholder value

By Rana Foroohar

It used to be that there was just one metric for corporate performance – share price. These days, not so much. In the age of Donald Trump and #MeToo, companies are expected to wade into the murky waters of politics.

The most recent mass high school shooting in Florida has added urgency to the issue, with BlackRock, the asset manager, floating the idea of leaving gun makers out of index funds and retailers like Dick's and Walmart taking assault-style weapons off their shelves.

This follows months of corporate stands on everything from immigration to sexual harassment to LGBT rights, a wave of activism punctuated by Merck chief executive Ken Frazier's resignation from the president's manufacturing council following Mr Trump's failure to condemn a white supremacist rally in Charlottesville last August. A few days later, the council was disbanded.

The calls for companies to be judged on something more than share price have been growing for some time. Larry Fink's most recent annual letter to BlackRock shareholders, which included a demand for more 'purpose-driven companies', was a big turning point in the backlash against the shareholder value theory that has been the guiding force for companies for four decades. It is one thing when liberal academics and politicians call for a new kind of 'stakeholder' capitalism. It's another when the largest asset manager in the world does it.

Vignette **1.1** *(continued)*

I surveyed a number of chief executives about Mr Fink's letter at the World Economic Forum in Davos. While all were supportive of the general principle, most also expressed some frustration, not because Mr Fink wasn't right but because he wasn't clear. Senior executives know that judging companies only by share performance does not work because it engenders short-termism – research and development as a percentage of revenue has declined since the 1980s, in part because the share price usually suffers when companies announce this kind of spending. But they do not know what the new playbook is.

'What does this really mean in practice?' asked the chief financial officer of a large multinational. 'What are the new metrics that we are being judged on? And what happens if we fall short?'

One of the things going for shareholder value was that it was precise. As long as shares rise quarter on quarter, you are doing your job. It is also clear it was a limited metric, one that has arguably resulted in far less corporate risk taking and innovation, and also one that disproportionately benefits senior executives, particularly large company chief executives who typically get more than half their compensation in stock. This incentivises short-term decision making.

Perhaps most importantly, it's a philosophy that does not appeal nearly as much to millennial consumers or workers, who demand that companies think about a broader group of stakeholders and a more complex set of political and social issues. A study released last week by the Global Strategy Group shows that two-thirds of Americans believe that corporations have a responsibility to address key social and political issues. It also found that those that do have far higher favourability ratings than those that don't. Lockheed Martin, a company that said and did nothing following Charlottesville, had a significant drop in favourability ratings.

Some of this depends on your politics. Corporate activism is far more popular among Democrats than Republicans (among the few memorable examples of any right-wing activism were arts and crafts store Hobby Lobby's fight against mandatory birth control coverage by corporate insurance, and restaurant chain Chick-fil-A's opposition to same-sex marriage). But the risks of non-action seem to outweigh those of action. Recent research shows that issues like Apple's stand on LGBT rights made liberals much more likely to want to buy Apple products, but it did not make opponents less likely to purchase them.

While I'm all for chief executives speaking out on issues that matter to them, I'm less keen on activism as a metric for corporate performance. This is not to say that we do not need to move beyond the mythology of shareholder value – we do. But my own guidelines would be more quantitative.

Here are two things that boards might take into account, aside from share price, when judging corporations. First, executives should manage human resources as well as they manage capital. In a world awash with cash but facing a talent shortage, we need to start thinking of labour as an asset rather than simply a cost liability (this could be encouraged by changes in the tax code and accounting standards).

Second, we should look more closely at corporate R&D as a percentage of revenues. Academics have found that private companies spend about twice as much on productive capital expenditure as public ones of the same type and size. It is a measure of how the pressure of adhering to shareholder value theory can kill innovation in its crib.

Companies clearly need to think about more than investors. Consumers and workers are demanding, and getting, more political engagement from corporate America. But politics is risky. Investors should stick to economic metrics when they value corporations. They just need broader and better ones.

Source: Foroohar, R. (2018) 'The backlash against shareholder value', *Financial Times*, 4 March. ©The Financial Times Ltd, 4 March 2018. All Rights Reserved.

Questions

1 What are the issues of judging corporate performance on just share price alone?

2 If share price alone is no longer an appropriate metric of corporate performance, what other factors should be considered?

1.3.1 Maximisation of profits

The classical economic view of the firm, as put forward by Hayek (1960) and Friedman (1970), is that it should be operated in a manner that maximises its **economic profits**. The concept of *economic profit* is far removed from the *accounting profit* found in a company's income statement. While economic profit broadly equates to cash, accounting profit does not. There are many examples of companies going into liquidation shortly after declaring high profits. Polly Peck plc's dramatic failure in 1990 is one such example.

There are three fundamental problems with profit maximisation as an overall corporate goal. The first problem is that there are *quantitative difficulties* associated with profit. Profit maximisation as a financial objective requires that profit be defined and measured accurately, and that all the factors contributing to it are known and can be taken into account. It is very doubtful that this requirement can be met on a consistent basis. If five auditors go into the same company, it is possible that each may come out with a different profit figure.

The second problem concerns the *timescale* over which profit should be maximised. Should profit be maximised in the short term or the long term? Given that profit considers one year at a time, the focus is likely to be on short-term profit maximisation at the expense of long-term investment, putting the long-term survival of the company into doubt.

The third problem is that profit does not take account of, or make an allowance for, risk. It would be inappropriate to concentrate our efforts on maximising accounting profit when this objective does not consider one of the key determinants of shareholder wealth.

Shareholders' dividends are paid with cash, not profit, and the timing and associated risk of dividend payments are important factors determining shareholder wealth. Considering this fact together with the problems just discussed, we can conclude that profit maximisation is not a suitable substitute objective for shareholder wealth maximisation. That is not to say that a company does not need to pay attention to its profit figures, since the financial markets take falling profits or profit warnings as a sign of financial weakness. In addition, profit targets can serve a useful purpose in helping a company to achieve short-term (operational) objectives within its overall strategic plan.

1.3.2 Maximisation of sales

If a company were to pursue sales maximisation (either in terms of volume or value) as its *only* overriding long-term objective, then it is likely to reach a stage where it is overtrading (see 'Overtrading', Section 3.4) and might eventually have to go into liquidation. Sales may not necessarily be at a profit, and sales targets could be disastrous if products are not correctly priced. Sales maximisation can be useful as a short-term objective, however. As an example, a company seeking to establish sustainable market share on entering a new market could follow a policy of sales maximisation.

1.3.3 Survival

Survival cannot be accepted as a satisfactory long-term objective. Will investors want to invest in a company whose main objective is merely to survive? The answer is, of course, an emphatic no. In the long term, a company must attract capital investment by holding out the prospect of gains which are at least as great as those offered by comparable alternative investment opportunities. Survival may be a key short-term objective, however, especially in times of economic recession. If a company were to be liquidated, there may be little, if any, money to distribute to ordinary shareholders by the time assets have been distributed to stakeholders higher up the **creditor hierarchy**. If liquidation were a possibility, short-term survival as an objective *would* be consistent with shareholder wealth maximisation.

1.3.4 Social responsibility

Some companies adopt an altruistic social purpose as a corporate objective. They may be concerned with improving working conditions for their employees, providing a healthy product for their customers or avoiding antisocial actions such as environmental pollution or undesirable promotional practices. Corporate social responsibility (CSR), as it is also sometimes known, can take the form of donating goods and services to various beneficiaries in society. UK drugs companies including AstraZeneca and GlaxoSmithKline (GSK) donate billions of pounds to CSR annually. While it is important not to upset stakeholders such as employees and the local community, social responsibility should play a supporting role within the framework of corporate objectives rather than acting as a company's primary goal. Although a company does not exist solely to please its employees, managers are aware that having a demotivated and unhappy workforce will be detrimental to the company's long-term prosperity. Equally, an action group of local residents unhappy with a company's environmental impact can decrease its sales by inflicting adverse publicity on the company. Consider the negative impact on BP's corporate image of the 2010 explosion on the Deep Water Horizon drilling rig in the Gulf of Mexico, where more than half of the company's market value was wiped out in March and June of that year. Or, more recently, Volkswagen's emissions cover-up in March 2015, where it was found to have installed software designed to manipulate the emissions details of its diesel cars. The German car manufacturer lost nearly 60 per cent of its market value in the ensuing six-month period after the scandal had broken.

1.4 HOW IS SHAREHOLDER WEALTH MAXIMISED?

We noted earlier that shareholder wealth maximisation is a rather vague and complicated concept. We also stated that shareholders' wealth is increased by the cash they receive in dividend payments and by capital gains arising from increasing share prices. It follows that shareholder wealth can be maximised by maximising the purchasing power that shareholders derive through dividend payments and capital gains over time. This view of shareholder wealth maximisation suggests three factors that directly affect shareholders' wealth:

- the *magnitude* of cash flows accumulating to the company;
- the *timing* of cash flows accumulating to the company;
- the *risk* associated with the cash flows accumulating to the company.

Having established the factors that affect shareholder wealth we can now consider what to take as an indicator of shareholder wealth. The indicator usually taken is a company's ordinary share price, as mentioned in Vignette 1.1, since this will reflect expectations about future dividend payments and investor views about the long-term prospects of the company and its expected cash flows. The substitute or surrogate objective to shareholder wealth maximisation, therefore, is to *maximise the current market* price of the company's ordinary shares and hence to maximise the company's total market value. Figure 1.4 illustrates the link between cash flows arising from a company's projects all the way through to the wealth of its shareholders.

At stage 1, a company takes on all investment projects with a positive NPV. By using NPV to appraise the financial acceptability of potential projects the company is considering the three factors that affect shareholder wealth, i.e. the magnitude of expected cash flows, their timing (through discounting) and their associated risk (through the selected discount rate). At stage 2, given that NPV is additive, the corporate NPV should equal the sum of the NPVs of the projects it has undertaken. At stage 3 the corporate NPV is accurately reflected by the market value of the company through its share price. The link between stages 2 and 3 (i.e. the market value of the company reflecting the true value of the company) will depend heavily on the *efficiency* of the stock market and hence on the speed and accuracy with which share price changes reflect new information about companies. (The importance to corporate finance of stock market efficiency is considered in Chapter 2.) Finally, at stage 4, the share price is taken to be a substitute for shareholder wealth and so shareholder wealth maximisation (SHWM) will occur when the market value (**market capitalisation**) of the company is maximised.

Now that we have identified the factors that affect shareholder wealth and established share price maximisation as a surrogate objective for shareholder wealth maximisation, we need to consider how a financial manager can achieve this objective. The factors identified as affecting shareholder wealth are largely under the control of the financial manager, even though the outcome of their decisions will also be affected by the conditions prevailing in the financial markets. From our earlier discussion, a company's value will be maximised if the financial manager makes 'good' investment, financing and dividend decisions.

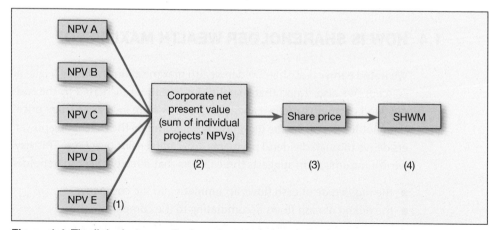

Figure 1.4 The links between the investment projects of a company and shareholder wealth

Examples of 'good' financial decisions, in the sense of decisions that promote share price maximisation, include the following:

- managing a company's working capital efficiently by striking a balance between the need to maintain liquidity and the opportunity cost of holding liquid assets;
- raising finance using the most appropriate mixture of debt and equity in order to minimise a company's **cost of capital**;
- using NPV to assess all potential investment projects and then accepting all projects with a positive NPV;
- adopting the most appropriate dividend policy, which reflects the amount of dividends a company can afford to pay, given its level of profit and the amount of **retained earnings** it requires for reinvestment;
- taking account of the risk associated with financial decisions and where possible guarding against it, e.g. hedging interest and exchange rate risk.

1.5 AGENCY THEORY

1.5.1 Why does agency exist?

While managers should make decisions that are consistent with the objective of maximising shareholder wealth, whether this happens in practice is another matter. The *agency problem* is said to occur when managers make decisions that are not consistent with the objective of shareholder wealth maximisation. Three important factors that contribute to the existence of the agency problem within public limited companies are as follows:

- There is divergence of ownership and control, whereby those who own the company (shareholders) do not manage it but appoint agents (managers) to run the company on their behalf.
- The goals of the managers (agents) differ from those of the shareholders (principals). Human nature being what it is, managers are likely to maximise their own wealth rather than the wealth of shareholders.
- **Asymmetry of information** exists between agent and principal. Managers run the company on a day-to-day basis and consequently have access to management accounting data and financial reports, whereas shareholders receive only annual reports, which may be subject to manipulation by the management.

When these three factors are considered together, it should be clear that managers are able to maximise their own wealth without necessarily being detected by the owners of the company. Asymmetry of information makes it difficult for shareholders to monitor managerial decisions, allowing managers to follow their own welfare-maximising decisions. Examples of possible management goals include:

- growth, or maximising the size of the company;
- increasing managerial power;
- increasing managerial job security;

- increasing managerial pay and rewards;
- pursuing their own social objectives or pet projects.

The potential agency problem between a company's managers and its shareholders is not the only agency problem that exists. Jensen and Meckling (1976) argued that the company can be viewed as a series of agency relationships between the different interest groups involved. These agency relationships are shown in Figure 1.5. The arrows point away from the principal towards the agent. For example, as customers pay for goods and services from the company, they are the principal and the supplying company is their agent. While a company's managers are the agents of the shareholders, the relationship is reversed between creditors and shareholders, with shareholders becoming, through the actions of the managers they appoint and direct, the agents of the creditors.

From a corporate finance perspective an important agency relationship exists between shareholders, as agents, and the providers of debt finance, as principals. The agency problem here is that shareholders will prefer debt to be used for progressively riskier investment projects, as it is shareholders who gain from the success of such projects, but debt holders who bear the risk.

1.5.2 How does agency manifest within a company?

The agency problem manifests itself in the investment decisions managers make. Managerial reward schemes are often based on short-term performance measures and managers therefore tend to use the payback method when appraising possible projects, as this technique emphasises short-term returns. With respect to risk, managers may make investments that diversify business operations and hence decrease **unsystematic risk**, in order to reduce the risk to the company. Unsystematic risk (see 'The concept of diversification', Section 8.2) is the risk associated with undertaking specific business activities. By reducing risk through diversification, managers hope to secure their own jobs. However, most investors will already have diversified away unsystematic risk themselves by investing in portfolios

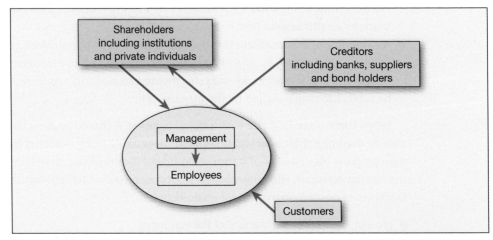

Figure 1.5 The agency relationships that exist between the various stakeholders of a company

containing the shares of many different companies. Shareholder wealth is not, therefore, increased by the diversifying activities of managers. Another agency problem relating to risk can arise if managers undertake low-risk projects when the preference of shareholders is for higher-risk projects.

The agency problem can also manifest in financing decisions. Managers will prefer to use equity finance rather than debt finance, even though equity finance is more expensive than debt finance, as lower interest payments mean lower bankruptcy risk and higher job security. This will be undesirable from a shareholder point of view because increasing equity finance will increase the cost of the company's capital.

Agency conflict arises between shareholders and debt holders because shareholders have a greater preference for higher-risk projects than debt holders. The return to shareholders is unlimited, whereas their loss is limited to the value of their shares, hence their preference for higher-risk (and therefore higher-return) projects. The return to debt holders, however, is limited to a fixed-interest return: they will not benefit from the higher returns from riskier projects.

1.5.3 Dealing with the agency problem between shareholders and managers

Jensen and Meckling (1976) suggested that there are two ways of optimising managerial behaviour in order to encourage **goal congruence** between shareholders and managers. The first way is for shareholders to monitor the actions of managers. There are a number of possible monitoring devices that can be used, although they all incur costs in terms of both time and money. These monitoring devices include using independently audited financial statements and additional reporting requirements, shadowing senior managers and using external analysts. The costs of monitoring must be weighed against the benefits accruing from a decrease in suboptimal managerial behaviour (i.e. managerial behaviour which does not aim to maximise shareholder wealth). A major difficulty associated with monitoring as a method of solving the agency problem is the existence of **free riders**. Smaller investors allow larger shareholders, who are more eager to monitor managerial behaviour owing to their larger stake in the company, to incur most of the monitoring costs while sharing in the benefits of corrected management behaviour. Hence the smaller investors obtain a free ride.

An alternative to monitoring is for shareholders to incorporate clauses into managerial contracts which encourage goal congruence. Such clauses formalise constraints, incentives and punishments. An optimal contract will be one which minimises the total costs associated with agency. These **agency costs** include:

- financial contracting costs, such as transaction and legal costs;
- the opportunity cost of any contractual constraints;
- the cost of managers' incentives and bonus fees;
- monitoring costs, such as the cost of reports and audits;
- the loss of wealth owing to suboptimal behaviour by the agent.

It is important that managerial contracts reflect the needs of individual companies. For example, monitoring may be both difficult and costly for some companies.

Managerial contracts for such companies may therefore include bonuses for improved performance. Owing to the difficulties associated with monitoring managerial behaviour, such incentives could offer a more practical way of encouraging goal congruence. The two most common incentives offered to managers are performance-related pay (PRP) and executive **share option schemes**. These methods are not without their drawbacks.

Performance-related pay (PRP)

The major problem here is finding an accurate measure of managerial performance. For example, managerial remuneration can be linked to performance indicators such as profit, **earnings per share** or return on capital employed (see 'Assessing financial performance', Section 2.4). However, the accounting information underpinning these three performance measures is open to manipulation by the same managers who stand to benefit from PRP. Profit, earnings per share and return on capital employed may also not be good indicators of wealth creation as they are not based on cash and so do not have a direct link to shareholder wealth maximisation.

Executive share option schemes

Given the problems associated with PRP, executive share option schemes represent an alternative way to encourage goal congruence between senior managers and shareholders. Share options allow managers to buy a specified number of their company's shares at a fixed price over a specified period. The options have value only when the market price of the company's shares exceeds the price at which they can be bought by using the option. The aim of executive share option schemes is to encourage managers to maximise the company's share price, and hence to maximise shareholder wealth, by making managers potential shareholders through their ownership of share options.

Share option schemes are not without their problems. First, while good financial management does increase share prices, there are a number of external factors affecting share prices. If a country is experiencing an economic boom, share prices will increase (a **bull market**). Managers will then benefit through increases in the value of their share options, but this is not necessarily down to their good financial management. Equally, if share prices in general are falling and/or volatile, share options may not reward managers who have been doing a good job in difficult conditions. This has been an issue for UK companies since the financial crisis of 2008. Second, problems with share option schemes arise because of their terms. Share options are not seen as an immediate cost to the company and so the terms of the options (i.e. the number of shares that can be bought, the price at which they can be bought and when they can be bought) may sometimes be set at too generous a level. The difficulty of quantifying the cost of share options and the introduction of new accounting treatment of their costs has led to a decline in their popularity.

Long-term incentive plans (LTIPs)

These types of executive compensation schemes are common in the UK and typically reward participants with free shares after a predetermined period of time (normally three years or more) provided defined performance targets are met. Remuneration committees award them to senior executives, although they can also be awarded to other employees. The advantage of LTIPs over share options is that free shares will still have value, even when share prices are falling, while share options have no incentive value when they are 'out of the money'.

In addition to using monitoring and managerial incentives, shareholders have other ways of keeping managers on their toes. For example, they have the right to remove directors by voting them out of office at the company's annual general meeting (AGM). Whether this represents a viable threat to managers depends heavily on the ownership structure of the company, for example whether a few large influential shareholders hold more than half of the company's ordinary shares. Alternatively, shareholders can 'vote with their feet' and sell their shares on the capital markets. This can have the effect of depressing the company's share price, making it a possible takeover target. The fact that target company managers usually lose their jobs after a takeover may provide an incentive for them to run their company more in the interests of shareholders.

1.5.4 The agency problem between debt holders and shareholders

The simplest way for debt holders to protect their investment in a company is to secure their debt against the company's assets. Should the company go into liquidation, debt holders will have a prior claim over assets, which they can then sell to recover their investment.

Another way for debt holders to protect their interests and limit the amount of risk they face is for them to use **covenants**. These are clauses written into debt agreements which restrict a company's decision-making process. They may prevent a company from investing in high-risk projects, or from paying out excessive levels of dividends, or may limit its future gearing levels. (Covenants are discussed in 'Bonds, loan notes, loan stock and debentures', Section 5.1).

1.5.5 The influence of institutional investors

We have already implied that an increase in the concentration of share ownership might lead to a reduction in the problems associated with agency. In the UK from the late 1970s to the middle of the 1990s there was an increase in shareholdings by large institutional investors. This trend has reversed somewhat in recent years. As Table 1.1 shows, UK institutional shareholders account for the ownership of only 29.4 per cent of all ordinary share capital. One marked change in recent years has been the steep decline in the number of shares held by pension funds and insurance companies. The pension fund decrease can be explained by the UK government's 1997 abolition of the favourable tax treatment enjoyed by pension funds up to that date which had enabled them to reclaim the tax paid on dividends. Once this tax benefit was lost, ordinary shares became a less attractive investment.

In the past, while institutional investors had not been overtly interested in becoming involved with companies' operational decisions, they had put pressure on companies to maintain their dividend payments even in adverse macroeconomic conditions. Ironically, rather than reducing the agency problem, institutional investors may have been exacerbating it by pressing companies to pay dividends they could not afford. However, recent years have seen institutional investors becoming more interested in corporate operational and

Table 1.1 Ownership of UK quoted ordinary shares according to owner classification (1975–2016)

	1975 %	1981 %	1997 %	2001 %	2006 %	2014 %	2016 %
Insurance companies	15.9	20.5	23.5	20.0	14.7	5.9	4.9
Pension funds	16.8	26.7	22.1	16.1	12.7	3.0	3.0
Other financial institutions*	15.3	10.7	10.7	15.2	17.1	19.3	21.5
Institutional investors (total)	48.0	57.9	56.3	51.3	44.5	28.2	29.4
Private companies	3.0	5.1	1.2	1.0	1.8	2.0	2.2
Personal sector	37.5	28.2	16.5	14.8	12.8	11.9	12.3
Overseas sector	5.6	3.6	24.0	31.9	40.0	53.8	53.9
Other	5.9	5.2	2.0	1.0	0.9	4.1	2.2
Total	100.0	100.0	100.0	100.0	100.0	100.0	100.0

*Includes banks, unit and investment trusts.
Source: National Statistics. © Crown copyright 2017. Reproduced by permission of the Office for National Statistics, licensed under the Open Government Licence v.3.0.

governance issues. The number of occasions where institutional investors have got tough with companies in which they invest when those companies did not comply with governance standards has increased steadily. The UK Financial Reporting Council introduced a new Stewardship Code in July 2010 to try to 'improve the effectiveness of interactions between companies and institutional investors in order to facilitate the attainment of long-term returns for shareholders.' The implications of a high level of share-ownership by institutional investors and the UK corporate governance code are the subject of Vignette 1.2.

Vignette 1.2

Investors falling short as active owners

By Ruth Sullivan

Expectations of improved engagement between institutional investors and the companies in which they invest have been high following the roll-out of the UK Stewardship Code. But more than a year on, just how successful has it been in promoting shareholder stewardship? Since the launch, 131 asset managers, 31 asset owners and 11 service providers have produced statements declaring how far they follow the code and exercise their voting rights, according to the Financial Reporting Council, which oversees the code. Yet in spite of such progress, doubts remain over the extent to which the guidance actually changes investor behaviour. 'The code has not turned investors into active owners, at least not yet,' says Harlan Zimmerman, a senior partner at Cevian Capital, a European activist investor. Out of those asset managers disclosing the information, 'nowhere near that number have increased the attention they pay to the ownership aspects of their investments,' he maintains.

Mr Zimmerman believes a critical area that typically gets less attention from investors than remuneration and succession issues is board composition. 'Voting on board candidates is perhaps the area where shareholders have the greatest ability to influence and exercise stewardship, but is an area where facts show widespread stewardship has been lacking,' he says. He points to FTSE 100 boards where, between 2006 and 2010, all of nearly 2,500 directors proposed were elected or re-elected without opposition, according to a survey by PIRC, the corporate governance group. 'You can count on one hand the number of companies where shareholders have voted down a board member,' he says. 'Either boards are doing a superb job or, for many investors, voting has been primarily a rubber-stamping exercise,' he says.

Outside the UK, the lack of meaningful change on the board of News Corp – Rupert Murdoch's media empire, listed in the US – in spite of the phone-hacking scandal

Vignette 1.2 (*continued*)

in part of its UK operations, is a case in point. However, Alan MacDougall, PIRC's managing director, says the power of voting should not be underestimated. 'It is a valuable part of engagement, more important in some situations as it brings shareholders around the table [at annual general meetings].' Individual shareholder engagement behind closed doors is less effective, he adds. A long-term investment approach and more active engagement are needed, says Mr Zimmerman. But barriers remain, preventing this.

One of these is that pension funds and insurance companies, the end asset owners in many cases, largely fail to give a specific mandate to asset managers to engage with companies, merely requiring 'asset managers to vote and little more,' he says. Colin Melvin, chief executive of Hermes Equity Ownership Services, agrees: 'Pension funds need to do more than ask asset managers whether they comply with the code,' he says. 'For the Stewardship Code to work, it requires a clearer link between pension funds and the asset managers they select.' At the moment the responsibility of stewardship falls on the asset manager whereas it should be linked to trustees' fiduciary duty, he argues. He believes the UK pensions regulator needs to issue a clear statement to support the code. 'If pension funds became more interested it would lead to more accountable companies,' Mr Melvin adds.

There is some glimmer of change as more pension funds are beginning to scrutinise – through surveys – how their asset managers, including international players investing in UK companies, comply with the stewardship code, says Mr Melvin. 'Larger funds are using a traffic light system to assess their managers' application of the code and there are still lots of red lights,' he adds.

Another barrier to engaging effectively with companies is the difficulty shareholders encounter in the UK in working together to tackle issues. 'Fear of breaking **concert party** rules often hinders this,' says Mr Zimmerman. But unless shareholders get together 'boards will play them off against each other,' he adds. The code encourages shareholders to act collectively where it is appropriate, but there is still concern it is not specific enough and such engagement could be seen as working together to control a company. 'Other countries such as Italy have introduced legislation to clarify this but it remains a grey area in the UK,' he argues.

However, some progress on shareholder participation in the companies in which they invest is being attributed to the code. A new report on voting trends carried out by Institutional Shareholder Services shows an increase in investor turnout at FTSE 350 general meetings in the first six months of 2011 across European Union countries, with the UK among those in the lead, with a 71 per cent turnout compared with the European average of 63 per cent. 'Shareholder participation at UK meetings significantly increased for 2011 [up from 68 per cent in 2010] following the implementation of the Stewardship Code,' according to Jean-Nicolas Caprasse, European governance head at ISS.

Activist investors believe there is still much to be done to engage with companies, particularly as share prices head south in volatile markets and shareholders become unhappy. 'This environment where there is dramatic share price volatility is helping to force issues on the agenda,' says David Trenchard, managing director at Knight Vinke. Mr Zimmerman takes it further. He believes it is 'a good environment for true active owners to get things done'.

Source: Sullivan, R. (2011) Investors falling short as active owners, *Financial Times*, 11 September.
© The Financial Times Limited 2011. All rights reserved.

Questions

1 Why is it important for institutional investors to become actively involved with the management of the companies they invest in?

2 Do you consider the UK Stewardship Code has been successful in promoting shareholder stewardship?

A significant development in the USA has been the increase in pressure on companies, from both performance and accountability perspectives, generated by shareholder coalitions such as the Council of Institutional Investors (CII) and the California Public Employees' Retirement System (CalPERS), the largest US pension fund with $355bn of assets under its control in March 2018. In the past these organisations used to publish a 'focus list' of companies which they considered to have been underperforming due to bad management. The publication of these lists was a tactic to force such companies to take steps to improve their future performance. CalPERS stopped publishing the list in 2011, preferring instead to engage directly with underperforming companies. While this kind of shareholder 'vigilantism' has yet to take root in the UK, CalPERS is actively seeking to increase investments in Europe, and large investment companies such as UK-based Hermes Investment Management are both firm and outspoken about what they see as acceptable (and not acceptable) stewardship of the companies in which they invest.

1.5.6 The influence of international investors

The pattern of UK share ownership over the past decade and a half has seen a steady increase in the proportion of shares held by overseas investors. Foreign investors now account for the ownership of 53.9 per cent of shares listed on the UK stock market, over twice the level it was in 1997. The increase in UK share ownership by foreign investors has come predominantly from international fund management groups (such as BlackRock and Capital International), international mergers, new UK subsidiaries being set up by overseas companies, and companies moving their headquarters to the UK. This increase has been at the expense of domestic pension funds, insurance companies and individual investors who have sought to diversify their shareholdings internationally. This change in UK share ownership has made it more difficult for companies to identify and understand who their shareholders are and has led to a wider array of shareholder objectives for companies to consider.

1.6 CORPORATE GOVERNANCE

Until now we have considered solutions to the agency problem at an individual company level. In recent years, however, a more overarching solution to the corporate governance problem has come through self-regulation. This approach has sought to influence the structure and nature of the mechanisms by which owners govern managers in order to promote fairness, accountability and transparency.

1.6.1 Corporate governance in the UK

The importance of good standards of corporate governance has been highlighted by the collapse of a number of large companies, including Polly Peck in 1990 and Maxwell Communications Corporation in 1991 in the UK, and Enron and WorldCom in 2002 in the USA. More recently, the global banking crisis that began in 2007 and its effect on the UK financial services sector have raised fresh concerns about the effectiveness of UK corporate governance, and the manner in which remuneration packages for senior executives have been determined.

The UK corporate governance system has traditionally stressed the importance of internal controls, and the role of financial reporting and accountability, focusing on the market-based process of self-regulation. This is the opposite approach to that used in the USA where firms face large amounts of external legislation (see Section 1.6.2). The issue of corporate governance was first addressed in the UK in 1992 by a committee chaired by Sir Adrian Cadbury. The resulting Cadbury Report (Cadbury Committee 1992) recommended a voluntary Code of Best Practice which the London Stock Exchange (LSE) subsequently required member companies to comply with. Listed companies had to state in their financial reports whether or not they complied with the Cadbury Code of Best Practice and, if not, explain the reasons behind their non-compliance. The Code was not intended to be a rigid set of rules, but a guide to good board practice that was likely to best facilitate 'efficient, effective and entrepreneurial management that can deliver shareholder value of the longer term'. The Code was subsequently revised and reinforced by the Greenbury Report in 1995 to produce the 'Combined Code' and by the Hampel Committee in 1998. The latter established a 'super code' made up of a combination of its own recommendations and the findings of the previous two committees, again overseen by the LSE, which continued to include compliance with the provisions of the code in its listing requirements. A summary of the key provisions of the Combined Code is provided later in this section.

The Combined Code was developed further in 2000 as a consequence of the findings of the Turnbull Report (published in September 1999), which focused on systems of internal control and the wide-ranging types of significant risk that companies need to control. Additionally, after the collapses of Enron and WorldCom in 2002, the UK government decided to investigate both the effectiveness of **non-executive directors (NEDs)** and the independence of audit committees in UK companies. The resulting Higgs Report in 2003 dealt with the first of these two issues and made recommendations designed to enhance the independence and effectiveness of NEDs. It also commissioned the Tyson Report (2003) to investigate how companies could recruit NEDs with varied backgrounds and skills to enhance board effectiveness. In the same year the Smith Report examined the role of audit committees and, while stopping short of recommending that auditors should be rotated periodically (e.g. every five years), gave authoritative guidance on how audit committees should operate and be structured. The recommendations of the Higgs and Smith reports were incorporated into an extended version of the Combined Code in July 2003. The Financial Reporting Council (FRC) has reviewed and amended the Combined Code seven times since 2005. At the time of writing, the current version of the Combined Code (the UK Corporate Governance Code) came into force in June 2016. However, the latest version of the Code, published in July 2018, came into force in January 2019.

The 2016 version of the UK Corporate Governance Code (the Code) lays out recommendations in terms of a company's board of directors, the remuneration they receive, their accountability, the audit committee and the company's relationship with shareholders, including institutional investors. A summary of the Code's key provisions is provided here.

Leadership

- The board should be effective and be collectively responsible for the long-term success of the company.

21

- The posts of chief executive officer and chairman, the two most powerful positions within a company, should not be held by the same person.
- A chief executive officer should not go on to be the chairman of the same company.
- One independent non-executive director is to be appointed as a senior independent director.

Effectiveness

- The board should have the appropriate balance of experience, skills and knowledge so it can discharge its duties effectively.
- Half of the board, excluding the chairman, should be made up of independent non-executive directors (NEDs) of sufficient calibre.
- The election of new directors to the board should be formal, rigorous and transparent. The majority of the nomination committee should be independent NEDs.
- The nomination committee's work should be detailed in the annual report, including the company's policy on diversity.
- All directors need to be able to allocate sufficient time to discharge their duties.
- All directors should receive an induction to the company on joining and thereafter develop and update their skills on an ongoing basis.
- Information must be supplied to the board in an appropriate and timely manner.
- The board should formally and rigorously evaluate its own performance, facilitated externally, every three years.
- All directors of FTSE 350 companies should be put up for re-election every year. Non-executive directors should seek annual re-election once they have served nine years.

Accountability

- The board should present a balanced, fair and understandable assessment of the company's performance and future prospects.
- The board should determine the nature and extent of the risks it is prepared to take to achieve its strategic objectives, and then maintain sound internal control and risk management systems via an annual review.
- The board should establish an audit committee of at least three independent non-executive directors who monitor the integrity of financial statements and review internal financial controls.
- The audit committee should also monitor the internal audit committee and the external auditor's independence, as well as being responsible for auditor appointment, re-appointment and removal.
- There should be full disclosure of directors' remuneration, including any pension contributions and share options.

Remuneration

- The remuneration of the chairman and all executive directors should be set by a remuneration committee made up of at least three independent non-executive directors.
- Directors' notice or contract periods should be no longer than one year.
- Remuneration should be designed to achieve long-term success. Any performance-related elements should be stretching and transparent, and should not reward poor performance.

Relations with shareholders

- The board should facilitate dialogue with shareholders based on a mutual understanding of objectives.
- The board should communicate with investors via general meeting and actively encourage their participation.

While debate about the effectiveness of the Code was stimulated in the wake of the banking crisis of late 2007 and continued in the economic slump that followed, recent signs have been very encouraging. According to Grant Thornton (2018), 72 per cent of FTSE 350 companies were claiming full compliance (up from 66 per cent in 2017). While this shows a movement in the right direction, there is still some way to go (only 27 per cent of companies gave a detailed account of how the principles were applied). The greatest area of non-compliance surrounded the independence of directors and chairmen. Additionally, shareholder engagement was also an area of concern with only 31 per cent of FTSE 350 companies found to be clearly explaining how they work with and engage with shareholders. As mentioned earlier, in July 2018 the FRC published proposed revisions to create a shorter, sharper UK Corporate Governance Code, to come into effect in January 2019. Five key areas of the proposed change were identified: stakeholder engagement, board composition, diversity, remuneration and how companies respond to a significant vote against a resolution. The impact of one of the proposed changes on board tenure is the subject of Vignette 1.3.

Vignette 1.3

UK corporate governance code changes to hit dozens of chairmen

By Madison Marriage

The chairmen of more than 60 of Britain's largest listed companies risk falling foul of proposed corporate governance reforms that aim to put an end to stale and insular boardrooms.

The proposed rules, set out in the UK's revised corporate governance code last week, state for the first time that chairmen should step down from their role after nine years on the board. This includes time spent in previous non-executive director roles.

The change would catch out the chairs of 67 listed companies, of which 19 are in the FTSE 100 index. This includes John McAdam, who heads both Rentokil Initial and United Utilities; and Alison Carnwath, of commercial property developer Land Securities.

Both have already spent more than nine years in their current role, something that is frowned upon by shareholders but has not previously been formally discouraged by the Financial Reporting Council, the watchdog that oversees the code.

Although the code is not mandatory, most listed UK companies comply rather than exercise their option to explain to shareholders why they are not doing so.

The tenure proposal is particularly controversial for chairmen of FTSE 100 companies who have not yet served nine years in their current role but previously held non-executive director positions that bring total tenure beyond that point.

This includes Richard Gillingwater of energy supplier SSE and Sarah Bates of wealth manager St James's Place. Mr Gillingwater was appointed chair of SSE just two years ago but was first appointed to the board as a non-executive director in 2007. Ms Bates was made chair of SJP in 2014, a decade after she was first appointed to board as a non-executive director.

Vignette 1.3 (continued)

A corporate governance expert, speaking on condition of anonymity, said the proposals were likely to alarm both boardrooms and shareholders. 'This provision may get a lot of pushback from both corporates and investors. The FRC is right to focus upon the issue of chairman tenure, but I don't think it should be so mechanistic,' he said.

'If you have someone who has been on the board for five years and is a natural person to go on to become chairman, you don't want to acknowledge that they can only be chairman for four years.'

Another 48 chairmen of FTSE 250 companies would be affected, according to analysis of board tenure at the UK's largest listed companies by the Financial Times and Manifest, a research firm.

This includes Brian Mattingley, who was a non-executive director at betting company 888 for 11 years before becoming chair just 18 months ago.

The chairman of one of the affected FTSE 250 companies, speaking privately, agreed that the changes were too prescriptive, particularly because non-executive directors are not closely involved with the day-to-day running of companies.

However Richard Buxton, chief executive of Old Mutual Global Investors, one of the UK's largest fund companies, said it was a 'positive' move by the FRC to look at the total tenure of chairs.

He said he was 'surprised' by the number of chairmen who have spent more than nine years on a board because 'you really can't be deemed to be independent after that length of service'.

A public consultation on the proposed changes to the code is taking place until February. It is expected to be finalised by June.

 Source: Marriage, M. (2017) 'UK corporate governance code changes to hit dozens of chairmen', *Financial Times*, 11 December.
©The Financial Times Limited 2018. All Rights Reserved.

Question

What do you consider to be the pros and cons of having a maximum tenure of nine years for the members of a company's board?

The rate of increase of directors' salaries continues to be a contentious issue and was again put into the spotlight when the bosses of the UK's largest companies received average pay rises of 20 per cent during 2017. New legislation was consequently proposed in May 2018, requiring companies to justify the pay gap between CEOs and staff, and this is the subject of Vignette 1.4.

Vignette 1.4

UK to force companies to justify pay gap between CEOs and staff

By Tom Belger

The UK will require large listed companies to publish and justify the pay gap between chief executives and their staff from 2020 under new legislation to be presented to parliament on Monday.

Listed companies will also be required to show how future share price rises will affect executive pay as part of the sweeping reform of corporate governance unveiled by the Department for Business, Energy and Industrial Strategy (BEIS).

Vignette **1.4** (continued)

The law will see large public and private companies required to show how directors take into account the interests of employees as well as investors, and to report on their responsible business arrangements.

All listed companies with more than 250 employees in the UK will not only have to disclose the ratio of chief executives' salaries to their average workers every year, but also be required to explain the difference.

Matthew Fell, the CBI's chief UK policy officer, gave the measures a qualified welcome. 'High pay for mediocre or poor performance is unacceptable. This legislation can help to develop a better dialogue between boards and employees about the goals and aspirations of their business, and how pay is determined to achieve this shared vision.

'Ratio comparisons between sectors and firms will be as meaningless as comparing apples and oranges. What's most important is that all businesses make progress towards fair and proportionate pay outcomes.'

James Jarvis, corporate governance analyst at the Institute of Directors, said: 'Ratios are a pretty blunt tool, which will generate plenty of heat but not necessarily much light on the issue of executive pay.

'Large companies shouldn't perhaps be surprised they have come under this additional political pressure, however, given the examples we've seen of

bumper packages based on opaque long-term incentive plans.'

The new measures are part of a push by the government to address public anger over corporate behaviour after the collapse of Carillion and BHS, and reflect Theresa May's call for responsible capitalism shortly before she became prime minister.

The new regulations would come into effect from the start of next year, and companies would start reporting their pay ratios in 2020.

Greg Clark, the business secretary, said: 'One of Britain's biggest assets in competing in the global economy is our deserved reputation for being a dependable and confident place in which to do business.

'Most of the UK's largest companies get their business practices right but we understand the anger of workers and shareholders when bosses' pay is out of step with company performance.'

Frances O'Grady, general secretary of the TUC said: 'Publishing and justifying pay ratios is a first step, but more is needed. Fat cat bosses are masters of self-justification and shrugging off public outcry. New rules are needed to make sure they change.

'We need guaranteed places for worker representatives on boardroom pay committees. That would bring a bit of common sense and fairness to decision-making when boardroom pay packets are approved.'

 Source: Belger, T. (2018) 'UK to force companies to justify pay gap between CEOs and staff', *Financial Times*, 10 June.
©The Financial Times Limited 2018. All Rights Reserved.

Question

Do you consider the above proposal will be an effective mechanism to close the gap between executive pay and that of their staff?

1.6.2 Corporate governance in the USA

Traditionally the USA's approach to corporate governance has been driven more by legislation compared to the UK's 'comply or explain' philosophy. Since 2002 and the high-profile collapse of companies such as Enron and WorldCom, this is now even more the case. The USA's response in 2002 to these corporate failures and several major corporate scandals was to pass the Sarbanes-Oxley Act (also known as 'SOX'). This far-reaching legislation, detailed in 11 sections or mandates, overhauled existing financial reporting standards as well as establishing new ones. The Act created an overseer for all auditors (the Public Company Accounting Oversight Board), established auditor independence to limit conflicts of interest, and restricted auditing companies from providing consulting services to their audit clients. Under Section 302 it also required senior executives to take personal responsibility for both the accuracy and completeness of their company's financial reports. Section 404 of the Act introduced enhanced reporting requirements for financial transactions and internal controls to assure the accuracy of financial reports and disclosures. SOX was backed up in 2002 with stiff criminal penalties for financial fraud via the Corporate and Criminal Fraud Act and the Corporate Fraud Accountability Act.

Its supporters argue that SOX has restored confidence in US companies and financial markets, and in the US corporate accounting framework. Detractors argue that it has eroded the USA's international competitive advantage by introducing an excessively complex regulatory environment into US financial markets, causing companies to incur significant compliance costs in both time and money terms. Undoubtedly compliance costs are direct and easy to quantify, while the benefits are more indirect in nature. Butler and Ribstein (2006) argued that reducing investment risk by means of individual investors diversifying their investments was more efficient than reducing risk by means of companies spending significant amounts of time and money on SOX compliance. The Act, as with much US legislation, has had an extraterritorial impact as it affects all US subsidiaries outside of the USA. Some commentators have argued that SOX drove many non-US companies away from New York to London. Piotroski and Srinivasan (2008) found evidence that small foreign firms, post SOX, were choosing the UK's Alternative Investment Market (AIM) over the USA's NASDAQ exchange. This finding was consistent with prevailing opinion that SOX impacted more acutely on small firms. This was believed to be particularly true with respect to Section 404 (assessment of internal control by both company management and the external auditor) due to the significant fixed costs of compliance.

While the debate continues over whether SOX has brought net benefits to the USA, it is certain that the Act is here to stay. A significant development in US corporate governance since the introduction of SOX has been the signing by President Obama of the Dodd-Frank Wall Street Reform and Consumer Protection Act in July 2010. This requires US public companies to give shareholders a 'say on pay' with respect to their senior executives every three years. Since the adoption of this Act in January 2011, in only 2 per cent of cases have companies (such as Hewlett-Packard) had their executive pay packages rejected by shareholders.

1.7 CONCLUSION

In this chapter we have introduced two key concepts in financial management, namely the relationship between risk and return, and the time value of money. We have linked the time value of money to compounding and future values, and to discounting and present values. We clarified the role of the financial manager within a public company and established that their main aim should be to maximise the wealth of the company's shareholders. Other often-cited objectives, such as profit maximisation, survival and social responsibility, are of secondary importance. Shareholder wealth is maximised through financial managers making sound investment, financing and dividend decisions, taking account of the amount, timing and associated risk of future company cash flows, as these are the key variables driving shareholder wealth.

Unfortunately, managers are able to maximise their own wealth rather than that of shareholders. The agency problem can be tackled internally and externally. Internally, the two most common approaches are to offer performance-related pay or executive share option schemes to managers. These are far from perfect solutions, however. Externally, the terms and conditions of executive pay and the topical issues of corporate governance have been the subject of reports by a number of committees, including Cadbury, Greenbury, Hampel, Turnbull and Higgs. The recommendations of these committees are based on a principles-driven 'comply or explain' approach and differ greatly to the rule-based stance in the USA (the differences in corporate stewardship cultures in the USA and the UK are further highlighted in Vignette 1.5). While corporate governance requirements have undoubtedly helped to reduce the problem of agency in the UK, managerial remuneration continues to be a contentious issue. 'Fat cat' headlines in the financial press are unlikely to become a thing of the past without a significant change in human nature.

Finally, it would be appropriate to consider how Brexit will affect corporate governance in future years. Many commentators consider the impact of Brexit on UK corporate governance to be relatively low. The UK's governance system is considered to be robust and at the forefront of good practice around the globe. However, it will need to continually evolve and change in response to any new demands placed upon it by the impact of Brexit if the UK is to maintain its leading position.

Vignette 1.5

A very British split at the top

By Geoffrey Owen

'I'm the chairman, you're the managing director, and you will do what I tell you.' That statement, dating from the 1960s, belongs to an era in which many of Britain's biggest companies were led by a chairman who had near-absolute power. He – almost never she – was in effect chairman and chief executive, although the latter title was not widely used at that time. Today, the situation could hardly be more different. Most companies are run by a chief executive and alongside him or her is a chairman who is usually both part-time and 'independent' – that is, not someone who worked for the company before the appointment or had commercial links with it.

This has been one of the biggest changes in British corporate governance to have taken place since the 1960s and it has put the UK on a different path from other industrial countries. In the US, in spite of a recent increase in the number of independent chairmen, most companies combine the two posts in one person. There is some scepticism about the British approach, among academics as well as business leaders, mainly on the grounds that it can lead to conflict and confused responsibilities at the top. Has the UK got it right? Does the split structure make for better-performing companies? The answer, as shown by a study I have conducted on behalf of Spencer Stuart, the executive recruitment firm, of how boards have evolved over the past 50 years, is by no means clear.

Most of the current and former British chairmen and institutional investors who were interviewed for the study believe the British system is best. Their view is that too much concentration of power at the top is dangerous and that this cannot be offset by the US practice of appointing a lead director from among the outside board members to act as a partial counterweight to the chairman/chief executive. 'You've got to have a chairman whose job is to hire and fire the chief executive,' one interviewee said.

Another recalled how lonely he felt when he served both as chairman and chief executive. 'You end up talking to yourself and that is not a very healthy position. You think you have lots of friends but actually you haven't,' he said. Yet there was also frank recognition that the interface between chairman and chief executive in the British system is difficult to manage. Several chairmen had served on dysfunctional boards, and the source of the problem often lay in an unsatisfactory relationship between the two people at the top.

A newly appointed chairman may be taking on the job soon after serving as chief executive in another company, and this can be an awkward transition that needs more preparation and training than is usually provided. As chief executive, he or she was used to ruling the roost and probably enjoyed the limelight and status that went with the job.

To retreat to an advisory role takes a degree of self-restraint that can be unwelcome. This may be why some companies have appointed former chief financial officers as chairmen rather than former chief executives – although a background in finance does not necessarily provide the broad strategic overview needed in a chairman.

The dilemma that all chairmen face is how much or how little to intervene. At one extreme are chairmen who, perhaps for personality reasons or because of insufficient knowledge of the business, are unable to stand up to a dominant chief executive. At the other are chairmen who are tempted to second-guess the executive team.

'It is a very tricky balance,' one interviewee pointed out. 'The chairman has to be close to the chief executive while every now and then making it quite clear to the board that he is sceptical about a proposal. You trust him when he sides with the CEO but you know it will not always happen.'

It is hard to predict in advance how someone new to the chairman's role will perform. As one chairman said: 'Ideally, you want a dynamic CEO and a wiser, more prudent chairman, but whether you get that combination is pretty fortuitous – it does not happen in many cases.'

Another commented: 'The single most important thing is that the chairman has the interests of the company at heart and not other interests – not political interests, not personal interests over and above that.' The chairman needs to be qualified by ability and experience to run the company in an emergency, if for some reason the chief executive is unable to do the job and no successor is yet in place.

How important is knowledge of the sector in which the company is competing?

One interviewee said that the necessary mutual respect between chairman and chief executive 'can't happen if the chairman does not understand the industry. If you are ignorant, you can end up becoming a puppet.'

Sir David Walker's recent review of corporate governance in financial institutions suggested that in appointing board members some banks had overstressed independence at the expense of knowledge. Sir David pointed out that bank boards that had appointed the retiring chief executive as chairman, thus departing from the independence criteria laid down in the corporate governance code, had performed relatively well in the financial crisis.

Banking is special and it does not follow that, say, a pharmaceutical company will do better if its chairman is a pharmaceutical expert. Having worked in the industry is no guarantee that the appointee will be a good chairman; that depends much more on the individual's personal qualities.

Nevertheless, the study suggests that knowledge of the business, or at least experience in a related or similar business, should be given greater weight in the appointment of a new chairman. Two other conclusions emerged: the first is that the role of chairman has acquired greater importance in recent years. As one of the interviewees put it: 'Chairmen are having to work a lot harder and sometimes they have to take on the requirement to be the face of the company, dealing with external stakeholders as well as shareholders.'

This is most obvious at times of crisis, as at BP last year, but whenever a big company comes under attack in the media, the chairman often finds himself or herself in the line of fire. The second conclusion is that too many chairmen have been appointed who lack the necessary capabilities to do the job well. Those capabilities, which were usefully set out in the Walker review, are partly innate, such as stamina, courage and openness to new ideas, and partly learnable, including empathy, listening to all points of view, reaching conclusions without appearing to dominate, and building confidence in colleagues.

Good chairmen will always be hard to find but better preparation and more emphasis on the learnable parts of the job make it more likely that the board will function well.

Vignette 1.5 (continued)

Some US companies are looking to separate, too. Companies in the S&P 500 in which the chairman is:

	2010	2005
The current CEO	60%	71%
Independent	19%	9%
Non-executive, former CEO	5%	15%
Executive, former CEO	14%	3%
Outside-related	2%	2%

Source: Spencer Stuart 2010 Board Index.

The tendency in recent years has been for more US companies to separate the two top posts, and in a growing number of such cases the chairmanship has gone to an independent outsider.

Where the former CEO becomes chairman, he or she may continue to be employed by the company in an executive capacity, working alongside the new CEO or – less commonly – become non-executive chairman.

The 'outside-related' category includes individuals such as a controlling shareholder or someone who has a significant business relationship with the company but is not an employee.

 Source: Owen, G. (2011) 'A very British split at the top', *Financial Times*, 14 March. ©The Financial Times Limited 2011. All Rights Reserved.

Question

Given the two very different relationships that exist between chairman and CEO in US and UK companies, which do you consider will promote better corporate governance?

■ ■ ■ KEY POINTS

1   Two key concepts in corporate finance are the time value of money and the relationship between risk and return.

2   Compounding calculates future values from an initial investment. Discounting calculates present values from future values. Discounting can also calculate the present values of annuities and perpetuities.

3   While accountancy has an important role in corporate finance, the fundamental problem addressed by corporate finance is how best to allocate the scarce resource of cash.

4   Financial managers are responsible for making decisions about raising funds (the financing decision), allocating funds (the investment decision) and how much to distribute to shareholders (the dividend decision).

5   While objectives such as profit maximisation, social responsibility and survival represent important supporting objectives, the overriding objective of a company must be that of shareholder wealth maximisation.

6   Share price maximisation is a substitute objective to shareholder wealth maximisation.

7   A financial manager can maximise a company's market value by making investment, financing and dividend decisions consistent with shareholder wealth maximisation.

8   Managers do not always act in the best interests of their shareholders, giving rise to the agency problem.

9   The agency problem is likely to arise when there is a divergence of ownership and control, when the goals of managers differ from those of shareholders, and when asymmetry of information exists.

10 An example of the agency problem in a company is where managers diversify away unsystematic risk to reduce the company's risk, thereby increasing their job security.

11 Monitoring and performance-related benefits are potentially two ways to optimise managerial behaviour and encourage goal congruence with shareholders.

12 Owing to difficulties associated with monitoring, incentives such as performance-related pay and executive share options are a more practical way to encourage goal congruence.

13 UK institutional shareholders, who own approximately 29 per cent of all UK ordinary shares, have brought pressure to bear on companies that do not comply with corporate governance standards.

14 Corporate governance problems have received a lot of attention due to some high-profile corporate collapses and the publicising of self-serving executive pay packages.

15 The UK corporate governance system has traditionally stressed internal controls and financial reporting rather than external legislation.

16 In the UK, corporate governance is addressed by the Combined Code. In the US it is addressed by the Sarbanes-Oxley Act.

SELF-TEST QUESTIONS

Answers to these questions can be found on pages 451–2.

1 Explain how the concept of the time value of money can assist a financial manager in deciding between two investment opportunities.

2 Calculate the following values assuming a discount rate of 12 per cent:
   (a) £500 compounded for five years;
   (b) the present value of £500 received in five years' time;
   (c) the present value of £500 received each year forever;
   (d) the present value of £500 to be received each year for the next five years.

3 What are the functions and areas of responsibility under the control of the financial manager?

4 Give examples to illustrate the high level of interdependence between the decision areas of corporate finance.

5 Given the following corporate objectives, provide a reasoned argument explaining which of them should be the main goal of the financial manager:
   (a) profit maximisation;
   (b) sales maximisation;
   (c) maximisation of benefit to employees and the local community;
   (d) maximisation of shareholder wealth.

6 Explain how a financial manager can, in practice, maximise the wealth of shareholders.

7 What is meant by the 'agency problem' in the context of a public limited company? How is it possible for the agency problem to be reduced in a company?

8 Which of the following will not reduce the agency problem experienced by shareholders?
   (a) increased monitoring by shareholders;
   (b) salary bonuses for directors based on financial performance;
   (c) granting share options to directors;
   (d) including covenants in bond deeds;
   (e) using shorter contracts for management.

9 What goals might be pursued by managers instead of maximising shareholder wealth?

10 Do you consider the agency problem to be relevant to UK public limited companies?

QUESTIONS FOR REVIEW

1 The primary financial objective of a company is stated by corporate finance theory to be maximising shareholder wealth, but this objective is usually replaced by the surrogate objective of maximising a company's share price. Discuss how this substitution can be justified.

2 Explain why maximising a company's share price is preferred as a financial objective to maximising its sales.

3 Discuss how the concepts of agency theory can be used to explain the relationship that exists between the managers of a listed company and its shareholders. Your answer should include an explanation of the following terms:

   (a) asymmetry of information;

   (b) agency costs;

   (c) the free-rider problem.

4 You are given the following details about Facts of Life plc, a company in the conglomerate sector.

   Breakdown of activities by percentage of total annual company turnover:

Department stores:	30%
Clothing:	24%
Building materials:	20%
Hotels and catering:	16%
Electronics:	10%

Current share price:	£2.34
Average annual share price growth over the past five years:	5%
Conglomerate sector average annual share price growth over the past five years:	9%
Level of gearing based on market values (debt/debt + equity):	23%
Conglomerate sector gearing level based on market values (debt/debt + equity):	52%

   The directors of the company were given share options by its remuneration committee five years ago. In one year's time the share options will allow each director to buy 100,000 shares in the company at a price of £2.00. The directors' average annual salary currently stands at £200,000 on a five-year rolling contract basis, while average annual salaries in the conglomerate sector are £150,000 and tend to be three-year rolling contracts.

   (a) Using the above information to illustrate your answer, critically discuss the extent to which Facts of Life plc can be said to be suffering from the agency problem.

   (b) Discuss how the issues you have identified in part (a) can be addressed to reduce the agency problem.

QUESTIONS FOR DISCUSSION

1 Discuss ways in which a company's shareholders can encourage its managers to act in a way which is consistent with the objective of maximising shareholder wealth.

2 The primary financial objective of corporate finance is usually taken to be the maximisation of shareholder wealth. Discuss what other objectives may be important to a public limited company and whether such objectives are consistent with the primary objective of shareholder wealth maximisation.

3 Discuss whether recent UK initiatives in the area of corporate governance have served to diminish the agency problem with respect to UK listed companies.

4 Critically evaluate the differing approaches taken by the US and UK governments to address the shortcomings of their corporate governance systems.

References

Butler, H. and Ribstein, L. (2006) *The Sarbanes–Oxley Debacle: What We've Learned; How to Fix it*, Washington: AEI Press.

Cadbury Committee (1992) *Committee on the Financial Aspects of Corporate Governance: Final Report*, December.

Financial Reporting Council (2005) *Review of the Turnbull Guidance on Internal Control*, June.

Financial Reporting Council (2010) *The UK Stewardship Code*, July.

Financial Reporting Council (2016) *The UK Corporate Governance Review*, June.

Friedman, M. (1970) 'The social responsibility of business is to increase its profits', *New York Magazine*, 30 September.

Grant Thornton (2018) *Corporate Governance Review*, October.

Greenbury, R. (1995) *Directors' Remuneration: Report of a Study Group Chaired by Sir Richard Greenbury*, London: Gee & Co.

Hampel Committee (1998) *Final Report*, January.

Hayek, F. (1960) 'The corporation in a democratic society: in whose interest ought it and should it be run?', in Asher, M. and Bach, C. (eds) *Management and Corporations*, New York: McGraw-Hill.

Higgs Report (2003) *Review of the Role and Effectiveness of Non-executive Directors*, January.

Jensen, M. and Meckling, W. (1976) 'Theory of the firm: managerial behaviour, agency costs and ownership structure', *Journal of Financial Economics*, vol. 3, pp. 305–60.

Piotroski, J. and Srinivasan, S. (2008) 'Regulation and bonding: the Sarbanes-Oxley Act and the flow of international listings', *Journal of Accounting Research*, vol. 46, no. 2, May, pp. 383–425.

Smith Report (2003) *Audit Committees: Combined Code Guidance*, January.

Turnbull Report (1999) *Internal Control: Guidance for Directors on the Combined Code,* London: Institute of Chartered Accountants in England and Wales.

Tyson Report (2003) *Tyson Report on the Recruitment and Development of Non-executive Directors,* June, London Business School.

Recommended reading

For an informative chapter which gives a US perspective on the problem of agency and how it can be solved by financial contracting see:

Emery, D., Stowe, J. and Finnerty, J. (2012) *Corporate Financial Management,* 4th edn, Tennessee: Ingram, Chapter 14: Agency Theory.

For a comprehensive insight into the world of corporate governance see:

Tricker, B. (2015) *Corporate Governance: Principles, Policies and Practices,* 3rd edn, New York: Oxford University Press.

Important and informative papers and articles recommended for further reading include:

Charkham, J. (1993) 'The Bank and corporate governance: past, present and future', *Bank of England Quarterly Bulletin,* August, pp. 388–92.

Fama, E. (1980) 'Agency problems and the theory of the firm', *Journal of Political Economy,* vol. 88, April, pp. 288–307.

Gompers, P., Ishii, J. and Metrick, A. (2003) 'Corporate governance and equity prices', *Journal of Economics,* vol. 118, no. 1, February, pp. 107–55.

Grinyer, J. (1986) 'Alternatives to maximization of shareholder wealth', *Accounting and Business Research,* Autumn.

Srinivasan, S. and Coates, J. (2014) 'SOX after ten years: a multidisciplinary review', *Accounting Horizons,* vol. 28, no. 3, September, pp. 627–71.

A useful website for information on corporate governance in the UK is that of the Financial Reporting Council at: http://www.frc.org.uk

For a broader, more international take on corporate governance see the International Corporate Governance Network website: http://www.icgn.org

2 CAPITAL MARKETS, MARKET EFFICIENCY AND RATIO ANALYSIS

Learning objectives

After studying this chapter, you should have achieved the following learning objectives:

- an appreciation of the range of internal and external sources of finance available to a company, and of the factors influencing the relative proportions of internal and external finance;

- an understanding of the significance of the capital markets to a company;

- an understanding of the importance of the efficient market hypothesis to corporate finance and an ability to explain the difference between the various forms of market efficiency;

- an appreciation of the empirical research that has been undertaken to establish the extent to which capital markets may be efficient in practice;

- the ability to calculate key ratios from corporate financial statements and an understanding of their significance in corporate finance;

- an appreciation of the difficulties relating to calculating and interpreting financial ratios;

- an appreciation of the concepts of economic profit and economic value added and their relationship with shareholder wealth.

■ ■ ■ INTRODUCTION

Capital markets are places where companies needing long-term finance can meet investors who offer finance. This finance may be equity finance from issuing new ordinary shares or debt finance, in which case companies can choose from a wide range of loans and debt securities. Capital markets are also places where investors buy and sell company and government securities. Their trading decisions reflect information on company performance provided by financial statements and financial analysis, dividend announcements by companies, market expectations on future levels of interest rates and inflation and investment decisions made by companies.

Both companies and investors want capital markets to assign fair prices to the securities being traded. In the language of corporate finance, companies and investors want the capital markets to be *efficient*. The characteristics of an efficient capital market can be described by considering the relationship between market prices and the information available to the market. Whether capital markets are in fact efficient is a question that has been studied for many years and, in the first part of this chapter, we focus on the key topic of the efficient market hypothesis.

Shareholders make decisions on which shares to add or remove from their portfolios. Investors such as banks and other financial institutions make decisions about whether, and at what price, to offer finance to companies. Financial managers make decisions in the key areas of investment, financing and dividends. Shareholders, investors and financial managers can inform their decisions by evaluating the financial performance of companies using information from financial statements, financial databases, the financial press and the Internet. Ratio analysis of financial statements can provide useful historical information on the profitability, solvency, efficiency and risk of individual companies. By using performance measures such as economic profit and **economic value added** (EVA®), company performance can be linked more closely with shareholder value and shareholder wealth, and attention can be directed to ways in which companies can create more value for shareholders.

2.1 SOURCES OF BUSINESS FINANCE

One of the key decision areas for corporate finance is the question of how a company finances its operations. If finance is not raised efficiently, the ability of a company to accept desirable projects will be adversely affected and the profitability of its existing operations may suffer. An efficient financing policy aims to raise the amount of funds needed, at the time they are needed, at the lowest possible cost. There is clearly a link between the financing decisions made by a company's managers and the wealth of the company's shareholders. For a financing policy to be efficient, however, companies need to be aware of the sources of finance available to them.

2.1.1 Internal finance

Sources of finance can be conveniently divided into external finance and internal finance. By internal finance we mean cash generated by a company which is not needed to meet operating costs, interest payments, tax liabilities, cash dividends or replacement of non-current assets. This surplus cash is commonly called *retained earnings* in corporate finance. The statement of profit or loss shows the profit generated by a company rather than the cash available for investment, which is best indicated by the statement of cash flows. Retained earnings in the financial position statement does not represent funds that can be invested. Only cash can be invested. A company with substantial retained earnings in its financial position statement, no cash in the bank and a large overdraft will not be able to finance investment from retained earnings.

Another internal source of finance that is often overlooked is savings generated by more efficient management of working capital. This is the capital associated with short-term assets and liabilities (see 'Working capital and the cash conversion cycle', Section 3.3). More efficient management of inventories, trade receivables, cash and trade payables can reduce investment in working capital, thereby reducing a bank overdraft and its interest charges, or increasing the level of cash.

2.1.2 External finance

The many kinds of external finance available can be split broadly into debt and equity finance. External finance can also be classified according to whether it is short-term (less than one year), medium-term (between one year and five years) or long-term (more than five years), and according to whether it is traded on a stock exchange (e.g. ordinary shares and **bonds**) or untraded (e.g. bank loans). An indication of the range of financial instruments associated with external finance and their interrelationships is given in Figure 2.1. You will find it useful to refer to this figure as you study this and subsequent chapters.

The distinction between equity finance and debt finance is of key importance in corporate finance and for this reason we devote whole chapters to these external sources of long-term finance: equity finance (ordinary shares and **preference shares**) is discussed in detail in 'Long-term finance: equity finance' (Chapter 4) and debt finance (corporate bonds, bank debt and leasing) is discussed in 'Long-term finance: debt finance, hybrid finance and leasing' (Chapter 5). Short-term finance is discussed in 'Short-term finance and managing working capital' (Chapter 3).

2.1.3 The balance between internal and external finance

Retained earnings, the major source of internal finance, may be preferred to external finance by companies for several reasons:

■ Companies view retained earnings as a ready source of cash.
■ The decision on how much to pay shareholders (and hence on how much to retain) is an internal one and does not require a company to present a funding case to a third party.

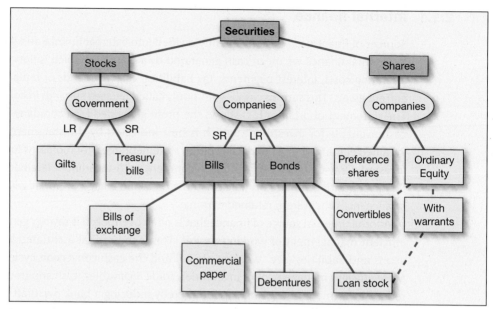

Figure 2.1 The variety of financial instruments that can be used by a company to raise finance

- Retained earnings have no issue costs.
- There is no dilution of control as might occur with issuing new equity shares.
- There are no restrictions on business operations as might arise with issuing new debt.

The amount of retained earnings available will be limited by the cash flow from business operations. Most companies will therefore need at some stage to consider external sources of finance if they need to raise funds for investment projects or to expand operating activities. The decision concerning the relative proportions of internal and external finance to be used for a capital investment project will depend on the following factors.

The level of finance required

It may be possible for a company to finance small investments from retained earnings, for example replacing existing non-current assets or undertaking minor new investment projects. Larger projects are likely to require funds from outside the company.

The cash flow from existing operations

If the cash flow from existing operations is strong, a higher proportion of the finance needed for investment projects can be found internally. If the cash flow from existing operations is weak, a company will be more dependent on external financing.

The opportunity cost of retained earnings

Retained earnings are cash funds that belong to shareholders (as the owners of the company) and so can be classed as equity financing. This means they have a required rate of return which is equal to the best return that shareholders could obtain on their funds if they were invested elsewhere in the financial markets. The best alternative return available to shareholders is called the *opportunity cost* of retained earnings and, as discussed in 'Equity finance' (Section 4.1) and 'Calculating the cost of individual sources of finance' (Section 9.1), the required return on equity (the **cost of equity**) is greater than the required return on debt (the **cost of debt**).

The costs associated with raising external finance

By using retained earnings, companies can avoid the issue costs associated with raising external finance and will not make commitments to servicing fixed-interest debt.

The availability of external sources of finance

The external sources of finance available to a company will depend on its circumstances. A company which is not listed on a stock exchange, for example, will find it difficult to raise large amounts of equity finance, while a company with a large proportion of debt finance and therefore seen as risky will find it difficult to raise further debt.

Dividend policy

The dividend policy of a company (Chapter 10) will have a direct impact on the amount of retained earnings available for investment. A company which consistently pays out a high proportion of **distributable profits** as dividends will not have much by way of retained earnings and so is likely to use a higher proportion of external finance when funding investment projects.

2.2 CAPITAL MARKETS

Capital markets are markets for trading long-term financial securities, illustrated in Figure 2.1. The most important ones for companies are ordinary shares, long-term debt securities such as secured bonds or loan notes (**debentures**), unsecured bonds and **convertible bonds**, and, to a much lesser extent, preference shares. Eurobonds and public-sector securities, such as **Treasury bills** and gilts (gilt-edged bonds), also trade on capital markets.

Capital markets have two main functions. First, they are where long-term funds can be raised by companies from those with funds to invest, such as financial institutions and private investors. In fulfilling this function, they are **primary markets** for new issues of equity and debt. Second, capital markets allow investors to sell their shares and bonds, or buy new ones to place in their portfolios; here, capital markets act as **secondary markets** for dealing in existing securities. The secondary market plays a key role in corporate finance, because by facilitating the buying and selling of securities it increases their liquidity and hence their value. Investors would pay more for a security that will be easy to sell in the future. The secondary market is also a source of pricing information for the primary market and consequently helps to increase the efficiency with which the primary market allocates new funds to their best use.

The London Stock Exchange is the main UK market for equity and bonds. Ways of obtaining a listing (quotation) on this market are considered in 'New issue methods' (Section 4.2.2).

Smaller companies that are unable to seek a listing on the main market of the LSE can apply for a listing on the **Alternative Investment Market (AIM)**, which has been operated by the LSE since 1995. The average market value of AIM companies is approximately £140m. The AIM is both a primary and a secondary market for the shares of small and growing companies and has enjoyed a debatable degree of success to date. Unlike the LSE's main market, the AIM does not have any qualifying restrictions on market capitalisation, length of trading record or percentage of shares required to be held in public hands. The number of companies listed on the AIM has declined in recent years and the market has been experiencing volatility, as indicated in Vignette 2.1. Decisions on whether to invest in companies listed on the AIM or elsewhere depend on having access to relevant information, which is the one of the topics considered in the next section on market efficiency.

Vignette 2.1

Aim investors should hold their nerve despite volatility

Analysts recommend reassessing risks and targeting established companies

By Andy Bounds

The FTSE has had a rough ride over the past three weeks as volatility returned to the market. But what of its little brother, Aim? Investors tend to dump smaller companies first when trouble threatens, believing multinationals are the safer harbour in a storm.

The Aim Allshare fell faster and further than the FTSE 100. The slide started on January 29 and accelerated in early February. There was a rally before it hit its floor on Feb 6. The index dropped 5.8 per cent from 1,076 to 1,013. It has since recovered and on Friday closed at 1,039.

The FTSE 100 meanwhile dropped 4.4 per cent from peak to trough. However, the FTSE 350 index of the biggest 350 businesses was down 7.4 per cent. So is it time abandon the minnows and back the bigger fish? Russ Mould, investment director at AJ Bell, which helps people invest directly, said it is time for a reappraisal of risk – but not to go too far. After an eight-year bull run, 'this is the beginning of the end rather than the end,' he said. He detects signs of

2006 and 1996, when ripples began after years of calm, eventually leading to a crash.

Short of a sudden economic shock he expects gradual decline. And after the liquidation of Carillion – the outsourcer that until last year was making good money and paying dividends – he warned that other big companies could hold nasty surprises.

'People will naturally gravitate towards profitable cash-generative stocks but are you going to get a tap on the shoulder for more money?'

He points to Galliford Try – a construction group that has moved to shore up its balance sheet in the wake of Carillion's collapse – and Cineworld, which needs to raise money to buy US rival Regal. 'There will be more cash calls. Many finance directors are thinking: If winter is coming we might need a bit more security.'

He suggests concentrating on established Aim-listed companies with profits and dividend flows. Scapa, a maker of adhesive tape, retailer Hotel

Vignette 2.1 (continued)

Chocolat, and pub company Young's have all put in decent performances, he said.

'There is still scope for growth at a reasonable price on Aim.' Gervais Williams, the small-cap fund manager at Miton Group, believes investors should hold their nerve.

He manages stakes in about 250 Aim companies across three funds. He cites the performance of early-stage, pre-profit stocks – such as AI software company Blue Prism – which have tracked the market. In past slumps they would have dropped far faster as investors fled risk, he said. 'Companies with established business models should still do well.'

There are some obvious examples: online retailers Asos and Boohoo are worth billions but remain on Aim. Meanwhile, fewer companies are coming on to the market: the number of Aim-listed companies fell to 960 at the end of the year, a 14-year low. With a dearth of new arrivals, investors are backing existing companies.

'The big surprise has been the vibrancy of secondary issues,' said Mr Williams: 166 companies raised £278m from secondary issues in January. In December, 196 companies raised £755m, including £150m from just one company, Smart Metering Systems. Last January, 136 companies raised £161m.

In all, 2017 was the best year since 2010 for money raising on Aim, with a total of £6.4bn, of which £4.8bn came in secondary issues.

Mr Williams said the low prices of many thinly traded Aim stocks have put companies off listing. So the lightly regulated market looks increasingly like its staid big brother, with established companies raising investment money.

Source: Bounds, A. (2018) 'Aim investors should hold their nerve despite volatility', *Financial Times,* 18 February. © The Financial Times Limited 2018. All Rights Reserved.

Question

Can the Alternative Investment Market be described as successful?

2.3 CAPITAL MARKET EFFICIENCY

What are the desirable features of capital markets such as the LSE's main market and the AIM? Dixon and Holmes (1992) suggest that transaction costs should be as low as possible, so that barriers to trading on capital markets are reduced and *operational efficiency* is promoted. Primary markets should direct funds to their most productive uses so that capital markets have *allocational efficiency.* This calls for fair prices to be provided by the secondary market, so activity on the primary market should have only a minimal effect on secondary market prices. This points to the need for *pricing efficiency,* which means that the prices of securities should reflect all relevant available information. Relevant information must be cheap to obtain and freely available to all, highlighting the need for *informational efficiency.*

2.3.1 Perfect markets and efficient markets

There are many references in corporate finance theory to perfect markets and efficient markets. According to Megginson (1997), a perfect market has the following characteristics:

■ the absence of factors inhibiting buying and selling, such as taxes or transaction costs;

■ all participants have the same expectations regarding asset prices, interest rates and other economic factors;

- entry to and exit from the market is free;
- information has no cost and is freely available to all market participants;
- many buyers and sellers, none of whom dominates the market.

Clearly, no stock market anywhere in the world is a perfect market. However, companies and investors do not need capital markets to be perfect; rather, they need capital markets to be efficient and to offer fair prices, so they can make reasoned investment and financing decisions. From our earlier discussion, we therefore expect an efficient capital market to have the following features:

- Operational efficiency: transaction costs in the market should be as low as possible and any trading can be quickly achieved.
- Pricing efficiency: the prices of capital market securities, such as shares and bonds, fully and fairly reflect all information concerning past events and all events that the market expects to occur in the future. The prices of securities are therefore fair prices.
- Allocational efficiency: the capital market, through the medium of pricing efficiency, allocates funds to where they can best be used.

The efficient market hypothesis is concerned with establishing the prices of capital market securities and states that the prices of securities fully and fairly reflect all relevant available information (Fama 1970). Market efficiency therefore refers to both the speed and the quality (i.e. direction and magnitude) of the price adjustment to new information. Testing markets for efficiency has led to the recognition of three different forms of market efficiency.

2.3.2 Different forms of market efficiency

Empirical tests of the efficiency of capital markets have investigated the extent to which share prices (security prices) reflect relevant information (i.e. pricing efficiency) because of a lack of data for testing allocational efficiency and operational efficiency. Many studies have investigated the extent to which it is possible for investors to make abnormal returns, which are returns greater than expected returns, or returns greater than those predicted by valuation methods such as the dividend growth model (see 'The dividend growth model', Section 10.4.3) and the capital asset pricing model (see Chapter 8).

Weak form efficiency

Capital markets are weak form efficient if current share prices reflect all *historical* information, such as past share price movements. This means it is not possible to make abnormal returns in such a market by using **technical analysis** to study past share price movements (see below). Empirical evidence strongly supports the view that capital markets are weak form efficient.

Semi-strong form efficiency

Capital markets are semi-strong form efficient if current share prices reflect all historical information and all publicly available information, and if share prices react quickly and accurately to incorporate any new information as it becomes available. This means abnormal returns cannot be made in a semi-strong form efficient market by studying publicly available company information or by using **fundamental analysis** (see below). Empirical studies support the proposition that well-developed capital markets are semi-strong form efficient.

Strong form efficiency

Capital markets are said to be strong form efficient if share prices reflect all information, whether it is publicly available or not. If markets are strong form efficient, no one can make abnormal returns from share dealing, not even investors who act on 'insider information'. Capital markets clearly do not meet all the conditions for strong form efficiency, since some investors do make abnormal returns by insider dealing, as shown by occasional prosecutions for this offence. However, the number of these is small compared with the volume of transactions in the capital market as a whole.

2.3.3 Testing for market efficiency

Weak form tests

If a capital market is weak form efficient, so that share prices reflect completely all past information, it will not be possible for investors to predict future share prices by studying past share price movements. Share prices will change as new information arrives on the market and, since new information arrives at random, share price movements will also appear to be random (Samuelson 1965). Many empirical studies have supported the proposition that the movement of share prices over time represents a random walk. This **random walk hypothesis** states that, if we know the share price at the end of one period, we cannot predict accurately the share price at the end of the next period. Research strongly supports the view that the relationship between share prices in different periods on well-developed capital markets is random, although no consensus view has been reached (Shamshir and Mustafa 2014), in which case we can say that research strongly supports the view that well-developed capital markets are weak form efficient.

Empirical studies of weak form efficiency have used serial correlation tests, run tests and filter tests. One of the earliest studies testing for *serial correlation* looked for any correlation between security price changes at different points in time (Kendall 1953). The evidence from this and other studies tends to support the random walk hypothesis. Studies using *run tests* (e.g. Fama 1965) consider whether any significance can be attached to the direction of price changes by examining the length of the runs of successive price changes of the same sign. The empirical evidence indicates that the direction of price changes on any one day was independent of the direction of price changes on any other day. The distribution of directions was found to be based on pure chance, adding further support to the view that capital markets are weak form efficient. *Filter tests* try to identify any significant long-term relationships in security price movements by filtering out short-term price changes. One early study found that while filter tests could provide abnormal returns compared with a simple *buy and hold* strategy, gains were cancelled out when transaction costs were considered (Alexander 1961).

More recent studies have found weak evidence that a period of above-average returns may follow a long period of below-average returns (mean reversion), but the weak form of the efficient market hypothesis is still broadly supported (Beechey et al. 2000; Hudson et al. 1996; Megginson 1997; Timmerman and Granger 2004). It has also been argued from an insider perspective that trading strategies based on anomalies do not generate abnormal returns (Roll 1994).

Recent research has indicated that emerging capital markets may be weak form inefficient (Gupta and Basu 2007; Magnus 2008; Shamshir and Mustafa 2014; Worthington and Higgs 2006), with the lower levels of liquidity and turnover associated with such markets suggested as contributory factors.

Semi-strong form tests

Tests for semi-strong form efficiency look at the speed and accuracy of share price responses to new information (event studies). In general, event studies support the view that capital markets are semi-strong form efficient.

An examination of the adjustment of share prices to the release of information about share splits (see 'Scrip issues and share splits', Section 4.4.1) found it was not possible to profit from the information because the market seemed to incorporate it efficiently and effectively (Fama et al. 1969). Similar findings were reached regarding earnings announcements (Ball and Brown 1968) and merger announcements (Keown and Pinkerton 1981). In fact, possible benefits arising from mergers were found to be anticipated by the capital market up to three months prior to any announcements (Franks et al. 1977). While event studies support the semi-strong form of the efficient market hypothesis, they also offer evidence of anomalies, such as the observation that share prices continue to rise (or fall) for a substantial period following the release of positive (or negative) information (Beechey et al. 2000). It has also been found that the more frequently a share is traded, the shorter is the time required for its price to return to equilibrium having absorbed new information (Manganelli 2002).

Strong form tests

Because some people have access to information before other investors and so can make abnormal gains, it can be argued that capital markets are not strong form efficient. It is not possible to test for strong form efficiency directly by investigating the market's use of insider information, since, by definition, this information is unknown. Tests for strong form efficiency are therefore *indirect* in approach: they examine how *expert users* of information perform when compared against a yardstick such as a stock market index or the average return on the market.

Fund managers with resources to invest in discovering and analysing information may be in a position to make abnormal gains. If their funds achieved above-average performances on a regular basis, this would be evidence that capital markets are not strong form efficient. A classic study of 115 mutual funds found that the majority did not make above-average returns when management costs were considered: in fact, their performance was inferior to a passive *buy and hold* strategy (Jensen 1968). Research continues to show that actively managed funds underperform the market after accounting for management costs, and in many cases before accounting for management costs as well (Beechey et al. 2000; Megginson 1997).

The interaction between stock market indices, management costs and fund manager performance is the subject of Vignette 2.2.

It has also been shown that investors could not benefit from the investment advice of financial tipsters (insider information becoming public information) due to the speed with which the market factored new information into share prices (Firth 1972).

Vignette 2.2

Indices don't just measure markets – they drive performance

Expectation of lower future returns focuses attention on fees charged by active funds

By John Authers

Indices no longer merely measure markets. They move them.

This has been growing clearer for years, as both individual savers and big institutions yank money from 'active' managers, who attempt to outperform the market using good stock selection, and into 'passive' funds, which try only to track a benchmark index. Both 'active' and 'passive' are in many ways misnomers and the dividing line between them is no longer clear, but the terms have stuck so I will use them.

This week saw three big developments in index world and in all cases, changes in the index moved the market and not vice versa. Tuesday brought news that General Electric was to be booted from the Dow Jones Industrial Average. GE had been a member of the Dow for more than a century, and its departure means that the Dow no longer holds any of its original members.

The Dow Industrials is only a historical curiosity. Although widely quoted, only about $29.5bn of funds are benchmarked against it. More than 300 times as much tracks the S&P 500, of which GE remains a member. But investors were so excited to see that Walgreens Boots Alliance, a chain of pharmacies, had taken GE's place that they bid its stock up by 3 per cent, on Wednesday.

Wednesday brought the annual reclassification of countries by MSCI, the indexing group that in effect controls the definition of which countries are 'emerging markets'. Its decision to re-promote Argentina, and grant Saudi Arabia EM status for the first time, was a big deal. Argentina's Merval index rallied 6 per cent on Thursday.

Friday brought 'Russell Recon', the day when the Russell indices, part of FTSE Russell, shuffle companies between indices of small- and large-cap stocks, demoting some and promoting others. This is now annually the day when the heaviest trading is done on the New York Stock Exchange. Before trading began on Friday, some $57bn was expected to change hands, as funds adjusted for companies that had moved in and out of the Russell 2000 small-cap index.

With some $8.5tn benchmarked against Russell indices, according to Melissa Roberts of KBW in New York, and with $1tn following them passively, changes in the index can only have a big effect. As Russell's method of selection is particularly transparent (unlike for the Dow or the MSCI indices where more judgment is involved), investors can trade ahead of the changes – meaning that on average, stocks that move index trade 45 times their normal volume on the day of reconstitution. Generally, new additions to the Russell 2000 handily beat the market in the days leading up to reconstitution.

If it is clear that indices move the market, it is not obvious that anything will stop them. Evidence continues to mount that active funds tend to lag their benchmark over time, largely because of the

Vignette 2.2 (continued)

fees they need to charge to pay for the considerable costs involved in attempting to beat the market.

For big institutions such as pension funds, the risk-adjusted return matters most – not just how well a fund did by the end of a journey, but how volatile the ride was to get there. One argument by active managers is that they also do active risk management, ensuring a smoother ride, albeit possibly at the expense of a little return. Index funds have no choice but to track the market's every lurch; so active funds can show their worth in times of greater volatility.

S&P's SPIVA project compares active funds' performance to their benchmarks and has found that over long periods less than 10 per cent outperform. It has now produced a risk-adjusted return – dividing both the index and active fund returns by the standard deviation of those returns, a standard measure of their volatility.

It turned out funds were no more likely to beat their benchmark on a risk-adjusted basis than on a comparison of returns. Net of fees, 95 per cent of US large-cap funds lagged behind the S&P 500. Even before fees, 84 per cent lagged behind. More than 80 per cent of global funds lagged behind after fees. Exceptions included loan participation

funds, where only 28 per cent have lagged behind their benchmark after fees for the last five years. But the exercise confirms that the index is difficult to beat, even on a risk-adjusted basis, and that the costs of undertaking the attempt tend to doom it to failure.

This does not mean that the big pension funds who have been buying up passive funds in recent years are convinced of the traditional case for passive investing. Amin Rajan of Create-Research interviewed 153 pension managers in 25 countries on the issue and found that many expected to increase their use of passives still further.

This was largely out of a pragmatic belief that when macro factors such as central bank policy are driving markets (as they have done for a decade), then allocating assets is far more important than selecting stocks. Even when this changes, investors doubt that they will pile back into active funds, because total returns will be much lower, so fees will matter more. As one manager put it: 'Fees have become the North Star of investing.'

Indices are leading and distorting markets, in ways that worry many investors who buy passive funds. There is no reason to expect this to change.

 Source: Authers, J. (2018) 'Indices don't just measure markets – they drive performance', *Financial Times,* 23 June. © The Financial Times Limited 2018. All Rights Reserved.

Questions

1 Does the movement of cash into passive funds suggest that a 'buy and hold' strategy is best?

2 If the costs of undertaking to beat the index 'tend to doom it to failure', can we say the market is strong form efficient?

2.3.4 Implications of the efficient market hypothesis

What are the implications for investors if the stock market is efficient?

- Paying for investment research will not produce above-average returns.
- Studying published accounts and investment tips will not produce above-average returns.
- There are no bargains (underpriced shares) to be found on the stock market.

For a company and its managers, the implications of stock market efficiency are as follows:

- The share price of a company fairly reflects its value and market expectations about its future performance and returns. The financial manager should therefore focus on making 'good' financial decisions which increase shareholder wealth as the market will interpret these decisions correctly and the share price will adjust accordingly.

■ Cosmetic manipulation of accounting information, whether by window dressing financial statements or by massaging earnings per share, will not mislead the market.

■ The timing of new issues of shares is not important since shares are never mispriced.

2.3.5 Technical and fundamental analysis

The efficient market hypothesis suggests that future share prices cannot be predicted by studying past prices and, as we have seen, there is extensive evidence to support this view. Despite the evidence, investment strategies based on the study of past share prices, or on the analysis of published information such as financial statements, are common, and the view held by many financial analysts therefore seems to be that capital markets are inefficient.

Technical analysis involves the use of charts (**Chartism**) and other methods to predict future share prices and share price trends, clearly implying that a relationship exists between past and future prices. For technical analysis to lead to abnormal returns on a regular basis, capital markets cannot even be weak form efficient. Fundamental analysis uses public information to calculate a fundamental value for a share and then offers investment advice by comparing the fundamental value with the current market price. It is not possible to make abnormal gains from fundamental analysis if capital markets are semi-strong form efficient, since all publicly available information will already be reflected in share prices.

Note that both technical analysis and fundamental analysis, by seeking abnormal returns, increase the speed with which share prices absorb new information and reach equilibrium, thereby preventing abnormal returns from being achieved.

2.3.6 Anomalies in share price behaviour

Even though there is widespread acceptance that share prices respond quickly and accurately to new information, we have noted that research into market efficiency has produced evidence of anomalies in share price behaviour. Many such anomalies have been reported and investigated in the quest to understand share price behaviour (Fama 1998), of which the following are examples.

Calendar effects

It has been reported that trading at particular times of the day can lead to negative or positive returns. For example, it appears that trading during the first 45 minutes on Monday mornings produces negative returns (the 'weekend effect'), whereas share prices tend to rise during the last 15 minutes of trading. While these effects have been reported, no satisfactory explanation has been offered. One suggestion is that investors evaluate their portfolios at weekends and sell on Monday mornings, whereas brokers initiate buy decisions regularly during the week. However, a 'reverse' weekend effect has been reported in a study (Brusa et al. 2005) that concluded that the weekend effect was related to both firm size and the nature of Friday trading.

High returns have also been noted in particular months, for example April in the UK and January in the USA. It is possible that these high returns are due to selling strategies designed to crystallise capital losses for tax purposes (known as bed and breakfasting) as the start of April is the end of the UK tax year. Share prices will be depressed at the start of April by such selling, but will recover as the new tax year begins. A trading strategy of buying at the start of the month and selling at the end may produce high returns in the UK in April.

Size anomalies

The returns from investing in smaller companies have been shown, in the long run, to be greater than the average return from all companies. One study, for example, found that small firms outperformed large firms by 6 per cent per year (Dimson and Marsh 1986). It has been suggested that above-average returns from small companies may compensate for the greater risk associated with them, such as the risk of financial distress (Beechey et al. 2000). It is possible that the growth prospects of smaller companies are better because they start from a lower base. However, it has been noted that small companies account for only a small proportion of the equity trading on major stock exchanges and so studies of small-firm effects have little macroeconomic significance (Fama 1991).

Value effects

Above-average returns can apparently be gained by investing in *value stocks,* which are shares with high earnings, cash flows or tangible assets relative to current share price, i.e. by investing in shares with low price/earnings ratios, as summarised by Beechey et al. (2000). It has also been shown that abnormal returns can be gained by investing in a portfolio of shares with poor past returns (De Bondt and Thaler 1985).

2.3.7 Behavioural finance

Behavioural finance suggests that investors do not appear in practice to be consistently able to make decisions that have as their objective the maximisation of their own wealth. This may be because they fail to update their information correctly (Small and Smith 2007) or because they do not make utility-maximising choices. Behavioural finance seeks to understand the market implications of the psychological factors underlying investor decisions and offers an alternative view of financial market activity to the efficient market hypothesis. It suggests that irrational investor behaviour can have significant and long-lasting effects on share price movements. While behavioural finance has not yet provided a unified theory of investor behaviour, it has had some success in explaining some anomalies in share price behaviour such as over-reaction to past price changes. A detailed discussion of behavioural finance is beyond the scope of this text; interested readers are referred to the excellent books by Shleifer (2000) and Haugen (2009), and to the survey by Barberis and Thaler (2002).

2.3.8 Summary

The existence of anomalies in share price behaviour suggests there are times when some share prices are not fair. Support for the efficient market hypothesis was almost universal before 1980. Since then, the theory has been regarded as an *incomplete* explanation of share price behaviour, with behavioural finance offering a growing challenge to the efficient market hypothesis.

Research suggests that the UK and US stock markets, as well as many other world-class stock markets, respond quickly and accurately to new information, and that only through insider dealing can investors make abnormal gains. Since such cases are rare compared with the total volume of trading activity, and since legislation makes insider dealing illegal, it is likely that well-developed capital markets are at least semi-strong form efficient. However, there is evidence that emerging capital markets are weak form inefficient. The continuing existence of anomalies in share price behaviour cannot be ignored, though it has been suggested that some anomalies disappear when reasonable changes in research methodology are made (Fama 1998).

2.4 ASSESSING FINANCIAL PERFORMANCE

In the introduction to this chapter, we said that shareholders, investors and financial managers obtain a great deal of information about companies from their financial statements, financial databases, the financial press and the Internet. In this section we look at ratio analysis, which can be applied to financial statements and similar data to assess the financial performance of a company. In 'Economic profit and economic value added (EVA®)' (Section 2.4.10) we look at ways of assessing financial performance, which have closer links to shareholder wealth maximisation.

Analysis of financial performance can provide useful financial information for a wide range of user groups or stakeholders.

Shareholders

Shareholders can use analysis of financial performance to assist them in making buy and sell decisions, comparing the performance of their investments with that of similar companies, and assessing whether managers as their agents (see 'Agency theory', Section 1.5) have been increasing shareholder wealth.

Investors

Investors such as banks and other financial institutions can use analysis of financial performance to inform decisions about whether to agree to requests for debt finance from companies and the terms and conditions to be attached to such finance.

Company managers

Managers can use analysis of financial performance to assess and compare the performance of different divisions and the performance of the company as a whole. They can compare their company's current performance with its performance in previous years, and against the performance of competitors.

Information sources for analysis of financial performance

Information for analysis of financial performance is derived initially from company financial statements (company accounts), but is now readily available through a variety of media. Financial databases are commonly used as a source of financial information on companies – for example, Datastream, Fame, Bloomberg and LexisNexis. One advantage of using such databases is that ratio analysis can be performed by the software, although users must take care to ensure they are familiar with the definitions of the ratios provided. Useful company information can also be found on company websites and on the Internet. Free company accounts can be obtained via the Internet for many companies listed on the London Stock Exchange.

Financial statements

Table 2.1 shows two of the financial statements of Boater plc: a statement of profit or loss and a financial position statement. The ability to calculate and understand accounting ratios rests on an understanding of financial statements such as these and what they represent.

The statement of profit or loss reports the *financial performance* for an accounting period, which is usually one calendar year ending on the date given in the financial position statement. The statement of profit or loss begins with revenue (sales or turnover) and subtracts costs incurred in producing the goods sold or the services delivered (cost of sales) to give gross profit. Costs incurred by supporting activities such as administration and distribution are then subtracted to give profit from operations, also known as *profit before interest and tax.* This is the profit left after all operating costs have been deducted, hence the term 'profit from operations'.

Financial costs such as interest payments are then subtracted to give profit before tax and the annual tax liability is subtracted to give profit after taxation (PAT). *Earnings* is the term given to profit that can be distributed to ordinary shareholders (distributable profit): in the absence of preference shares, earnings are equal to PAT; if preference shares have been issued, as in this case, earnings are equal to profit after tax and after preference dividends.

While the statement of profit or loss shows the financial performance of a company during an accounting period, the financial position statement shows the financial position of the company at the end of the accounting period. The financial position statement records the assets and liabilities of the company. Assets are divided into *non-current assets,* which are expected to be a source of financial benefit to the company over several accounting periods, and *current assets* (see Section 3.2.3), which are used or sold within an accounting period. These assets are balanced by current (short-term) liabilities, such as trade payables and overdrafts, and non-current liabilities, such as debt, shareholders' funds and preference shares. Ordinary shareholders' funds are divided into the *ordinary share account* (ordinary shares), where the nominal value or **face value** of issued shares is recorded; the *share premium* account, which records the difference between the nominal value of shares issued and the finance raised by selling them; and reserves, the most common of which is the cumulative *retained earnings reserve,* which increases each year by the

Table 2.1 Financial statements of Boater plc

Statements of profit or loss for the year ended 31 December		
	Year 2 £000	Year 1 £000
Revenue	5,700	5,300
Cost of sales	4,330	4,000
Gross profit	1,370	1,300
Administration cost	735	620
Profit before interest and tax	635	680
Interest	220	190
Profit before taxation	415	490
Taxation	125	147
Profit after taxation	290	343
Ordinary dividends	230	230
Retained profits	60	113

Financial position statements as at 31 December				
	Year 2		Year 1	
	£000	£000	£000	£000
Non-current assets		5,405		4,880
Current assets:				
Inventory	900		880	
Trade receivables	460		460	
Cash	55		60	
		1,415		1,400
Total assets		6,820		6,280
Equity:				
Ordinary shares (£1 nominal)	1,500		1,500	
Reserves	1,410	2,910	1,350	2,850
Non-current liabilities				
Bank loan	2,000		1,000	
Bonds	1,100	3,100	1,100	2,100
Current liabilities:				
Trade payables	425		190	
Overdraft			800	
Taxation	155		110	
Dividends	230	810	230	1,330
Total liabilities		6,820		6,820

Annual depreciation: £410,000 (Year 2) and £380,000 (Year 1)

Bond market price: £102 (Year 2) and £98 (Year 1) per £100 bond

Ordinary share price: £1.35 (Year 2) and £2.20 (Year 1)

retained profit from the statement of profit or loss. If land and buildings are revalued, any gain or loss in value is recorded in a *revaluation reserve.*

Another financial statement produced by companies, which is not illustrated in Table 2.1, is the *statement of cash flows,* which shows in a formal way the sources and uses of cash during the accounting period. Financial statements are published at least once each year as part of company accounts.

Profit, EBITDA and cash

In assessing financial performance, it is important to consider the quality of the returns generated by companies. While useful information is provided by the level of profit reported in the financial statements of a company, whether before or after tax, corporate finance tends to focus on cash flows. There is a fundamental difference between accounting profit and cash flows because accounting profit is prepared by applying *accruals accounting* and *accounting policies.* An example of the significance of accruals accounting here is that reported profit includes credit sales, which become cash flows only when trade receivables settle their accounts. The significance of accounting policies is that companies with similar cash flows can report different accounting profits if their accounting policies are different.

To remedy some of the deficiencies of accounting profit, it has become common for companies and analysts to consider earnings before interest, tax, depreciation and amortisation (**EBITDA**). Since EBITDA represents profit from operations excluding non-cash expenses such as depreciation and amortisation (a regular provision writing down intangible assets such as goodwill), it is similar to cash flow from operating activities, ignoring the effect of changes in working capital. As a measure of financial performance, EBITDA eliminates the effects of financing and capital expenditure, and hence can indicate trends in sustainable profitability. EBITDA can be compared with capital employed, as well as indicating the cash flow available to meet interest payments. It has also been suggested that EBITDA can be compared with the market value of equity plus debt, less working capital (Rutterford 1998).

EBITDA can be criticised as a measure of cash flow since it ignores the fact that earnings and revenue are not cash flows. Simply adding back interest, depreciation and amortisation will not turn earnings into cash. EBITDA also ignores the contribution to cash flow made by changes in working capital.

Vignette 2.3 illustrates the need to think carefully about the financial information made available by companies.

2.4.1 The need for benchmarks

When analysing financial performance, it is important to recognise that performance measures and financial ratios in isolation have little significance. To interpret the meaning of performance measures and ratios, they must be compared against suitable benchmarks, of which the following are examples:

■ financial targets set by a company's strategic plan, e.g. a target return on capital employed or a target earnings per share;

■ performance measures and ratios of companies engaged in similar business activities;

Vignette 2.3

Financial reporting relativism is running deeper and deeper

It is not just quarterly reports that companies are using to polish their figures

By Alexandra Scaggs

Analysts and writers have long expressed concern about financial-metric relativism in corporate earnings reports. But instead of fretting about the figures that underpin valuations, they should direct their worries instead towards the documents underlying transactions.

Sanford C Bernstein's global quantitative strategy team were the latest to voice anxiety about corporate earnings in a note that decried the broader blurring of lines between fact and opinion in popular discourse.

'The frequency of usage of the words "fact" and "evidence" appears to have gone into decline,' the team of strategists, led by Inigo Fraser-Jenkins, noted.

More specifically, they took aim at the increased usage of profit metrics that do not fit within standards set by the US's generally accepted accounting principles, or GAAP.

'The reporting of non-GAAP earnings by companies and the alacrity within which investors use them is worrying as it is an example of exactly the triumph of opinions over facts that is the subject of this essay.'

The impression conveyed by the authors is that social media and changing attitudes have created a pernicious relativism that has reached into the worlds of finance and commerce. Yet those who follow trends in financial reporting and accounting know that companies have been in the vanguard of such informational gamesmanship – and that the battleground has moved on from earnings per share and into bond documents and proxy statements.

Financial analysts and writers started raising concerns about corporate earnings reports well before any elected official used the phrase 'fake news'. It was late 2015 when researchers at Audit Analytics found that 88 per cent of companies reported non-

GAAP metrics in their financial reports. And of the companies that reported a non-GAAP measure of income, 82 per cent had higher income than would have been reported otherwise, the study found.

The Securities and Exchange Commission in 2016 issued guidance that effectively limited the ability of companies to use non-GAAP measures in a misleading way. And regulators appear to be pushing back against in other ways, as General Electric has reported an investigation into its accounting practices.

But the massaging of market narratives is not limited to the numbers in companies' financial reports. Executives can – and often do – manage investor and analyst expectations as well. In the so-called 'guidance game', company management teams give conservative estimates about future performance to Wall Street, to improve perceptions of their own performance. The popularity of this shows in the numbers: over the past five years, an average 70 per cent of companies have beaten Wall Street analyst estimates for their earnings each quarter, according to FactSet.

The most troublesome cases of financial-metric relativism do not occur via quarterly reports, however. Companies often make opaque adjustments to metrics used to set executive benchmarks and targets and disclose the terms of mergers and acquisitions. Those documents are not always required to use GAAP metrics or show investors how the chosen metrics match up. And even when they do reconcile their calculations to GAAP, in bond documents and similar offerings, companies can still 'add back' figures which raise leverage.

For example, the covenants for a bond offering from workspace operator WeWork feature 'highly unusual' add-backs to ebitda-based metrics. Covenants are meant to set limitations on the company's ability to borrow under certain circumstances,

Vignette 2.3 *(continued)*

according to analysts at Covenant Review, an independent credit research firm.

Deals with ebitda 'add-backs', which make companies appear more creditworthy, hit a multi-decade high of about 25 per cent in the first quarter, according to S&P Global Market Intelligence. The practice means that leverage in corporate debt markets is probably higher than reported. That coincided with a record start to the year for mergers and acquisitions, fuelled in large part by debt. Taking such ebitda add-backs into account, a 'conservative' estimate for total leverage on new deals was probably 6.2× ebitda in March, rather than 5× as otherwise reported, according to UBS analysts.

In a recent report, expert witness and economic consulting firm Cornerstone Research found there were four times as many class-action lawsuits about M&A accounting in 2017 as there were the year

before. All of the cases claimed the deal documents did not include reconciliations between GAAP and non-GAAP figures even though such disclosures are not required by law, Cornerstone found.

Audit Analytics finds that the number of proxy statements with non-GAAP language rose to 60 per cent in 2016 from less than 20 per cent in 2012. That matters because the sections of proxy statements that set executives' performance targets are not required to comply with GAAP standards or reconcile them.

Of course, transactions and deals themselves require boards, counterparties and investors to cooperate. So as financing costs and interest rates rise, these stakeholders might demand more from their management teams. Otherwise, executives risk eroding their credibility while raising their leverage levels, which can be a truly worrisome combination.

 Source: Scaggs, A. (2018) 'Financial reporting relativism is running deeper and deeper', *Financial Times* 4 May. © The Financial Times Limited 2018. All Rights Reserved.

Questions

1 What might managers gain by using 'non-GAAP metrics' in financial statements?
2 Why is it important to have reporting standards for financial statements?

- average performance measures and ratios for the company's operations, i.e. sector averages;
- performance measures and ratios for the company from previous years, adjusted for inflation if necessary.

The benchmarks selected will depend on the purpose of the analysis. Comparing the calculated performance measures or ratios against appropriate benchmarks is not an end in itself, as there is still the difficult task of interpreting or explaining any differences found.

2.4.2 Categories of ratios

When using ratios for analysing financial performance, some sort of analytical framework is required to assist in calculation and interpretation. We have divided ratios into groups or categories which are linked to particular areas of concern. There is widespread agreement on the main ratios included in each category, even though the same category may be given different names by different authors.

- Profitability ratios: return on capital employed, net profit margin, net asset turnover, gross profit margin, etc.

■ Activity ratios: trade receivables days, trade payables days, inventory days, sales/net current assets, etc. These ratios are important in the management of working capital.
■ Liquidity ratios: **current ratio**, quick ratio, etc.
■ Gearing ratios: **capital gearing** ratio, debt/equity ratio, interest cover, etc. These ratios are measures of **financial risk** (see 'Gearing: its measurement and significance', Section 9.8).
■ Investor ratios: return on equity, dividend per share, earnings per share, **dividend cover**, price/earnings ratio, payout ratio, **dividend yield**, **earnings yield**, etc.

A detailed introduction to ratio analysis can be found in Elliott and Elliott (2017). Because some ratios can be defined in different ways, it is important when comparing ratios to make sure that they have been calculated on a similar basis. The golden rule is always to compare like with like.

The ratios discussed in the following sections are illustrated by calculations based on the financial statements of Boater in Table 2.1.

2.4.3 Profitability ratios

Profitability ratios indicate how successful the managers of a company have been in generating profit. Return on capital employed is often referred to as the *primary ratio.*

Return on capital employed (ROCE)

$$\frac{\text{Profit before interest and tax} \times 100}{\text{Capital employed}}$$

This ratio relates the overall profitability of a company to the finance used to generate it. It is also the product of net profit margin and asset turnover:

$$\text{ROCE} = \text{Net profit margin} \times \text{Asset turnover}$$

Profit before interest and tax is often called *profit from operations.* The meaning of *capital employed* can cause confusion, but it is simply *total assets less current liabilities* (or equity plus non-current liabilities, which has a similar meaning). Another definition of capital employed with the same meaning is *non-current assets plus net working capital.* This ratio is clearly sensitive to investment in non-current assets, to the age of non-current assets (since older assets will have depreciated more than younger ones) and to when assets were last revalued. There is a close link between ROCE and **accounting rate of return (ARR)** (see 'The return on capital employed method', Section 6.2). For Boater:

Capital employed (year 1) = 6,280 − 1,330 = £4,950
Capital employed (year 2) = 6,820 − 810 = £6,010

ROCE (year 1) = 100 × (680/4,950) = 13.7%
ROCE (year 2) = 100 × (635/6,010) = 10.6%

Net profit margin

$$\frac{\text{Profit before interest and tax} \times 100}{\text{Revenue or turnover}}$$

This ratio, also called *profit from operations margin,* indicates the efficiency with which costs have been controlled in generating profit from sales. It does not distinguish between operating costs, administrative costs and distribution costs. A fall in ROCE may be due to a fall in net profit margin, in which case further investigation may determine whether an increased cost or a fall in profit margin is the cause. For Boater:

Net profit margin (year 1) $= 100 \times (680/5,300) = 12.8\%$
Net profit margin (year 2) $= 100 \times (635/5,700) = 11.1\%$

Net asset turnover

$$\frac{\text{Revenue or turnover}}{\text{Capital employed}}$$

Capital employed is defined here in the same way as for ROCE, i.e. *total assets less current liabilities,* and so the asset turnover ratio is also sensitive to non-current asset values. This ratio gives a guide to productive efficiency, i.e. how well assets have been used in generating sales. A fall in ROCE may be due to a fall in asset turnover rather than a fall in net profit margin. For Boater:

Asset turnover (year 1) $= 5,300/4,950 = 1.07$ times
Asset turnover (year 2) $= 5,700/6,010 = 0.95$ times

Gross profit margin

$$\frac{\text{Gross profit} \times 100}{\text{Revenue or turnover}}$$

This ratio shows how well costs of production have been controlled, as opposed to distribution costs and administration costs. For Boater:

Gross profit margin (year 1) $= 100 \times (1,300/5,300) = 24.5\%$
Gross profit margin (year 2) $= 100 \times (1,370/5,700) = 24.0\%$

EBITDA/capital employed

$$\frac{\text{EBITDA} \times 100}{\text{Capital employed}}$$

This ratio relates earnings before interest, tax, depreciation and amortisation to the equity and debt finance used to generate it. The meaning of capital employed is as for ROCE, i.e. *total assets less current liabilities.* For Boater:

EBITDA (year 1) $= (680 + 380) = £1,060,000$
EBITDA (year 2) $= (635 + 410) = £1,045,000$

$$\text{EBITDA/capital employed (year 1)} = 100 \times (1{,}060/4{,}950) = 21.4\%$$
$$\text{EBITDA/capital employed (year 2)} = 100 \times (1{,}045/6{,}010) = 17.4\%$$

2.4.4 Activity ratios

Activity ratios show how efficiently a company has managed short-term assets and liabilities, i.e. working capital, and they are closely linked to the liquidity ratios. With each ratio, the average value for the year should be used (e.g. average level of trade receivables should be used in calculating the trade receivables ratio), but it is common for the year-end value to be used to obtain figures for comparative purposes. As ratios must be calculated on a consistent basis, either year-end values or average values must be used throughout your analysis.

Trade receivables days or trade receivables ratio

$$\frac{\text{Trade receivable} \times 365}{\text{Credit sales}}$$

The value of credit sales is usually not available and it is common for revenue or turnover to be used as a substitute. The trade receivables days ratio gives the average period of credit being taken by customers. If it is compared with a company's allowed credit period, it can give an indication of the efficiency of trade receivables administration (see 'Managing receivables', Section 3.7). For Boater:

$$\text{Trade receivable (year 1)} = 365 \times (460/5{,}300) = 32 \text{ days}$$
$$\text{Trade receivable (year 2)} = 365 \times (460/5{,}700) = 29 \text{ days}$$

Trade payables days or trade payables ratio

$$\frac{\text{Trade payables} \times 365}{\text{Cost of sales}}$$

Trade payables should be compared with credit purchases, but as this information is not always available, cost of sales is often used instead. The trade payables days ratio gives the average time taken for suppliers of goods and services to receive payment. For Boater:

$$\text{Trade payables days (year 1)} = 365 \times (190/4{,}000) = 17 \text{ days}$$
$$\text{Trade payables days (year 2)} = 365 \times (425/4{,}330) = 36 \text{ days}$$

Inventory days or inventory turnover

$$\frac{\text{Stock or inventory} \times 365}{\text{Cost of sales}}$$

This ratio shows how long it takes for a company to turn its inventories into sales. Several other ratios can be calculated by separating the total inventory figure into its component parts, i.e. raw materials, work-in-progress and finished goods (see 'Working capital and the cash conversion cycle', Section 3.3). The shorter the inventory days ratio, the lower the cost to the company of holding inventory. The value of this ratio is very dependent on the need for inventory and so will vary significantly depending on the nature of a company's business (see 'Managing inventory', Section 3.5). For Boater:

$$\text{Inventory days (year 1)} = 365 \times (880/4,000) = 80 \text{ days}$$
$$\text{Inventory days (year 2)} = 365 \times (900/4,330) = 76 \text{ days}$$

Cash conversion cycle

The cash conversion cycle (also called the operating cycle or working capital cycle) is found by adding inventory days and trade receivables days and then subtracting trade payables days. It indicates the length of time for which working capital financing is needed. The longer the cash conversion cycle, the higher the investment in working capital. For Boater:

$$\text{Cash conversion cycle (year 1)} = 32 \text{ days} + 80 \text{ days} - 17 \text{ days} = 95 \text{ days}$$
$$\text{Cash conversion cycle (year 2)} = 29 \text{ days} + 76 \text{ days} - 36 \text{ days} = 69 \text{ days}$$

Non-current asset turnover

Net asset turnover (see above) is based on capital employed, but an alternative view of asset use can be found by separating non-current assets from capital employed.

$$\frac{\text{Revenue or turnover}}{\text{Non-current assets}}$$

Non-current asset turnover indicates the sales being generated by the non-current asset base of a company. Like ROCE, it is sensitive to the **acquisition**, age and valuation of non-current assets. For Boater:

$$\text{Non-current asset turnover (year 1)} = 5,300/4,880 = 1.09 \text{ times}$$
$$\text{Non-current asset turnover (year 2)} = 5,700/5,405 = 1.05 \text{ times}$$

Revenue/net working capital

The companion ratio to non-current asset turnover compares revenue with net working capital (net current assets).

$$\frac{\text{Revenue or turnover}}{\text{Net-current assets}}$$

This ratio shows the level of working capital supporting sales. Working capital must increase in line with sales if undercapitalisation (overtrading) is to be avoided (see 'Overtrading', Section 3.4) and so this ratio can be used to forecast the level of working capital needed for a given level of sales when projecting financial statements. For Boater:

$$\text{Sales/net working capital (year 1)} = 5,300/(880 + 460 - 190) = 4.6 \text{ times}$$
$$\text{Sales/net working capital (year 2)} = 5,700/(900 + 460 - 425) = 6.1 \text{ times}$$

2.4.5 Liquidity ratios

Current ratio

$$\frac{\text{Current assets}}{\text{Current liabilities}}$$

This ratio measures a company's ability to meet its financial obligations as they fall due. It is often said that the current ratio should be around two, but what is normal will in fact vary from industry to industry: sector averages are a better guide than a rule of thumb. For Boater:

Current ratio (year 1) = 1,400/1,330 = 1.1 times
Current ratio (year 2) = 1,415/810 = 1.8 times

Quick ratio

$$\frac{\text{Current assets less inventory}}{\text{Current liabilities}}$$

It is argued that the current ratio may overstate the ability to meet financial obligations because it includes inventory in the numerator. This argument has merit if it takes more than a short time to convert inventory into sales, i.e. if the inventory days ratio is not small. It is not true, however, where inventory is turned over quickly and where sales are mainly on a cash or near-cash basis, for example in the retail food trade. The quick ratio compares liquid current assets with short-term liabilities. While a common rule of thumb is that it should be close to one, in practice the sector average value should be used as a guide. For Boater:

Quick ratio (year 1) = (1,400 − 880)/1,330 = 0.4 times
Quick ratio (year 2) = (1,415 − 900)/810 = 0.6 times

2.4.6 Gearing ratios

Gearing ratios or leverage ratios relate to how a company is financed with respect to debt and equity and can be used to assess the financial risk that arises with increasing debt (see 'Gearing: its measurement and significance', Section 9.8) for a more detailed discussion of gearing and its implications).

Capital gearing ratio

$$\frac{\text{Long-term debt} \times 100}{\text{Capital employed}}$$

The purpose of this ratio is to show the proportion of long-term debt used by a company. When comparing calculated values to benchmarks it is essential to confirm that the same method of calculation is used because other definitions of this ratio are found. One alternative uses prior charge capital (preference shares plus debt finance) rather than debt finance alone.

A company may be thought *highly geared* if capital gearing is greater than 50 per cent using book values for debt and equity, but this is only a rule of thumb. For Boater:

$$\text{Capital gearing (year 1)} = 100 \times (2,100/4,950) = 42.4\%$$
$$\text{Capital gearing (year 2)} = 100 \times (3,100/6,010) = 51.6\%$$

It is usual in corporate finance to calculate gearing using market values for debt and equity. Reserves are not included in the calculation of the market value of equity. Note also that the total value of debt is the sum of the market value of the bonds and the book value of the bank loan because bank loans have no market value. For Boater:

$$\text{Market value of equity (year 1)} = 1,500,000 \times 2.20 = £3,300,000$$
$$\text{Market value of equity (year 2)} = 1,500,000 \times 1.35 = £2,025,000$$

$$\text{Market value of bonds (year 1)} = 1,100,000 \times 98/100 = £1,078,000$$
$$\text{Market value of bonds (year 2)} = 1,100,000 \times 102/100 = £1,122,000$$

$$\text{Total value of debt (year 1)} = 1,078,000 + 1,000,000 = £2,078,000$$
$$\text{Total value of debt (year 2)} = 1,122,000 + 2,000,000 = £3,122,000$$

$$\text{Capital gearing (year 1)} = 100 \times (2,078/(2,078 + 3,300)) = 38.6\%$$
$$\text{Capital gearing (year 2)} = 100 \times (3,122/(3,122 + 2,025)) = 60.7\%$$

Debt/equity ratio

$$\frac{\text{Long-term debt} \times 100}{\text{Share capital and reserves}}$$

This ratio serves a similar purpose to capital gearing. A company could be said to be highly geared if its debt/equity ratio were greater than 100 per cent using book values, but again this is only a rule of thumb. For Boater:

$$\text{Debt/equity ratio (year 1)} = 100 \times (2,100/2,850) = 73.7\%$$
$$\text{Debt/equity ratio (year 2)} = 100 \times (3,100/2,910) = 106.5\%$$

Using market values:

$$\text{Debt/equity ratio (year 1)} = 100 \times (2,078/3,300) = 63.0\%$$
$$\text{Debt/equity ratio (year 2)} = 100 \times (3,122/2,025) = 154.2\%$$

Interest coverage ratio and interest gearing

$$\frac{\text{Profit before interest and tax}}{\text{Interest charges}}$$

The interest coverage ratio shows how many times a company can cover its current interest payments (finance charges) out of current profits and indicates whether servicing debt may be a problem. An interest coverage ratio of more than seven times is usually regarded as safe, and an interest coverage ratio of more than three times as acceptable. These are only rules of thumb, however, and during periods of low and stable interest rates, lower levels of interest cover may be deemed acceptable. The interest coverage ratio is a clearer indication of financial distress than either capital gearing or the debt/equity ratio, since inability to meet interest payments will lead to corporate failure no matter what the level of gearing may be. For Boater:

$$\text{Interest coverage ratio (year 1)} = 680/190 = 3.6 \text{ times}$$
$$\text{Interest coverage ratio (year 2)} = 635/220 = 2.9 \text{ times}$$

The inverse of the interest coverage ratio is known as interest gearing or **income gearing** and some analysts prefer this to the interest coverage ratio. For Boater:

$$\text{Interest gearing (year 1)} = 100 \times (190/680) = 27.9\%$$
$$\text{Interest gearing (year 2)} = 100 \times (220/635) = 34.7\%$$

2.4.7 Investor ratios

Investor ratios are used in corporate finance for a variety of purposes, including valuing a target company in a takeover (e.g. using the price/earnings ratio: see 'Income-based valuation methods', Section 11.4.3), analysing dividend policy (e.g. using the payout ratio: see 'Dividend policies', Section 10.6), predicting the effect of a **rights issue** (e.g. using earnings yield: see 'Market price after a rights issue', Section 4.3.4) and assessing the effects of proposed financing (e.g. on earnings per share: see 'Evaluating the financial effect of financing choices', Section 5.9).

Return on equity

$$\frac{\text{Earnings after tax and preference dividends}}{\text{Shareholders funds}}$$

Whereas ROCE looks at overall return to all providers of finance, return on equity compares the earnings attributable to ordinary shareholders with the book value of their investment in the business. *Shareholders' funds* are equal to ordinary share capital plus reserves, but excluding preference share capital. For Boater:

$$\text{Return on equity (year 1)} = 100 \times (343/2,850) = 12.0\%$$
$$\text{Return on equity (year 2)} = 100 \times (290/2,910) = 10.0\%$$

Dividend per share

$$\frac{\text{Total dividend paid to ordinary shareholders}}{\text{Number of issued ordinary shares}}$$

While the total dividend paid may change from year to year, individual shareholders will expect that dividend per share will not decrease (see 'Dividend relevance or irrelevance?', Section 10.5). For Boater:

$$\text{Dividend per share (year 1)} = 100 \times (230/1,500) = 15.3 \text{ pence}$$
$$\text{Dividend per share (year 2)} = 100 \times (230/1,500) = 15.3 \text{ pence}$$

Earnings per share

$$\frac{\text{Earnings after tax and preference dividends}}{\text{Number of issued ordinary shares}}$$

Earnings per share is regarded as a key ratio by stock market investors. Take care when looking at this ratio in company accounts as there are several ways it can be calculated. These complications are beyond the scope of this text: for further discussion, see for example Elliott and Elliott (2017). We shall calculate earnings per share by simply using earnings attributable to ordinary shareholders, so for Boater:

$$\text{Earnings per share (year 1)} = 100 \times (343/1,500) = 22.9 \text{ pence}$$
$$\text{Earnings per share (year 2)} = 100 \times (290/1,500) = 19.3 \text{ pence}$$

Dividend cover

$$\frac{\text{Earnings per share}}{\text{Dividend per share}}$$

Dividend cover indicates how safe a company's dividend payment is by calculating how many times the total dividend is covered by current earnings. The higher the dividend cover, the more likely it is that a company can maintain or increase future dividends. For Boater:

$$\text{Dividend cover (year 1)} = 22.9/15.3 = 1.5 \text{ times}$$
$$\text{Dividend cover (year 2)} = 19.3/15.3 = 1.3 \text{ times}$$

Price/earnings ratio

$$\frac{\text{Market price per share}}{\text{Earnings per share}}$$

Like earnings per share, the price/earnings (P/E) ratio is seen as a key ratio by stock market investors. It shows how much an investor is prepared to pay for a company's shares, given its current earnings per share (EPS). The ratio can therefore indicate the confidence of investors in the expected future performance of a company: the higher the P/E ratio relative to other companies, the more confident the market is that future earnings will increase. A word of caution, though: a high P/E ratio could also be due to a low EPS, perhaps due to a one-off cost in the statement of profit or loss. The P/E ratio can also be used to determine the value of a company, as discussed in 'Income-based valuation methods' (Section 11.4.3). For Boater:

$$\text{Price/earnings ratio (year 1)} = 220/22.9 = 9.6 \text{ times}$$
$$\text{Price/earnings ratio (year 2)} = 135/19.3 = 7.0 \text{ times}$$

Payout ratio

$$\frac{\text{Total dividend paid to ordinary shareholders} \times 100}{\text{Earnings after tax and preference dividends}}$$

The payout ratio is often used in the analysis of dividend policy. For example, some companies may choose to pay out a fixed percentage of earnings every year and finance any investment needs not covered by retained earnings from external sources. For Boater:

$$\text{Payout ratio (year 1)} = 100 \times (230/343) = 67.1\%$$
$$\text{Payout ratio (year 2)} = 100 \times (230/290) = 79.3\%$$

Dividend yield

$$\frac{\text{Dividend per share} \times 100}{\text{Market price of share}}$$

Dividend yield gives a measure of how much an investor expects to gain in exchange for buying a given share, ignoring any capital gains that may arise. It is commonly quoted on a gross (before tax) basis in the financial press. For Boater, on a net (after tax) basis:

$$\text{Net dividend yield (year 1)} = 100 \times (15.3/220) = 7.0\%$$
$$\text{Net dividend yield (year 2)} = 100 \times (15.3/135) = 11.3\%$$

Gross dividend yield is found by 'grossing up' net dividend yield at the basic rate of income tax. Assuming a tax rate of 20 per cent, for Boater, on a gross (before tax) basis:

$$\text{Gross dividend yield (year 1)} = 7.0 \times (100/80) = 8.8\%$$
$$\text{Gross dividend yield (year 2)} = 11.3 \times (100/80) = 14.1\%$$

Earnings yield

$$\frac{\text{Earnings per share} \times 100}{\text{Market price of share}}$$

Earnings yield gives a measure of the potential return shareholders expect to receive in exchange for purchasing a given share; it is the reciprocal of the price/earnings ratio. The return is a potential one since few companies pay out all their earnings as dividends. Earnings yield can be used as a discount rate to capitalise future earnings in calculating the value of a company, as discussed in 'Income-based valuation methods' (Section 11.4.3). For Boater:

$$\text{Earnings yield (year 1)} = 100 \times (22.9/220) = 10.4\%$$
$$\text{Earnings yield (year 2)} = 100 \times (19.3/135) = 14.3\%$$

2.4.8 Interpreting the financial ratios of Boater

The ratios calculated for Boater are given in Table 2.2. If this had been a focused analysis, only a selection of ratios would have been calculated. For example, if the focus had been on working capital management, no purpose would have been served by calculating the investor ratios. What is the overall assessment of financial performance indicated by Boater's ratios? The following comments are a guide to some of the issues raised in each of the ratio categories and should be studied in conjunction with Table 2.2.

Table 2.2 Comparative financial ratios for Boater

	Year 2	Year 1
Return on capital employed	10.6%	13.7%
Net profit margin	11.1%	12.8%
Asset turnover	0.95 times	1.07 times
Gross profit margin	24.0%	24.5%
EBITDA/capital employed	17.4%	21.4%
Trade receivables days	29 days	32 days
Trade payables days	36 days	17 days
Inventory days	76 days	80 days
Cash conversion cycle	69 days	95 days
Non-current asset turnover	1.05 times	1.09 times
Sales/net working capital	6.1 times	4.6 times
Current ratio	1.8 times	1.1 times
Quick ratio	0.6 times	0.4 times
Capital gearing (book value)	51.6%	42.4%
Capital gearing (market value)	60.7%	38.6%
Debt/equity ratio (book value)	106.5%	73.7%
Debt/equity ratio (market value)	154.2%	63.0%
Interest coverage ratio	2.9 times	3.6 times
Interest gearing	34.7%	27.9%
Return on equity	10.0%	12.0%
Dividend per share	15.3 pence	15.3 pence
Earnings per share	19.3 pence	22.9 pence
Dividend cover	1.3 times	1.5 times
Price/earnings ratio	7.0 times	9.6 times
Payout ratio	79.3%	67.1%
Net dividend yield	11.3%	7.0%
Gross dividend yield	14.1%	8.8%
Earnings yield	10.4%	14.3%

Profitability

Boater's overall profitability has declined, and this is due both to a decline in revenue in relation to capital employed and to a decline in profit margins. This decline has occurred despite an increase in revenue and seems to be partly due to a substantial increase in administration costs. The decline in ROCE and EBITDA/capital employed can also be linked to replacement of the overdraft with a bank loan and substantial investment in non-current assets.

Activity and liquidity

The exchange of the overdraft for a long-term bank loan has improved both the current ratio and the quick ratio, but cash reserves have fallen. There has been little change in trade receivables days or inventory days, but trade payables days have more than doubled. Although Boater is no longer heavily reliant on an overdraft for working capital finance, the company has increased its dependence on trade payables as a source of short-term finance.

Gearing and risk

The new loan has increased gearing substantially and gearing now looks to be risky whether book values or market values are used. Interest coverage now looks to be low and income gearing is increasing owing to the fall in profit from operations and the increase in interest payments.

Investor interest

Even though earnings have fallen, the dividend has been maintained and, since the share price has fallen, dividend yield has increased as a result. The decrease in price/earnings ratio may indicate that investors feel that the company is unlikely to improve in the future.

2.4.9 Problems with ratio analysis

When using ratio analysis to evaluate financial performance, you must treat the results with caution for several reasons. One problem is that the financial position statement relates to a company's position on one day of the year. If the financial position statement had been prepared three months earlier, a different picture might have been presented and key financial ratios might have had different values. Tax payable and dividends due might not have been included in current liabilities, for example, and the current ratio could have looked much healthier. Should we exclude such temporary items when calculating working capital ratios?

It can be difficult to find a similar company as a basis for intercompany comparisons. No two companies are identical in every respect and so differences in commercial activity must be allowed for. As a minimum, differences in accounting policies should be considered.

The reliability of ratio analysis in the analysis of financial performance naturally depends on the reliability of the accounting information on which it is based. Financial statements have become increasingly complex and it is difficult to determine whether **creative accounting** has taken place. Company accounting has been described as 'a jungle with many species of animal – some benign, some carnivorous – and its own rules' (Smith 1996). Care must be taken to identify any complex financial instruments which may distort a company's true financial position. As shown by occasional high-profile corporate failures, identifying the financial position of a company can be difficult, even for experts.

In conclusion, ratio analysis must be regarded as only the beginning of the analysis of financial performance, serving mainly to raise questions which require deeper investigation before understanding begins to appear. Shareholders, investors and company managers use ratio analysis as only one of many sources of information to assist them in making decisions.

2.4.10 Economic profit and economic value added (EVA®)

It has long been recognised that reported earnings are an incomplete measure of company performance, since positive earnings do not guarantee that a company is increasing shareholder wealth. What is missing is an opportunity cost for the capital employed in the business, since a company must earn at least the average required rate of return on its capital employed if it is going to create an increase in value for its shareholders. A performance measure which addresses this deficiency in reported earnings is economic profit, which can be defined as profit from operations after tax less a cost of capital charge on capital employed:

$$\text{Economic profit} = (\text{Operating profit} \times (1 - t)) - (K_0 \times \text{CE})$$

where: t = company taxation rate
  K_0 = average rate of return required by investors
  CE = book value of capital employed

An almost identical concept which is familiar to management accountants is residual income, defined as controllable contribution less a cost of capital charge on controllable investment (Drury 2015), although contribution here is before taxation.

Economic profit as defined above corrects the deficiency in earnings of failing to allow for a charge on capital employed, but it still relies on accounting data, which is open to subjective adjustment and manipulation in its preparation. There is also the problem that the book value of capital employed fails to capture accurately the capital invested in a company. For example, research and development costs produce benefits for a company over several years but are treated as an annual expense rather than a financial position statement asset. We cannot rely on a financial position statement to give us an accurate measure of a company's tangible and intangible capital. The difficulty of extracting a fair value for invested capital from financial statements is addressed by the topical performance measure known as EVA.

EVA was trademarked and introduced by the Stern Stewart company in the 1990s with the objective of providing an overall measure of company performance that would focus managers' attention on the drivers that lead to the creation of shareholder wealth. It refined and amended the information used in the calculation of economic profit so that the two terms have become largely synonymous (Hawawini and Viallet 2002). In fact, EVA can be seen as an attempt to measure a company's economic profit rather than its accounting profit (Keown et al. 2003). EVA calculates an adjusted value for invested capital by making rule-based changes to the book value of capital employed. For example, it capitalises expenditure on marketing and research and development, thereby treating these expenses as assets and spreading their costs over the periods benefiting from them. EVA also calculates an adjusted value for profit from operations by making complementary changes to those it makes to the value of invested capital. For example, research and development expenses included in accounting profit must be reduced to balance the amount included in invested capital. By making these changes to invested capital and profit from operations after tax, EVA corrects the effect of financial accounting rules that ignore the ways a company creates value for shareholders. EVA can be defined as:

$$EVA = (AOP \times (1 - t)) - (WACC \times AVIC)$$

where: AOP = adjusted operating profit
t = company taxation rate
WACC = weighted average cost capital (see 'Calculation of weighted average cost of capital', Section 9.2)
AVIC = adjusted value of invested capital

Alternatively:

$$EVA = (RAVIC - WACC) \times AVIC$$

where: RAVIC = required after-tax return on adjusted value of invested capital
WACC = weighted average cost of capital
AVIC = adjusted value of invested capital

While open to criticism on the subjectivity of some of the adjustments it makes to accounting information, many large organisations have adopted EVA and some positive results have been claimed from its use as a performance measure (Leahy 2000). However, it has been suggested that there is a very low empirical correlation between increases in market value and EVA (Fernandez 2003), and that EVA could be used as one of a range of performance measures, including traditional accounting-based performance measures (Kumar and Low 2002). Ideally, managerial performance should be evaluated on the present value of expected future cash flows, while EVA is a short-term concept that looks at the current reporting period (Johnson and Bamber 2007).

The usefulness of EVA lies in the attention it directs towards the *drivers* of shareholder value creation. Reflecting on the definition of EVA points to several ways in which company managers can seek to generate increased value for shareholders. This leads on to the extensive topic of value management, which is beyond the scope of this text. Briefly, the value drivers that managers may be able to influence can be seen in the following value-creating strategies:

- Look for ways to increase net profit from operations after tax without increasing the amount of capital invested in the company.
- Undertake investment projects which are expected to generate returns greater than the company's cost of capital.
- Take steps to reduce the opportunity cost of the capital invested in the company, either by reducing the company's cost of capital or by reducing the amount of invested capital.

You will find it useful to think of examples of how these value-creating strategies can be applied in practice. For example, net profit from operations after tax can be increased by eliminating unnecessary costs. Undertaking projects which generate returns greater than the company's cost of capital can be achieved by using net present value (NPV) and internal rate of return (IRR) as investment appraisal methods (see 'The net present value method' and 'The internal rate of return method', Sections 6.3 and 6.4). A company's cost of capital can be reduced by the sensible use of debt (see 'Pecking order theory', Section 9.15). The amount of invested capital can be reduced by disposing of unwanted assets and by returning unwanted cash to shareholders via a share repurchase scheme (see 'Share repurchases', Section 10.7.2).

2.5 CONCLUSION

In this chapter we have looked at some key aspects of the financing decision in corporate finance – the balance between internal and external finance, the different sources of finance available to a company, the importance of the capital markets – and have discussed at some length the key topic of capital market efficiency. The debate about market efficiency is a continuing one and you should consider carefully the implications of market efficiency for corporate finance theory as you continue your studies.

The analysis of financial performance is a key activity providing financial information for a wide range of user groups, and we considered both ratio analysis and a currently topical performance measure, economic value added (EVA). Later chapters will discuss key ratios in more detail, especially those concerned with working capital and gearing.

■ ■ ■ KEY POINTS

1 An efficient financing policy raises required funds at the required time and at the lowest cost.

2 Internal finance or retained earnings must not be confused with retained profit as only cash can be invested. Retained earnings are a major source of funds for investment.

3 The mix of internal and external finance depends on the amount of finance needed: the cash flow from existing operations; the opportunity cost of retained earnings; the cost and availability of external finance; and the company's dividend policy.

4 There are many kinds of external finance available to a company, including ordinary shares, preference shares, bonds (debentures, loan stock and convertibles) and bank loans.

5 New issues of equity and debt are made in the primary market. Already-issued securities are traded in the secondary market, which is therefore a source of pricing information.

6 Smaller companies not ready for a full market listing can seek a listing on the Alternative Investment Market (AIM).

7 An efficient market needs operational efficiency, allocational efficiency and pricing efficiency. A perfect market requires the absence of factors inhibiting buying and

selling; identical expectations of participants; free entry and exit; free and readily available information; and many buyers and sellers, none of whom dominates.

8 Operational efficiency means low transaction costs and quickly executed sales. Pricing efficiency means that share prices fully and fairly reflect all relevant information, and so are fair prices. Allocational efficiency means that capital markets allocate funds to their most productive use.

9 Markets are weak form efficient if share prices reflect all past price movements. In such a market, abnormal returns cannot be made by studying past share price movements. Research suggests well-developed capital markets are weak form efficient.

10 The random walk hypothesis suggests there is no connection between movements in share price in successive periods. A substantial amount of research supports this view. Weak form tests include serial correlation tests, run tests and filter tests.

11 Markets are semi-strong form efficient if share prices reflect all past information and all publicly available information. In such a market, abnormal returns cannot be made by studying available company information. Research suggests well-developed capital markets are to a large extent semi-strong form efficient.

12 Tests for semi-strong form efficiency look at the speed and accuracy of share price movements to new information (event studies).

13 Markets are strong form efficient if share prices reflect all information. In such a market, no one can make abnormal returns. While well-developed capital markets are not totally strong form efficient, research suggests these stock markets are very efficient.

14 Strong form efficiency can only be tested indirectly, for example by investigating whether fund managers can regularly make abnormal returns.

15 The implications of capital market efficiency for investors are that research is pointless and no bargains exist.

16 The implications of capital market efficiency for companies are that share prices value companies correctly, the timing of new issues is irrelevant and manipulating accounts is pointless.

17 Technical analysts try to predict share prices by studying their historical movements, while fundamental analysts look for the fundamental value of a share. Neither activity is worthwhile (theoretically) in a semi-strong form efficient market.

18 A significant body of research has examined anomalies in share price behaviour, such as calendar effects, size anomalies and value effects.

19 Behavioural finance seeks to understand the market implications of the psychological factors underlying investor decisions and has had some success explaining anomalies.

20 Shareholders, investors and financial managers can analyse financial performance to help them in their decisions.

21 To remedy perceived deficiencies in accounting profit, reporting EBITDA (earnings before interest, tax, depreciation and amortisation) has become more common.

22 Performance measures and ratios mean little in isolation: they must be compared with benchmarks such as financial targets, performance measures and ratios of similar companies, sector averages, or performance measures and ratios from previous years.

23 A systematic approach to ratio analysis could look at ratios relating to profitability, activity, liquidity, gearing and investment.

24 Problems with ratio analysis include the following: financial position statement figures are single-point values; similar companies for comparison are hard to find; accounting policies may differ between companies; creative accounting may distort financial statements; and complex financing methods can make accounts difficult to interpret.

25 The terms 'economic profit' and 'economic value added' have a similar meaning. EVA is the difference between profit from operations after tax and a cost of capital charge on invested capital. Many large companies use EVA.

26 EVA focuses attention on the drivers of shareholder value creation. Financial managers should seek to increase net profit from operations, undertake projects with a return greater than the cost of capital, and reduce the opportunity cost and amount of invested capital.

SELF-TEST QUESTIONS

Answers to these questions can be found on pages 452–3.

1 Describe the factors influencing the relative proportions of internal and external finance used in capital investment.

2 What is the relevance of the efficient market hypothesis for the financial manager?

3 Which of the following statements about capital market efficiency is not correct?

(a) If a stock market is weak form efficient, chartists cannot make abnormal returns.

(b) If a stock market is strong form efficient, only people with insider information can make abnormal returns.

(c) In a semi-strong form efficient market, fundamental analysis will not bring abnormal returns.

(d) If a stock market is semi-strong form efficient, all past and current publicly available information is reflected in share prices.

(e) If a stock market is weak form efficient, all historical information about a share is reflected in its current market price.

4 Explain the meaning of the following terms: allocational efficiency, pricing efficiency and operational efficiency.

5 Why is it difficult to test for strong form efficiency?

6 Describe three anomalies in share price behaviour.

7 Describe benchmarks that can be used when assessing financial performance.

8 Describe the five categories of ratios, list and define the ratios in each category and, without referring to the calculations in the text, calculate each ratio for Boater.

9 What are the potential problems associated with using ratio analysis to assess the financial health and performance of companies?

10 Explain the meaning of economic value added. How can EVA help financial managers to create value for shareholders?

QUESTIONS FOR REVIEW

1 Distinguish between a primary and a secondary capital market and discuss the role played by these markets in corporate finance. What are the desirable features of primary and secondary capital markets?

2 Recent capital market efficiency research has explored anomalies in share price behaviour. Briefly describe some of these anomalies and suggest possible explanations.

3 The following financial statements are extracts from the accounts of Hoult Ltd:

Statements of profit or loss for years ending 31 December

	Year 1	Year 2	Year 3
	£000	£000	£000
Revenue	960	1,080	1,220
Cost of sales	670	780	885
Gross profit	290	300	335
Administration expenses	260	270	302
Profit before interest and tax	30	30	33
Interest	13	14	18
Profit before tax	17	16	15
Taxation	2	1	1
Profit after tax	15	15	14
Dividends	0	0	4
Retained profit	15	15	10

Financial position statements for years to 31 December

	Year 1		Year 2		Year 3	
	£000	£000	£000	£000	£000	£000
Non-current assets		160		120		100
Current assets						
Inventory	200		210		225	
Trade receivables	160	360	180	390	250	475
Total assets		520		510		575
Equity						
Ordinary shares	160		160		160	
Profit and loss	95	255	110	270	120	280
Non-current liabilities						
8% bonds		120		80		40
Current liabilities						
Trade payables	75		80		145	
Overdraft	70	145	80	160	110	255
		520		510		575

Annual depreciation was £18,000 in year 1, £13,000 in year 2 and £11,000 in year 3. The 8 per cent bonds are redeemable in instalments: the final payment is due in year 4.

The finance director is concerned about rising short-term interest rates and the poor liquidity of Hoult Ltd. After calculating appropriate ratios, prepare a report that comments on the recent performance and financial health of Hoult Ltd.

4 Discuss the following statement:

'It is not possible to test whether a stock market is strong form efficient. In fact, the existence of insider trading proves otherwise.'

5 Discuss the following statement:

'Ratio analysis using financial statements is pointless. Only economic value added gives a true measure of the financial performance of a company.'

QUESTIONS FOR DISCUSSION

1 Dayton has asked you for advice about his investment portfolio. He is considering buying shares in companies listed on the Alternative Investment Market. Green, a friend of Dayton, has told him he should invest only in shares that are listed on an efficient capital market as otherwise he cannot be sure he is paying a fair price. Dayton has said to you that he is not sure what an 'efficient' capital market is.

(a) Explain to Dayton what characteristics are usually required to be present for a market to be described as efficient.

(b) Discuss whether the Alternative Investment Market is an efficient market.

(c) Discuss the extent to which research has shown capital markets to be efficient.

2 Critically discuss the following statements about stock market efficiency:

(a) The weak form of the efficient market hypothesis implies that it is possible for investors to generate abnormal returns by analysing changes in past share prices.

(b) The semi-strong form of the efficient market hypothesis implies that it is possible for an investor to earn superior returns by studying company accounts, newspapers and investment journals, or by purchasing reports from market analysts.

(c) The strong form of the efficient market hypothesis implies that, as share prices reflect all available information, there is no way that investors can gain abnormal returns.

3 Discuss the importance of the efficient market hypothesis to the following groups:

(a) shareholders concerned about maximising their wealth;

(b) corporate financial managers making capital investment decisions;

(c) investors analysing the annual reports of listed companies.

4 Tor plc is a large company listed on the main market of the London Stock Exchange. The objectives of the company, in the current year and in recent years, are stated by its Annual Report to be as follows:

(1) To maximise the wealth of our shareholders.

(2) To give shareholders an annual return of 15 per cent per year.

(3) To increase real dividends by 4 per cent per year.

The shares of Tor plc are owned as follows:

	%
Chief executive officer	17
Managing director	6
Other directors	4
UK institutional investors	44
Foreign institutional investors	10
Small shareholders	19
	100

The following information relates to the recent performance of Tor plc.

Year (most recent last)	1	2	3	4	5
Revenue (£m)	144	147	175	183	218
Earnings per share (pence)	46.8	50.7	53.3	53.7	63.7
Dividend per share (pence)	18.7	20.0	21.4	22.9	24.5
Annual inflation (%)		2.5	2.7	3.1	2.9
Price/earnings ratio (times)	8	8	10	13	15

Average values for year 5 for Tor plc's business sector are:

Dividend yield	4.2%
Total shareholder return	35%
Price/earnings ratio	14 times

(a) Using the information provided, evaluate the recent performance of Tor plc and discuss the extent to which the company has achieved its declared financial objectives.

(b) Critically discuss how the agency problem may be reduced in a company listed on the main market of the London Stock Exchange, illustrating your answer by referring to the information provided.

References

Alexander, S. (1961) 'Price movements in speculative markets: trends or random walks', *Industrial Management Review*, May, pp. 7–26.

Ball, R. and Brown, P. (1968) 'An empirical evaluation of accounting income numbers', *Journal of Accounting Research*, Autumn, pp. 159–78.

Barberis, N. and Thaler, R. (2002) 'A survey of behavioral finance', *Social Science Research Network Economic Library*, available at *https://ssrn.com/en/*

Beechey, M., Gruen, D. and Vickery, J. (2000) 'The efficient market hypothesis: a survey', Research Discussion Paper, Economic Research Department, Reserve Bank of Australia.

Brusa, J., Liu, P. and Schulman, C. (2005) 'Weekend effect, "reverse" weekend effect, and investor trading activities', *Journal of Business Finance and Accounting*, vol. 32, nos. 7 and 8, pp. 1495–517.

De Bondt, W. and Thaler, R. (1985) 'Does the stock market overreact?', *Journal of Finance*, vol. 40, pp. 793–805.

Dimson, E. and Marsh, P. (1986) 'Event study methodologies and the size effect: the case of UK press recommendations', *Journal of Financial Economics*, vol. 17, no. 1, pp. 113–42.

Dixon, R. and Holmes, P. (1992) *Financial Markets: An Introduction*, London: Chapman & Hall.

Drury, C. (2015) *Management and Cost Accounting*, 9th edn, Andover: Cengage Learning EMEA.

Elliott, B. and Elliott, J. (2017) *Financial Accounting and Reporting*, 18th edn, Harlow: Pearson.

Fama, E. (1965) 'The behaviour of stock market prices', *Journal of Business*, January, pp. 34–106.

Fama, E. (1970) 'Efficient capital markets: a review of theory and empirical work', *Journal of Finance*, vol. 25, pp. 383–417.

Fama, E. (1991) 'Efficient capital markets: II', *Journal of Finance*, vol. 46, pp. 1575–617.

Fama, E. (1998) 'Market efficiency, long-term returns and behavioural finance', *Journal of Financial Economics*, vol. 49, pp. 283–306.

Fama, E., Fisher, L., Jensen, M. and Roll, R. (1969) 'The adjustment of stock prices to new information', *International Economic Review*, vol. 10, February, pp. 1–21.

Fernandez, P. (2003) 'EVA, economic profit and cash value added do not measure shareholder value creation', *Journal of Applied Finance*, vol. 9, no. 3, pp. 74–94.

Firth, M. (1972) 'The performance of share recommendations made by investment analysts and the effects on market efficiency', *Journal of Business Finance*, Summer, pp. 58–67.

Franks, J., Broyles, J. and Hecht, M. (1977) 'An industry study of the profitability of mergers in the United Kingdom', *Journal of Finance*, vol. 32, pp. 1513–25.

Gupta, R. and Basu, P.K. (2007) 'Weak form efficiency in Indian stock markets', *International Journal of Business and Economics Research*, vol. 6, no. 3, pp. 57–64.

Haugen, R. (2009) *The New Finance: Overreaction, Complexity and Other Consequences*, 4th edn, Upper Saddle River, NJ: Prentice Hall.

Hawawini, G. and Viallet, C. (2002) *Finance for Executives: Managing for Value Creation*, Cincinnati, OH: South-Western/Thomson Learning.

Hudson, R., Dempsey, M. and Keasey, K. (1996) 'A note on the weak form efficiency of capital markets: the application of simple trading rules to UK stock prices – 1935 to 1994', *Journal of Banking and Finance*, vol. 20, pp. 1121–32.

Jensen, M. (1968) 'The performance of mutual funds in the period 1945–64', *Journal of Finance*, May, pp. 389–416.

Johnson, S. and Bamber, M. (2007) 'Creating value: economic value added', *ACCA Student Accountant*, October, pp. 40–3.

Kendall, R. (1953) 'The analysis of economic time series, part 1: prices', *Journal of the Royal Statistical Society*, vol. 69, pp. 11–25.

Keown, A. and Pinkerton, J. (1981) 'Merger announcements and insider trading activity', *Journal of Finance*, vol. 36, September, pp. 855–70.

Keown, A., Martin, J., Petty, J. and Scott, D. (2003) *Foundations of Finance: The Logic and Practice of Financial Management*, Upper Saddle River, NJ: Prentice Hall.

Kumar, S. and Low, W.L. (2002) 'Economic value added versus traditional accounting measures of performance of the companies listed on the Singapore stock exchange', *Working Paper No. 2002-5*, Strathclyde: Graduate School of Business, University of Strathclyde.

Leahy, T. (2000) 'Capitalizing on economic value added', *Business Finance*, July.

Magnus, F.J. (2008) 'Capital market efficiency: an analysis of weak form efficiency on the Ghana stock exchange', *Journal of Money, Investment and Banking*, Issue 5, pp. 5–12.

Manganelli, S. (2002) 'Duration, volume and volatility impact of trades', European Central Bank Working Paper 125.

Megginson, W.L. (1997) *Corporate Finance Theory*, Reading, MA: Addison-Wesley.

Roll, R. (1994) 'What every CEO should know about scientific progress in economics: what is known and what remains to be resolved', *Financial Management*, vol. 23, pp. 69–75.

Rutterford, J. (ed.) (1998) *Financial Strategy*, Chichester: Wiley.

Samuelson, P. (1965) 'Proof that properly anticipated prices fluctuate randomly', *Industrial Management Review*, vol. 6, pp. 41–9.

Shamshir, M. and Mustafa, K. (2014) 'Efficiency in stock markets: a review of the literature', *International Journal of Economics, Commerce and Management*, vol. 2, issue 12.

Shleifer, A.S. (2000) *Inefficient Markets: An Introduction to Behavioural Finance*, Oxford: Oxford University Press.

Small, K. and Smith, J. (2007) 'The hot stock tip from Debbie: implications for market efficiency', *The Journal of Behavioral Finance*, vol. 8, no. 4, pp. 191–7.

Smith, T. (1996) *Accounting for Growth: Stripping the Camouflage from Company Accounts*, 2nd edn, London: Century Business.

Timmerman, A. and Granger, C.W.J. (2004) 'Efficient market hypothesis and forecasting', *International Journal of Forecasting*, vol. 20, pp. 15–27.

Worthington, A. and Higgs, H. (2006) 'Weak form efficiency in Asian emerging and developed capital markets: comparative tests of random walk behaviour', *Accounting Research Journal*, vol. 19, no. 1, pp. 54–63.

Recommended reading

A lucid treatment of efficient markets is found in:

Arnold, G. (2012) *Corporate Financial Management*, 5th edn, Harlow: Pearson.

A practical and lucid discussion of ratio analysis can be found in:

Walsh, C. (2008) *Key Management Ratios*, 4th edn, Harlow: FT Prentice Hall.

Useful journal articles and other material include the following:

Fama, E. (1970) 'Efficient capital markets: a review of theory and empirical work', *Journal of Finance*, vol. 25, pp. 383–417.

Fama, E. (1991) 'Efficient capital markets II', *Journal of Finance*, vol. 46, pp. 1575–617.

A wealth of business information can be obtained from the FT.com homepage (*https://www.ft.com/*) and its related web pages.

A wealth of information on equity is available from the London Stock Exchange: *https://www.lseg.com/*

Another useful website is LexisNexis: *http://www.lexisnexis.co.uk/en-uk/home.page*

3 SHORT-TERM FINANCE AND WORKING CAPITAL MANAGEMENT

Learning objectives

After studying this chapter, you should have achieved the following learning objectives:

- an appreciation of the importance of working capital management in ensuring the profitability and liquidity of a company;

- the ability to describe the cash conversion cycle and to explain its significance to working capital management;

- an understanding of the need for working capital policies concerning the level of investment in current assets, and of the significance of aggressive, moderate and conservative approaches to working capital management;

- an understanding of the link between the sources of short-term finance available to a company and working capital policies concerning the financing of current assets;

- the ability to describe and discuss a range of methods for managing inventory, cash, trade receivables and trade payables;

- the ability to evaluate, at an introductory level, the costs and benefits of proposed changes in working capital policies;

- an understanding of how factoring and invoice discounting can assist in managing working capital.

▓ ▓ ▓ INTRODUCTION

Long-term investment and financing decisions give rise to future cash flows which, when discounted by an appropriate cost of capital, determine the market value of a company. However, such long-term decisions will result in the expected benefits for a company only if attention is also paid to short-term decisions regarding current assets and liabilities. *Current assets and liabilities,* that is, assets and liabilities with maturities of less than one year, need to be carefully managed. *Net working capital* is the term given to the difference between current assets and current liabilities: current assets may include inventories of raw materials, work-in-progress and finished goods, trade receivables, short-term investments and cash, while current liabilities may include trade payables, overdrafts and short-term loans.

The level of current assets is a key factor in a company's liquidity position. A company must have, or be able to generate, enough cash to meet its short-term needs if it is to continue in business. Therefore, working capital management is a key factor in the company's long-term success: without the 'oil' of working capital, the 'engine' of non-current assets will not work. The greater the extent to which current assets exceed current liabilities, the more solvent or liquid a company is likely to be, depending on the nature of its current assets.

3.1 THE OBJECTIVES OF WORKING CAPITAL MANAGEMENT

To be effective, working capital management must have its objectives clearly specified. The two main objectives of working capital management are to increase the profitability of a company and to ensure that it has sufficient liquidity to meet short-term obligations as they fall due and so continue in business (Pass and Pike 1984). Profitability is related to the goal of shareholder wealth maximisation, so investment in current assets should be made only if an acceptable return is obtained. While liquidity is needed for a company to continue in business, a company may choose to hold more cash than is needed for operational or transaction needs, for example, for precautionary or speculative reasons. The twin goals of profitability and liquidity will often conflict since liquid assets give the lowest returns. Cash kept in a safe will not generate a return, for example, while a six-month bank deposit will earn interest in exchange for loss of access for the six-month period.

3.2 WORKING CAPITAL POLICIES

Because working capital management is so important, a company will need to formulate clear policies concerning the various components of working capital. Key policy areas relate to the level of investment in working capital for a given level of operations and the extent to which working capital is financed from short-term funds such as a bank overdraft.

A company should have working capital policies on managing inventory, trade receivables, cash and short-term investments to minimise the possibility of managers making decisions which are not in the best interests of the company. Examples of such suboptimal decisions are giving credit to customers who are unlikely to pay and ordering unnecessary inventories of raw materials. Sensible working capital policies will reflect corporate decisions on the *total* investment needed in current assets, i.e. the overall level of investment; the amount of investment needed in each *type* of current asset, i.e. the mix of current assets; and the way in which current assets are to be financed.

Working capital policies should reflect the nature of a company's business, as different businesses will have different working capital requirements. A manufacturing company will invest heavily in spare parts and components and might be owed large amounts of money by its customers. A food retailer will have large inventories of goods for sale but will have very few trade receivables. The manufacturing company clearly has a need for a carefully thought-out policy on receivables management, whereas the food retailer may not grant any credit at all.

Working capital policies will also need to reflect the credit policies of a company's close competitors, since it would be foolish to lose business from an unfavourable comparison of terms of trade. Any expected fluctuations in the supply of or demand for goods and services, for example due to seasonal variations in business, must also be considered, as must the impact of a company's manufacturing period on its current assets.

3.2.1 Working capital investment policy

An *aggressive* policy on the level of investment in working capital means that a company chooses to operate with lower levels of inventory, trade receivables and cash for a given level of activity or sales. An aggressive policy will increase profitability since less cash will be tied up in current assets, but it will also increase risk since the possibility of cash shortages or running out of inventory is increased. A *conservative* and more flexible working capital policy for a given level of turnover would be associated with maintaining a larger cash balance, perhaps even investing in short-term securities, offering more generous credit terms to customers and holding higher levels of inventory. Such a policy will give rise to a lower risk of financial problems or inventory problems, but at the expense of reducing profitability. A *moderate* policy would tread a middle path between the aggressive and conservative approaches. All three working capital investment policies are shown in Figure 3.1.

It should be noted that working capital investment policies can only be classified as aggressive, moderate or conservative by comparing them with the working capital investment policies of similar companies. While there are no absolute benchmarks of what may be regarded as aggressive or otherwise, these classifications are useful for describing the ways in which individual companies approach the operational problem of working capital investment.

3.2.2 Short-term finance

Short-term sources of finance include overdrafts, short-term bank loans and trade credit.

An *overdraft* is an agreement by a bank to allow a company to borrow up to a certain limit without the need for further discussion. The company will borrow as much or as little as it needs, up to the overdraft limit, and the bank will charge daily interest at a variable

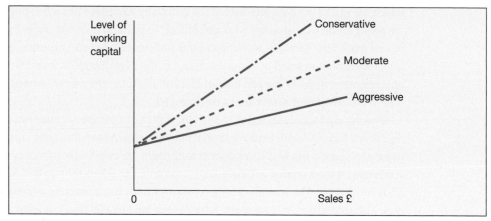

Figure 3.1 Working capital investment policies

rate on the debt outstanding. The bank may also require security or collateral as protection against the risk of non-payment by the company. An overdraft is a flexible source of finance in that a company uses it only when the need arises. However, an overdraft is technically repayable on demand, even though in practice a bank is likely to give warning of its intention to withdraw agreed overdraft facilities.

A *short-term loan* is a fixed amount of debt finance borrowed by a company from a bank, with repayment to be made in one year or less. The company pays interest on the loan at either a fixed or a floating (i.e. variable) rate at regular intervals, for example, quarterly. A short-term bank loan is less flexible than an overdraft, since the full amount of the loan must be borrowed over the loan period and the company takes on the commitment to pay interest on this amount, whereas with an overdraft interest is paid only on the amount borrowed, not on the agreed overdraft limit. As with an overdraft, however, security may be required as a condition of the short-term loan being granted.

Trade credit is an agreement to defer payment for goods and services to a date (the settlement date) later than that on which the goods and services are supplied to the purchasing company (the delivery date). It is common to find one, two or even three months' credit being offered on commercial transactions, and trade credit is a major source of short-term finance for most companies.

Short-term sources of finance are usually cheaper and more flexible than long-term ones. Short-term interest rates are usually lower than long-term interest rates, for example, and an overdraft is more flexible than a long-term loan on which a company is committed to pay fixed amounts of interest every year. However, short-term sources of finance are riskier than long-term sources from the borrower's point of view in that they may not be renewed (an overdraft is, after all, repayable on demand) or may be renewed on less favourable terms (e.g. when short-term interest rates have increased). Another source of risk for the short-term borrower is that interest rates are more volatile in the short term than in the long term and this risk is compounded if floating rate short-term debt (such as an overdraft) is used. A company must clearly balance *profitability* and *risk* in reaching a decision on how the funding of current and non-current assets is divided between long-term and short-term sources of funds.

The difficulty faced by small and medium-sized enterprises (SMEs) in gaining access to finance, short-term or otherwise, is highlighted by Shanahan (2013) and is the subject of Vignette 3.1.

Vignette 3.1

Banks 'reluctant to lend' to small businesses, MPs told

SMEs struggle in face of onerous borrowing terms and mistreatment

By Caroline Binham

Despite recent small business scandals at the Royal Bank of Scotland and Lloyds Banking Group, small and medium-sized enterprises (SME) are finding it tougher than ever to take out loans, according to evidence submitted to a parliamentary inquiry.

The SME Alliance, which represents thousands of small businesses in Britain who say they were mistreated by lenders – including RBS and Lloyds – told MPs on the Commons Treasury select committee that big banks are more reluctant to lend to them, while challenger banks are reverting to classic business models.

The group also alleged that banks' large legal teams are able to delay and frustrate small businesses' claims and complaints beyond the six-year statute of limitations.

The complaints were made in written evidence submitted to the select committee on Friday as part of its inquiry into whether enough is being done to protect SMEs from unfair treatment.

'Commercial lending is still unregulated and, other than large fines, we have seen little that has changed – except perhaps the fact lenders seem even more reluctant to lend and are even more keen to ensure terms of lending are onerous and biased in their favour,' the SME Alliance said.

SMEs make up 99 per cent of private businesses in the UK and account for more than half of all turnover and employment.

Lending to small businesses over 2017 remained fairly static, with the £5.6bn of new loans drawn in the fourth quarter some 11 per cent down compared to the same period in 2016, according to the most recent data from UK Finance, the banking lobby group.

UK Finance claims that this was owing to subdued demand from SMEs rather than banks taking a tougher line; it says eight out of 10 loan applications were approved, with a higher rate of loans approved for exporters and larger SMEs.

The select committee launched its inquiry into whether SMEs are being ripped off last month, following the scandal at RBS's Global Restructuring Group, which stands accused of 'widespread and inappropriate treatment' of the thousands of SMEs it was meant to help after the financial crisis. The Financial Conduct Authority's investigation into the matter is continuing.

Six people were jailed last year for a total of 47 years over a fraud at HBOS's Reading office between 2002 and 2007, when struggling small businesses were referred to a turnround consultancy then saddled with unmanageable debts. Lloyds bought HBOS in 2009. The FCA is investigating whether HBOS's senior executives knew of the fraud at the time.

SME Alliance has also called for regulation of the practice of banks forcing SME owners to make personal guarantees – such as their home – as a prerequisite for loans, and has asked the select committee to scrutinise these arrangements.

UK Finance has launched its own SME inquiry, which it says will be an evidence-based assessment of how disputes are resolved.

Source: Binham, C. (2018) 'Banks "reluctant to lend" to small businesses, MPs told', *Financial Times*, 30 March. © The Financial Times Limited 2018. All Rights Reserved.

Question
Why might SMEs have difficulty in securing finance?

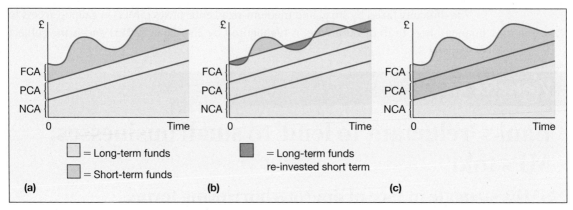

Figure 3.2 The (a) matching, (b) conservative and (c) aggressive working capital funding policies

3.2.3 Financing working capital

The trade-off between risk and return which occurs in working capital investment policy is also significant in the policy decision on the relative amounts of finance of different maturities in the balance sheet, i.e. on the choice between short- and long-term funds to finance working capital. To assist in the analysis of policy decisions on the financing of working capital, we can divide a company's assets into three different types: non-current assets, permanent current assets and fluctuating current assets (Cheatham 1989). *Non-current assets* are long-term assets from which a company expects to derive benefit over several periods, for example, factory buildings and production machinery. **Permanent current assets** represent the core level of investment needed to sustain normal levels of business or trading activity, such as investment in inventories and investment in the average level of a company's trade receivables. **Fluctuating current assets** correspond to the variations in the level of current assets arising from normal business activity.

A *matching working capital funding policy* is one that finances fluctuating current assets with short-term funds and permanent current assets and non-current assets with long-term funds. The maturity of the funds roughly matches the maturity of the different types of assets. A *conservative working capital funding policy* uses long-term funds to finance not only non-current assets and permanent current assets but some fluctuating current assets as well. As there is less reliance on short-term funding, the risk of such a policy is lower, but the higher cost of long-term finance means that profitability is reduced as well. An *aggressive working capital funding policy* uses short-term funds to finance not only fluctuating current assets but also some permanent current assets. This policy carries the greatest risk of insolvency, but also offers the highest profitability and increases shareholder value. These three working capital funding policies are illustrated in Figure 3.2.

3.3 WORKING CAPITAL AND THE CASH CONVERSION CYCLE

Working capital can be viewed *statically* as the balance between current assets and current liabilities, for example, by comparing the financial position statement figures for inventory, trade receivables, cash and trade payables. Alternatively, working capital can be viewed *dynamically* as an equilibrium between the income-generating and resource-purchasing activities of a company (Pass and Pike 1984), in which case it is closely linked to the cash conversion cycle (see 'Activity ratios', Section 2.4.4).

The *cash conversion cycle,* which represents the interaction between the components of working capital and the flow of cash within a company, can be used to determine the amount of cash needed for any sales level. It is the period of time between the outlay of cash on raw materials and the inflow of cash from the sale of finished goods, and represents the number of days of operation for which financing is needed. The longer the cash conversion cycle, the greater the amount of investment required in working capital. The length of the cash conversion cycle depends on the length of:

■ the inventory conversion period;
■ the trade receivables collection period;
■ the trade payables deferral period.

The *inventory conversion period* is the average time taken to use up raw materials, plus the average time taken to convert raw materials into finished goods, plus the average time taken to sell finished goods to customers. The inventory conversion period might be several months for an engineering or manufacturing company, but negligible for a service company. The *trade receivables period* is the average time taken by credit customers to settle their accounts. The *trade payables deferral period* is the average time taken by a company to pay its trade payables, i.e. its suppliers. If we approximate these three periods with the financial ratios of inventory days, trade receivables days and trade payables days (see 'Activity ratios', Section 2.4.4), the length of the cash conversion cycle (CCC) is given by:

$$\text{CCC} = \text{Inventory days} + \text{Trade receivables days} - \text{Trade payable days}$$

Example   Calculating working capital required

The amount of working capital required by a company can be estimated from information on the value of relevant working capital inputs and outputs, such as raw material costs and credit purchases, together with information on the length of the components of the cash conversion cycle. Assume that Carmed plc expects credit sales of £18m in the next year and has budgeted production costs as follows:

	£m
Raw materials	4
Direct labour	5
Production overheads	3
Total production costs	12

➡

Raw materials are in inventory for an average of three weeks and finished goods are in inventory for an average of four weeks. All raw materials are added at the start of the production process, which takes five weeks and incurs labour costs and production overheads at a constant rate. Suppliers of raw materials allow four weeks' credit, whereas customers are given 12 weeks to pay. If production takes place evenly throughout the 52-week year, what is the total working capital requirement?

Suggested answer

		£	£
Raw materials	4m × (3/52) =		230,769
Work-in-progress			
Raw materials	4m × (5/52) =	384,615	
Labour costs	5m × (5/52) × 0.5 =	240,385	
Overheads	3m × (5/52) × 0.5 =	144,231	
			769,231
Finished goods	12m × (4/52) =		923,077
Trade receivables	18m × (12/52) =		4,153,846
Trade payables	4m × (4/52) =		(307,692)
Working capital required			5,769,231

Labour costs and overheads are incurred at a constant rate during production so if work-in-progress is on average half-finished, labour and overheads have to be multiplied by 0.5 as only half the amounts of these costs are present in the work in progress.

On the information given, Carmed needs £5.77m of working capital. The proportions of long- and short-term finance used will depend on the working capital policies of the company. Note that Carmed's cash conversion cycle is $(3 + 5 + 4) + 12 - 4 = 20$ weeks.

3.3.1 The cash conversion cycle and working capital needs

Forecasts of working capital requirements can be based on forecasts of sales if a relationship between net working capital and sales is assumed to exist. Such a relationship is quantified by the *sales/net working capital ratio* described in 'Activity ratios' (Section 2.4.4) and made explicit by a working capital investment policy (see Section 3.2.1). However, even with such a policy in place, the relationship between sales and working capital is unlikely to remain static as levels of business and economic activity change. Since budgeted production is based on forecast sales, care must be taken in periods of reduced economic activity to ensure that overinvestment in inventories of raw materials, work-in-progress and finished goods does not occur. Although the overall amount of working capital needed can be estimated from forecast sales and the cash conversion cycle, there is likely to be a difference between forecast activity and actual activity. There can therefore be no substitute for regularly reviewing **working capital** needs in the light of changing levels of activity.

The cash conversion cycle also shows where managers should focus their attention if they want to decrease the amount of cash tied up in current assets. Apart from reducing sales and reducing the cost per unit sold, cash invested in current assets can be reduced by shortening the cash conversion cycle (Cheatham 1989). This can be done by decreasing the inventory conversion period (inventory days), by reducing the trade receivables collection period (trade receivables days) or by increasing the trade payables deferral period (trade payables days).

The inventory conversion period can be reduced by shortening the length of the production cycle, for example by more effective production planning or by outsourcing part of the production process. The amount of inventory within the production process can be reduced by using **just-in-time** (JIT) production methods (see below) or by employing production methods which are responsive to changing sales levels.

The trade receivables conversion period can be shortened by offering incentives for early payment such as early settlement discounts, by reducing the period of credit offered to customers, by chasing slow or late payers and by more stringent assessment of customers' creditworthiness to screen out slow payers. The minimum trade receivables conversion period is likely to be the credit offered by competitors.

The trade payables deferral period is less flexible as it is determined to a large extent by a company's suppliers. If a company delays payables payments past their due dates, it runs the risk of paying interest on overdue accounts, losing its suppliers or being refused credit in future.

3.4 OVERTRADING

Overtrading (also called undercapitalisation) occurs if a company is trying to support too large a volume of trade from too small a working capital base. It is the result of the supply of funds failing to meet the demand for funds within a company and it emphasises the need for adequate working capital investment. Even if a company is operating profitably, overtrading can result in a liquidity crisis, with the company being unable to meet its debts as they fall due because cash has been absorbed by growth in non-current assets, inventory and trade receivables. Serious and sometimes fatal problems for a company can therefore arise from overtrading.

Overtrading can be caused by a rapid increase in turnover, perhaps because of a successful marketing campaign where funding was not put in place for the necessary associated investment in non-current assets and current assets. Overtrading can also arise in the early years of a new business if it starts off with insufficient capital. This may be due to a mistaken belief that sufficient capital could be generated from trading profits and ploughed back into the business, when in fact the early years of trading are often difficult ones. Overtrading may also be due to erosion of a company's capital base, perhaps due to the non-replacement of long-term loans following their repayment.

There are several strategies that are appropriate for dealing with overtrading:

■ *Introducing new capital*: this is likely to be an injection of equity finance rather than debt since, with liquidity under pressure due to overtrading, managers will be keen to avoid straining cash flow further by increasing interest payments.
■ *Improving working capital management*: overtrading can also be attacked by better control and management of working capital, for example, by chasing overdue accounts. Since overtrading is more likely if an aggressive funding policy is being followed, adopting a matching policy or a more relaxed approach to funding could be appropriate.
■ *Reducing business activity*: as a last resort, a company can choose to level off or reduce the level of its planned business activity to consolidate its trading position and allow time for its capital base to build up through retained earnings.

Ratio analysis can assess whether a company is overtrading and indications of overtrading could include:

■ rapid growth in sales over a relatively short period;
■ rapid growth in the amount of current assets and perhaps non-current assets;
■ deteriorating inventory days and trade receivables days ratios;
■ using trade credit to finance current asset growth (increasing trade payables days);
■ declining liquidity, indicated perhaps by a falling quick ratio;
■ declining profitability, perhaps due to using discounts to increase sales;
■ decreasing amounts of cash and liquid investments, or a rapidly increasing overdraft.

3.5 MANAGING INVENTORY

Significant amounts of working capital can be invested in inventories of raw materials, work-in-progress and finished goods. Inventories of raw materials and work-in-progress can act as a buffer between different stages of the production process, ensuring its smooth operation. Inventories of finished goods allow the sales department to satisfy customer demand without unreasonable delay and potential loss of sales. These benefits of holding inventory must be weighed against any costs incurred if optimal inventory levels are to be determined. Costs which may be incurred in holding inventory include:

■ holding costs, such as insurance, rent and utility charges;
■ replacement costs, including the cost of obsolete inventory;
■ the cost of the inventory itself;
■ the opportunity cost of cash tied up in inventory.

3.5.1 The economic order quantity

This classical inventory management model calculates an optimum order size by balancing the costs of holding inventory against the costs of ordering fresh supplies. This optimum order size is the basis of a minimum cost procurement policy. The economic order quantity model assumes that, for the period under consideration (usually one year), costs and demand are constant and known with certainty. It is also called a *deterministic* model because it makes these steady-state assumptions. It makes no allowance for the existence of **buffer inventory**.

If we assume a constant demand for inventory, holding costs will increase as average inventory levels and order quantity increase, while ordering costs will decrease as order quantity increases and the number of orders falls. The total cost is the sum of the annual holding cost and the annual ordering cost. The total cost equation is therefore:

> Total annual cost = Annual holding cost + Annual ordering costs

Algebraically:

$$TC = \frac{(Q \times H)}{2} + \frac{(S \times F)}{Q}$$

where:

Q = order quantity in units
H = holding cost per unit per year
S = annual demand in units per year
F = ordering cost per order

The annual holding cost is the average inventory level in units ($Q/2$) multiplied by the holding cost per unit per year (H). The annual ordering cost is the number of orders per year (S/Q) multiplied by the ordering cost per order (F). This relationship is shown in Figure 3.3.

The minimum total cost occurs when holding costs and ordering costs are equal (as can be shown by differentiating the total cost equation with respect to Q and setting to zero). Putting holding costs equal to ordering costs and rearranging gives:

$$Q = \sqrt{\frac{2 \times S \times F}{H}}$$

Q is now the economic order quantity, which minimises the sum of holding costs and ordering costs. This formula is called the economic order quantity (EOQ) model.

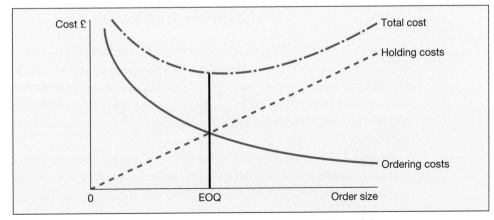

Figure 3.3 Inventory costs and the economic order quantity model

Example	**Using the EOQ model**

Oleum plc sells a soap called Fragro, which it buys in boxes of 1,000 bars with ordering costs of £5 per order. Retail sales are 200,000 bars per year and holding costs are £2.22 per year per 1,000 bars. What are the economic order quantity and average inventory level for Fragro?

Suggested answer

$$F = \text{£5 per order}$$
$$S = 200{,}000 \text{ bars per year}$$
$$H = \text{£2.22 per 1,000 bars}$$

So:

$$Q = (2 \times 200{,}000 \times 5/(2.22/1{,}000))^{1/2}$$
$$= 30{,}015 \text{ bars, or approximately 30 boxes}$$

The average inventory level = $Q/2$ = 30,000/2 = 15,000 bars.

More sophisticated inventory management models have been developed which relax some of the classical model's assumptions, whereas some modern approaches, such as just-in-time methods (see below) and material resource planning (MRP), question the need to hold any inventory at all.

3.5.2 Buffer inventory and lead times

There will usually be a delay between ordering and delivery, known as **lead time**. If demand and lead time are assumed to be constant, new inventory should be ordered when the inventory in hand falls to a level equal to the demand during the lead time. For example, if demand is 10,400 units per year and the lead time for delivery of an order is two weeks, the amount used during the lead time is:

$$10{,}400 \times (2/52) = 400 \text{ units}$$

New units must be ordered when the level of inventory falls to 400 units. If demand or lead times are uncertain or variable, a company may choose to hold buffer inventory to reduce or eliminate the possibility of running out of supplies. It could optimise the level of buffer inventory by balancing holding costs against the potential costs of running out of inventory. However, the EOQ model can still be used to determine an optimum order size.

Figure 3.4 shows the pattern of inventory levels where a company chooses to operate with buffer inventory OB. Regular economic orders of size BQ are placed, based on average annual demand. Because lead time is known and is equal to ab, new orders are placed

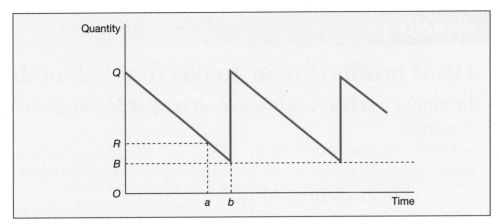

Figure 3.4 Average inventory levels, reorder level and buffer inventory

when inventory levels fall to *OR*. The company can meet unexpected demand during the lead time from the buffer inventory held. The average inventory level will be:

Buffer inventory + Half of regular order quantity = *OB* + (*BQ/2*)

This can be used to calculate the expected holding cost for the year.

3.5.3 Just-in-time inventory policies

Many companies in recent years have reduced inventory costs by minimising inventory levels. The main purpose of a just-in-time purchasing policy is to minimise or eliminate the time which elapses between the delivery and use of inventory. Such policies have been applied in a wide range of commercial operations and call for a close relationship between the supplier and the purchaser of both raw materials and bought components. The purchaser requires guarantees on both quality and reliability of delivery from the supplier to avoid disruptions to production. In return for these commitments, the supplier can benefit from long-term purchase agreements since a company adopting JIT purchasing methods will focus on dealing with suppliers who are able to offer goods of the required quality at the required time. The purchaser will benefit from a reduction in the costs of holding, ordering and handling inventory since materials will move directly from reception to the production line.

The main purpose of a JIT manufacturing policy is to minimise inventory acting as a buffer between different stages of production. Apart from developing closer relationships with suppliers, this can be achieved by changing factory layout to reduce queues of work-in-progress and by reducing the size of production batches. Good production planning is also essential if a JIT manufacturing policy is to be successful.

The problems of managing inventory in the challenging environment of the fashion industry are the subject of Vignette 3.2.

Vignette 3.2

H&M profits dive in 'tough' first half of the year

Inventory levels at world's second-largest fashion retailer still 'too high'

By Camilla Hodgson and Richard Milne

Trouble shifting stock sent profits at fast-fashion chain H&M Hennes & Mauritz down by a third in the first six months of its financial year, the Swedish retailer said on Thursday.

H&M said profits 'after financial items' were SKr7.3m (€702,000) over the period to May 31, and SKr6m in the quarter between March and the end of May, while the group's profit after tax for the half-year fell by nearly a third, to SKr6m from SKr8.4m last year.

Sales at the world's second-largest fashion retailer remained broadly flat over the period, though poor trading at the start of the year was helped by a 2 per cent rise in the second quarter. Pre-tax profit for the quarter was also in line with last year's figure.

'As we signalled previously, it was going to be a tough first half-year. We went into the second quarter carrying too much stock and we still had some imbalances in the H&M assortment – something that we are gradually correcting,' said chief executive Karl-Johan Persson.

The company strikingly refused to confirm its full-year guidance of a 'somewhat better result' this year compared with 2017, leading some to wonder if it had issued an implicit profit warning. Mr Persson told a press conference: 'It has become tougher to reach the full-year guidance, but there is still half a year to go.'

H&M shares recovered after initially falling 4.6 per cent to stand 0.5 per cent higher on Thursday morning.

Analysts focused on H&M's intensifying inventory problems after two years of persistently high stock levels. Stock-in-trade as a percentage of sales reached 18.2 per cent, up 2 percentage points from a year ago, and one of its highest ever levels despite Mr Persson vowing to cut it.

Although investments in online platforms were 'starting to have results', H&M said, total sales for the quarter 'were not satisfactory, which meant that inventory levels were still too high at the end of the period'. Overall, the first half of the year was 'somewhat more challenging than we initially thought'.

Nils Vinge, head of investor relations, said the high level of stock compared with revenues was in large part due to a stagnant top line. 'It had been a long time since the growth has been so slow in the business. Of course, it's a concern. We work hard to get back to a leaner level.'

But he added that there was a 'difficult balance' between introducing new products and marking down products that do not sell fast enough. 'What we need is stronger growth of full-price garments,' he said.

Mr Persson said updates to logistics systems over the second quarter of the year had hurt sales and profits, particularly in major markets such as the US, France, Italy and Belgium.

H&M has been particularly vulnerable to changes in customer habits and the boom in online shopping, given its reliance on opening large numbers of stores, and said on Thursday that it was 'going through a period of transformation'.

In February, the retailer cautioned that sales for 2018 were likely to be disappointing, while in March the group reported a 60 per cent drop in profits for the first quarter of the year, as higher markdowns hurt margins and sales flagged. Shares tumbled to a 10-year low on the news.

Source: Hodgson, C. and Milne, R. (2018) 'H&M profits dive in "tough" first half of the year', *Financial Times*, 28 June. © The Financial Times Limited 2018. All Rights Reserved.

Questions

1 Discuss why 'persistently high stock levels' can lead to financial problems.

2 What business reasons are suggested for high inventory levels?

3.6 MANAGING CASH

Cash management, which is part of the wider task of treasury management, is concerned with optimising the amount of cash available, maximising the interest earned by spare funds not required immediately and reducing losses caused by delays in the transmission of funds. Holding cash to meet short-term needs incurs an opportunity cost equal to the return which could have been earned if the cash had been invested or put to productive use. However, reducing this opportunity cost by operating with small cash balances will increase the risk of being unable to meet debts as they fall due, so an optimum cash balance should be found.

3.6.1 The need for cash

There are three reasons why companies choose to hold cash.

Transactions motive

Companies need a cash reserve to balance short-term cash inflows and outflows as these are not perfectly matched. This is called the transactions motive for holding cash, and the approximate size of the cash reserve can be estimated by forecasting cash inflows and outflows and by preparing cash budgets. In addition to the cash reserve held for day-to-day operational needs, cash may be built up to meet significant anticipated cash outflows, for example, those arising from investment in a new project or the redemption of debt.

Precautionary motive

Forecasts of future cash flows are subject to uncertainty and it is possible that a company will experience unexpected demands for cash. This gives rise to the precautionary motive for holding cash. Reserves could be held for precautionary reasons in the form of liquid short-term investments, which are discussed below.

Speculative motive

Companies may build up cash reserves to take advantage of any attractive investment opportunities that may arise, for example, in the mergers and acquisitions market. Such reserves are held for speculative reasons. If a company has significant speculative cash reserves for which it cannot see an advantageous use, it may choose to enhance share-holder value by returning them to shareholders, for example, by means of a share buy-back or a special cash dividend (see 'Alternatives to cash dividends', Section 10.7).

3.6.2 Optimum cash levels

Given the variety of needs a company may have for cash and the different reasons it may have for holding cash, the optimum cash level will vary both over time and between companies. The optimum amount of cash held by a company will depend on the following factors:

- forecasts of the future cash inflows and outflows of the company;
- the efficiency with which the cash flows of the company are managed;
- the availability of liquid assets to the company;
- the borrowing capability of the company;
- the availability and cost of short-term finance;
- the company's tolerance of risk (risk appetite).

3.6.3 Cash flow problems

A company may experience cash-flow problems for several reasons. It may, for example, be making losses. While this need not be a problem in the short term, making losses on a regular basis will lead to serious cash-flow problems, and perhaps even liquidation or acquisition. Inflation may also be a source of cash-flow problems since historical profit may prove to be insufficient to fund replacement of necessary assets. As we saw in our discussion of overtrading, growth requires investment in non-current assets and working capital; if the funds needed for this investment are not forthcoming, cash-flows can be severely strained. Managing cash is particularly difficult in a seasonal business as cyclical sales patterns can lead to cash-flow imbalances. Finally, cash-flow problems may arise due to sizable one-off items of expenditure, such as redemption of debt or investment in non-current assets. Companies could plan for the redemption of debt capital by setting up a *sinking fund* in which regular contributions of cash and accumulated interest combine to produce the required lump sum, although refinancing with new debt is more common.

When faced with cash-flow shortages, a company may choose one or more possible remedies. It may, for example, postpone non-essential capital expenditure. It may be able to accelerate the rate at which cash flows into the business, for example by offering customers early settlement discounts, by chasing overdue accounts or by reducing prices to move out unwanted inventory. If a company has investments, bought perhaps with surplus cash from an earlier period, it may choose to sell them to generate cash. Finally, a company may be able to identify ways to reduce or postpone cash outflows, for example, by taking longer to pay suppliers or by rescheduling loan repayments. As a last resort, it may decide to reduce or not pay a dividend, although this is usually seen by the capital markets as a sign of financial weakness (see 'Dividends are signals to investors', Section 10.4.1).

3.6.4 Cash budgets

Cash budgets are central to managing cash. They show expected cash inflows and outflows over a budget period and highlight anticipated cash surpluses and deficits. Preparing cash budgets assists managers in planning borrowing and investment, and facilitates control of expenditure. Computer spreadsheets allow managers to undertake 'what if' analysis to anticipate possible cash-flow difficulties as well as to examine possible future scenarios. To be useful, cash budgets should be regularly updated by comparing estimated figures with actual results, using a *rolling cash budget* system. Significant variances from planned figures must always be investigated.

3.6.5 Managing cash flows

Cash flows must be managed efficiently. This means that debts should be collected in line with agreed credit terms and cash should be quickly banked. Prompt banking will either reduce the interest charged on an outstanding overdraft or increase the interest earned on cash deposits. Credit offered by suppliers should be used to the full and payments made as late as possible, provided the benefit of these actions is greater than the benefit of taking any early payment discounts available.

The *float* is the time between initiating payment and receiving cash in a company's bank account. The float can be several days and consists of:

- transmission delay: the time taken for a payment to pass from payer to payee;
- lodgement delay: the delay in banking any payments received;
- clearance delay: the time taken by a bank to clear a presented instruction to pay.

Float can be reduced by minimising lodgement delay (e.g. by using electronic payment methods) and by simplifying and speeding up cash handling. Good cash management will aim to keep the float to a minimum.

3.6.6 Investing surplus cash

As discussed above, companies have several reasons for holding funds in liquid or near-liquid form. Cash which is surplus to immediate needs should earn a return by being invested on a short-term basis. There must be no risk of capital loss, since these funds are required to support a company's continuing working capital needs. To reduce the risk of loss, it is important for large companies to set limits on the amounts they deposit with individual banks as banks can, and do, fail.

The factors that should be considered when choosing an appropriate investment method for short-term cash surpluses are:

- the size of the surplus, as some investment methods have minimum amounts;
- the ease with which an investment can be turned into cash;
- when the investment is expected to mature;
- the risk and yield of the investment;
- any penalties which may be incurred for early liquidation.

Short-term methods that can be useful in managing corporate liquidity include money market deposits, certificates of deposit, Treasury bills and gilt-edged government securities.

Term deposits

Cash can be put on deposit with a bank to earn interest, with the interest rate depending on the size of the deposit, its maturity and the notice required for withdrawals. To maximise return, companies should obtain quotations from several banks before making a deposit since interest rates vary between banks as they compete for funds. **Money market** deposits are useful where cash-flow needs are predictable with a high degree of certainty.

In the UK, large companies can lend directly to banks on the interbank market at rates close to the London Interbank Offered Rate (LIBOR). Smaller companies lend indirectly onto the market through term deposits with their banks.

Sterling certificates of deposit

Sterling certificates of deposit are debt securities issued by banks and building societies. They are for a minimum amount of £100,000 and have maturities ranging from 28 days to 5 years, although most certificates have maturities of less than six months. At maturity, the holder of an interest-bearing sterling certificate of deposit is entitled to receive both principal and interest. Zero coupon certificates can also be issued on a discount basis.

Because certificates of deposit can be sold before maturity and so are more liquid than money market deposits, they carry a lower rate of interest. They may be useful if a company's cash flows are not predictable enough for a money market deposit to be made.

Treasury bills

Treasury bills are zero coupon debt securities of one-, three-, six- and 12-month maturities that are issued on a discounted basis by the UK Debt Management Office of the UK government. They are bought and sold on the discount market (part of the money market). The yield on Treasury bills is lower than on other money market instruments because of the lower **default risk** associated with government borrowing. In fact, the Treasury bill yield is often used as an approximation of the *risk-free rate of return* (see Section 8.6.2).

Gilt-edged government securities

Gilt-edged government securities (gilts) are the long-term interest-bearing debt securities that are used by the UK Debt Management Office on behalf of HM Treasury, with maturities of 5, 10, 30 and 50 years. Short-term cash surpluses should not be invested in newly issued gilts, since their long maturities make their market prices sensitive to interest rate changes and the risk of capital loss in the short term could be high. Gilts close to maturity may be regarded as liquid assets, however, and can be bought as short-term investments.

3.7 MANAGING TRADE RECEIVABLES

A company's credit management policy should help it to maximise expected profits. The policy will need to reflect the company's current and desired cash position, as well as its ability to satisfy expected demand. To put the credit management policy into effect successfully, managers and staff may need training or new staff may need to be recruited.

Key variables affecting the level of trade receivables will be the terms of sale prevailing in a company's area of business and the ability of the company to match and service comparable terms of sale. There is also a relationship between the level of trade receivables and a company's pricing policy: for example, it may keep selling prices relatively high while offering attractive early payment terms. The effectiveness of trade receivables follow-up procedures will also influence the overall level of trade receivables and the likelihood of bad debts arising.

The trade receivables management policy formulated by senior managers should also consider the administrative costs of debt collection, how the policy can be implemented and the costs and effects of easing credit. It should balance the benefits to be gained from offering credit to customers against the costs of offering credit. Longer credit terms may increase sales but will also increase the risk of bad debts. The cost of increased bad debts and the cost of any additional working capital required should be less than the increased profits generated by the higher turnover. To operate its trade receivables policy, a company needs to set up a credit analysis system, a credit control system and a trade receivables collection system.

3.7.1 Credit analysis system

To make a sensible decision about whether to trade with a company or not, information about the business is needed. The risk of bad debts can be minimised if the creditworthiness of new customers is carefully assessed before credit is granted and if the creditworthiness of existing customers is reviewed on a regular basis. Relevant information can be obtained from a variety of sources. New customers can be asked to provide bank references to confirm their financial standing and trade references to indicate satisfactory conduct of business affairs. Published information, such as the audited annual report and accounts of a prospective customer, may also provide a useful indication of creditworthiness. A company's own experience of similar companies will also be useful in forming a view on credit worthiness, as will the experience of other companies within a group.

For a fee, a report may be obtained from a credit reference agency, such as Experian, Equifax or Callcredit. A credit report may include a company profile, recent accounts, financial ratios and industry comparisons, analysis of trading history, payment trends, types of borrowing, previous financial problems and a credit limit.

Bearing in mind the cost of assessing creditworthiness, the magnitude of likely regular sales could be used as a guide to determine the depth of the credit analysis.

3.7.2 Credit control system

Once creditworthiness has been assessed and a credit limit agreed, the company should take steps to ensure the customer keeps to the credit limit and the terms of trade. Customer accounts should be kept within the agreed credit limit and credit granted should be reviewed periodically to ensure that it remains appropriate. To encourage prompt payment, invoices and statements should be checked carefully for accuracy and dispatched promptly. Under no circumstances should customers who have exceeded their credit limits be able to obtain goods.

3.7.3 Trade receivables collection system

Since the purpose of offering credit is to maximise profitability, the costs of debt collection should not be allowed to exceed the amounts recovered. A company should regularly prepare an *aged trade receivables analysis* and take steps to chase late payers. It is helpful to establish clear procedures for chasing late payers, to set out the circumstances under which credit control staff should send out reminders and initiate legal proceedings. Some thought could also be given to charging interest on overdue accounts to encourage timely payment, depending on the likely response of customers. Vignette 3.3 illustrates the problem of late payment and how large companies can put pressure on their suppliers, while Vignette 3.4 offers an international perspective on late payment.

Vignette 3.3

Large UK companies accused of 'supply chain bullying'

FSB urges FTSE 100 groups to tackle late payments

By Sarah Gordon

The head of one of Britain's leading small business groups has called for FTSE 100 companies to change the way they deal with their suppliers, notably by tackling the practice of late payments.

'Many large firms appear to be using the disparity of power in business relationships to squeeze their suppliers, delaying payments to improve their own cash flow,' said Mike Cherry, chair of the Federation of Small Businesses, in a letter to chairs and chief executives of all FTSE 100 companies. 'This is supply chain bullying, pure and simple.'

The collapse of the construction company Carillion in January highlighted the willingness of large groups to put pressure on their suppliers.

Mr Cherry said he had written to Carillion last July after he learnt that payment terms were being extended to 120 days, adding that the company's behaviour was not a one-off.

The FSB letter said Carillion's failure showed the 'frailty' of the prompt-payment code. The government-backed code, to which 2,174 companies have signed up, commits groups to pay suppliers within a maximum of 60 days, and to 'work towards' adopting 30 as the norm.

Mr Cherry called on those in charge of Britain's largest companies to 'personally shine a light' on their own company's practices, confirming, for example, that they regularly report on their payment terms.

These terms were lengthening across the UK economy, said the FSB, with common practices including retrospective discounting, where companies paid less than the full amount due, but with a shorter delay.

The FSB said that more than four-fifths of its 165,000 members reported being paid late, with more than a third finding terms had deteriorated over the past two years. Only 4 per cent had seen any improvement.

Nearly a third of all payments were late, with an average value of £6,142, and about 50,000 UK companies failed each year owing to poor payment practices.

The government has introduced a number of initiatives to address the problem of suppliers being paid late, but without much success.

Adam Marshall, director-general of the British Chambers of Commerce, said he heard from many suppliers who had been subjected to unfair terms. 'Culture change is needed from top to bottom. It's not something that can be solved overnight by any government policy,' he said.

Josh Hardie, deputy director-general of the CBI, said fair payment terms were a critical part of the strong supply chain partnerships that were essential for big and small companies.

Source: Gordon, S. (2018) 'Large UK companies accused of "supply chain bullying"', *Financial Times*, 29 May. © The Financial Times Limited 2018. All Rights Reserved.

Questions

1 Discuss the financial effects of late payment of invoices on a small company.

2 Discuss the problem of larger companies using their suppliers as a source of finance.

Vignette 3.4

Longer customer payment terms spark corporate fears

Research finds growing trend that raises insolvency risk as global economy slows

By Oliver Ralph

Companies around the world are taking longer to collect payments from customers, leading to a growing risk that they could hit trouble as the global economy slows.

Research from trade credit insurer Euler Hermes shows that companies are accepting much longer payment terms from their customers than they were a decade ago.

The average global days sales outstanding, or the number of days it takes for suppliers to be paid for their goods or services, has grown by one-tenth since 2008 to 66 days and is likely to increase again this year.

Ludovic Subran, chief economist at the Euler Hermes, said the trend increases the risk of insolvencies: 'This is one of the dark sides of the recovery. Companies are extending a lot of trust in the way that clients pay them – it is a loosening of discipline.'

He added: 'The longer you wait, the more the risk that your clients hit trouble. When there is a cyclical downturn the companies with longer payment terms are those that get hit first.' One in four insolvencies, said Mr Subran, is because of non-payment from customers.

The global days sales outstanding figure increased by 2 days last year, and the increase was widespread. It grew in two out of three countries, and in two out of three sectors.

The increases were sharpest in the US, China and the Eurozone, where Spain, Portugal, Greece and the Netherlands stood out as registering particularly large rises in days sales outstanding.

Euler Hermes looked at 25,000 listed companies in 36 countries. The research reveals sharp differences in payment behaviour around the world.

Companies in China have to wait an average of 92 days to be paid by their customers while Turkey and Greece also registered high scores. Companies in New Zealand only have to wait for 43 days on average, while South Africa, Denmark and Austria also recorded low numbers.

'Companies are using this "invisible bank" as a way to finance themselves,' said Mr Subran. 'In some sectors, everyone accepts late payments but in others, such as consumer industries, they want shorter payment times because margins are thin and they need the money to buy more supplies.'

In the UK, where days sales outstanding is below average at 53, the government has pledged to tackle what it calls the 'late payment culture'.

In his spring statement in March, chancellor Philip Hammond called for evidence 'on how we can eliminate the continuing scourge of late payments – a key ask from small business.'

Source: Ralph, O. (2018) 'Longer customer payment terms spark corporate fears', *Financial Times*, 3 May. © The Financial Times Limited 2018. All Rights Reserved.

3.7.4 Insuring against bad debts

Insurance against the risk of bad debts is available and can be arranged through brokers or intermediaries. *Whole turnover insurance* will cover any debt below an agreed amount against the risk of non-payment. *Specific account insurance* will allow a company to insure key accounts against default and may be used for major customers.

3.7.5 Early settlement discounts

Cash discounts may encourage early payment, but the cost of such discounts must be less than the total financing savings resulting from lower trade receivables balances, any administrative or financing savings arising from shorter trade receivables collection periods and any benefits from lower bad debts.

| Example | Evaluating a change in trade receivables policy |

Mine plc has annual credit sales of £15m and allows 90 days' credit. It is considering introducing a 2 per cent discount for payment within 15 days and reducing the credit period to 60 days. It estimates that 60 per cent of its customers will take advantage of the discount, while the volume of sales will not be affected. The company finances working capital from an overdraft at a cost of 10 per cent. Is the proposed change in policy worth implementing?

Suggested answer

	£000	£000
Current level of receivables: 15,000 × (90/365) =		3,699
Proposed level of receivables:		
15,000 × (60/365) × 40% =	986	
15,000 × (15/365) × 60% =	370	
		1,356
Reduction in receivables		2,343

	£
Saving in finance costs: 2,343,000 × 0.10 =	234,300
Cost of discount: 15,000,000 × 2% × 60% =	180,000
Net benefit of proposed policy change	54,300

The policy change is financially attractive. However, the difficulty of forecasting accurately the effects of a change in trade receivables policy should be considered when deciding whether or not to introduce it.

3.7.6 Factoring

Factoring companies offer a range of services in sales administration and collecting amounts due from trade receivables. A factor can take over the administration of sales invoicing and accounting for a client company, together with collecting amounts due from trade receivables and chasing up any slow payers. A factor can offer a cash advance against the security of trade receivables, allowing a company ready access to cash as soon as credit sales are made. For an additional fee, a factor can take on any bad debts that may arise through non-payment. This is called **non-recourse factoring**, since here the factor does not have **recourse** to the company for compensation in the event of non-payment.

While a factor will advance up to 100 per cent of the face value of invoices, interest will be charged on the sum advanced. In exchange for accelerated cash receipts, therefore, a company incurs an interest charge, which can be compared with the cost of short-term borrowing. This charge is in addition to the service fee levied by the factor, which is usually between 0.5 per cent and 3 per cent of gross annual turnover. Administration costs will be reduced, however, and the company will have access to the factor's expertise in credit analysis and credit control.

The advantages that factoring offers to a company may include the following:

- prompt payment of suppliers, perhaps leading to early payment discounts;
- a reduction in the amount of working capital tied up in trade receivables;
- financing growth through sales;
- savings on sales administration costs;
- benefits arising from the factor's experience in credit analysis and credit control.

3.7.7 Invoice discounting

Invoice discounting involves the sale of selected invoices to a third party while retaining full control over the sales ledger; it is a service often provided by factoring companies. The main cost of invoice discounting is a discount charge linked to bank base rates, although a fee of between 0.2 per cent and 0.5 per cent of turnover is often levied. Invoice discounting is useful to a company because it results in an improvement in cash flow.

Evaluating the costs and benefits of factoring and invoice discounting is similar to evaluating discounts for early payment, as discussed earlier.

Example	**Cost–benefit analysis of factoring**

Trebod plc has annual credit sales of £4.5m. Credit terms are 30 days, but its management of trade receivables has been poor and the average collection period is 50 days, with 0.4 per cent of sales resulting in bad debts. A factor has offered to take over the task of debt administration and credit checking, at an annual fee of 1 per cent of credit sales. Trebod estimates that it would save £35,000 per year in administration costs as a result. Due to the efficiency of the factor, the average collection period would fall to 30 days and bad debts would be eliminated. The factor would advance 80 per cent of invoiced debts at an annual interest rate of 11 per cent. Trebod currently finances trade receivables from an overdraft costing 10 per cent per year.

If credit sales occur smoothly throughout the year, determine whether the factor's services should be accepted.

Suggested answer

	£
Current level of trade receivables is £4.5m × (50/365) =	616,438
Under the factor, trade receivables would fall to £4.5m × (30/365) =	369,863

The costs of the current policy are as follows:

	£
Cost of financing current receivables: £616,438 × 10% =	61,644
Cost of bad debts: £4.5m × 0.4% =	18,000
Costs of current policy:	79,644

The costs under the factor are as follows:

	£
Cost of financing new receivables through factor: (£369,863 × 0.8 × 0.11) + (£369,863 × 0.2 × 0.10) =	39,945
Factor's annual fee: £4.5m × 0.01 =	45,000
Saved administration costs:	(35,000)
Net cost under factor:	49,945

Cost–benefit analysis shows the factor's services are cheaper than current practice by £29,699 per year. On financial grounds, the services of the factor should be accepted.

3.8 CONCLUSION

Managing working capital effectively lies at the heart of a successful company, playing a crucial role in increasing shareholder wealth and achieving benefits from capital investment. In fact, poor management of working capital is one of the more common reasons for corporate failure. It is essential that company managers understand this key area of corporate finance.

■ ■ ■ KEY POINTS

1 The main objectives of working capital management are profitability and liquidity.

2 Short-term sources of finance include overdrafts, short-term bank loans and trade credit.

3 Companies may adopt aggressive, moderate or conservative working capital investment policies and working capital funding policies.

4 The cash conversion cycle can be used to find a company's working capital requirement as well as to help managers find ways of decreasing cash invested in current assets.

5 Overtrading can lead to business failure and must be corrected if found. Corrective measures include introducing new capital, improving working capital management and reducing business activity.

6 Because large amounts of cash can be tied up in inventories of finished goods, raw materials and work-in-progress, the amount of inventory and the time it is held for must be monitored.

7 The economic order quantity model can be used to determine an optimum order size and directs attention to the costs of holding and ordering inventory. However, there is a growing trend for companies to minimise the use of inventory.

8 Cash may be held for transactions, precautionary and speculative reasons, but companies should optimise holdings of cash according to their individual needs.

9 Cash-flow problems can be anticipated by forecasting cash needs, for example, by using cash-flow forecasts and cash budgets.

10 Surplus cash should be invested to earn a return in appropriate short-term instruments.

11 Managing trade receivables effectively requires assessing customers' Creditworthiness, controlling credit granted and collecting money due efficiently. Factoring and invoice discounting can assist effective management of receivables.

SELF-TEST QUESTIONS

Answers to these questions can be found on pages 452–3.

1 Explain the different working capital funding policies that a company may adopt.

2 Describe the cash conversion cycle and explain its significance in determining the working capital needed by a company.

3 Describe the main sources of short-term finance for a company.

4 Describe the strategies that could be followed by a company dealing with the problem of overtrading.

5 Discuss the possible reasons why a company might experience cash-flow problems and suggest ways in which such problems might be alleviated.

6 Explain why a company may choose to have reserves of cash.

7 Discuss ways in which a company might invest its short-term cash surpluses, explaining briefly the factors which it should consider in making its selection.

8 How might the creditworthiness of a new customer be checked?

9 Is it worth offering early settlement discounts to trade receivables to encourage prompt payment?

10 Explain the difference between factoring and invoice discounting.

QUESTIONS FOR REVIEW

1 Sec uses 60,000 tons of salt over a 50-week working year. It costs £100 to order salt and delivery follows two weeks later. Storage costs for the salt are expected to be £0.10 per ton per year. The current practice is to order twice a year when inventory falls to 10,000 tons (all orders are equal in size). Recommend an ordering policy for Sec using the Economic Order Quantity model and contrast its cost with the cost of the current policy.

2 MW has sales of £700,000 per year. Its costs as a percentage of sales are as follows:

	%
Raw materials	20
Direct labour	35
Overheads	15

Raw materials are carried in inventory for two weeks and finished goods are held in inventory for three weeks. Production takes four weeks. MW takes four weeks' credit from suppliers and gives eight weeks' credit to its customers. If both overheads and production are incurred evenly throughout the year, what is MW's total working capital requirement?

3 MC has current sales of £1.5m per year. Cost of sales is 75 per cent of sales and bad debts are 1 per cent of sales. Cost of sales comprises 80 per cent variable costs and 20 per cent fixed costs. The company finances working capital from an overdraft at a rate of 7 per cent per year. MC currently allows customers 30 days' credit but is considering increasing this to 60 days' credit to boost sales.

  It has been estimated that this change in policy will increase sales by 15 per cent, while bad debts will increase from 1 per cent to 4 per cent of sales. It is not expected that the policy change will result in an increase in fixed costs and payables and inventory will be unchanged. Should MC introduce the proposed policy?

4 A company is planning to offer a discount for payment within 10 days to its customers, who currently pay after 45 days. Only 40 per cent of credit customers would take the discount, although administrative cost savings of £4,450 per year would be gained. If credit sales, which are unaffected by the discount, are £1.6m per year and the cost of short-term finance is 8 per cent, what is the maximum discount that could be offered?

1 Stenigot's finance director is concerned about the lax management of the company's trade receivables. Stenigot's trade terms require settlement within 30 days, but its customers take an average of 60 days to pay their bills. In addition, out of total credit sales of £20m per year, the company suffers bad debts of £200,000 per year. Stenigot finances working capital needs with an overdraft at a rate of 8 per cent per year. The finance director is reviewing two options:

■ *Option 1*: offering a discount of 1 per cent for payment within 30 days. It is expected that 35 per cent of customers will take the discount, while the average time taken to pay by the remaining customers will remain unchanged. As a result of the policy change, bad debts would fall by £60,000 per year and administration costs would fall by £20,000 per year.

■ *Option 2*: Stenigot's debt administration and credit control could be taken over by a factor. The annual fee charged by the factor would be 1.75 per cent of sales. Stenigot would gain administration cost savings of £160,000 per year and an 80 per cent reduction in bad debts. The factor would reduce Stenigot's average trade receivables days to 30 days and would advance 80 per cent of invoices at an interest rate of 12 per cent.

(a) Calculate the benefit, if any, to Stenigot of the two suggested options and recommend an appropriate course of action to the finance director.

(b) Critically discuss whether it is possible for a company to optimise its working capital position. Your answer should include a discussion of the following matters:
   (i)   the risk of insolvency;
   (ii) the return on assets;
   (iii) the level, mix and financing of current assets.

2 Saltfleet is a supply company which operates through its stores and depots throughout the UK. Its subsidiary, Irby, manufactures scaffolding and security fences. Saltfleet's finance director has been reviewing its working capital management and is considering several proposals which he hopes will increase efficiency and effectiveness in this area:

■ appointing a credit controller to oversee credit management in the stores and depots;

■ appointing a factor to take over the sales administration and trade receivables management of Irby;

■ investing short-term cash surpluses on the London Stock Exchange. The finance director is interested in buying shares of a small company recently tipped by an investment magazine.

(a) Critically discuss the importance of credit management to a company like Saltfleet, explaining the areas to be addressed by a credit management policy.

(b) Distinguish between factoring and invoice discounting and explain the benefits which Irby may receive from a factoring company.

(c) Discuss whether Saltfleet should invest short-term cash surpluses on the London Stock Exchange.

3 The following information has been extracted from the financial statements of Rowett:

Statement of profit or loss extracts

	£000	£000
Sales		12,000
Cost of sales:		
Raw materials	5,800	
Labour	3,060	
		8,860
Gross profit		3,140
Administration/distribution costs		1,680
Profit before interest and tax		1,460

Financial position statement extracts

	£000	£000
Current assets:		
Inventories of raw materials	1,634	
Inventories of finished goods	2,018	
Trade receivables	1,538	
Cash and bank	500	5,690
Current liabilities:		
Trade payables	1,092	
Overdraft	300	
Other expenses	76	1,468

Powell, a factoring company, has offered to take over Rowett's debt administration and credit control on a non-recourse basis for an annual fee of 2 per cent of sales. This would save Rowett £160,000 per year in administration costs and reduce bad debts from 0.5 per cent of sales to nil. Powell would reduce trade receivables days to 40 days and would advance 75 per cent of invoiced debts at an interest rate of 10 per cent.

Rowett finances working capital from an overdraft at 8 per cent.

(a) Calculate the length of Rowett's cash conversion cycle and discuss its significance to the company.

(b) Discuss ways in which Rowett could improve the management of its receivables.

(c) Using the information given, assess whether Rowett should accept the factoring service offered by Powell. What use should the company make of any finance provided by the factor?

4 The finance director of Menendez is trying to improve the company's slack working capital management. Although Menendez's trade terms require settlement within 30 days, its customers take an average of 45 days to pay. In addition, out of total credit sales of £15m per year, the company suffers bad debts of £235,000 annually.

It has been suggested that the average settlement period could be reduced if an early settlement discount were offered and the finance director is considering a reduction of 1.5 per cent of the face value of invoice for payment within 30 days. It is expected that

40 per cent of customers would use the discount, but that the average time taken by the remaining customers would not be affected. It is also expected that, if the new credit terms are introduced, bad debts will fall by £60,000 per year and administration costs will fall by £15,000 per year.

(a) If total sales are unchanged and if working capital is financed by an overdraft at 9 per cent per year, are the new credit terms of any benefit to Menendez?

(b) Discuss whether Menendez should finance its working capital needs from an overdraft.

(c) It has been suggested by the managing director of Menendez that the way to optimise the company's overall level of working capital is by minimising its cash conversion cycle. Critically discuss whether the finance director should follow this suggestion.

(d) Briefly discuss ways in which Menendez could use its trade receivables as a source of finance.

References

Cheatham, C. (1989) 'Economizing on cash investment in current assets', *Managerial Finance*, vol. 15, no. 6, pp. 20–5.

Pass, C. and Pike, R. (1984) 'An overview of working capital management and corporate financing', *Managerial Finance*, vol. 10, nos. 3/4, pp. 1–11.

Shanahan, B. (2013) *Working Capital – What's Next?*, Marston Gate: Informita Limited.

Recommended reading

An interesting discussion of cash management can be found in:

Van Horne, J.C. and Wachowicz, Jr, J.M. (2009) *Fundamentals of Financial Management*, 13th edn, Harlow: FT Prentice Hall.

An interesting discussion of inventory management methods can be found in:

Titman, S.J., Martin, J.D. and Keown, A.J. (2013) *Financial Management: Principles and Applications*, 12th edn, Harlow: Prentice Hall.

An excellent discussion of working capital management from an American perspective can be found in:

Gitman, L.J. and Zutter, C.J. (2014) *Principles of Managerial Finance*, 14th edn, Boston, MA: Pearson Education.

4 LONG-TERM FINANCE: EQUITY FINANCE

Learning objectives

After studying this chapter, you should have achieved the following learning objectives:

- a knowledge of the key characteristics of equity finance;

- an understanding of the different ways that a company can issue new equity finance and the reasons why a stock market quotation may or may not be desirable;

- an understanding of rights issues, their importance to companies and their effect on shareholder wealth;

- the ability to estimate the theoretical effect of rights issues on share prices;

- an appreciation of the difference between share splits, **bonus issues**, scrip dividends and share repurchases, and their importance to companies;

- an understanding of preference shares as a source of finance for a company.

■ ■ ■ INTRODUCTION

Ordinary share capital or equity finance is the foundation of the financial structure of a company and should be the source of most of its long-term finance. Since a company is owned by its ordinary shareholders, raising additional finance by issuing new ordinary shares has ownership and control implications which merit careful consideration.

In this chapter we look at some of the key areas concerning ordinary share capital, such as ways in which a company can raise finance through issuing new shares and the implications for a company of obtaining a stock market listing. Rights issues (issuing new shares to existing shareholders) are discussed, and their impact on shareholder wealth. We examine some of the ways in which a company can increase or decrease the number of ordinary shares in issue, and the implications for both companies and investors. We also discuss preference shares, which have characteristics in common with both equity and debt, and consider the relative merits of ordinary shares and preference shares.

4.1 EQUITY FINANCE

Equity finance is raised through the sale of ordinary shares to investors. This may be a sale of shares to new owners, perhaps through the stock market as part of a company's initial listing, or it may be a sale of shares to existing shareholders by means of a rights issue. Ordinary shares are bought and sold regularly on stock exchanges throughout the world and ordinary shareholders, as owners of a company, want a satisfactory return on their investment. This is true whether they are the original purchasers of the shares or investors who have subsequently bought the shares on the stock exchange.

The ordinary shares of a company must have a *nominal value* (par value) by law and cannot be issued for less than this amount. The nominal value of an ordinary share, usually 1p, 5p, 10p, 25p, 50p or £1, bears no relation to its *market value*, and ordinary shares with a nominal value of 25p may have a market price of several pounds. New shares, whether issued at the foundation of a company or subsequently, are almost always issued at a *premium* to their nominal value. The nominal value of shares issued by a company is represented in the financial position statement by the *ordinary share account*. The additional funds raised by selling shares at an issue price greater than the nominal value are represented by the *share premium account*. This means that the cash raised from the sale of shares on the asset side of the financial position statement is equally matched with shareholders' funds on the liability side of the financial position statement.

4.1.1 The rights of ordinary shareholders

Ownership of ordinary shares gives rights to ordinary shareholders on both an individual and a collective basis. For corporate finance, some of the most important rights of shareholders are:

■ to attend general meetings of the company;
■ to vote on the appointment of directors of the company;

- to vote on the appointment, remuneration and removal of auditors;
- to receive the annual accounts of the company and the report of its auditors;
- to receive a share of any dividend agreed to be distributed;
- to vote on important company matters such as permitting the repurchase of its shares, using its shares in a takeover bid or a change in its **authorised share capital**;
- to receive a share of any assets remaining after the company has been liquidated;
- to participate in a new issue of shares in the company (the **pre-emptive right**).

While individual shareholders have influence over who manages a company and can express an opinion on decisions relating to their shares, it is rare for shareholders to exercise their power collectively. This is due partly to the division between small shareholders and institutional shareholders, partly to real differences in opinion between shareholders and partly to shareholder apathy. There is evidence in recent years of an increasingly active approach by shareholders (see 'The influence of institutional investors', Section 1.5.5).

4.1.2 Equity finance, risk and return

Ordinary shareholders are the ultimate bearers of the risk associated with the business activities of the companies they own. This is because an order of precedence governs the distribution of the proceeds of liquidation in the event of a company going out of business. The first claims settled are those of *secured creditors,* such as bond holders and banks, who are entitled to receive in full both unpaid interest and outstanding debt capital or principal. The next claims settled are those of *unsecured creditors,* such as suppliers of goods and services. *Preference shareholders* are next in order of precedence and their claims are settled if any proceeds remain once the claims of secured and unsecured creditors have been met in full. *Ordinary shareholders* are not entitled to receive any of proceeds of liquidation until the amounts owing to secured and unsecured creditors and preference shareholders have been satisfied in full. The position of ordinary shareholders at the bottom of the *creditor hierarchy* (see Figure 9.1) means there is a significant risk of their receiving nothing or very little from liquidation. This is especially true when it is recognised that liquidation is likely to occur after a protracted period of unprofitable trading. It is also possible, however, for ordinary shareholders to make substantial gains from liquidation as they are entitled to all that remains once the fixed claims of creditors and preference shareholders have been met.

Since ordinary shareholders carry the greatest risk of any of the providers of long-term finance, they expect the highest return in compensation. In terms of regular returns on capital, this means that ordinary shareholders expect the return they receive through capital gains and ordinary dividends to be higher than either interest payments or preference dividends. In terms of the cost of capital (see 'The cost of capital and capital structure', Chapter 9), it means that the cost of equity is always higher than either the cost of debt or the cost of preference shares.

4.2 THE STOCK EXCHANGE

Financial securities are bought and sold on a stock exchange. The ordinary shares of many large UK companies are traded on the London Stock Exchange (LSE). Companies pay an annual fee to have the price of their ordinary shares listed (quoted) on the stock exchange and undergo a rigorous financial assessment before being granted a listing. The LSE is a market not only for ordinary shares but also for bonds and depositary receipts. Bonds such as loan stock and debentures are discussed in 'Bonds, loan notes, loan stock and debentures' (Section 5.1). Depositary receipts, which are certificates representing ownership of a given company's shares that can be listed and traded independently of those shares, are not discussed in this text.

Trading in shares on a stock exchange is subject to statutory regulation to ensure fair trading. Trading on the LSE is regulated by the Financial Conduct Authority (FCA) under powers granted to it under the Financial Services and Markets Act 2000, as amended. In carrying out this market regulatory role it is referred to as the UK Listing Authority (UKLA). The responsibilities of the UKLA include:

- admitting securities to listing;
- maintaining the **Official List**;
- the regulation of sponsors (see Section 4.2.1);
- imposing and enforcing continuing obligations on issuing companies;
- suspending and cancelling listings where necessary.

4.2.1 The new equity issues market

A company that is planning to issue new equity will need advisers to guide it through the process. A company seeking a listing on the LSE or the Alternative Investment Market (AIM) will need to appoint a range of advisers, including a sponsor, a reporting accountant, a broker or bookrunner, and lawyers. The sponsor, who will help the listing company to meet and abide by all relevant regulations, will be largely responsible for putting out the prospectus, managing the listing process and liaising with the UKLA and the LSE. The broker will advise on an appropriate issue price for the new shares and market the issue to institutional and other investors. The sponsor and the bookrunner may in fact be the same firm. Sponsors are regulated by the UKLA.

4.2.2 New issue methods

A company may issue shares and/or obtain a listing on the LSE, the AIM and other stock exchanges by several methods. Issuing shares to obtain a listing is called an **initial public offering (IPO)**. European tech (technology) companies raising funds through IPOs is the subject of Vignette 4.1.

A placing

There are two main methods of issuing ordinary shares in the UK, and the one used most frequently is called a *placing.* Here, the shares are issued at a fixed price to several

Vignette 4.1

European tech IPOs begin to rival US successes

At its debut Dutch group Adyen achieved a valuation that would be the envy of Silicon Valley

By Aliya Ram and Richard Waters

The day before Adyen's stock market listing this week, the Dutch financial technology group's co-founder sent a message to employees: 'We won't be ringing the bell – or sounding the gong – tomorrow,' Pieter van der Does wrote. 'While it's definitely important to celebrate successes, investor liquidity is not something we celebrate.'

He failed to stop the party, though. Adyen shares soared more than 90 per cent on their debut on Wednesday. Having achieved a market value of almost €14bn, the payments group boasts a multiple that would be the envy of most Silicon Valley stars: more than 12 times revenues and 170 times earnings.

It is the latest sign of ebullience among European-based tech companies, which have been long overshadowed by US juggernauts. A month before Adyen came Avast, a Czech cyber security company, listed in one of the five largest tech flotations on the London Stock Exchange. That came two days after Swedish payments company iZettle's abortive plans for what would have been Europe's biggest fintech IPO.

The announcements – which follow Swedish music streaming group Spotify's much-anticipated New York listing in April – are being taken as a sign that Europe's tech sector has matured, with better access to late-stage capital and the infrastructure to go public.

Still to come are flotations from online luxury fashion marketplace Farfetch and Funding Circle, the peer-to-peer lender, according to several people familiar with the companies' plans. Data from Dealogic show the number of IPOs of European-headquartered tech companies outpaced those from the US in each of the past four years and surged 34 per cent last year to 59.

But just before iZettle was due to list in Stockholm, US payments giant PayPal swooped in and snapped it up at double the IPO price. The start-up's owners, like so many others from Europe, traded in a public listing for a bigger cheque and a future under the auspices of a Silicon Valley owner.

For Europe-focused investors and politicians eager to build the next Google, Apple or Tencent, iZettle's sale reignited concerns over the ability of the continent's private tech companies to grow big and develop sustainable business models independently. Over the past decade a succession of trailblazing European tech companies have been bought by US peers, including Skype and Mojang (Microsoft), DeepMind (Google) and Shazam (Apple).

'Selling to a strategic partner you get a much higher price,' said Shing Lo at law firm Bird & Bird, who advises technology companies on deals and flotations. 'Start-ups are starting to think about listing . . . but more of them are actually doing trade sales.'

However, the near doubling of Adyen's shares on its trading debut pointed to huge untapped appetite for technology companies in Europe's public markets. European investors have found it hard to get large stock allocations in US-listed IPOs, leaving them on the sidelines of a hot market, said Lise Buyer, an IPO adviser who worked on Google's 2004 stock market listing. She said that had created pent-up demand that probably added to the spike in Adyen's share price.

Neil Rimer, co-founder of Index Ventures, an early backer of iZettle, Adyen, Farfetch and Funding Circle, pointed to 'a coincidence of a big market need and technological platforms and tools like [the cloud] that enable you to serve that need in a way that is very compelling and scaleable'.

The increase in IPOs from European companies comes against a backdrop of the most active tech IPO market in the US since the dotcom boom that

Vignette 4.1 (continued)

peaked at the turn of the century. Twenty tech companies have gone public in the US this year, including cloud storage company Dropbox.

Farfetch plans to list in New York with a targeted valuation of up to $5bn this year, while Funding Circle will float in London with a valuation of up to £2bn, according to people familiar with the two companies' plans. The run of listings by venture-backed European companies will bring a windfall for investors such as Index Ventures and General Atlantic, and should boost confidence that early-stage funds can find easy exit opportunities.

Despite the strong recovery in appetite for buying into IPOs – typically among the most volatile stock market investments – investors have been far more cautious than they were during the dotcom boom. The IPO wave on Wall Street has been led by 'software as a service' companies, which charge monthly subscriptions for access to their technology, making

their financial performance highly predictable. Adyen, which strikes multiyear contracts with merchants, also receives recurring revenues.

Institutional investors caution that listings do not always translate into success on the public markets, especially if flotations are used by venture capital investors to offload companies beyond the typical seven-year timescale for an investment. Rovio, the Finnish mobile gamily company, has lost almost half its value since it listed in Helsinki last year.

'We are scrutinising the IPOs to try to establish positions in the companies that we might, on a longer-term basis, build a position [in] at a reasonable valuation,' said Walter Price, fund manager of the Allianz Technology Trust. 'The issue with the IPO market is that there is a large part of the initial demand for these stocks from people that are just trying to flip the stock, often causing the valuation to get extended on the initial offering.'

 Source: Ram, A. and Waters, R. (2018) 'European tech IPOs begin to rival US successes', *Financial Times,* 14 June. © The Financial Times Limited 2018. All Rights Reserved.

Questions

1 Why might owners prefer a trade sale to an IPO?

2 Why might investors be more cautious than in the dotcom boom?

institutional investors who are approached by the broker prior to the issue. The issue is underwritten by the issuing company's sponsor. This issue method carries very little risk since it is essentially a way of distributing a company's shares to institutional investors. Consequently, it has a low cost in comparison with other issue methods.

A public offer

The other main method of raising funds by issuing shares is called a public offer for sale or *public offer,* which is usually made at a fixed price. It is normally used for a large issue when a company is coming to the market (seeking a listing) for the first time. In this listing method, the shares are offered to the public with the help of the sponsor and the bookmaker, who will help the company to decide on an issue price. The issue price should be low enough to be attractive to potential investors but high enough to allow the required finance to be raised without the issue of more shares than necessary. The issue is underwritten, usually by institutional investors, so that the issuing company is guaranteed to receive the finance it needs. Any shares on offer which are not taken up are bought by the underwriters (see below) at an agreed price.

An introduction

A stock exchange listing may also be gained via an *introduction*. This is where a listing is granted to the existing ordinary shares of a company, which already have a wide ownership base. It does not involve selling any new shares and so no new finance is raised. A company may choose an introduction to increase the marketability of its shares, to obtain access to capital markets or simply to determine the value of its shares.

4.2.3 Listing regulations

New issues of unlisted ordinary shares are governed by the Financial Services and Markets Act 2000, and the Prospectus Regulation 2017, which require that a prospectus is issued, the contents of which comply with the regulations. Securities are admitted to the Official List by the UK Listing Authority, which is a division of the Financial Services Authority, and admitted to trading by the London Stock Exchange itself under its own Admission and Disclosure Standards. The UKLA Listing Rules contain listing requirements that must be met by companies seeking a listing, some of which are as follows:

- Audited historical financial information for up to three years prior to admission.
- At least 25 per cent of the company's shares must be in public hands (free float requirement) when trading in its shares begins.
- The company must be able to conduct its business independently of any shareholders with a controlling interest.
- The company must publish a prospectus containing a forecast of expected performance and other detailed information to assist investors in assessing its prospects.
- The company must have a minimum market capitalisation of £700,000.

4.2.4 Relative importance of placing and public offer

A public offer is currently the most frequent method of raising cash from the LSE's Main Market, although more cash tends to be raised via placings. The relative importance of public offers and placings varies between markets. Essentially, placings are used more frequently in smaller markets where the amounts raised cannot usually justify the additional costs (e.g. marketing, advertising and underwriting costs) incurred by a public offer.

4.2.5 Underwriting

In the period between the announcement of a new equity issue and its completion, there is the possibility of adverse share price movements which may lead to the issue being unsuccessful. An unsuccessful equity issue is one where a company fails to raise the finance it is seeking or where it is left with shares that investors did not wish to purchase. A company will wish to avoid an unsuccessful equity issue because of the damage it may cause to its reputation. An unsuccessful equity issue is also likely to make raising equity finance more expensive in the future. For these reasons, companies insure against the possibility of a new issue being unsuccessful by having it underwritten.

For each new issue, one or more *main underwriters* will be appointed, who will further spread the risk by appointing several *sub-underwriters*. While the main underwriter is usually the issuing house or merchant bank advising on the equity issue, most underwriters are financial institutions such as insurance companies and pension funds. In return for a fee of about 2–3 per cent of the proceeds of the new equity issue, underwriters will accept the shares not taken up by the market, each underwriter taking unsold shares in proportion to the amount of fee income received. Through underwriting, therefore, a company is certain of raising the finance that it needs.

4.2.6 Advantages of obtaining a stock exchange quotation

There are some benefits that may be obtained by a company through becoming listed on a stock exchange, and any one of them may encourage the directors of a company to decide to seek a listing. Broadly speaking, these benefits include the raising of finance by coming to market, easier access to finance and the uses to which listed shares can be put.

Raising finance through coming to market

The owners of a private company may decide to seek a listing so that, as part of the process of becoming listed, they can sell some of their shares and thereby realise some of the investment they have made in the company. An unlisted company whose growth has been due in part to an investment of venture capital may seek a stock market listing to give the venture capitalists an *exit route* by which to realise their investment. This is particularly true of management buyouts (see 'Management buyouts', Section 11.7.3). In both situations, some or most of the funds raised by selling shares pass to a third party rather than to the company obtaining the listing. But a company may also decide to seek a listing primarily to raise funds for its own use, for example, to fund an expansion of business activities.

Access to finance

By being listed on a recognised stock exchange, a company will have easier access to external sources of equity capital, whether through the new issues market or by a rights issue, since a listed company is likely to be more attractive to institutional investors. This means that a listed company can more easily obtain any long-term equity funds it needs for expansion. Unlisted companies, in contrast, may find their growth opportunities limited because of difficulties in raising the finance they need. This gap is filled to some extent by venture capitalists, who take an equity stake in companies they invest in. As far as debt finance is concerned, lenders tend to look more favourably on listed companies since both credibility and reputation are enhanced by a listing, increasing a company's security and lowering its perceived risk. This may result in a lower cost of debt.

Uses of shares

Taking over another company can be a relatively straightforward way to achieve corporate growth and issuing new shares is a common way of financing a takeover. The shares of a listed company are more likely to be accepted by target company shareholders in exchange for their existing shares than shares in a private company. This is partly because the shares of listed companies are easier to sell because a ready market exists in them since, to satisfy listing rules, at least 25 per cent of their shares must be in public hands. The shares of a private company may not have a ready market. Marketability also increases the value of the shares and hence the value of the company. The use of shares as a means of payment for acquisitions is discussed further in 'Mergers and takeovers' (Chapter 11).

4.2.7 Disadvantages of obtaining a stock market quotation

The benefits derived from a listing naturally have a cost and the disadvantages associated with being listed must be considered if a balanced view is to be presented. There are, after all, many other ways to obtain funds or to establish a reputation: a stock market listing will not be the best option for all companies.

Costs of a quotation

Obtaining and maintaining a stock exchange quotation is expensive. The costs of obtaining a listing will reduce the amount of finance raised by a new issue. Initial listing costs will include the admission fee (typically between £9,000 and £500,000), the sponsor's fee, legal fees and the reporting accountant's fee. The ongoing annual costs of satisfying listing requirements must also be met (typically between £7,000 and £75,000). Another cost is that of increased financial disclosure since stock exchange disclosure requirements are more demanding than those of company law. This will lead to increased public scrutiny of the company and its performance.

Shareholder expectations

The directors of a private company may have been used to satisfying their own needs but, once the company becomes listed, they will need to consider the expectations of new shareholders. These will include the expectations of institutional shareholders, which may include a focus on short-term profitability and dividend income. The possibility of being taken over is increased if the company fails to meet shareholder expectations since dissatisfied shareholders are likely to be more willing to sell their shares to a bidding company. The stock exchange is therefore seen as a *market for corporate control,* meaning that poor performance by a listed company may be corrected by removing its managers through a takeover. The increased financial transparency resulting from the stock exchange requirement to produce regular reports and accounts means that bidders are more easily able to select likely acquisition targets, whose shares they can then seek to acquire on the open market.

4.3 RIGHTS ISSUES

If a company wishes to issue new shares, it is required by law to offer them first to its existing shareholders, unless those shareholders have already agreed in a meeting of the company to waive the right for a period. Because of this legal right to be offered the shares before other investors, such an issue of new shares is called a *rights issue*. To preserve existing patterns of ownership and control, a rights issue is offered on a *pro rata basis,* such as one new share for every four existing shares (referred to as a *1 for 4 issue*).

As a way of raising finance, rights issues are cheaper in terms of issuing costs than a public offer. In addition, there is no dilution of ownership and control if the rights issue shares are fully taken up. However, a rights issue is not appropriate if the amount of finance to be raised is large, as the funds available to individual shareholders are likely to be limited.

Rights issues are offered at a discount to the current market price, commonly in the region of 15–20 per cent. This discount makes the new shares more attractive to shareholders and allows for any adverse share price movements prior to the issue. The current market price will normally be quoted *ex dividend,* which means that buying the share will not confer the right to receive a dividend about to be paid (see 'Dividends: operational and practical issues', Section 10.1). The price of an already issued share may increase to reflect the value of the right to receive new shares at a discount; this new price is called the **cum rights price.** When buying shares on the open market no longer gives the buyer the right to participate in the rights issue because the list of shareholders has closed, the share price will fall as it goes *ex rights.*

4.3.1 The theoretical ex-rights price

After the issue, both old and new shares will trade at the *theoretical ex-rights price,* which is a weighted average of the cum rights price and the rights issue price. We have:

$$P_e = P_P \frac{N_O}{N} + P_N \frac{N_N}{N}$$

where: P_e = the theoretical ex-rights price
P_P = cum rights price
P_N = rights issue price
N_O = number of old shares
N_N = number of new shares
N = total number of shares after the issue

4.3.2 The value of the rights

An ordinary shareholder can *detach* the rights from their shares and sell them. There is an active market in rights, with prices quoted regularly in the financial press. The value of the rights is the maximum price that a buyer is prepared to pay for them: this will be the theoretical gain the buyer could make by exercising them. It is the difference between the theoretical ex-rights price and the rights issue price. For Nolig plc (see example below), the value of the rights attached to four Nolig shares is £2.05 − £1.85 = £0.20 or 20p. This is the amount that an investor would be prepared to pay for the rights attached to the four shares, as he could then pay £1.85 for a share that would be worth £2.05 on the equity market. The value of the rights can also be expressed as 20p/4 = 5p per existing share.

Example	Calculation of the theoretical ex-rights price

Nolig plc has in issue 2m ordinary shares of nominal value £1.00, currently trading at £2.20 per share. The company decides to raise new equity funds by offering its existing shareholders the right to buy one new share at £1.85 for every four shares already held. After the announcement of the issue, the ordinary share price falls to £2.10 and remains at this level until the time of the rights issue. What is the theoretical ex-rights price?

Suggested answer

Cum rights price, P_P = £2.10
New issue price, P_N = £1.85
Number of old shares, N_O = 2.0 million
Number of new shares, N_N = 2.0/4 = 0.5 million
Total number of shares, N = 2.5 million

and so:
$$\text{Theoretical ex-rights price, } P_e = \frac{(2 \times 2.10) + (0.5 \times 1.85)}{2.5} = £2.05$$

Alternatively, using the terms of the 1 for 4 rights issue:
$$\text{Theoretical ex-rights price, } P_e = \frac{(4 \times 2.10) + (1 \times 1.85)}{5} = £2.05$$

4.3.3 Rights issues and shareholder wealth

If we regard cash in a shareholder's bank account as equivalent in wealth terms to the ordinary shares that could be bought in exchange for it, then the wealth of the shareholder need not be affected by a rights issue. If shareholders subscribe for their full entitlement of new shares or if they sell all the rights attached to their existing shares (or any combination of these two alternatives), their wealth position will be unchanged. If they do nothing and allow their rights to lapse, however, their wealth will fall. We can show this with a simple example (see below).

Choosing neither to subscribe for new shares offered nor to sell the rights attached to existing shares held will lead to a decrease in shareholder wealth, as the example shows. If appropriate action is taken, however, the effect on shareholder wealth is, in theory at least, a neutral one. This will be true no matter how great a discount is attached to the new shares.

4.3.4 Market price after a rights issue

The actual ex-rights price is likely to be different from the price predicted by theory. This is primarily due to differing investor expectations, which influence their buying and selling preferences and hence market prices. Investors will have expectations about the future

Example	Wealth effect of a rights issue

Nolig plc has 2m ordinary shares of nominal value £1.00 in issue. The company decided (see above) to make a 1 for 4 rights issue at £1.85 per new share and the cum rights share price was £2.10. The theoretical ex-rights price was found to be £2.05 and the value of the rights was found to be 5p per existing share. If Rose, a shareholder, owns 1,000 shares in Nolig plc, she has the right to subscribe for 250 new shares and her shareholding is currently worth £2,100 (1,000 × £2.10). How will Rose's wealth be affected in each of the following scenarios?

1 Rose subscribes for 250 new shares.
2 Rose sells all her rights.
3 Rose takes no action over the rights issue.

1 Rose subscribes for 250 new shares

	£
1,000 shares cum rights @ £2.10 =	2,100.00
Cash for 250 new shares @ £1.85 =	462.50
1,250 shares ex-rights @ £2.05 =	2,562.50

Rose's overall wealth position is unchanged if she subscribes for the new shares, although some of her wealth has changed from cash into ordinary shares.

2 Rose sells her rights

	£
1,000 shares ex-rights @ £2.05 =	2,050.00
Sale of rights, 1,000 @ 5 pence =	50.00
Wealth position after rights issue =	2,100.00

Rose's wealth position is also unchanged if she sells her rights: the effect here is that some of her wealth has changed from ordinary shares into cash.

3 Rose takes no action over the rights issue

	£
Initial position, 1,000 shares @ £2.10 =	2,100.00
Final position, 1,000 shares @ £2.05 =	2,050.00
Decline in wealth by doing nothing =	50.00

Rose's wealth has declined because the price of her shares has fallen from the cum rights value to the ex-rights value.

state of the economy; they may be expecting interest rates or inflation to increase, for example, or may be anticipating a downturn in economic activity. Investors may also have formed opinions about the proposed use of the new funds by the company. If these opinions are favourable, the share price will increase accordingly.

As far as earnings are concerned, if these are expected to be maintained or increased after the new issue, then the share price may be unchanged or even increase, even though there will be more shares in circulation. This points to the need to consider the effect of a proposed rights issue on *earnings yield* (see 'Investor ratios', Section 2.4.7) as well as earnings per share. If the earnings yield on existing funds remains unchanged, the key variable affecting the ex-rights price will be the expected earnings yield on the funds raised.

We can modify our earlier formula for the theoretical ex-rights price (P_e) to enable it to consider the expected earnings yield on the new funds raised (γ_N), compared with the earnings yield on existing funds (γ_O). We have:

$$P_e = P_P \frac{N_O}{N} + P_N \frac{N_N \gamma_N}{N \gamma_O}$$

where:
P_P = cum rights price
P_N = rights issue price
N_O = number of old shares
N_N = number of new shares
N = total number of shares
γ_N / γ_O = ratio of earnings yield on new capital to earnings yield on old capital

If γ_N / γ_O is greater than one, reflecting the situation where investors expect earnings to increase after the rights issue, the ex-rights share price will be greater than the price predicted by the simple weighted average considered earlier. If γ_N / γ_O is less than one, representing the situation where investors expect earnings to fall, then the ex-rights share price will be less than a simple weighted average.

Returning to the earlier example of Nolig plc, you will recall that the theoretical ex-rights price was found to be £2.05. If we now assume that the earnings yield on existing funds is 18 per cent and the earnings yield on the funds raised is expected to be is 25 per cent, we have:

$$\text{Ex-rights price, } P_e = \frac{(2 \times 2.10)}{2.5} + \frac{(0.5 \times 1.85) \times 25}{(2.5 \times 18)} = £2.19$$

The increased earnings yield has led to a higher predicted ex-rights share price.

The ex-rights share price will also be affected by the expected level of dividends. If dividends are expected to fall, the share price will decline. While earnings from the new investment may take some time to come on stream, the decision on how much to pay out as dividends rests with the directors of the company. To reassure shareholders, who are being asked to subscribe further funds to the company, an announcement about the expected level of dividends may accompany an announcement of a rights issue.

Empirical evidence suggests that the market assumes that companies will be able to maintain their level of dividend payments and that the formula for determining the theoretical ex-rights price is a reasonably accurate reflection of the real world.

4.3.5 Underwriting and deep discount rights issues

In theory, shareholder wealth is not affected by a rights issue since the value of the rights is equivalent to the difference between the value of the original shares held and the theoretical ex-rights price. We also noted that one of the reasons why a rights issue is issued at a discount to the current market price to make it attractive to existing shareholders and thereby help to ensure the issue's success. Why, in that case, is it common for a company to seek a further guarantee of the success of a rights issue by having it underwritten? Since the size of the discount is irrelevant, the cost of underwriting could be reduced, and the success of a rights issue could be assured by increasing the size of the discount, i.e. by offering the new shares at a *deep discount* to the current share price.

The use of a rights issue to aid restructuring is the subject of Vignette 4.2.

Vignette 4.2

Mothercare to close more stores as it seeks to raise £32.5m

Struggling retailer looks to pay down debt while number of planned closures rises to 60

By Katie Martin, Naomi Rovnick and Jonathan Eley

Baby goods retailer Mothercare is seeking to raise £32.5m from existing shareholders and will increase the number of store closures as it struggles to adapt to challenging conditions on the UK's high streets.

The capital raising, which is larger than originally planned, will be at 19p a share, well below Friday's closing level of 28.6p, and the proceeds will be used to reduce debt.

Mothercare's shares fell 9 per cent in early London trade to 26p. The company said it was 'likely there may be short-term impacts on our business operations' from the restructuring, which will result in 60 UK stores closing against an earlier target of 50.

Some of that increase comes from the decision to put its Childrens World subsidiary, which houses 22 of its stores, into administration. Mothercare will transfer 13 Childrens World outlets to other parts of its business.

In May, the group announced a £73m loss for the year to March 24, largely because of restructuring costs, store closures and expensive leases.

The restructuring will help generate £10m in savings a year, the company said. It is seeking to find

another £9m of annual savings through a root and branch review of the business. Entering a company voluntary arrangement with landlords and other unsecured creditors allows Mothercare to accelerate the pace of store closures. 'It basically means we can do three years' work in a year,' said chief executive Mark Newton-Jones.

The company is one of several retailers to have struck CVAs, which are resented by many landlords, and close stores. Other companies to have taken this route include floor coverings specialist Carpetright, department store operator House of Fraser, and fast-fashion chain New Look.

Mr Newton-Jones, who was reappointed to the top job at Mothercare in May, a month after the retailer abruptly ousted him, said he expected market conditions to remain challenging, with customers trading down to cheaper options for products such as pushchairs and car seats.

But he added that medium-term prospects were better: 'Our customer base is very unusual, in that there is a new generation of shoppers coming through each year.' Around four-fifths of expectant parents visit a Mothercare store or the group's website.

Vignette 4.2 (continued)

John Stevenson, equity analyst at Peel Hunt, said Mothercare differed from some other high street casualties in that it had a profitable and cash-generative overseas business, which accounted for two-thirds of group revenue and all of the operating profit. 'They just need to get the UK stores back to break-even,' he said, adding that sales per square foot were low while rents as a proportion of revenue were above average.

One key metric will be the proportion of sales that transfer from the closed stores, either to retained premises or to the website.

'Ten years ago we had 425 stores in the UK. Just in my time here [from 2014] we have closed over 100 but seen very little drop in total sales,' said Mr Newton-Jones. 'But this time we are going much faster.' By the end of its 2021 fiscal year, Mothercare will operate just 73 UK stores, located mostly in retail parks rather than town centres and offering services such as ultrasound scans and maternity bra fittings.

The fundraising, which will see important shareholders such as DC Thomson and the investment vehicle of former Evolution chief executive Richard Griffiths maintain their holdings, is still subject to shareholder approval. Without their assent, the group warned it could enter administration by October.

Source: Martin, K., Rovnick, N. and Eley, J. (2018) 'Mothercare to close more stores as it seeks to raise £32.5m', *Financial Times,* 9 July.
© The Financial Times Limited 2018. All Rights Reserved.

Question

Discuss why Mothercare may have preferred a rights issue to a new issue of debt.

4.4 SCRIP ISSUES, SHARE SPLITS, SCRIP DIVIDENDS AND SHARE REPURCHASES

4.4.1 Scrip issues and share splits

Scrip issues and share splits are both ways in which a company can increase the number of shares in issue, without raising any additional finance. A *scrip issue* (or bonus issue) converts existing capital reserves or retained earnings into additional shares, which are then distributed pro rata to existing shareholders. It is in effect a transfer from profit reserves to the ordinary share account in a financial position statement. A **share split** (a **stock split** in the USA) involves simultaneously reducing the nominal value of each share and increasing the number of shares in issue so that the financial position statement value of the shares is unchanged. For example, a company with 1 million shares of nominal value 50p could, following a share split, have 2 million ordinary shares of nominal value 25p.

Several possible explanations for share splits have been advanced. One suggestion is that share splits increase the ease with which ordinary shares can be traded by moving them into a more acceptable price range. More investors will be willing to buy shares trading at £5, it is argued, than shares trading at £10. Under this theory, share splits increase liquidity. Research by Copeland (1979), however, suggests that liquidity declines following a share split, since trading volume is proportionately lower and transactions costs are proportionately higher.

Another explanation of why share splits occur is that they have, in some unexplained way, a positive effect on shareholder wealth. The effect of share splits on shareholder wealth has been the subject of much research, but the results are inconclusive. Some researchers, such as Firth (1973), have found that share splits do not have any beneficial effects resulting from share price movements. Other researchers, such as Grinblatt et al. (1984), have detected a positive effect on shareholder wealth and suggest that investors might interpret the announcement of a share split as a positive signal about a company's future cash flows. Grinblatt et al. (1984) also found positive effects on shareholder wealth resulting from of scrip issue announcements.

Pressure for Nintendo to undertake a share split as a step towards improving corporate governance is the subject of Vignette 4.3.

The opposite of a share split is a share consolidation or reverse stock split, where the nominal value of each share is increased at the same time as the number of shares in issue is decreased, so that the financial position statement value of the shares is unchanged.

Vignette 4.3

Nintendo faces calls to split stock to aid governance

Group's shares priced beyond most retail investors on back of Switch console success

By Leo Lewis and Kana Inagaki

Nintendo is facing calls from investors to split its stock and broaden its shareholder base as the global success of the Switch games console re-ignites concerns over corporate governance at the Japanese group.

The pressure has arisen because the stock has climbed above ¥45,000 per share – a near 10-year high that leaves them beyond the reach of average retail investors because of a minimum trading limit of 100 shares.

A wider shareholder base, say investors planning to push for the stock-split, would underscore a commitment to greater transparency. Macquarie analyst David Gibson described the move as 'a good first step'.

Nintendo is Japan's richest company, and by some estimates is sitting on nearly ¥1tn ($9.4bn) of cash reserves. It has sold more than 12m units of the Switch console since its launch last March.

The unit's success has delivered a turnaround from the disappointment of its predecessor console the

Wii U, triggered an increase in full-year profit forecasts and been a reminder of Nintendo's capacity to surprise.

But despite presenting itself as the ultimate family-friendly company with a commitment to diversity, the creator of Mario, Princess Peach and Donkey Kong has yet to break its tradition of an all-male board.

Its enthusiasm for corporate governance reform has also always been low, said one person who has worked directly with the company, and the market's rediscovered love of the shares could produce the sort of complacency that will lower it further.

Yutaka Suzuki, a governance expert at Daiwa Institute of Research (DIR), warned momentum for governance improvement was generally reduced in times of strong corporate earnings.

In Nintendo's case, its shares have nearly doubled in the past year, giving investors little reason to complain about its board structure or stance on information disclosure.

Vignette 4.3 (continued)

'Shareholders will not be satisfied if stock prices are low even if the company's governance structure is perfect. Likewise, they will be content if stock prices are high even if the company's governance is horrible,' Mr Suzuki said.

Fears of a broader pushback by Japan Inc are mounting as the Financial Services Agency prepares to make revisions to strengthen the 2015 corporate governance code.

One of the country's foremost advocates of reform, Kazuhiko Toyama, chief executive of Industrial Growth Platform, said last week that companies that claim it is too much trouble to implement the code 'should de-list or not list in the first place'.

Nintendo is often cited by many investors as a prime example of a company whose stunning success has come despite foot-dragging on corporate governance reforms.

The group's introduction of three outside members to its board failed to impress critics. Mr Gibson of Macquarie is among a number of analysts who point to the fact all three men had previously served as auditors of the company.

Nintendo is among about 22 per cent of publicly traded Japanese companies that have switched to a new governance structure that has allowed them to appoint their statutory auditors as outside directors.

Critics of the structure, introduced in 2015, say it has made it easier for these groups to address pressure to appoint independent directors without actually giving them influence over key issues such as compensation and powers to nominate the chief executive.

'It's questionable how seriously companies want their external directors to be active in their roles,' said the DIR's Mr Suzuki.

Masaaki Tanaka, an adviser to PwC International, told the FSA's committee on revising the corporate governance code last week that independent committees charged with nominating chief executives should be made up entirely of people from outside the company, noting that nearly all of the companies embroiled in corporate scandals have been those using the board of auditors' format.

Resistance to reform, say seasoned asset managers, is especially obstinate in Nintendo's home city of Kyoto. One investor said some companies in the city believe 'there is no such thing as too much cash and have no concept of being owned by shareholders'.

But demands for a share split at Nintendo, which has been raised or is being planned by at least three large shareholders, are expected to intensify in the lead-up to its annual meeting in June.

Nintendo's sometimes eccentric corporate nature means that observers look for unusual gauges that change may be afoot. In December, Kellogg's announced a deal to launch a Super Mario breakfast cereal.

Serkan Toto, a Tokyo-based games industry analyst, said the licensing tie-up with the US group was one of a number of signals that a company once notoriously protective of its intellectual property was becoming more open. Other deals include an agreement with Nvidia to distribute Nintendo games in China and plans for an animated Mario movie.

However, he warned non-transparency is among a number of governance shortcomings Nintendo is unlikely to shed.

'When you look at Nintendo from the outside, there is a clear sense of change towards greater openness . . . it is involved in deals that it would not have considered in the past,' he said. 'But internally, I do not see any real signs of change. The lack of transparency at Nintendo is part of its DNA.'

Nintendo said it had been taking measures to communicate with investors, and its stance has not changed.

Source: Lewis, L. and Inagaki, K. (2018) 'Nintendo faces calls to split stock to aid governance', *Financial Times*, 19 February.
© The Financial Times Limited 2018. All Rights Reserved.

Question

Discuss the reasons why a stock split might help to improve corporate governance.

4.4.2 Scrip dividends

Another method of issuing new equity which does not raise additional finance is the issuing of a **scrip dividend** (also known as a share dividend). Here, a shareholder accepts more ordinary shares in a company as a partial or total alternative to a cash dividend (see 'Scrip dividends', Section 10.7.1).

There are cash-flow advantages to the company in offering a scrip dividend, since if investors choose to take up the scrip dividend there will be less cash paid out by the company as dividends. A further benefit to the company is that because of the increase in equity, there will be a small decrease in gearing (see 'Gearing ratios', Section 2.4.6). Since the scrip dividend replaces a cash dividend that would have been paid anyway, there is no reason why a scrip dividend should cause a share price fall in an efficient capital market.

If ordinary shareholders wish to increase their shareholdings, a scrip dividend allows them to do so cheaply, without incurring dealing costs. For a tax-paying ordinary shareholder, there is no difference in the UK between a scrip dividend and a cash dividend since a scrip dividend is taxed as though it were income. For tax-exempt ordinary shareholders, however, there is a difference. With a cash dividend, tax-exempt shareholders can benefit by reclaiming the tax paid by the company on the profits distributed. With a scrip dividend, this benefit is lost since no corporation tax liability arises when a scrip dividend is issued. As a cash dividend and any scrip dividend alternative offered by a company are required by regulation to be similar in value, there is a financial disincentive for tax-exempt ordinary shareholders to accept scrip dividends.

4.4.3 Share repurchases

Share repurchases (or share buybacks) are one way of returning cash to ordinary shareholders. A UK company can purchase its own shares if permission has been given by shareholders in a general meeting of the company. To protect the interests of creditors and the remaining shareholders, though, share repurchases are carefully regulated.

There are several reasons for returning surplus capital to shareholders. One rationale is that shareholders will be able to invest the cash more effectively than the company. Another is that the value of the remaining shares will be enhanced after shares have been repurchased. Since the capital employed by a company is reduced by repurchasing shares, return on capital employed (see 'Profitability ratios', Section 2.4.3) will increase. The number of shares will fall, resulting in an increase in earnings per share. While share repurchases also lead to an increase in gearing, it is argued that any increase in financial risk is negligible and so, if the cost of equity is unaltered, the value of both shares and company will be increased. The transfer of cash from a company to its shareholders may be ill-advised when credit is tight and liquidity is at a premium, however.

Other reasons than returning cash to shareholders may drive a share buyback, as illustrated by Vignette 4.4.

Glencore launches $1bn share buyback

Miner and commodity trader responds to fall in stock price after DoJ subpoena

By Neil Hume

Glencore has responded to a sharp fall in its stock price following a subpoena from US regulators by announcing plans to repurchase up to $1bn of its shares.

The London-listed miner and commodity trader, run by billionaire Ivan Glasenberg, said the share buyback programme would commence immediately and run until the end of the year.

The buyback will be a two-stage process. Ahead of half year results in early August, Citigroup will buy £350m of shares on behalf of the company. After that, the repurchases will be undertaken in accordance with directions from Glencore. The company last announced a buyback in August 2014 when its shares were trading at 359p.

Analysts said the buyback signalled management's confidence in its underlying business and the value of its shares.

'This serves to provide a message to the market that management sees value in the shares at current level, at a time where perceived external uncertainty is high, and where impact from the Department of Justice subpoena specifically is difficult to judge,' said Tyler Broda of RBC Capital Markets.

Shares in Glencore dropped to a 12-month low on Tuesday following news that it could be facing a wide-ranging US government investigation into bribery and corruption after federal prosecutors demanded details of its business dealings in some of the world's most volatile countries.

Glencore has been ordered by the Department of Justice to hand over records related to its compliance with US money-laundering laws and the Foreign Corrupt Practices Act (FCPA). The subpoena covers Glencore's operations in Nigeria, the Democratic Republic of Congo and Venezuela dating back to 2007.

Glencore's share price has dropped 18 per cent this year, underperforming its peers that include Anglo American, BHP Billiton and Rio Tinto, as it has wrestled with a number of problems, chiefly in the Democratic Republic of Congo.

The central African nation is home to some of Glencore's most important growth assets: large copper and cobalt mines. However, the prospects for those operations have been clouded by legal fights with Gécamines, the DRC's state mining company, and also Dan Gertler, a former business partner who is under US sanctions. The DRC has also pushed through a new mining code, which will lead to increased royalties and taxes.

'Glencore shares are down 18 per cent year to date versus peers up an average 5 to 6 per cent over the same period. This is despite the underlying commodity basket of Glencore remaining relatively resilient,' said Eugene King, Goldman Sachs analyst.

'Expectations of a buyback among investors we have spoken with had increased more recently as the shares had continued to underperform, however most had expected a buyback to be announced with the first-half results in August.'

While investors have been focused on Glencore's problems in the DRC, and now the prospect of a DoJ investigation, its underlying business has been performing well.

Bankers said Glencore's thermal coal business would be generating large profits at the moment with prices for the fossil fuel in Asia at a six-year high of about $115 a tonne.

In metals, strong global growth and supply constraints following years of under-investment by cash-strapped mining companies have created lucrative arbitrage opportunities for Glencore's trading business.

The lowly valuation of Glencore and other miners is something that Mr Glasenberg has been keen to address this year. At conferences he has told investors the sector has 'never been' cheaper compared

Vignette 4.4 (continued)

with the wider market and new dividend and capital return policies would ensure they 'receive a greater share of earnings' in the future.

'We expect a positive response to the additional capital return, which shows the success of Glencore's completed balance sheet deleveraging programme,' said analysts at Numis Securities.

'However, the company faces significant regulatory and geopolitical noise with respect to the recent US DoJ subpoena, the new DRC mining code and several lawsuits in the DRC with regards to its operations in the country.'

Shares in Glencore were up 4 per cent at 332p on Thursday morning, the biggest riser in the FTSE 100.

 Source: Hume, N. (2018) 'Glencore launches $1bn share buyback', *Financial Times,* 5 July.
© The Financial Times Limited 2018. All Rights Reserved.

Questions

1 What are the objectives of the buyback offer?

2 Discuss whether shareholder wealth will be increased by accepting the buyback offer or by remaining a shareholder.

4.5 PREFERENCE SHARES

Preference shares differ from ordinary shares in giving the holder preferential rights to receive a share of annual profits. An ordinary dividend cannot be paid unless all preference dividends due have been paid in full. Preference shares are also higher in the creditor hierarchy than ordinary shares and have a preferential right to receive the proceeds of disposal of the assets in the event of a company going into liquidation. They are therefore less risky than ordinary shares, even though they are legally share capital as well. Like ordinary shares, preference shares are normally permanent (i.e. irredeemable) but, unlike ordinary shares, they do not usually give voting rights. However, preference shares carry a higher risk than debt, for several reasons:

- Preference shares, unlike debt, are not secured on company assets.
- Preference dividends cannot be paid until interest payments on debt have been covered.
- In the event of liquidation, preference shareholders will not be paid off until the claims of debt holders have been satisfied.

Both preference shares and debt are treated as 'prior charge capital' when calculating gearing (see 'Gearing ratios', Section 2.4.6). The LSE allows preference shares to be listed as either equity or debt.

Preference shares may be either non-cumulative or cumulative with respect to preference dividends which, like ordinary dividends, are a distribution of taxed profits and not a payment of interest. With *non-cumulative* preference shares, if distributable profits are insufficient to pay the preference dividend, the dividend is lost; with *cumulative* preference shares, if distributable profits are insufficient to pay the preference dividend, the right to receive it is carried forward and unpaid preference dividends must be settled before any ordinary dividend can be paid in subsequent years. If preference shares are *non-participating,* the preference dividend represents the sole return to the holders of the shares, irrespective of the company's earnings growth. *Participating* preference shares, in addition to paying a fixed preference dividend, offer the right to receive an additional dividend if profits in the year exceed an agreed amount.

4.5.1 Variable rate preference shares

Preference shares commonly pay investors a fixed rate dividend, but preference shares paying a variable rate dividend have become more common in recent years. Two methods of periodically resetting the preference dividend rate are used. In the first method, the preference dividend rate is a *floating rate* or an adjustable rate determined by adding a fixed percentage to a market interest rate such as **London Interbank Offered Rate (LIBOR)**. With the second method, the preference dividend rate is adjusted periodically to the rate which allows the preference shares to trade at a *constant stated market value.* An example of the second method of resetting the dividend rate is given by **auction market preferred stock (AMPS)**.

4.5.2 Convertible preference shares

Other features may be added to preference shares to make them attractive or to satisfy company financing needs. Convertible preference shares, for example, give the holder the option to convert them into ordinary shares on prescribed terms in prescribed circumstances.

4.5.3 The popularity of preference shares

The cost disadvantage of preference shares relative to debt has led to a decline in their popularity in the UK. It is unlikely that the dividend rate on preference shares would be less than the after-tax interest cost of a bond issue due to the relative risks associated with the two securities. Convertible redeemable preference shares have been a popular financing method with providers of venture capital, however. If the company supported by the venture finance is doing well, the preference shares can be converted into ordinary shares, leading to higher returns. If the company is not doing well, the preference shares can be redeemed. The 1980s saw preference shares growing in popularity with bank issuers, whereas AMPS proved attractive to corporate issuers in the 1990s. The AMPS market collapsed in February 2008 when underwriters refused to buy stock back from investors, although some investors were subsequently compensated for their losses.

4.5.4 The advantages and disadvantages of preference shares

One of the main advantages to companies of preference shares compared with debt – an advantage also of ordinary shares – is that preference dividends do not need to be paid if profits are insufficient to cover them. This is less of a problem for holders of cumulative preference shares (although the real value of unpaid preference dividends will decline), but owners of non-cumulative preference shares will be unhappy about not receiving a dividend. For this reason, holders of non-cumulative preference shares will demand a higher return. Further advantages to companies of preference shares are:

- they do not carry general voting rights and so will not dilute ownership and control;
- they preserve debt capacity, since they are not secured;
- non-payment of preference dividends does not give preference shareholders the right to appoint a receiver.

The major disadvantage of preference shares to companies is their cost relative to, say, the cost of bonds. Because of the higher risk associated with preference shares the percentage dividend may, for example, be 10 per cent when the interest rate on bonds stands at 7 per cent. This cost differential is exacerbated when the tax efficiency of debt is considered. Assuming an issuing company is not in a tax-exhausted position, its after-tax cost of debt with a corporate tax rate of 30 per cent and an interest rate of 7 per cent will be $7 \times (1 - 0.3)$ or 4.9 per cent. Given these relative costs, companies will choose debt finance rather than preference shares.

Irredeemable preference shares may perhaps not be irredeemable, as illustrated by Vignette 4.5.

Vignette 4.5

Aviva drops plan to cancel preference shares
Insurer abandons idea after investor backlash as it faces probe

By Oliver Ralph and Katie Martin

Aviva has ditched a controversial plan to cancel its preference shares following an outcry from investors and politicians and amid a probe by regulators.

The insurer raised the possibility that it could cancel preference shares earlier this month, which sent their price crashing by almost a third. The £450m of preference shares, which carry a coupon of 8–9 per cent and rank above ordinary share dividends in terms of priority, represent an expensive form of funding for Aviva.

On Friday, the company said that it 'had received strong feedback and criticism' and so had 'decided to take no action to cancel its preference shares'.

Mark Taber, who campaigns on behalf of preference shareholders, said that Aviva had 'done the right thing' by dropping the idea. He added that 'it was an ill-conceived plan in the first place'.

Aviva is looking to use £3bn of excess cash this year and had planned to use some of it to cancel the shares. But there was a backlash from investors. In a letter to the Financial Times this week, two shareholder groups wrote: 'Individual shareholders are deeply upset and appalled at the reckless and cavalier announcements by Aviva.'

They argued that the shares were irredeemable and that the company should not try to use 'an obscure loophole' to cancel them.

Nicky Morgan MP, chair of the Treasury select committee, asked the Financial Conduct Authority to look into how the preference shares were originally marketed to retail investors.

The FCA had already said that it was 'seeking to understand the basis upon which the firm is taking this action'.

Vignette 4.5 (continued)

Announcing the decision to ditch the plan, chief executive Mark Wilson said: 'I am very aware that Aviva is in a position of trust with our customers and investors. To maintain that trust it is critical that we listen to and act on feedback . . . I hope our decision today goes some way to restoring that trust.'

A group of investors including M&G, Invesco, GAM and BlackRock, which between them own 29 per cent of the preference shares and 15 per cent of the ordinary shares, met Aviva chairman Sir Adrian Montague on Wednesday.

On Friday, the investor group said: 'The announcement by Aviva today goes a long way towards addressing our concerns and we thank Sir Adrian and the board for engaging constructively with us and being willing to reverse their course.'

Mr Taber now wants regulators to take a look at the loophole in the Companies Act that would have allowed Aviva to cancel the shares. 'They shouldn't be able to do this,' he said. 'Aviva will have some work to do to rebuild trust.'

 Source: Ralph, O. and Martin, K. (2018) 'Aviva drops plan to cancel preference shares', *Financial Times*, 23 March. © The Financial Times Limited 2018. All Rights Reserved.

Question

Discuss whether shareholder reaction to the proposal to cancel the preference shares was consistent with the objective of maximising shareholder wealth.

4.6 CONCLUSION

In this chapter we have discussed some important issues in connection with equity finance and preference shares. Since equity finance is truly permanent capital which does not normally need to be repaid, it gives a company a solid financial foundation. Ordinary shareholders, as the owners of the company and the carriers of the largest slice of risk, expect the highest returns. Their position and rights as owners are protected by both government and stock market regulations, and any new issue of shares must take these into account.

■ ■ ■ KEY POINTS

1 Ordinary shares have a nominal value, which is different from their market value, and are usually issued at a premium. They confer individual and collective rights on their owners.

2 Ordinary shareholders, being at the bottom of the creditor hierarchy, are the ultimate bearers of risk because they stand to lose everything in a company liquidation. They therefore expect the greatest return.

3 To help it to satisfy regulations governing new equity issues and to advise it on listing procedures, a company will appoint a sponsor.

4 A placing involves issuing blocks of new shares at a fixed price to institutional investors and is a low-cost issue method involving little risk.

5 A public offer is usually used for large issues of new equity and involves offering shares to the public through an issuing house or sponsoring merchant bank.

6 An introduction grants a listing to the existing shares of a company and does not involve a new share issue.

7 The UK Listing Authority enforces Listing Regulations, which are designed to protect investors and screen companies seeking a listing.

8 Companies insure against the failure of a new equity issue through underwriting. The main underwriter is usually the issuing house and most underwriters are financial institutions.

9 The benefits arising from obtaining a listing are raising finance via an IPO, easier access to equity and other finance, and uses to which shares can be put, including payment in a takeover bid.

10 The disadvantages of being listed include the costs of obtaining and maintaining a listing, increased financial transparency, the need to meet shareholder expectations, the need to maintain dividends and the risk of takeover.

11 A rights issue involves the issue of new shares to existing shareholders in proportion to their existing holdings. It can preserve existing patterns of ownership and control and is cheaper than a public offer but it is unsuitable for raising large amounts of finance.

12 Rights issue shares are usually offered at a 15–20 per cent discount to current market price, making them attractive to shareholders and allowing for adverse share price movements.

13 After a rights issue, shares should trade at the theoretical ex-rights price.

14 Rights can be sold to investors. The value of rights is the difference between the theoretical ex-rights price and the rights issue price. If shareholders either buy the offered shares or sell their rights, their wealth is not affected by the rights issue.

15 The actual ex-rights price may be different from the theoretical ex-rights price because of market expectations and because of the expected yield on new funds.

16 A scrip issue (bonus issue) converts existing reserves into additional shares. A share split (stock split) reduces the nominal value of shares while at the same time increasing the number issued, so that the total nominal value of shares is unchanged.

17 It has been suggested that share splits increase liquidity, but research has not supported this view. It has also been suggested that share splits increase shareholder wealth, but the evidence is inconclusive.

18 A scrip dividend involves offering ordinary shares as an alternative to a cash dividend. It has cash-flow advantages for a company.

19 Share repurchases are a way of returning cash to shareholders. They are carefully regulated to protect creditors.

20 Preference shares carry a right to receive a dividend before ordinary shareholders, but a dividend may not need to be paid if profits are low.

21 Preference shares are less risky than ordinary shares, but riskier than debt. They do not usually give voting rights and are unsecured. While preserving debt capacity, they are not tax efficient.

22 Preference shares may be either cumulative or non-cumulative with respect to preference dividends. Preference shares can also be variable rate, participating and non-participating, and convertible.

23 In practice, ordinary preference shares tend to be less attractive than debt.

SELF-TEST QUESTIONS

Answers to these questions can be found on pages 454–5.

1 Explain why the return required by ordinary shareholders is different from the return required by bondholders.

2 Briefly outline some of the important rights of ordinary shareholders.

3 Briefly explain the various ways in which a company may obtain a listing for its ordinary shares on the London Stock Exchange.

4 Outline the advantages and disadvantages that should be considered by a currently unquoted company which is considering obtaining a listing on a stock exchange.

5 What are pre-emptive rights and why are they important to shareholders?

6 Discuss the advantages and disadvantages of a rights issue to a company.

7 XTC is planning a 1 for 4 rights issue at a 20 per cent discount to the current market price of £2.50. If investors wish to sell their 'rights per existing share', how much should they sell them for?

(a) 10p

(b) 20p

(c) 30p

(d) 40p

(e) 50p

8 'A conversion of existing capital reserves into ordinary shares, which are then distributed pro rata to existing shareholders.' This statement best defines:

(a) scrip dividends;

(b) a rights issue;

(c) bonus bonds;

(d) scrip issues;

(e) share splits.

9 Explain why preference shares are not popular as a source of finance for companies.

10 Which one of the following statements best describes a cumulative preference share?

(a) It has the right to be converted into ordinary shares at a future date.

(b) It entitles the shareholder to a share of residual profits.

(c) It carries forward to the next year the right to receive unpaid dividends.

(d) It entitles the shareholder to a fixed rate of dividend.

(e) It gives its holder voting rights at a company's annual general meeting.

QUESTIONS FOR REVIEW

1 Brand plc generates profit after tax of 15 per cent on shareholders' funds. Its current capital structure is as follows:

	£
Ordinary shares of 50p each	200,000
Reserves	400,000
	600,000

The board of Brand plc plans to raise £160,000 from a rights issue to expand existing operations. Return on shareholders' funds will be unchanged. The current ex dividend share price of Brand plc is £1.90. Three different rights issue prices have been suggested by the finance director: £1.80, £1.60 and £1.40.

Calculate the number of shares to be issued, the theoretical ex-rights price, the expected earnings per share and the form of the issue for each issue price. Comment on your results.

2 Maltby plc, a company quoted on the London Stock Exchange, has been making regular annual after-tax profits of £7 million for some years and has the following capital structure.

	£000
Ordinary shares, 50p each	4,000
12 per cent bonds	9,000
	13,000

The bond issue is not due to be redeemed for some time and the company has become increasingly concerned about the need to continue paying interest at 12 per cent when the interest rate on newly issued government bonds of a similar maturity is only 6 per cent.

A proposal has been made to issue 2m new shares in a rights issue at a discount of 20 per cent to the current share price of Maltby plc, and to use the funds raised to pay off part of the bond issue. The current share price of Maltby plc is £3.50 and the current market price of the bonds is £112 per £100 bond.

Alternatively, the funds raised by the rights issue could be invested in a new project giving an annual after-tax return of 20 per cent. Maltby's price/earnings ratio will remain unchanged whichever option is chosen. Maltby plc pays corporation tax at a rate of 30 per cent.

By considering the effect on the share price of the two alternative proposals, discuss whether the proposed rights issue can be recommended as being in the best interests of the ordinary shareholders of Maltby plc. Your answer should include all relevant calculations.

3 Companies often offer their shareholders a cash dividend and an equivalent scrip dividend. Briefly consider the advantages of scrip dividends from the point of view of:

(a) the company;

(b) the shareholders.

QUESTIONS FOR DISCUSSION

1 Hanging Valley plc has issued share capital of 2m ordinary shares, nominal value £1.00. The board of the company has decided it needs to raise £1m, net of issue costs, to finance a new product and a 1 for 4 rights issue has been suggested. The issue price will be at a 20 per cent discount to the current market price of £2.75 and issue costs will be £50,000. Calculate and explain the following:

(i) the theoretical ex-rights price per share;

(ii) the net cash raised;

(iii) the value of the rights.

2 Brag plc is raising finance through a rights issue and the current ex dividend market price of its shares is £3.00. The rights issue is on a 1 for 6 basis and the new shares will be offered at a 20 per cent discount to the current market price.

(a) Discuss the relative merits of the following ways of raising new equity finance:
(i) a placing;
(ii) a public offer.

(b) Explain why, in general, rights issues are priced at a discount to the prevailing market price of the share.

(c) Calculate the theoretical ex-rights share price of Brag plc and the value of the rights per share using the above information.

(d) Discuss the factors that determine whether the actual ex-rights share price is the same as the theoretical ex-rights price.

3 Mansun plc is a listed company with the following capital structure.

	£000
Ordinary shares, £1 each	20,000
Reserves	10,000
8% unsecured bonds (redeemable in 7 years)	2,000
13% bonds (redeemable in 2 years)	16,000
	48,000

The 13 per cent bonds give Mansun plc the right to redeem them at any time before maturity by paying full market value to bondholders. The unsecured bonds have just been issued and their cost is indicative of current financial market conditions. The current share price of Mansun plc is £4.27 and the current market price of the 13 per cent bonds is £105 per £100 bond. Mansun plc has been making regular annual after-tax profits of £10m for some years and pays corporation tax at a rate of 30 per cent.

At a recent board meeting, the finance director suggested that 4m new shares be issued in a rights issue, at a discount of 15 per cent to the company's current share price, and that the funds raised should be used to redeem part of the 13 per cent bond issue. Issue costs are expected to be £660,000. The managing director, however, feels strongly that the proceeds of the rights issue should be invested in a project yielding an annual return before tax of 22 per cent.

The board agreed that the price/earnings ratio of the company would be unchanged whichever option was selected and agreed to proceed with the rights issue. One week later, the company announced the rights issue and explained the use to which the funds were to be put.

(a) If capital markets are semi-strong form efficient, determine the expected share price on the announcement of the rights issue under each of the two alternative proposals.

(b) Discuss, with the aid of supporting calculations, whether the rights issue is in the best interests of the shareholders of Mansun plc.

4 Freeze plc is a listed company. It has been advised that its proposed 1 for 4 rights issue should be at a 15 per cent discount to its current ordinary share price of £4.20. The proposed rights issue is for £3m to expand existing business activities.

(a) Mr Tundra is a small investor who owns 10,000 shares of Freeze plc. Using the information provided, discuss the effect of the proposed rights issue on the personal wealth of Mr Tundra.

(b) Critically discuss the factors to be considered by Freeze plc in using a rights issue as a way of raising new equity finance. Your answer should include a discussion of the following points:
(i) the difference between actual and theoretical ex-rights price;
(ii) other ways in which Freeze plc could raise the new equity finance.

References

Copeland, T. (1979) 'Liquidity changes following stock splits', *Journal of Finance*, vol. 34, March, pp. 115–41.

Firth, M. (1973) 'Shareholder wealth attendant upon capitalization issues', *Accounting and Business Research*, vol. 4, no. 13, pp. 23–32.

Grinblatt, M., Masulis, R. and Titman, S. (1984) 'The valuation effects of stock splits and stock dividends', *Journal of Financial Economics*, December, pp. 461–90.

Recommended reading

A useful discussion of equity finance, new issue methods and preference shares can be found in:

Arnold, G. (2012) *Corporate Financial Management*, 5th edn, Harlow: FT Prentice Hall.

It is interesting to look at equity from an international perspective. See, for example:

McGuigan, J., Kretlow, W., Moyer, R. and Rao, R. (2011) *Contemporary Corporate Finance,* 12th edn, London: South-Western Cengage Learning.

The topics covered in this chapter can be followed through the Financial Times website: *https://www.ft.com/*

Useful and up-to-date information on the stock market listing process can be found on the website of the London Stock Exchange: *https://www.londonstockexchange.com/home/homepage.htm*

The regulatory environment relating to stock market listing can be studied on the UK Listing Authority website: *https://www.fca.org.uk/markets/ukla*

5 LONG-TERM FINANCE: DEBT FINANCE, HYBRID FINANCE AND LEASING

Learning objectives

After studying this chapter, you should have achieved the following learning objectives:

- a knowledge of the key features of long-term finance;

- an appreciation of the kinds of long-term debt finance available to companies, including bank debt, loan notes, ordinary bonds, loan stock, debentures, **deep discount bonds**, zero coupon bonds, convertible debt and Eurobonds;

- the ability to value redeemable debt, irredeemable debt, convertible debt and warrants;

- an understanding of the relative attractions of different kinds of long-term debt finance to a company, and an appreciation of the relative attractions of debt and equity finance;

- the ability to compare leasing with borrowing to buy as a source of finance for a company and an appreciation of how the financing decision can interact with the investment decision;

- an understanding of the reasons for the popularity of leasing as a source of finance.

■ ■ ■ INTRODUCTION

Long-term debt finance, for example, a bank loan or an issue of fixed interest securities such as bonds, has significant differences from equity finance. The interest paid on long-term debt finance is an allowable deduction from profit chargeable to tax, whereas dividends paid to ordinary and preference shareholders are not an allowable deduction from profit; dividends are in fact a share of the after-tax profit itself. Interest must be paid to providers of debt finance, but dividends are paid to shareholders only if directors choose to do so. In the event of liquidation, debt holders are paid off before shareholders because they rank higher in the creditor hierarchy. Thus, in liquidation, shareholders may receive only part-payment and in some cases nothing at all. Long-term debt finance therefore carries less risk for investors than equity finance and this is reflected in its lower required return. The future interest and capital payment from a debt security such as a bond can be discounted by the rate of return required by providers of debt finance to estimate a fair price for the security.

Debt can be engineered to suit the requirements of issuing companies and investors. For example, a new issue of bonds can be made more attractive to investors by attaching *warrants* to each bond. These give the holder the right to subscribe for ordinary shares at an attractive price in the future. Alternatively, bonds may be convertible into ordinary shares at a future date, in which case they may pay a lower interest rate because of the higher capital and dividend returns that may be available following conversion.

A further source of finance discussed in this chapter is leasing, which is a popular method of gaining access to a wide range of assets. We compare leasing with borrowing to buy and examine recent trends in lease finance.

5.1 BONDS, LOAN NOTES, LOAN STOCK AND DEBENTURES

Loan notes, loan stock and debentures are examples of long-term bonds or debt securities with a nominal value which is usually (in the UK) £100 and a market price determined by buying and selling in the bond markets. The interest rate (or coupon) is based on the nominal value and is usually paid once or twice each year. For example, a fixed interest 10 per cent bond will pay the holder £10 per year in interest, although this might be in the form of £5 paid twice each year. Interest is an allowable deduction in calculating taxable profit and so the effective cost to a company of servicing debt is lower than the interest (or coupon) rate. On a fixed interest 10 per cent bond with corporate tax at 20 per cent, for example, the servicing cost is reduced to 8 per cent per year ($10 \times (1 - 0.2)$). In corporate finance, this is referred to as the *tax efficiency* of debt. If the bond is redeemable, the principal (the nominal value) will need to be repaid on the redemption date.

Loan note is another term for bond. While the terms *debenture* and *loan note* can be used interchangeably, as a debenture is simply a written acknowledgement of indebtedness, a debenture is usually a bond that is *secured* by a trust deed against corporate assets, whereas loan stock is usually taken to refer to an *unsecured* bond. The debenture trust deed will cover in detail such matters as any charges on the assets of the issuing company (security), the way in which interest is paid, procedures for redemption of the issue, the production of regular reports on the position of the issuing company, the power of trustees to appoint a receiver and any restrictive covenants intended to protect the investors of debt finance.

The debenture may be secured against assets of the company by either a fixed or a floating charge. **Fixed charge security** will be on specified non-current assets which cannot be disposed of while the debt is outstanding. If the assets are land and buildings, the debenture is called a mortgage debenture. **Floating charge security** will be on a class of assets, such as current assets, and so disposal of some assets is permitted. In the event of default, for example, non-payment of interest, a floating charge will crystallise into a fixed charge on the specified class of assets.

5.1.1 Covenants

Restrictive (or banking) covenants are conditions attached to bonds as a means by which providers of long-term debt finance can restrict the actions of the managers of the issuing company. The purpose of covenants is to prevent any significant change in the *risk profile* of the company which existed when the bonds were first issued. This was the risk profile which was reflected in the cost of debt (i.e. the required return) at the time of issue. For example, a covenant might limit the amount of additional debt that could be issued by the company, or it might require a target *gearing ratio* to be maintained (see Section 2.4.6). To guard against insolvency and liquidity difficulties, it is possible for a covenant to specify a target range for the *current ratio* (see Section 2.4.5) in the hope of encouraging good working capital management. If the terms agreed in the covenant are breached, asset disposal may be needed to satisfy the bond holders, although the actual course of events following such a breach is likely to be determined by negotiation.

5.1.2 Redemption and refinancing

Bond redemption represents a significant demand on the cash flow of a company and calls for careful financial planning. Because of the large amount of finance needed, some companies may choose to invest regularly in a fund which has the sole purpose of providing for redemption. The amounts invested in such a **sinking fund**, together with accrued interest, will be sufficient to allow a company to redeem a bond issue without placing undue strain on its liquidity position.

Alternatively, a company may replace an issue of bonds due for redemption with a new issue of long-term debt or a new issue of equity. This *refinancing* choice has the advantage that it allows the company to maintain the relationship between long-term assets and long-term liabilities, i.e. the matching principle is upheld (see Section 3.2.3). The problems that can be associated with refinancing are illustrated in Vignette 5.1.

The cash-flow demands of redemption can also be eased by providing in the trust deed for redemption over a period of time, rather than on a specific date. This *redemption window* allows a company to choose the best time for redemption in light of prevailing conditions (e.g. the level of interest rates). A choice about when to redeem can also be gained

Vignette 5.1

House of Fraser on hunt for financing

Struggling department store chain says so far no talks have progressed

By Scheherazade Daneshkhu and Javier Espinoza

House of Fraser, the struggling department store group, has held refinancing talks with Alteri Investors, the London-based turnround specialist, in the latest sign of financial stress at the 169-year company.

The talks, first reported in the *Sunday Times,* have ended but they come as the company seeks to refinance or extend the terms of £224m of debt that matures in July 2019, four months after the UK leaves the EU.

The retailer which was bought by China's Sanpower in 2014 on the promise of expanding the brand in that country, sought to allay concerns on Sunday, saying: 'House of Fraser is a privately-owned business and we have the full financial support of our shareholders.'

British retailers have had a dismal start to the year – the worst since 2013 – as they grapple with rising business rates and other costs, while struggling to fill their stores with customers who are increasingly buying online.

Maplin, the electronics retailer and the UK arm of Toys R Us, both fell into administration while Mothercare, Carpetright and New Look have all been renegotiating terms with landlords or lenders.

House of Fraser also had a tough Christmas trading period with sales 2.9 per cent lower in the six weeks to December 23 than the same period in 2016. It promised £16m of cost cuts this year on top of last year's £10m. The group has also been seeking rent reductions from some of its landlords.

Alteri, which is backed by US buyout giant Apollo Global Management, was involved in the sale of struggling Jones Bootmaker to Endless in 2017 and in the acquisition of CBR Fashion Group from EQT earlier this year.

House of Fraser said: 'As you'd expect in the current market, finance providers are keen to talk to retailers,' but added that 'under the terms of the current banking facilities, the talks did not progress'.

The stumbling block appears to have been that most of House of Fraser's assets are already held as security by its existing lenders, led by HSBC bank.

The lenders recently hired EY, the professional services group, as an adviser, according to Sky News on Friday. The group was brought in to assess whether the lenders' investment in the business is safe, according to one person familiar with the situation.

Moody's, the rating agency, in December downgraded its rating on House of Fraser to Caa1, from B3, meaning that it deemed the group's creditworthiness had deteriorated to 'very high credit risk' from 'speculative'.

House of Fraser has a £175m bond maturing in 2020, which trades at a significant discount to face value. Net debt at the beginning of last year, the last publicly available figure, was £224m.

Sanpower injected further uncertainty into the retailer's future this month when it unexpectedly announced the sale of a 51 per cent stake in House of Fraser to Wuji Wenhua, a Chinese tourism group.

Source: Daneshkhu, S. and Espinoza, J. (2018) 'House of Fraser on hunt for financing', *Financial Times,* 25 March. © The Financial Times Limited 2018. All Rights Reserved.

Questions

1 Explain why refinancing is important to House of Fraser.

2 Discuss why House of Fraser is having difficulty refinancing its debt.

by attaching a **call option** to the bond issue, as this gives the company the right, but not the obligation, to buy (i.e. redeem) the issue before maturity. Early redemption might be gained in exchange for compensating investors for lost interest by paying a premium over nominal value. Redemption *at a premium* can also be used to obtain a lower interest rate (coupon) on a bond.

It is possible, but rare, for a bond to be *irredeemable.* The permanent interest-bearing shares (PIBs) and perpetual sub bonds (PSBs) issued by some building societies are an example. However, as Vignette 5.2 shows, strong companies can issue bonds with very long redemption dates.

Vignette 5.2

Petrobras century bond makes more sense than first appears

By Ralph Atkins

Petrobras is a Brazilian state oil company engulfed last year by a multibillion-dollar bribery and kick-back scandal. Would global investors really lend it money for 100 years? Well, yes, they would. Bids this week for a 'century bond' issued by Petrobras were more than five times higher than the $2.5bn issued.

Century bonds are not unprecedented. Past big issu-ers have included France's EDF utility. In April, Mexico's government issued 100-year bonds denomi-nated in euros. Petrobras, however, has extended further the boundaries of corporate bond markets, which have expanded rapidly in an era of historic borrowing costs. It allowed the troubled Brazilian energy group to lock in financing until 2115 – by when the world might be using energy beamed back from Mars.

Doubtless, it also left many scratching their heads about what the new issue told us about the post-2007 crisis financial system. One wrong conclusion would be that investors acted crazily. True, Petrobras has problems, as does Brazil's economy. The bonds, however, yielded a temptingly high 8.45 per cent. Rather, the deal highlighted how ultra-low global interest rates and quantitative easing are reshaping the corporate debt market, breaking down bonds' traditional role as supposedly safer alternatives to equities.

Investing in a bond that will not be redeemed until way beyond a normal human's lifespan might seem to imply reckless assumptions about the issuer's survival chances. The beauty of bond market maths, however, means such existential questions are largely irrelevant when proper account is taken of payments to be made so far into the future. If this week an investor bought Petrobras bonds with a par value of $1,000 and used 8.45 per cent as the 'discount rate', the present value of the final 2115 payment on the bond – the return of the $1,000 plus a coupon – would be just 26 cents. So whether the bond is eventually redeemed or not makes scant difference. Similar calculations explain why Mexico could issue a €1.5bn 100-year bond – even though some would question whether Europe's single cur-rency will be around in a decade let alone a century.

What matters instead for the nearer-term perfor-mance of Petrobras's bonds as tradable securities will be trends in its perceived creditworthiness, and global interest rates. The latter could push bond yields higher – and prices down – but improvements in the energy group's fortunes would work in the opposite direction, justifying lower yields and higher bond prices.

Petrobras's century bond may still be sending warn-ing signals. It did not help calm fears about the large inflows in recent years into emerging market corpo-rate bonds – and the risk of a disruptive correction if the US Federal Reserve starts lifting interest rates later this year. 'It is a sign of euphoria,' warns Alberto Gallo, head of credit research at Royal Bank of Scotland. 'It is a clear sign that the market has disconnected from macro and micro fundamentals.'

Longer bonds allow pension and insurance compa-nies to better match their future liabilities. But they may amplify market swings; bond maths means

---

Vignette 5.1 (continued)

small changes in interest rates produce proportionally bigger price movements on longer-dated bonds.

Century bonds strengthen the trend towards company and government debt maturing ever further into the future. The proportion of new issuance with maturities longer than 10 years is the highest since 2007, according to JPMorgan.

In the sell-offs that have punctuated recent market activity, bonds have appeared to act more like equities. 'We have to get more used to thinking of bonds as 'risky' assets,' says Stephanie Flanders, chief market strategist for Europe at JPMorgan Asset

Management. 'When you see a bond with a high yield, you know it is going to have particular risk attached.'

If investor interest is understandable, a harder question is why Petrobras wanted to issue 100-year debt. The answer is: because it could. Massive investor demand gave it a chance to storm back to capital markets with a headline grabbing bond issue, boosting confidence and setting a benchmark that should make future issues easier. Shorter-term bonds might not have been much cheaper. These are difficult times for Petrobras but global financial conditions are in its favour.

 Source: Atkins, R. (2015) 'Petrobras century bond makes more sense than first appears', *Financial Times*, 4 June. © The Financial Times Limited 2015. All Rights Reserved.

Questions

1 Explain why the capital repayment on the century bond is currently of little value.

2 Discuss the reasons why investors were attracted to the century bond issue.

5.1.3 Floating interest rates

While it is usual to think of bonds as fixed interest securities, they may be offered with a *floating interest rate* linked to a current market interest rate, for example, 3 per cent (300 basis points) over the three-month LIBOR or 2 per cent (200 basis points) above bank **base rate**. A floating rate may be attractive to investors who want a return that is consistently comparable with prevailing market interest rates or who want to protect themselves against unanticipated inflation. A fixed interest rate protects investors against anticipated inflation since this was part of the fixed rate set on issue. Floating rate debt is also attractive to a company for hedging against falls in market interest rates (see 'Interest rate risk', Section 12.1.1) since, when interest rates fall, the company is not burdened by fixed interest rates higher than market rates.

5.1.4 Bond ratings

A key feature of a bond is its rating, which measures its investment risk by considering the degree of protection offered on interest payments and repayment of principal, both now and in the future. The investment risk is rated by reference to a standard risk index. Bond rating is carried out by commercial organisations such as Moody's Investors Service, Standard & Poor's Corporation and Fitch Group. Each rating is based on analysis of the expected financial performance of the issuing company as well as on expert forecasts of the economic environment. Institutional investors may have a statutory or self-imposed requirement to invest only in *investment-grade* bonds; a downgrading of the rating of a particular

Table 5.1 Moody's Investors Service's bond ratings

Aaa	Obligations rated Aaa are judged to be of the highest quality, with minimal credit risk
Aa	Obligations rated Aa are judged to be of high quality, with very low credit risk
A	Obligations rated A are considered upper-medium grade, with low credit risk
Baa	Obligations rated Baa are considered medium grade, with moderate credit risk and so may possess certain speculative characteristics
Ba	Obligations rated Ba are considered speculative, with substantial credit risk
B	Obligations rated B are considered speculative, with high credit risk
Caa	Obligations rated Caa are considered speculative, with very high credit risk
Ca	Obligations rated Ca are highly speculative and in or close to default, with some prospect of recovering principal and interest
C	Obligations rated C are the lowest rated and typically in default, with little prospect of recovering either principal or interest

Note: Moody's appends numerical modifiers 1, 2 and 3 to each generic rating classification from Aa through Caa, indicating higher-end ranking, mid-range ranking and lower-end ranking respectively of its generic rating category.

bond to speculative (or junk) status can therefore lead to an increase in selling pressure, causing a fall in the bond's market price and an increase in its required yield (see 'The valuation of fixed interest bonds', Section 5.6). The standard ratings issued by Moody's Investors Service for long-term fixed interest corporate debt are summarised in Table 5.1, while Vignette 5.3 illustrates how increased gearing can change credit ratings.

Vignette 5.3

AT&T downgraded after Time Warner deal closes

By Alexandra Scaggs

AT&T's credit rating was downgraded to two notches above junk by two rating agencies on Friday, after the US telecommunication giant completed its $80bn acquisition of Time Warner.

Analysts at Moody's and S&P Global Ratings each cut their ratings one level – to Baa2 and BBB, respectively – because of the significant amount of debt the acquisition adds to AT&T's balance sheet. The combined company's net debt will total $180bn, and the analysts estimate that is more than 3.5 times its earnings before interest, tax, depreciation and amortisation, or ebitda.

The deal will also make AT&T the largest non-financial debt issuer in the US by far, they said. Such scale introduces the risk that bond fund managers' demand will be damped by limits on how much debt they can hold from any individual company

'Investors can only have a certain amount of exposure to any particular issuer, which reduces demand and puts pressure on pricing of debt,' said Allyn Arden, credit analyst with S&P Global Ratings.

Its tie-up with Time Warner is expected to offer just $1.5bn of annualised cost savings, which is 'minimal' even with the expected revenue synergies of $1bn, Mr Arden said.

The combined company has $2bn of debt maturing this year and nearly $9bn maturing next year, according to filings. Moody's analysts expect AT&T to maintain good liquidity over the next year, but added that it may eventually need to cut its dividend to compete with new media and technology industry competitors.

Vignette 5.3 (continued)

'The sheer amount of debt commits AT&T to sizeable annual maturity obligations for the long term thereby making the company beholden to the health of the capital markets,' the analysts said in their downgrade note Friday.

As part of the cash- and equity-funded acquisition, AT&T will take on Time Warner's debt, which totals more than $15bn. To strengthen its current rating, the company could take other actions besides cutting its dividend, the analysts said. Those include selling assets, delaying or reducing its capital expenditures or issuing more equity.

The downgrade follows the Department of Justice's decision not to seek to further delay the acquisition pending a possible appeal. The DOJ had initially challenged the deal on antitrust concerns, but a federal judge approved it earlier this week.

 Source: Scaggs, A. (2018) 'AT&T downgraded after Time Warner deal closes', *Financial Times*, 15 June. © The Financial Times Limited 2018. All Rights Reserved.

Questions

1 Explain why AT&T has been downgraded.

2 What effect will the downgrading have on AT&T's ability to raise further debt?

5.1.5 Deep discount and zero coupon bonds

There is clearly a relationship between redemption the terms, the **coupon rate** and the issue price of bonds. This relationship is explored in more detail in 'The valuation of fixed interest bonds' (see Section 5.6), which deals with valuating debt securities. It is possible for a company to issue a bond at a price well below its nominal value in exchange for a lower interest rate coupled with redemption at nominal (or at a premium to nominal) on maturity. Such a security, referred to as a *deep discount bond*, will be attractive to investors who prefer to receive a higher proportion of their return in the form of capital gains, as opposed to interest income. Different personal taxation treatment of interest income and capital gains will also be a factor influencing the preferences of individual investors.

The lower servicing cost of deep discount bonds may be attractive if cash-flow problems are being experienced or are anticipated, for example if the cash raised by the new issue is to be used in an investment project whose returns are expected to be low in its initial years. If no interest at all is paid on a bond issued at a deep discount, so that all of the return to investors is in the form of capital appreciation, it is called a **zero coupon bond**. The general attractions of zero coupon bonds to the issuing company are similar to those of deep discount bonds. However, these advantages must be weighed against the high cost of redemption compared with the amount of finance raised.

5.1.6 New issues

Debt finance is raised in the new issues market (the primary market) through lead banks, which will seek to place blocks of new bonds with clients through advance orders prior to the issue date. This process is referred to as book building. Several banks may join forces in a syndicate in order to spread the risk associated with providing debt finance.

5.2 BANK AND INSTITUTIONAL DEBT

Long-term loans are available from banks and other financial institutions at both fixed and floating interest rates, provided the issuing bank is convinced that the purpose of the loan is a good one. The cost of bank loans is usually an agreed amount above bank base rate, depending on the perceived risk of the borrowing company. The issuing bank charges an arrangement fee on bank loans, which are usually secured by a fixed or floating charge, the nature of the charge depending on the availability of assets of good quality to act as security. A *repayment schedule* is often agreed between the bank and the borrowing company, structured to meet the specific needs of the borrower and in accordance with the lending policies of the bank. Payments on long-term bank loans will include both interest and capital elements.

Example	Interest and capital elements of annual loan payments

Consider a £100,000 bank loan at 10 per cent per year, repayable in equal annual instalments over five years. The annual repayment can be found by dividing the amount of the loan by the cumulative present value factor for five years at 10 per cent:

$$\text{Annual repayment} = 100,000/3.791 = £26,378.26$$

Table 5.2 Interest elements of loan repayments

Year	Opening balance (£)	Add 10% interest (£)	Less repayment (£)	Closing balance (£)
1	100,000	10,000	26,378.26	83,621.74
2	83,621.74	8,362.17	26,378.26	65,605.65
3	65,605.65	6,560.57	26,378.26	45,787.96
4	45,787.96	4,578.79	26,378.26	23,988.50
5	23,988.50	2,398.85	26,378.26	9.09

The interest elements of the annual repayments are calculated in Table 5.2. The capital elements are the difference between the interest elements and the annual repayments. The small residual difference is due to rounding of the cumulative present value factor.

Long-term bank loans cannot be sold on directly by the company to a third party. The growth of *securitisation*, however, means that banks, financial institutions and large companies can, in some circumstances, parcel up debts as securities and sell them on the securitised debt market, as illustrated by Vignette 5.4.

The problems faced by small businesses in raising debt finance can be partially mitigated by government assistance, for example, the Enterprise Finance Guarantee Scheme managed by British Business Financial Services, a subsidiary of the UK government's British Business Bank. This scheme allows smaller companies to obtain bank loans even if they lack adequate security for a commercial loan and they are facing tight credit conditions.

Vignette 5.4

Barclays and Pimco to securitise £5.3bn of UK mortgages

Robust investor demand will enable groups to sell bonds backed by 'bad bank' mortgages

By Robert Smith

Barclays and Pimco are planning a multibillion pound securitisation of the mortgages they recently agreed to acquire from the UK government's 'bad bank', taking advantage of buoyant demand from investors for structured debt.

UK Asset Resolution (UKAR), which borrowed £48.7bn to take on the loans of failed lenders Northern Rock and Bradford & Bingley in 2010, announced on Thursday that it was selling a £5.3bn portfolio of mortgages to a group of investors led by Barclays.

The sale of the mortgages, which were originally made by Bradford & Bingley, will allow UKAR to repay the last of the so-called Financial Service Compensation Scheme (FSCS) loan that the UK Treasury made in 2008 and 2009 to cover the collapse of high street lenders.

'This is a strategically important transaction for the UK government, as it enables the repayment of the remaining £4.7bn of the FSCS loan,' said Cecile Hillary, head of asset finance solutions at Barclays.

Barclays and Pimco are planning to launch a securitisation of the mortgages shortly after the portfolio sale formally closes in a few weeks, according to a person familiar with the matter. Securitisation is a process where loans such as mortgages are transferred to a special-purpose vehicle, which then sells bonds secured against these assets to fund managers and other investors.

These bonds are sliced into different 'tranches' that carry more or less risk depending on the order in which they will be repaid. The 'senior' piece at the top typically carries a triple-A credit rating and a relatively low interest rate, while the riskiest 'equity' slice at the bottom generates much higher returns but is more exposed to potential losses.

The £5.3bn of loans are split into two portfolios of buy-to-let and owner-occupied mortgages, that will be transferred into two separate securitisation vehicles called Dorset Home Loans and Cornwall Home Loans.

US asset manager Pimco is taking on the riskiest 'equity' piece on both of these deals. Barclays, meanwhile, will hold 5 per cent of each tranche of the securitisations to meet 'risk retention' requirements, a post-financial crisis rule that means sellers of asset-backed securities must keep a certain amount of 'skin in the game'.

A consortium of banks made up of Barclays, HSBC, Lloyds, Nationwide, NatWest and Santander UK has committed to buying investment grade bonds from the securitisation. This finance package was a so-called 'staple', a term for debt financing that is offered to all bidders in an auction.

This structure closely mirrors the one UKAR used when it sold an even larger slug of Bradford & Bingley mortgages to Blackstone and Prudential in 2017. Blackstone's nearly £10bn securitisation deal saw £5.5bn of senior notes sold to the same consortium of banks, with much of the remaining debt publicly sold to third-party investors. Goldman Sachs held the risk retention piece on that deal, called Ripon.

One asset-backed securities investor said that when it emerged Pimco's consortium was in pole position to win the bid earlier this week, many in the market wrongly assumed that the UKAR's latest sale would not result in a public securitisation deal. This is because Pimco was the sole buyer of a £1.7bn securitisation of the Co-operative bank's mortgages in October, in a deal called Warwick Finance Three.

Source: Smith, R. (2018) 'Barclays and Pimco to securitise £5.3bn of UK mortgages', *Financial Times,* 27 April. © The Financial Times Limited 2018. All Rights Reserved.

5.3 INTERNATIONAL DEBT FINANCE

The international operations of companies directly influence their financing needs. For example, a company may finance business operations in a foreign country by borrowing in the local currency to hedge against exchange rate losses (see 'Internal management of exchange rate risk', Section 12.2.2). It may also borrow in a foreign currency because of comparatively low interest rates (although it is likely that exchange rate movements will eliminate this advantage over time). Foreign currency borrowing can enable a company to diminish the effect of restrictions on currency exchange. One way of obtaining long-term foreign currency debt finance is by issuing Eurobonds.

5.3.1 Eurobonds

Eurobonds are bonds outside the control of the country in whose currency they are denominated and they are sold in different countries at the same time by large companies and governments. A Eurodollar bond, for example, is outside of the jurisdiction of the USA. Eurobonds typically have maturities of 5–15 years and interest on them, which is payable gross (i.e. without deduction of tax), may be at either a fixed or a floating rate. The Eurobond market is not as tightly regulated as domestic capital markets and so Eurobond interest rates tend to be lower than those on comparable domestic bonds.

Eurobonds are *bearer securities*, meaning that their owners are unregistered, and so they offer investors the attraction of anonymity. Because Eurobonds are unsecured, companies issuing them must be internationally known and have an excellent credit rating. Common issue currencies are US dollars (Eurodollars), yen (Euroyen) and sterling (Eurosterling). The variety of Eurobonds mirrors the variety on domestic bond markets: for example, fixed rate, floating rate, zero coupon and convertible Eurobonds are available.

Companies may find Eurobonds useful for financing long-term investment, or as a way of balancing their long-term asset and liability structures in terms of exposure to exchange rate risk. Investors, for their part, may be attracted to Eurobonds because they offer both security and anonymity, but will be concerned about achieving an adequate return, especially as the secondary market for Eurobonds has been criticised for poor liquidity in recent years.

5.4 CONVERTIBLE BONDS

Convertible bonds have characteristics of both debt and equity and so are an example of *hybrid finance.* They are fixed interest debt securities which can be converted into ordinary shares of a company at the option of the holder, on a predetermined date and at a predetermined rate. If they are not converted, they are redeemed at a date which is usually several years after the conversion date. The conversion rate is stated either as a *conversion price* (the nominal value of the bond that can be converted into one ordinary share) or as a *conversion ratio* (the number of ordinary shares obtained from one bond). Conversion terms may vary over time, with the conversion ratio decreasing in line with the expected increase in the value of ordinary shares. For example, conversion terms may say that one

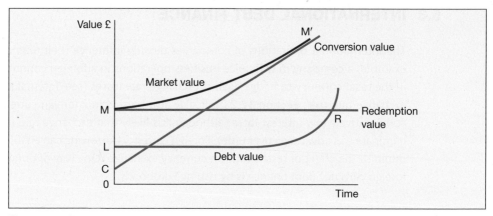

Figure 5.1 Factors influencing the market value of a convertible security

bond can be converted into 35 ordinary shares and also say that three years later one bond can be converted into only 30 ordinary shares.

Conversion value is the market value of ordinary shares into which one bond may be converted and is equal to the conversion ratio multiplied by the market price per ordinary share. When convertible bonds are first issued, the conversion value is less than the issue value of the bond. As the conversion date approaches, it is expected that the conversion value will have increased due to the growth of the ordinary share price so that converting into equity becomes an attractive choice for investors. The **conversion premium** (Section 5.7.3) is the difference between the market price of the convertible bond and its conversion value. In Figure 5.1 the conversion premium is represented by the vertical distance between the lines MM′ and CM′. The conversion premium is proportional to the time remaining before conversion takes place and, as conversion approaches, the market value and the conversion value converge, and the conversion premium becomes negligible. The conversion premium is often expressed on a per-share basis. The difference between the market value of a convertible bond and its value as straight debt is called the *rights premium*. In Figure 5.1, the rights premium is represented by the vertical distance between the lines MM′ and LR.

Example	Convertible bond terms

Consider a 12 per cent convertible bond, redeemable at nominal value of £100 in six years' time, which can be converted at any time in the next three years into 30 ordinary shares. The bond is currently trading ex-interest (buying the bond does not confer the right to receive the next interest payment) at £115.50 and the current ordinary share price is £3.20. The ex-interest market value of ordinary bonds of a similar risk class and maturity is £105.00.

Current conversion value: 30 × £3.20 = £96.00
Current conversion premium: £115.50 − £96.00 = £19.50 or 65p per share
Current rights premium: £115.50 − £105.00 = £10.50 or 35p per share

The interest on a convertible bond is less than that on an unconvertible bond (also called an ordinary, vanilla or straight bond) due to the value to the investor of the conversion rights. The minimum price (floor value) of a convertible bond is equal to its value as an ordinary bond with the same interest rate, maturity and risk. The *actual* market value of a convertible bond will depend on:

- the current conversion value;
- the time to conversion;
- the expected conversion value;
- whether the market expects that conversion is likely.

Valuing convertible bonds is considered in Section 5.7.

5.4.1 The attractions of convertible bonds for companies

Companies can view convertible bonds as *delayed equity*. Issuing such debt securities may be attractive when, in the directors' view, the company's ordinary share price is depressed and so does not reflect company's the true value. Alternatively, the directors may turn to convertible bonds as a way of raising finance because they feel that an immediate issue of new equity would cause an unacceptably large fall in earnings per share (EPS).

Convertible bonds are also attractive to companies because, like ordinary bonds, they pay fixed interest, making financial forecasting and planning somewhat easier. Furthermore, issuing convertible bonds allows a company to pay a lower rate of interest than it would pay if it were to issue straight bonds of a similar maturity, thereby helping its cash-flow situation. As interest payments on bonds are tax-deductible, issuing convertible bonds can decrease the average cost of capital. Convertible bonds also allow companies to push their gearing beyond a level normally considered acceptable by creditors, owing to the expectation that conversion, with a consequent reduction in gearing, is likely to occur. One of the main attractions of convertible bonds is that if conditions governing conversion were assessed correctly at the time of issue, they are *self-liquidating* in that the issuing company does not have to find cash to redeem them, whereas straight bonds must be redeemed or refinanced on maturity.

As for disadvantages, gearing will be increased while convertible bonds are outstanding, which will affect the overall risk profile of the company. Dilution of earnings per share may also occur on conversion, as well as dilution of the control of existing shareholders. Finally, convertibles are hard to issue in a bear market.

5.4.2 The attractions of convertible bonds to investors

The convertible bond mixture of fixed interest in the short term and an option to convert into equity in the longer term may be attractive to some investors, as it offers a lower-risk investment in the short term with the possibility of greater gains in the longer term. An advantage over ordinary bonds is that convertibles offer investors the opportunity to participate financially in the growth of the company, rather than receiving a fixed return. An advantage over ordinary equity is that convertible bond holders can evaluate the performance of a company and its shares before deciding whether to become ordinary shareholders by converting.

It is not certain, however, that bond holders will exercise their option to convert. They are under no obligation to do so if conversion is unattractive, for example, if expected share price growth has not occurred and so the conversion value is less than the floor value. This lack of growth may be due entirely to factors which are outside the control of the company, for example, a general downturn in overall economic conditions. If conversion does not occur, the bond will run its full term and will need to be redeemed at maturity. The popularity of convertible bonds is illustrated by Vignette 5.5.

Vignette 5.5

Convertible bonds surge highlights late stage of credit cycle

Market on pace for the biggest volume of issuance since financial crisis

By Alexandra Scaggs

There are plenty of signs the credit cycle is advancing into its later stages and one more can be added to the list – companies are issuing more convertible debt (which has features of both bonds and equities) for their financing needs.

Twitter Inc is the latest member of this group. Last week's news that the social media platform would be added to the S&P 500 index sparked a share price rally of almost 9 per cent, as the benchmark is widely followed by passive investors.

Perhaps to celebrate the institutional stamp of approval, the company went to market with $1bn of securities that could dilute the current shareholders' stake in the company.

When the notes, which yield 0.25 per cent, reach maturity in June 2024, owners will have the option to exchange them for either their cash principal or shares of Twitter at $57.14. The company said it had entered into hedging transactions that could reduce the dilution but the extent of such a reduction was not clear. The shares fell for a session but still looked set to close the week sharply higher.

The market is heating up for convertible debt, which was created in the US during the late-1800s railroad financing boom and pays regular coupons like a bond. But in exchange for a lower interest rate

– and often, subordination to other bondholders in a default – investors can choose whether to exchange them for stock at a pre-determined price.

'What we're seeing is a huge amount of new issuance,' said Odell Lambroza, a portfolio manager at Advent Capital. 'I think companies are trying to get ahead of rising interest rates and using convertibles as growth capital.'

So far this year, companies have issued 62 convertible bonds worth $22.9bn, according to Dealogic, putting the market on pace for the highest volume of issuance since the financial crisis.

This is, in part, because the Federal Reserve is raising interest rates, a defining feature of the late stages of the US credit cycle. Convertible bonds are more appealing to corporate treasurers during periods of rising rates because the lower coupons reduce the costs of interest payments.

In fact, the last time Twitter issued debt, it was riding a wave of increased convertible bond issuance back in 2014, Dealogic data shows. This was driven by the rise in interest rates in the wake of 2013's taper tantrum, brought about by the announcement of the reduction in the Fed's quantitative easing programme. Sliding oil prices and a drop in yields led issuance to decline again.

Vignette 5.5 (continued)

For investors, the conditions that characterise the later stages of the credit cycle make convertible bonds more interesting as well. For one, the securities are actively traded around mergers and acquisitions, because certain features allow for a wide range of outcomes. And while there has been some uncertainty about regulatory treatment of deals, the upcoming decision about AT&T's proposed purchase of Time Warner could spark more activity, depending on the outcome.

Secondly, the equity market has become pricier and corporate credit spreads have remained relatively narrow, shrinking the range of reasonable options to deploy investors' cash. Convertible bonds can be used for sophisticated trades that do not depend on the direction of a company's equity or debt, known as arbitrage.

Twitter shares boast high valuations as the company's stock trades at 51 times its expected earnings for the next 12 months, according to FactSet data. The S&P 500, in comparison, is trading at 17 times its earnings forecasts.

While the company has reported two consecutive quarters of growth, investors may still have hesi-tated to buy equity – those were the only two quarters of positive earnings it has reported in the nearly five years it has spent as a public company.

That is part of the reason why convertible bonds are especially popular among companies like Twitter, which aim for high growth and experience variable cash flows. But those types of companies tend to be more speculative bets than other issuers. And it is important to note convertible bonds historically have had poor recovery rates in cases of default. In the case of a tech bust, investors could end up losing money.

The tech sector is the biggest issuer of convertible debt by far. At about 40 per cent of the market, its share is more than twice as large as much any other sector, according to ICE BofAML data. That consti-tutes a significant amount of shareholder dilution if the tech boom continues.

Shareholders may be able to take heart from a sta-tistic reported by Goldman Sachs. During periods of rising rates going back to 2003, convertible bonds have outperformed high-yield bonds but underper-formed the S&P 500.

 Source: Scaggs, A. (2018) 'Convertible bonds surge highlights late stage of credit cycle', *Financial Times*, 8 June. © The Financial Times Limited 2018. All Rights Reserved.

Questions

1 Discuss why Twitter Inc might have chosen convertible bonds rather than ordinary bonds as a source of finance.

2 What dilution might be experienced in 2024?

5.5 WARRANTS

A warrant is the right to buy new ordinary shares in a company at a future date, for a fixed, predetermined price known as the **exercise price**. Warrants are usually issued as part of a package with bonds as an **equity sweetener**, a phrase which signifies that attaching war-rants to the bond issue can make it more attractive to investors. Warrants can be separated from the underlying bonds and traded, however, both before and during the specified exercise period. The buyer of bonds with warrants attached can therefore reduce the invest-ment cost by selling the warrants.

The *intrinsic value* of a warrant (V_w) is the current ordinary share price (P) less the exercise price (E), multiplied by the number of shares obtained for each warrant exercised (N):

$$V_w = (P - E) \times N$$

For example, if a warrant entitles the holder to purchase five ordinary shares at an exercise price of £1 and the ordinary share price is currently £1.25, the intrinsic value is:

$$V_w = (1.25 - 1.00) \times 5 = £1.25$$

The actual warrant price on the market will be higher than the intrinsic value owing to the possibility of future share price growth. The difference between the actual warrant price and the intrinsic value is called *time value* and so:

Actual warrant price = Intrinsic value + Time value

Warrants may therefore have a market value even when they have no intrinsic value.

Continuing our example, suppose that the ordinary share price increases from £1.25 to £2.50 over a six-month period. The intrinsic value of the warrant increases to:

$$V_w = (2.50 - 1.00) \times 5 = £7.50$$

The value of the underlying ordinary share increases by 100 per cent, but the value of the warrant increases by 500 per cent. This means that a greater proportionate gain can be obtained by buying and holding the warrant than by buying and holding the ordinary share. If the ordinary share price decreases from £1.25 to £1.00 over the six-month period, the intrinsic value of the warrant is zero. The value of the underlying share decreases by 20 per cent, but the value of the warrant decreases by 100 per cent. In this case a greater proportionate loss is sustained by holding the warrant than by holding the ordinary share. This phenomenon of proportionately higher gains and losses is known as the *gearing effect* of warrants. The absolute loss on the warrant is limited to £0.25, however, while the loss on the ordinary share can be as high as £1.00.

For investors, the attractions of warrants therefore include a low initial outlay, a lower loss potential than that entailed by purchasing ordinary shares and a higher relative profit potential due to the gearing effect of warrants.

From a company point of view, the interest rate on sweetened bonds will be lower than that on ordinary bonds of similar maturity, while attaching warrants will make the issue more attractive to investors. Warrants may even make possible an issue of bonds when the available security is insufficient. Unlike convertible bonds, warrants lead to the subscription of a small amount of additional equity funds in the future, provided that satisfactory share price growth is achieved, and the warrants are exercised.

5.6 VALUING FIXED INTEREST BONDS

5.6.1 Irredeemable bonds

Valuing irredeemable bonds, where the principal or capital amount is never repaid, is straightforward. It is the sum to infinity of the discounted future interest payments, as follows:

$$P_0 = \frac{I}{K_d}$$

where: P_0 = ex-interest market value (£)
          I = annual interest paid (£)
          K_d = rate of return required by debt investors (%)

| Example | **Valuing an irredeemable bond** |

Consider an 8 per cent irredeemable bond where debt investors require a return of 11 per cent. The theoretical market value of the bond will be:

$$P_0 = \frac{I}{K_d} = £8/0.11 = £72.73$$

The market price is less than the nominal value of £100 because the bond offers annual interest of only 8 per cent while the return required is 11 per cent. If the bond had offered more than 11 per cent interest, its theoretical value would be at a premium to its nominal value.

It is important to remember that this valuation model gives the *ex-interest* market price of irredeemable bonds since it represents the present value of *future* cash flows. Any current interest or interest which is shortly to be paid is not included in the valuation. The rate of return (K_d) on bonds required by investors is the cost of debt (see Section 9.1.3) and is also known as the *yield* of the bond. If the current market value (P_0) and interest rate are known, therefore, the model can be used to calculate the current cost of irredeemable debt.

5.6.2 Redeemable bonds

Redeemable bonds can be valued by discounting the future interest payments and the future redemption value by the debt holders' required rate of return (K_d). Interest payments are usually made on an annual or semi-annual basis, while redemption value is usually at the nominal value of £100.

$$P_0 = \frac{I}{(1 + K_d)} + \frac{I}{(1 + K_d)^2} + \frac{I}{(1 + K_d)^3} + \dots + \frac{I + RV}{(1 + K_d)^n}$$

where: P_0 = ex-interest market value
         I = interest paid (£)
         K_d = rate of return required by debt investors (%)
         RV = redemption value (£)
         n = time to maturity (years)

| Example | Valuing a redeemable bond with annual interest |

Consider a bond that pays annual interest of 10 per cent and which is redeemable at nominal value of £100 in four years' time. Assume investors in this bond require an annual return of 12 per cent. Because the bond is redeemed at nominal value and the required rate of return is greater than its interest rate, we would expect its market value to be less than its nominal value. We can calculate the theoretical market value as follows:

$$P_0 = \frac{10}{(1.12)} + \frac{10}{(1.12)^2} + \frac{10}{(1.12)^3} + \frac{(10 + 100)}{(1.12)^4} = £93.93$$

If interest is paid semi-annually, the valuation model can be modified by dividing both the annual discount rate and the annual interest rate by 2, while leaving the treatment of the redemption value unchanged. While not mathematically accurate, this approximation is good enough for most purposes.

| Example | Valuing a redeemable bond with semi-annual interest |

We repeat our earlier calculation with semi-annual interest payments of £5 discounted at a six-monthly required rate of return of 6 per cent. The theoretical market value now becomes:

$$P_0 = \frac{5}{(1.06)^2} + \frac{5}{(1.06)^2} + \cdots + \frac{5}{(1.06)^8} + \frac{100}{(1.12)^4} = £94.60$$

The increase in theoretical market value occurs because half of each year's interest payment is received sooner and therefore it has a higher present value.

5.7 VALUING CONVERTIBLE BONDS

Because convertible bonds give the holder the option to convert them into ordinary equity at a future date, valuing them is more complex than valuing ordinary bonds. The bond can be valued from two different perspectives:

- Convertible bonds can be valued as ordinary bonds if conversion at some future date appears unlikely. The market value will be the sum of the present values of the future interest payments and the principal to be repaid on maturity.
- Alternatively, convertible bonds can be valued on the assumption that they will be converted into ordinary shares. The market value will be the sum of the present values of the future interest payments up to the conversion date and the present value of the shares into which each bond is converted.

Which perspective is adopted depends on the expectations of investors with respect to the future price of the underlying ordinary share.

5.7.1 Conversion value

If investors expect the company's share price to increase at an average annual rate sufficient to make future conversion into ordinary shares an attractive option, the current market value of a convertible bond depends primarily on its future conversion value. The conversion value depends on the estimated share price on the conversion date, as follows:

$$CV = P_0(1 + g)^n R$$

where: CV = conversion value of the convertible bond (£) after n years
P_0 = current ex-dividend ordinary share price (£)
g = expected annual growth rate of ordinary share price (%)
n = time to conversion (years)
R = number of shares received on conversion

5.7.2 Market value

The theoretical market value of a convertible bond where conversion is expected is the sum of the present values of the future interest payments and the present value of the bond's conversion value, as follows:

$$P_0 = \frac{I}{(1 + K_d)} + \frac{I}{(1 + K_d)^2} + \frac{I}{(1 + K_d)^3} + \cdots + \frac{I + CV}{(1 + K_d)^n}$$

where: P_0 = ex-interest market value (£)
I = interest paid (£)
K_d = rate of return required by investors (%)
CV = conversion value of the convertible bond (£) after n years
n = time to conversion (years)

This can also be expressed as follows:

$$P_0 = \sum_{i=1}^{i=n} \frac{I}{(1 + K_d)^i} + \frac{P_0(1 + g)^n R}{(1 + K_d)^n}$$

Example	Valuing a convertible bond

A 10 per cent convertible bond can be converted in four years' time into 25 ordinary shares or redeemed at nominal value of £100 on the same date. The return required on the bond is 11 per cent. The current ex dividend market price of the underlying share is £3.35 and this is expected to grow by 5 per cent per year.

The conversion value of the bond in four years' time will be:

$$CV = P_0(1 + g)^n R = 3.35 \times 1.05^4 \times 25 = £101.80$$

Conversion looks likely since a rational investor, faced by a choice between the conversion value of £101.80 and the nominal value of £100, will choose to convert.

The theoretical market value of the bond will be the sum of the present values of the expected future cash flows. From discount tables, the cumulative present value factor (CPVF) for four years at 11 per cent is 3.102 and the present value factor (PVF) for four years at 11 per cent is 0.659. Using the valuation model gives:

$$
\begin{aligned}
P_0 &= (I \times CPVF_{11,4}) + (CV \times PVF_{11,4}) \\
&= (10 \times 3.102) + (101.80 \times 0.659) \\
&= 31.02 + 67.09 \\
&= £98.11
\end{aligned}
$$

If conversion were unlikely, redemption would still be guaranteed and the theoretical value of the bond would be its minimum value (floor value) of £96.92 ((10 $\times$ 3.102) + (100 $\times$ 0.659)).

5.7.3 Factors influencing the market value of a convertible bond

The factors influencing the market value of a convertible bond were illustrated in Figure 5.1. The market value is shown by the line MM'. Initially, the floor price of the convertible bond will reflect its redemption value. As the ordinary share price rises over time, however, the conversion value (CM') will become greater than the redemption value, and the conversion value will then become the floor price. The actual market value (MM') is greater than the conversion value (CM') because of the expectation of investors that the share price will increase even further in the future, therefore increasing the future conversion value.

The conversion premium is represented by the vertical distance between the curve MM' and the line CM', whereas the rights premium is represented by the vertical distance between the curves MM' and LR. Conversion should take place only after M' since conversion before this point will result in a loss in potential profit to the investor.

If the underlying share price rises slowly or falls and conversion is not anticipated, the convertible bond will have value only as debt and its market value will fall to that of an ordinary bond, where it will remain until redemption at point R, as shown in Figure 5.2. At point A, the right to convert has ceased to have any value and the convertible bond is valued thereafter as ordinary debt.

5.8 LEASING

Leasing is a form of financing which essentially refers to hiring an asset under an agreed contract. The company hiring the asset is called the **lessee**, whereas the company owning the asset is called the **lessor**. In corporate finance, we are concerned on the one hand with

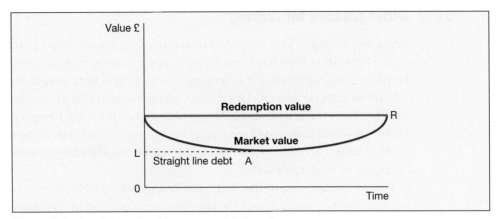

Figure 5.2 The debt value of a convertible bond

the reasons why leasing is a popular source of finance and on the other with how we can evaluate whether leasing is an attractive financing alternative to debt.

With leasing, the lessee obtains the use of an asset for a period of time while legal ownership of the leased asset remains with the lessor. This is where leasing differs from hire purchase, a form of instalment finance, since legal title passes to the purchaser under hire purchase when the final payment is made. For historical reasons, banks and their subsidiaries are by far the biggest lessors.

5.8.1 Reporting leases

International Financial Reporting Standard 16 (IFRS 16), enforceable from January 2016, takes away the distinction between operating leasing and finance leases that existed before that date. Lessees must report leases as financial assets and associated financial liabilities in their financial position statements. Both the asset and the liability are based on the present value of contracted future lease payments, discounted at the rate of interest implicit in the lease. Leases for periods less than 12 months and leases for low-value items may be exempt from the requirements of IFRS 16.

5.8.2 Tax reasons for leasing

If a company is not producing sufficient taxable profits at the time that a decision to acquire an asset is taken, it will not be able to take immediate advantage of available **capital allowances** (tax-allowable depreciation). Leasing would be an attractive alternative to buying for a company in such circumstances, especially if a lessor with adequate profits were able to pass on the benefit of capital allowances in the form of lower lease payments.

Tax advantages can occur if the tax-paying positions of the lessor and lessee differ. For example, a tax-paying lessor could buy an asset, use the capital allowance and then lease the asset to a non-tax-paying lessee, setting the lease payments at a level where both lessor and lessee benefit. Tax benefits can also arise due to year-end effects as different accounting year-ends may allow a lessor to capture tax benefits more quickly than a lessee. This benefit can be enhanced by lessors having several subsidiaries with different year-ends.

5.8.3 Other reasons for leasing

Drury and Braund (1990) suggested several possible reasons why companies choose to lease assets rather than buy them outright. Leasing can provide a source of finance if a company is short of liquidity. If a company has difficulty in borrowing to finance the acquisition of an asset because of a lack of good quality assets to offer as security, leasing can be used to access the asset instead. Since ownership of the leased asset remains with the lessee, the leased asset is itself security for the leasing contract and can be reclaimed in the event of default on lease payments. For this reason, leasing provides an attractive source of finance for small companies.

Due to the fast pace of technological change and development, some assets may become obsolete relatively quickly. Leasing offers a solution to this *obsolescence problem* since assets leased under short-term cancellable leases can be replaced with newer models. By leasing rather than buying, companies can ensure their assets are up to date.

The flexibility of lease contracts in respect to choice of equipment and scheduling of lease payments means that the popularity of leasing is well-established.

5.8.4 Evaluating leasing as a source of finance

Evaluating leasing as a source of finance may involve both an investment decision and a finance decision. The optimal overall decision can be reached in several ways, as follows:

- make the financing decision first, then evaluate the investment decision;
- make the investment decision first, then optimise the financing method;
- combine the investment and financing decisions.

If the investment decision is made first, an investment project might be rejected which would have been accepted if the lowest-cost financing method had been used. Combining the investment and financing decision involves investment appraisal methods beyond the scope of this text. For these reasons, the first method, where the financing method is determined before the investment decision is evaluated, is recommended. This means that the financing decision can be separated from the investment decision and we need not consider the investment decision any further in this section.

If we assume that a company's debt capacity is limited and if we assume a commitment to a series of regular payments arises under both leasing and borrowing, we can regard leasing as being equivalent to borrowing as a way of acquiring use of an asset (Myers et al. 1976). Discounted cash-flow methods can then be used to compare the relative costs of the two financing alternatives. To make this comparison, we first need to identify the relevant cash flows, as follows:

- *Taxation*: capital allowances (tax-allowable depreciation) are available to the buyer if an asset is purchased, while if an asset is leased, the lessee can set off lease payments against taxable profits. The relevant cash flows are therefore the tax benefits arising from capital allowances and lease payments, possibly taken one year in arrears.
- *Maintenance costs*: allowable deductions against profits for tax purposes such as maintenance costs may be payable by the lessor or the lessee, depending on the lease contract.

- *Lease payments*: lease payments may be payable in advance or in arrears, and their amount and timing are clearly important.
- *Purchase price and disposal value*: if the asset is purchased through borrowing, the purchase price (equivalent to the present value cost of the loan) must be considered, together with any disposal value. Balancing allowances or charges will be affected by any disposal value expected to arise at the end of the useful life of the purchased

These cash flows must be discounted by an appropriate discount rate. Since leasing is seen as a direct substitute for borrowing as a source of finance, an appropriate discount rate to use is the cost of borrowing to the company. We could use, for example, the *before-tax interest rate* on the loan the company would need to take out to purchase the asset. This rate is appropriate if the company is **tax-exhausted** and cannot take advantage of available tax benefits. If the company is profitable (i.e. not tax-exhausted), the *after-tax interest rate* on the loan should be used as the discount rate.

If the net present value method is used to compare leasing with borrowing to buy, then cash flows can be discounted by the after-tax cost of borrowing. If the internal rate of return (IRR) method is used, the IRR of leasing can be compared with the cost of borrowing (Tan 1992). Here, we shall consider only the net present value method.

Example	Evaluating leasing versus borrowing to buy

DDX plc is trying to decide whether to lease or to buy a machine with a useful life of six years. DDX could borrow £90,000 to buy the machine or lease it for annual lease rentals of £20,000 per year for six years, payable at the start of each year. If the machine is bought, maintenance costs of £1,000 per year will be incurred. These costs will not be incurred if the machine is leased. The machine has zero scrap value. DDX pays tax at a rate of 30 per cent one year in arrears and can claim capital allowances on a 25 per cent reducing balance basis. The company's before-tax cost of borrowing is 10 per cent. Should DDX lease or buy the machine?

Suggested answer

As leasing is an alternative to borrowing, the relevant cash flows of the two alternatives can be compared using the after-tax cost of borrowing, i.e. $10 \times (1 - 0.30)$ = 7 per cent.

The capital allowances are calculated as follows:

Year		£
1	$90{,}000 \times 0.25 =$	22,500
2	$22{,}500 \times 0.75 =$	16,875
3	$16{,}875 \times 0.75 =$	12,656
4	$12{,}656 \times 0.75 =$	9,492
5	$9{,}492 \times 0.75 =$	7,119
6	(by difference)	21,358
		90,000

Table 5.3 Tax relief computation for DDX plc if buying is used

Year	Capital allowances (£)	Operating costs (£)	Total deductions (£)	30% tax relief (£)	Taken in year
1	22,500	1,000	23,500	7,050	2
2	16,875	1,000	17,875	5,363	3
3	12,656	1,000	13,656	4,097	4
4	9,492	1,000	10,492	3,148	5
5	7,119	1,000	8,119	2,436	6
6	21,358	1,000	22,358	6,707	7

The tax benefits of borrowing to buy are calculated in Table 5.3. Notice that the maintenance costs give rise to tax relief, a point that is often overlooked.

We can now calculate the present values of the costs of leasing and borrowing to buy, as shown in Table 5.4. From this table we can see that the present cost of leasing (£75,276) is slightly higher than the present cost of borrowing (£73,063), and so on financial grounds we recommend that the machine should be bought. The present cost of borrowing to buy is included in the evaluation of the investment decision using the net present value method (Section 6.3).

Table 5.4 The present values of costs of leasing and borrowing to buy for DDX plc

Present value of cost of leasing				
Years	Cash flow	(£)	7% discount factors	Present value (£)
0–5	lease payments	(20,000)	(4.100 + 1.000) = 5.100	(102,000)
2–7	tax relief	6,000	(5.389 − 0.935) = 4.454	26,724
				(75,276)

Present value of cost of borrowing to buy					
Year	Capital (£)	Operating costs (£)	Tax relief (£)	Net cash flow (£)	7% discount factors	Present value (£)
0	(90,000)			(90,000)	1.000	(90,000)
1		(1,000)		(1,000)	0.935	(935)
2		(1,000)	7,050	6,050	0.873	5,282
3		(1,000)	5,363	4,363	0.816	3,560
4		(1,000)	4,097	3,097	0.763	2,363
5		(1,000)	3,148	2,148	0.713	1,532
6		(1,000)	2,436	1,436	0.666	956
7			6,707	6,707	0.623	4,179
						(73,063)

5.8.5 The distribution of financial benefits

For a leasing contract to go ahead, both parties to the lease must benefit. If both lessee and lessor pay taxes at the same rate, then from a taxation perspective there are no overall financial benefits to be distributed and leasing appears to be a **zero sum game** (Drury and Braund 1990). For tax benefits to arise, lessee and lessor must be faced to some extent with differences in their respective cash-flow situations, arising from some or all of the following factors:

- different costs of capital for the lessor and lessee;
- different tax rates between the lessor and lessee;
- different abilities to benefit from available capital allowances.

Different costs of capital may arise because the cost of equity and the cost of borrowing of a large leasing company are likely to be lower than those of a small company wanting to lease an asset from it. Different tax rates may arise because the UK tax system differentiates between small and large companies. Different abilities to benefit from capital allowances can arise, for example, if a lessor sets up multiple subsidiaries with different year-ends. Non-tax financial benefits can also lead to lower lease payments, for example, if a discount is gained by a lessor making bulk purchases of assets to lease.

The distribution of financial benefits depends on the size and timing of lease payments. The lessor will have a minimum amount it wishes to receive, and the lessee will have a maximum amount it is prepared to pay. The actual lease payments will be between these limits and will be determined by the relative bargaining power of the two parties.

5.9 EVALUATING THE FINANCIAL EFFECTS OF FINANCING CHOICES

Selecting from the range of financing choices available to a company calls for a financial evaluation of the effects of selecting a given source of finance. One such financial evaluation looks at the effect on shareholder wealth of a given financing decision.

Example	**Evaluation of equity finance versus debt finance**

PXP plc is a listed company that has made an offer of £3.20 per share for the ordinary share capital of VVM plc. Details of the two companies are as follows:

	PXP	*VVM*
	£000	*£000*
Ordinary shares (25p nominal value)	2,500	900
Reserves	1,750	1,000
	4,250	1,900
Current ordinary share price	£5.10 per share	£2.50 per share
After-tax cost of capital	9 per cent	13 per cent
Current earnings per share	23p	19p

PXP is not sure whether to finance the offer by a rights issue or by an issue of bonds. It expects that, after the acquisition, it will make savings in after-tax operating costs of £250,000 per year. PXP pays tax on profits at a rate of 30 per cent.

If the price/earnings ratio of PXP remains constant, calculate the post-acquisition share price of PXP under the following methods of finance and comment on the effect on the wealth of its shareholders:

1 a rights issue at an issue price of £4.00 per share;
2 an issue of 12 per cent bonds.

Suggested answer

The post-acquisition market value of PXP, ignoring the financing method is as follows:

	£m
Current market value of PXP = 2.5m × 4 × £5.10 =	51.00
Current market value of VVM = 0.9m × 4 × £2.50 =	9.00
Combined market value	60.00
Less purchase price = 0.9m × 4 × £3.20 =	11.52
Market value of PXP before savings	48.48
Present value of cost savings = 250,000/0.09 =	2.78
Post-offer market value of PXP	51.26

Financed by a rights issue

Number of shares issued = £11.52m/4.0 = 2.88m

Total number of shares after acquisition = 10m + 2.88m = 12.88m

PXP earnings before acquisition = 0.23 × 10m = £2.30m

VVM earnings before acquisition = 0.19 × 3.6m = £0.68m

Increase in earnings from cost savings = £0.25m

Total earnings after acquisition = 2.30m + 0.68m + 0.25m = £3.23m

The post-acquisition market value can be found by multiplying the post-acquisition earnings by the P/E ratio.

P/E ratio before acquisition = 5.10/0.23 = 22 times

Post-acquisition market value = 3.23m × 22 = £71.06m

Post-acquisition share price = 71.06m/12.88m = £5.52 per share

The theoretical ex-rights price is (51m + 11.52m)/12.88m = £4.85 per share

Since the post-acquisition share price is greater than the theoretical ex-rights price per share, the wealth of PXP shareholders has increased by 67p per share.

Financed by a bond issue

The number of shares remains at 10m

Post-acquisition earnings ignoring bond interest = £3.23m (see above)

Interest on bonds = 11.52m × 12% = £1.382m

Tax saved = 1.382m × 0.3 = £0.415m

Decrease in earnings from debt finance = 1.382m − 0.415m = £0.967m

Post-acquisition earnings = 3.23m − 0.967m = £2.263m

Post-acquisition market value = 2.263m × 22 = £49.79m

Post-acquisition share price = 49.79m/10m = £4.98 per share

Since the post-acquisition share price is less than the current market price per share of £5.10, the wealth of PXP shareholders has decreased by 12p per share.

Conclusion

Financing by a rights issue can be recommended as it leads to an increase in the wealth of shareholders, while financing by an issue of bonds cannot be recommended.

5.10 CONCLUSION

We have seen in this chapter that ordinary debt, bank loans, convertible debt (hybrid finance) and leasing can all be useful ways for a company to obtain the financing it needs to acquire assets for use in its business. Each of these financing methods has advantages and disadvantages which a company must consider carefully before reaching a final decision as to the most suitable method to use. In theory it should be possible, given the wide range of methods available, for a company to satisfy its individual financing requirements.

■ ■ ■ KEY POINTS

1 Bonds or loan notes are interest-paying debt securities which must be redeemed on maturity (unless irredeemable). Interest paid is tax-deductible, reducing the cost of debt finance. Debentures are bonds secured on assets of the company.

2 Restrictive covenants are a way of protecting providers of debt finance and may, for example, limit how much further debt can be raised, set a target gearing ratio or set a target current ratio.

3 Bond redemption needs careful financial planning and can be over a period of time rather than on a specific date. Companies may use refinancing, upholding the matching principle, or a sinking fund.

4 Bond ratings measure the risk of corporate bonds as an investment.

5 A deep discount bond is issued at a price well below nominal in exchange for a lower interest rate. It may attract investors who prefer capital growth to interest, and companies who prefer lower servicing costs to match expected investment returns.

6 A zero coupon bond pays no interest and is issued at a deep discount to its nominal value.

7 Fixed and floating rate long-term loans are available from banks and other financial institutions, secured by either a fixed or a floating charge on the assets of a company.

8 Debt finance may be raised in a specific currency to hedge exchange rate risk, to exploit interest rate differentials or to get around restrictions on currency movements.

9 Eurobonds are long-term international debt finance issued as bearer securities, with fixed or floating rate interest that can be lower than domestic rates.

10 Eurobonds can be used to finance international investment or to hedge exchange rate risk. Investors may find them attractive because they offer anonymity.

11 Convertible bonds can be converted, on predetermined dates and at a predetermined rate, at the option of the holder, into ordinary shares of the company.

12 Conversion value is the market value of shares into which a bond can be converted. Conversion premium is the difference between a convertible's market price and its conversion value. Rights premium is the difference between a convertible's market value and its value as ordinary debt.

13 Convertible bond interest is usually lower than interest on unconvertible bonds.

14 The floor value of a convertible bond is its value as an ordinary bond. Its actual value depends on its current conversion value, the time to conversion and market expectations.

15 Issuing convertible bonds can be attractive if a company's share price is depressed or if diluting EPS by new equity is unacceptable. It can also decrease the overall cost of capital. A major attraction of convertible bonds is that they can be self-liquidating.

16 Convertible bonds offer a lower-risk medium-term investment coupled with the possibility of greater long-term gains. Unlike ordinary bonds, they offer the opportunity to participate in company growth.

17 A warrant is the right to buy new shares at a future date, at a fixed, predetermined price. Warrants are often issued with bonds as an equity sweetener.

18 The gearing effect of warrants means that a greater proportionate gain can be obtained by holding the warrant than by holding the ordinary share. The initial outlay is also lower.

19 The interest rate on 'sweetened' bonds will be lower than on ordinary bonds, while the attached warrants may make the bond issue easier to sell.

20 The theoretical market value of a fixed interest bond can be found by discounting interest payments and redemption value by the cost of debt.

21 A convertible bond is valued in the same way as an ordinary bond, except its value is the greater of its value as an ordinary bond and its value if converted into equity.

22 Leasing is a source of financing where the lessee obtains use of an asset for a period of time, while ownership of the asset remains with the lessor.

23 Leases must be reported in the financial position statement as an asset and an associated liability, based on the present value of contracted future lease payments.

24 Tax reasons for leasing include low lessee profitability and differing tax positions of lessor and lessee.

25 Non-tax reasons for leasing include:

(a) leasing is a source of finance if a company is short of liquidity;

(b) leasing allows small companies access to expensive assets;

(c) leases can allow a company to avoid obsolescence of some assets;

(d) the lessor may be able to borrow at a cheaper rate than the lessee.

26 The present value of leasing can be compared to the present value of the cost of borrowing to buy, using the before- or after-tax cost of debt as a discount rate.

27 For tax benefits to arise, the cash flows of lessee and lessor must be different due to different costs of capital, different tax rates or different abilities to use capital allowances.

SELF-TEST QUESTIONS

Answers to these questions can be found on pages 456–8.

1 Discuss briefly the key features of bonds such as debentures and loan stock.

2 Explain what is meant by the following terms that refer to bonds:

(a) covenant;

(b) refinancing;

(c) redemption window.

3 Explain the following items and state the circumstances under which their issue would be beneficial to (i) lenders and (ii) borrowers:

(a) deep discount bonds;

(b) zero coupon bonds;

(c) warrants;

(d) convertible bonds.

4 What are the advantages and disadvantages to a company of financing via Eurobonds?

5 Explain the difference between a conversion premium and a rights premium.

6 A company has in issue a 10 per cent bond, redeemable at the option of the company between one and five years from now. What factors will be considered by the company in reaching a decision on when to redeem the bond?

7 Outline the advantages and disadvantages to a company of issuing convertible bonds.

8 What is the gearing effect of warrants?

9 A company has in issue some 9 per cent bonds which are redeemable at nominal value of £100 in three years' time. Investors require a yield of 10 per cent. What will be the current ex-interest market value of each bond? What would be the current ex-interest market value if the bonds had been irredeemable?

10 Explain the attractions of leasing as a source of finance.

QUESTIONS FOR REVIEW

1 Bugle plc has some surplus funds it wishes to invest. It requires a return of 15 per cent on bonds and you have been asked to advise whether it should invest in either of the following bonds:

(a) *Bond 1*: 12 per cent bonds redeemable at nominal at the end of two more years. The current market value per £100 bond is £95.

(b) *Bond 2*: 8 per cent bonds redeemable at £110 at the end of two more years. The current market value per £100 bond is also £95.

2 Discuss, with the aid of a diagram, the relationship between the conversion premium, the rights premium and the market value of a convertible bond.

3 Laursen plc has in issue 10 per cent convertible bonds which will be redeemed in 10 years' time. The bonds have a nominal value of £100 and are currently selling at £93 per bond. Interest on the bonds is paid annually and each bond is convertible into 25 shares at any time over the next two years. The current market price of Laursen plc's ordinary shares is £3.20 per share and this is expected to increase by 14 per cent per year for the foreseeable future. Laursen plc has a cost of debt of 12 per cent.

(a) Advise an investor holding some of Laursen's convertible bonds as to which of the following courses of action to take:
(i)   sell the convertible bond now;
(ii) convert the bond now or within the next two years;
(iii) hold the bond to maturity.

(b) Explain the importance to an investor of the distinction between convertible bonds and bonds with warrants attached.

4 Discuss the reasons for the popularity of leasing as a source of finance.

5 Turner plc is considering whether to buy a machine costing £1,000 through a three-year loan with interest at 14 per cent per year. The machine would have zero scrap value at the end of its three-year life. Alternatively, the machine could be leased for £320 per year, payable in arrears. Corporate tax is payable at 30 per cent and capital allowances are available over the life of the machine on a 25 per cent reducing balance basis. Calculate whether Turner should lease or buy the machine.

1 (a) Discuss the factors which determine the market price of convertible bonds.

(b) Marlowe plc has in issue bonds which are convertible in three years' time into 25 ordinary shares per bond. If not converted, they will be redeemed in six years' time at nominal value of £100 per bond. The bonds pay interest of 9 per cent per year and have a current market price of £90.01 per bond. Marlowe's current share price is £3.24. If the cost of debt of Marlowe plc is 13 per cent, calculate:

(i) the minimum expected annual share price growth that would be needed to ensure that conversion takes place in three years' time;

(ii) the implicit conversion premium.

2 Utterby is considering the purchase of a new machine which would enable the company to cut annual salaries by £130,000 per year.

The machine would cost £480,000 if bought from the manufacturers, Fotherby. Annual service costs would be £14,500. The machine would need to be replaced after five years, but at that time could be sold on by Utterby for spare parts, yielding 2.5 per cent of the purchase price of the machine.

Fotherby has offered to lease the machine to Utterby for a lease payment of £98,000 per year, payable in advance at the start of each year. This lease payment would also cover service costs, with the lease contract renewable on an annual basis.

Utterby could finance the purchase of the machine by a medium-term bank loan at an interest rate of 11 per cent per year.

Utterby pays tax at a rate of 30 per cent per year, one year in arrears, and has been making a small profit after tax in each of the last two years. The company can claim 25 per cent reducing balance capital allowances on machinery.

(a) Using a present value analysis, calculate whether Utterby should buy or lease the new machine, considering:

(i) the case where tax benefits are considered; and

(ii) the case where tax benefits are ignored.

(b) Critically discuss the reasons why leasing has been a popular source of finance in recent years, illustrating your answer by referring to the information given.

3 Cold plc has decided to acquire equipment with a current market value of £700,000. A bank has offered a five-year loan at an interest rate of 13 per cent per year, provided it can reach agreement with Cold plc on ways to protect its investment. The equipment would be scrapped after five years and at that time would have negligible scrap value.

Cold plc could also lease the equipment for £180,000 per year, payable at the start of each year. The lessor would be responsible for servicing the equipment whereas, if the equipment were bought, Cold plc would incur annual servicing costs of £25,000.

Cold plc is a profitable company that pays tax one year in arrears at an annual rate of 30 per cent and can claim annual capital allowances on a 25 per cent reducing balance basis.

(a) Discuss ways in which the bank could protect its loan of £700,000 to Cold plc for the equipment purchase.

(b) Calculate the present value of the tax benefits arising on capital allowances if Cold plc decides to purchase the new equipment.

(c) Calculate whether Cold plc should lease or buy the new equipment.

(d) Critically discuss what other factors may influence the decision of Cold plc to lease or buy the new equipment, apart from financial considerations.

4 Permafrost plc needs a new computer network but is uncertain whether to buy the system or to lease it from Slush plc. The system will cost £800,000 if bought and Permafrost plc would borrow to finance this. Information on the two options is as follows:

Option 1
If the system is leased, Slush plc will receive an annual lease payment of £150,000, paid in advance. Slush plc will service the system, at no additional cost, over its eight-year life.

Option 2
1 If the system is bought, Permafrost plc will service the system at an annual cost of £10,000. It has a choice of three financing methods:
2 It could issue 12 per cent bonds, secured on existing non-current assets, to be redeemed in eight years' time at nominal value of £100 per bond.
3 It could raise an eight-year floating rate bank loan, secured on existing non-current assets, to be repaid in equal instalments over its life.
It could issue zero coupon bonds, to be redeemed at £100 nominal in eight years.
Permafrost plc pays tax one year in arrears at an annual rate of 30 per cent and can claim capital allowances on a 25 per cent reducing balance basis. The before-tax cost of debt of the company is 10 per cent and this is not expected to change as a result of the financing choice made in connection with the new computer network.

(a) Calculate the market values of the 12 per cent bond issue and the zero coupon bond issue, and analyse and critically discuss the relative merits of the three debt finance methods to Permafrost plc.

(b) Evaluate whether Permafrost plc should lease or buy the new computer network.

References

Drury, C. and Braund, S. (1990) 'The leasing decision: a comparison of theory and practice', *Accounting and Business Research*, vol. 20, no. 79, pp. 179–91.

Myers, S.C., Dill, D.A. and Bautista, A.J. (1976) 'Valuation of financial lease contracts', *Journal of Finance*, vol. 31, June, pp. 799–819.

Tan, C. (1992) 'Lease or buy?', *Accountancy*, December, pp. 58–9.

Recommended reading

Hillier, D., Ross, S., Westerfield, R., Jaffe, J. and Jordan, B. (2013) *Corporate Finance*, 2nd European edn, Maidenhead: McGraw-Hill Education, offers a useful discussion of leasing and adds an international perspective in chapter 21.

Useful information on bond ratings can be found on the websites of the rating organisations themselves, for example:

Moody's Investors Service: *https://www.moodys.com/*

Standard & Poor's Corporation: https://www.standardandpoors.com/en_US/web/guest/home

Fitch Ratings: https://www.fitchratings.com/site/home

Information on benchmark yields for short-term and long-term debt can be found on the website of the UK Government Debt Management Office: https://www.dmo.gov.uk/

A useful website for further information on leasing is that of the Finance and Leasing Association, found at: https://www.fla.org.uk/

Bonds that are trading on the London Stock Exchange can be searched at: http://www.londonstockexchange.com/exchange/prices-and-markets/retail-bonds/retail-bonds-search.html

Details of the UK government's Enterprise Finance Guarantee Scheme can be found at https://www.british-business-bank.co.uk/ourpartners/supporting-business-loans-enterprise-finance-guarantee/understanding-enterprise-finance-guarantee/

6 AN OVERVIEW OF INVESTMENT APPRAISAL METHODS

Learning objectives

After studying this chapter, you should have achieved the following learning objectives:

- to be able to define and apply the four main investment appraisal methods of payback, return on capital employed, net present value and internal rate of return;

- to be able to explain the reasons why discounted cash-flow methods are preferred to the more traditional techniques of payback and return on capital employed;

- to be able to explain why net present value is considered superior to internal rate of return as an investment appraisal method;

- an understanding of the techniques to be employed to arrive at the best investment decision if investment capital is rationed.

■ ■ ■ INTRODUCTION

Companies need to invest in wealth-creating assets to renew, extend or replace the means by which they carry on their business. Capital investment allows companies to continue to generate cash flows in the future and maintain the profitability of existing business activities. Typically, capital investment projects will require significant cash outflows at the beginning and will then produce cash inflows over several years. Capital investment projects require careful evaluation because they need very large amounts of cash to be raised and invested, and because they will determine whether the company is profitable in the future.

A company seeks to select the best or most profitable investment projects so that it can maximise the return to its shareholders. It also seeks to avoid the negative strategic and financial consequences which could follow from poor or sub-optimal investment decisions.

Capital investment decisions affect a company for a long time, and a company and its statement of financial position represent the sum of the previous investment and financing decisions taken by its directors and managers.

6.1 THE PAYBACK METHOD

While research has shown that payback is the most popular investment appraisal method, it suffers from such serious shortcomings that it should really be regarded only as a first screening method. The *payback period* is the number of years it is expected to take to recover the original investment from the net cash flows resulting from a capital investment project. The decision rule when appraising investments using the *payback method* is to accept a project if its payback period is equal to or less than a predetermined target value. It is possible to estimate the payback period to several decimal places if cash flows are assumed to occur evenly throughout each year, but a high degree of accuracy in estimating the payback period is not needed, since it does not offer useful information. A value to the nearest half-year or month is usually sufficient.

6.1.1 Example of the payback method

Consider an investment project with the cash flows given in Table 6.1. The cash flows of this project are called *conventional* cash flows and the project is called a *conventional* project. A conventional project is defined as one which requires a cash investment at the start of the project, followed by a series of cash inflows over the life of the project. Table 6.1

Table 6.1 Simple investment project, showing a significant initial investment followed by a series of cash inflows over the life of the project

Year	0	1	2	3	4	5
Cash flow (£000)	(450)	100	200	100	100	80

Table 6.2 Cumulative cash flows for the conventional project of the previous table, showing that the payback period is between three and four years

Year	Cash flow (£)	Cumulative cash flow (£)
0	(450)	(450)
1	100	(350)
2	200	(150)
3	100	(50)
4	100	50
5	80	130

shows that the project generates total cash inflows of £400,000 after three years. In the fourth year, the remaining £50,000 of initial investment will be recovered. As the cash inflow in this year is £100,000 and assuming even cash flow during the year, it will take a further six months or 0.5 years for the final £50,000 to be recovered. The payback period is therefore 3.5 years.

It can be helpful to draw up a table of cumulative project cash flows to determine the payback period, as shown in Table 6.2.

6.1.2 The advantages of the payback method

The advantages of the payback method are that it is simple and easy to apply and, as a concept, straightforward to understand. The payback period is calculated using cash flows, not accounting profits, and so should not be open to manipulation by managerial preferences for different accounting policies. If we accept that more distant cash flows are more uncertain, and that increasing uncertainty is the same as increasing risk, we could argue that a further advantage of the payback method is that it takes account of risk, in that payback implicitly assumes that a shorter payback period is superior to a longer one.

It has been argued that payback period is a useful investment appraisal method when a company is restricted in the amount of finance it has available for investment, since the sooner cash is returned by a project, the sooner it can be reinvested into other projects. While there is some truth in this claim, it ignores the fact that there are better investment appraisal methods available to deal with **capital rationing** (see Section 6.6).

6.1.3 The disadvantages of the payback method

There are several difficulties in using the payback method to assess capital investment projects and these are sufficiently serious for it to be generally rejected by corporate finance theory as a credible investment appraisal method. One major disadvantage is that the approach ignores the *time value of money* (see Section 1.1.3), so that it gives equal weight to cash flows whenever they occur within the payback period. The example in Table 6.1

illustrates this point. You can see that the payback period remains 3.5 years even if the project generates no cash inflows in the first and second years, but then a cash inflow of £400,000 occurs in the third year. In fact, any combination of cash inflows in the first three years which totals £400,000 would give the same payback period.

The problem of ignoring the time value of money is addressed by using the *discounted payback method* (see Section 6.7).

Another serious disadvantage of the payback method is that it ignores all cash flows outside the payback period and so does not consider the whole project. If a company rejected all projects with payback periods greater than three years, it would reject the project in Table 6.1. Suppose this project had been expected to have a cash inflow of £1m in year 4. This expected cash inflow would have been ignored and the project would still have been rejected if the *only* investment appraisal method being used was the payback method. Would this have been a wealth-maximising decision for the company concerned? Hardly! In fact, the choice of the maximum payback period acceptable to a company is quite arbitrary since it is not possible to say why one payback period is preferable to any other. Why accept a project with a payback period of three years but reject a project with a payback period of three-and-a-half years?

In fairness, we should recognise that in practice when the payback method is used, cash flows outside of the payback period are not ignored but taken into consideration as part of the exercise of managerial judgement. However, this serves only to reinforce the inadequacy of the payback method as the *sole* measure of project acceptability.

The general conclusion of this discussion is that the payback method does not give any indication of whether an investment project increases the value of a company. Consequently, it has been argued that, despite its well-documented popularity, the payback method is not really an investment appraisal method at all, but rather a means of assessing the effect on a company's liquidity position of accepting an investment project.

6.2 THE RETURN ON CAPITAL EMPLOYED METHOD

There are several different definitions of return on capital employed (ROCE), which is also called return on investment (ROI) and accounting rate of return (ARR). All definitions relate accounting profit to some measure of the capital employed in a capital investment project. One definition that is widely used is:

$$\text{ROCE} = \frac{\text{Average annual accounting profit}}{\text{Average investment}} \times 100$$

The average investment must take account of any scrap value. Assuming straight-line depreciation from the initial investment to the terminal scrap value, we have:

$$\text{Average investment} = \frac{\text{Initial investment} + \text{Scrap value}}{2}$$

Another common definition of ROCE (see 'Profitability ratios', Section 2.4.3) uses the initial or final investment rather than the average investment, for example:

$$\text{ROCE} = \frac{\text{Average annual accounting profit}}{\text{Initial (or final) investment}} \times 100$$

It is important to remember that return on capital employed is calculated using accounting profits, which are before-tax operating cash flows adjusted to take account of depreciation. *Accounting profits are not cash flows* because depreciation is an accounting adjustment which does not correspond to an annual movement of cash. The *decision rule* here is to accept an investment project if its return on capital employed is greater than a target (or hurdle) rate of return set by the investing company. If only one of two investment projects can be undertaken (i.e. if the projects are *mutually exclusive*), the project with the higher return on capital employed should be accepted.

Example	Calculating return on capital employed

Carbon plc is planning to buy a new machine and has found two that meet its needs. Each machine has an expected life of five years. Machine 1 would generate annual cash flows (receipts less payments) of £210,000 and would cost £570,000. Its scrap value at the end of five years would be £70,000. Machine 2 would generate annual cash flows of £510,000 and would cost £1,616,000. The scrap value of this machine at the end of five years would be £301,000. Carbon plc uses the straight-line method of depreciation and has a target return on capital employed of 20 per cent.

Calculate the return on capital employed for both Machine 1 and Machine 2 on an average investment basis, and state which machine you would recommend, giving reasons.

Suggested answer

For Machine 1:	£
Total cash flow = 210,000 × 5 =	1,050,000
Total depreciation = 570,000 − 70,000 =	500,000
Total accounting profit	550,000
Average annual accounting profit = 550,000/5 =	£110,000 per year
Average investment = (570,000 + 70,000)/2 =	£320,000
Return on capital employed = 100 × (110,000/320,000) =	34.4%

For Machine 2:	£
Total cash flow = 510,000 × 5 =	2,550,000
Total depreciation = 1,616,000 − 301,000 =	1,315,000
Total accounting profit	1,235,000
Average annual accounting profit = 1,235,000/5 =	£247,000 per year
Average investment = (1,616,000 + 301,000)/2 =	£958,500
Return on capital employed = 100 × (247,000/958,500) =	25.8%

Both machines have a return on capital employed greater than the target rate and so are financially acceptable, but as only one machine is to be bought, the recommendation is that Machine 1 should be chosen, as it has a higher return on capital employed than Machine 2.

6.2.1 Advantages of the return on capital employed method

There are several reasons for the popularity of the return on capital employed method, even though it has little theoretical credibility as a method of making investment decisions. For example, it gives a value in percentage terms, a familiar relative measure of return, which can be compared with a company's existing ROCE, the primary accounting ratio used by financial analysts in assessing company performance (see 'Profitability ratios', Section 2.4.3). It is also a reasonably simple method to apply and can be used to compare mutually exclusive projects. Unlike the payback method, it considers all cash flows arising during the life of an investment project and it can indicate whether a project is acceptable by comparing the ROCE of the project with a target rate, for example, a company's current ROCE or the ROCE of a division.

6.2.2 Disadvantages of the return on capital employed method

While it can be argued that the return on capital employed method provides useful information about a project, as an investment appraisal method it has significant drawbacks. For example, it is not based on cash, but uses accounting profit, which is open to manipulation. The approach is not linked directly to the fundamental objective of maximising shareholder wealth.

Because the method uses *average* profits, it also ignores the *timing* of profits. Consider the two projects A and B in Table 6.3. Both projects have the same initial investment and zero scrap value and hence the same average investment:

$$£45,000/2 = £22,500$$

Both projects have the same average annual accounting profit:

$$\text{Project A: } (-250 + 1,000 + 1,000 + 20,750)/4 = £5,625$$
$$\text{Project B: } (6,000 + 6,000 + 5,500 + 5,000)/4 = £5,625$$

So their return on capital employed values are identical too:

$$\text{ROCE} = (100 \times 5,625)/2,500 = 25\%$$

Table 6.3 Illustration of how return on capital employed, which uses average accounting profit, ignores the timing of project cash flows

Year	0 £000	1 £000	2 £000	3 £000	4 £000
Project A Cash flows Depreciation Accounting profit	(45,000)	11,000 11,250 (250)	12,250 11,250 1,000	12,250 11,250 1,000	32,000 11,250 20,750
Project B Cash flows Depreciation Accounting profit	(45,000)	17,250 11,250 6,000	17,250 11,250 6,000	16,750 11,250 5,500	16,250 11,250 5,000

But Project B has a smooth pattern of returns, whereas Project A offers little in the first three years and a large return in the final year. Although they have the same ROCE, we see that Project B is preferable to Project A, due to the pattern of its profits.

A more serious drawback is that the return on capital employed method does not consider the time value of money and gives equal weight to cash flows whenever they occur. It also fails to take account of the length of the project life and, being a relative measure expressed in percentage terms, it ignores the size of the investment. For these reasons, the return on capital employed method does not offer sensible advice about whether a project creates wealth or not. To find such advice, we need to use discounted cash-flow methods, the most widely accepted of which is net present value.

6.3 THE NET PRESENT VALUE METHOD

The net present value (NPV) method of investment appraisal uses *discounted cash flows* to evaluate capital investment projects and is based on the sound theoretical foundation of the investment-consumption model developed by Hirshleifer (1958). It uses a *cost of capital* (see Chapter 9) or target rate of return to discount all cash inflows and outflows to their *present values* (see Section 1.1.3), then compares the present value of all cash inflows with the present value of all cash outflows. A *positive* NPV indicates that an investment project is expected to give a return greater than the cost of capital and therefore increase shareholder wealth. We can represent calculating NPV algebraically as follows:

$$\text{NPV} = -I_0 + \frac{C_1}{(1+r)} + \frac{C_2}{(1+r)^2} + \frac{C_3}{(1+r)^3} + \cdots + \frac{C_n}{(1+r)^n}$$

where: I_0 is the initial investment

$C_1, C_2, \ldots, C_n$ are the project cash flows occurring in years $1, 2, \ldots, n$

r is the cost of capital or required rate of return

By convention, cash flows occurring *during* a time period are assumed to occur at the *end* of that time period (this avoids the mathematics of continuous discounting). The initial investment occurs at the start of the first time period. The NPV *decision rule* is to accept all independent projects with a positive net present value. If two capital investment projects are not independent but mutually exclusive, so that of the two projects available only one project can be undertaken, the project with the higher net present value should be selected

---

Example   **Calculating net present value**

Clement plc is evaluating three investment projects, whose expected cash flows are given in Table 6.4. Calculate the net present value for each project if Clement's cost of capital is 10 per cent. Which project should be selected?

Table 6.4 Three investment projects with different cash-flow profiles to illustrate calculating net present value

Clement plc: cash flows of proposed investment projects			
Period	Project A (£000)	Project B (£000)	Project C (£000)
0	(5,000)	(5,000)	(5,000)
1	1,100	800	2,000
2	1,100	900	2,000
3	1,100	1,200	2,000
4	1,100	1,400	100
5	1,100	1,600	100
6	1,100	1,300	100
7	1,100	1,100	100

Project A

The cash inflows of this project are identical and so do not need to be discounted separately. Instead, we can use the cumulative present value factor (CPVF) or annuity factor for seven years at 10 per cent ($CPVF_{10,7}$), which is found from CPVF tables (see pages 479–80) to have a value of 4.868. We have:

	£000
Initial investment	(5,000)
Present value of cash inflows = £1,100 × 4.868 =	5,355
Net present value	355

Project A has a positive net present value of £355,000.

Project B

Because the cash inflows of this project are all different, it is necessary to discount each one separately. The easiest way to organise this calculation is by using a table, as in Table 6.5.

Using a table to organise net present value calculations is especially useful when dealing with the more complex cash flows which arise when taking account of taxation, inflation and a range of costs or project variables. A tabular approach also aids clear thinking and methodical working in examinations. From Table 6.5, we can see that Project B has a positive net present value of £618,000.

Project C

The cash flows for the first three years are identical and can be discounted using the cumulative present value factor for three years at 10 per cent ($CPVF_{10,3}$), which is found from cumulative present value factor (CPVF) tables to be 2.487. The cash flows for years 4 to 7 are also identical and can be discounted using a cumulative present value factor. To find this, we subtract the cumulative present value factor for three years at

Table 6.5 Calculating net present value of Project B using a tabular approach
This approach organises the calculation and information used in a clear, easily
understood format which helps to avoid errors during the calculation process

Year	Cash flow (£000)	10% present value factors	Present value (£000)
0	(5,000)	1.000	(5,000)
1	800	0.909	727
2	900	0.826	743
3	1,200	0.751	901
4	1,400	0.683	956
5	1,600	0.621	994
6	1,300	0.564	733
7	1,100	0.513	564
		Net present value	618

10 per cent from the cumulative present value factor for seven years at 10 per cent.
From the CPVF tables, we have:

$$CPVF_{10,7} - CPVF_{10,3} = 4.868 - 2.487 = 2.381$$

	£000
Initial investment	(5,000)
Present value of cash inflows, years 1 to 3 = £2,000 × 2.487 =	4,974
Present value of cash inflows, years 4 to 7 = £100 × 2.381 =	238
Net present value	212

Project C has a positive net present value of £212,000. If the annual cash flows are
discounted separately, as in Table 6.7, the NPV is £209,000, the difference being due
to rounding.

The decision on project selection

We can now rank the projects in order of decreasing net present value:

Project B	NPV of £618,000
Project A	NPV of £355,000
Project C	NPV of £212,000

Which project should be selected? If the projects are mutually exclusive, then Project B
should be selected as it has the highest NPV and will lead to the largest increase in
shareholder wealth. If the projects are not mutually exclusive and there is no restriction
on capital available for investment, all three projects should be undertaken since all
three have a positive NPV and will increase shareholder wealth. However, the cash
flows in years 4 to 7 of Project C should be investigated; they are not very large and
they are critical to the project, since without them it would have a negative NPV and
would therefore lead to a decrease in shareholder wealth.

6.3.1 Advantages of the net present value method

The net present value method of investment appraisal, being based on discounted cash flows, takes account of the *time value of money* (see Section 1.1.3), one of the key concepts in corporate finance. Net present value uses cash flows rather than accounting profit, takes account of both the amount and the timing of project cash flows, and takes account of all relevant cash flows over the life of an investment project. For all these reasons, net present value is the *academically preferred method* of investment appraisal. In all cases where there are no constraints on capital, the net present value decision rule offers sound investment advice.

6.3.2 Disadvantages of the net present value method

It has been argued that net present value is conceptually difficult to understand, but this is hardly a realistic criticism. It has also been pointed out that it is difficult to estimate the future cash inflows and outflows of a project needed to calculate its net present value, but the difficulty of forecasting future cash flows is a problem of investment appraisal in general and not specific to any one investment appraisal technique. A more serious criticism is that it is only possible to accept all projects with a positive NPV in a perfect capital market, because only in such a market is there no restriction on the amount of finance available. capital is restricted or rationed in the real world (see Section 6.6) and this can limit the applicability of the NPV decision rule.

When calculating NPV, we tend to assume not only that the company's cost of capital is known, but also that it remains constant over the life of a project. In practice, the cost of capital of a company may be difficult to estimate (see Section 9.5) and selecting an appropriate discount rate to use in investment appraisal is also not straightforward (see Sections 9.3 and 9.4). The cost of capital is also likely to change over the life of the project, since it is influenced by the dynamic economic environment within which companies operate. However, if changes in the cost of capital can be forecast, the net present value method can accommodate them with ease (see Section 6.5.3).

6.4 THE INTERNAL RATE OF RETURN METHOD

If the cost of capital used to discount future cash flows is increased, the net present value of an investment project with conventional cash flows will fall. Eventually, as cost of capital continues to increase, the NPV will become zero, and then negative. This is illustrated in Figure 6.1.

The *internal rate of return* (IRR) of an investment project is the cost of capital or required rate of return which, when used to discount the project cash flows, produces a net present value of zero. The internal rate of return investment appraisal method involves calculating the IRR of a project, usually by linear interpolation, and then comparing it with a target rate of return or hurdle rate. The internal rate of return decision rule is to accept all independent investment projects with an IRR greater than the company's cost of capital or target rate of return.

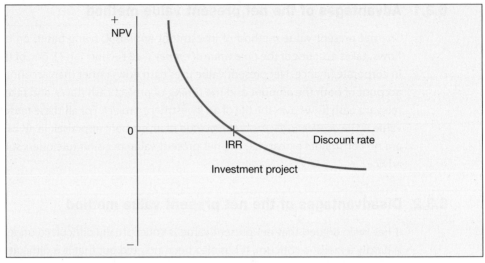

Figure 6.1 The relationship between conventional project net present values and discount rate. The internal rate of return produces a net present value of zero

We can restate the net present value formula in terms of the internal rate of return as follows:

$$\frac{C_1}{(1 + r^*)} + \frac{C_2}{(1 + r^*)^2} + \frac{C_3}{(1 + r^*)^3} + \cdots + \frac{C_n}{(1 + r^*)^n} - I_0 = 0$$

where: $C_1, C_2, \ldots, C_n$ are the project cash flows occurring in years $1, 2, \ldots, n$
r^* is the internal rate of return
I_0 is the initial investment

Example   Calculating internal rates of return

Clement plc is evaluating three investment projects, whose expected cash flows were given in Table 6.4. Calculate the internal rate of return for each project. If Clement's cost of capital is 10 per cent, which project should be selected?

Project A

In the previous example we found that (all values in £000):

$$(£1,100 \times CPVF_{10,7}) - £5,000 = (1,100 \times 4.868) - 5,000 = £355$$

Where project cash inflows are identical, we can determine the cumulative present value factor for a period corresponding to the life of the project and a discount rate equal to the internal rate of return (r^*). If we represent this by ($CPVF_{r^*,7}$), then from the formula above:

$$(£1,100 \times CPVF_{r^*,7}) - £5,000 = 0$$

Rearranging:

$$CPVF_{r*,7} = 5,000/1,100 = 4.545$$

From CPVF tables (see pages 479–80), looking along the row corresponding to seven years, we find that the discount rate corresponding to this cumulative present value factor is approximately 12 per cent. Project A therefore has an internal rate of return of 12 per cent.

Project B

The cash flows of Project B are all different and so to find its IRR we must use linear interpolation. This technique relies on the fact that, if we know the location of any two points on a straight line, we can find any other point which also lies on that line. The procedure is to make an estimate (R_1) of the internal rate of return, giving a net present value of NPV_1. We then make a second estimate (R_2) of the internal rate of return: if NPV_1 was positive, R_2 should be higher than R_1; if NPV_1 was negative, R_2 should be lower than R_1. We then calculate a second net present value, NPV_2, from R_2. The values of R_1, R_2, NPV_1 and NPV_2 are then put into the following formula:

$$IRR = R_1 + \frac{(R_2 - R_1) \times NPV_1}{(NPV_1 - NPV_2)}$$

We calculated earlier that the NPV of Project B was £618,000 at a discount rate of 10 per cent. If we now increase the discount rate to 20 per cent, since 10 per cent was less than the internal rate or return, we can recalculate the NPV, as shown in Table 6.6. The earlier NPV calculation is included for comparison.

Interpolating, using the method discussed earlier:

$$IRR = 10 + \frac{(20 - 10) \times 618}{618 - (-953)} = 10 + 3.9 = 13.9\%$$

So the internal rate of return of Project B is approximately 13.9 per cent.

Table 6.6 Calculating the NPV of Project B at discount rates of 10 per cent and 20 percent as preparation for determining its IRR by linear interpolation

Year	Cash flow (£)	10% PV factors	Present value (£)	20% PV factors	Present value (£)
0	(5,000)	1.000	(5,000)	1.000	(5,000)
1	800	0.909	727	0.833	666
2	900	0.826	743	0.694	625
3	1,200	0.751	901	0.579	695
4	1,400	0.683	956	0.482	675
5	1,600	0.621	994	0.402	643
6	1,300	0.564	733	0.335	436
7	1,100	0.513	564	0.279	307
			618		(953)

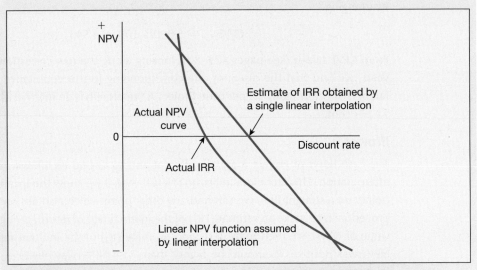

Figure 6.2 Illustration of why IRR estimated by a single linear interpolation calculation is only an approximation of the actual IRR of an investment project

We say 'approximately' since in using linear interpolation we have drawn a straight line between two points on a project NPV line that is in fact a curve. As shown in Figure 6.2, the straight line will not cut the x-axis at the same place as the project NPV curve, so the value we have obtained by interpolation is not the actual value of the IRR, but only an estimated value (and, for conventional projects, an overestimate). We would have obtained a different value if we had used a different estimate for R_2; for example, if we had used $R_1 = 10$ per cent and $R_2 = 15$ per cent, we would have obtained a value for the IRR of 13.5 per cent. To determine the actual IRR the interpolation calculation must be repeated, feeding successive approximations back into the calculation until the value produced no longer changes significantly. A financial calculator or a spreadsheet IRR function can do this task easily.

Project C

A calculation of the NPV of Project C at Clement's cost of capital of 10 per cent and a first estimate of the project IRR at 15 per cent is given in Table 6.7.

Interpolating:

$$\text{IRR} = 10 + \frac{15 - 10 \times 209}{209 - (-244)} = 10 + 2.3 = 12.3\%$$

The internal rate of return of Project C is approximately 12.3 per cent.

The decision on project selection

We can now summarise our calculations on the three projects:

Project A	IRR of 12.0 per cent	NPV of £355,000
Project B	IRR of 13.9 per cent	NPV of £618,000
Project C	IRR of 12.3 per cent	NPV of £209,000

Table 6.7 Calculating the NPV of Project C at discount rates of 10 per cent and 15 per cent as preparation for determining its IRR by linear interpolation

Year	Cash flow (£)	10% PV factors	Present value (£)	15% PV factors	Present value (£)
0	(5,000)	1.000	(5,000)	1.000	(5,000)
1	2,000	0.909	1,818	0.870	1,740
2	2,000	0.826	1,652	0.756	1,512
3	2,000	0.751	1,502	0.658	1,316
4	100	0.683	68	0.572	57
5	100	0.621	62	0.497	50
6	100	0.564	56	0.432	43
7	100	0.513	51	0.376	38
			209		(244)

All three projects have an IRR greater than Clement's cost of capital of 10 per cent, so all are acceptable capital is not restricted. If the projects are mutually exclusive, however, it is not possible to choose the best project by using the internal rate of return method. Notice that, although the IRR of Project C is higher than that of Project A, its NPV is lower. This means that the projects are ranked differently using IRR than they are using NPV. The problem of mutually exclusive investment projects is discussed in Section 6.5.1.

6.5 COMPARING THE NPV AND IRR METHODS

There is no conflict between these two discounted cash-flow methods when a *single* investment project with *conventional* cash flows is being evaluated. In the following situations, however, the net present value method may be preferred:

- where mutually exclusive projects are being compared;
- where the cash flows of a project are not conventional;
- where the discount rate changes during the life of the project.

6.5.1 Mutually exclusive projects

Consider two mutually exclusive projects, A and B, whose cash flows are given in Table 6.8. The net present value decision rule recommends accepting Project B, since it has the higher NPV at a cost of capital of 14 per cent. However, if the projects are compared using internal rate of return, Project A is preferred as it has the higher IRR. If the projects were independent so that both could be undertaken, this conflict of preferences would not be relevant. Since the projects are mutually exclusive, however, which should be accepted?

Table 6.8 The cash flows, net present values at a cost of capital of 14 per cent and internal rates of return of two mutually exclusive projects

	Project A	Project B
Initial investment (£)	13,000	33,000
Year 1 net cash flow (£)	7,000	15,000
Year 2 net cash flow (£)	6,000	15,000
Year 3 net cash flow (£)	5,000	15,000
Net present value (£)	+1,128	+1,830
Internal rate of return (%)	19.5	17

Table 6.9 The net present values of two mutually exclusive projects at different discount rates

Discount rate (%)	12	14	16	18	20	22
Project A (£)	1,593	1,128	697	282	(113)	(473)
Project B (£)	3,030	1,830	690	(390)	(1,410)	(2,370)

In all cases where this conflict occurs, the correct decision is to choose the project with the higher NPV. This decision supports the primary corporate finance objective of maximising shareholder wealth since selecting the project with the highest NPV leads to the greatest increase in company value. Although Project A has the highest IRR, this is only a *relative* measure of return. NPV measures the *absolute* increase in the company's value.

To illustrate the conflict between the two investment appraisal methods in more detail, Table 6.9 shows the NPV of the two projects at different discount rates and Figure 6.3 displays the same information in the form of a graph. Figure 6.3 shows that the two projects,

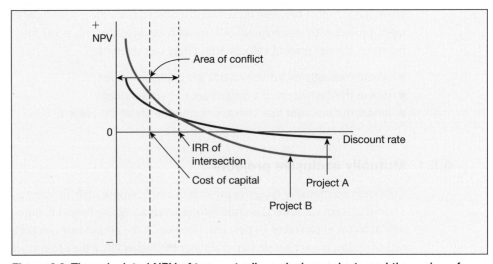

Figure 6.3 The calculated NPV of two mutually exclusive projects and the region of conflict

A and B, have project lines with different slopes. For costs of capital *greater* than the IRR of the intersection of the two project lines, which occurs at approximately 16 per cent, the two methods give the same advice, which is to accept Project A. For costs of capital *less* than the IRR of the intersection, the advice offered by the two methods is in conflict and the net present value method is preferred.

6.5.2 Non-conventional cash flows

If an investment project has cash flows of different signs in successive periods (e.g. a cash inflow followed by a cash outflow, followed by a further cash inflow), it may have more than one internal rate of return. Such cash flows are called non-conventional cash flows, and the existence of multiple internal rates of return may result in incorrect decisions being taken if the IRR decision rule is applied. The NPV method has no difficulty in accommodating non-conventional cash flows, as shown in Figure 6.4. The non-conventional project in Figure 6.4 has two internal rates of return, at IRR_1 and IRR_2. This kind of project is not unusual: for example, a mineral extraction project, with heavy initial investment in land, plant and machinery and significant environmental costs towards the end of the project life, might have this kind of NPV profile. Using the internal rate of return method, which IRR should be used to assess the project?

If the cost of capital is R_A, the project would be accepted using the internal rate of return method, since both IRR_1 and IRR_2 are greater than R_A. If the net present value method is used, it will be rejected, because at this discount rate it has a negative NPV and would decrease shareholder wealth. However, if the cost of capital used to assess the project is R_B, it will be accepted using the net present value method because at this discount rate it has a positive NPV. The internal rate of return method cannot offer any clear advice since R_B is between IRR_1 and IRR_2.

In each case, the net present value method gives the correct investment advice.

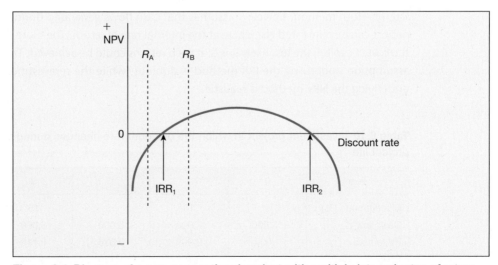

Figure 6.4 Diagram of a non-conventional project with multiple internal rates of return

6.5.3 Changes in the discount rate

If there are changes in the cost of capital over the life of an investment project, the net present value method can easily accommodate them. Consider the net present value formula described earlier, with the symbols having the same meaning:

$$NPV = -I_0 + \frac{C_1}{(1+r)} + \frac{C_2}{(1+r)^2} + \frac{C_3}{(1+r)^3} + \cdots + \frac{C_n}{(1+r)^n}$$

If the discount rates in successive years are r_1, r_2, etc., we have:

$$NPV = -I_0 + \frac{C_1}{(1+r_1)} + \frac{C_2}{(1+r_1)(1+r_2)} + \cdots$$

Consider the investment project in Table 6.10, where the discount rate increases in year 3 from 10 per cent to 15 per cent. The present value factor for year 3 is the present value factor for two years at 10 per cent multiplied by the present value factor for one year at 15 per cent. Using present value tables (see pages 479–80), we have:

$$PVF_{10,2} \times PVF_{15,1} = 0.826 \times 0.870 = 0.719$$

The NPV of the project is £1,807 while the IRR is approximately 18.8 per cent. The IRR, however, ignores the fact that the discount rate in year 3 is different from that in years 1 and 2.

6.5.4 Reinvestment assumptions

The net present value method assumes that cash flows generated during the life of a project can be reinvested elsewhere at a rate equal to the cost of capital. This seems to be a sensible reinvestment assumption since the cost of capital represents an opportunity cost, i.e. the best return that could have been obtained on an alternative investment. The internal rate of return method, however, assumes that cash flows generated during the life of the project can be reinvested elsewhere at the internal rate of return. The more the IRR exceeds the cost of capital, the less likely it is that such returns could be achieved. The reinvestment assumption underlying the IRR method is dubious, while the reinvestment assumption underlying the NPV method is realistic.

Table 6.10 Investment project in which the discount rate changes during the project life

Year	0	1	2	3
Discount rate (%)		10	10	15
Cash flow (£)	(13,000)	7,000	5,000	6,000
PV factors	1.000	0.909	0.826	0.719
Present value (£)	(13,000)	6,363	4,130	4,314

6.5.5 The superiority of the net present value method

We can now summarise the arguments in favour of the net present value method of investment appraisal:

1 The NPV method gives correct advice about mutually exclusive projects.

2 The NPV method can accommodate non-conventional cash flows, when the internal rate of return method may offer multiple solutions.

3 The reinvestment assumption underlying the NPV method is realistic, but the reinvestment assumption underlying the internal rate of return method is not.

4 The NPV method can easily incorporate changes in the discount rate, whereas the internal rate of return method ignores these changes.

For these reasons, the net present value method is held to be technically superior to the internal rate of return method.

The internal rate of return method, however, enjoys comparable popularity (see Section 7.6). It is obviously to be preferred to both payback period and accounting rate of return as an investment appraisal method, since it takes account of the time value of money, is based on cash flows and considers the whole of the project. The IRR or *yield* of an investment project is also a concept widely understood by financial analysts, investors and managers, and indicates the extent to which a project offers returns greater than a minimum required level, i.e. it indicates a margin of safety.

This chapter has argued that discounted cash-flow investment appraisal methods (i.e. NPV and IRR) are superior to simplistic investment appraisal methods (i.e. payback and return on capital employed) and this is widely accepted. Companies using discounted cash flow (DCF) investment appraisal methods should therefore perform better than those using simplistic methods. Empirical research on this question has produced mixed results, however, and Haka et al. (1985) found evidence that adoption of sophisticated investment appraisal methods may not necessarily lead to improved performance. Since most companies now use more than one investment appraisal method (see Section 7.6.1), it is in practice difficult to isolate any beneficial effects that may be solely due to using DCF methods. This does not invalidate the academic superiority of NPV and IRR, however. As illustrated by Vignette 6.1, it may be difficult to find values to use in a DCF analysis, such as the discount rate.

6.6 THE PROFITABILITY INDEX AND CAPITAL RATIONING

If a company does not have sufficient funds to undertake all projects that have a positive net present value, it is in a *capital rationing* situation. It will need to find a way of choosing between investment opportunities which maximise the return on the funds invested, i.e. it needs to *rank* investment projects in terms of financial desirability. The NPV method, which requires a company to invest in *all* projects with a positive NPV to maximise shareholder wealth, needs a perfect market to provide any investment funds that may be required. The NPV method cannot be used to rank investment projects if capital is rationed,

Vignette 6.1

A realistic discount rate for pensions
Changing the discount rate could be storing future problems

By Robert Pozen and Theresa Hamacher

Private pension funds across the world are finding it more difficult to meet their obligations to future retirees. In July 2012, the 100 largest US private pension funds faced a $533bn shortfall, according to the consulting firm Milliman. In the same month, private pensions in the UK faced a £283bn shortfall, according to the government's insurer of pension plans.

The current plight of corporate pension funds is the result of several factors: poor stock market returns over the past five years, a shift from stocks to bonds, and historically low interest rates over the past year. Low interest rates play a critical role in calculating pension plan obligations. Specifically, the interest rates on high-quality corporate bonds are used to determine the plan's expected risk-free return in the future – a metric known as the "discount rate". If the discount rate decreases, a pension plan needs more assets today in order to be sure it can generate sufficient investment returns to pay a projected amount of benefits in the future. Therefore, today's low discount rate places a burden on pension plans.

Corporate executives believe this burden is unfair: they argue that the current low rates do not truly reflect expected risk-free returns, but rather the policy measures taken by central banks. Some governments have eased this burden by dictating higher discount rates. In June, Denmark and Sweden took direct approaches, setting floors or specific values for the discount rates applicable to certain obligations. Nevertheless, it is unclear what an accurate discount rate should be.

A less contrived approach would be to use actual interest rates, averaged over several years. The US recently took this step: Congress allowed corporations to use a discount rate based on high-quality bond yields averaged over 25 years, instead of an average over two years as under the previous rules. This change is estimated to increase discount rates by at least 100 basis points, which would significantly reduce how much US corporations must contribute to their pension funds. For instance, David Zion of

Credit Suisse estimates that a 100 basis point increase in the discount rate would cause UPS's required contribution to drop in 2013 from $1.6bn to $47m.

UK regulators have yet to follow on the heels of their American counterparts, but British companies are making their case. The Confederation of British Industry, a group representing over 200,000 businesses, has called for a smoothing of interest rates "over a number of years".

While an averaging period of five to 10 years might better reflect more "normal" conditions, a 25-year averaging period, as enacted in the US, clearly goes too far. Interest rates in 1988 are unlikely to have much predictive value for the next 10 to 20 years. In any case, obligations that are payable in the next few years should not be afforded any higher discount rates. Even if current interest rates do not reflect long-term expectations, they do represent risk-free expected returns in the short-term.

For obligations further in the future, we would ideally prefer a discount rate that utilises expectations about the future, rather than data from the past. To a rough approximation, we can measure future expectations by calculating the forward interest rate on risk-free assets, such as US Treasuries or UK gilts. This forward rate, adjusted for the historic spread between Treasuries or gilts and the relevant corporate bond yields, might be a reasonable reflection of expected risk-free returns in the future.

As a specific example, consider an investor deciding between (1) buying a 20-year Treasury today and holding until maturity or (2) buying two 10-year Treasuries in succession (once in 2012, and again in 2022). The "10-year Treasury rate 10 years forward" would be the rate on the second 10-year Treasury that would make the investor indifferent between those two options. Currently, that rate is roughly 3 per cent.

In short, low interest rates make the obligations of pension plans seem more daunting, because plan trustees cannot rely on expectations of strong invest-

Vignette 6.1 (continued)

ment returns. But policy makers must be careful when considering what the "correct" discount rate should be. What if today's historically low interest rates are not some aberration that will quickly disappear? If so, temporary increases in the discount rate will only delay, rather than prevent, the day or reckoning for pensions.

 Source: Pozen, R. and Hamacher, T. (2012) A realistic discount rate for pensions, *Financial Times,* 19 August.
© The Financial Times Limited 2018. All Rights Reserved.

Questions

1 Discuss the origin of DCF approaches to investment appraisal techniques.

2 What is the relationship between pension obligations, the discount rate and future returns?

however, since ranking by NPV may lead to incorrect investment decisions. This is because a *combination* of smaller projects may collectively offer a higher NPV than a single project in return for investing the available capital, even if the smaller projects are ranked lower in NPV terms.

6.6.1 Hard and soft capital rationing

We can distinguish between hard and soft capital rationing. Hard capital rationing occurs when the limitation on investment funds is imposed externally by the capital market. Soft capital rationing occurs when the limitation on investment funds is imposed internally by a company's managers.

Hard capital rationing

A company may be unable to raise investment finance because capital markets are depressed or because investors consider the company to be too risky. If only a small amount of finance is needed, for example, to meet a marginal funding requirement, issue costs might make raising this finance unacceptably expensive. Most capital rationing is self-imposed and therefore soft in nature. While it has been unusual historically for hard capital rationing to occur, the onset of the 'credit crunch' in 2008 meant that it became more difficult to obtain suitable finance for capital investment. As illustrated by Vignette 6.2, hard capital rationing can be can be a problem for some companies.

Soft capital rationing

Investment funds may be restricted internally by managers for several reasons. They may decide against issuing equity finance, for example, because they wish to avoid dilution (reduction) of control, or because they wish to avoid any potential dilution (reduction) of

Vignette 6.2

China's war on debt hits heart of private enterprise glut

Zhejiang firms shelve investment plans as banks cut lending

By Sun Yu

Lying just to the south of Shanghai, Zhejiang province is the historical centre of Chinese private enterprise. But now the credit taps are being turned off, forcing private companies to cut their debt loads after years of state-sanctioned borrowing.

This deleveraging push is in line with the leadership's new-found appetite for curbing risk in the financial system, but the cost is reduced investment, which will drag on growth in one of China's most vibrant economic centres.

In a survey of 72 small and medium-sized private companies in this eastern province, just 16.7 per cent said their long-term debt had increased over the past 12 months, while 36.1 per cent said it had not risen. When we last surveyed Zhejiang companies in 2016, 35 per cent said their long-term debt had increased from a year earlier.

Start-up spirit

Hangzhou, Zhejiang's capital, is home to the headquarters of tech giant Alibaba, and the province has long hosted thousands of smaller private companies that got their start as lower-cost competitors to Pearl River Delta manufacturers in the south.

Analysts had hoped that some of Zhejiang's entrepreneurial spirit had rubbed off on Xi Jinping when he served there in the 2010s as governor and party secretary. Instead, China's president has pledged to 'inspire and protect' entrepreneurship while articulating a vision of state-owned companies at the heart of a more prosperous Chinese economy.

An important step towards this has been forcing the financial system to curb risky lending, a campaign aimed at lowering corporate leverage that has had a disproportionately negative impact on private companies. Only one of the 14 companies that have defaulted in the onshore bond market this year has been state owned.

Liquidity dries up

Nearly a quarter of the Zhejiang private companies surveyed said they were facing large debt pressure, compared with none when we last surveyed them in 2016.

At the time, local banks were helping companies to extend and pretend in collusion with local officials. But banks have come under the regulatory cosh since China's reshuffled leadership stepped up the campaign to curb lending excesses.

Officials at Zheshang Bank and Hangzhou Union Bank, two major Zhejiang lenders, said they had cut lending to smaller – read private – borrowers. They complained that a shortage of deposits limited their ability to lend and acknowledged that they were doing less off-balance-sheet lending as regulations have tightened.

One Zheshang Bank official said that last year he worked on more than Rmb4bn ($603m) in entrusted, or intercompany, loans and trust loans but had done none so far in 2018.

'We've gone from making great leaps to making small steps,' he said.

The small and medium-sized firms surveyed – on average, their revenues last year were less than Rmb20m – are among the companies that the government is pledging to help as it eases the strains of its deleveraging push.

The People's Bank of China has insisted at each of its most recent cuts in reserve requirement ratios that at least some of the funding released be used to support small companies. This reflects both the central bank's recognition that such firms are underserved by the state-dominated financial system, and that releasing additional liquidity has tended to do more to inflate asset prices than to support real economic activity. For its two most recent cuts, the bank explicitly earmarked a total of Rmb600bn for lending to small and micro-sized

Vignette 6.2 (continued)

firms, warning lenders that this would count towards their quarterly assessments.

But this additional liquidity is not yet being felt in Zhejiang. Surveyed firms said they were less willing or able to borrow to service outstanding loans, with 40.3 per cent taking out formal loans and 33.9 per cent of respondents borrowing from non-traditional channels to pay down debt, lower than the 81.8 per cent and 80.3 per cent that reported doing so in 2016.

Zhao Youlong, general manager of a jewellery maker in Zhuji, a pearl-farming centre in the north of the province, said the same banks that had been supportive only recently have turned down his loan applications three times, even though his company is profitable. In an industry-wide slowdown, lenders have stopped financing jewellery manufacturers regardless of their creditworthiness, he said.

Mr Zhao is paying 50 per cent more to borrow than he did two years ago. Among all survey respondents, 48.4 per cent reported a year-over-year increase in funding costs – 39.4 per cent said so in 2016 – while just 9 per cent reported a fall.

Although business has recovered from the turmoil of 2015 and 2016, private companies have become more cautious. Among respondents to our survey, 35 per cent have no long-term debt and 14 per cent reported no short-term debt either. Zhang Xulin,

general manager of Yucai Holding Co, an educational toy maker in Wenzhou, said the firm would take advantage of currently stable business conditions to lower its debt of about Rmb60m by a third this year. 'We don't want to grow by increasing debt,' Mr Zhang said.

The cost

Deleveraging leads to slower growth. Nearly 52 per cent of the companies surveyed said they had cut capital expenditure to reduce debt, with redundancies the second most used method.

The province's factories are generally in traditional industrial sectors, where barriers to entry are low and competition is fierce. Rising labour and land costs compound the problems. Jiang Xiaojun, owner of Dinggu Mold Co in Taizhou, decided against a new plant because salaries have risen 20 per cent in two years while the land would cost the equivalent of 150 per cent of Dinggu's 2017 revenues. 'We're not at the state where we need to finance expansion by borrowing,' he said.

Although national data have showed some improvement in the investment appetite of private companies since 2016, Zhejiang firms surveyed expressed caution, with 27.4 per cent warning they expect their leverage ratio to have a negative impact on their business.

 Source: Sun Yu (2018) 'China's war on debt hits heart of private enterprise glut', *Financial Times*, 5 July. © The Financial Times Limited 2018. All Rights Reserved.

Questions

1 Discuss the nature of the capital rationing described in the vignette.

2 Discuss the reasons why companies in Zhejiang province face capital rationing.

earnings per share (EPS). They may decide against raising debt finance through a desire to avoid increased interest payment commitments, perhaps because they are concerned about their company's existing level of gearing or financial risk. If a company is small or family-owned, its managers may limit the investment funds available as part of a policy of seeking steady growth through retained earnings, as opposed to a policy of rapid expansion.

It is also possible that self-imposed capital rationing, by fostering a competitive *internal market* for available investment funds, will weed out marginal or borderline investment projects and encourage the generation of better, more robust, investment proposals.

6.6.2 Single-period capital rationing

In single-period capital rationing the available funds are only restricted initially, i.e. in year 0. A company needs to choose the combination of projects that maximises the total NPV. Depending on the circumstances, this can be done either by ranking projects using the **profitability index** or by finding the NPV of possible combinations of projects.

Divisible, non-deferrable investment projects

To clarify the circumstances in which the profitability index can be used, we can define three kinds of investment project. A *divisible project* is one where any portion of the project may be undertaken; a *non-deferrable project* is one which, if it is not undertaken now, cannot be undertaken later; a *non-repeatable project* is one that may be undertaken only once.

If the available investment projects are divisible, non-deferrable and non-repeatable and if capital is rationed in the initial period only, ranking projects by their absolute NPV may not lead to the correct decision since, as pointed out earlier, a project with a large NPV will be preferred over a combination of several smaller projects with a larger collective NPV. The correct approach here is to calculate a *profitability index* or benefit to cost ratio for each project and then to rank them using this measure. The profitability index tells us how much we can expect to receive, in present value terms, for each unit of currency invested in the project:

$$\text{Profitability index} = \frac{\text{Present value of future cash flows}}{\text{Value of initial capital invested}}$$

If there is no restriction on investment capital, all projects with a profitability index greater than one should be accepted. This corresponds to the NPV decision rule of accepting all projects with a positive NPV. If investment capital is restricted, the project with the highest profitability index should be undertaken: funds should then be allocated to the project with the next highest profitability index, and so on until there is no longer a whole project that can be undertaken. As the projects are divisible, the remaining funds are invested pro rata in the next best project. The total NPV arising from this investment schedule is the sum of the NPV of the complete projects, added to the pro rata share of the NPV of the partly undertaken project. This procedure is illustrated in Table 6.11.

From Table 6.11 we can see that, if we have £1,650,000 available to invest in the divisible Projects A, B, C and D, the optimum investment is to undertake all of Projects A and B and 62.5 per cent of Project C, giving a total NPV of £1,865,000. This is preferable to investing £1,650,000 in Projects C and D, even though these have the highest NPV, since their total NPV is only £1,565,000. If Project A had been repeatable, the optimum investment schedule would have been to repeat Project A 3.3 times, giving a total NPV of £2,145,000.

The profitability index can also be defined as the ratio of NPV to initial capital invested: the optimum investment schedule decision process and optimum NPV are the same regardless of the definition of profitability index used.

Table 6.11 Ranking divisible projects by profitability index to find the optimum investment schedule under single-period capital rationing

Project	A	B	C	D
Initial investment (£000)	500	650	800	850
Net present value (£000)	650	715	800	765
PV of future cash flows (£000)	1,150	1,365	1,600	1,615
Profitability index	2.3	2.1	2.0	1.9
Ranking by NPV	4	3	1	2
Ranking by profitability index	1	2	3	4

Capital available = £1,650,000

Optimum investment schedule:	NPV (£000)	Cumulative investment (£000)
£500,000 invested in Project A	650	500
£650,000 invested in Project B	715	1,150
£500,000 invested in Project C	500	1,650
Total NPV for £1,650,000 invested:	1,865	

Indivisible, non-deferrable investment projects

If investment projects are not divisible, profitability indices still provide useful information, but the selection of projects can only be found by examining the total NPV of all possible combinations of projects. The combination with the highest NPV which does not exceed the available investment capital is optimal. Taking the projects in Table 6.11 as indivisible, the optimum investment schedule is a combination of Projects C and D.

Projects A and B	Total NPV = £1,365,000
Projects A and C	Total NPV = £1,450,000
Projects A and D	Total NPV = £1,415,000
Projects B and C	Total NPV = £1,515,000
Projects B and D	Total NPV = £1,480,000
Projects C and D	Total NPV = £1,565,000

6.6.3 Multiple-period capital rationing

If investment funds are expected to be restricted in more than one period, the decision about which projects to select cannot be based on ranking projects by profitability index or by trying different combinations of projects since neither of these methods accommodates the restriction on finance in future periods. The complexity of this problem means that linear programming is needed for its solution. With only two variables, the linear programming problem can be solved graphically, but, if there are more than two variables, the simplex method or a computer must be used. The solution of multiple-period capital rationing problems is not considered in this text (but see, for example, Drury 2018).

Table 6.12 How cumulative NPV can be used to determine discounted payback period

Year	Cash flow (£)	15% PV factor	Present value (£)	Cumulative NPV (£)
0	(5,000)	1.000	(5,000)	(5,000)
1	2,300	0.870	2,001	(2,999)
2	2,500	0.756	1,890	(1,109)
3	1,200	0.658	790	(319)
4	1,000	0.572	572	253
5	1,000	0.497	497	750

6.7 THE DISCOUNTED PAYBACK METHOD

The payback method discussed previously (Section 6.1) can be modified by discounting the project cash flows by the company's cost of capital to take account of the time value of money. Consider the example given in Table 6.12, where a company with a cost of capital of 15 per cent is evaluating an investment project.

The discounted payback period is approximately 3.6 years, compared with an undiscounted payback period of approximately 2.2 years. The discounted payback method has the same advantages and disadvantages as before except that the shortcoming of failing to account for the time value of money has been overcome.

6.8 CONCLUSION

In this chapter we have considered at an introductory level the methods used by corporate finance to evaluate investment projects. While there is a wide range of techniques that can be used, the net present value method enjoys the support of academics and is regarded as superior to the other investment appraisal methods discussed.

■ ■ ■ KEY POINTS

1 Payback period is the number of years taken to recover the original investment from the cash flows generated by a capital investment project.

2 Payback takes account of risk (if risk means the uncertainty that increases as cash flows become more distant) and is a simple method to apply and understand. However, it ignores the time value of money, the timing of cash flows within the payback period and any cash flows after the payback period. It does not say whether a project is a 'good' one.

3 Return on capital employed is the ratio of average annual profit to capital invested. It is simple to apply, looks at the whole of an investment project and can be used to compare mutually exclusive projects. A project is acceptable if the ROCE exceeds a target value.

4 Return on capital employed ignores the time value of money, fails to take account of the size and timing of cash flows and uses profits rather than cash flows.

5 Net present value is the difference between the present value of future benefits and the present value of capital invested, discounted at a company's cost of capital. The NPV decision rule is to accept all projects with a positive net present value.

6 The NPV method takes account of the time value of money and the amount and timing of all relevant cash flows over the life of the project.

7 The NPV method can take account of both conventional and non-conventional cash flows, can accommodate changes in the discount rate during a project's life and gives an absolute rather than a relative measure of financial acceptability.

8 Problems with using the NPV method include difficulty in estimating future project cash flows; difficulties in estimating the discount rate; and possible changes in the discount rate during the life of the project.

9 The internal rate of return method involves calculating the discount rate which gives an NPV of zero. The IRR decision rule is to accept all projects with an IRR greater than the company's target rate of return.

10 The NPV method gives correct investment advice when comparing mutually exclusive projects, but IRR may not do so.

11 The NPV method assumes that cash flows can be reinvested at the cost of capital, while the IRR method assumes that cash flows are reinvested at the internal rate of return. Only the reinvestment assumption underlying the NPV method is realistic.

12 Capital rationing can be either hard (externally imposed) or soft (internally imposed).

13 Hard capital rationing might occur because capital markets are depressed or because a company is thought to be too risky.

14 Soft capital rationing might occur because a company wishes to avoid dilution of control, dilution of EPS or further fixed interest commitments. The company may wish to pursue a policy of steady growth or believe that restricting funds will encourage better projects.

15 In single-period capital rationing, divisible, non-deferrable and non-repeatable investment projects can be ranked using the profitability index to find the optimal investment schedule. The profitability index is the ratio of the present value of future cash flows divided by the initial capital invested.

16 Multiple-period capital rationing can be solved using linear programming.

SELF-TEST QUESTIONS

Answers to these questions can be found on pages 458–60.

1 Explain why the payback method cannot be recommended as the main method used by a company to assess potential investment projects.

2 Calculate the return on capital employed (average investment basis) for projects A, B and C, and show which would be chosen if the target ROCE is 12 per cent. Scrap value is zero.

	Project A (£)	Project B (£)	Project C (£)
Initial investment	10,000	15,000	20,000
Net cash inflows:			
Year 1	5,000	5,000	10,000
Year 2	5,000	5,000	8,000
Year 3	2,000	5,000	4,000
Year 4	1,000	10,000	2,000
Year 5		5,000	

3 Explain the shortcomings of return on capital employed as an investment appraisal method and suggest reasons why it may be used by managers.

4 Three investment projects have the following net cash flows. Decide which of them should be accepted using the NPV decision rule if the discount rate is 12 per cent.

Year	Project A (£)	Project B (£)	Project C (£)
0	(10,000)	(15,000)	(20,000)
1	5,000	5,000	10,000
2	5,000	5,000	10,000
3	2,000	5,000	4,000
4	1,000	10,000	2,000
5		5,000	

5 List the advantages of the net present value investment appraisal method.

6 Explain how NPV and IRR deal with non-conventional cash flows.

7 Discuss the problem of choosing between mutually exclusive projects with respect to their net present values and internal rates of return.

8 Show with the aid of a numerical example how linear interpolation can be used to determine the internal rate of return of a project.

9 Explain the distinction between hard and soft capital rationing, and outline the reasons why these conditions might occur.

10 How can a company's optimum investment schedule be determined under conditions of capital rationing?

1 The expected cash flows of two projects are given below. The cost of capital is 10 per cent.

Period	Project A (£)	Project B (£)
0	(5,000)	(5,000)
1	1,000	2,000
2	2,500	2,000
3	2,500	2,000
4	1,500	1,000

   (a) Calculate the payback period, net present value, internal rate of return and return on capital employed (average investment basis) of each project.

   (b) Show the rankings of the projects by each of the four methods and comment on your findings.

2 LJH plc is planning to buy a machine which will cost £900,000 and which is expected to generate new cash sales of £600,000 per year. The expected useful life of the machine will be eight years, at the end of which it will have a scrap value of £100,000. Annual costs are expected to be £400,000 per year. LJH plc has a cost of capital of 11 per cent.

   (a) Calculate the payback period, return on capital employed, net present value and internal rate of return of the proposed investment.

   (b) Discuss the reasons why net present value is preferred by academics to other methods of evaluating investment projects.

3 Brown Ltd is considering buying a new machine which would have a useful economic life of five years, a cost of £125,000 and a scrap value of £30,000, with 80 per cent of the cost being payable at the start of the project and 20 per cent after one year. The machine would produce 50,000 units per year of a new product with an estimated selling price of £3 per unit. Direct costs would be £1.75 per unit and annual fixed costs, including depreciation calculated on a straight-line basis (equal annual amounts), would be £40,000 per year.

   In years 1 and 2, special sales promotion expenditure, not included in the above costs, would be incurred, amounting to £10,000 and £15,000, respectively.

   Evaluate the project using the NPV method of investment appraisal, assuming the company's cost of capital is 10 per cent.

4 Better plc is comparing two mutually exclusive projects, whose details are given below. The company's cost of capital is 12 per cent.

	Project A (£m)	Project B (£m)
Year 0	(150)	(152)
Year 1	40	80
Year 2	50	60
Year 3	60	50
Year 4	60	40
Year 5	80	30

(a) Using the net present value method, which project should be accepted?

(b) Using the internal rate of return method, which project should be accepted?

(c) If the cost of capital increases to 20 per cent in year 5, would your advice change?

5 The finance director of Park plc is preparing financial plans and different departments have submitted capital investment applications. The managing director has said that no more than £1m is available for new investment projects. Cashflow forecasts from the capital investment applications are as follows:

	Project A (£000)	Project B (£000)	Project C (£000)	Project D (£000)
Year 0	(340)	(225)	(350)	(275)
Year 1	105	75	90	115
Year 2	110	75	90	115
Year 3	115	75	140	115
Year 4	110	75	140	115
Year 5	105	90	140	nil

The cost of capital of Park plc is 15 per cent per year.

(a) If investment projects are divisible but not repeatable, calculate the optimum investment schedule and the net present value of the optimum investment schedule.

(b) If investment projects are not divisible and not repeatable, calculate the optimum investment schedule and the net present value of the optimum investment schedule.

(c) Discuss why the managing director of Park plc may have limited the funds available for investment projects at the start of the next financial year, even if this results in rejecting projects which may increase the value of the company.

QUESTIONS FOR DISCUSSION

1 Willow plc is evaluating two mutually exclusive projects with the following cash flows.

Year	Project A (£)	Project B (£)
0	(110,000)	(200,000)
1	45,000	50,000
2	45,000	50,000
3	30,000	50,000
4	30,000	100,000
5	20,000	55,000

Willow's cost of capital is 10 per cent and both investment projects have zero scrap value. The company's current return on capital employed is 12 per cent (average investment basis) and the company uses straight-line depreciation over the life of projects.

(a) Advise Willow which project should be undertaken if:
   (i)   the net present value method of investment appraisal is used;
   (ii) the internal rate of return method of investment appraisal is used;
   (iii) the return on capital employed method of investment appraisal is used.

(b) Discuss the problems that arise in using net present value if investment capital is limited and explain how these problems may be resolved in practice.

2 The finance director of RM plc is considering several investment projects and has collected the following information about them.

Project	Estimated initial outlay (£)	Cash inflow Year 1 (£)	Cash inflow Year 2 (£)	Cash inflow Year 3 (£)
A	200,000	50,000	150,000	150,000
B	450,000	357,000	357,000	357,000
C	550,000	863,000	853,000	853,000
D	170,000	278,000	278,000	nil
E	200,000	250,000	250,000	250,000
F	330,000	332,000	332,000	nil

Projects D and E are mutually exclusive. The capital available for investment is limited to £1m in the first year. All projects are divisible and none may be postponed or repeated. The cost of capital of RM plc is 15 per cent.

(a) Discuss the possible reasons why RM plc may be limited as to the amount of capital available for investment in its projects.

(b) Determine which investment projects the finance director of RM plc should choose to maximise the return on the capital available for investment. If the projects were not divisible, would you change your advice to the finance director?

(c) Critically discuss the reasons why net present value is the method of investment appraisal preferred by academics. Is the internal rate of return method now redundant?

3 The finance manager of Wide plc is evaluating two capital investment projects which may assist the company in achieving its business objectives. Both projects will require an initial investment of £500,000 in plant and machinery, but it is not expected that any additional investment in working capital will be needed. The expected cash flows of the two projects are as follows:

Period	Broad project (£)	Keeling project (£)
1	60,000	220,000
2	90,000	220,000
3	140,000	50,000
4	210,000	50,000
5	300,000	50,000
6	140,000	50,000
7	100,000	200,000

The cost of capital of Wide plc is 10 per cent.

(a) For both the Broad and Keeling projects, calculate the return on capital employed (average investment basis), the net present value and the internal rate of return.

(b) If the Broad and Keeling projects are mutually exclusive, advise Wide plc which project should be undertaken.

(c) Critically discuss the advantages and disadvantages of return on capital employed as an investment appraisal method.

References

Drury, C. (2018) *Management and Cost Accounting*, 10th edn, London: Cengage Learning EMEA, Chapter 26.

Haka, S., Gordon, L. and Pinches, G. (1985) 'Sophisticated capital budgeting selection techniques and firm performance', *The Accounting Review*, vol. 60, no. 4, pp. 651–69.

Hirshleifer, J. (1958) 'On the theory of optimal investment decisions', *Journal of Political Economy*, vol. 66, pp. 329–52.

Recommended reading

Many textbooks offer the opportunity to read further on the topic of investment appraisal techniques. A useful text is:

Arnold, G. (2018) *Corporate Financial Management*, 6th edn, Harlow: Pearson Education.

7 INVESTMENT APPRAISAL: APPLICATIONS AND RISK

Learning objectives

After studying this chapter, you should have achieved the following learning objectives:

- an understanding of the influence of taxation on investment decisions and a familiarity with the calculation of tax liabilities and benefits;

- an understanding of the influence of general and specific inflation on investment decisions;

- a familiarity with both the real-terms and nominal-terms approaches to investment appraisal under conditions of inflation;

- an understanding of the distinction between risk and uncertainty;

- a familiarity with the application of sensitivity analysis to investment projects;

- a general understanding of the ways in which risk can be incorporated into the investment appraisal process;

- an understanding of the differences between domestic and international investment appraisal and the ability to evaluate international investment decisions;

- an appreciation of the general results of empirical research into the capital investment decision making process.

■ ■ ■ INTRODUCTION

To make optimal capital investment decisions, the investment appraisal process must take account of the effects of taxation and inflation on project cash flows and on the required rate of return, since the influence of these factors is inescapable. In addition, expected future cash flows are subject to both risk and uncertainty. In this chapter we consider some of the suggested methods for the investment appraisal process to take these factors into account. We also consider the appraisal of foreign direct investment, which is more complex than the appraisal of domestic investment. Exchange rates must be forecast and the effect on project cash flows of different taxation systems must be considered. Finally, we look at what research says about the way in which investment appraisal is conducted in the real world. Do companies take the advice of academics on the best investment appraisal methods to use, or do they have their own ideas about how to evaluate investment projects?

7.1 RELEVANT PROJECT CASH FLOWS

In 'An overview of investment appraisal methods' (Chapter 6) we gave little thought to which costs and revenues should be included in project appraisal, although using cash flows rather than accounting profits was emphasised. A key concept to grasp is that only *relevant* cash flows should be included. One test of relevance is to ask whether a cash flow occurs as a result of undertaking a project. If the answer is no, the cash flow is not relevant. It is useful to think in terms of *incremental* cash flows, which are the changes in a company's overall cash flows that result directly from undertaking an investment project. Cash flows such as initial investment, cash from sales and direct cost of sales are clearly incremental and relevant. The following costs, however, need careful consideration.

7.1.1 Sunk costs

Costs incurred before the start of an investment project are called *sunk costs* and are not relevant to project appraisal, even if they have not yet been paid, since such costs will be paid whether or not the project is undertaken. Examples of sunk costs are market research, the historical cost of machinery already owned, and research and development expenditure. Vignette 7.1 shows that a sunk cost can be quite large!

7.1.2 Apportioned fixed costs

Costs which will be incurred regardless of whether a project is undertaken or not, such as apportioned fixed costs (e.g. rent and building insurance) or apportioned head office costs, are not relevant to project evaluation and must be excluded. Only *incremental* or *additional* fixed costs that arise as a result of taking on a project should be included as relevant project cash flows.

Vignette 7.1

RBS: never mind the price

By Lex

In deciding when to sell, what you paid to buy is not a good starting point.

By George, she's got it. The UK government caught the sales bug this week, announcing plans to start returning its 79 per cent stake in Royal Bank of Scotland to the private sector, and placing half of its remaining 30 per cent stake in Royal Mail. Lest anyone misses the irony: privately owned RBS had to be rescued by the state in a £45bn bailout, while state-owned Royal Mail was surrendered to the private sector because it could not compete in a changed postal market.

George Osborne, chancellor, needs to sell assets to cut the UK's public debt. This week's Royal Mail placing has harvested £750m. The postal service's 2013 flotation drew criticism for being priced too low; similar criticism is now levelled at the decision to sell RBS – valued at £32bn – at a loss. RBS shares would have to go for an average 455p, against 360p now, to recoup the outlay.

The hand-wringing over whether taxpayers get all their money back is wrong-headed. What one paid should not influence the decision to sell. It is a sunk cost. And the investment in RBS was not about profit. If then-chancellor Alistair Darling had not saved RBS, Lloyds Banking Group and others, the collapse of confidence would have cost incalculably more. Taxpayers bought stability.

Finally, the sale process could take years. RBS could increase in value as the UK recovery gains pace and as state ownership declines. The state's stake in Lloyds, already reduced from 41 per cent to 18 per cent, shows what can be done. With greater liquidity and less interference comes investability and higher demand.

RBS has set aside £1.9bn for a settlement with US regulators for mis-selling subprime mortgage securities. There will be further costs as RBS scales back its operations. But asset shrinkage and its exit from Citizens Financial Group will boost its already decent common equity tier one capital ratio, raising hopes of buybacks or dividends in a year or so. That might just drive up the share price. Enough moaning.

Source: Lex (2015) 'RBS: never mind the price', *Financial Times*, 11 June. © The Financial Times Limited 2015. All Rights Reserved.

7.1.3 Opportunity costs

An *opportunity cost* is the benefit lost by using an asset for one purpose rather than another. If an asset is used for an investment project, we must ask what benefit has thereby been lost, since this lost benefit or opportunity cost is the relevant cost as far as the project is concerned. An example using raw materials will illustrate this point.

Suppose a company has 1,000 kg of raw material A in inventory, bought for £2,000 in cash six months ago. The supplier is now offering material A for £2.20 per kg. The existing inventory could be sold on the second-hand market for £1.90 per kg, the lower price being due to deterioration in storage. Two-thirds of the inventory of material A is needed for a project which begins in three weeks' time. What is the relevant cost of material A to the project?

Since material A has already been bought, the original cost of £2,000 is a sunk cost and is irrelevant. If the company has no other use for material A and uses it for the new project, the benefit of selling it on the second-hand market is lost and the relevant cost is the resale price of £1.90 per kg. If material A is used regularly in other production processes, any material used in the new project must be replaced and the relevant cost is the current market price of £2.20 per kg.

7.1.4 Incremental working capital

As activity levels increase due to investment in non-current assets and company growth, a company's inventories of raw materials, inventories of finished goods and levels of trade receivables will also increase. These increases will be partly financed by increases in trade payables. The net incremental increase in working capital represents cash flowing out of the company and it is a relevant cash flow which must be included in the investment appraisal process. Additional investment in working capital may be needed in the future as sales levels continue to rise, if the problem of *overtrading* or undercapitalisation is to be avoided (see 'Overtrading', Section 3.4). At the end of a project, however, levels of trade receivables, inventories and trade payables will fall (unless the project is sold as a going concern) and investment in working capital will be recovered. The recovery of working capital will be a cash inflow, either in the final year of the project or in the year immediately following the end of the project.

7.2 TAXATION AND CAPITAL INVESTMENT DECISIONS

At the start of this chapter we noted that the effect of taxation on capital investment decisions could not be ignored. To determine the net cash benefits gained by a company from an investment project, the benefits or liabilities that arise from corporate taxation must be estimated. We now discuss the factors to consider when estimating these benefits or liabilities.

7.2.1 Tax-allowable depreciation

In financial accounting, capital expenditure appears in the statement of profit or loss in the form of annual depreciation charges. These charges are determined by company management in accordance with relevant accounting standards. For taxation purposes, capital expenditure is written off against taxable profits in a manner laid down by government and enforced by the tax authorities. Under this system, companies write off capital expenditure by means of annual capital allowances (also known as tax-allowable depreciation).

Capital allowances are a matter of government policy, as illustrated by Vignette 7.2. In the UK the standard tax-allowable depreciation on plant and machinery is 18 per cent on a reducing balance basis for total investment exceeding an annual investment allowance (£200,000 at the time of writing). UK businesses also have access to 100 per cent first-year allowances for specified investments, for example in approved energy-saving equipment. A *balancing adjustment* is needed in addition to a capital allowance in the last year of an investment project to ensure that the capital value consumed by the business over the life of the project (capital cost minus scrap value) has been deducted in full and not exceeded in calculating taxable profits.

At the time of writing the UK main corporation tax rate is 19 per cent, regardless of size of profits. The rate is expected to be cut further, although Vignette 7.2 suggests that continuing cuts may be unwelcome.

Vignette 7.2

Tax experts call for 'rethink' of UK corporation tax in Budget

By Jim Pickard, Vanessa Houlder and Madison Marriage

Tax experts have urged UK chancellor Philip Hammond to 'rethink' plans to cut corporation tax to 17 per cent by the end of the decade in order to free up £5bn a year for other spending priorities. When David Cameron became prime minister in 2010, the headline corporation tax rate was 28 per cent. Mr Hammond's predecessor, George Osborne, repeatedly cut the tax rate to its current level of 19 per cent. In 2016, Mr Osborne announced plans for the rate to drop a further two percentage points, to 17 per cent, in April 2020. In his March Budget this year, Mr Hammond underlined his commitment to reducing the rate further, saying cutting it to 17 per cent would send the 'clearest possible signal that Britain is open for business'. But now some tax experts say the chancellor should redirect the money earmarked for a corporation tax cut to tackle other policy challenges. 'I hope [the chancellor] does rethink,' said Bill Dodwell, head of tax policy at Deloitte. 'Business welcomed the drop to 20 per cent. Nobody seems to welcome the cut to 17 per cent.' The British Chambers of Commerce has also urged Mr Hammond to 'pause' and keep the corporate tax rate at 19 per cent until after UK leaves the EU. The lobby group has said that the resulting revenue could be ringfenced to ease other burdens on business. Chris Sanger, global head of tax policy at EY, professional services firm, said many companies were talking about the possibility of the corporate tax rate cut being delayed. But he said there would be negative reaction if the resulting funds were not redeployed to help business.

Mr Hammond is already expected to use this week's Budget to address concerns about business rates by switching next year's increase in the tax for business owners from RPI to CPI, meaning the rate will go up by 3 per cent, instead of 3.9 per cent. But the chancellor is loath to abandon the 'corporation tax road map', fearing that a change of tack would breach a Tory manifesto promise and require the reversal of existing legislation. The Treasury has sought to reassure business leaders in recent weeks that it is still committed to cutting the tax. Some tax experts have said it would be a mistake to slow or cancel the rate cut, particularly as the US has plans to reduce its own corporate tax rate to 20 per cent. 'There has been speculation whether he might rein back reduction in corporate tax rate,' said Stella Amiss, tax partner at PwC. 'We don't think he will. A slowdown would send negative signals.' Jeff Soar, UK head of financial services tax at EY, said that companies were hoping to be 'spared' any big announcements in the Budget. 'With the ongoing market uncertainty Brexit has brought, a period of calm on the tax front would be welcome,' he said. Mr Soar added that reversing any corporation tax cuts 'would be an unwelcome move that would see companies having to recalculate their deferred tax provisions and would likely end up hitting their bottom lines'. The gradual cuts in the corporate tax rate from 28 per cent to 17 per cent between 2010 and 2020 are estimated to reduce government revenues by at least £16.5bn a year in the short to medium term, according to the Institute for Fiscal Studies think-tank. However, some of the lost revenue will eventually be recaptured through higher investment on the part of businesses. In a 2013 report, HM Revenue & Customs suggested that within 20 years, between 45 and 60 per cent of lost corporate tax receipts would be recouped as a result of higher investment and increased economic activity.

Source: Pickard, J., Houlder, V. and Marriage, M. (2017) 'Tax experts call for 'rethink' of UK corporation tax in Budget', *Financial Times*, 12 July. © The Financial Times Limited 2017. All Rights Reserved.

Table 7.1 Capital allowances on a 25 per cent reducing balance basis on a machine costing £200,000 which is purchased at year 0. The expected life of the machine is four years and its scrap value after four years will be £20,000. Corporation tax is 20 per cent, payable one year in arrears

	£	£
Calculation of capital allowances:		
Year 1: 200,000 × 0.25 =		50,000
Year 2: (200,000 − 50,000) × 0.25 =		37,500
Year 3: (200,000 − 50,000 − 37,500) × 0.25 =		28,125
Year 4: (200,000 − 50,000 − 37,500 − 28,125) × 0.25 =		21,094
Initial value =	200,000	
Scrap value =	20,000	
Value consumed by the business over 4 years =	180,000	
Sum of capital allowances to end of Year 4 =	136,719	
Year 4 balancing allowance =		43,281
Total capital allowances over 4 years =		180,000
Calculation of taxation benefits:	£	
Year 1 (taken in Year 2): 50,000 × 0.2 =	10,000	
Year 2 (taken in Year 3): 37,500 × 0.2 =	7,500	
Year 3 (taken in Year 4): 28,125 × 0.2 =	5,625	
Year 4 (taken in Year 5): (21,094 + 43,281) = 64,375 × 0.2 =	12,875	
Total benefits (should equal 180,000 × 0.2 = 36,000)	36,000	

It is useful to calculate taxable profits and tax liabilities separately before calculating the net cash flows of a project. Performing the two calculations at the same time can lead to confusion. Since a worked example makes these concepts easier to grasp, an example of the calculation of capital allowances on plant and machinery on a 25 per cent reducing balance basis, together with the associated tax benefits at a corporation tax rate of 20 per cent, is given in Table 7.1.

7.2.2 Tax allowable costs

Tax liabilities will arise on the taxable profits generated by an investment project. Liability to taxation is reduced by deducting allowable expenditure from annual revenue when calculating taxable profit. Relief for capital expenditure is given by deducting capital allowances from annual revenue, as already discussed. Relief for revenue expenditure is given by deducting tax-allowable costs. Tax-allowable costs include the costs of materials, components, wages and salaries, production overheads, insurance, maintenance, lease rentals and so on.

7.2.3 Are interest payments a relevant cash flow?

While interest payments on debt are an allowable deduction in calculating taxable profit, it is a mistake to include interest payments as a relevant cash flow in the appraisal of a domestic capital investment project. The reason for excluding interest payments is that the required return on any debt finance used in an investment project is accounted in the cost of capital used to discount the project cash flows. If a company has sufficient taxable profits, the tax-allowability of interest payments is accommodated by using the after-tax weighted average cost of capital (see 'Bonds and convertibles', Section 9.1.3) to discount after-tax net cash flows.

7.2.4 The timing of tax liabilities and benefits

UK companies with annual taxable profits less than £1.5m pay corporation tax on taxable profits nine months after the end of the relevant accounting year. In investment appraisal, cash flows arising during a period are taken as occurring at the end of that period, so in this case *tax liabilities* are taken as being paid one year after the originating taxable profits. Any *tax benefits*, for example, from capital allowances, are also received one year in arrears. There is some variation in the way that different authors allow for capital allowances in appraising investment projects where tax is paid in arrears. The method used here is as follows:

■ Capital investment occurs at Year 0.
■ The first capital allowance affects cash flows arising in Year 1.
■ The benefit from the first capital allowance arises in Year 2.
■ The number of capital allowances equals the number of years in the life of the project.

UK companies with annual taxable profits greater than £1.5m are required to pay corporation tax in instalments and pay two out of four instalments of their estimated tax liabilities during the accounting year in which they arise. Larger UK companies therefore pay their (average) tax liabilities close to the end of the relevant accounting year. For such companies, tax liabilities and benefits can be treated as arising in the same year as the originating taxable profits.

Example   NPV calculation involving taxation

Bent plc is considering buying a new machine costing £200,000 which would generate the following before-tax cash flows from the sale of goods produced.

Year	Before-tax cash flow
1	£65,000
2	£70,000
3	£75,000
4	£98,000

Bent pays corporation tax of 20 per cent per year one year in arrears and claims capital allowances on a 25 per cent reducing balance basis. The machine would be sold after four years for £20,000. If Bent's after-tax cost of capital is 10 per cent, is the purchase of the machine financially acceptable?

Suggested answer

The capital allowances were calculated in Table 7.1. The tax liabilities can be found by subtracting the capital allowances from the before-tax cash flows to give taxable profits and then multiplying taxable profits by the corporation tax rate, as follows:

	£
Year 1 (taken in Year 2): (65,000 − 50,000) × 0.2 =	3,000
Year 2 (taken in Year 3): (70,000 − 37,500) × 0.2 =	6,500
Year 3 (taken in Year 4): (75,000 − 28,125) × 0.2 =	9,375
Year 4 (taken in Year 5): (98,000 − 64,375) × 0.2 =	6,725

The calculations of the net cash flows and the net present value of the proposed investment are shown in Table 7.2. The NPV of £35,886 is a positive value and so purchase of the machine by Bent plc is financially acceptable.

Table 7.2 Calculating net cash flows and net present value for Bent plc

Year	Capital (£)	Operating cash flows (£)	Taxation (£)	Net cash flows (£)
0	(200,000)			(200,000)
1		65,000		65,000
2		70,000	(3,000)	67,000
3		75,000	(6,500)	68,500
4	20,000	98,000	(9,375)	108,625
5			(6,725)	(6,725)

Year	Net cash flows (£)	10% discount factor	Present value (£)
0	(200,000)	1.000	(200,000)
1	65,000	0.909	59,085
2	67,000	0.826	55,342
3	68,500	0.751	51,444
4	108,625	0.683	74,191
5	(6,725)	0.621	(4,176)
		Net present value	35,886

7.2.5 Can taxation be ignored?

If an investment project is found to be viable using the net present value method, introducing tax liabilities on profits is unlikely to change the decision, even if these liabilities are paid one year in arrears (Scarlett 1993, 1995). Project viability can be affected, however, if the profit on which tax liability is calculated is different from the cash flows generated by the project. This situation arises when capital allowances are introduced into the evaluation, although it has been noted that the effect on project viability is still only a small one. The effect is amplified under inflationary conditions since capital allowances are based on historical investment costs and their real value will therefore decline over the life of the project. This decline in the real value of capital allowances is counteracted to some extent, in the case of plant and machinery, by the availability of enhanced first-year capital allowances.

We may conclude our discussion of taxation, therefore, by noting that, while introducing the effects of taxation into investment appraisal makes calculations more complex, it also makes the appraisal more accurate and should lead to better investment decisions.

7.3 INFLATION AND CAPITAL INVESTMENT DECISIONS

Inflation can have a serious effect on capital investment decisions, both by reducing the *real value* of future cash flows and by increasing their *uncertainty*. Future cash flows must be adjusted to take account of any expected inflation in the prices of goods and services and so express them in *nominal* (or money) terms, i.e. in terms of the actual cash amounts to be received or paid in the future. Nominal cash flows are discounted by a nominal cost of capital using the net present value method of investment appraisal.

As an alternative to the nominal approach to dealing with inflation in investment appraisal, it is possible to deflate nominal cash flows by the general rate of inflation and so obtain cash flows expressed in real terms, i.e. with inflation stripped out. These *real* cash flows can then be discounted by a real cost of capital to determine the net present value of the investment project. Whichever method is used, whether nominal terms or real terms, care must be taken to determine and apply the correct rates of inflation to the correct cash flows.

7.3.1 Real and nominal costs of capital

The real cost of capital is obtained from the nominal (or money) cost of capital by removing the effect of inflation. Since:

$$(1 + \text{Nominal cost of capital}) = (1 + \text{Real cost of capital}) \times (1 + \text{Inflation rate})$$

rearranging gives:

$$(1 + \text{Real cost of capital}) = \frac{(1 + \text{Nominal cost of capital})}{(1 + \text{Inflation rate})}$$

For example, if the nominal cost of capital is 15 per cent and the rate of inflation is 9 per cent, the real cost of capital will be 5.5 per cent:

$$(1 + 0.15)/(1 + 0.09) = 1.055$$

7.3.2 General and specific inflation

It is likely that individual costs and prices will inflate at different rates and so individual cash flows will need to be inflated by *specific* rates of inflation. These specific rates will need to be forecast as part of the investment appraisal process. There will also be an expected *general* rate of inflation, calculated, for example, by reference to the **consumer price index (CPI)**, which represents the average increase in consumer prices. The general rate of inflation can be used to deflate a nominal cost of capital to a real cost of capital and to deflate nominal cash flows to real cash flows.

7.3.3 Inflation and working capital

Working capital recovered at the end of a project (Section 7.1.4) will not have the same nominal value as the working capital invested at the start. The nominal value of the invest-ment in working capital needs to be inflated each year in order to maintain its value in real terms. If the inflation rate applicable to working capital is known, we can include in the investment appraisal an annual capital investment equal to the incremental annual increase in the nominal value of working capital. At the end of the project, the full nominal value of the investment in working capital is recovered.

7.3.4 The golden rule for dealing with inflation in investment appraisal

The golden rule is to discount real cash flows with a real cost of capital and to discount nominal cash flows with a nominal cost of capital. Cash flows which have been inflated using either specific or general rates of inflation are nominal cash flows and so should be discounted with a nominal cost of capital. Nominal cash flows may, if desired, be deflated with a general rate of inflation to produce real cash flows, which should then be discounted with a real cost of capital. A little thought will show that the net present value obtained by discounting real cash flows with a real cost of capital is identical to the net present value obtained by discounting nominal cash flows with a nominal cost of capital. After all, the real cost of capital is obtained by deflating the nominal cost of capital by the general rate of inflation and the same rate of inflation is also used to deflate the nominal cash flows to real cash flows.

In reality, while inflation will influence the discount rate used in investment appraisal, it may not be a major factor in investment appraisal decisions.

Example	NPV calculation involving inflation

Thorne plc is planning to sell a new electronic toy. Non-current assets costing £700,000 would be needed, with £500,000 payable at once and the balance payable after one year. Initial investment in working capital of £330,000 would also be needed. Thorne expects that, after four years, the toy will be obsolete and the residual value of the non-current assets will be zero. The project would incur incremental total fixed costs of £545,000 per year at current prices, including annual depreciation of £175,000. Expected sales of the toy are 120,000 units per year at a selling price of £22 per toy and a variable cost of £16 per toy, both in current price terms. Thorne expects the following annual increases because of inflation:

Fixed costs	4 per cent
Selling price	5 per cent
Variable costs	7 per cent
Working capital	7 per cent
General prices	6 per cent

If Thorne's real cost of capital is 7.5 per cent and taxation is ignored, is the project financially acceptable?

Suggested answer

Depreciation is not a cash flow: we must deduct it from total fixed costs to find cash fixed costs:

$$\text{Cash fixed costs per year} = 545,000 - 175,000 = £370,000$$

Inflating by 4 per cent per year:

$$\text{Year 1 cash fixed costs} = 370,000 \times 1.04 = £384,800$$
$$\text{Year 2 cash fixed costs} = 384,800 \times 1.04 = £400,192$$
$$\text{Year 3 cash fixed costs} = 400,192 \times 1.04 = £416,200$$
$$\text{Year 4 cash fixed costs} = 416,200 \times 1.04 = £432,848$$

The contribution per unit is the difference between the selling price and the variable cost per unit, inflated by their respective inflation rates. The nominal net operating cash flow for each year is then the difference between the total contribution and the inflated fixed costs for that year, as shown in Table 7.3.

Table 7.3 Net operating cash flows and net present value for Thorne plc

Year	1	2	3	4
Selling price per unit (£)	23.10	24.25	25.47	26.74
Variable cost per unit (£)	17.12	18.32	19.60	20.97
Contribution per unit (£)	5.98	5.93	5.87	5.77
Contribution per year (£)	717,600	711,600	704,400	692,400
Fixed costs per year (£)	384,800	400,192	416,200	432,848
Net operating cash flow (£)	332,800	311,408	288,200	259,552

Year	0	1	2	3	4
Operating cash flow (£)		332,800	311,408	288,200	259,552
Working capital (£)	(330,000)	(23,100)	(24,717)	(26,447)	404,264
Capital (£)	(500,000)	(200,000)			
Net cash flow (£)	(830,000)	109,700	286,691	261,753	663,816
14% discount factors	1.000	0.877	0.769	0.675	0.592
Present value (£)	(830,000)	96,207	220,465	176,683	392,979

$$\text{NPV} = 96,207 + 220,465 + 176,683 + 392,979 - 830,000 = £56,334$$

Investment in working capital in Year 0 = £330,000
Incremental investment in working capital:

in Year 1 = 330,000 × 1.07 = £353,100, an incremental investment of £23,100
in Year 2 = 353,100 × 1.07 = £377,817, an incremental investment of £24,717
in Year 3 = 377,817 × 1.07 = £404,264, an incremental investment of £26,447
working capital recovered at the end of Year 4 = £404,264

We could deflate the nominal cash flows by the general rate of inflation to give real cash flows and then discount them by Thorne's real cost of capital. It is simpler and quicker to inflate Thorne's real cost of capital into nominal terms and use it to discount our nominal cash flows. Thorne's nominal cost of capital is 1.075 × 1.06 = 1.1395 or 14 per cent.

The nominal (money terms) net present value calculation is given in Table 7.3.

Since the NPV is positive, the project can be recommended on financial grounds. The NPV is not very large however, so we must ensure that forecasts and estimates are as accurate as possible. In particular, a small increase in inflation during the life of the project might make the project uneconomical. Sensitivity analysis (see Section 7.4.1) can be used to determine the key project variables on which success may depend.

7.4 INVESTMENT APPRAISAL AND RISK

While the words *risk* and *uncertainty* tend to be used interchangeably, they do have different meanings. Risk refers to sets of circumstances which can be quantified and to which probabilities can be assigned, for example on the basis of past experience. Uncertainty implies that probabilities cannot be assigned to sets of circumstances. In the context of investment appraisal, risk refers to the business risk of an investment, which increases with the variability of expected returns, rather than to financial risk, which is reflected in a company's weighted average cost of capital since it derives from its capital structure (see Section 9.2). Risk is thus distinct from uncertainty, which increases proportionately with project life. However, the distinction between the two terms has little significance in actual business decisions, as managers are neither completely ignorant nor completely certain about the probabilities of future events, although they may be able to assign probabilities with varying degrees of confidence (Grayson 1967). For this reason, the distinction between risk and uncertainty is usually neglected in the practical context of investment appraisal.

A risk-averse company is concerned about the possibility of receiving a return less than expected, i.e. with *downside risk,* and will therefore want to assess the risk of an investment project. There are several methods of assessing project risk and of incorporating risk into the decision-making process.

7.4.1 Sensitivity analysis

Sensitivity analysis is a way of assessing the risk of an investment project by evaluating how responsive the NPV of the project is to changes in the variables from which it has been calculated. There are several ways this sensitivity can be measured. In one method, each project variable in turn is changed by a set amount, say, 5 per cent, and the NPV is recalculated. Only one variable is changed at a time. Since we are more concerned with downside risk, the 5 per cent change is made to adversely affect the NPV calculation. In another method, the relative amounts by which each project variable would have to change to make the NPV become zero are determined. Again, only one variable is changed at a time.

Both methods of sensitivity analysis give an indication of the *key variables* associated with an investment project. Key or critical variables are those variables where a relatively small change can have a significant adverse effect on project NPV. These variables merit further investigation, for example, to determine the extent to which their values can be relied upon, and their identification will also serve to indicate where management should focus its attention to ensure the success of the proposed investment project.

Both methods suffer from the disadvantage that only one variable at a time can be changed. This implies that all project variables are independent, which is clearly unrealistic. A more fundamental problem is that sensitivity analysis is not really a method of assessing the risk of an investment project at all. This may seem surprising since sensitivity analysis is always included in discussions of investment appraisal and risk, but the method does nothing more than indicate *which* are the key variables. It gives no information as to the *probability of changes* in the key variables, which is the information that would be needed if the risk of the project were to be estimated. If the values of all project variables are certain, a project will have zero risk, even if sensitivity analysis has identified its key variables. In such a case, however, identifying the key variables will still help managers to monitor and control the project to ensure that the desired financial objectives are achieved.

Example | **Application of sensitivity analysis**

Swift has a cost of capital of 12 per cent and plans to invest £7m in a machine with a life of four years. The units produced will have a selling price of £9.20 each and will cost £6 each to make. It is expected that 800,000 units will be sold each year. By how much will each variable have to change to make the NPV zero? What are the key variables for the project?

Suggested answer

The relative change in each project variable that makes the NPV zero can be calculated as:

$$\frac{\text{NPV}}{\text{Present value of cash flows linked to project variable}}$$

Calculating the net present value of the project:

	£
Present value of sales revenue = 9.20 × 800,000 × 3.037 =	22,352,320
Present value of variable costs = 6.00 × 800,000 × 3.037 =	14,577,600
Present value of contribution	7,774,720
Initial investment	7,000,000
Net present value	774,720

We can now calculate the relative change needed in each variable to make the NPV zero.

Initial investment

The NPV becomes zero if the initial investment increases by an absolute amount equal to the NPV (£774,720), which is a relative increase of 11.1 per cent:

$$100 \times (774{,}720/7{,}000{,}000) = 11.1\%$$

Sales price

The relative decrease in sales revenue or selling price per unit that makes the NPV zero is the ratio of the NPV to the present value of sales revenue:

$$100 \times (774{,}720/22{,}352{,}320) = 3.5\%$$

This is an absolute decrease of £9.20 $\times$ 0.035 = 32 pence, so the selling price that makes the NPV zero is 9.20 − 0.32 = £8.88.

Variable cost

Since a decrease of 32 pence in selling price makes the NPV zero, an increase of 32 pence or 5.3 per cent in variable cost will have the same effect. Confirming this:

$$100 \times (774{,}720/4{,}577{,}600) = 5.3\%$$

Sales volume

The relative decrease in sales volume that makes the NPV zero is the ratio of the NPV to the present value of contribution:

$$100 \times (774{,}720/7{,}774{,}720) = 10.0\%$$

This is an absolute decrease of 800,000 $\times$ 0.1 = 80,000 units, so the sales volume that makes the NPV zero is 800,000 − 80,000 = 720,000 units.

Project discount rate

What is the cumulative present value factor that makes the NPV zero? We have:

$$((9.20 - 6.00) \times 800{,}000 \times CPVF) - 7{,}000{,}000 = 0$$

and so:

$$CPVF = 7{,}000{,}000/((9.20 - 6.00) \times 800{,}000) = 2.734$$

Using the table of cumulative present value factors on page 479–80, and looking along the row of values for a life of four years (project life remains constant), we find that 2.734 corresponds to a discount rate of almost exactly 17 per cent, an increase in the discount rate of 5 per cent in *absolute* terms or 41.7 per cent in *relative* terms (100 $\times$ 5/12). Note that this is the method for finding the internal rate of return of an investment project that was described in Section 6.4.

Our sensitivity analysis is summarised in Table 7.4. The project is most sensitive to changes in selling price and variable cost per unit and so these are the key project variables.

Table 7.4 Sensitivity analysis of the proposed investment by Swift

Variable	Change to make NPV zero		Sensitivity
	absolute	relative	
Selling price per unit	−32p	−3.5%	High
Sales volume	−80,000 units	−10.0%	Low
Variable cost per unit	+32p	+5.3%	High
Initial investment	+£774,720	+11.1%	Low
Project discount rate	+5%	+41.7%	Very low

7.4.2 Payback

The payback method discussed earlier (see Section 6.1) is the oldest and most widely used method of explicitly recognising uncertainty in capital investment decisions. It does this by focusing on the near future, thereby emphasising liquidity, and by promoting short-term projects over longer-term (and therefore perhaps riskier) ones. While it may be criticised for its shortcomings as an investment appraisal method, it is harder to criticise *shortening payback* as a way of dealing with risk. After all, since the future cash flows on which both payback and net present value are based are only estimates, it may be sensible to consider whether better advice can be offered by focusing on the near future. Furthermore, the effect of investment on liquidity cannot be ignored, especially by small firms. However, payback has such serious shortcomings as an investment appraisal method that its use as a method of adjusting for risk cannot be recommended.

7.4.3 Conservative forecasts

Also known as the *certainty-equivalents* method, this traditional way of dealing with risk in investment appraisal reduces estimated future cash flows to more conservative values 'just to be on the safe side', then discounts these conservative or risk-free cash flows by a risk-free rate of return.

This approach cannot be recommended. First, such reductions are subjective and may be applied differently between projects. Second, reductions may be anticipated by managers and cash flows increased to compensate for potential reduction before investment projects are submitted for evaluation. Finally, attractive investment opportunities may be rejected due to the focus on pessimistic (conservative) cash flows, especially if further methods of adjusting for risk are subsequently applied.

7.4.4 Risk-adjusted discount rates

It is widely accepted that investors need a return greater than the risk-free rate to compensate for taking on a risky investment; this concept is used in both portfolio theory and the capital asset pricing model (see Chapter 8). The greater the risk attached to future returns, the greater the **risk premium** required. When using discounted cash flow (DCF) investment appraisal methods, the discount rate can be regarded as having two components (Grayson 1967). The first component allows for *time preference* or *liquidity preference*, meaning that investors prefer cash now rather than later and want compensation for being unable to use their cash now. The second component allows for *risk preference*, meaning that investors prefer low-risk to high-risk projects and want compensation (a risk premium) for taking on higher-risk projects. However, it is very difficult to decide on the size of the risk premium to be applied to different investment projects.

One solution is to assign investment projects to *risk classes* and then to discount them using the discount rate selected as appropriate for that class. This solution gives rise to problems with both the assessment of project risk and the determination of appropriate discount rates for the different risk classes. Another solution is to assume that the average risk of a company's investment projects will be similar to the average risk of its current business. In these circumstances a single overall discount rate – typically the company's weighted average cost of capital – can be used.

The use of a risk-adjusted discount rate implicitly assumes *constantly increasing risk* as project life increases. This may accurately reflect the risk profile of an investment project. If, however, the assumption of increasing risk is not appropriate, incorrect decisions may result. There are situations where the use of a *constant risk* allowance could be appropriate, in which case the risk-adjusted discount rate should decline over time. With the launch of a new product, a *higher initial risk premium* may be appropriate, with progressive reduction as the product becomes established.

7.4.5 Probability analysis and expected net present value

So far, we have discussed investment projects with single-point estimates of future cash flows. If instead a probability distribution of expected cash flows can be estimated, it can be used to obtain a mean or *expected net present value*. The risk of an investment project can be examined in more detail by calculating the probability of the worst case and the probability of failing to achieve a positive NPV. Probability analysis is increasing in popularity as a method of assessing the risk of investment projects (see 'Risk analysis', Section 7.6.3).

In its simplest form, a probability distribution may consist of estimates of the probabilities of the best, most likely and worst cases, as follows:

Forecast	Probability	Net present value
Best case	0.2	£30,000
Most likely case	0.7	£20,000
Worst case	0.1	£10,000

Calculating the mean or expected net present value (ENPV):

$$(0.2 \times 30{,}000) + (0.7 \times 20{,}000) + (0.1 \times 10{,}000) = £21{,}000$$

It is argued that this approach may give more useful information than single-point NPV estimates, but we should note that the single-point estimates are future states that are expected to occur, while the ENPV, being a mean or average value, does *not* represent an expected future state. Calculations of the probability of the worst case and of the probability of failing to achieve a positive NPV are illustrated in the example below.

The probabilities being discussed here are the probability estimates made by managers based on the project data available to them. While such estimates are subjective, this is not grounds for their rejection, since they only make explicit the assessments of the likelihood of future events which are made by expert managers in the normal course of business.

Example | Calculating expected net present value

Star has a cost of capital of 12 per cent and is evaluating a project with an initial investment of £375,000. The estimated net cash flows of the project under different economic circumstances and their respective probabilities are as follows:

Net cash flows for Year 1

Economic conditions	Probability	Cash flow (£)
Weak	0.2	100,000
Moderate	0.5	200,000
Good	0.3	300,000

Net cash flows for Year 2

Economic conditions	Probability	Cash flow (£)
Moderate	0.7	250,000
Good	0.3	350,000

If economic conditions in Year 2 are not dependent on economic conditions in Year 1, what is the expected value of the project's NPV? What is the risk that the NPV will be negative?

Suggested answer

The first step is to calculate the present values of each individual cash flow.

Year	Economic conditions	Cash flow (£000)	12% discount factor	Present value (£000)
1	Weak	100	0.893	89.3
1	Moderate	200	0.893	178.6
1	Good	300	0.893	267.9
2	Moderate	250	0.797	199.2
2	Good	350	0.797	279.0

The next step is to calculate the *total* present value of the cash flows of each *combination* of Year 1 and Year 2 economic conditions by adding their present values.

Year 1		Year 2		Overall
Economic conditions	Present value of cash flow (£000)	Economic conditions	Present value of cash flow (£000)	Total present value of cash flow (£000)
Weak	89.3	Moderate	199.2	288.5
Weak	89.3	Good	279.0	368.3
Moderate	178.6	Moderate	199.2	377.8
Moderate	178.6	Good	279.0	457.6
Good	267.9	Moderate	199.2	467.1
Good	267.9	Good	279.0	546.9

The total present value of the cash flows of each combination of economic conditions is now multiplied by the *joint probability* of each combination of economic conditions, and these values are then added to give the expected present value of the cash flows of the project.

Total present value of cash flow (£000)	Year 1 probability	Year 2 probability	Joint probability	Expected present value of cash flows (£000)
A	B	C	D = B × C	A × D
288.5	0.2	0.7	0.14	40.4
368.3	0.2	0.3	0.06	22.1
377.8	0.5	0.7	0.35	132.2
457.6	0.5	0.3	0.15	68.6
467.1	0.3	0.7	0.21	98.1
546.9	0.3	0.3	0.09	49.2
				410.6

	£
Expected present value of cash inflows	410,600
Less: Initial investment	375,000
Mean or expected value of NPV	35,600

The probability that the project will have a negative NPV is the probability that the total present value of the cash flows is less than £375,000. Using the column in the table headed 'Total present value of cash flow' and picking out values less than £375,000, we can see that the probability that the project will have a negative NPV is 0.14 + 0.06 = 0.20, or 20 per cent.

7.4.6 Simulation models

It is possible to improve the decision-making process involving the calculation of NPV by estimating probability distributions for each project variable. Sensitivity analysis changes one project variable at a time, but some of the project variables, for example selling price and market share, may be interdependent. A simulation model can be used to determine, by repeated analysis, how simultaneous changes in more than one variable may influence the expected net present value. The procedure is to assign random numbers to ranges of values in the probability distribution for each project variable. A computer then generates a set of random numbers and uses these to randomly select a value for each variable. The NPV of that set of variables is then calculated. The computer repeats the process many times and builds up a frequency distribution of the NPV. From this frequency distribution, the expected NPV and its standard deviation can be determined. Spreadsheet software and cheap computing power have combined to make this approach more accessible for investment appraisal.

This simulation technique does not give investment advice. From a corporate finance point of view, managers must still decide whether an investment is acceptable, or whether it is preferable to a mutually exclusive alternative. They will be able to consider both the return of the investment (its expected ENPV) and the risk of the investment (the standard deviation of the expected NPV). The rational decision (see 'Investor attitudes to risk', Section 8.3) would be to prefer the investment with the highest return for a given level of risk or with the lowest risk for a given level of return.

7.5 APPRAISAL OF FOREIGN DIRECT INVESTMENT

Foreign direct investment is a long-term investment in a country other than that of the investing company, where the investing company has control over the business invested in. The main example of such an investment is the setting up or purchase of a foreign subsidiary.

7.5.1 The distinctive features of foreign direct investment

Foreign direct investment decisions are not conceptually different from domestic investment decisions and can be evaluated using the same investment appraisal techniques, such as the net present value method. However, foreign direct investment decisions do have some distinctive features which make their evaluation more difficult:

- project cash flows will need to be evaluated in a foreign currency;
- exchange rate movements create currency risk, which may need hedging;
- the foreign taxation system may differ from the domestic taxation system;
- project cash flows and parent company cash flows will be different;
- remittance of project cash flows may be restricted;
- the investment decision can be evaluated from more than one point of view.

7.5.2 Methods of evaluating foreign direct investment

The financial evaluation of foreign direct investment proposals can help to eliminate poor projects, check whether marketing assumptions are valid, and give an indication as to the amount and type of finance needed. The academically preferred method of evaluating foreign direct investment proposals is the net present value method, since shareholder wealth will be increased by the selection of projects with a positive net present value. This also suggests that, as it is shareholders of the parent company whose wealth is of paramount importance, it is the NPV of the after-tax cash flows remitted to the parent company that should be used to judge the financial acceptability of a foreign direct investment proposal. We should note, however, that evaluation at the level of the host country is also possible.

7.5.3 Evaluation of foreign direct investment at local level

A foreign direct investment project can be evaluated in local terms and in local currencies, for example, by comparing it with similar undertakings in the host country. This evaluation ignores the extent to which cash flows can be remitted back to the parent company and also ignores the overall value of the project to parent company shareholders. Whether foreign direct investment is evaluated at local level or parent company level, local currency project cash flows need to be determined, however. These project cash flows can be classified as follows:

Initial investment

This will be the outlay on non-current assets such as land, buildings, plant and machinery. Funding for this may be from an issue of equity or debt, and debt finance may be raised locally or from the parent company. The initial outlay may include transfer of assets such as plant and equipment, in which case transferred assets should be valued at the opportunity cost to the parent company.

Investment in working capital

This may be part of the initial investment or may occur during the start-up period as the project establishes itself in operational terms. Investment in working capital may be achieved in part by transfer of inventories of components or part-finished goods from the parent company.

Local after-tax cash flows

These cash flows will be the difference between cash received from sales and any local operating costs for materials and labour, less local taxation on profits. Interest payments may need to be deducted in determining taxable profit to the extent that the investment is financed by locally raised debt, such as loans from local banks or other financial institutions. One difficulty will be the treatment of goods provided by the parent company, when the price charged to the subsidiary (**transfer price**) must be seen by local taxation authorities as a fair one. In cash-flow terms, such transferred goods will be an operating cost at local level but a source of revenue to the parent company and will have tax implications at both levels.

The terminal value of the project

A **terminal value** for the project will need to be calculated, either because the evaluation will be cut short for ease of analysis or because it is expected that the parent company's interest in the foreign direct investment will cease at some future date, for example, through sale of the subsidiary. The expected market value of the subsidiary at the end of the parent company's planning horizon is one possible terminal value.

Even though evaluating the investment project solely in terms of the cash flows accruing in the foreign country (the local level) may indicate that it is financially acceptable, making a decision to invest on these grounds may be incorrect. The NPV of the project to the parent company depends on the future cash flows which can be remitted. If remittance of funds to the parent company is restricted, this value may be reduced. The effect of the project on existing cash flows, for example, existing export sales, must also be considered.

7.5.4 Evaluation of foreign direct investment at parent company level

At the parent company level, project cash flows will be the actual cash receipts and payments in the parent company's own currency, together with any incremental changes in the parent company's existing cash flows. These project cash flows are as follows:

Initial investment

This will consist of cash that has been invested by the parent company and may be in the form of debt or equity. It will also include transferred plant and equipment at opportunity cost. It may be the price paid to take over or acquire a foreign company.

Returns on investment

The parent company will receive dividends from the project and, if debt finance has been provided, interest payments and repayment of principal.

Receipts from intercompany trade

The parent company may receive cash payments in exchange for goods and services provided to the project. Goods sold to the project will generate income based on agreed transfer prices. Royalties may be received on patents. Management fees may be received for the services of experienced personnel.

Accumulated contributions

If remittances have been subject to exchange controls, the parent company will at some point receive accumulated (accrued) cash, perhaps at the end of the project.

Taxation

Cash flows remitted to the parent company will be liable to taxation under the domestic tax system. Tax relief may be given at parent company level for tax paid overseas.

Cash flows from the foreign direct investment will need to be converted into the home currency, which means that exchange rates will need to be forecast over the life of the project, probably from forecast differences in inflation rates between home country and host country using purchasing power parity theory (Buckley 2012). A further problem (see 'The cost of capital for foreign direct investment', Section 9.7) is that an appropriate discount rate for the project will need to be determined.

Example	Foreign direct investment evaluation

WK plc is a UK company which plans to set up a manufacturing subsidiary in the small country of Parland, whose currency is the dollar. An initial investment of $5m in plant and machinery is needed. Initial investment in working capital of $500,000 would be financed by a loan from a local bank, at an annual interest rate of 10 per cent per year. At the end of five years, the subsidiary would be sold as a going concern for $12m and part of the proceeds would be used to pay off the bank loan.

The subsidiary is expected to produce net cash flows from operations of $3m per year in current price terms over the five-year period, before allowing for Parland inflation of 8 per cent per year. Capital allowances on the initial investment in plant and machinery are available on a straight-line basis at 20 per cent per year. As a result of setting up the subsidiary, WK plc expects to lose after-tax export income from Parland of £80,000 per year in current price terms, before allowing for UK inflation of 3 per cent per year.

Profits in Parland are taxed at a rate of 20 per cent after interest and capital allowances. All after-tax cash profits are remitted to the UK at the end of each year. UK tax of 24 per cent is charged on UK profits, but a tax treaty between Parland and the UK allows tax paid in Parland to be set off against any UK liability. Taxation is paid in the year in which the liability arises. WK plc requires foreign investments to be discounted at 15 per cent. The current exchange rate is $2.50/£1 and the dollar is expected to depreciate against sterling by 5 per cent per year.

Should WK plc undertake the investment in Parland?

Suggested answer

Initial investment in Parland		= $5,000,000
Annual capital allowance	$5,000,000 × 0.2	= $1,000,000
Annual interest payment	$500,000 × 0.1	= $50,000

The calculation of the subsidiary's cash flows is given in Table 7.5. The net cash flows from operations have been inflated by 8 per cent per year. Note that a separate tax calculation has not been carried out: instead, capital allowances have been deducted

Table 7.5 Calculating the project cash flows for WK plc's subsidiary in Parland

Year	0 ($000)	1 ($000)	2 ($000)	3 ($000)	4 ($000)	5 ($000)
Cash flows from operations		3,240	3,499	3,779	4,081	4,408
Capital allowances		(1,000)	(1,000)	(1,000)	(1,000)	(1,000)
Interest		(50)	(50)	(50)	(50)	(50)
Profit before tax		2,190	2,449	2,729	3,031	3,358
Local tax		(438)	(490)	(546)	(606)	(672)
Profit after tax		1,752	1,959	2,183	2,425	2,686
Add back CAs		1,000	1,000	1,000	1,000	1,000
		2,752	2,959	3,183	3,425	3,686
Initial investment	(5,000)					
Working capital	(500)	(40)	(43)	(47)	(50)	(54)
Loan capital	500					(500)
Sale of subsidiary						12,000
Project cash flows	(5,000)	2,712	2,916	3,136	3,375	15,132

from net cash flows from operations to give taxable profit and then added back to after-tax profit to give after-tax cash flows. The capital allowances must be added back because they are not cash flows. Note also that, as the subsidiary is sold as a going concern, working capital is not recovered.

The first step to determining the acceptability of the project to WK plc is to translate the remitted cash flows into sterling. The exchange rates have been increased by 5 per cent each year because the dollar is expected to depreciate against sterling by 5 per cent per year. UK tax payable on the sterling cash flows has been calculated by applying the UK tax rate to the profit before tax of the Parland subsidiary and then deducting local tax paid, as follows:

Year 1 taxable profit ($) = 2,190,000
Year 1 taxable profit (£) = 2,190,000/2.63 = 832,700
UK tax liability = 832,700 × 0.24 = £199,848
Local tax paid = 832,700 × 0.20 = £166,540
UK tax payable = 199,848 − 166,540 = £33,308

This calculation is repeated for subsequent years, bearing in mind that the exchange rate changes each year. After incorporating the after-tax value of the lost export sales, the parent company cash flows and their present values can be determined, as shown in Table 7.6.

We have:

NPV = − 2,000,000 + 797,000 + 708,000 + 628,000 + 560,000 + 2,291,000
= £2,984,000

At the parent company level, the NPV is strongly positive and so the project should be accepted. The following observations can be made:

Table 7.6 Calculating the project cash flows and present values for WK plc's subsidiary at parent company level

Year	0	1	2	3	4	5
Project cash flows ($000)	(5,000)	2,712	2,916	3,136	3,375	15,132
Exchange rate ($/£)	2.50	2.63	2.76	2.90	3.04	3.19
	(£000)	(£000)	(£000)	(£000)	(£000)	(£000)
UK cash received	(2,000)	1,031	1,057	1,081	1,110	4,744
UK tax		(33)	(36)	(38)	(40)	(42)
	(2,000)	998	1,021	1,043	1,070	4,702
Lost exports after tax		(82)	(85)	(88)	(91)	(93)
Parent cash flows	(2,000)	916	936	955	979	4,609
15% discount factors	1.000	0.870	0.756	0.658	0.572	0.497
Present values	(2,000)	797	708	628	560	2,291

■ The evaluation assumes that both sales volume and inflation rates are constant over the five-year period, but in reality these will change due to market forces. Is it possible to forecast these project variables more accurately?
■ The discount rate of 15 per cent must be justified. Has the risk of the project been taken into account in calculating the discount rate?
■ Are there any benefits that are non-financial in nature or that are difficult to quantify which have not been included in the evaluation, for example, the existence of '**real options**', like the possibility of continuing in production with different products rather than selling the business to a third party?

7.5.5 Taxation and foreign direct investment

The taxation systems of the host country and the home country are likely to be different. If profits were subjected to tax in both countries, i.e. if *double taxation* existed, there would be a strong disincentive to investment. *Double taxation relief* is usually available, either by treaty between two countries or on a unilateral basis, whereby relief is given for tax paid abroad on income received. The net effect of a double taxation treaty is that the parent company will pay *in total* the higher of local tax or domestic tax on profits generated by the foreign subsidiary. Taxes paid abroad will not affect the total amount of tax paid but will affect the division of tax between the two countries. If the local tax rate is greater than the domestic tax rate, no domestic tax is paid.

For calculation purposes, the UK tax liability can be found from the taxable profits of the foreign subsidiary. This is easier than grossing up receipts from foreign investments and avoids the possibility of wrongly assessing capital cash flows to profit tax. The UK tax liability can then be reduced by any tax already paid in the foreign country to give the UK tax payable.

7.6 EMPIRICAL INVESTIGATIONS OF INVESTMENT APPRAISAL

There have been many studies that help to build up a picture of the investment appraisal methods actually used by companies, such as Pike (1983, 1996), McIntyre and Coulthurst (1986), Lapsley (1986), Drury et al. (1993), Arnold and Hatzopoulos (2000), Ryan and Ryan (2002), Verbeeten (2006) and Burns and Walker (2009). Their findings can be summarised as follows:

- While for many years payback was the most commonly used investment appraisal method, DCF methods now appear to be more popular.
- In large organisations, payback is used in conjunction with other investment appraisal methods. In smaller organisations, using payback as the sole investment appraisal method continues to decline.
- Internal rate of return is more popular than net present value in small companies, but net present value is now the most popular investment appraisal method in large companies.
- Using experience and qualitative judgement is an important complement to quantitative methods.
- Although return on capital employed is the least popular investment appraisal method, it continues to be used in conjunction with other methods.
- Companies tend not to use sophisticated methods to account for project risk.
- Where companies do take account of risk, sensitivity analysis is most often used.
- Research has focused on the selection stage of the capital budgeting process.

We have noted that the academically preferred approach is to use DCF methods, with net present value being preferred to internal rate of return. This conclusion is rooted in the fact that DCF methods take account of both the time value of money and corporate risk preferences. Earlier cash flows are discounted less heavily than more distant ones, while risk can be incorporated by applying a higher discount rate to more risky projects. There are a number of drawbacks with the payback and return on capital employed methods (as discussed earlier in Chapter 6).

7.6.1 Investment appraisal techniques used

Drury et al. (1993) found that payback was the most frequently used investment appraisal technique, followed by net present value and accounting rate of return, with internal rate of return the least popular. In contrast, Arnold and Hatzopoulos (2000) found that net present value and internal rate of return were almost equal in overall popularity, with both being more popular than payback, indicating that the gap between theory and practice in investment appraisal methods had diminished.

A similar change can be noted in the relative preferences of small and large companies for different investment appraisal methods. Drury et al. (1993) found that larger companies tended to prefer DCF methods to payback and accounting rate of return, with 90 per cent of larger companies using at least one DCF method compared with 35 per cent of smaller companies; smaller companies preferred payback. Arnold and Hatzopoulos (2000) found that acceptance of DCF methods by small companies had increased, with internal rate of return being more popular than payback, and that large companies preferred internal rate of return to payback.

Drury et al. (1993) found that only 14 per cent of all companies used payback alone and suggested that, after using payback as an initial screening device to select suitable projects, companies then subjected those projects to a more thorough screening using net present value or internal rate of return. Arnold and Hatzopoulos (2000) found that 68 per cent of all companies used payback in conjunction with one or more investment appraisal methods. They also found that 90 per cent of companies used two or more investment appraisal methods.

Why should most companies use multiple investment appraisal methods? One possible explanation is that using multiple evaluation techniques may reinforce the justification for the decision and increase the feeling of security or comfort derived from the use of analytical investment appraisal methods (Kennedy and Sugden 1986). Another possible explanation is that evaluating investment projects from several different perspectives compensates for the breakdown of some of the assumptions of the net present value method in real-world situations (Arnold and Hatzopoulos 2000). There appears to be little difference between US and European capital budgeting practices (Burns and Walker 2009, citing Brounen et al. 2004).

7.6.2 The treatment of inflation

It is important to account for inflation in the investment appraisal process to prevent sub-optimal decisions being made. The techniques to deal with the problem of inflation discussed earlier are:

- using nominal discount rates to discount nominal cash flows that have been adjusted to take account of expected future inflation (nominal-terms approach);
- using real discount rates to discount real cash flows (real-terms approach).

Drury et al. (1993) found that most companies discounted unadjusted cash flows using a nominal discount rate and that, overall, only one quarter of all companies allowed for inflation using a theoretically correct method. The findings of this survey were consistent with those of earlier surveys, which indicated that most companies did not account for inflation in the investment appraisal process in an appropriate manner. In contrast, Arnold and Hatzopoulos (2000) reported that 81 per cent of companies correctly accounted for inflation in investment appraisal, lending support to their overall conclusion that the gap between theory and practice in capital budgeting had narrowed.

7.6.3 Risk analysis

It is generally agreed (see Section 7.4) that risk should be considered in the capital investment process and that project risk should be reflected in the discount rate. Prior to the 1970s, companies took account of risk by shortening the target payback period or by using conservative cash flows. Some companies used probability analysis and simulation. These models address the risk attached to future cash flows, but give no guidance on selecting an appropriate discount rate. This problem is addressed by the capital asset pricing model (see Chapter 8), which enables the systematic risk of a project to be considered and reflected in an appropriate discount rate.

Drury et al. (1993) found a very low level of use of the more sophisticated methods of allowing for risk, with 63 per cent of companies either very unlikely to use probability analysis or never having used it at all, and with more than 95 per cent of companies rejecting simulation and the use of the capital asset pricing model. The most popular approach, they found, was sensitivity analysis, used by 82 per cent of companies surveyed. Similar results were reported by Arnold and Hatzopoulos (2000), who found that 85 per cent of all companies used sensitivity analysis and that very few companies used the capital asset pricing model. They did find, however, that 31 per cent of companies used probability analysis; the increased use of this technique perhaps being a consequence of the widespread availability of information technology. The need for further research into the low usage of sophisticated risk analysis methods such as Monte Carlo analysis (simulation) was noted by Burns and Walker (2009).

7.6.4 Foreign direct investment

Several empirical studies of international investment appraisal have been summarised by Demirag and Goddard (1994), Kim and Ulferts (1996) and Buckley (2003). The evidence suggests that, rather than using NPV alone, companies evaluate international decisions using a range of different methods. We can summarise the main findings as follows:

- Most multinational companies use discounted cash flow (DCF) methods of investment appraisal as the primary method for evaluating foreign investment projects, with internal rate of return being preferred to net present value.
- Use of DCF investment appraisal methods does not seem to have increased in recent years.
- A large proportion of companies do not use after-tax cash flows to the parent company as the main measure of income in the evaluation.
- A number of companies appear to base the required rate of return for foreign investment decisions on the cost of debt.
- Smaller firms tend to use less sophisticated investment appraisal methods such as return on capital employed and payback.

The divergence between the methods used by companies and the methods recommended by theory is worth noting.

7.6.5 Conclusions of empirical investigations

We can conclude that most companies use a combination of investment appraisal techniques and that there are differences between the practices of small and large companies, although these differences are not great. Most companies now deal with inflation correctly, removing possible distortions in DCF calculations and resulting in better investment decisions. Companies were found to be more likely to use simple approaches to dealing with risk such as sensitivity analysis than theoretically correct methods such as the capital asset pricing model. There are differences between theory and practice in relation to appraisal of foreign direct investment.

7.7 CONCLUSION

In this chapter we have considered some of the problems in evaluating 'real-world' investment projects, including the difficulties in allowing for the effects of taxation and inflation. We have considered the need to take account of project risk in the investment appraisal process and examined different ways by which this has been attempted. Some of these methods were found to be more successful than others. We considered the specific difficulties arising with evaluation of foreign direct investment. We concluded our discussion by considering empirical research on investment appraisal methods used by companies in the real world, noting that the gap between theory and practice appears to be diminishing.

■ ■ ■ KEY POINTS

1 Only relevant cash flows, which are the incremental cash flows arising as the result of an investment decision, should be included in investment appraisal. Relevant cash flows include opportunity costs and incremental investment in working capital.

2 Non-relevant cash flows, such as sunk costs and apportioned fixed costs, must be excluded from the investment appraisal.

3 Tax relief for capital expenditure is given through capital allowances, which are a matter of government policy and depend on the type of asset for which allowances are claimed.

4 Tax liability is reduced by expenses that can be deducted from revenue in calculating taxable profit. Relief for such expenses is given by allowing them to be deducted in full.

5 Taxation does not alter the viability of simple projects unless taxable profit is different from the cash flows generated by the project.

6 Inflation can have a serious effect on investment decisions by reducing the real value of future cash flows and by increasing their uncertainty.

7 Inflation can be included in investment appraisal by discounting nominal cash flows by a nominal cost of capital or by discounting real cash flows by a real cost of capital.

8 The real cost of capital can be found by deflating the nominal cost of capital by the general rate of inflation.

9 Both specific and general inflation need to be considered in investment appraisal.

10 Risk refers to situations where the probabilities of future events are known. Uncertainty refers to circumstances where the probabilities of future events are not known.

11 Sensitivity analysis examines how responsive the NPV of a project is to changes in the variables from which it has been calculated.

12 One problem with sensitivity analysis is that only one variable can be changed at a time, but real-world project variables are unlikely to be independent.

13 Sensitivity analysis identifies key project variables but does not indicate the probability that they will change. For this reason, it is not a method of assessing project risk.

14 Payback reduces risk and uncertainty by focusing on the near future and by promoting short-term projects.

15 Conservative forecasts can be criticised because they are subjective, because they may be applied inconsistently and because cash-flow reductions may be anticipated.

16 Despite difficulties in assessing project risk and determining risk premiums, risk-adjusted discounted rates are a preferred way of incorporating risk into investment appraisal.

17 Probability analysis can be used to find the expected (mean) NPV of a project, the probability of the worst case NPV and the probability of a negative NPV.

18 Simulation can generate a frequency distribution of the NPV, the expected NPV and its standard deviation.

19 NPV at parent company level should be used to evaluate foreign direct investment.

20 While taxation systems of countries may differ, double taxation relief is usually available.

21 Research has shown that DCF methods are now the most common investment appraisal techniques, often used in conjunction with other methods.

22 Companies tend to use simple approaches to risk, such as sensitivity analysis, rather than sophisticated methods.

23 The majority of companies correctly account for inflation in investment appraisal.

SELF-TEST QUESTIONS

Answers to these questions can be found on pages 460–1.

1 Discuss which cash flows are relevant to investment appraisal calculations.

2 Explain the difference between the nominal-terms approach and the real-terms approach to dealing with inflation in investment appraisal.

3 Explain whether general inflation or specific inflation should be included in investment appraisal.

4 Explain the difference between risk and uncertainty.

5 Discuss how sensitivity analysis helps managers to assess the risk of an investment project.

6 Why is payback commonly used as a way of dealing with risk in investment projects?

7 Discuss the use of risk-adjusted discount rates in evaluating investment projects.

8 Explain the meaning of 'simulation' in the context of investment appraisal.

9 How do foreign direct investment decisions differ from domestic investment decisions?

10 Discuss whether all companies use the same investment appraisal methods.

QUESTIONS FOR REVIEW

1 Logar plc is considering buying a machine which will increase sales by £110,000 per year for a period of five years. At the end of the five-year period, the machine will be scrapped. Relevant financial information on two machines being considered is as follows:

	Machine A	Machine B
Initial cost (£)	200,000	250,000
Labour cost (£ per year)	10,000	7,000
Power cost (£ per year)	9,000	4,000
Scrap value (£)	nil	25,000

The following average annual rates of inflation are expected:

Sales prices	6 per cent per year
Labour costs	5 per cent per year
Power costs	3 per cent per year

Logar pays corporation tax of 30 per cent one year in arrears and has a nominal after-tax cost of capital of 15 per cent. Capital allowances are available on a 25 per cent reducing balance basis.

Advise Logar on the choice of machine.

2 Mr Smart has £75,000 invested in relatively risk-free assets returning 10 per cent per year. He has been approached by a friend with an idea for a business venture. This would take the whole of the £75,000. Market research has revealed that it is not possible to be exact about the returns of the project, but that the following can be inferred from the study:
   − There is a 20 per cent chance that returns will be £10,000 per year.
   − There is a 60 per cent chance that returns will be £30,000 per year.
   − There is a 20 per cent chance that returns will be £50,000 per year.
   − If returns are £10,000 per year, there is a 60 per cent chance that the life of the project will be five years and a 40 per cent chance that it will be seven years.

- If returns are £30,000 per year, there is a 50 per cent chance that the life of the project will be five years and a 50 per cent chance that it will be seven years.
- If returns are £50,000 per year, there is a 40 per cent chance that the life of the project will be five years and a 60 per cent chance that it will be seven years. Assume that cash flows occur at the end of each year.

(a) Calculate the worst likely return and the best likely return on the project, along with the probabilities of these events happening.

(b) Calculate the expected net present value of the investment.

3 Bing plc is evaluating the purchase of a machine and has the following information:

Initial investment	£350,000
Residual value	nil
Expected life	10 years
Sales volume	20,000 units per year
Sales price	£8.50 per unit
Variable cost	£3.50 per unit
Fixed costs	£24,875 per year
Cost of capital	15 per cent

(a) Calculate the internal rate of return of the project.

(b) Assess the sensitivity of the net present value to a change in project life.

(c) Assess the sensitivity of the net present value to a change in sales price.

4 Scot plc is planning to invest in Glumrovia and because it is risky to invest there the company will require an after-tax return of at least 20 per cent on the project.

Market research suggests that cash flows from the project in the local currency (the dollar) will be as follows:

Year	1	2	3	4	5
$000	250	450	550	650	800

The current exchange rate is $3.00/£1; in subsequent years it is expected to be:

Year	1	2	3	4	5
$/£	4.00	5.00	6.00	7.00	8.00

The project will cost $600,000 to set up, but the Glumrovian government will pay $600,000 to Scot plc for the business at the end of the five-year period. It will also lend Scot plc the $250,000 required for initial working capital at the advantageous rate of 6 per cent per year, to be repaid at the end of the five-year period.

Scot plc will pay Glumrovian tax on the after-interest profits at the rate of 20 per cent, while UK tax is payable at the rate of 30 per cent per year. All profits are remitted at the end of each year. There is a double taxation treaty between the two countries. Tax in both countries is paid in the year in which profits arise.

(a) Calculate the net present value of the project and advise on its acceptability.

(b) Discuss the possible problems that might confront a company making the type of decision facing Scot plc.

5 Brinpool plc has been invited to build a factory in the small state of Gehell by the government of that country. The local currency is the Ked (K) and data on current and expected exchange rates are as follows:

Year	0	1	2	3	4	5
K/£	3.50	4.00	4.40	4.70	4.90	5.00

Initial investment will be K250,000 for equipment, payable in sterling, and K1m for working capital. Working capital will be financed by a local loan at 10 per cent per year, repayable in full after five years. Gehell's government has also expressed a wish to acquire the factory from Brinpool plc as a going concern after five years and has offered K4.2m in compensation. Their loan would be repaid from the compensation payment.

Brinpool plc estimates that cash profits will be K3m per year, but also expects to lose current annual export sales to Gehell of £50,000 after tax. All after-tax cash profits are remitted to the UK at the end of each year.

Profits in Gehell are taxed at a rate of 15 per cent after interest and capital allowances, which are available on the £1.5m initial investment on a straight-line basis at a rate of 20 per cent per year. UK taxation of 30 per cent is charged on UK profits and a double taxation agreement exists between Gehell and the UK. Taxation is paid in the year in which it arises.

Brinpool plc feels that, due to the political risk of Gehell, it should apply a cost of capital of 18 per cent.

Advise whether the proposed investment is financially acceptable to Brinpool plc.

QUESTIONS FOR DISCUSSION

1 DK plc is evaluating the purchase of a freeze dryer. Packets of frozen food will be sold in boxes of eight and the following information applies to each box:

	£ per box
Selling price	9.70
Packaging and labour	2.20
Frozen food and processing	4.80

The selling price and cost of the frozen food are expected to increase by 6 per cent per year, while packaging and labour costs are expected to increase by 5 per cent per year. Investment in working capital will increase by £90,000 at the start of the first year and by 4 per cent per year in subsequent years. The freeze dryer will have a useful life of five years before being scrapped, the net cost of disposal being £18,000. Sales in the first year are expected to be 80,000 boxes, but sales in the second and subsequent years will be 110,000 boxes.

The freeze dryer will cost £1m, with 60 per cent to be paid initially and the 40 per cent to be paid one year later. The company's nominal cost of capital is 14 per cent. Ignore taxation.

(a) Assess whether DK plc should invest in the freeze dryer.

(b) Explain the choice of discount rate used in part (a).

2 R plc plans to invest £1m in new machinery to produce Product GF. Advertising costs in the first two years of production would be £70,000 per year and quality control costs would be 3 per cent of sales revenue.

Sales revenue from Product GF would be £975,000 per year and production costs would be £500,000 per year. Both sales revenue and production costs are at current prices and annual inflation is expected to be as follows:

Sales revenue inflation	4 per cent per year
Production cost inflation	5 per cent per year
General inflation	3 per cent per year

Initial investment in working capital of £80,000 will be made and this investment will rise in line with general inflation. At the end of four years, production of Product GF will cease.

Capital allowances on the initial investment in machinery are available on a 25 per cent reducing balance basis. The equipment used to make Product GF is expected to have a scrap value of £50,000. R plc pays profit tax at a rate of 30 per cent per year and has a real weighted average after-tax cost of capital of 8.7 per cent.

(a) Calculate the net present value of investing in production of Product GF. Show all your workings and explain clearly any assumptions you make.

(b) Calculate the sensitivity of the net present value of investing in production of Product GF to a change in selling price.

(c) Explain the difference between risk and uncertainty in relation to investment appraisal, and discuss the usefulness of sensitivity analysis as a way of assessing the risk of investment projects.

3 Ring plc is evaluating the purchase of a machine to produce Product MP3, to which the following information applies:

	£ per box
Selling price	11.00
Packaging and production	3.00
Components	5.50

Incremental fixed costs will be £25,000 per year. The machine will cost £850,000 and will last for four years. At the end of four years it is expected to have a scrap value of £40,000. Additional initial investment in working capital of £80,000 will be required. Annual sales of 150,000 units per year of Product MP3 are expected.

Ring plc has a nominal cost of capital of 10 per cent and a real cost of capital of 7 per cent. Taxation may be ignored.

(a) Calculate the net present value of the proposed investment and the sensitivity of this net present value to changes in the following project variables:
   (i) selling price;
   (ii) variable costs;
   (iii) sales volume.

Comment on your findings. Ignore inflation in this part of the question.

(b) Further investigation reveals that the proposed investment will be subject to the following specific inflation rates:
   (i) Selling price: 4 per cent
   (ii) Variable costs: 4 per cent

(iii) Fixed costs: 5 per cent

(iv) Working capital: 4 per cent

Calculate the net present value of the proposed investment using a nominal (money) terms approach.

(c) Briefly discuss ways in which the evaluation in part (b) could be improved to support better decision-making.

4 GZ plc plans to build a factory in the USA for $3.4m. Additional investment in working capital of $500,000 would be needed and this would be financed by a loan from a US bank of $500,000. Annual before-tax cash flows of $1m per year in current price terms would be expected from the sale of goods made in the new factory.

Tax in the USA would be at a concessionary rate of 15 per cent per year for a period of five years, which is also the planning horizon used by GZ plc. The company can claim capital allowances on the investment of $3.4m on a 25 per cent reducing balance basis. Tax in the UK is at an annual rate of 30 per cent per year. A double taxation agreement exists between the two countries and tax liabilities are paid in the year in which they arise in both the USA and the UK. The current exchange rate is $1.70/£ and the US dollar is expected to depreciate against sterling by 5 per cent per year.

GZ plc has a nominal after-tax cost of capital of 15 per cent. Annual inflation in the USA is expected to be 3 per cent per year for the foreseeable future. At the end of its five-year planning horizon, GZ plc expects the US factory to have a nominal market value of $5m.

(a) Calculate whether GZ plc should build the factory in the USA.

(b) Calculate and discuss whether $5m is an acceptable estimate of the market value of the factory in five years' time.

5 Ice plc has decided to expand sales in Northland because of pressure in its domestic market. It is evaluating two alternative expansion proposals.

Proposal 1

Ice plc could increase production from an existing UK site. This would require initial investment of £750,000 and give export sales worth £280,000 per year before tax.

Proposal 2

Ice plc could build a factory in Northland at a cost of N$2.7m. Annual sales from the factory would initially be N$1m before tax, but these are expected to increase each year. The rate of increase each year will depend on economic conditions in Northland, as follows:

Economic conditions in Northland	Good	Moderate	Poor
Probability of these conditions occurring	25%	60%	15%
Annual increase in sales	6%	5%	4%

Forecast exchange rates

Year	0	1	2	3	4	5	6	7	8
N$/£	3.60	3.74	3.89	4.05	4.21	4.34	4.55	4.74	4.92

Further information

Ice plc pays UK corporation tax one year in arrears at a rate of 30 per cent per year. For investment appraisal purposes the company uses a seven-year planning period and ignores terminal values. Its weighted-average cost of capital is 12 per cent after tax. Any foreign company investing in Northland pays profit tax to the Northland government one year in arrears at a rate of 30 per cent per year.

(a) Using the information provided, calculate which proposal should be adopted, explaining any assumptions that you make.

(b) Critically discuss the evaluation process used in part (a) and suggest what further information could assist Ice plc in evaluating the two investment proposals.

References

Arnold, G.C. and Hatzopoulos, P.D. (2000) 'The theory–practice gap in capital budgeting: evidence from the United Kingdom', *Journal of Business Finance and Accounting*, vol. 27, no. 5.

Brounen, D., de Jong, A. and Koedijk, K. (2004) 'Corporate finance in Europe: confronting theory with practice' *Financial Management*, vol. 33, no. 4.

Buckley, A. (2003) *Multinational Finance*, 5th edn, Harlow: FT Prentice Hall.

Buckley, A. (2012) *International Finance: A Practical Perspective*, Harlow: FT Prentice Hall.

Burns, R.M. and Walker, J. (2009) 'Capital Budgeting Surveys: The Future is Now', *Journal of Applied Finance*, Issues 1 and 2.

Demirag, I. and Goddard, S. (1994) *Financial Management for International Business*, London: McGraw-Hill.

Drury, C., Braund, S., Osborn, P. and Tayles, M. (1993) *A Survey of Management Accounting Practices in UK Manufacturing Companies*, Certified Research Report 32, ACCA.

Grayson, C. (1967) 'The use of statistical techniques in capital budgeting', in Robicheck, A. (ed.), *Financial Research and Management Decisions*, New York: Wiley, pp. 90–132.

Kennedy, A. and Sugden, K. (1986) 'Ritual and reality in capital budgeting', *Management Accounting*, February, pp. 34–7.

Kim, S. and Ulferts, G. (1996) 'A summary of multinational capital budgeting studies', *Managerial Finance*, vol. 22, no. 1, pp. 75–85.

Lapsley, I. (1986) 'Investment appraisal in UK non-trading organizations', *Financial Accountability and Management*, Summer, vol. 2, pp. 135–51.

McIntyre, A. and Coulthurst, N. (1986) *Capital Budgeting in Medium-sized Businesses*, London: CIMA Research Report.

Pike, R. (1983) 'A review of recent trends in formal capital budgeting processes', *Accounting and Business Research*, Summer, vol. 13, pp. 201–8.

Pike, R. (1996) 'A longitudinal survey of capital budgeting practices', *Journal of Business Finance and Accounting*, vol. 23, no. 1.

Ryan, P. and Ryan, G. (2002) 'Capital budgeting practices of the Fortune 1000: how have things changed?', *Journal of Business and Management*, vol. 8, no. 4.

Scarlett, R. (1993) 'The impact of corporate taxation on the viability of investment', *Management Accounting*, November, p. 30.

Scarlett, R. (1995) 'Further aspects of the impact of taxation on the viability of investment', *Management Accounting,* May, p. 54.

Verbeeten, F. (2006). 'Do organizations adopt sophisticated capital budgeting practices to deal with uncertainty in the investment decision? A research note', *Management Accounting Research,* vol. 17.

Recommended reading

A more detailed analysis of risk and uncertainty in the context of investment appraisal can be found in:

Arnold, G. (2018) *Corporate Financial Management,* 6th edn, Harlow: Pearson Education.

8 PORTFOLIO THEORY AND THE CAPITAL ASSET PRICING MODEL

Learning objectives

After studying this chapter, you should have achieved the following learning objectives:

■ an ability to calculate the standard deviation of an investment's returns and to calculate the risk and return of a two-share portfolio;

■ a firm understanding of both systematic and unsystematic risk and the concept of risk diversification using portfolio investment;

■ the ability to explain the foundations of Markowitz's portfolio theory and to discuss the problems associated with its practical application;

■ a critical understanding of the capital asset pricing model and the assumptions on which it is based;

■ the ability to calculate the required rate of return of a security using the capital asset pricing model;

■ an appreciation of the empirical research that has been undertaken to establish the applicability and reliability of the capital asset pricing model in practice.

■ ■ ■ INTRODUCTION

Risk–return trade-offs have an important role to play in corporate finance theory – from both a company and an investor perspective. Companies face variability in their project cash flows whereas investors face variability in their capital gains and dividends. Risk–return trade-offs were met earlier in this text in the form of risk-adjusted hurdle rates in Chapter 7 and will be met again later, in Chapter 9, where required rates of return for different securities will be seen to vary according to the level of risk they face. Until now, however, we have not given risk and return a formal treatment.

Assuming that companies and shareholders are rational, their aim will be to minimise the risk they face for a given return they expect to receive. To do this they will need a firm understanding of the nature of the risk they face. They will then be able to quantify the risk and hence manage or control it. Traditionally, risk has been measured by the standard deviation of returns, the calculation of which is considered below. In 'The concept of diversification' (Section 8.2) we examine how investors, by 'not putting all their eggs in one basket', are able to reduce the risk they face given the level of their expected return. Next (Section 8.3), we consider how an investor's attitude to risk and return is mirrored in the shape of their utility curves. The final part of the jigsaw is to introduce an investor's utility curves to the assets available for investment, allowing them to make an informed choice of portfolio: this is the essence of the portfolio theory developed by Markowitz in 1952 (Section 8.4).

Having considered portfolio theory, we turn to the capital asset pricing model developed by Sharpe in 1964 (Section 8.5 and subsequent sections). This provides a framework in which to value individual securities according to their level of 'relevant' risk, having already eradicated their 'non-relevant' risk through holding a diversified portfolio.

8.1 THE MEASUREMENT OF RISK

Risk plays a key role in the decision-making processes of both investors and companies, so it is important that the risk associated with an investment can be quantified. Risk is measured by the *standard deviation* (σ) of returns of a share, calculated using either historical returns or the expected future returns.

8.1.1 Calculating risk and return using probabilities

Table 8.1 gives the forecast returns and associated probabilities of shares A and B, where:

$$P_A = \text{probability of return on A}$$
$$R_A = \text{the corresponding return on A}$$
$$P_B = \text{probability of return on B}$$
$$R_B = \text{the corresponding return on B}$$

Table 8.1 The forecast returns and associated probabilities of two shares, A and B

Share A		Share B	
P_A	R_A (%)	P_B	R_B (%)
0.05	10	0.05	12
0.25	15	0.25	18
0.40	22	0.40	28
0.25	25	0.25	32
0.05	30	0.05	38
1.00		1.00	

The mean returns and standard deviations of the two shares are given by the following formulae:

$$\text{Mean return of a share } \bar{R} = \sum_{i=1}^{n} P_i \times R_i$$

$$\text{Standard deviation } (\sigma) = \sqrt{\sum_{i=1}^{n} P_i \times (R_i - \bar{R})^2}$$

where: $P_1, \ldots, P_n$ = the probabilities of the n different outcomes

$R_1, \ldots, R_n$ = the corresponding returns of the n different outcomes

By using the above formulae and the information provided we can calculate the mean return and the standard deviation of forecast returns for shares A and B.

Mean return of share A

$(0.05 \times 10) + (0.25 \times 15) + (0.40 \times 22) + (0.25 \times 25) + (0.05 \times 30) = 20.8$ per cent

Mean return of share B

$(0.05 \times 12) + (0.25 \times 18) + (0.40 \times 28) + (0.25 \times 32) + (0.05 \times 38) = 26.2$ per cent

Standard deviation of share A

$((0.05 \times (10 - 20.8)^2) + (0.25 \times (15 - 20.8)^2) + (0.40 \times (22 - 20.8)^2)$
$+ (0.25 \times (25 - 20.8)^2) + (0.05 \times (30 - 20.8)^2))^{1/2} = 4.84$ per cent

Standard deviation of share B

$((0.05 \times (12 - 26.2)^2) + (0.25 \times (18 - 26.2)^2) + (0.40 \times (28 - 26.2)^2)$
$+ (0.25 \times (32 - 26.2)^2) + (0.05 \times (38 - 26.2)^2))^{1/2} = 6.60$ per cent

Here we can see that while share B has a higher mean return compared with A, it also has a correspondingly higher level of risk.

8.1.2 Calculating risk and return using historical data

The mean and standard deviation of the annual historical returns of a share can be found using the following equations.

$$\text{Mean return } \bar{R} = \frac{\sum\limits_{i=1}^{n} R_i}{n}$$

$$\text{Standard deviation } (\sigma) = \sqrt{\frac{\sum\limits_{i=1}^{n} (R_i - \bar{R})^2}{n}}$$

The standard deviation formula given here applies where the historical data relates to a whole population. If the standard deviation of a sample of a population is being calculated, the denominator becomes $(n - 1)$ rather than n.

Table 8.2 shows data detailing the historical returns of two shares, S and T, over the past five years.

Using the historical returns and the formulae above:

Mean return of share S

$$(6.6 + 5.6 + (-9.0) + 12.6 + 14.0)/5 = 5.96 \text{ per cent}$$

Mean return of share T

$$(24.5 + (-5.9) + 19.9 + (-7.8) + 14.8)/5 = 9.10 \text{ per cent}$$

Standard deviation of share S

$$(((6.6 - 5.96)^2 + (5.6 - 5.96)^2 + (-9.0 - 5.96)^2$$
$$+ (12.6 - 5.96)^2 + (14 - 5.96)^2)/5)^{1/2} = 8.16 \text{ per cent}$$

Standard deviation of share T

$$(((24.5 - 9.10)^2 + (-5.9 - 9.10)^2 + (19.9 - 9.10)^2$$
$$+ (-7.8 - 9.10)^2 + (14.8 - 9.10)^2)/5)^{1/2} = 13.39 \text{ per cent}$$

We can see that while share T has a higher mean return than security S, it also has a higher standard deviation of returns. In Figure 8.1 we can see a graphical representation of

Table 8.2 The historical returns of two shares, S and T

Year (t)	S return (%)	T return (%)
−4	6.6	24.5
−3	5.6	−5.9
−2	−9.0	19.9
−1	12.6	−7.8
0	14.0	14.8

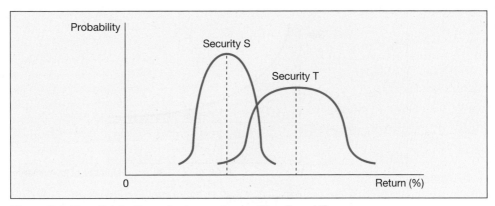

Figure 8.1 The distribution of returns of securities S and T

the distribution of the expected returns of the two shares. T has a higher mean return but a flatter normal distribution curve when compared with S, due to its higher standard deviation.

8.2 THE CONCEPT OF DIVERSIFICATION

Earlier we mentioned that for investors to control and manage risk it is important for them to understand the *nature* of the risk they face. The overall risk that investors and companies face can be separated into systematic and unsystematic risk. **Systematic risk** (also known as non-diversifiable, non-specific, unavoidable or market risk) relates to how a share's returns are affected by systematic factors such as business cycles, government policy and changes in interest rates. According to Solnik (1974), systematic risk accounts in the UK for roughly 34 per cent of an individual share's total risk.

Unsystematic risk (also known as **diversifiable**, specific, avoidable or non-market risk) is the risk specific to a particular share, i.e. the risk of the individual company performing badly or going into liquidation. While this type of risk accounts in the UK for approximately 66 per cent of an individual share's total risk, unsystematic risk can be diversified away.

8.2.1 Diversifying unsystematic risk: at company level or investor level?

There are two ways that unsystematic risk can be diversified away. First, companies can reduce unsystematic risk by diversifying their operations into unrelated lines of business. Alternatively, investors can reduce unsystematic risk through holding a *diversified portfolio* of shares (the basis of Markowitz's portfolio theory). As there is no need to diversify unsystematic risk at both company level and investor level the question is: 'Which is the most effective way of dealing with unsystematic risk?' The universally accepted answer is that it is better to diversify away unsystematic risk at an investor level due to several undesirable side-effects of corporate diversification. First, if business operations are scaled down,

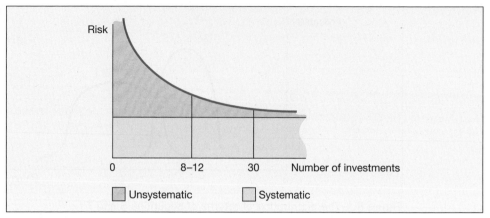

Figure 8.2 The amount of unsystematic risk diversification obtained as the number of investments increases

valuable **economies of scale** will be lost. Second, diversified companies will have to operate in areas of business in which they have little or no expertise. Finally, diversification is likely to complicate and increase the cost of company management. Hence it is more efficient for investors to diversify away unsystematic risk through holding a diversified portfolio of shares. An illustration of the relationship between systematic and unsystematic risk relative to the number of investments held in a portfolio is shown in Figure 8.2. On average about 90 per cent of unsystematic risk can be diversified away by investing in 8–12 shares (in different sectors). This rises to 95 per cent if around 30 shares are used. Vignette 8.1 considers why some investors over-diversify their portfolios.

A counter-argument put forward to support corporate diversification at an international (or cross-border) level is that it allows companies to protect themselves against over-exposure to any one economy. Since different economies are unlikely to move in parallel, a company can reduce the volatility of its cash flows by investing in projects in different countries. Reducing cash-flow volatility reduces business risk, so one consequence of international diversification is a reduction of risk. There is no reason, however, why investors should limit their investments to UK shares. Investors who include in their portfolio shares from major stock exchanges around the world can further reduce unsystematic risk. While the fortunes of the world's stock exchanges are closely linked, there is significantly less than perfect correlation between many of them. This is particularly true for the stock exchanges of Europe and their South East Asian counterparts. Solnik (1974) estimated that an internationally diversified portfolio reduced the proportion of systematic risk to a mere 11 per cent of total risk.

8.2.2 Diversifying unsystematic risk using a two-share portfolio

The simplest portfolio to consider is that containing two shares. The extent to which a two-share portfolio will reduce unsystematic risk depends on the correlation between the two shares' returns. This correlation is quantified by the correlation coefficient (ρ) of the returns of the two shares, which can take any value in the range -1 to $+1$.

Messy portfolios and the 'be busy' syndrome

By Merryn Somerset Webb

Imagine you are a primary school head teacher. You are looking for a new job and there are two alternatives. The first involves a small school – there are a mere 20 pupils.

It isn't an easy job. You will be responsible for keeping a very close eye on the children, analysing their every move every day and hoping they reach their potential. You also have to endlessly liaise with the school governors and with parents about each child. To add to your trying admin burden, you also have to keep a long waiting list of the children who you will take on when the ones you have moved on.

The second job comes with the same responsibilities, boring admin tasks and reporting duties. The difference is that it houses 60 children – you have triple the number of needy kids to keep an eye on at any time and triple the number on your waiting (or watch) list. The pay is the same for both and both offer the same level of general social and professional status, as well as the same opportunities for advancement.

Which would you choose – the one which makes you responsible for a small number of carefully chosen clever children, or the one where you take charge of an unruly rabble of some clever and some not so clever kids?

I wouldn't need to think about this for long. I'd take the first – fewer children would allow me more time to get to know each child better and, hopefully, also give me more free time of my own. However, I am not a fund manager. Look at the way most of them do their jobs and it seems likely that most would choose the second.

There is a huge amount of academic and practical research available into the optimum number of stocks that should be held in a portfolio (from Harry Markowitz's Modern Portfolio Theory down). The results are pretty consistent.

They tell us that you must diversify a portfolio. If you only hold a couple of stocks you run the risk of losing a large percentage of your money if one goes horribly wrong. However, they also tell us that there is no point in diversifying too much: all the benefits of diversification in terms of cutting your risks can be gained by holding 15–20 stocks and there is

almost no more benefit to be had from holding more than 25. Holding more than 25 is therefore nothing more than a make-work scheme for junior fund managers and analysts.

Yet, despite this volume of research and the fact that (unusually) almost everyone agrees with its premise, the average fund manager holds more like 40–50 stocks in his portfolio and some hold 100 plus. That means huge trading expenses (the average fund manager turns over about 80 per cent of his portfolio ever y year and the more stocks he has the more he is likely to trade) and research expenses (all those company visits for starters). It also means hours of extra work: instead of having 20 stocks to analyse and another 20-odd on their watch list, they have hundreds to keep an eye on.

So why do they do it? We need make-work schemes for clever young people in the UK at the moment. But given that it's hard to accuse very many fund management firms of intense focus on altruism and social usefulness, I don't think that's what is going on here.

I am amused by the idea that our fund managers might all be great believers in the homeopathic approach to investment (the more you dilute a portfolio, the better it works) but I don't think that's it either.

Instead it is a mixture of things. Some are technical. Managers worry about liquidity. If they have large positions in a stock, will they be able to liquidate it should investors redeem in volume? And funds are subject to rules about how much of the portfolio any one stock makes up. These can be valid problems – particularly at the small-cap end of the market. But I suspect the biggest factors in here are more psychological rather than technical.

There's the fact that everyone hates to sell stocks that have gone up and replace them with new ones (what if the old ones go up further?). There is novelty. If you have new money coming into your fund it is more fun to buy new holdings than top up old. There is the 'be busy' syndrome – it's hard to sit at a desk all day doing almost nothing and feeling you justify your rather too high salary when everyone else is buying new stuff.

Vignette **8.1** (continued)

There is the herding (whereby managers are more comfortable owning the stocks other managers own too) and there is, of course, career risk. I've written about this before but there is more benefit to a manager in tracking their index (almost inevitable if you hold 100 stocks) than in underperforming it, even in the short term. Finally, there is the fact that holding a smaller number of stocks with conviction requires a certain amount of mental stamina (idleness isn't easy). Fund investors may think that stamina is what they pay for, but I'm told it's just too hard.

So what do you do? You can approach this in a simple way and just reject all funds with more than 25 holdings as being run by mentally weak lemmings, an approach that would probably end with you buying the excellent Fundsmith fund. But you could also accept funds with 30–40 holdings on the basis that in a good fund only 25 or so of those will be core holdings – the rest will be positions in the process of being built up or sold down. This might take you to the Troy Income and Growth Fund.

Finally, you might make the odd exception for funds with 50–100 holdings. This sounds silly under the circumstances but if you look at, say, the excellent Scottish Mortgage Investment Trust, you will see that it has 70 holdings. However, the top 25–30 make up 80 per cent of the portfolio so in that sense it almost fits the bill. The rest are companies in which a bigger position might be taken later or a spread in a newish sector in which it isn't clear who will be the winner. It's a bit like taking the first job above but insisting on being allowed to run the nursery too.

Source: Somerset Webb, M. (2014) 'Messy portfolios and the "be busy" syndrome', *Financial Times*, 9 May. © The Financial Times Limited 2014. All Rights Reserved.

Question

Critically discuss why many investors diversify their portfolios beyond the number of shares that is deemed appropriate by portfolio theory.

If $p_{x,y} = +1$	no unsystematic risk can be diversified away
If $p_{x,y} = -1$	all unsystematic risk will be diversified away
If $p_{x,y} = 0$	no correlation between the two securities' returns

Therefore, when picking a two-share portfolio it is most beneficial to choose two shares whose correlation coefficient is as close to −1 as possible. However, as long as the correlation coefficient is less than +1, some unsystematic risk will be diversified away. In practice it is difficult to find two securities whose correlation coefficient is exactly −1, but the most commonly quoted example is that of an umbrella manufacturer and an ice-cream company.

The *correlation coefficient* of two shares x and y ($\rho_{x,y}$) can be calculated by the formula:

$$\rho_{x,y} = \frac{\text{Cov}_{x,y}}{\sigma_x \sigma_y}$$

where $\text{Cov}_{x,y}$ is the covariance of returns of securities x and y.

If using expected return data, $\rho_{x,y}$ is given by:

$$\rho_{x,y} = \frac{\sum_{i=1}^{n} P_i(R_{ix} - \bar{R}_x) \times (R_{iy} - \bar{R}_y)}{\sigma_x \sigma_y}$$

and if using historical data, is given by:

$$\rho_{x,y} = \frac{\sum_{i=1}^{n} (R_{ix} - \bar{R}_x) \times (R_{iy} - \bar{R}_y)}{n\sigma_x\sigma_y}$$

The formulae to calculate the return and risk of a two-share portfolio are given below. The return of a two-share portfolio is the weighted average of the two shares' returns. The standard deviation formula is more complex owing to the diversification of unsystematic risk that occurs.

Return of a two-share portfolio (R_p):

$$R_p = (W_xR_x) + (W_yR_y)$$

Standard deviation of a two-share portfolio σ_p:

$$\sigma_p = \sqrt{(W_x)^2(\sigma_x)^2 + (W_y)^2(\sigma_y)^2 + 2W_xW_y\sigma_x\sigma_y\rho_{x,y}}$$

where: W_x = proportion of funds invested in share x
W_y = proportion of funds invested in share y
R_x = mean return of share x (per cent)
R_y = mean return of share y (per cent)
σ_x = standard deviation of share x's returns (per cent)
σ_y = standard deviation of share y's returns (per cent)
$\rho_{x,y}$ = correlation coefficient between x and y's returns
σ_p = standard deviation of portfolio containing x and y (per cent)

Using annual returns of the two shares S and T from our earlier example, we can calculate the return and standard deviation (risk) of a series of portfolios consisting of differing amounts of S and T. First we calculate the correlation coefficient between the returns of the two shares:

$$\begin{aligned}
\rho_{S,T} = &((6.6 - 5.96) \times (24.5 - 9.10) + (5.6 - 5.96) \times (-5.9 - 9.10) \\
&+ (-9.0 - 5.96) \times (19.9 - 9.10) + (12.6 - 5.96) \times (-7.8 - 9.10) \\
&+ (14.0 - 5.96) \times (14.8 - 9.10))/(5 \times 8.16 \times 13.39) \\
= &-0.389
\end{aligned}$$

The return and risk of a portfolio consisting of 80 per cent of S and 20 per cent of T are as follows:

$$\begin{aligned}
\text{Return of portfolio} &= (0.8 \times 5.96) + (0.2 \times 9.1) = 6.59 \text{ per cent} \\
\text{Risk of portfolio} &= ((0.8^2 \times 8.16^2) + (0.2^2 \times 13.39^2) \\
&\quad + (2 \times 0.8 \times 0.2 \times 8.16 \times 13.39 \times -0.389))^{1/2} \\
&= 6.02
\end{aligned}$$

Table 8.3 Diversification of risk in a portfolio containing securities S and T

	All S	A	B	C	D	All T
Mean return (%)	5.96	6.59	7.21	7.84	8.47	9.10
Standard deviation (%)	8.16	6.02	5.68	7.40	10.18	13.39

The results of these calculations are given in Table 8.3, where:

$$A = 80\% \, S + 20\% \, T$$
$$B = 60\% \, S + 40\% \, T$$
$$C = 40\% \, S + 60\% \, T$$
$$D = 20\% \, S + 80\% \, T$$

The results of these calculations are illustrated graphically in Figure 8.3. We can see that an investor can locate anywhere along the arc SABCDT according to how the portfolio is divided between the shares S and T. The points along this arc, by offering a higher return for the same risk or a lower risk for the same return, are *superior* to those on the straight line between security S and security T due to the diversification of unsystematic risk that occurs when more than one security is held.

8.2.3 Diversifying unsystematic risk using a three-share portfolio

With the introduction of an additional share into the portfolio there is even further scope for the diversification of unsystematic risk. The introduction of a higher risk and return share R into the earlier example is represented graphically in Figure 8.4, where:

ST represents portfolios of securities S and T
SR (dotted line) represents portfolios of securities S and R
TR represents portfolios of securities T and R
SR (bold line) represents portfolios of securities T, S and R

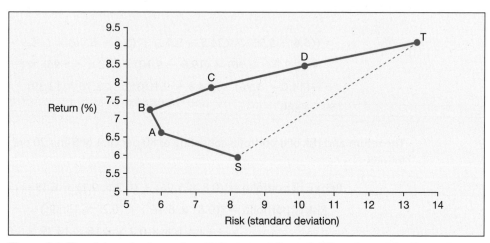

Figure 8.3 The risk and return of portfolios consisting of different combinations of securities S and T

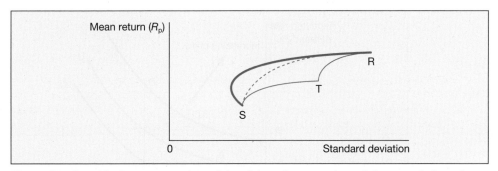

Figure 8.4 Graphical representation of the risk and return of portfolios consisting of combinations of securities S, T and R

Here we can see that the optimal set of portfolios is achieved when all three shares are invested in (i.e. the bold line SR). This *optimal frontier* is superior to investing in just S and T owing to a greater ability to diversify away unsystematic risk when investing in all three shares. As more shares are added to the investment portfolio, progressively more and more unsystematic risk will be diversified away. This principle is the basis of Markowitz's portfolio theory, where the investor's choice of investments is not limited to three shares but includes all available risky securities. Before we consider Markowitz's theory, however, let us consider investor attitudes to risk and return.

8.3 INVESTOR ATTITUDES TO RISK

How much risk will an investor accept in the first place? The answer to this question depends on how much utility an individual investor or company receives from taking risk. The attitudes that investors and companies have towards risk can be summarised as follows:

- *Risk-loving*: where the preference is for high return in exchange for a high level of risk.
- *Risk-neutral*: where the investor is indifferent to the level of risk faced.
- *Risk-averse*: where the preference is for low-risk, low-return investments.

While attitudes towards risk may differ, we expect investors to act rationally and not expose themselves to higher risk without the possibility of higher returns. A common misconception often levelled at risk-loving investors is that they are acting irrationally. This is not the case, however, as investors with a preference for taking risks will be prepared to incur higher risk only if it is accompanied by correspondingly higher returns.

The attitude of an investor to different combinations of risk and return is reflected by the shape of their *utility curves* (**indifference curves**). These are adapted from microeconomics and the concept of *utility maximisation,* which uses utility curves to analyse consumer demand for combinations of goods and services. Here, we apply utility curve analysis to portfolios rather than to goods and services, in terms of investors receiving positive utility from increasing returns and negative utility from increasing risk.

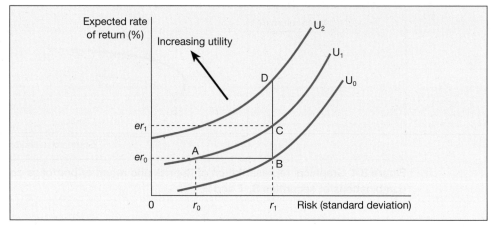

Figure 8.5 Graphical representation of investor utility curves

Utility curves are similar to contour lines on a map, but instead of joining up points of equal height, utility curves map out points of equal utility. Consider utility curve U_1 in Figure 8.5. At point A, the combination of expected return of er_0 and risk of r_0 gives the investor a certain level of utility that corresponds to utility curve U_1. If the investor is faced with an increased level of risk r_1, he would require an increase in expected return equivalent to $(er_1 - er_0)$ in order to preserve his original level of utility, corresponding to point C on U_1. Utility curves slope upwards at an increasing rate because to persuade an investor to take on progressively more risk, progressively higher rates of expected return are required to compensate and keep their utility constant. This is referred to as an *increasing marginal rate of substitution.*

Rational investors will always try to increase their level of utility by seeking the highest return for a given level of risk, or by seeking the lowest risk for a given level of return. Hence moving from utility curve U_1 onto U_2 (i.e. from point C to point D) represents an increase in utility for the investor. Subsequent movements in a north-westerly direction will further increase investor utility. Conversely, a movement from point C to point B would represent a decrease in investor utility as they find themselves on U_0, which represents a lower utility curve compared with U_1.

Just as contour lines on a map differ with the type of terrain, utility curves differ in shape according to investors' differing preferences for risk and return. The key difference here is the slope of the utility curves. In Figure 8.6, V_0 represents the utility curve of risk-loving investor V while U_0 corresponds to investor U who is **risk averse**. Initially both investors are located at point D and derive an equal level of utility given an expected return of er_2 and risk of r_2. Assume both investors are faced with an increase in risk to point r_3. To maintain his utility, investor V requires an increase in expected return of $(er_3 - er_2)$. However, given investor U's risk aversion, he requires a much higher increase in expected return $(er_4 - er_2)$ to maintain his utility.

Hence, as indicated in Figure 8.7, a risk-averse investor's utility curves (U_0, U_1 and U_2) quickly steepen at low levels of risk whereas the opposite is true for a risk-loving investor,

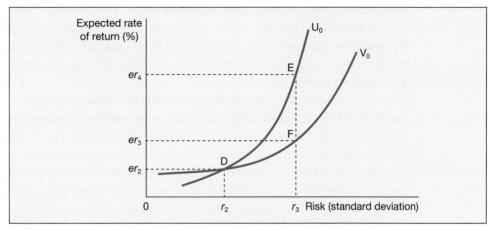

Figure 8.6 Comparison of a risk-averse investor's utility curve (U_0) with that of a risk-loving investor (V_0)

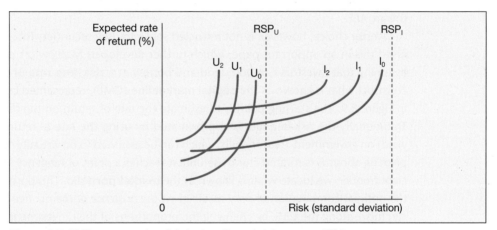

Figure 8.7 Utility curves for risk-loving (I) and risk-averse (U) investors

whose curves (I_0, I_1 and I_2) are much flatter. The risk saturation point, i.e. the level of risk beyond which an investor will not go, is much lower for investor U (indicated by the vertical line RSP_U) compared with that of investor I (RSP_I).

Having considered earlier the portfolio choices available to investors, we can now combine these choices with their utility curves, thereby allowing investors to select portfolios which satisfy their preference for risk and return.

8.4 MARKOWITZ'S PORTFOLIO THEORY

The cornerstone of Markowitz's seminal 1952 theory, for which he was awarded a Nobel Prize in Economics in 1990, is the ability of investors to diversify away unsystematic risk by holding portfolios consisting of a number of different shares. Markowitz's starting point is to construct what is known as the **envelope curve**. This represents the set of portfolio choices available to investors when investing in different combinations of risky assets. In Figure 8.8 the envelope curve is represented by the shaded area AEFCDG. Investors can construct portfolios anywhere in this shaded area by holding different combinations of available risky assets.

While investors can locate themselves anywhere within the envelope curve, rational investors will invest only in those portfolios on the **efficient frontier** represented by the arc AEF. It is called the efficient frontier because all portfolios on this arc are superior to (i.e. more efficient than) all other portfolios within the envelope curve, giving either the *maximum return* for a given level of risk or the *minimum risk* for a given level of return. For example, if we compare portfolios B and E, which both have the same level of risk, we can see that portfolio E on the boundary of the envelope curve offers a higher return without incurring any additional risk. Portfolio E is said to *dominate* portfolio B. Equally, while portfolio A has the same expected return as portfolios B and C, it dominates them as both B and C incur a higher level of risk. Using the same rationale, portfolios on the arc between A and G cannot be regarded as efficient as they are dominated by those on the arc AEF.

Investor choice, however, is not restricted solely to risky securities. Tobin (1958) recognised this in an important paper which further developed Markowitz's earlier work. By assuming that investors can both lend and borrow at a **risk-free rate of return**, we can construct what is known as the **capital market line** (CML), represented by the line R_fMN in Figure 8.9. The starting point is to estimate the rate of return on the risk-free asset, R_f. Traditionally the risk-free rate is approximated by using the rate of return (redemption yield) on government Treasury bills, which can be assumed to be virtually risk-free. If a line pivoting about R_f is rotated clockwise until it reaches a point of tangency M with the efficient frontier, we locate what is known as the **market portfolio**. This portfolio represents the optimal combination of risky assets *given the existence of the risk-free asset*. Investors can move along the CML by changing the proportions of their investment in the risk-free

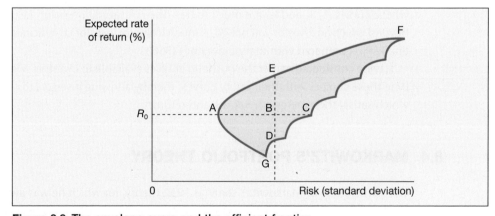

Figure 8.8 The envelope curve and the efficient frontier

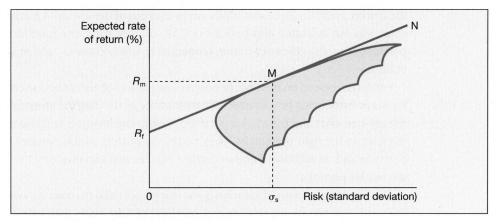

Figure 8.9 Identifying the capital market line

asset and in the market portfolio in what is in effect a two-share portfolio. This results in a straightforward linear trade-off between risk and return.

Investors will always choose a portfolio on the CML because the CML portfolios are more efficient than those on the efficient frontier (shown by AEF in Figure 8.8). The CML portfolio chosen by an investor will depend on the investor's risk preference. Risk-averse investors will choose portfolios closer to R_f by investing most of their money in the risk-free asset; less risk-averse investors will choose portfolios closer to M, putting most of their funds into the market portfolio. Theoretically, the precise portfolio that an investor will choose on the CML will be determined by the point of tangency of their utility curves with the CML. In Figure 8.10 we consider a moderately risk-averse investor with utility curves U_0, U_1, U_2 and U_3. He will locate at point P on the CML, tangential to utility curve U_2, by investing the majority of his funds into the risk-free asset and the remainder into

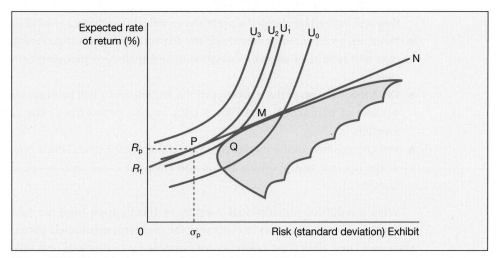

Figure 8.10 Graphical representation of Markowitz's theory

the market portfolio (note that utility curve U_3 is out of the investor's grasp). If the risk-free asset was not available and hence the CML did not exist, the investor would choose portfolio Q on the efficient frontier, tangential to utility curve U_1, and enjoy a lower level of utility.

Portfolios located on the CML between points R_f and M are of constant value, the choice for the investor being how to maximise their utility by dividing the invested funds between the risk-free asset and the market portfolio. Risk-loving investors will choose portfolios on the CML to the right of point M. They do this by putting all their money into the market portfolio and, in addition, *borrowing at the risk-free rate* and investing their borrowings in the market portfolio.

The two-stage process of identifying the market portfolio (to diversify away unsystematic risk) and then combining this optimal portfolio of risky assets with lending or borrowing at the risk-free rate (to satisfy the individual investor's preference for risk and return) is often referred to as *Tobin's separation theory*.

Furthermore, the risk-free asset is significant from the perspective of calculating the risk of a portfolio containing a large number of shares in order to facilitate an optimal investment decision. This calculation involves incorporating correlation coefficients for every possible pair of shares, with the number of correlation coefficients growing exponentially with the number of shares in the portfolio. The introduction of the risk-free asset simplifies enormously the calculation of portfolio risk since the returns of the shares are not correlated with the return on the risk-free asset.

8.4.1 Problems with the practical application of portfolio theory

There are problems associated with trying to apply portfolio theory in practice, some of which are as follows:

- It is unrealistic to assume that investors can borrow at the risk-free rate. Individuals and companies are not risk free and will therefore not be able to borrow at the risk-free rate; they will instead be charged a premium to reflect their higher level of risk.
- There are problems with identifying the market portfolio as this requires knowing the risks and returns of all risky investments and their corresponding correlation coefficients.
- Once the make-up of the market portfolio is identified it will be expensive to construct because of transaction costs. These costs will be prohibitive in the case of smaller investors.
- The composition of the market portfolio changes over time. This is due to shifts both in the risk-free rate of return and in the envelope curve, and hence in the efficient frontier.

While it is difficult for individual investors to directly apply portfolio theory in practice, one way for smaller investors to overcome the problems mentioned above is by buying a stake in a large, diversified portfolio, for example by buying into unit trusts, investment trusts or *index tracker funds*. This is the subject of Vignette 8.2.

Vignette 8.2

Diversification made easy

By David Stevenson

A few months back, I had the good fortune to sit in on a customer panel session at a leading stockbroking firm. My primary purpose was to quiz the poor unfortunate clients on their behavioural vices for an up-and-coming book – I wanted the truth about their overtrading and their overconfidence in their ability to pick shares in the style of Warren Buffett.

But what I actually got was a bunch of fairly level-headed folk who were largely terrified of making mistakes and who looked to people like me (sadly) to provide them with clues. More to the point, when I started talking about diversification they all – to a man and woman – said, to paraphrase one very charming lady: 'How much is enough? We all understand that you have to diversify but how exactly should you do it?' It was a cracking question to which there's a proper answer – and a real answer.

The proper answer is to listen to the collective wisdom of generations of investment academics and use modern portfolio theory, as devised by professor Harry Markowitz. This suggests that you look at risks and returns, alongside volatility, and then compute something called 'an efficient frontier' of different assets, allocated sensibly, in an optimised fashion. It's what the big wealth managers claim to do (although they actually don't in most cases). It's also what many fine and upstanding financial planners will do for a very fair fee.

Unfortunately, it's not what anyone I've ever talked to actually does. It's not the *real* answer. Here's Professor Markowitz at a conference in Chicago on what he invested in: 'I should have computed co-variances of the asset classes and drawn an efficient frontier – instead I split my contributions 50/50 between bonds and equities'. Just to ram the point home, it's also worth pointing out that he's not alone. Take the father of modern risk analysis in economics, Bill Sharpe, on the subject of how he builds his portfolio: 'I invest in various funds, large stocks, small stocks and international stocks'. Or Eugene Fama, the father of the index funds movement – when asked by a publication called *Investment News* what he invested in, he replied by detailing a fund invested in the broad-based US Wilshire 5000 index, plus small cap and international index funds, and just over a third in value-oriented stock indexes and short-term bond funds.

The vast majority of UK-based academics that I talk to also maintain a very sensible 60/40 split between equities and bonds, with just a couple of funds of each. The odd few go a little further, adding a few additional asset categories and maybe getting up to 6 funds – but that's it.

Over in the US, the idea of a simple, small number of funds has been taken to an extreme degree by one commentator: Paul Farrell. He recommends so-called 'lazy' portfolios with between just 2 and maybe 8 funds. This lazy portfolio proposition is built on four simple principles:

1   Use funds to capture the market, not individual shares

2   Use index tracking funds to track the market efficiently and cheaply

3   Keep portfolios simple with no more than ten individual funds

4   Buy and hold – don't overtrade, just stick with the portfolio for the very long term.

Some enthusiasts for this approach maintain that just two funds could do it: 60 per cent in an equity index fund (tracking, say, the FTSE All Share) and 40 per cent in a bond fund (tracking the FTSE All Stock Gilts index). Just these two funds could give you all the diversification you need!

But I suspect that most of us would want a little bit more spice than that. James Norton of UK financial planning firm Evolve has studied returns between 1988 and 2008 to work out just how many funds you probably need. He started with a classic 60/40 split (Citi Bond index and FTSE all Share) which produced an average annualised return of 8.83 per cent a year with volatility (standard deviation) of 9.58 per cent. He then progressively added funds until he got to eight (FTSE All Share, MSCI World index excluding UK, emerging markets, value and small cap for both the UK and the World), which produced a higher annual return – 9.91 per cent – but with almost exactly the same volatility: 9.69 per cent.

Norton's conclusions are backed up by a separate study from American commentators Paul Merriman and Richard Buck, who ran a similar analysis back in September 2005. They ended up with a nine-way split and similar results.

Vignette 8.2 (continued)

So, between 4 and 9 asset classes or funds should just about do it. However, there are still analysts who think you need fewer. One of them is US analyst Rob Arnott who says: 'Most of the advantage of diversifying happens with three or four significant positions in seriously cheap assets. If you go beyond ten, you're deluding the opportunity set. You're reducing your ability to add value.'

Tim Bond at BarCap also cautions against over-diversification, favouring a focus on China's infrastructure boom and the new carbon-lite economy. 'Under those circumstances, diversification, is literally the worse possible solution to your investment needs . . . it's the worst possible thing to do. Actually, you need a really narrowly-focused portfolio, where you're investing specifically on that theme.'

Source: Stevenson, D. (2009) 'Diversification made easy', *Financial Times,* 21 August.
© The Financial Times Limited 2009. All Rights Reserved.

Question

Critically discuss whether the fact that leading academics do not use portfolio theory when choosing their investment portfolios implies that portfolio theory is of no relevance.

8.5 INTRODUCTION TO THE CAPITAL ASSET PRICING MODEL

The fact that the capital asset pricing model (CAPM), a development based on Markowitz's portfolio theory, owes its conception to William Sharpe, a PhD student unofficially supervised by Markowitz, is perhaps no great surprise. Sharpe developed this method of share valuation in his seminal 1964 paper in which he attempted to 'construct a market equilibrium theory of asset prices under conditions of risk'. Sharpe, like Markowitz, was in 1990 awarded the Nobel Prize for Economics.

While the CAPM is the next logical step from portfolio theory and is based on the foundations provided by Markowitz, there are subtle differences between the two. *Normative* portfolio theory considers the *total* risk and return of portfolios and advises investors on which portfolios to invest in, whereas the *positive* CAPM uses the *systematic* risk of individual securities to determine their fair price. In order to ignore the influence of unsystematic risk on the valuation of securities, it is assumed that investors have eradicated unsystematic risk by holding diversified portfolios.

As with most academic models, the CAPM is based on a simplified world using the following assumptions:

- Investors are rational and want to maximise their utility; they do not take risk for risk's sake.
- All information is freely available to investors and, having interpreted it, investors arrive at similar expectations.
- Investors can borrow and lend at the risk-free rate.
- Investors hold diversified portfolios, eliminating all unsystematic risk.
- Capital markets are perfectly competitive. The conditions required for this are: a large number of buyers and sellers; no one participant can influence the market; no

taxes and transaction costs; no entry or exit barriers to the market and securities are divisible.

■ Investment occurs over a single, standardised holding period.

While these assumptions are clearly at odds with the real world, we should refrain from dismissing the CAPM as unrealistic and impractical. As Sharpe (1964) observed: 'The proper test of a theory is not the realism of its assumptions, but the acceptability of its implications.' The issue of the CAPM's applicability and usefulness is considered later in the chapter.

8.6 USING THE CAPM TO VALUE SHARES

Central to the CAPM is the existence of a *linear relationship* between risk and return. The linear relationship is defined by what is known as the *security market line* (SML), where the systematic risk of a security is compared with the risk and return of the market and the risk-free rate of return in order to calculate a required return for the security and hence a fair price. A graphical representation of the SML is given in Figure 8.11. The equation of the SML can be defined as:

$$R_j = R_f + \beta_j(R_m - R_f)$$

where: R_j = the rate of return of security J predicted by the model.

R_f = the risk-free rate of return

β_j = the beta coefficient of security J

R_m = the return of the market

In order to use the CAPM in valuing shares, we need to understand the components that make up the SML and how they can be calculated or approximated. First, we consider the beta coefficient, which is used to quantify a security's level of systematic risk.

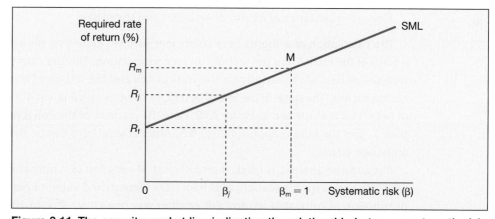

Figure 8.11 The security market line indicating the relationship between systematic risk (measured by beta) and the required rate of return on capital assets

8.6.1 The meaning and calculation of beta

The beta (β) of a security can be defined as an *index of responsiveness* of the changes in returns of the security relative to a change in the stock exchange or market. By definition, the *beta of the market* is always 1 and acts as a benchmark against which the systematic risk of securities can be measured. The *beta of a security* measures the sensitivity of the returns on the security to changes in systematic factors. For example, if a security has a beta of 0.8 (i.e. less systematic risk than the market) and the market return *increases* by 10 per cent, the security's return will increase by 8 per cent. If the market return *decreases* by 10 per cent, the return of the security decreases by 8 per cent. This security is commonly called a *defensive* security and is most attractive to investors when the stock exchange is falling. Alternatively, for a security with a beta of 1.5 (i.e. more systematic risk than the market), if the return of the market increases by 10 per cent, the security's return will increase by 15 per cent. If the market return decreases by 10 per cent, the return of the security decreases by 15 per cent. This security is commonly called an *aggressive* security and is most attractive to investors when the stock exchange is rising.

As we will see later in 'Equity betas and asset betas' (Section 9.4.1) , betas can be classified as either liability or **asset betas**. *Liability betas* (or equity betas as they are more commonly known) take into account a security's total systematic risk, i.e. risk arising from the nature of a company's business (business risk) and risk arising from the way in which a company finances itself (financial risk). *Asset betas* reflect only systematic business risk. In subsequent paragraphs when we talk of beta we are in fact referring to equity betas.

The relationship between the beta of a security, and the risk and return of the security and the market is given by the following equation:

$$\beta_j = \frac{\text{Cov}_{j,m}}{(\sigma_m)^2} = \frac{\sigma_j \times \sigma_m \times \rho_{j,m}}{(\sigma_m)^2} = \frac{\sigma_j \times \rho_{j,m}}{\sigma_m}$$

where: σ_j = standard deviation of security *J*'s returns

σ_m = standard deviation of return of the market

$\rho_{j,m}$ = correlation coefficient between the security's returns and the market returns

$\text{Cov}_{j,m}$ = covariance of returns of security *J* and the market.

The calculation of a share's beta coefficient involves collecting data on the periodic returns of the market and the security under consideration. This data can then be plotted with the returns of the security on the vertical axis and the returns of the market on the horizontal axis. The slope of the line of best fit, or *characteristic line,* will then give the value of beta. This is illustrated in Figure 8.12. Here the gradient of the line is positive and less than 1, and the beta is approximately 0.5. Alternatively, beta can be determined using regression analysis.

If regression analysis is used, the *coefficient of variation* (R^2) indicates the extent to which the regression equation, and hence the determined value of beta, explains the distribution of correlated returns. Put another way, the closer R^2 is to 100 per cent, the more of the total variability of a security's returns is explained by systematic risk as

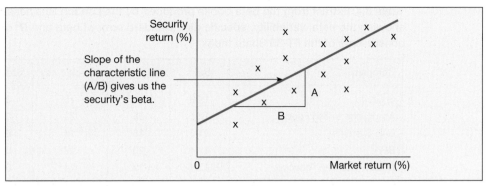

Figure 8.12 Finding the beta of a security by plotting the security's returns against those of the market

measured by beta, as opposed to other factors. Hence the higher the value of R^2, the stronger the case for a unifactor model like the CAPM, rather than multifactor models such as **arbitrage pricing theory**.

An easier way to find a security's beta is to leave it to the experts. The Risk Measurement Service of the London Business School publishes quarterly *beta books* of companies' equity beta coefficients. It calculates the betas of all major companies by regressing their monthly returns against the monthly returns of the FT actuaries' all-share index over the previous five years. An extract from one of the pages of the beta books is shown in Table 8.4.

Not only do the beta books give equity betas, they also provide other important information. The *variability* column indicates the total variability of a share's returns (σ_j) as measured by standard deviation. The *specific risk* column gives the variability of a share's returns ($\sigma_{j,sp}$), which is explained by specific factors measured by standard deviation. The *standard error* column indicates the reliability of the beta coefficient calculated – the closer this is to zero the better. Finally, the *R-squared* column indicates the percentage of a share's total variability of returns that is explained by systematic factors as measured by beta. The relationship between the total variability, the systematic variability (representing the variance of market returns) and the specific variability of a share's returns is:

$$Total\ variability\ of\ returns\ =\ Systematic\ variability\ +\ Specific\ variability$$
$$\sigma_j^2 = (\beta_j^2 \times \sigma_m^2) + \sigma_{j,sp}^2$$

Algebraically, *R-squared* is represented by:

$$R^2 = \frac{\beta_j^2 \times \sigma_m^2}{\sigma_j^2}$$

A frequency distribution of FTSE 100 company betas is shown in Figure 8.13. Most company betas (90 per cent) lie in the range 0.8 to 1.2, with a beta of 1.0 being the most common. While it is mathematically possible for beta to be negative, it is very rare in

Table 8.4 Extract from the beta books produced by the London Business School, showing the beta, variability, specific risk, standard error of beta and R^2 of the constituents of the FT-30 Share Index

Company	Beta	Variability	Specific risk	Std error	R sq.
3i Group	1.29	20	16	0.18	37
Associated British Foods	1.05	25	23	0.22	16
BAE Systems	0.90	18	16	0.13	22
BP	1.14	20	17	0.18	31
British American Tobacco	1.24	19	14	0.16	41
BT Group	1.02	20	17	0.18	24
Burberry Group	1.28	23	19	0.20	29
Compass Group	0.92	16	13	0.15	32
Diageo	0.91	16	13	0.15	32
Experian	1.20	18	13	0.15	43
Ferguson	0.85	16	14	0.16	26
GKN	0.97	23	21	0.20	17
GlaxoSmithKline	1.05	18	15	0.16	33
GVC Holdings	0.80	23	22	0.21	11
International Consolidated Airlines	0.89	28	27	0.23	9
ITV	0.97	25	23	0.21	14
Land Securities Group	1.07	19	17	0.17	31
Lloyds Banking Group	0.78	24	23	0.21	10
Man Group	1.16	32	30	0.24	12
Marks and Spencer Group	1.07	23	21	0.20	20
National Grid	0.84	18	16	0.17	21
Prudential	1.06	19	16	0.17	30
Reckitt Benckiser Group	1.01	17	14	0.16	33
Royal Bank of Scotland Group	0.95	31	29	0.24	9
RSA Insurance Group	0.91	25	23	0.22	13
Smith Group	0.90	18	16	0.17	24
Tate & Lyle	0.82	23	22	0.21	11
Tesco	0.97	26	24	0.22	13
Vodafone Group	1.07	19	16	0.17	30
WPP Group	1.02	19	16	0.18	27

Source: London Business School, Risk Measurement Service, vol. 40, no. 4, April–June 2018.

practice as few companies experience increasing returns in times of economic downturn. The most important determinant of a company's beta is the industry in which it operates. Companies with betas greater than 1 tend to be those in industries such as consumer durables, leisure and luxury goods. Companies with betas less than 1 usually come from industries such as food retailers, utilities and other necessity goods producers. A useful exercise is to look through the industrial betas sections that the London Business School includes in its beta books.

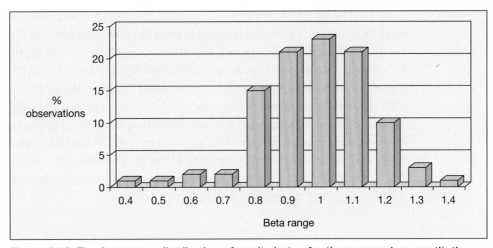

Figure 8.13 The frequency distribution of equity betas for the companies constituting the FTSE 100, June 2018

Table 8.5 Calculating the beta of a portfolio by weighting the betas of its constituent securities by their relative market value in the portfolio

Security	Beta	Weighting (%)	Weighted beta
Barclays	1.43	20	0.286
BP	1.49	35	0.522
Kingfisher	0.84	15	0.126
Severn Trent	0.53	20	0.106
Tesco	0.94	10	0.094
Portfolio beta		100	1.134

An important feature of equity betas is that they can be used to find the beta of a portfolio of shares. This allows the calculation of the required rate of return from the whole portfolio. An example is given in Table 8.5.

The *portfolio beta* is obtained by weighting the individual security betas by their relative market value (i.e. the number of shares multiplied by their market price and divided by the total market value of the portfolio). In the example in Table 8.5, the portfolio beta is 1.134, indicating that the portfolio has more systematic risk than the market portfolio (i.e. it is an aggressive portfolio). It must be noted, however, that a portfolio of only five shares will not diversify away all unsystematic risk and therefore the risk of this portfolio will not consist solely of systematic risk (see Figure 8.2).

Having now built up a firm understanding of what beta represents and how it can be determined, we can go on to consider the other variables used in the CAPM.

8.6.2 Determining the risk-free rate and the return of the market

The risk-free rate R_f represents the rate of return earned by investing in the risk-free asset. Two conditions must be met before an asset can be considered completely risk free. First, there must be no risk of default associated with the asset. Second, the asset's actual return must be equal to its expected return (i.e. there is no reinvestment risk). While no investments are actually totally risk free, bonds issued by the governments of politically and economically stable countries are generally considered to be free from the risk of default. Therefore, the risk-free rate can be approximated by taking the current rate of return or yield on short-dated government bonds. In the UK this equates to the yield on short-dated Treasury bills, which is reported regularly in the *Financial Times*. The recent financial crisis, however, had serious implications for government debt. In the USA, increasing borrowing levels and the subsequent downgrading of the US government's credit rating in August 2011 (from AAA to AA+) raised issues as to whether US government debt can be considered risk free. Vignette 8.3 considers the implications of this.

Vignette 8.3

Get used to a world without a 'risk-free' rate

By Gillian Tett

Earlier this week, I pointed out in a column that the cost of insuring the US government against default in the credit **derivatives** markets is now higher than for many major companies. More specifically, data from Markit shows that no less than 70 US corporate names currently command lower credit default swap (CDS) spreads than the sovereign contract (currently running at 50 basis points). A few years ago, there were none.

Unsurprisingly, that observation prompted a flurry of e-mails: some readers suggested that this pattern simply demonstrated what a poor guide CDS prices can be; others argued that it showed instead what a poor job American politicians were doing in relation to US debt.

However, one of the most interesting observations came from Bruce Tozer, a senior official at Crédit Agricole Investment Bank, who suggested that the most important aspect of this swing is that it should force investors to rethink their concept of the 'risk free' rate.

More specifically, in recent decades, western investors and asset managers have been raised to assume that the US Treasury yield was the 'risk free' benchmark, against which other assets could be measured; this consequently formed the bedrock for their investment approaches, such as their use of the capital asset pricing model.

But, these CDS swings, Tozer adds, raise three questions: firstly, can we really consider Treasuries an appropriate 'risk-free' rate today? Secondly, is this concept of 'risk free' even appropriate in today's world? And thirdly – and most crucially – if the answer to the first two questions is 'no', then 'what does that mean for portfolio theory and the capital asset pricing model?' It is worth considering each of these three questions in turn, since they are absolutely fundamental.

On the first issue – namely whether US Treasuries really offer a good 'risk-free' rate – I personally think that there does need to be an investment rethink. On paper, the idea that the US would actually default on its debts currently looks odd; quite apart from the fact that the dollar is the world's reserve currency, the US fiscal problems would not be impossible to solve if only politicians could produce an intelligent, collaborative fiscal plan.

But therein lies the rub: what matters in the US today is not economic and financial volatility, but rising political volatility too. Hence the fact that S&P recently downgraded US debt (entirely understandably, in my view) and the widening of those CDS spreads.

Of course, some observers might retort that even amid these woes, the US still looks less risky than most rivals. True enough. Japan's debt to gross

Vignette 8.3 (continued)

domestic product ratio, after all, is heading over 200 per cent. Germany's fiscal situation is better, but clouded by turmoil in the eurozone. And while a country such as Switzerland is now being treated by investors as a safe haven, its bond markets are too small to provide any alternative 'risk-free' benchmarks.

And there are not many obvious candidates elsewhere. At a meeting of chief investment officers that I attended in New York, for example, some CIOs suggested – half in jest – that the investment community should start asking whether some large companies (such as IBM) could provide an alternative benchmark. Another leading CIO proposed coal as the best new risk-free asset: after all, he argued, coal (unlike food) does not depreciate over time; however, it (unlike gold) has a tangible use that transcends cultures.

But unless asset managers are ready to start loading up on the black stuff, the more realistic conclusion is that we could be moving into a world where there is no real 'risk-free' rate at all. If so, as Tozer says, it may now also be time to recognise that all of those capital asset pricing model techniques to which 20th century finance was so addicted need to be reconsidered too.

Would that be such a bad thing? Some might argue not. After all, as Emanuel Derman, the well-respected financial 'quant', argues in a powerful book that will be published next month, while models are essential for the modern world, they are always illusory to some degree. And in the case of that 'risk-free' benchmark, that always incorporated some element of fiction. If the current debate about US debt – and the CDS spreads – is now forcing investors to clearly recognise this, then it might be a positive thing in the long term.

But in the short term, at least, the main impact of these swings is that it has left many investors feeling profoundly uneasy, albeit in ways that they cannot always articulate. After all, nobody likes losing their long-cherished compass, when the landscape around them looks scary; risk is a four-letter word.

 Source: Tett, G. (2011) 'Get used to a world without a "risk-free" rate', *Financial Times*, 1 September. © The Financial Times Limited 2011. All Rights Reserved.

Questions

1 Critically discuss whether the yield on US Treasury bills provides an accurate estimate for the 'risk-free' rate today.

2 Critically discuss the implications for portfolio theory and the capital asset pricing model if government securities can no longer be considered 'risk free'.

The return on the market, R_m, is more difficult to calculate. It is usually approximated by using *stock exchange indices* such as the FTSE 100 or the FTSE All Share Index as a representation of the market. To find the return of the market, the capital gains of the chosen index over a one-year period should be added to the dividend yield of the shares in the index over the same period. This is given by the following formula, which allows us to approximate the return of the market over the year:

$$R_m = \frac{P_1 - P_0}{P_0} + \text{Div}$$

where: P_0 = the stock exchange index at the beginning of the period

P_1 = the stock exchange index at the end of the period

Div = average dividend yield of the stock exchange index over the period

Because of short-term fluctuations in stock exchange indices it is advisable to use a *time-smoothed average* to estimate the return of the market. For instance, if using monthly data, calculate the monthly return of the index over, say, a three-year period. Alternatively, if using annual data, calculate a moving average by shifting the one-year period back a month at a time to cover a number of years.

A large number of empirical studies have attempted to quantify the market or **equity risk premium** $(R_m - R_f)$, which represents the excess of market returns over those associated with investing in risk-free assets. Results vary considerably (typically between 3 per cent and 12 per cent) according to the time period used as a basis: whether a geometric or arithmetic mean is calculated (Jenkinson (1994) found that the latter tends to give higher results); and whether gilts or Treasury bills are used to represent the risk-free asset (again the latter gave higher results).

Using historical UK market returns over the period 1918–77, Dimson and Brealey (1978) found an average equity risk premium of 9 per cent. A similar result (9.1 per cent) was found by Allan et al. (1986) over a longer period, 1919–84. A study by Dimson et al. (2002) yielded a range of results including a geometric mean equity risk premium for the UK of 4.5 per cent based on the period 1900–2001 and using Treasury bills to represent risk-free assets. This increased significantly to 7.2 per cent when the period 1951–2001 was considered. In the USA, Ibbotson Associates (2003) arrived at an arithmetic mean equity risk premium of 8.4 per cent using data over the period 1926–2002. Hence, while an equity risk premium of between 8 and 9 per cent has traditionally been put forward by academics, others have argued that this is an overstatement and that a figure of around 5 per cent gives a more appropriate current premium for equity risk.

Using a lower premium is further supported if we consider the effects on equity returns of the tragic events of 11 September 2001. In 2007, Barclays Global Investors arrived at an **arithmetic mean** UK equity risk premium of 4.2 per cent using gilts and a 107-year data period (Barclays Capital 2007). This is broadly in line with UK industry watchdogs such as Ofwat, Ofgem and Ofcom which, in the past, have applied an equity risk premium of between 3.5 per cent and 5 per cent when making their weighted average cost of capital (WACC) calculations (see 'WACC in the real world', Section 9.6). A further complication in quantifying the equity risk premium is that an equity **bear market** in 2007 saw massive falls in share prices and as a result 2008 saw UK gilt returns massively outperform their equity counterparts. The implications of this for the equity risk premium are that if shorter time periods are taken, the equity risk premium becomes negative for data samples up to 20 years.

Coming right up to date, the Credit Suisse (2018) *Global Investment Returns Yearbook* estimated the UK equity risk premium for the period 1968–2017 to be 4.8 per cent (using UK Treasury bills); for the extended period 1900–2017 to be a little lower at 4.5 per cent; and for the more recent period 2000–2017 to be lower still at 2.4 per cent. Damodaran (2018) calculated the implied year-end US equity risk premium for the period 1961-2017 to be 5.08 per cent. Finally, KPMG NL (2018) estimated the 'global' equity risk premium to be 5.5 per cent. The issue of the equity risk premium is discussed further in Vignette 8.4.

Vignette 8.4

Developed world returns set to weaken

By Steve Johnson

Future returns from developed world equities and bonds are set to fall below those seen in the past 110 years, according to two heavyweight annual reports. A year ago Barclays Capital predicted that the equity risk premium, the excess return over cash investors need to compensate for the risk of stock market investing, would rise from a historical 4 percentage points a year to 5 points in the next decade. However, it is now forecasting this premium will slide to just 3 per cent.

This finding broadly tallies with that from academics at London Business School who, writing in this year's Credit Suisse Global Investment Returns Sourcebook, estimate the equity risk premium is set to fall to between 3 and 3.5 per cent, comfortably below a long-term average they calculate at 4.5 per cent. 'Believing the future [for equities] will match the past is optimistic,' the LBS team said, while the prospects for fixed income may be worse still. 'Hoping bond returns will match the period since 1982 is fantasy.' BarCap is also predicting a future of lower nominal returns from bonds, of about 3 per cent a year, compared with long-run nominal returns from UK gilts of 5.1 per cent. However, real returns, at 1 per cent, may not be too far below those of the past, given an assumption of muted inflation.

The bank's pessimism about prospects for developed world equities is driven by demographics, particularly the likelihood that the baby boomer generation will de-risk by shifting their pension savings from equities to bonds as they retire, reversing the trend seen between 1980 and 2000, when a bulge of workers in the high-saving 35–54 age group coincided with a two-decade equity bull market.

The LBS team of Elroy Dimson, Paul Marsh and Mike Staunton used a different approach to conclude that the historical global equity risk premium of 4.5 per cent will not be replicated in the future. They calculate that more than 80 basis points of this premium resulted from real dividend growth and almost 50 points from a re-rating of equities, specifically a rise in the price/dividend ratio, neither of which are repeatable, they argue. 'Since 1900 dividend yields have fallen; investors are willing to pay more per unit of dividend than before. We think that is because equity investment has become less risky, for example mutual funds mean it is easier to invest across industries. We don't think this multiple expansion can go much further, if it is due to diversification,' said Professor Marsh. 'Many investment books still cite figures as high as 7 per cent [for the equity risk premium]. 'Investors who rely on such numbers are likely to be disappointed.'

However, BarCap remains upbeat on emerging market equities, where it is forecasting real total returns of 10.5 per cent a year for foreign investors (factoring in currency gains), and commodities, where it believes demand will outstrip supply. As a result, Michael Dicks, chief economist at Barclays Wealth, said developed world equity investors needed to diversify. 'There has always been a very strong home bias in most developed markets. What this really tells us is you have got to look at the rest of the world and think more about alternative asset classes.'

Source: Johnson, S. (2011) 'Developed world returns set to weaken', *Financial Times,* 13 February.
© The Financial Times Limited 2011. All Rights Reserved.

Questions

1 Critically discuss whether the equity risk premium can be predicted accurately.

2 What have been the implications of economic recession for the equity risk premium?

8.6.3 Using the CAPM: A numerical example

Now that we have a firm understanding of the components of the CAPM, we can work through an example to illustrate its use. Consider the following data:

Beta of Burberry Group plc (β_j)   = 1.14
Yield of short-dated Treasury bills (R_f) = 1.0 per cent
Equity risk premium ($R_m - R_f$)   = 4.5 per cent

Using $R_j = R_f + \beta_j(R_m - R_f)$ we have

$$R_j = 1.0 + (1.14 \times 4.5) = 1.0 + 5.1 = 6.1 \text{ per cent}$$

From the data provided, the CAPM predicts that the required rate of return of Burberry Group's shareholders and hence Burberry Group's cost of equity is 6.1 per cent.

8.6.4 Summary of the implications of the CAPM

The implications of using the CAPM to price securities such as shares can be summarised as follows:

■ Investors calculating the required rate of return of a security consider only systematic risk to be relevant, as unsystematic risk can be eradicated by portfolio diversification.
■ Shares with higher levels of systematic risk are expected, on average, to yield higher rates of return.
■ There should be a linear relationship between systematic risk and return, and securities that are correctly priced should plot on the security market line (SML).

A graphical representation of the final implication is shown in Figure 8.14. Share B is correctly priced and plots on the SML. Share A is *underpriced*, giving higher returns compared with those required by investors given its level of systematic risk. Share A will

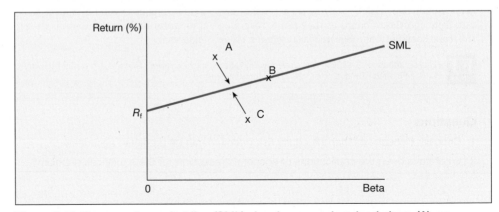

Figure 8.14 The security market line (SML) showing an underpriced share (A), an overpriced share (C) and a correctly valued share (B)

therefore be bought by investors, causing its price to rise and its return to decrease, and the share will move onto the SML. Share C is *overpriced* and hence the opposite will occur. If shares take a long time moving onto the SML, the linear relationship between risk and systematic return will be weakened. We therefore see the importance of the assumption made by the CAPM that capital markets are perfect, as under these conditions share prices will move accurately and quickly to reflect information about shares.

8.7 EMPIRICAL TESTS OF THE CAPM

Earlier in this chapter we acknowledged that the CAPM's assumptions are unrealistic from a real-world perspective and we noted the key assumption of the CAPM that capital markets are perfect. But capital markets are not perfect as transaction costs and taxes clearly do exist in practice. However, capital markets have been shown by empirical tests to exhibit high levels of efficiency. In fact, although the CAPM's assumptions do not totally mirror reality, reality may not be so far away from the assumptions as to invalidate the model. The CAPM, therefore, should not be prejudged on its assumptions but assessed on the results of its application.

There have been many tests of the validity of the CAPM's applications and uses. Research has concentrated on two main areas: the stability of beta coefficients over time, and the strength and nature of the linear relationship between risk and return.

8.7.1 Tests of the stability of beta

While the CAPM is a forward-looking model, the availability of only historical data means that betas are calculated using historical returns of shares in relation to historical returns of the market. Therefore the usefulness of historical betas in both pricing shares and appraising investment projects will depend heavily on the stability of beta coefficients over time. This was investigated by Sharpe and Cooper (1972), who examined the stability of US equity betas over the period 1931–67. They started by splitting their sample of shares into 10 risk classes, each class containing an equal number of shares, allocated according to their beta at the start of the test period. As a rule of thumb, stability was defined as any share that either remained in its existing class or moved by only one class over a five-year period. Their results suggested that shares with high and low betas demonstrated higher levels of stability when compared with shares with mid-range betas. They additionally found that approximately 50 per cent of shares' betas could be considered stable (according to their earlier definition) over a five-year period.

While empirical evidence on the stability of individual betas is inconclusive, there is general agreement that the betas of portfolios of shares exhibit much higher levels of stability over time. The most common explanation offered for this is that any errors associated with the estimation of an individual share's beta or any actual changes in the systematic risk characteristics of individual shares will tend to average out when shares are combined in a portfolio.

8.7.2 Tests of the security market line

Many empirical tests have used regression analysis to derive a *fitted* security market line (SML) which is then compared with the *theoretical* SML. Deriving the fitted SML involves a two-stage process. The first stage is to select a wide-ranging sample of shares and using market returns and security returns over a specified period (say monthly data over a five-year period), calculate the average return of the securities and their beta coefficients using a series of regressions. The second stage is to derive a fitted SML by regressing individual shares' beta coefficients against their average returns. The theoretical SML is located by estimating the risk-free rate of return (R_f) to give the intercept on the vertical (y) axis and then calculating the return of the market (R_m) and plotting it against a beta of 1 on the horizontal (x) axis. Some of the best-known tests include those carried out by Jacob (1971), Black et al. (1972) and Fama and Macbeth (1973). The conclusions of their tests can be summarised as follows:

- The fitted SML intercept with the y-axis was above the theoretical SML intercept with the y-axis, indicating that systematic risk was not the only factor determining rates of return.
- The slope of the fitted SML was flatter than the slope of the theoretical SML.
- The fitted SML indicated a strong linear relationship between systematic risk and return, albeit a different relationship to that suggested by the theoretical SML.

Figure 8.15 illustrates these points.

The broad conclusion drawn from these tests is that the CAPM does not fully explain observed data, although systematic risk does go a long way towards explaining expected returns of individual securities. More recent tests have been far less kind to the CAPM. Black (1993) considered the strength of the risk–return relationship in the USA over the periods 1931–65 and 1966–91. In his simulation he constructed 10 portfolios, the first containing

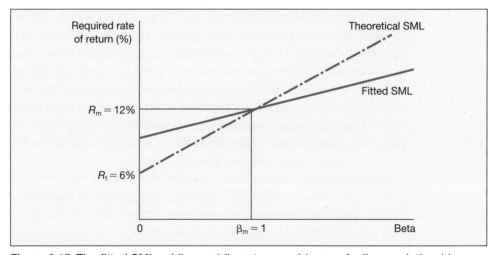

Figure 8.15 The fitted SML, while providing strong evidence of a linear relationship between risk and return, suggests a less steep linear relationship when compared with the theoretically derived SML

shares with beta values in the highest 10 per cent right category down to the final portfolio made up of shares with beta values in the lowest 10 per cent category. He then calculated the returns for the 10 portfolios over the previous five years. This process was repeated year on year with the 10 portfolios' compositions changing to maintain their risk profile. When results for the period 1931–65 were examined, the 10 portfolios plotted close to the theoretical SML with the highest risk portfolio yielding the highest return and the lowest risk portfolio the lowest return. When the period 1966–91 was considered, however, the relationship broke down completely. Fama and French (1992) also found against the CAPM. Focusing on US equity returns over the period 1963–90, they concluded that no meaningful relationship could be found between market betas and average returns on shares. They did find, however, that average returns on shares were negatively correlated with company size and positively correlated with company book-to-market values. Comparative studies based on returns of share from major European stock markets were equally unsupportive of the CAPM.

While recent tests question the validity of the CAPM, Roll (1977) argued that the CAPM is difficult, if not almost impossible, to test. The reason is that the stock exchange indices that are used to approximate the market return are poor surrogates. Not only do stock exchange indices fail to include all tradeable shares, they also omit untradeable shares and other financial and non-financial assets (such as bonds, property, land, antiques and so on). Roll therefore concluded that it is impossible to create a truly diversified market portfolio which accurately reflects all risky assets, making it is impossible to test the validity of the CAPM.

Is the CAPM worthless and are students of corporate finance wasting their time by studying it? The answer to this question, from an educational, if not an academic, perspective, must be no. Despite Fernandez (2015) recently referring to the CAPM as 'an absurd model' we should only discard a theory or model if there is a better one with which to replace it. Ross (1976) proposed a potential 'heir to the throne' of the CAPM in the shape of the arbitrage pricing model (APM). This multi-factor model has until now remained ill-defined in terms of both the type and the number of variables relevant to explaining equity returns, hence the APM has some way to go before it replaces the CAPM. That said, Fama and French (1992) proposed a three-factor regression model adding company size and book-to-market value as independent variables. More recently, they proposed a five-factor model (Fama and French 2014), adding profitability and investment to further improve the model's performance. While the CAPM may be limited in its practical value to companies, it does provide a framework with which to quantify and translate risk into an easily understandable required rate of return. We should also note that the CAPM is superior to the dividend growth model (see Chapter 9) as a way of calculating a company's cost of equity.

8.8 CONCLUSION

In this chapter we considered the important relationship between risk and return. We started by looking at how the risk and return of individual investments can be measured and then went on to show that investors can, by holding well-diversified portfolios, eradicate the unsystematic risk they face, which is the basis of Markowitz's portfolio theory. We then located the optimal portfolio of risky shares (the market portfolio) when risk-free assets are available to investors and identified the linear relationship between risk and return known as the capital market line (CML). Investors can select portfolios on the CML according to their risk preferences.

The capital asset pricing model (CAPM) is a development of Markowitz's portfolio theory. This model identifies a linear relationship between the returns on individual securities and their systematic risk as measured by their beta factor. This relationship allows investors to calculate the required return for a share given its systematic risk and hence determine whether it is fairly priced. While the CAPM's assumptions are not realistic, empirical evidence suggests that a linear relationship exists between systematic risk and return, albeit one which is slightly different from that suggested by theory.

■ ■ ■ KEY POINTS

1 The relationship between risk and return has an important role in corporate finance. The risk of an investment is measured by the standard deviation of its historical or forecast returns.

2 The risk of an investment can be divided into systematic and unsystematic risk. Unsystematic risk can be diversified away by investing in a range of different shares.

3 The simplest form of diversification is to invest in a two-share portfolio. The key determinant of the amount of risk that can be diversified away is the degree of correlation between the returns on the two shares.

4 The greater the variety of shares in a portfolio, the more unsystematic risk will be diversified away.

5 Markowitz's portfolio theory provides the basis from which investors can, by combining the most efficient portfolio of risky assets with the risk-free asset, construct a portfolio which satisfies their risk and return requirements, and hence maximises their utility.

6 One difficulty in practice for smaller investors using portfolio theory is that transaction costs can be high. However, they can overcome this problem by investing in diversified portfolios, e.g. investment trusts and unit trusts.

7 The CAPM, which builds on portfolio theory, defines a linear relationship between the systematic risk of a security and its required rate of return. This linear relationship is represented by the security market line (SML).

8 Systematic risk is measured by beta, which indicates the sensitivity of a security's returns to systematic factors, relative to the market return and the risk-free rate of return.

9 If securities are correctly priced, they should plot on the security market line.

10 While empirical tests do not reinforce the validity of the CAPM, the model does provide a useful aid to understanding the relationship between systematic risk and the required rate of return of securities.

SELF-TEST QUESTIONS

Answers to these questions can be found on pages 461–3.

1 Explain why risk continues to exist even in a well-diversified portfolio.

2 Discuss whether diversification at company level has any value to a company's ordinary shareholders.

3 Distinguish between an efficient portfolio and an optimal portfolio.

4 Explain the importance of risk-free assets to portfolio theory.

5 How do we approximate the risk-free rate in practice? In reality, will the capital market line be a straight line?

6 List the limitations of portfolio theory as an aid to investment decisions.

7 Explain whether you consider the assumptions upon which the capital asset pricing model is based to be unrealistic.

8 Explain what is measured by beta.

9 Identify the problems associated with determining the equity risk premium.

10 The market return is 10 per cent and UK Treasury bills yield 4 per cent. Lime Spider plc shares have a covariance of 7.5 with the market whereas the market has a variance of 4.5. What is the required rate of return for Lime Spider plc's shares?

QUESTIONS FOR REVIEW

1 Discuss how portfolio theory can help individual investors maximise their utility.

2 You are looking to invest in two shares, X and Y, and have the following information:

Share	Possible return (%)	Probability
X	30	0.3
	25	0.4
	20	0.3
Y	50	0.2
	30	0.6
	10	0.2

(a) Calculate the expected return for each share and for a portfolio of 60 per cent X and 40 per cent Y.

(b) Calculate the expected risk of each share and of the portfolio as defined above if the correlation coefficient of the two returns is +0.15.

3 Lampard plc has been investing surplus funds in a small portfolio of shares over the past few years. Details of the portfolio are as follows:

Company	No. of shares	Beta	Share price (£)	Dividend yield (%)	Expected return (%)
Martin	70,000	1.27	3.75	5.6	12
Jerome	150,000	1.53	4.25	3.5	16
Carson	100,000	1.01	2.50	4.2	14
Lawrence	80,000	0.95	4.50	6.2	9.5
Thorne	130,000	0.82	3.50	4.8	15

The current market return is 12 per cent and the yield on Treasury bills is 5 per cent.

(a) Is Lampard's portfolio more or less risky than that of the market portfolio? Support your answer with appropriate calculations.

(b) Give Lampard plc advice on how it should change the composition of its portfolio, giving a rationale for the changes that you recommend.

4 You are given the following data which refers to the performance of the FTSE 100 and two companies over the last financial year.

FTSE 100 Index at start of year	5,447
FTSE 100 Index at the end of year	5,905
Dividend yield on FTSE 100 Index for the year	4.55%
Current redemption yield for 7% Treasury bills	3.78%

	Aardvark plc	Bear plc
Share price at start of year	201p	260p
Share price at end of year	224p	307p
Dividend payment for year	8p	9p
Equity beta	1.3	0.87

Required:

(a) Using the data above, calculate whether a diversified investor with shareholdings in the two companies will be satisfied with the returns they are receiving.

(b) Critically discuss how useful you consider the analysis in part (a) to be when making portfolio management decisions.

5 Mr Magoo plans to invest £18m in one of two short-term portfolios. Both portfolios consist of four short-term securities from diverse industries. The correlation between the returns of the individual securities is thought to be close to zero.

Portfolio A investments	Equity beta	Expected return (%)	Standard deviation of return (%)	Invested amount (£m)
1	1.5	17	8	3.6
2	0.0	5	1	5.4
3	0.8	10	4	5.8
4	1.0	13	12	3.2

Portfolio B investments	Equity beta	Expected return (%)	Standard deviation of return (%)	Invested amount (£m)
1	1.2	12	10	7.4
2	0.7	10	4	2.6
3	0.3	6	2	5.2
4	1.6	17	14	2.8

(a) Mr Magoo's financial adviser has suggested that he use the capital asset pricing model (CAPM) to compare the portfolios. The current equity risk premium is 5.5 per cent and the yield on short-dated Treasury bills is 4.5 per cent. Using the information provided, recommend which of the two portfolios should be selected.

(b) Briefly explain whether the CAPM and portfolio theory use the same measure of risk.

(c) Discuss whether you consider portfolio theory or the CAPM to be most appropriate when choosing between the portfolios in part (a).

QUESTIONS FOR DISCUSSION

1 The shares of companies Z and Y have the following expected returns and standard deviations:

	Z	Y
Expected return (%)	15	35
Standard deviation (%)	20	40

If the correlation coefficient between the two securities is +0.25, calculate the expected return and standard deviation for the following portfolios:

(a) 100 per cent Z;

(b) 75 per cent Z and 25 per cent Y;

(c) 50 per cent Z and 50 per cent Y;

(d) 25 per cent Z and 75 per cent Y;

(e) 100 per cent Y.

2 Ms Moroley has just finished reading a textbook on portfolio theory and is keen to put her newfound knowledge into action by investing £1,000. She has identified the efficient frontier for portfolios of risky assets according to the following table:

Portfolio	Expected return (%)	Standard deviation (%)
A	4.0	5.0
B	6.0	4.0
C	8.0	5.0
D	10.0	8.0
E	10.6	11.0
F	11.0	14.0

She has estimated the yield on short-dated Treasury bills as 7 per cent and has identified the shape of a typical utility curve, given her own attitude towards risk. Points that plot on this utility curve are as follows:

Expected return (%)	Standard deviation (%)
8.8	1.0
9.0	3.0
9.5	5.0
10.2	6.0
11.2	7.0

Using this information, construct a diagram that allows you to identify how Ms Moroley will split her investment between Treasury bills and the market portfolio.

3   Loring plc has paid the following dividends in recent years:

Year	Year 1	Year 2	Year 3	Year 4	Year 5
Dividend per share	64p	nil	7p	69p	75p

The dividend for Year 5 has just been paid. The risk-free rate of return is 6 per cent and the market rate of return is 15 per cent.

(a) If Loring plc has an equity beta of 1.203, what will be the market price of one of its shares?

(b) Discuss the meaning of the term 'equity beta' and explain how the equity beta of a public limited company may be determined.

4   Critically discuss whether the CAPM makes portfolio theory redundant.

5   You have the following information about the returns for the shares of Super Lux plc and the returns for the market:

Time	Return of Super Lux (%)	Return of the market (%)
t_1	18	10
t_2	21	11
t_3	20	8
t_4	25	12
t_5	26	14

Given that the rate of return on Treasury bills is 8 per cent and that the correlation coefficient between the returns on Super Lux's shares and the market is +0.83, calculate the rate of return on Super Lux's shares predicted by the CAPM.

References

Allan, D., Day, R., Hirst, I. and Kwiatowski, J. (1986) 'Equity, gilts, treasury bills and inflation', *Investment Analyst*, vol. 83, pp. 11–18.

Barclays Capital (2007) *Barclays Capital Equity Gilt Study: 52nd edn*, London: Barclays Capital.

Black, F. (1993) 'Beta and returns', *Journal of Portfolio Management*, vol. 20, pp. 8–18.

Black, F., Jensen, M. and Scholes, M. (1972) 'The capital asset pricing model: some empirical tests', in Jensen, Frederick A. (ed.) *Studies in the Theory of Capital Markets*, New York: Praeger.

Credit Suisse (2018) *Credit Suisse Global Investment Returns Year Book*, February, Zurich: Credit Suisse.

Damodaran, A. (2018) 'Implied Equity risk premiums', available at: *http://people.stern.nyu.edu/adamodar*

Dimson, E. and Brealey, R. (1978) 'The risk premium on UK equities', *Investment Analyst*, vol. 52, pp. 14–18.

Dimson, E., Marsh, P. and Staunton, M. (2002) *Triumph of the Optimists: 101 Years of Global Investment Returns*, Princeton, NJ, and Oxford: Princeton University Press.

Fama, E. and French, K. (1992) 'The cross-section of expected stock returns', *Journal of Finance*, vol. 47, pp. 427–65.

Fama, E. and French, K. (2014) 'A five-factor asset pricing model', *Journal of Financial Economics*, vol. 116, issue 1, April, pp. 1–22.

Fama, E. and Macbeth, J. (1973) 'Risk, return and equilibrium: empirical tests', *Journal of Political Economy*, vol. 81, May/June, pp. 607–36.

Fernandez, P. (2015) 'CAPM: an absurd model', *Business Valuation Review*, vol. 34, issue 1, Spring, pp. 4–23.

Ibbotson Associates (2003) *Stocks, Bonds, Bills, and Inflation Yearbook: Valuation Edition*, Chicago, IL: Ibbotson Associates.

Jacob, N. (1971) 'The measurement of systematic risk for securities and portfolios: some empirical results', *Journal of Financial and Quantitative Analysis*, vol. 6, pp. 815–33.

Jenkinson, T. (1994) 'The equity risk premium and the cost of capital debate in the UK regulated utilities', University of Oxford, mimeo.

KPMG NL (2018) *Equity Market Risk Premium – Research Summary*, January, Netherlands: KPMG.

Markowitz, H. (1952) 'Portfolio selection', *Journal of Finance*, vol. 7, pp. 13–37.

Roll, R. (1977) 'A critique of the asset pricing theory's tests, part 1: on past and potential testability of the theory', *Journal of Financial Economics*, vol. 4, pp. 129–76.

Ross, S. (1976) 'The arbitrage theory of capital asset pricing', *Journal of Economic Theory*, vol. 13, pp. 341–60.

Sharpe, W. (1964) 'Capital asset prices: a theory of market equilibrium under conditions of risk', *Journal of Finance*, vol. 19, pp. 768–83.

Sharpe, W. and Cooper, G. (1972) 'Risk–return classes of New York Stock Exchange common stocks 1931–67', *Financial Analysts Journal*, vol. 28, pp. 46–54.

Solnik, B. (1974) 'Why not diversify internationally rather than domestically?', *Financial Analysts Journal*, vol. 30, July/August, pp. 48–54.

Tobin, J. (1958) 'Liquidity preference as behaviour towards risk', *Review of Economic Studies*, 26 February, pp. 65–86.

Recommended reading

For an in-depth account of risk and return, portfolio theory and the CAPM see:

Arnold, G. (2014) *Corporate Financial Management*, 5th edn, Harlow: Pearson.

For a most definitive accounts of portfolio theory, the CAPM and their application see:

Elton, E., Gruber, M. and Brown, S. (2017) *Modern Portfolio Theory and Investment Analysis*, 9th edn, Hoboken, NJ: Wiley & Sons Inc.

Although the following book has not been reprinted for some time, it includes a number of readable and interesting articles, including both Markowitz's and Sharpe's seminal articles and an excellent overview article of the CAPM by Mullins:

Ward, K. (ed.) (1994) *Strategic Issues in Finance,* Oxford: Butterworth-Heinemann.

This publication is an extremely usefully quarterly for getting data on the equity betas of listed UK companies:

London Business School (2018) Risk Measurement Service: Beta Books, London.

The next publication gives an interesting overview of the CAPM and the challenges associated with its use. It also considers Fama and French's enhanced CAPM, which includes variables to allow for the effect of small companies and firms with low book-to-market equity values:

Davies, R., Unni, S., Draper, P. and Paudyal, K. (1999) *The Cost of Equity Capital,* London: CIMA Publishing, chapters 2– 4.

Informative papers, reports and articles recommended for further reading include the following:

Appleyard, A. and Strong, N. (1989) 'Beta geared and ungeared: the case of active debt management', *Accounting and Business Research,* vol. 19, no. 74, pp. 170–4.

Credit Suisse (2018) *Credit Suisse Global Investment Returns Year Book,* February, Zurich: Credit Suisse.

Damodaran, A. (2010) 'Into the abyss: what if nothing is risk free?', available at: http://people.stern.nyu.edu/adamodar/pdfiles/papers/nothingisriskfree.pdf

Damodaran, A. (2015) 'Equity risk premiums: determinants, estimation and implications', available at: https://papers.ssrn.com/sol3/papers.cfm?abstract_id=2581517

Dimson, E., Marsh, P. and Staunton, M. (2003) 'Global evidence on the equity risk premium', *Journal of Applied Corporate Finance,* vol. 15, no. 4, pp. 27–38.

Head, A. (2008) 'The Capital Asset Pricing Model', *Student Accountant,* January, pp. 69–70.

Head, A. (2008) 'CAPM: theory, advantages and disadvantages', *Student Accountant,* July, pp. 50–2; both papers are available from the ACCA in the technical papers section at: http://www.accaglobal.com

9 THE COST OF CAPITAL AND CAPITAL STRUCTURE

Learning objectives

After studying this chapter, you should have achieved the following learning objectives:

- a firm understanding of how to calculate a company's cost of capital and how to apply it appropriately in the investment appraisal process;

- the ability to calculate the costs of different sources of finance used by a company and to calculate the company's weighted average cost of capital;

- an appreciation of why, when calculating the weighted average cost of capital, it is better to use market values than book values;

- an understanding of how the capital asset pricing model can be used to calculate risk-adjusted discount rates for use in investment appraisal;

- the ability to discuss critically whether a company can, by adopting a particular capital structure, influence its cost of capital.

■ ■ ■ INTRODUCTION

The concept of the cost of capital, which is the rate of return required on invested funds, plays an important role in corporate finance theory and practice. A company's cost of capital is (or could be) used as the discount rate in the investment appraisal process when using techniques such as net present value and internal rate of return. If we assume that a company is rational, it will want to raise capital by the cheapest and most efficient methods, thereby minimising its average cost of capital. This will have the effect of increasing the net present value of the company's projects and hence its market value. For a company to try to minimise its average cost of capital, it first requires information on the costs associated with the different sources of finance available to it. Second, it needs to know how to combine these different sources of finance to reach its optimal capital structure.

The importance of a company's capital structure, like the importance of dividend policy, has been the subject of intense academic debate. As with dividends, Miller and Modigliani argued, somewhat against the grain of academic thought at the time, that a company's capital structure was irrelevant in determining its average cost of capital. They later revised their views to take account of the tax implications of debt finance. If market imperfections are also considered, it can be argued that capital structure does have relevance to the average cost of capital. In practice, calculating a company's cost of capital can be extremely difficult and time-consuming; it is also difficult to identify or prove that a given company has an optimal financing mix.

9.1 CALCULATING THE COST OF INDIVIDUAL SOURCES OF FINANCE

A company's overall or **weighted average cost of capital (WACC)** can be used as a *discount rate* in investment appraisal and as a *benchmark* for company performance, so being able to calculate it is a key skill in corporate finance. The first step in calculating WACC is to find the cost of capital of each source of *long-term* finance used by a company. That is the purpose of this section.

9.1.1 Ordinary shares

Equity finance can be raised either by issuing new ordinary shares or by using retained earnings. We can find the cost of equity (K_e) by rearranging the dividend growth model (considered later in this book in Section 10.4.3):

$$K_e = \frac{D_0(1 + g)}{P_0} + g$$

where: K_e = cost of equity

D_0 = current dividend or dividend to be paid shortly

g = expected annual growth rate in dividends

P_0 = ex dividend share price

Retained earnings have a cost of capital equal to the cost of equity. A common misconception is to see retained earnings as a source of finance with no cost. It is true that retained earnings do not have servicing costs, but they do have an *opportunity cost* equal to the cost of equity, since if these funds were returned to shareholders they could have achieved a return equivalent to the cost of equity through personal reinvestment.

An alternative and arguably more reliable method of calculating the cost of equity is to use the *capital asset pricing model* (CAPM), considered earlier in Chapter 8. The CAPM allows shareholders to determine their required rate of return, based on the risk-free rate of return and an equity risk premium. The *equity risk premium* reflects both the systematic risk of the company and the excess return generated by the market relative to risk-free investments.

Using the CAPM, the cost of equity is given by the following linear relationship:

$$R_j = R_f + [(\beta_j \times (R_m - R_f))]$$

where: R_j = the rate of return of share j predicted by the model
R_f = the risk-free rate of return
b_j = the beta coefficient of share j
R_m = the return of the market

9.1.2 Preference shares

Calculating the cost of preference shares is usually easier than calculating the cost of ordinary shares. This is because the dividends paid on preference shares are usually constant. Preference shares tend to be irredeemable and preference dividends are not tax-deductible since they are a distribution of after-tax profits. The cost of irredeemable preference shares (K_{ps}) can be calculated by dividing the dividend payable by the ex dividend market price as follows:

$$K_{ps} = \frac{\text{Dividend payable}}{\text{Market price(ex dividend)}}$$

When calculating the cost of raising new preference shares, the above expression can be modified, as can the dividend growth model, to take issue costs into account.

9.1.3 Bonds and convertibles

There are three major types of bonds or loan notes: irredeemable bonds, redeemable bonds and convertible bonds. The cost of irredeemable bonds is calculated in a similar way to that of irredeemable preference shares. In both cases, the model being used is one that values a perpetual stream of cash flows (a perpetuity). Since the interest payments made on an irredeemable bond are tax deductible, it will have both a before- and an after-tax cost of debt. The *before-tax* cost of irredeemable bonds (K_{ib}) can be calculated as follows:

$$K_{ib} = \frac{\text{Interest rate payable}}{\text{Market price of bond}}$$

The *after-tax* cost of debt is then easily obtained if the corporate taxation rate (C_T) is assumed to be constant:

$$K_{ib}(\text{after tax}) = K_{ib}(1 - C_T)$$

To find the cost of redeemable bonds we need to find the overall return required by providers of debt finance, which combines both revenue (interest) and capital (principal) returns. This is equivalent to the *internal rate of return* (K_d) of the following valuation model:

$$P_0 = \frac{I(1 - C_T)}{(1 + K_d)} + \frac{I(1 - C_T)}{(1 + K_d)^2} + \frac{I(1 - C_T)}{(1 + K_d)^3} + \cdots + \frac{I(1 - C_T) + RV}{(1 + K_d)^n}$$

where: P_0 = current ex interest market price of bond
  I = annual interest payment
  C_T = corporate taxation rate
  RV = redemption value
  K_d = cost of debt after tax
  n = number of years to redemption

Note that this equation will give us the after-tax cost of debt. If the before-tax cost is required, I and not $I(1 - C_T)$ should be used. Linear interpolation can be used to estimate K_d (see 'The internal rate of return method', Section 6.4).

As an alternative to linear interpolation, the before-tax cost of debt can be estimated using the bond yield approximation model developed by Hawawini and Vora (1982):

$$K_d = \frac{I + \left[\dfrac{P - NPD}{n} \right]}{P + 0.6(NPD - P)}$$

where: I = annual interest payment
  P = par value (nominal value) or face value
  NPD = net proceeds from disposal (market price of bond)
  n = number of years to redemption

The after-tax cost of debt can be found using the company taxation rate (C_T):

$$K_d(\text{after tax}) = K_d(1 - C_T)$$

The cost of capital of convertible debt is more difficult to calculate. To find its cost we must first determine whether conversion is likely to occur (see 'The valuation of convertible bonds', Section 5.7). If conversion is *not* expected, we ignore the conversion value and treat the bond as redeemable debt, finding its cost of capital using the linear interpolation or bond approximation methods described above.

If conversion is expected, we find the cost of capital of convertible debt using linear interpolation and a *modified* version of the redeemable bond valuation model given earlier. We modify the valuation model by replacing the number of years to redemption (n) with the number of years to conversion, and by replacing the redemption value (RV) with the expected future conversion value (CV) (see 'Market value', Section 5.7.2).

It must be noted that an *after-tax* cost of debt is appropriate only if the company is in a profitable position, i.e. it has taxable profits against which to set its interest payments.

9.1.4 Bank borrowings

The sources of finance considered so far have all been tradeable securities and have a market price to which interest or dividend payments can be related to calculate their cost. This is not the case with bank borrowings, which are not in tradeable security form and which do not have a market value. To approximate the cost of bank borrowings, therefore, the average interest rate paid on the loan should be taken, adjusted to allow for the tax deductibility of interest payments. The average interest rate can be found by dividing the interest paid on bank borrowings by the average amount of bank borrowings for the year. Alternatively, the cost of debt of any bonds or traded debt issued by a company can be used as an approximate value for the cost of debt of its bank borrowings.

9.1.5 The relationship between the costs of different sources of finance

When calculating the costs of the different sources of finance used by a company, a logical relationship should emerge between the cost of each source of finance on the one hand and the *risk* faced by each supplier of finance on the other. Equity finance represents the highest level of risk faced by investors. This is due both to the *uncertainty* surrounding dividend payments and capital gains, and to the *ranking* of ordinary shares at the bottom of the creditor hierarchy (see Figure 9.1) should a company go into liquidation. New equity issues therefore represent the most expensive source of finance, with retained earnings working out slightly cheaper owing to the savings on issue costs over a new equity issue.

The cost of preference shares will be less than the cost of equity for two reasons. First, preference dividends must be paid before ordinary dividends, hence, there is less risk of their not being paid. Second, preference shares rank higher in the creditor hierarchy than ordinary shares and so there is less risk of failing to receive a share of liquidation proceeds.

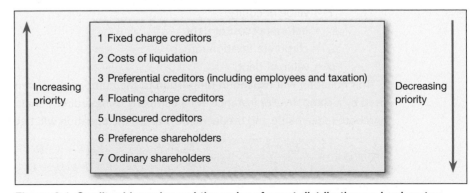

Figure 9.1 Creditor hierarchy and the order of asset distribution on bankruptcy

There is no uncertainty with respect to interest payments on debt unless a company is likely to be declared bankrupt. Debt is further up the creditor hierarchy than both preference shares and ordinary shares, implying that debt finance has a lower cost of capital than both. Whether bank borrowings are cheaper than bonds will depend on the relative costs of obtaining a bank loan and issuing bonds, on the amount of debt being raised, and on the extent and quality of security used. Generally speaking, the longer the period over which debt is raised, the higher will be its cost of capital: this is because lenders require higher rewards for giving up their purchasing power for longer periods of time. The risk of default also increases with time. The cost of convertible debt depends on when and whether the debt is expected to convert into shares. If convertible debt is *not* expected to convert, its cost will be similar to the cost of redeemable bonds of a similar maturity. If convertible debt *is* expected to convert, its cost will be between the costs of redeemable bonds and ordinary shares. The longer the time to conversion, the closer will be the cost of convertible debt to that of redeemable bonds (and vice versa).

The relationships discussed above are illustrated in the WACC calculation example given below.

9.2 CALCULATING THE WEIGHTED AVERAGE COST OF CAPITAL

Once the costs of a company's individual sources of finance have been found, the overall WACC can be calculated. To calculate WACC, the costs of the individual sources of finance are weighted according to their relative value as sources of finance. The WACC can be calculated either for the existing capital structure (average basis) or for additional incremental finance (marginal basis). The problem of average versus marginal WACC is discussed in the next section.

The WACC calculation for a company financed solely by debt and equity finance is represented by:

$$\text{WACC} = \frac{K_e \times E}{(D + E)} + \frac{K_d(1 - C_T) \times D}{(D + E)}$$

where: K_e = cost of equity
E = value of equity
K_d = before-tax cost of debt
C_T = corporate taxation rate
D = value of debt

This equation will expand in proportion to the number of different sources of finance used by a company. For instance, for a company using ordinary shares, preference shares and both redeemable and irredeemable bonds, the equation will become:

$$\text{WACC} = \frac{K_e \times E}{E + P + D_i + D_r} + \frac{K_{ps} \times P}{E + P + D_i + D_r} + \frac{K_{ib}(1 - C_T)D_i}{E + P + D_i + D_r} + \frac{K_{rb}(1 - C_T)D_r}{E + P + D_i + D_r}$$

where P, D_i and D_r are the value of preference shares, irredeemable bonds and redeemable bonds, respectively.

9.2.1 Market value weightings or book value weightings?

We now need to determine the weightings to be attached to the costs of the different sources of finance. The weightings allow the calculated average to reflect the relative proportions of capital used by a company. We must choose between book values or market values. Book values are easily obtained from a company's accounts whereas market values can be obtained from the financial press and from a range of financial databases.

While book values are easy to obtain, using them to calculate the WACC cannot be recommended. Book values are based on historical costs and rarely reflect the current required return of providers of finance, whether equity or debt. The nominal value of an ordinary share, for example, is usually only a fraction of its market value. In the following example, an ordinary share with a nominal value of £1 has a market value of £4.17. Using book values will therefore understate the impact of the cost of equity finance on the average cost of capital. As the cost of equity is *always* greater than the cost of debt, this will lead to the WACC being underestimated. This can be seen in the following example by comparing the WACC calculated using market values with the WACC calculated using book values. If the WACC is underestimated, unprofitable projects might be accepted. As mentioned earlier, some sources of finance, such as bank loans, do not have market values. There is no reason, theoretically, why book values and market values cannot be used in conjunction with each other. Hence when making WACC calculations it is recommended to use as many market values as possible.

Example | **Calculating weighted average cost of capital**

Strummer plc is calculating its current weighted average cost of capital on both a book value and a market value basis. You have the following information:

Year-end financial position statement

	£000	£000
Non-current assets	33,344	
Current assets	15,345	48,689
Ordinary shares (50p nominal value)	6,400	
Reserves	7,200	
7% preference shares (£1 nominal value)	9,000	22,600
Long-term liabilities		
5% bonds (redeemable in 6 years)	4,650	
9% irredeemable bonds	8,500	
Bank loans	3,260	16,410
Current liabilities		9,679
		48,689

1 The current dividend, shortly to be paid, is 23p per share. Dividends in the future are expected to grow at a rate of 5 per cent per year.
2 Corporation tax is currently 30 per cent.
3 The interest rate on bank borrowings is currently 7 per cent.
4 Year-end market prices (all ex dividend or ex interest):

Ordinary shares	£4.17
Preference shares	89p
5% bonds	£96 per £100 bond
9% irredeemable bonds	£108 per £100 bond

Step one: Calculating the costs of individual sources of finance

1 *Cost of equity*: using the dividend growth model:

$$K_e = [D_0(1 + g)/P_0] + g$$
$$= [23 \times (1 + 0.05)/417] + 0.05$$
$$= 10.8 \text{ per cent}$$

2 *Cost of preference shares*:

$$K_{ps} = \frac{8}{89} = 9.0 \text{ per cent}$$

3 *Cost of redeemable bonds (after tax)*: using the Hawawini–Vora bond yield approximation model:

$$K_{rb} = \frac{5 + (100 - 96)/6}{100 + 0.6(96 - 100)}$$

K_{rb}(before tax) = 5.8%
K_{rb}(after tax) = 5.8 × (1 − 0.30) = 4.1 per cent

4 *Cost of bank loans (after tax)*:

$$K_{bl}(\text{after tax}) = 7 \times (1 - 0.30) = 4.9 \text{ per cent}$$

5 *Cost of irredeemable bonds (after tax)*:

$$K_{ib}(\text{after tax}) = 9 \times (1 - 0.30)/108 = 5.8 \text{ per cent}$$

Step two: Calculating book and market values of individual sources of finance

Source of finance	Book value (£000)	Market value (£000)
Ordinary shares	6,400 + 7,200 = 13,600	6,400 × 4.17 × 2 = 53,376
Preference shares	9,000	9,000 × 0.89 = 8,010
Redeemable bonds	4,650	4,650 × 96/100 = 4,464
Irredeemable bonds	8,500	8,500 × 108/100 = 9,180
Bank loans	3,260	3,260
Total	39,010	78,290

Step three: Calculating WACC using book values and market values

WACC (book values) = (10.8% × 13,300/39,010) + (9.0% × 9,000/39,010)
+ (4.1% × 4,650/39,010) + (4.9% × 3,260/39,010)
+ (5.8% × 8,500/39,010)
= 8.0 per cent

WACC (market values) = (10.8% × 53,376/78,290) + (9.0% × 8,010/78,290)
+ (4.1% × 4,464/78,290) + (4.9% × 3,260 × 78,290)
+ (5.8% × 9,180/78,290)
= 9.4 per cent

9.3 AVERAGE AND MARGINAL COST OF CAPITAL

As mentioned earlier, the cost of capital can be calculated in two ways. If it is calculated on an average basis using balance sheet data and book values or market values as weightings, as in the above example, it represents the average cost of capital currently employed. This cost of capital represents historical financial decisions. If it is calculated as the cost of the next increment of capital raised by a company, it represents the marginal cost of capital. The relationship between average (AC) cost of capital and marginal (MC) cost of capital is shown in Figure 9.2.

The relationship between the average cost and marginal cost curves can be explained as follows. When the marginal cost of capital is less than the average cost of capital, the average cost of capital will fall if incremental finance is raised. Once the marginal cost rises above the average cost of capital, however, the average cost of capital will increase if incremental finance is raised, albeit at a slower rate than that at which the marginal cost of capital is rising.

Should we use the marginal or the average cost of capital when appraising investment projects? Strictly speaking, the marginal cost of capital raised to finance an investment project should be used rather than an average cost of capital. One problem with calculating

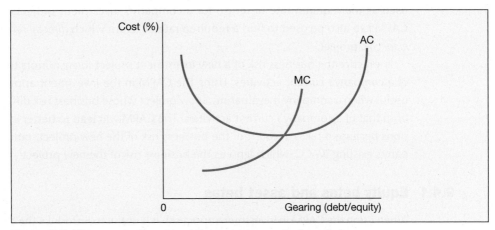

Figure 9.2 The marginal cost and the average cost of capital

the marginal cost of capital, however, is that it is often difficult to allocate specific funding to a specific project. Furthermore, companies with a target capital structure will often raise marginal finance by using only one source of finance at a time. For example, assume a company has a target capital structure of equal amounts of equity and debt. If in one year the company needs £10m, it might prefer to raise this as debt finance, incurring one issue fee, rather than raising £5m each of debt and equity. In the next year, the company can raise £10m of equity finance, restoring its target capital structure. The problem here is that the marginal cost of capital will fluctuate from a low level when marginal debt financing is used to a high level when marginal equity financing is used. It could be argued therefore that a *rolling average* marginal cost of capital is more appropriate than an *incremental* marginal cost of capital.

Using an average cost of capital as the discount rate in investment appraisal is appropriate only if the following three restrictive assumptions are satisfied:

- The business risk of an investment project is similar to the business risk of the company's current activities as a whole.
- Incremental finance is raised in proportions which preserve the existing capital structure of the company.
- The investment project does not disturb the existing risk/return relationships between providers of finance, whether by synergy, scale economies or other effects.

If these restrictive assumptions are *not* satisfied, using a marginal cost of capital may be more appropriate. Any effect on the existing average cost structure must also be reflected in the marginal cost of capital.

9.4 THE CAPM AND INVESTMENT APPRAISAL

In Chapter 8 we discussed using the CAPM in security valuation and saw that the model can be used to calculate the security's required return. This required return of shareholders is the cost of equity of the company and it can therefore be used in calculating the company's WACC. The WACC calculated using a CAPM-derived cost of equity can be used as the required rate of return for a company's investment projects. However, the CAPM can also be used to find a required rate of return which *directly* reflects the risk of a *specific* project.

In practice the business risk of a new investment project *rarely* mirrors the business risk of a company's current activities. Using the CAPM in the investment appraisal process is useful when a company is evaluating a new project whose business risk differs significantly from that of a company's current activities. The CAPM will lead to better investment decisions because it takes account of the business risk of the new project, rather than a company's existing WACC, which ignores the business risk of the new project.

9.4.1 Equity betas and asset betas

When using the CAPM in investment appraisal, it is useful to introduce the concept of asset and liability betas. There are two liability betas: an equity beta and a debt beta. The betas discussed earlier in Chapter 8 were equity betas (also known as geared betas) which represent the total systematic risk of a company. This systematic risk has two components:

- *Business risk*: this represents the sensitivity of a company's cash flows to changes in the economic climate and depends on the industry within which the company operates.
- *Financial risk*: this represents the sensitivity of a company's cash flows to changes in the interest it pays on its debt finance. The level of financial risk faced by a company increases with its level of gearing.

Both types of risk are reflected in a company's equity beta. The *asset beta* or *ungeared beta*, however, reflects only a company's business risk. A company's asset beta is the weighted average of the asset betas of the company's individual projects. For example, a company with only two projects, both equal in value, one with an asset beta of 1.2 and the other with an asset beta of 0.8, will have an overall company asset beta of 1.

A company's asset beta is also the weighted average of its liability betas, weighted to reflect the market values of its liabilities, whether debt or equity finance. This is represented by the following equation:

$$\beta_a = \left[\beta_e \times \frac{E}{E + D(1 - C_T)} \right] + \left[\beta_d \times \frac{D(1 - C_T)}{E + D(1 - C_T)} \right]$$

where: β_a = asset beta or ungeared beta
β_e = equity beta or geared beta
E = market value of equity
D = market value of debt
C_T = corporate tax rate
β_d = debt beta

We can see from this equation that a company's equity beta will always be greater than its asset beta, unless of course a company is all-equity financed, in which case its equity beta is equal to its asset beta. If we assume that companies do not default on their interest payments we can take the beta of debt to be zero. The last term of the equation therefore disappears to leave the following equation (the ungearing formula):

$$\beta_a = \beta_e \times \frac{E}{E + D(1 - C_T)}$$

Rearranging this gives the following alternative equation (the regearing formula):

$$\beta_e = \beta_a \times \frac{E + D(1 - C_T)}{E}$$

9.4.2 Using the CAPM to calculate a project's discount rate

Using the CAPM in investment appraisal is very similar to using it in security valuation. Once again only the systematic risk of a project is relevant since shareholders of the company are assumed to have diversified portfolios. To use the CAPM to find a discount rate to use in investment appraisal, we need estimates of the risk-free rate and the equity risk premium (see Section 8.6.2) and, in addition, the *beta of the project.* It is the last of these three components which is the most difficult to find. We can now outline the steps involved in using the CAPM to derive a discount rate for using in investment appraisal.

1 Identify listed companies engaged mainly or entirely in the same type of business operation as the project under appraisal. These companies will have similar systematic business risk to the project and so their equity betas can be used as suitable *proxies* for the project beta.

2 Once the proxy companies and their equity betas have been identified, these proxy equity betas must be adjusted (ungeared) to eliminate gearing effects (i.e. financial risk) and hence give proxy *asset* betas. This is because the proxy companies' gearing will be different from the appraising company's gearing and is therefore not relevant. The formula to *ungear* an equity beta was given earlier (see Section 9.4.1).

3 The next step is either to calculate an average of the proxy asset betas or to select the proxy asset beta considered most appropriate. This beta must then be *regeared* to reflect the financial risk of the appraising company. The formula to regear an asset beta was given earlier (see Section 9.4.1).

4 The *regeared equity beta* will now reflect the *business risk* of the project and the *financial risk* of the appraising company. This beta can now be inserted into the CAPM to yield a cost of equity (required rate of return) which reflects the project's systematic risk.

The cost of equity calculated by this method is an appropriate discount rate for appraising the new project if financing is wholly from retained earnings or from a new equity issue. If the project is financed by a mixture of debt and equity, however, the cost of equity will need to be combined with the cost of new debt finance to give a *project-specific* WACC.

9.4.3 The benefits of using the CAPM instead of the WACC

We suggested earlier that using the CAPM in project appraisal would lead to better investment decisions. This is illustrated in Figure 9.3.

Consider two projects, A and B, where X marks the plot of their expected level of return and level of systematic risk as measured by beta. Project A would be rejected using the WACC since its expected return is less than the company's WACC. However, using the CAPM, which takes account of the lower systematic risk of the project, Project A would be accepted since its expected return is above the security market line. The opposite is true of Project B. This would be accepted using the WACC but rejected using the CAPM. Using the CAPM, therefore, which takes account of the systematic risk of projects, leads to better investment decisions in two areas:

■ the area shaded in pink, where we find low systematic-risk, low-return projects, previously rejected using the WACC, but which will now be accepted;

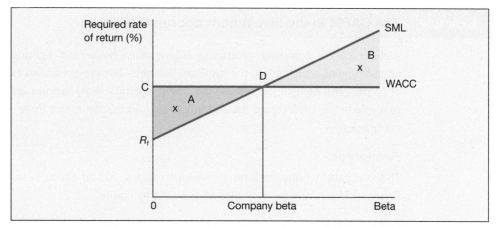

Figure 9.3 How using the CAPM instead of the existing WACC in investment appraisal will lead to better investment decisions

- the area shaded in blue, where we find high systematic-risk, high-return projects, previously accepted using WACC, but which will now be rejected.

9.4.4 Problems using the CAPM in investment appraisal

While the CAPM leads to better investment decisions, there are many problems associated with using it in investment appraisal, as follows:

- The CAPM's assumptions are not applicable to the real world and so may undermine the applicability of the model.
- There is a problem in identifying suitable proxy companies with similar systematic risk to the project under consideration. Companies often undertake a diversified range of activities rather than undertaking only the activity specific to the project being appraised.
- Companies may have difficulty identifying capital structure data with which to ungear proxy companies' equity betas.
- The CAPM assumes that transactions take place over a single period, which is usually taken to be no more than a year.

Clearly, the last point represents a difficulty as investment projects span multiple time periods. Two problems arise. First, equity betas calculated using historical data may not be appropriate for making future decisions, as they often exhibit instability over long time periods. This problem can be reduced by taking the betas of several proxy companies and averaging them to give a portfolio beta (see 'Using the CAPM to calculate a project's hurdle rate', Section 9.4.2, step 3). Second, using the yield of short-dated government securities to approximate the risk-free rate of return will no longer be appropriate. The rate used will need to be tailored to the duration of the project under consideration. For example, if the project spans five years, the yield on gilts (government bonds) maturing in five years could be used to approximate the risk-free rate of return.

Example	The CAPM in the investment appraisal process

Arclight plc, a company producing high-quality household lighting products, is considering diversifying into the furniture business. The project has an expected return of 15 per cent. Arclight plc will use the CAPM to establish an appropriate discount rate to apply to the project and has the following information about three suitable proxy companies.

Furnisure plc

This company, wholly involved in furniture making, has an equity beta of 1.23 and is financed 35 per cent by debt and 65 per cent by equity.

Home Furnish plc

This company, wholly involved in furniture making, has an equity beta of 1.27 and is financed 40 per cent by debt and 60 per cent by equity.

Lux Interior plc

This company has an equity beta of 1.46 and is financed 30 per cent by debt and 70 per cent by equity. It is split into two divisions of equal size: one division produces furniture and the other produces luxury wallpaper. The wallpaper division has 50 per cent more systematic risk than the furniture division.

Other information

- Arclight plc has traditionally adopted a target capital structure of 33 per cent debt and 67 per cent equity, although the project, if accepted, will be financed entirely by equity.
- The current yield on Treasury bills is 4 per cent and the current return on the stock market is 10 per cent.
- The corporation tax rate is 30 per cent.
- Corporate debt can be assumed to be risk-free.

Using the above information, calculate an appropriate discount rate to apply to the project and decide whether it is financially acceptable.

Suggested answer

1 Ungearing the proxy equity betas to give proxy asset betas using the equation:

$$\beta_a = \beta_e \times \left[\frac{E}{E + D(1 - C_T)} \right]$$

Furnisure plc

$$\beta_a = 1.23 \times 65/(65 + 35 \times (1 - 0.30)) = 0.89$$

Home Furnish plc

$$\beta_a = 1.27 \times 60/(60 + 40 \times (1 - 0.30)) = 0.87$$

Lux Interior plc

$$\beta_a = 1.47 \times 70/(70 + 30 \times (1 - 0.30)) = 1.12$$

We have to make a further calculation as Lux Interior's asset beta partly reflects the business risk of its wallpaper division, which is of no relevance to the project under consideration. As the wallpaper division has 50 per cent more systematic risk than the furniture division, its asset beta is 1.5 times the asset beta of the furniture division. We can find the asset beta of its furniture division (b_{af}) as follows:

Lux Interior asset beta $= (0.5 \times$ Wallpaper asset beta$) + (0.5 \times$ Furniture asset beta$)$
$$1.15 = (0.5 \times 1.5 \times \beta_{af}) + (0.5 \times \beta_{af})$$

Hence:

$$\beta_{af} = 1.12/1.25 = 0.90$$

2 Taking an average of the three proxy asset betas:

$$\text{Proxy asset beta} = (0.89 + 0.87 + 0.90)/3 = 0.89$$

3 Regearing the proxy asset beta to reflect Arclight's financial risk using the equation:

$$\beta_e = \beta_a \times \left[\frac{E + D(1 - C_T)}{E} \right]$$

$$\text{Proxy equity beta} = 0.89 \times (67 + 33 \times (1 - 0.30))/67 = 1.20$$

4 Inserting the proxy equity beta into the CAPM to calculate the discount rate:

$$R_j = 0.04 + 1.20 \times (0.10 - 0.04) = 0.112, \text{ i.e. } 11.2\%$$

The expected rate of return of the project (15 per cent) is greater than the discount rate (11.2 per cent) and so Arclight plc should accept the project.

9.4.5 Splitting the cost of equity into its determinants

In Section 8.6.3 we saw how a company's cost of equity finance could be calculated using the CAPM. The ability to ungear a company's equity beta to find its asset beta allows us to divide the cost of equity into three determinants: the risk-free rate of return, business risk and financial risk. This is considered later in the context of capital structure in Section 9.9.1 and Figure 9.1. The following example shows how these determinants can be calculated.

Example	Dividing the cost of equity into its determinants

Yell plc wants to find the relative importance of the determinants of its cost of equity, namely the risk-free rate of return, business risk and financial risk. You have the following information:

	£000
Ordinary shares (nominal value £1)	2,300
Reserves	3,200
Bank loans	3,500
6% bonds (nominal value £100)	3,000
	12,000

1 The return on the market is 8.21 per cent per year.
2 The current yield of treasury bills is 4.34 per cent per year.
3 Corporation tax is currently 30 per cent.
4 The company's current equity beta is 1.21.
5 The ex dividend ordinary share price is £3.98 per share.
6 The ex interest bond price is £123 per bond.

Analysis

1 Calculate the cost of equity using the CAPM:

$$K_e = R_f + \beta_j(R_m - R_f)$$
$$K_e = 4.34 + 1.21\,(8.21 - 4.34) = 4.34 + 4.68 = 9.02 \text{ per cent}$$

2 Ungear the equity beta to give the asset beta. Market values of the company's debt and equity are needed to ungear the equity beta:

Market value of equity	= 2.3m × £3.98	= £9.15m
Market value of bonds	= £3m × 1.23	= £3.69m
Total value of debt	= £3.69m + £3.5m	= £7.19m

Using the ungearing equation:

$$\beta_a = \beta_e \times \left[\frac{E}{E + D(1 - C_T)} \right]$$

We have:

$$\text{Asset beta} = 1.21 \times 9.15/(9.15 + 7.19 \times (1 - 0.3)) = 0.781$$

3 Calculate the ungeared cost of equity:

$$K_e = 4.34 + 0.781\,(8.21 - 4.34) = 7.36 \text{ per cent}$$

4 Calculate the relative importance of the three determinants:

The risk-free rate contributes 100 × 4.34/9.02 =   48% of the cost of equity
Business risk contributes 100 × (7.36 − 4.34)/9.02 =   34% of the cost of equity
Financial risk contributes 100 × (9.02 − 7.36)/9.02 =   18% of the cost of equity

9.5 PRACTICAL PROBLEMS WITH CALCULATING WACC

In addition to the problem of deciding between an average or a marginal cost of capital, there are several practical difficulties in calculating and using a company's WACC.

9.5.1 Calculating the cost of sources of finance

Calculating the cost of capital of a source of finance is not always straightforward. For example, certain securities may not be traded regularly and therefore do not have a market price. This is particularly true for the ordinary shares of private companies. One way to overcome this problem is to calculate the cost of equity for a listed company with similar business activities and then add a premium to reflect the higher risk of the private company. A similar problem may be experienced in finding the market value of bonds, even when the issuing company is listed. One solution is to find the market value of bonds issued by another company with similar maturity, risk and interest rate, and use this market value as a substitute.

The cost of capital of convertible bonds can be very difficult to calculate owing to their complex nature. Convertible bonds start life as debt and so initially have a cost of capital in line with ordinary bonds of a similar maturity and interest rate. Later in their life, however, the bonds are likely to convert into ordinary shares and hence have an equity-related cost of capital. If conversion is near, the market value of the bonds will reflect, not redemption value, but the value of the ordinary shares gained on conversion. It would be incorrect to use this market value in a cost of capital calculation assuming redemption, as this will understate the cost of debt.

Leasing can also provide problems when we wish to calculate the WACC. Many leases provide finance on a medium- to long-term basis and therefore should be included in WACC calculations. While it may be relatively easy to identify the lease payments, which should be taken after tax due to their tax deductibility, the capital value to which these payments relate is difficult to determine. Viewing leasing is as an alternative to debt finance, however, means that the cost of secured debt can be used as a substitute for the cost of capital of leasing, given that leases are secured on the leased assets.

Another problem with respect to the cost of sources of finance relates to debt where interest payments are subject to swap agreements (see 'Interest rate swaps', Section 12.6.1). The main issue here is whether the cost of the debt should reflect the interest rate when the loan was first raised, or the interest rate agreed in the swap. There is no clear answer to this problem.

Finally, the accuracy of the calculated cost of equity depends heavily on the reliability and applicability of the models used. For example, if a company increases its dividends at a very low but constant rate, perhaps due to a low payout ratio, the cost of equity calculated by the dividend growth model is likely to be greatly understated. Alternatively, if a company's beta is unstable and unreliable, the cost of equity calculated using the CAPM will also be unstable and unreliable. The authors recommend using the CAPM for calculating the cost of equity, not only because it is more theoretically sound than the dividend growth model, but also because it does not depend on estimating the future dividend growth rate of a company. It is very difficult to predict dividend growth rates with any real credibility.

9.5.2 Which sources of finance should be included in the WACC?

A major question is which sources of finance to include in the WACC calculation and which to leave out. The general rule is that if finance is being used to fund the long-term investment strategy of a company, it should be included in the calculation. Equity finance, preference shares, medium- and long-term debt and leasing should all therefore be included. Short-term debt should not in general be included in the WACC calculation as it is linked to financing short-term rather than long-term assets. However, if a short-term source of finance, for example, a bank overdraft, is used on an ongoing basis, it can be argued that it is being used to finance long-term assets such as permanent current assets and hence should be included in the WACC calculation.

9.5.3 Problems associated with weighting the sources

Difficulties in finding the market values of securities will also impact on cost of capital through the weightings applied to the costs of the different sources of finance. Market values are preferred to book values, as discussed earlier. However, market values may be hard to find or, in the case of bank loans, may simply not exist. In practice, therefore, both market values and book values are used as weightings when calculating weighted average cost of capital.

Additional problems will be experienced by companies that have raised debt finance denominated in foreign currencies. The values of these debts will have to be translated into sterling to include them in the WACC calculation. Two problems arise here. First, the exchange rate used to convert the debt into sterling is difficult to identify. Second, as exchange rates move, the sterling value of the weightings will also move.

9.5.4 WACC is not constant

A company's WACC is not fixed. As the market values of securities change, so will a company's WACC. Not only will weightings change, but the costs of capital of the different sources of finance will also change as macroeconomic conditions and investor preferences and attitudes change. It is therefore both advisable and necessary for companies to recalculate their WACC frequently to reflect such changes. In investment appraisal we usually assume that WACC is constant in future periods, but this is clearly not true. While this assumption makes calculations easier, it is one of the reasons why investment appraisal is an imperfect mirror of the real world.

It should be apparent from this section that in practice the WACC is both hard to calculate and difficult to apply to the investment appraisal process. The application of WACC in the real world is the subject of the next section.

9.6 WACC IN THE REAL WORLD

Do companies calculate their weighted average cost of capital in practice? Increasingly, the answer to this question is yes and some companies now include cost of capital estimates in their financial statements. Increasing attention is being paid to the WACC due to its close association with concepts such as economic value added (Section 2.4.10), an overall measure of company performance linked to shareholder wealth. Whether WACC can be calculated accurately, given the problems identified earlier, is another matter. Clearly Fama and French (1997) did not think so, since after their US survey of industry cost of capital, they concluded that the chances of accurately calculating a company's WACC were 'fairly bleak' because 'estimates of the cost of equity are distressingly imprecise'. Their conclusions were echoed a decade later by Gregory and Michou (2009), who conducted similar research in the UK.

Despite these problems, WACC has received increasing attention from national regulatory bodies such as the UK Competition and Markets Authority (see 'Merger regulation and control', Section 11.6.1) and industry-specific regulatory bodies such as Oftel and Ofgem, regulators of the UK telecommunications and UK gas and electricity-generating industries respectively. WACC is pivotal in the regulatory process to help determine what is a 'fair' level of profit. Predictably, this has led to many companies claiming that the cost of capital calculated by a regulatory body underestimates their true cost of capital. In 1998 the Competition Commission (then called the Monopolies and Mergers Commission) investigated the price of calls to mobile telephones. It estimated Vodafone's nominal before-tax WACC to be between 14.9 per cent and 17.8 per cent, whereas Vodafone estimated it to be 18.5 per cent. It was a similar story in May 2011 when Ofgem set the pre-tax WACC for Independent Gas Transporters (IGTs) at 7.6 per cent. This was at odds with the IGTs' consultant London Economic's estimate of 8.8 per cent. Given the subjectivity surrounding many of the key variables used in calculating the WACC, these differences should not be surprising. To their credit, UK regulatory bodies and the Office of Fair Trading jointly commissioned an independent report, published in February 2003 (see Wright et al. 2003), which sought to establish the best and most consistent approach to determining the cost of capital for regulated utility companies. Despite this, conflict between regulators and utility companies continues to flare up, as evidenced by Vignette 9.1.

Vignette 9.1

Water operators hit by Ofwat's demands

By Michael Kavanagh

Ofwat has turned the screw on water industry operators across England and Wales by demanding they accept lower rates of return on equity and capital in the next five-year regulatory period that runs to 2020.

The statement by Ofwat follows complaints from lobby group Consumer Council for Water that plans put forward by companies in December, demanding returns averaging 4.3 per cent, could offer too much reward to investors at the expense of customers.

All but two of 19 water and sewage service operators governed by Ofwat put in pricing proposals that will see bills held or reduced in real terms in the five years from 2015. The exceptions are Thames Water,

Vignette 9.1 (continued)

the country's biggest operator, whose customers face the prospect of bill increases to help finance the £4.2bn Thames super sewer project, and industry minnow Dee Valley, which also faces unusually high projects costs.

However, in spite of the prospect of static or lower bills in real terms for most UK households, Ofwat said on Monday that business plans assuming an average cost of capital of 4.3 per cent across the sector for the period were too generous.

The regulator has instead concluded that an acceptable cost of debt to companies is in the range of 2.2 to 2.8 per cent for the period. It also set an acceptable average cost of equity at nearly one percentage point below companies' average claim of 6.6 per cent, stating 'current total equity return expectations should be below historical evidence on returns'.

Sonia Brown, head of regulation at Ofwat, said the overall guidance took account of an anticipated increase in gearing for most companies compared with the past, which would allow operators to benefit still more from access to historically low levels of interest rates.

'Outperformance should not just be about having a clever Treasury function,' she said.

Guidelines on Monday suggested that an increase of half a percentage point in WACC – close to the

spread between Ofwat's guidance of 3.85 per cent and average companies' assumption of 4.3 per cent – equated to a notional increase in annual bills of about £10.

Water UK, the body that represents operators, suggested it could be some time before companies made clear whether they accepted the calls for accepting lower returns and keener prices. 'Ofwat has published significant information and companies will take time to understand fully the implications,' it said.

In a note on Monday, analysts at Deutsche Bank described the lower guidance from Ofwat as 'a clear negative for the listed water companies', arguing that United Utilities and Severn Trent could face pressure to trim future dividend payments.

Shares in both companies, however, edged up on Monday as the move by Ofwat had been widely anticipated.

Companies that move to adopt acceptable levels of risk and reward on financing and operational targets face the prospect of having their business plans 'fast-tracked' for provisional approval as early as March, Ms Brown added. Operators that make this cut will also avoid the burden of facing further onerous scrutiny of their plans by Ofwat ahead of final pricing settlements being agreed next January.

 Source: Kavanagh, M. (2014) 'Water operators hit by Ofwat's demands', *Financial Times,* 27 January. © The Financial Times Limited 2014. All Rights Reserved.

Questions

1 Explain why the control of utility companies' cost of capital has a pivotal role in Ofwat's regulation of the industry.

2 Critically discuss why two parties may come up with different estimates for the same company's weighted average cost of capital.

An extensive sector-by-sector survey of US companies' costs of capital by Damodaran (2018) found an average nominal after-tax WACC of 6.69 per cent using a sample of 7,247 companies. Financial services (non-bank and insurance) companies were found to have the lowest WACC with a sector average of 2.99 per cent. At the opposite end of the spectrum, chemicals (diversified) provided the highest sector average WACC of 10.78 per cent.

9.7 THE COST OF CAPITAL FOR FOREIGN DIRECT INVESTMENT

The arguments for and against using the existing WACC or the CAPM as the source of a discount rate for use in investment appraisal were discussed earlier. Similar arguments are relevant when considering the appropriate discount rate to be used in evaluating foreign direct investment. The following alternative suggestions have been made concerning the cost of capital for foreign direct investment (Stanley 1990):

- A project-specific cost of capital should be used since the discount rate should reflect the value to the company of undertaking specific activities.
- The WACC should be used for projects of similar risk to existing activities; otherwise a project-specific cost of capital should be used.
- The appropriate cost of capital is that of local firms in the same industry.

All three suggestions point to the need for a cost of capital which reflects the risk and characteristics of individual projects. Each suggestion also implies that a single cost of capital can adequately take account of the complex interaction between sources of finance, taxation, exchange rates, exchange controls and risk, which is a feature of foreign direct investment.

In contrast, the *adjusted present value* (APV) method of investment appraisal suggests that the basic investment project, ignoring taxation and financing aspects, should be discounted at the parent company's ungeared cost of equity, and that taxation and financing implications can be treated as adjustments to this 'base-case NPV' by discounting their cash flows at an appropriate cost of debt. This investment appraisal method has the advantage of being able to deal with project-specific financing from different capital markets, but the disadvantage that estimating the side-effects of adjustments to the base-case NPV and their associated discount rates is difficult, calling for considerable expertise.

The CAPM was recommended as being the best way of finding the cost of equity for use in investment appraisal, but there are a number of difficulties that arise in applying the CAPM in foreign direct investment.

- The risk-adjusted discount rate found by using the CAPM takes account of systematic or market risk, but which market portfolio should be used in determining the project beta?
- The CAPM is sensitive to financial market prices and these will change frequently. Over what time frame should the cost of equity be determined?
- What is the value of the equity risk premium? Studies comparing the returns of capital markets of different countries, while offering some evidence of increasing integration, suggest that integration is by no means complete. Should a global risk premium be determined?

While the resolution of these problems lies in the future, steps have been taken towards the development of an *international capital asset pricing model* (ICAPM), for example, as discussed by Buckley (2003).

On the question of whether the cost of capital should in general be higher or lower for foreign direct investment than for domestic investment, common sense may suggest that foreign direct investment, especially in countries regarded as politically unstable, ought to require a higher risk premium. Holland (1990), however, suggests that if foreign investment provides otherwise unattainable diversification benefits to parent company shareholders, the cost of capital could be lower. The safe course may be to assume that the cost of capital for each foreign direct investment should be determined individually by selecting from the techniques available, depending on the sophistication of the analysis involved. A number of empirical studies of international investment appraisal have been summarised by Demirag and Goddard (1994), Kim and Ulferts (1996) and Buckley (2003). The evidence suggests that, for a large number of multinational companies, internal rate of return is the most common technique used for evaluating foreign direct investment. This may not be so surprising, given the difficulties in determining an appropriate cost of capital for such investment, although the question of determining a hurdle rate against which to compare the calculated internal rate of return remains.

9.7.1 The international financing decision

One of the main objectives of the international financing decision is to minimise the company's after-tax cost of capital at an acceptable level of risk, since minimising the cost of capital will maximise the market value of the company. A multinational company with access to international capital markets has a greater opportunity to reduce its cost of capital than a domestic company. The financing decision will need to consider:

- the relative proportions of equity and debt finance at both parent and subsidiary level;
- the relative proportions of long-term and short-term finance;
- the availability of different sources of funds;
- the effect of different sources of finance on the risk of the company;
- the direct and indirect costs of different sources of finance;
- the effect of taxation on the relative costs of equity and debt.

9.7.2 Factors influencing the choice and mix of finance

Key factors influencing the choice and mix of finance for international operations include gearing, taxation, political risk and currency risk.

Gearing

Both the total gearing of the company and the gearing of each subsidiary must be considered. If the holding company *guarantees* the debts of its subsidiaries, whether formally or informally, then as long as the group gearing is acceptable, the decision on the gearing of individual subsidiaries can be made independently. Advantage can then be taken of local interest rates, tax rules and subsidised finance as appropriate. If the holding company does not guarantee the debts of its subsidiaries, the gearing of each subsidiary must be considered separately to optimise its individual capital structure (see Section 9.9).

Taxation

Differences between the treatment in different tax systems of profit, gains, losses, interest and dividends can be exploited through the financing decision. In particular, since interest payments on debt are tax-deductible whereas dividends are not, there is an incentive to use debt as the main source of finance for a foreign subsidiary. Some countries counter this tendency by imposing a maximum allowable level of gearing for tax purposes.

Political risk

One kind of political risk is the possibility of *expropriation* or seizure of assets by a foreign government. Expropriation of assets is less likely if foreign direct investment is financed as much as possible from local sources, for example, using local debt, and if the financing arrangements involve international banks and government agencies. Buckley (2003) cites the example of investment along these lines by Kennecott in a Chilean copper mine project, on which the company was able to secure returns despite the subsequent coming to power of a regime committed to expropriating foreign-held assets without compensation. Political risk is discussed further in Section 12.8.

Currency risk

The financing mix chosen for foreign direct investment can be used by a company as part of its overall strategy of managing currency risk. The use of local debt finance, for example, will reduce translation exposure and allow the parent company to use the internal risk management technique called matching (see Section 12.2.2).

9.8 GEARING: ITS MEASUREMENT AND SIGNIFICANCE

The term *gearing* in a financial context refers to the amount of debt finance a company uses relative to its equity finance. A company with a high level of debt finance relative to equity finance is referred to as highly geared, and vice versa. The term *leverage* is used interchangeably with gearing, more often in the USA. Gearing can be measured using financial ratios, including:

- debt/equity ratio (long-term debt/shareholders' funds);
- capital gearing ratio (long-term debt/long-term capital employed).

The debt/equity ratio and the capital gearing ratio are both examples of financial position statement gearing ratios (see Section 2.4.6). It is possible to include short-term debt as well as long-term debt when calculating gearing ratios, especially if it is an overdraft which persists from year to year. As with the WACC, both the debt/equity ratio and the capital gearing ratio can be calculated using market values and book values. It is often argued that book values should be used rather than market values since book values are less volatile. The problem is that in most cases book values for securities, especially ordinary shares, are significantly different from their market values. As with the calculation of WACC, market values (rather than book values) are both more appropriate and more useful when calculating gearing ratios.

The nature of the industry within which a company operates is a major factor in determining what the market considers to be an appropriate level of gearing. Industries with lower levels of business risk, such as utilities, typically have higher levels of gearing than industries associated with high levels of business risk, such as retailers of luxury goods. The difference in average gearing levels between industries is apparent in Table 9.1. It must be appreciated, however, that gearing levels within a particular industry are not static but change in response to changing economic conditions. A good example of this was the trend, up until the late 1990s, for firms in the energy and water sectors to gear up after their privatisation in the early 1990s.

When discussing the significance of gearing, it is usual to focus on the implications of high gearing rather than low gearing. The implications of high gearing are described below.

9.8.1 Increased volatility of equity returns

The higher a company's level of gearing, the more sensitive are its profitability and earnings to changes in interest rates. This sensitivity is accentuated if the company has most of its debt based on floating interest rates.

If a company is financed partly by debt, its profits and distributable earnings will be at risk from increases in the interest rate charged on the debt. This risk is borne by shareholders (and not debt holders) as the company may have to reduce dividend payments to meet interest payments as they fall due. This kind of risk is referred to as financial risk. The more debt a company has in its capital structure, the higher will be its financial risk.

9.8.2 Increased possibility of bankruptcy

At very high levels of gearing, shareholders will start to face bankruptcy risk. This is defined as the risk of a company failing to meet its interest payment commitments and hence putting the company into liquidation. Interest payments may become unsustainable if profits

Table 9.1 Selected UK industrial sectors' capital gearing ratios (defined as preference shares plus short- and long-term debt/total capital employed plus short-term debt)

Industrial sector	Capital gearing ratio (%)
Transport (passenger)	70
Construction	56
Hotels	53
Food producers	52
Transport (road freight)	47
Pharmaceuticals	46
Retailers	44
Gas distribution	32
Engineering and contractors	32
Clothing	31

Source: FAME, published by Bureau van Dijk Electronic Publishing.

decrease or interest payments on variable rate debt increase. For shareholders, bankruptcy risk is the risk that they might lose the value of their initial investment owing to the position they occupy in the hierarchy of creditors. Debt holders face bankruptcy risk too, but, as we shall see later in the chapter, at a much-reduced level.

9.8.3 Reduced credibility on the stock exchange

Because of the extensive information requirements accompanying a stock exchange listing it is relatively straightforward for investors to calculate a company's level of gearing. Investors who have made this calculation may feel a company has too high a level of gearing, resulting in what they see as an unacceptable level of financial risk or even bankruptcy risk. They will be reluctant to buy the company's shares or to offer it further debt. This reluctance to finance the company is a loss of financial credibility that will exert downward pressure on its share price.

9.8.4 The encouragement of short-termism

If a company has a high level of gearing its primary financial objective may shift from shareholder wealth maximisation to survival, i.e. generating enough cash flow to meet its interest commitments and thereby staving off possible bankruptcy. Managers therefore focus on the short-term need to meet interest payments rather than the longer-term objective of maximising wealth: this managerial behaviour is called *short-termism*.

The difficulties for companies dealing with excessive levels of debt finance will clearly be influenced by the prevailing economic conditions and hence the associated uncertainty of income streams. The impact of the 2008 economic downturn on companies with high levels of debt finance is the subject of Vignette 9.2.

Vignette 9.2

Companies address the call for more equity

By Rachel Morarjee

Shortly before Lehman Brothers collapsed, one of its bankers warned of the consequences that companies could face if they buried their heads in the sand about their need to raise more money from investors. 'If you know you have a problem but just stand there like a deer in the headlights, you will find yourself in the middle of a car crash,' he said.

The advice came too late for Lehman. As the economic downturn accelerates, and mounting job losses prompt the world's consumers to keep their hands firmly in their pockets, many formerly healthy companies will see their working capital needs mount as orders collapse. Whether senior

management is looking at a heavily debt-laden balance sheet or has found that the flow of incoming orders no longer produces enough working capital, what is needed is a clear-eyed assessment of the company's capital requirements and swift planning about how to meet them.

One thing is certain: doing nothing and waiting for things to get better is a bad idea. Matthew Westerman, Global head of capital markets at Goldman Sachs, says: 'There is a sense that people are realistic about companies having debt problems, but they are not willing to accept that they are not being addressed. Investors are telling man-

Vignette 9.1 (continued)

agements they should come and talk to them now and not leave it.' 'Investors have had a dreadful year, and a lot of bad news in the financial and corporate sector has been priced in,' says Emmanuel Geroult, head of European equity capital markets at Morgan Stanley. 'However, one positive to take away is that there is a lot less stigma attached to raising capital. In the current macro environment, it is justifiable, in a way that it wasn't six months ago,' he adds.

During 2008, the financial sector raised $3,080bn to plug the gaping holes that opened in its balance sheets. On the one hand, it demonstrates the severity of the problem, but it also shows capital is there for companies that can explain why investors should back them. This year, financial companies have raised $14bn, while mines have raised $9.7bn and construction and real estate companies have both raised more than $5bn, according to Dealogic. Outside the financial sector, where it can be difficult to see the assets on a balance sheet clearly, companies that are heavily indebted are in a stronger position than many of their financial peers. 'The visibility that the market has on balance sheets, working capital and debt redemption schedules is generally a lot higher at corporates than at banks,' says Henrik Gobel, head of European equity syndicate at Morgan Stanley.

After almost a decade of debt-fuelled expansion, the credit crisis has forced companies of all sizes and in all industries to re-examine their dependence on bank financing. Even though many companies resisted the temptation to load themselves with large amounts of debt, the crisis has made debt more expensive and harder to come by, even for some of the world's largest companies. Combined with a severe, global economic downturn, the crisis is forcing executives to pay close attention to the shape of their balance sheets and their dependence on bank financing, and making them consider tapping equity markets instead.

Viswas Raghavan, head of international capital markets at JP Morgan, says: 'There is a shifting expectation about what an acceptable balance sheet looks like. You are seeing corporates accessing the credit markets at higher prices than they had to pay 18 months ago, and they may begin to look to the equity markets as another source of liquidity.' Investment grade companies can still raise debt, but for most other companies, equity markets will become a cheaper avenue to raise

capital to fortify their balance sheets. Furthermore, companies with debt-laden balance sheets are seeing their share prices hammered. 'The market is placing a strong valuation emphasis on the state of a company's balance sheet, often independently of the performance of the sector, and it is penalising those that are highly leveraged. We've had a decade of de-equitisation with share buy-backs and now the pendulum is swinging back. Companies need to rebuild their equity bases.' says Morgan Stanley's Mr Gobel.

In Europe, the most tried and tested way to raise money is the rights issue. By giving existing investors the right of first refusal on a share issue, the rights issue avoids diluting the holdings of existing investors. One lesson from the banking sector over the past year is that preparation is all-important. Before announcing a rights issue, companies should have their prospectus ready to minimise the time the rights are trading in the market, and thus the effect on their share price. In addition, Matthew Koder, co-head of Global Capital Markets at UBS, says companies can also lower the risk of a rights issue by building cornerstones of strategic investors before launching the process. 'In fact, for many companies, the rights issue may mark the beginning of a strategic relationship with another party,' he says.

UK bank HSBC announced a £12bn rights issue this month, becoming the latest in a long line of banks to tap the markets for fresh funds. Companies needing to raise less than 10 per cent of their existing market capital, will find accelerated primary placements over weekends and after market close an efficient way to raise capital and a method that reduces the risk to their share price. For those that have already raised money through rights issues, it may be difficult to raise more, so new avenues will have to be found. 'We could also see accelerated book-builds, and a bounce back in the convertibles market,' says JP Morgan's Mr Raghavan.

On the corporate side there will be a lot of activity. Real estate is a business that was built on leverage across the globe and has the shortest-dated debt maturities, and now has the least access to debt capital markets. There will be a huge premium for companies that choose to place themselves at the head of the queue to raise capital. Bankers say that in the coming years, businesses will need a much higher equity content than they have had in the

Vignette 9.2 (continued)

past, and will need to move fast to raise equity before conditions get too pressing and share prices are negatively impacted. 'Coming to market early will be more of a priority than ever and companies that act early will thank themselves later,' says Mr Raghavan.

 Source: Morarjee, R. (2009) 'Companies address the call for more equity', *Financial Times*, 25 March. © The Financial Times Limited 2009. All Rights Reserved.

Questions

1 Critically discuss what changes companies might want to make to their capital structures in times of economic recession.

2 What is the most efficient way for a company to make the changes you identified in question (1)?

9.9 THE CONCEPT OF AN OPTIMAL CAPITAL STRUCTURE

Earlier in this chapter we looked at how a company can determine its average cost of capital by calculating the costs of the various sources of finance it uses and weighting them according to their relative importance. The market value of a company clearly depends on its weighted average cost of capital. The lower a company's WACC, the higher the net present value of its future cash flows and therefore the higher its market value.

One issue that we have not considered so far is whether financing decisions can affect investment decisions and thereby affect the value of the company. Put another way, will the way in which a company finances its assets (i.e. how much debt it uses relative to equity) affect its WACC and hence the company's value? If an optimum financing mix exists (i.e. one that gives a minimum WACC), then it would be in a company's best interests to locate it and move towards this *optimal capital structure*. There has been a large amount of academic discussion on whether or not an optimal capital structure exists for individual companies. Before we go on to discuss the differing views on capital structure, we shall first consider the factors that determine the rate of return required by shareholders and debt holders.

9.9.1 Gearing and the required rate of return

The rate of return required by shareholders and debt holders on their investments reflects the risk they face. The required rate of return of shareholders will consequently *always* be higher than that of debt holders since shareholders face higher levels of risk. We shall now consider in detail the factors that determine the shape of the cost of debt curve and the cost of equity curve faced by a company, i.e. the relationship between these costs of capital and the level of gearing.

Let us consider first the cost of equity curve. Figure 9.4 illustrates the determinants of a company's cost of equity. As a minimum, shareholders require the risk-free rate of return

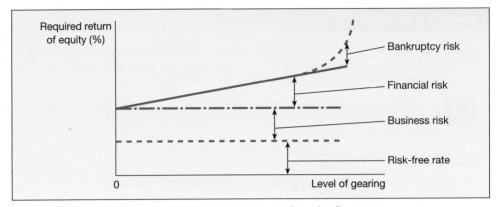

Figure 9.4 The determinants of a company's cost of equity finance

which can be approximated by the yield on short-dated government debt (Treasury bills). In addition, shareholders require a premium for business risk, which is the risk of a company's profits and earnings varying due to systematic influences on that company's business sector. The level of business risk faced by shareholders will vary from company to company and so, therefore, will the required premium. The combination of the risk-free rate and the business risk premium represents the cost of equity of a company financed entirely by equity.

As a company starts to gear up by taking on debt finance, its distributable profits will be reduced by the interest payments it is required to make, although this reduction in profitability is lessened by the **tax shield** on debt. Any volatility in operating profits will be amplified by the need to meet interest payments since these payments represent an additional cost. Further volatility in distributable profits arises if any of the interest payments are on floating rate rather than fixed rate debt, as the size of such payments will be determined by prevailing market interest rates. The volatility of distributable profits arising from the need to meet interest payments, which is called *financial risk,* will get progressively higher as a company's gearing level increases. Shareholders require a premium for facing financial risk and this premium increases with the level of a company's gearing.

Finally, at very high levels of gearing, the possibility of the company going into liquidation increases due to its potential inability to meet interest payments. At high levels of gearing, shareholders require compensation for facing *bankruptcy risk* in addition to compensation for facing financial risk, resulting in a steeper slope for the cost of equity curve.

Turning to the cost of debt curve, we note that the situation of debt holders is different from that of shareholders. The returns of debt holders are fixed in the sense that they do not vary with changes in a company's profit level. By definition, therefore, debt holders do not face financial risk. They do, however, face bankruptcy risk at very high levels of gearing, but they face a lower level of bankruptcy risk than shareholders since debt holders have a preferential position in the creditor hierarchy (see Figure 9.1) and can secure debts against corporate assets.

9.10 THE TRADITIONAL APPROACH TO CAPITAL STRUCTURE

The first view of capital structure we shall consider is usually called the traditional approach. This view or model, like other models, relies on simplifying assumptions:

- no taxes exist, either at a personal or a corporate level;
- companies have two choices of finance: perpetual debt finance or ordinary equity shares;
- companies can change their capital structure without incurring issue or redemption costs;
- any increase (decrease) in debt finance is accompanied by a simultaneous decrease (increase) in equity finance of the same amount;
- companies pay out all distributable earnings as dividends;
- the business risk associated with a company is constant over time;
- companies' earnings and hence dividends do not grow over time.

The proposition of the traditional approach to capital structure is that an optimal capital structure does exist and that a company can therefore increase its total value by the sensible use of debt finance within its capital structure. The traditional approach is illustrated in Figure 9.5.

Figure 9.5 can be explained as follows. The cost of equity curve (K_e) rises with increased gearing due to the increasing level of financial risk being faced by shareholders. The curve rises at a steeper rate at high gearing levels due to the risk of bankruptcy threatening the value of shareholders' investments. The cost of debt curve (K_d) will rise only at high levels of gearing, where bankruptcy risk threatens the value of debt holders' investments. A company financed entirely by equity will be located at point A in Figure 9.5. As a company starts to replace more expensive equity with cheaper debt finance, shareholders are initially indifferent to the introduction of a small amount of financial risk: their response to increasing financial risk is not a linear one. The WACC of the company will fall initially due to the benefit of the cheaper debt finance outweighing any increase in the cost of the company's remaining equity finance. Hence the company's WACC will fall to B, to give an optimal

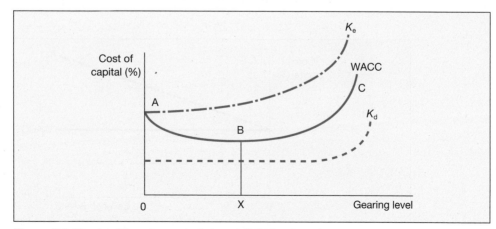

Figure 9.5 The traditional approach to capital structure

capital structure represented by the point X. If the company continues to gear up, increasing its gearing past X, the benefits associated with using cheaper debt finance are outweighed by the increase in the cost of the company's remaining equity finance. The company's WACC curve will therefore start to rise. At very high levels of gearing, bankruptcy risk causes the cost of equity curve to rise at a steeper rate and also causes the cost of debt to start to rise. At very high levels of gearing, therefore, the company's WACC curve will rise at an even faster rate.

The conclusion of the traditional approach to capital structure is that an optimal capital structure *does* exist for individual companies. A company should therefore use the combination of debt and equity finance that minimises its overall cost of capital and thereby maximise the wealth of its shareholders. This view is in sharp contrast to that put forward by Miller and Modigliani, which we now consider.

9.11 MILLER AND MODIGLIANI (I): NET INCOME APPROACH

As with their views on the importance of dividend policy (which are considered later in Chapter 10), the opinions of Miller and Modigliani on the importance of capital structure flew in the face of traditional beliefs. The proposition put forward by Miller and Modigliani (1958) was that a company's WACC remains unchanged at all levels of gearing, implying that no optimal capital structure exists for a company. They argued that the market value of a company depends on its expected performance and commercial risk: the company's market value and its cost of capital are independent of its capital structure. They came to this conclusion using a model based on the assumptions outlined in the previous section but added the extra assumption that capital markets are perfect. The assumption of perfect capital markets was central to their model as it implies that bankruptcy risk could be ignored. Companies in financial distress could always raise additional finance in a perfect capital market. A diagram of their model is shown in Figure 9.6.

The relationship between the curves in Figure 9.6 can be explained as follows. The cost of equity curve (K_e) increases at a constant rate to reflect the higher financial risk shareholders face at higher levels of gearing, so there is a *linear relationship* between the cost of equity

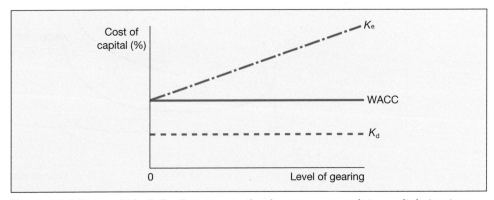

Figure 9.6 Miller and Modigliani's net operating income approach to capital structure

and financial risk (level of gearing). As debt holders do not face bankruptcy risk, the cost of debt curve (K_d) is horizontal and the cost of debt does not increase at high levels of gearing: the cost of debt is *independent* of the level of gearing. A company financed entirely by equity is represented by point A in Figure 9.6. As the company gears up by replacing equity with an equivalent amount of debt, the benefit of using an increasing level of cheaper debt finance is *exactly offset* by the increasing cost of the company's equity finance. The company's WACC therefore remains constant and, since its net income or earnings is assumed constant, its market value is also constant. Miller and Modigliani therefore state that the WACC of a geared company is identical to the cost of equity the company would have if it were financed entirely by equity. This cost of equity is determined by the risk-free rate of return and the business risk of the company; it is independent of financial risk (level of gearing). Miller and Modigliani supported their argument that capital structure was irrelevant in determining the market value and WACC of a company by using arbitrage theory.

9.11.1 The arbitrage approach to capital structure

Arbitrage theory states that goods which are perfect substitutes for each other should not sell at different prices in the same market. Applying this to companies, Miller and Modigliani argued that two companies identical in every way except for their gearing levels should have *identical average costs of capital* and hence should not have different market values. This argument is best illustrated with an example.

| **Example** | **Arbitrage process using two companies** |

Two companies, A and B, have similar net operating incomes (i.e. gross income less operating expenses) and similar levels of business risk. The only difference is that Company A is not geared, whereas Company B is partly financed by £3,000 of debt with an interest rate of 5 per cent. Financial data for the two companies are as follows:

	Company A	Company B
Net operating income (£)	1,000	1,000
Interest on debt (5% × £3,000)	nil	150
Earnings available to shareholders (£)	1,000	850
Cost of equity	10%	11%
Market value of equity (£)	10,000	7,727
Market value of debt (£)	nil	3,000
Total value of company (£)	10,000	10,727
WACC	10%	9.3%

Note: Market value of equity = earnings/cost of equity, e.g. 850/0.11 = £7,727

Company B has a higher cost of equity but a lower overall WACC and a higher market value. This is consistent with the traditional view of capital structure. Miller and Modigliani, however, would argue that, since the two companies have the same business risk and net operating income, they must have the same market values and WACC. Since this is not the case, they would consider Company A to be undervalued and Company B to be overvalued, and that arbitrage will cause the values of the two companies to converge. Using Miller and Modigliani's assumptions, which imply that companies and individuals can borrow at the same rate, we can illustrate how an investor can make a profit by exploiting the incorrect valuations of the two companies.

If a rational investor owned 1 per cent of the equity of the geared firm, Company B, i.e. £77.27, he/she could:

- sell his/her shares in Company B for £77.27;
- borrow £30 at 5 per cent. Here the investor emulates Company B's level of financial risk by making his/her personal gearing equal to the company's gearing (30/77.27 = 3,000/7,727);
- buy 1 per cent of the shares in Company A (the ungeared firm) for £100, thus leaving a surplus of £7.27.

If we compare the investor's income streams, we have the following results:

Original situation

$$\text{Return from Company B shares} = 11\% \times 77.27 = £8.50$$

New situation

Return from Company A shares	= 10% × £100	= £10.00
Less: Interest on debt	= 5% × £30	= (£1.50)
Net return		£8.50

We see that by selling shares in Company B and buying shares in Company A, the investor obtains the same annual income and generates a surplus of £7.27. This risk-free surplus of £7.27 is called an *arbitrage profit*. A rational investor would repeat this process until the opportunity to create a profit disappears. The consequence of this repetition would be the following sequence of events:

- Company B's share price will fall due to pressure to sell its shares.
- Since returns to its shareholders remain the same, its cost of equity will rise.
- Since its cost of equity increases, its WACC will increase.

For Company A the opposite would happen. This process of arbitrage will stop when the companies' WACCs are equal.

There are, however, serious flaws in Miller and Modigliani's arbitrage argument, owing mainly to their unrealistic assumptions. First, the assumption that individuals can borrow at the same rate as companies can be challenged. The costs of personal debt and corporate debt are not the same because companies have higher credit ratings than most individuals. Personal borrowing is therefore seen as riskier, and hence more costly, than corporate borrowing. Second, their assumption that there are no transaction costs in buying and selling shares is clearly untrue. Higher personal borrowing rates and transaction costs both undermine the ability of investors to make risk-free profits from arbitrage, therefore creating the possibility of identical companies being overvalued and undervalued. Miller and Modigliani (1958) acknowledged the rather unrealistic nature of their assumptions in their paper, stating: 'These and other drastic simplifications have been necessary in order to come to grips with the problem at all. Having served their purpose, they can now be relaxed in the direction of greater realism and relevance.'

Another simplification made by Miller and Modigliani was to ignore the existence of taxation. They amended their model to take account of corporate tax in a later paper, which is the subject of the next section.

9.12 MILLER AND MODIGLIANI (II): CORPORATE TAX

In their second paper on capital structure, Miller and Modigliani (1963) amended their earlier model by recognising the existence of corporate tax. Their acknowledgement of the existence of corporate tax and the tax deductibility of interest payments implies that, as a company gears up by replacing equity with debt, it shields more and more of its profits from corporate tax. The tax advantage of debt finance over equity finance means that a company's WACC decreases as gearing increases, suggesting an optimal capital structure for a company of 100 per cent debt finance. This is illustrated in Figure 9.7. The cost of debt curve (K_d) from Miller and Modigliani's first model shifts downwards to reflect the lower after-tax cost of debt finance ($K_d(1 - C_T)$). As a company gears up, its WACC curve now falls.

9.13 MARKET IMPERFECTIONS

There is clearly a problem with the model proposed in Miller and Modigliani's second paper since in practice companies do not adopt an all-debt capital structure. This indicates the existence of factors which *undermine* the tax advantages of debt finance and which Miller and Modigliani failed to take into account. These factors are now considered.

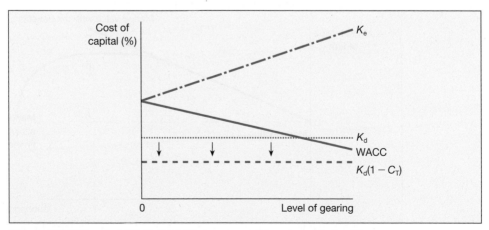

Figure 9.7 Miller and Modigliani (II), incorporating corporate taxation

9.13.1 Bankruptcy costs

The obvious omission from their second model is bankruptcy costs. This stems from their assumption that capital markets are perfect. In a perfect capital market, a company will always be able to raise finance and thereby prevent bankruptcy. In practice, while capital markets are considered to be efficient, they cannot be considered to be perfect. In reality, at high levels of gearing, there is a significant possibility of a company defaulting on its interest commitments and hence being declared bankrupt. At higher levels of gearing, then, where bankruptcy becomes a possibility, shareholders require a higher rate of return to compensate them for facing bankruptcy risk (see Section 9.8.2).

The costs of bankruptcy can be classified in two ways:

- *Direct bankruptcy costs* include the costs of paying lenders higher rates of interest to compensate them for higher risk and, if forced into liquidation, the cost of employing lawyers and accountants to manage the liquidation process.
- *Indirect bankruptcy costs* include loss of sales and goodwill as a consequence of operating the company at extreme levels of financial distress and, if forced into liquidation, the cost of having to sell assets at below their market value.

If we now combine the tax shield advantage of increasing gearing with the bankruptcy costs associated with very high levels of gearing (in effect Miller and Modigliani's 1963 view modified to account for bankruptcy risk) we again see an optimal capital structure emerging. This is illustrated in relation to company value in Figure 9.8.

Figure 9.8 can be explained in the following manner. As a company financed entirely by equity increases its gearing by replacing equity with debt, its market value increases due to the increasing value of its tax shield. This is given by the vertical distance between the dotted line DA and the line DC. Bankruptcy becomes a possibility when the gearing level increases beyond X and consequently the company's cost of equity starts to rise more steeply to compensate shareholders for facing bankruptcy risk, eating into the benefit of the tax shield. Beyond gearing level Y the marginal benefit of the tax shield is outweighed

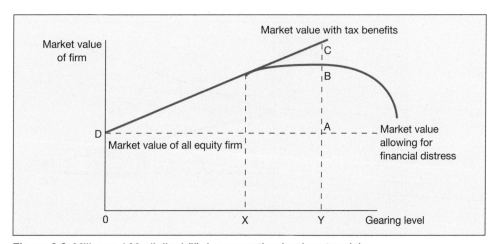

Figure 9.8 Miller and Modigliani (II), incorporating bankruptcy risk

by the marginal increase in the cost of equity due to higher bankruptcy risk. An optimal gearing level therefore exists at gearing level Y, where:

AC = value of the tax shield

BC = cost of bankruptcy risk

AB = net benefit of the geared company

Gearing levels beyond Y will increase the value of the tax shield but this is more than cancelled out by increasing bankruptcy costs, leading to a decline in the value of the company.

While there is little doubt about the existence of bankruptcy costs at high gearing levels, the size of such costs and the level of gearing at which they become relevant (indicated by point X in Figure 9.8) are less clear. Very little research has been done on bankruptcy costs. Baxter (1967) made a study of individual and small US company liquidations and found bankruptcy costs to be of sufficient magnitude to warrant consideration. Warner (1977) considered the bankruptcy of large public limited companies and found that direct bankruptcy costs were insignificant. Research by Altman (1984) into the bankruptcy of industrial companies found that the combined direct and indirect costs at the time of filing for bankruptcy averaged 16.7 per cent of a company's value. More recently Andrade and Kaplan (1998) estimated the combined effect of both economic and financial distress led to an average loss of 38 per cent of company value, based on 31 highly geared US companies over the period 1980–9. Financial distress accounted for 12 per cent of the total loss of value. These figures are clearly significant, even after allowing for the probability of bankruptcy occurring and its time of occurrence.

9.13.2 Agency costs

At higher levels of gearing, in addition to bankruptcy costs, there are costs associated with the problem of agency. If gearing levels are high, shareholders have a lower stake in a company and have fewer funds at risk if the company fails. They will therefore prefer the company to invest in high-risk/high-return projects since they will enjoy the benefit of the higher returns that arise. Providers of debt finance, however, will not share in the higher returns from such high-risk projects since their returns are not dependent on company performance. They will therefore take steps to prevent the company from taking on high-risk projects which might put their investment at risk. They may, for example, impose covenants on the management (see Section 5.1.1). Such covenants could restrict future dividend payments, place restrictions on ways of raising finance or impose minimum levels of liquidity. Alternatively, debt holders may increase the level of management monitoring and require a higher level of financial information with respect to the company's activities. These agency costs will eat further into the tax shield benefits associated with increasing gearing levels.

9.13.3 Tax exhaustion

Another explanation of why companies fail to adopt higher levels of gearing is that many companies have insufficient profits from which to derive all available tax benefits as they increase their gearing level (often referred to as 'tax exhaustion'). This will prevent them from enjoying the tax shield benefits associated with high gearing, but still leave them liable to incur bankruptcy costs and agency costs.

The existence of bankruptcy costs and agency costs, and the fact that companies may become tax-exhausted at high gearing levels, explain why companies do not adopt 100 per cent debt capital structures, in contradiction to Miller and Modigliani's second paper.

9.14 MILLER AND PERSONAL TAXATION

Although Miller and Modigliani amended their earlier paper to take account of the effects of corporate taxation in 1963, it was left to Miller (1977) to integrate the effects of personal taxes into their model. Miller's complex model considers the relationship between gearing levels, corporate taxation, the rate of personal taxation on debt and equity returns, and the amount of debt and equity available for investors to invest in. The following explanation represents a simplification of his model.

Investors choose investments in companies that suit their personal taxation situation, taking account of a company's capital structure and the amount of debt finance and equity finance that it and other companies have issued. For example, investors who pay income tax will be inclined to invest in equity rather than debt, due to the capital gains tax allowance associated with ordinary shares and the later payment date of capital gains tax compared with income tax. When the economy is in equilibrium, therefore, all investors will be holding investments that suit their personal tax situation. For a company to increase its debt finance and take advantage of the associated tax benefits, it will have to persuade equity holders to swap ordinary shares for debt securities. Because this will involve investors moving to a less favourable personal tax position, they will have to be 'bribed' by the company through a higher, more attractive interest rate on the new debt. According to Miller's model, this higher interest rate will cancel out the tax benefits of the additional debt, leaving the average cost of capital unchanged. The result is a horizontal WACC curve similar to that in Miller and Modigliani's first model (see Figure 9.6) . As with both Miller and Modigliani's previous models, Miller's 1977 paper did not take account of bankruptcy risk. If his model is modified to account for the bankruptcy costs which exist at high levels of gearing, we arrive at the WACC curve illustrated in Figure 9.9.

Miller's paper was applicable to the tax regime prevalent in the USA during the 1970s. Since then the US tax regime has changed so that, as in the UK, there is now only a small difference in the personal tax treatment of debt and equity returns. This implies that introducing personal tax into the capital structure debate reduces, but does not eradicate, the corporate tax savings associated with an increase in gearing level.

9.15 PECKING ORDER THEORY

Pecking order theory (Donaldson 1961) goes against the idea of companies seeking a unique combination of debt and equity finance which minimises their WACC. The theory suggests that when a company is looking at financing its long-term investments, it has a

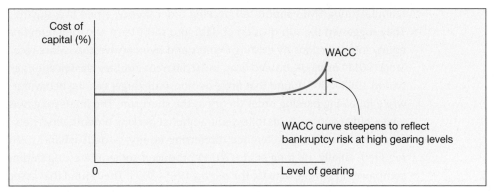

Figure 9.9 Miller's 1977 model, incorporating bankruptcy risk

well-defined order of preference with respect to the sources of finance it selects. Its first preference is to use internal finance or retained earnings rather than external sources of finance. If internal finance proves insufficient, bank borrowings and corporate bonds are the preferred source of external source of finance. After exhausting these possibilities, the final and least preferred source of finance is issuing new equity capital.

The initial explanation of these preferences involves issue costs and the ease with which sources of finance are accessed. Retained earnings are readily accessible, have no issue costs and do not involve dealing or negotiating with third parties such as banks. As for choosing between debt and equity finance, the cost of issuing new debt is much less than the cost of issuing new equity; it is also possible to raise small amounts of debt, whereas it is not usually possible to raise small amounts of equity. Additionally issuing debt avoids the potential ownership issues associated with the issue of new equity.

A more sophisticated explanation for the existence of a pecking order was put forward by Myers (1984). He suggested that the order of preference stemmed from the existence of asymmetry of information between the company and the capital markets. For example, suppose that a company wants to raise finance for a new project and the capital market underestimates the benefit of the project. The company's managers, with their inside information, will be aware that the market has undervalued the company. They will therefore choose retained earnings to finance the project so that, when the market recognises the true value of the project, existing shareholders will benefit. If retained earnings are insufficient, managers will choose debt finance in preference to issuing new shares as they will not want to issue new shares if they are undervalued by the market. The opposite is true if the company believes the capital market is overvaluing its shares in light of the new project they are about to accept. In this situation it will prefer to issue new shares at what it considers to be an overvalued price.

Baskin (1989) examined the relationship between profits and companies' gearing levels and found a significant negative relationship between high profits and high gearing levels. This finding contradicts the idea of the existence of an optimal capital structure and gives support to the insights offered by pecking order theory. Subsequent evidence has been mixed. US-based research by Frank and Goyal (2003) produced evidence contradicting pecking order theory while Watson and Wilson (2002), basing their research on UK shares, found in favour of the theory. Zoppa and McMahon's research (2002) on Australian manufacturing SMEs supported pecking order theory, albeit in a slightly modified form. They suggested the sub-division of debt into short-term and long-term financing and new equity into injections by existing owners and by new investors. More recently, Tucker and Stoja (2011) using UK-quoted firms in 10 different industry classifications and data over the period 1968–2006, found that firms demonstrate target gearing behaviour in the long run, while following pecking order theory in the short run. The interesting twist here was that while 'old economy' firms followed traditional pecking order theory, 'new economy' firms followed a modified preference, preferring equity to debt when external finance was required. Finally, de Jong et al. (2011) produced some interesting findings based on US companies in sample data for the period 1985–2005. They found that companies requiring finance who were above their target gearing but below their debt capacity closed the financing gap by issuing debt finance, thus supporting pecking order theory. In contrast, companies who were below their target gearing with surplus finance were found to close the gap by repurchasing equity finance rather than debt, thus discrediting pecking order theory.

9.16 CONCLUSION: DOES AN OPTIMAL CAPITAL STRUCTURE EXIST?

In this chapter we have seen that gearing is an important consideration for companies. Some academic theories (the traditional approach, Miller and Modigliani (II) with bankruptcy costs) support the existence of an optimal capital structure. Others academic theories (Miller and Modigliani (I), Miller) argue that one capital structure is as good as another. Market imperfections such as corporate and personal taxation, and bankruptcy and agency costs, lend support to the existence of an optimal capital structure. In practice, though, it is more likely that there exists a range of capital structures within which a company can minimise its WACC (i.e. between P and Q in Figure 9.10) rather than one specific combination of debt and equity (an optimal capital structure) that academic theories such as the traditional approach suggest. This implies that the WACC curve will be flatter in practice than the U-shaped curve suggested by theory.

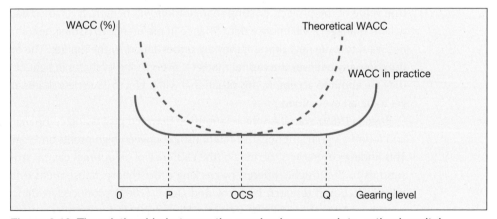

Figure 9.10 The relationship between the academic approach to optimal capital structure and the weighted average cost of capital in practice

In conclusion, it appears that by integrating sensible levels of debt into its capital structure a company can enjoy the tax advantages arising from debt finance and thereby reduce its weighted average cost of capital, while avoiding increasing its gearing to levels that give rise to concern among its investors about its possible bankruptcy.

■ ■ ■ KEY POINTS

1 A company's WACC is a fundamental determinant of its market value, since it is used as the discount rate in investment appraisal methods such as NPV and internal rate of return.

2 A major determinant of a company's WACC is its cost of equity, which can be calculated using either the dividend growth model or the capital asset pricing model.

3 The costs of capital of preference shares and irredeemable bonds can be calculated by dividing the dividend or interest payment by the security's market value.

4 The cost of debt of redeemable bonds can be found by using an internal rate of return calculation or a bond approximation formula.

5 The cost of debt of bank loans, which have no market value, is approximated by the interest rate paid on them or by the cost of debt of traded bonds with similar risk and maturity.

6 If a company is in a tax-paying position, the cost of debt finance must be adjusted to take account of the tax deductibility of interest payments.

7 The costs of individual sources of finance must be weighted according to their relative importance using either market or book values.

8 While book values are stable and easy to find, using market values is better as they reflect the true value of a company's securities.

9 A company can calculate its current average cost of capital or its marginal cost of capital, which represents the cost of incremental capital raised.

10 A company's WACC is only appropriate for appraising new projects if they are financed in similar proportions to its existing capital structure and have similar levels of risk to that of the company as a whole.

11 When new projects have significantly different risk characteristics to those of the investing company, the CAPM can be used to calculate a project-specific cost of equity by estimating an appropriate project equity beta from suitable proxy equity betas, and using this cost of equity in a project-specific discount rate.

12 It is difficult in practice to calculate a company's WACC. Problems include dealing with the wide variety of sources of finance used by a company, the existence of complex instruments such as convertibles and the volatility of a company's cost of capital.

13 The arguments for and against using the WACC and the CAPM in domestic investment appraisal also apply to the problem of finding the cost of capital for foreign

investment. A cost of capital which reflects the risk of the individual project should be used.

14 In using the CAPM with foreign investment, problems arise when considering: which market portfolio to use to find beta; over which time period to conduct the analysis and how to find the value of the market premium.

15 The international financing decision seeks to minimise the after-tax cost of capital at an acceptable level of risk and reflects key factors such as gearing, taxation, political risk and currency risk.

16 The optimal capital structure debate addresses the question of whether a company can minimise its cost of capital by adopting a specific combination of debt and equity.

17 The traditional approach to the optimal capital structure question argued that an optimal capital structure did exist for companies.

18 Miller and Modigliani argued that a company's market value depends on its expected performance and commercial risk; market value and WACC are therefore independent of capital structure, as shown by arbitrage theory. Their model was academically sound but based on restrictive and unrealistic assumptions.

19 Miller and Modigliani later modified their earlier model to take account of corporate tax and argued that companies should gear up to take advantage of the tax shield of debt. If this later model is modified to take account of bankruptcy and agency costs at high levels of gearing, an optimal capital structure emerges.

20 Miller amended their earlier model to take account of differences in the personal tax treatment of equity and debt returns. He argued that the need to 'bribe' investors into holding more debt cancelled out the tax benefits to companies of issuing extra debt, and concluded that all combinations of debt and equity finance were optimal.

21 Pecking order theory suggests that companies, rather than seeking an optimal capital structure, prefer retained earnings to external funds and prefer new debt to new equity.

22 In practice it seems plausible that companies can reduce their cost of capital by integrating sensible levels of debt finance into their balance sheet. Whether a company can accurately locate its range of optimal capital structures is debatable.

Answers to these questions can be found on pages 463–4.

1 Gorky has in issue 500,000 £1 ordinary shares whose current ex dividend market price is £1.50 per share. The company has just paid a dividend of 27p per share and dividends are expected to continue at this level for some time. If the company has no debt capital, what is its weighted average cost of capital?

2 The 8 per cent irredeemable bonds of Eranio plc are currently trading at £92 per £100 bond. If the company pays corporation tax of 30 per cent, what is the current after-tax cost of debt of the bonds?

3 Pollock has in issue 1 million ordinary shares, nominal value 25p and £100,000 of 8 per cent irredeemable bonds. The current ex dividend market price of the ordinary shares is 49p per share and the current ex-interest market price of the bonds is £82 per £100 nominal. The company has just paid a dividend of 6p per share and dividends are expected to continue at this level indefinitely. If the company pays corporation tax at a rate of 30 per cent, what is its weighted average cost of capital?

4 Should companies use their current weighted average cost of capital as the discount rate when assessing the acceptability of new projects?

5 Explain why the asset beta of a company will always be lower than its equity beta, unless the company is all-equity financed.

6 A company has an equity beta of 1.30 and is financed by 25 per cent debt and 75 per cent equity. What will be the company's new equity beta if it changes its financing to 33 per cent debt and 67 per cent equity? Assume corporation tax is 30 per cent.

7 What difficulties may be faced by analysts seeking to use the capital asset pricing model to determine a discount rate for foreign direct investment?

8 Describe the main factors influencing the choice and mix of financing used in foreign direct investment.

9 One-third of the total market value of Johnson plc consists of bonds with a cost of 10 per cent. York plc is identical in every respect to Johnson except that it is financed by equity alone. York's cost of equity is 16 per cent. According to Modigliani and Miller, if taxation and tax relief on interest are ignored, what is Johnson plc's cost of equity?

10 Briefly explain the traditional view of capital structure.

QUESTIONS FOR REVIEW

1 Calet plc pays corporation tax at 30 per cent and has the following capital structure:

   - *Ordinary shares*: 1,000,000 ordinary shares of nominal value 25p per share and market value of 79p per share. A dividend of 6p per share has just been paid and dividends are expected to grow by 5 per cent per year for the foreseeable future.
   - *Preference shares*: 250,000 preference shares of nominal value 50p per share and market value of 42p per share. The annual dividend of 7.5 per cent has just been paid.
   - *Bonds*: £100,000 of 7 per cent irredeemable bonds with a market price of £102 per £100 nominal. The annual interest has just been paid.

   Calculate the weighted average after-tax cost of capital of Calet plc.

2 Icicle Works plc is a frozen food company that intends to diversify into electronics. The project has a return of 12 per cent and Icicle Works is trying to decide whether it should be accepted. To help it decide it plans to use the CAPM to find a proxy beta for the project and has the following information on three electronics companies:

   (a) *Supertronic plc*: This company has an equity beta of 1.33 and is financed by 50 per cent debt and 50 per cent equity.

   (b) *Electroland plc*: This company has an equity beta of 1.30 and is financed by 40 per cent debt and 60 per cent equity. The company has just bought a non-electronics company with an asset beta of 1.4 that accounts for 20 per cent of its value.

   (c) *Transelectro plc*: This company has an equity beta of 1.05 and is financed by 35 per cent debt and 65 per cent equity.

   Assume that all debt is risk-free, and that corporation tax is 30 per cent. Icicle Works plc is financed by 30 per cent debt and 70 per cent equity. The risk-free rate of return is 5 per cent and the return on the market is 9 per cent. Should the company accept the project?

3 Carbon plc and Short plc operate in the same industry and have the same business risk. Financial information on the two companies is as follows.

	Carbon plc £000	Short plc £000
Annual operating income	500	1,000
Annual interest	nil	200
Annual cash flow	500	1,200
Equity market value	3,125	6,000
Debt market value	nil	2,000
Total market value	3,125	8,000
Cost of equity capital	16%	16.6%
Cost of debt capital		10%
WACC	16%	15%
No. of shares in issue	3.25m	5m
Market price per share	96p	120p

Kitson holds £1,000 worth of shares in Short and can borrow at the same rate as Short. Show how Kitson can increase his wealth through arbitrage. Ignore taxes and transaction costs.

4 Paisley Brothers plc, a company producing paisley shirts, has net operating income of £2,000 and is faced with three options of how to structure its debt and equity:

(a) to issue no debt and pay shareholders a return of 9 per cent;

(b) to borrow £5,000 at 3 per cent and pay shareholders a return of 10 per cent;

(c) to borrow £9,000 at 6 per cent and pay shareholders a return of 13 per cent.

Assuming no taxation and a 100 per cent payout ratio, determine which financing option maximises the market value of the company.

5 The calculation of the WACC is straightforward in theory, but difficult in practice. Outline possible difficulties that may be experienced when trying to calculate the WACC.

6 Discuss problems that may be met in using the CAPM in investment appraisal.

QUESTIONS FOR DISCUSSION

1 You are given the following financial position statement information about Jordan plc:

	£000	£000
Non-current assets		1,511
Current assets		672
Total assets		2,183
Equity finance		
Ordinary shares (50p nominal value)	200	
Reserves	150	350
Non-current liabilities		
7% preference shares (£1 nominal value)	300	
9% bonds (redeemable after 8 years)	650	
9% bank loan	560	1,510
Current liabilities		323
Total liabilities		2,183

You are also given the following information:

Yield on Treasury bills	7%
Jordan plc equity beta	1.21
Equity risk premium	9.1%
Current ex div ordinary share price	£2.35
Current ex div preference share price	66p
Current ex interest bond price	£105 per £100 bond
Corporation tax rate	30%

Calculate the company's WACC using market weightings.

2 The following information has been taken from the accounts of Merlin plc:

	£000	£000
Non-current assets		872
Current assets		573
Total assets		1,445
Equity finance		
Ordinary shares (£1 nominal) (i)	225	
Reserves	150	375
Non-current liabilities		
12% bonds (ii)	500	
9% convertible bonds (iii)	250	750
Current liabilities		320
Total liabilities		1,445

Notes:

(i) The current ex div ordinary share price of Merlin plc is £3.14. Both dividends and share price are expected to increase by 7 per cent per year for the foreseeable future.

(ii) The 12 per cent bonds are redeemable in five years' time at £100 nominal. The current ex interest market price of the bonds is £114.

(iii) The 9 per cent bonds are convertible in three years' time into 40 ordinary shares of Merlin plc per bond or in four years' time into 35 ordinary shares per bond. The current ex-interest market price of the convertible bonds is £119 per £100 bond. If not converted, the bonds will be redeemed at £100 nominal after four years.

(iv) The corporation tax rate is 30 per cent.

(a) Calculate the cost of debt of the 12 per cent redeemable bonds.

(b) Calculate the cost of debt of the convertible bonds.

(c) If a dividend of 35p per ordinary share has just been paid, calculate the cost of equity.

(d) Calculate the weighted average after-tax cost of capital of Merlin plc.

3 Critically discuss whether companies, by integrating a sensible level of debt into their capital structure, can minimise their weighted average cost of capital.

4 The finance director of Kingsize plc is currently reviewing the capital structure of the company. She believes that the company is not financing itself in a way that minimises its WACC. The company's financing is as follows:

	£000
Ordinary shares (£1 nominal)	15,000
Reserves	10,000
7% preference shares (£1 nominal)	10,000
10% bonds (redeemable after 7 years)	15,000
	50,000

Other information:

Ordinary share price (ex div)	£2.65
Preference share price (ex div)	75p
Bond price (ex interest)	£102 per £100 nominal
Last 5 years' dividends (most recent last)	22p, 23p, 25p, 27p, 29p

The finance director feels that by issuing more debt the company will be able to reduce its WACC. She proposes the issue of £15m of 11 per cent bonds. These bonds will be sold at a 5 per cent premium to their nominal value of £100 and will be redeemed after seven years. The cash raised will be used to repurchase ordinary shares which the company will then cancel. She expects the repurchase will cause the company's share price to rise to £2.78 and the future dividend growth rate to rise by 20 per cent (in relative terms). She expects the price of the 10 per cent bonds to be unaffected, but the price of the preference shares to fall to 68p. Corporation tax stands at 30 per cent.

(a) Calculate the current cost of capital (WACC) for Kingsize plc.

(b) Recalculate the company's cost of capital to reflect the proposed changes and comment on the finance director's projections.

(c) Identify and discuss possible inaccuracies that may occur with the finance director's estimates.

References

Altman, E. (1984) 'A further empirical investigation of the bankruptcy cost question', *Journal of Finance*, vol. 39, pp. 1067–89.

Andrade, G. and Kaplan, S. (1998) 'How costly is financial (not economic) distress? Evidence from highly leveraged transactions that became distressed', *Journal of Finance*, vol. 53, October, pp. 1443–93.

Baskin, J.B. (1989) 'An empirical investigation of the pecking order hypothesis', *Financial Management*, vol. 18, pp. 26–35.

Baxter, N. (1967) 'Leverage, risk of ruin and the cost of capital', *Journal of Finance*, vol. 26, pp. 395–403.

Buckley, A. (2003) *Multinational Finance*, 5th edn, Harlow: FT Prentice Hall.

Damodaran, A. (2018) 'Costs of capital by industrial sector', available at: http://pages.stern.nyu.edu/~adamodar/New_Home_Page/datafile/wacc.htm

de Jong, A., Verbeek, M. and Verwijmeren, P. (2011) 'Firms' debt–equity decisions when the static tradeoff theory and the pecking order theory disagree', *Journal of Banking & Finance*, vol. 35, pp. 1303–14.

Demirag, I. and Goddard, S. (1994) *Financial Management for International Business*, London: McGraw-Hill.

Donaldson, G. (1961) *Corporate Debt Capacity*, Boston, MA: Harvard University Press.

Fama, E. and French, K. (1997) 'Industry costs of equity', *Journal of Financial Economics*, vol. 43, pp. 153–93.

Frank, M. and Goyal, V. (2003) 'Testing the pecking order theory of capital structure', *Journal of Financial Economics*, vol. 67, pp. 217–48.

Gregory, A. and Michou, M. (2009) 'Industry cost of capital: UK evidence', *Journal of Business Finance and Accounting*, June/July, pp. 679–704.

Hawawini, G. and Vora, A. (1982) 'Yield approximations: an historical perspective', *Journal of Finance*, vol. 37, March, pp. 145–56.

Holland, J. (1990) 'Capital budgeting for international business: a framework for analysis', *Managerial Finance,* vol. 16, no. 2, pp. 1–6.

Kim, S. and Ulferts, G. (1996) 'A summary of multinational capital budgeting studies', *Managerial Finance,* vol. 22, no. 1, pp. 75–85.

Miller, M. (1977) 'Debt and taxes', *Journal of Finance,* vol. 32, pp. 261–75.

Miller, M. and Modigliani, F. (1958) 'The cost of capital, corporation finance and the theory of investment', *American Economic Review,* vol. 48, pp. 261–96.

Miller, M. and Modigliani, F. (1963) 'Taxes and the cost of capital: a correction', *American Economic Review,* vol. 53, pp. 43–33.

Myers, S. (1984) 'The capital structure puzzle', *Journal of Finance,* vol. 39, pp. 575–92.

Stanley, T. (1990) 'Cost of capital in capital budgeting for foreign direct investment', *Managerial Finance,* vol. 16, no. 2, pp. 13–16.

Tucker, J. and Stoja, E. (2011) 'Industry membership and capital structure dynamics in the UK', *International Review of Financial Analysis,* vol. 20, no. 4, pp. 207–14.

Warner, J. (1977) 'Bankruptcy costs: some evidence', *Journal of Finance,* vol. 26, pp. 337–48.

Watson, R. and Wilson, N. (2002) 'Small and medium size enterprise financing: some of the empirical implications of a pecking order', *Journal of Business Finance and Accounting,* vol. 29 (April), pp. 557–78.

Wright, S., Mason, R. and Miles, D. (2003) 'A study into certain aspects of the cost of capital for regulated utilities in the U.K.', London: Smithers and Co Ltd.

Zoppa, A. and McMahon, R. (2002) 'Pecking order theory and the financial structure of manufacturing SMEs from Australia's business longitudinal survey', *Small Enterprise Research,* vol. 10, no. 2, pp. 23–31.

Recommended reading

A text dedicated to the subject of cost of capital which is relatively up to date and extremely enlightening:

Armitage, S. (2012) *Cost of Capital: Intermediate Theory,* Cambridge: Cambridge University Press.

The following text critically discusses alternative models for estimating the cost of equity, including recent developments with respect to the capital asset pricing model:

Davies, R., Unni, S., Draper, P. and Paudyal, K. (1999) *The Cost of Equity Capital,* London: CIMA Publishing.

The following practitioner's guide from Ernst & Young is extremely useful in terms of applying the concept of the weighted average cost of capital to the real world:

Ernst & Young (2018) *Practitioner's Guide to Cost of Capital and WACC Calculation,* February.

A book in FT Prentice Hall's Corporate Financial Manual series, dedicated to determining the cost of capital and including a useful interactive software package:

Johnson, H. (1999) *Determining Cost of Capital: The Key to Firm Value,* London: FT Prentice Hall.

A practical guide to the cost of capital and its calculation can be found in this useful textbook:

Ogier, T., Rugman, J. and Spicer, L. (2004) *The Real Cost of Capital,* London: FT Prentice Hall.

Two relatively up-to-date and extensive texts focusing on the calculation and application of cost of capital:

Porras, E. (2010) *The Cost of Capital,* Basingstoke: Palgrave Macmillan.

Pratt, S. and Graboski, R. (2015) *Cost of Capital: Applications and Examples,* 5th edn, New Jersey: Wiley.

These texts collect together readable and interesting articles on the capital structure debate, including (in Ward) reprints of Miller and Modigliani's two seminal papers:

Barker, K. and Martin, G. (eds) (2011) *Capital Structure and Corporate Financing Decisions: Theory, Evidence, and Practice,* New Jersey: Wiley.

Stern, J. and Chew, D. (eds) (2003) *The Revolution in Corporate Finance,* 4th edn, Malden, MA: Blackwell.

Ward, K. (ed.) (1994) *Strategic Issues in Finance,* Oxford: Butterworth-Heinemann.

Important and informative papers and articles recommended for further reading on the cost of capital and capital structure include the following:

Brierley, P. and Bunn, P. (2005) 'The determination of UK corporate capital gearing', *Bank of England Quarterly Bulletin,* Summer, pp. 354–66.

Neish, S. (1994) 'Building the best balance sheet', *Corporate Finance,* March, pp. 26–31.

10 DIVIDEND POLICY

Learning objectives

The chapter looks at the key question of whether a company's dividend policy affects its share price and hence its value. It also examines the factors which determine a company's dividend policy. After studying this chapter, you should have achieved the following learning objectives:

■ an understanding of the arguments put forward by the 'dividend irrelevance' school;

■ a general understanding of the arguments put forward by those who believe that dividends are relevant to share valuation due to their informational, liquidity and taxation implications;

■ the ability to discuss the reasons why a financial manager disregards the importance of the dividend decision at his or her peril;

■ an appreciation of the alternative dividend policies that companies can operate and their significance to investors;

■ the ability to describe alternatives to cash dividends such as share repurchases, scrip dividends and non-pecuniary benefits.

■ ■ ■ INTRODUCTION

Traditionally, corporate finance was seen to involve two distinct areas of decision-making: the investment decision, where investment projects are evaluated and suitable projects selected, and the finance decision, where finance is raised to enable the selected projects to be implemented. The dividend decision, which considers the amount of earnings to be retained by the company and the amount to be distributed to shareholders, is closely linked to both the investment and financing decisions. For example, a company with few suitable projects should return unused earnings to shareholders via increased dividends. A company with several suitable projects that maintains high dividends will have to find finance from external sources.

In recent years, the decision on the amount of earnings to retain and the amount to pay out has become an increasingly important decision in its own right, so that it is now usual to talk about the three decision areas of corporate finance (as we did in Chapter 1). Managers need to consider the views and expectations of shareholders and other providers of capital when making dividend decisions. The attitude of shareholders to changes in the level of dividend paid must be balanced against the availability and cost of internal and external sources of finance (see Section 2.1).

10.1 DIVIDENDS: OPERATIONAL AND PRACTICAL ISSUES

A dividend is a cash payment made on a quarterly or semi-annual basis by a company to its shareholders. It is a distribution of after-tax profits. Most UK companies pay dividends twice a year, while US companies pay dividends on a quarterly basis. The UK *interim dividend*, paid midway through the company's financial year (and after publication of interim results), tends to be smaller than the *final dividend*. The final dividend requires shareholder approval at the company's annual general meeting (AGM) and so is paid after the end of the financial year to which the annual accounts relate. The size of the interim dividend relative to the final dividend can be partly explained by the company's need to link dividend payments with overall profitability for the period. At the end of the financial year the company is in a far better position to assess the level of dividend it can afford to pay. The mechanics of paying dividends, generally speaking, are governed by a company's Articles of Association.

The delay between the dividend announcement and the actual cash payment gives rise to the terms *cum dividend* and *ex dividend* when quoting share prices. When a dividend is announced, a company's share price will change. This change will reflect the market's attitude to the dividend that has just been declared. The share price will then continue to be cum dividend for a short period of time, meaning that anyone purchasing the share during this period is entitled to receive the dividend when it is paid. When the share price goes ex dividend, anyone purchasing the share on or after this date will not be entitled to the dividend payment, even though the payment has yet to be made. The entitlement to the dividend will remain with the previous owner of the share. The share price will change on the ex dividend date, falling by the value of the dividend to be paid, to reflect the

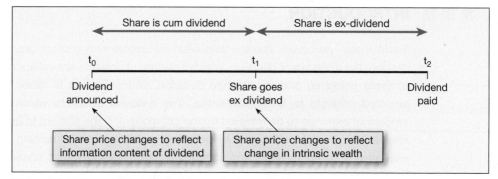

Figure 10.1 The relationship between the cum dividend and ex dividend share prices

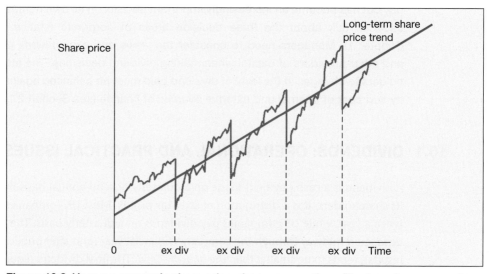

Figure 10.2 How a company's share price changes over time. The long-term upward trend is punctuated by falls in the share price on the company's ex dividend dates.

intrinsic change in the value of the share. Suppose, for example, that a share has a **cum dividend price** of £3.45 and the dividend to be paid is 23p per share. When the share goes ex dividend, the share price will fall by 23p to £3.22 per share.

The timings of dividend announcement and payment, and the corresponding cum dividend and ex dividend periods, are illustrated in Figures 10.1 and 10.2.

There are practical constraints that companies must consider when paying dividends to shareholders. These are described below.

10.1.1 Legal constraints

Companies are bound by the Companies Act 2006 to pay dividends solely out of *accumulated net realised profits.* This includes profits that have been realised in the current year and those that have been realised historically. Although the Act does not define clearly how accumulated net realised profit should be calculated, the Consultative Committee of Accountancy Bodies (CCAB) has issued guidance stating that dividends can be paid out of profit calculated using Financial Reporting Standards after accounting for any accumulated losses. A company whose net assets fall below the total of its called-up share capital and non-distributable reserves is prevented from paying a dividend.

The UK government has occasionally imposed direct restrictions on the amount of dividends that companies can pay. One example occurred in the 1960s when the UK government, as part of its prices and incomes policy, placed restrictions on the percentage increase that companies could make on their dividend payments. These restrictions were lifted in 1979.

Companies must also comply with any restrictions imposed on dividend policy by loan agreements or covenants (see Section 5.1.1) that protect the interests of the company's creditors.

10.1.2 Liquidity

Managers must consider carefully the effect of proposed dividends on the company's liquidity position since dividends and their associated tax payments are cash transactions. A common misconception is that a company with high levels of profits can afford to pay high dividends. As Chapter 1 stressed, profit is not the same as cash available to the company and so the dividends paid must reflect not just the company's profits but also its *ability* to pay dividends.

10.1.3 Interest payment obligations

Dividends are paid out of profits remaining after interest and tax liabilities have been accounted for. A company's level of gearing and its interest commitments are therefore a major constraint on its dividend policy. A highly geared company with high interest payments will have lower profits from which to pay dividends than a lower-geared company with similar overall profit levels. However, if the highly geared company has fewer issued shares than the lower-geared company with similar overall profit levels, it may actually pay the higher dividend per share.

10.1.4 Investment opportunities

Retained earnings are a major source of finance for companies. Hence, when companies are faced with attractive projects, there is pressure to reduce dividends in order to finance the projects as much as possible from retained earnings. Whether a company will choose to reduce dividend payments to finance new projects will depend on factors such as:

- the attitude of shareholders and capital markets to a reduction in dividends;
- the availability and cost of external sources of finance;
- the investment funds required by the company relative to its available distributable profits.

10.2 THE EFFECT OF DIVIDENDS ON SHAREHOLDER WEALTH

The objectives of a company's dividend policy should be consistent with the overall object-ive of shareholder wealth maximisation. A company should pay a dividend, therefore, only if it leads to such an increase in wealth. A simple model for analysing dividend payments was put forward by Porterfield (1965), who suggested that paying a dividend will increase shareholder wealth only when:

$$d_1 + P_1 > P_0$$

where: d_1 = cash value of dividend paid to shareholders
P_1 = expected ex dividend share price
P_0 = market price before the dividend was announced

It is important to consider the factors which influence these variables. For example, the value of d_1 is influenced by the marginal income tax rate of individual shareholders, while P_0 will reflect market expectations of the company's performance before the dividend is paid. P_1 will be influenced by any new information about the company's future prospects, which the market sees as signalled by the dividend decision. Porterfield's expression is consistent with dividend relevance, which is considered below. The expression can be modified to:

$$d_1 + P_1 = P_0$$

This implies that dividends do not affect shareholder wealth and hence are irrelevant. Dividend irrelevance is discussed in the next section.

10.3 DIVIDEND IRRELEVANCE

The question of the effect of dividends on share prices has been a controversial one for many years. The dividend irrelevance school first originated with a paper by Miller and Modigliani (1961). They argued that share valuation is a function of the level of corporate earnings, which reflects a company's investment policy, rather than a function of the pro-portion of earnings paid out as dividends. They also argued that, since a company's value does not depend on its capital structure, investment decisions were responsible for a com-pany's future profitability and hence were the only decisions determining its market value. Miller and Modigliani concluded that share valuation is *independent* of the level of dividend paid by a company.

To fully understand Miller and Modigliani's model we must first identify the assumptions on which it was based:

- converting shares into cash by selling them does not incur transactions costs;
- companies can issue shares without incurring flotation or transactions costs;
- there are no taxes at either a corporate or a personal level;
- capital markets are perfectly efficient (for the required characteristics, see 'Perfect mar-kets and efficient markets', Section 2.3.1).

Miller and Modigliani said that, under these assumptions, investors who are rational (i.e. always make choices that maximise their wealth) are indifferent to whether they receive capital gains or dividends on their shares. To maximise shareholder utility, what is important is that a company maximises its market value by adopting an optimal investment policy.

An optimal investment policy requires a company to invest in all projects with a positive net present value (NPV) and hence maximise the net present value of the whole company. Given the assumption that capital markets are perfect, capital rationing is eliminated and so does not hinder such an investment policy. A company with insufficient internal funds can raise equity funds on the capital markets, allowing it to finance all desirable projects. Alternatively, a company already investing in all projects with positive net present values available to it and with surplus internal funds (retained earnings) could adopt a residual dividend policy and pay the surplus to shareholders. A graphical representation of dividends as a residual payment is given in Figure 10.3. Here, a company is faced with six projects. Only the first three are attractive to the company, i.e. they have an internal rate of return greater than its cost of equity. The amount of investment required is therefore OA. If the company has profits OP then OA is retained and AP could be paid as a residual dividend. If the profits are only OP*, however, OP* is retained and P*A must be raised as equity finance from the capital markets.

Miller and Modigliani were not arguing that dividends are a residual payment. They were arguing that provided a company followed its optimal investment policy, its value was completely unaffected by its dividend policy. Hence, according to Miller and Modigliani, the investment decision is separate from the dividend decision; or, more precisely, a company's choice of dividend policy, given its investment policy, is really a choice of financing strategy.

Miller and Modigliani also did not argue, as is often assumed, that investors were not concerned whether they received a dividend or not. Rather, they argued that shareholders

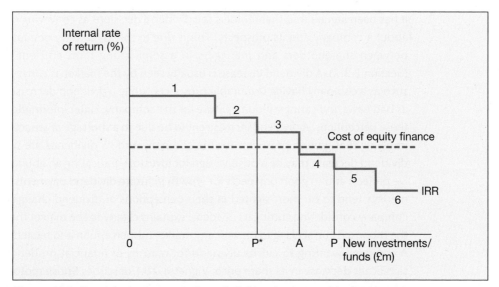

Figure 10.3 Graphical representation of dividends as a residual payment

were indifferent to the *timing* of dividend payments. If no dividends were paid, because all earnings had been consumed by the company's optimum investment schedule, the market value of the company would increase to reflect the expected future dividend payments or increasing share prices resulting from the investment returns. Shareholders who wanted cash when no dividend had been paid could, it was argued, generate a 'homemade' dividend by selling some of their shares.

10.4 DIVIDEND RELEVANCE

In contrast to the theory advanced by Miller and Modigliani is the view that dividend policies *are* relevant to company share valuations. This was the prevailing belief at the time that Miller and Modigliani published their paper, with the case for dividend relevance being put forward by Lintner (1956) and Gordon (1959). They argued that dividends are preferred to capital gains due to their certainty. This is often referred to as the *bird in the hand* argument and means that an investor will prefer to receive a certain dividend payment now, rather than leaving the equivalent amount in an investment of uncertain future value. Current dividends, on this analysis, represent a more reliable return than future capital gains.

If dividends are preferred to capital gains by investors, dividend policy has a vital role to play in determining the market value of a company. Companies that pay out low dividends may experience a fall in share price as investors exchange their shares for those of a different company with a more generous dividend policy.

Other arguments that have been advanced in support of dividend relevance will now be considered.

10.4.1 Dividends are signals to investors

It has been argued that shareholders see dividend decisions as conveying new information about a company and its prospects. This is due to the asymmetry of information existing between shareholders and managers in a semi-strong form efficient capital market (Section 2.3.2). A dividend increase is usually seen by the market as conveying good news, such as a company having favourable prospects, while a dividend decrease is usually seen as bad news, indicating a gloomy future for the company. Fuller information could reverse these perceptions. A dividend increase could be due to a shortage of attractive investments, implying that growth prospects for the company and its dividends are poor. Likewise, a dividend decrease may be a positive sign for investors, indicating an abundance of attractive projects and so good prospects for growth in future dividend payments. Unfortunately, markets tend to be short-sighted in their perceptions of dividend changes, even when a company considering cutting its dividend explains clearly to the market the reason behind the proposed cut, seeking to prevent any market misperception and related share price fall. A company wanting to cut its dividend for reasons of financial prudence often faces a significant decrease in its share price. Vignette 10.1 describes British motoring association AA plc's experiences over its dividend cut in 2018.

Vignette 10.1

AA shares tumble nearly 30% after dividend cut

By Pete Campbell

Shares in the AA fell almost 30 per cent after the breakdown cover provider slashed its dividend and warned of lower profits as it embarks on a technology drive. The company laid out a three-year plan to increase its use of vehicle-monitoring systems to spot breakdowns pre-emptively and expand its insurance business. It will spend an extra £45m this year in both operational and capital spending, as well as another £54m over the next two years, specifically developing new services.

As a result, the dividend has been cut from 9p to 2p, and it has cut full-year profit forecasts for next year to £335m–£345m, compared with expectations of £390m–£395m for the year until April. Simon Breakwell, chief executive, acknowledged that the investment would cut short-term profits but said it was 'vital to our long-term success'. Analysts at Morgan Stanley said the plan was 'necessary, but not without pain and risk'. AA shares, which fell 28 per cent to 83.6p on Wednesday, have lost two-thirds of their value since floating in 2014 as boardroom turmoil disrupts the former private equity-owned business.

The AA last year fired former executive chairman Bob Mackenzie following an altercation with a senior colleague. Mr Breakwell was named chief executive in September and has vowed to reinvent the 113-year-old business as a technology and product marketing company. The group aims to get more customers to install telematics technology, which monitors the car's engine and other systems. This will enable the detection of a problem before it happens, allowing a motorist to fix it and avoid calling out an AA van. It is trialling the systems in 5,000 vehicles, but hopes to roll them out eventually to as many customers as possible.

Mr Breakwell said the technology had the potential to 'profoundly change' the way the group operates, although the AA is expecting no additional revenues or profits from the service in the short term. It will also launch 65 more roadside vans, on top of the 2,100 already in service, in order to cut its reliance on third-party garages for call-outs that it cannot attend, as well as expanding its insurance business.

Mr Breakwell said margins in its insurance business were likely to slim slightly as it targeted growth by selling car and home insurance to non-AA customers, while also looking to sell more to existing users. The dividend will remain at 2p 'until such time as the board are satisfied that profit and free cash flow enable a change in dividend policy'. Some analysts had expected the dividend to be cancelled completely because of the need for higher investments.

Source: Campbell, P. (2018) 'AA shares tumble nearly 30% after dividend cut', *Financial Times*, 21 February. © The Financial Times Limited 2018. All Rights Reserved.

Questions

1 Explain why investors often see a cut in a company's dividend payment as a negative signal.

2 If a company is planning a cut in its dividend, how should it go about this?

Miller (1986) argued that it was not so much the *direction* of a dividend change that mattered but more the *difference* between the actual dividend payment and the market's expectations of what the dividend would be. The market, for instance, may be expecting a drop in a company's dividend payment, but if the *actual* decrease is greater than the *expected* decrease, this will lead to a fall in the company's share price. (Empirical evidence on the signalling properties of dividends will be considered in 'Alternatives to cash dividends', Section 10.7.)

10.4.2 The clientele effect

It has been argued that shareholders are not indifferent as to whether they receive dividends or capital gains. Preferences for one or the other can arise for two main reasons.

First, some shareholders need dividends as a source of regular income. This is true of small shareholders such as pensioners, and institutional investors such as pension funds and insurance companies: both have regular liabilities to meet. This need is balanced by stock exchange dealers, who over a small holding period prefer capital gains to dividend payments.

Second, preferences for dividends or capital gains may arise due to their different tax treatment. Capital gains in the UK are currently taxed at either 18 per cent or 28 per cent depending on the level of the investor's income, once investors have used up their annual capital gains allowance (£11,700 for the 2018/19 tax year). Dividends are treated as taxable income. In April 2016 new rules governing the taxation of dividends came into force. The UK system of tax credits was abolished and individuals received a £5,000 tax-free allowance. However, this has now been reduced and investors currently receive a tax-free allowance of £2,000 per year. Above that, the tax paid depends on an investor's income tax band. UK investors paying income tax at the basic rate (i.e. those with taxable income at or below £34,500 for the 2018/19 tax year) pay tax at 7.5 per cent. However, UK investors with taxable income over £34,500 and at or below £150,000 pay tax at a rate of 32.5 per cent and hence have a further 25 per cent to pay on dividend income. Investors with taxable income over £150,000 pay tax at a rate of 38.1 per cent and hence have a further 24.3 per cent to pay on dividend income. UK higher income taxpayers who have exhausted their capital gains allowance tend therefore to prefer further investment income in the form of capital gains (taxed at either 18 or 28 per cent) rather than dividends (taxed at either 32.5 or 38.1 per cent).

The existence of preferences for either dividends or capital gains means that investors will be attracted to companies whose dividend policies meet their requirements. Each company will therefore build up a clientele of shareholders who are satisfied by its dividend policy. The implication for a company is that a significant change in its dividend policy could dissatisfy its shareholders, resulting in downward pressure on its share price. (Empirical evidence on the clientele effect is considered in 'Empirical evidence on dividend policy', Section 10.8.)

10.4.3 The dividend growth model

The dividend growth model is a mathematical model that calculates the present value of a constantly increasing stream of cash flows (a perpetuity), allowing us to predict the value of ordinary shares. The model links the value of a share to the present value of the future dividend payments accruing to that share, and hence lends support to the dividend relevance view. The model holds that the market price of a share is equal to the sum of that share's discounted future dividend payments. Algebraically, we have:

$$P_0 = \frac{D_1}{(1+r)} + \frac{D_1(1+g)}{(1+r)^2} + \frac{D_1(1+g)^2}{(1+r)^3} + \cdots + \frac{D_1(1+g)^{n-1}}{(1+r)^n}$$

where: P_0 = current ex dividend market price of the share

$\quad\quad\;\; D_1$ = declared dividend at time t_1

$\quad\quad\;\; g\;$ = expected future growth rate of dividends

$\quad\quad\;\; n\;$ = number of years for which the share is held

$\quad\quad\;\; r\;$ = shareholders' required rate of return

This equation can be simplified by assuming that the share is held for a long time since as n tends towards infinity we have:

$$P_0 = \frac{D_0(1 + g)}{(r - g)} = \frac{D_1}{(r - g)}$$

This equation is called the *dividend growth model*.

How can we find the information needed by the right-hand side of the equation? The current year's dividend D_0 is usually known. The shareholders' required rate of return r (also called the cost of equity, K_e) can be calculated using the capital asset pricing model (see Chapter 8). The expected future growth rate of dividends g is difficult to estimate. One method of predicting it is by looking at historical dividend growth rates.

Example | **Calculating share price using the dividend growth model**

Shareholders require a 15 per cent return on their shares and a company has just paid a dividend of 80p per share. Over the past four years, the company has paid dividends of 68p, 73p, 74p and 77p per share (most recent dividend last). What is a fair price for the share using the dividend growth model?

Suggested answer

We need to estimate the dividend growth rate, g. Over the four-year period, dividends have grown from 68p to 80p per share and so:

$$68 \times (1 + g)^4 = 80$$

Rearranging:

$$1 + g = \sqrt[4]{\frac{80}{68}}$$

hence:

$$g = 4.1\%$$

Inserting D_0, g and r into the dividend growth model:

$$P_0 = \frac{80(1 + 0.041)}{(0.15 - 0.041)} = \frac{83.28}{(0.15 - 0.041)} = £7.64$$

Problems relating to using the dividend growth model to value shares include the following:

- It has been noted that dividends do not actually grow smoothly and so average historical g is only an approximation of the future dividend growth rate. This is a valid point and care must be taken when estimating g by calculating the average historic dividend growth rate that the sample of historic dividend payments used shows a stable trend. The assumption that the future dividend growth rate is the same as the average historic dividend growth rate may not be correct. Drawing a graph of historic dividend payments can help an analyst to determine whether a stable dividend trend exists.
- The model implies that if D_0 is zero, the share is worthless. This is not really a problem, since, presumably, dividend payments will begin at some point in the future. The dividend growth model can be applied to the future dividend stream and the calculated future value of the share price can be discounted to give a current share price.
- It is often said that the dividend growth model fails to take capital gains into account, i.e. it assumes investors buy shares and hold them for an infinite period. Again, this is not really a problem since, if a share is sold, the price paid will be the present value of its expected future dividends on the selling date. The dividend stream, and hence its present value, is not affected by the change in ownership.
- It has been noted that the dividend growth model makes no allowance for personal or other taxation. While this is true, the model can be modified to incorporate such tax effects.

In the model's favour though, if dividends have followed a specific growth pattern in the past, there may be no reason to assume it will change in the future, especially if a company follows a declared dividend policy. As dividends become distant (especially when the discount rate is high), small errors in dividend estimation become less significant as a progressively higher discount is applied.

10.5 DIVIDEND RELEVANCE OR IRRELEVANCE?

Who is right? It is possible to criticise some of the assumptions made by Miller and Modigliani as being unrealistic. Transaction costs are *not* zero and so there is a price to be paid by investors who sell their shares to create a 'home-made' dividend: this means that capital gains are not a perfect substitute for dividends in cash-flow terms. Taxation *does* exist in the real world, at both a corporate and a personal level, further distorting the required equivalence of dividends and capital gains. Securities *do* incur issue costs and information is *not* necessarily freely available: investors will have to expend time and money in acquiring and interpreting it.

While these shortcomings undermine Miller and Modigliani's argument, they do not totally invalidate it. In fact, empirical research since Miller and Modigliani published their paper has tended to support the dividend irrelevance school, for example, research by Black and Scholes (1974) and by Miller and Scholes (1978). (Further empirical evidence with respect to dividend policy is reviewed in 'Empirical evidence on dividend policy', Section 10.8.)

Ultimately it is the attitude of a company's shareholders that will determine whether dividends are paid and so the company's dividend policy is an important factor in determining the market price of its shares. In the current financial climate, where just under half of all ordinary shares are owned by institutional investors, the reactions of these shareholders to proposed dividend cuts certainly indicate they consider dividend payments to be very important. Because of their need for a constant stream of dividends from their shares, institutional investors have occasionally been accused of pressuring companies to maintain dividends they cannot afford to pay. Ironically, institutional investors might potentially be restricting future dividends by limiting the amount of retained earnings available for reinvestment.

10.6 DIVIDEND POLICIES

There are a number of different dividend policies or payout strategies that companies can adopt. These are considered in turn, as are the relative advantages and disadvantages of each policy.

10.6.1 Fixed percentage payout ratio policy

Here the company pays out a fixed percentage of annual profits as dividends, i.e. it maintains a constant *payout ratio* (Section 2.4.7). The advantages of this policy from the company's point of view are that it is relatively easy to operate and sends a clear signal to investors about the level of the company's performance. The disadvantage for a company is that it limits the amount of funds it retains for reinvestment. This dividend policy is unsuitable for companies with volatile profits that have shareholders requiring a stable dividend payment.

10.6.2 Zero dividend policy

A company could decide to pay no dividend at all. Such an extreme policy is likely to be highly beneficial to a small minority of investors while being totally unacceptable to the majority. Such a policy is easy to operate and will not incur the administration costs associated with paying dividends. A zero-dividend policy allows a company to reinvest all of its profits and so will be attractive to investors who, from a personal tax perspective, prefer capital gains to dividends.

Given that the majority of ordinary shareholders are institutional investors who rely on dividend payments for income, a zero-dividend policy is hardly likely to be acceptable on an ongoing basis. A zero-dividend policy, however, is often adopted by new companies that need large amounts of reinvestment in the first few years of their existence. Eurotunnel plc, for instance, when floated in 1987, indicated that a payment of dividends was unlikely to occur before 2005, although this was due to a large extent to the high level of interest payments arising out of inaccurate cost and revenue projections. Some high-profile US companies have refused to pay dividends in the past, including Internet-based companies Facebook, Google and Amazon.

10.6.3 Constant or steadily increasing dividend

A company may choose to pay a constant or steadily increasing dividend in either *money terms* or in *real terms* (i.e. with the effects of inflation removed: see 'Inflation and capital investment decisions', Section 7.3). A constant or increasing dividend in money terms may result in a declining or increasing dividend in real terms, depending on the level of inflation (or deflation). A constant or increasing dividend in real terms will usually result in an increasing dividend in money terms. In both policies, dividend increases are kept in line with long-term sustainable earnings. As mentioned earlier, it is important for a company to avoid volatility in dividend payments as doing so can help to maintain a stable share price. Cuts in dividends, however well-signalled or justified to the markets, are usually taken to mean financial weakness and result in downward pressure on a company's share price.

One drawback of paying constant or steadily increasing dividends is that investors may expect that dividend payments will continue on this trend indefinitely. This can cause major problems when companies wish to reduce dividend payments, either to fund re-investment or in the name of financial prudence (see Vignette 10.1). Because of the reaction of the market to a dividend cut, companies experiencing increases in profit tend to be cautious about a dividend increase. Rarely will a 20 per cent profit increase lead to a 20 per cent dividend increase. This is reinforced by the fact that a certain level of profit rarely equates to an equal amount of cash, which is ultimately what dividends are paid out of. Companies tend to increase dividends slowly over time, to reflect the new profit level, when they are confident that the new level is sustainable.

10.6.4 Dividend policies in practice

The dividend policies adopted by companies in practice tend to be influenced by three major factors. The first factor is the industry or commercial sector within which a company operates. Companies operating in industries that require large amounts of long-term re-investment are usually found to have lower payout ratios in order to facilitate higher levels of reinvestment. Additionally, companies operating in industries associated with high business risk, or industries susceptible to large cyclical swings in profit, tend to pay lower dividends and have lower payout ratios to avoid the risk of having to reduce dividend payments in the future. This view was supported by Rozeff (1986) in a paper that examined how companies determined their payout ratios. The wide variation in dividend **payout ratios** between different industries can clearly be seen in Table 10.1. Remember, however, that these ratios are merely snapshots: in a poorly performing sector, a high payout ratio may be a short-term phenomenon as companies with lower profits maintain their dividend payments, causing a temporary increase in the payout ratio. While no smooth trend can be identified in Table 10.1, eight of the ten listed sectors experienced an increase in their payout ratios between 2015 and 2018. The companies in two sectors (information technology and pharmaceuticals) were, on average, unable to cover their dividends in 2018 from their existing earnings while the extractive industries had the lowest payout ratio at 39 per cent.

Table 10.1 Average dividend payout ratios for a selection of UK industries in 2012, 2015 and 2018

Industry	Payout ratio in 2012 (%)	Payout ratio in 2015 (%)	Payout ratio in 2018 (%)
Food retailers	47	213	51
Banks (retail)	35	77	81
Telecommunications	39	52	87
Electronics	31	51	44
Information technology	41	46	118
General retail	42	42	54
Chemicals	36	42	48
Leisure and hotels	34	41	48
Extractive industries	13	36	39
Pharmaceuticals	56	28	110

Source: Adapted from *Financial Times*, 2 March 2012, 15 July 2015 and 6 July 2018.

The second factor affecting companies' dividend policies is the nature of the company and its individual characteristics. For example, a company which has reached the mature stage of its life cycle may choose to adopt a high payout ratio owing to its minimal reinvestment requirement. Alternatively, a company which has a high level of bank borrowings relative to the rest of the companies in its sector may, in response to an increase in interest rates, choose to decrease its level of dividend payout to meet its interest commitments.

The third factor is the state of a country's economy and the environment of the global economy. If a country's economy is booming and corporate liquidity levels are high, then there is a tendency for companies' dividend payouts to increase. Equally, in times of recession when corporate liquidity is low, companies are likely to pay lower dividends. The subject of the recent boom in dividend payouts in the UK in 2018 is the focus of Vignette 10.2.

Vignette 10.2

UK dividends look unsustainable, investors warned

By Kate Beioley

Investors should proceed with caution when buying UK income stocks, as the high dividends they offer may be unsustainable, according to broker AJ Bell. FTSE 100 companies are forecast to pay out £87.5bn in dividends in 2018, equating to a dividend yield of 4.4 per cent – far higher than the average return on cash savings and bonds. Dividend yield is a measure of a company's income payments relative to its share price.

Several companies have experienced a rise in dividend yield mainly as the result of sharp share price falls, meaning they may struggle to pay their high income in future. Companies such as Persimmon and Centrica are now sitting on forecast dividend yields of more than 9 per cent, signalling high potential income to investors. But many of the top payers have seen increases in their yields not because their dividends have risen but because

---

Vignette 10.2 (continued)

their share prices have fallen sharply. Many of those stocks are not on track to generate enough revenue to cover their dividends more than two times over, which analysts cite as the ideal minimum level. This means that if those stocks run into trouble this year, investors could see their dividends cut too.

According to AJ Bell, earnings cover improved over the first quarter of 2018 but remains at an average of 1.71 times, meaning companies could not pay out their planned dividends more than 1.71 times from current earnings. At the end of 2017, cover had been even more precarious, at a level of 1.63 times. Income among the highest-yielding companies looks shakier still. Average dividend cover across the 10 highest yielding stocks in the FTSE is just 1.42 times. AJ Bell said: 'Dividends cover of around 1.5 is less than ideal because it means a company has less room for manoeuvre if profits fall in one year. It will then need to decide whether to reduce its dividend, stop reinvesting in the business or take on more debt.'

Centrica, currently forecast to yield 8.4 per cent in 2018, was trading at more than 220p in April 2017 but is now below 140p. Its dividend is only covered 1.19 times by its earnings.

Shares in Micro Focus, a technology company, also shed half their value in March. The company revealed that sales were falling and announced the departure of its chief executive Chris Hsu last month, just two years after a £6.6bn merger with Hewlett-Packard. The company is currently yielding 7.5 per cent. AJ Bell said: 'The 10 highest forecast dividend yields in the FTSE 100 this year are starting to look questionably high.'

Investment trusts with assets in UK equities have similar dividend cover ratios, but according to data from Numis, investors in these are better protected due to the pots of cash that such trusts hold in reserve. The average UK equity income investment trust currently has dividend cover of 1.1 times and could cover dividends 0.7 times from their reserves.

Unlike mutual funds, investment trusts can hold back income each year to continue paying out dividends even if earnings fall. That means that they can cover their dividends each year both from earnings and revenue reserves. Sam Murphy, analyst at Numis, said: 'Investment trusts in the UK Equity income sector have been pretty prudent. Dividend cover on average is 1.1 so they're all putting away income for a rainy day.'

Across the sector, the average trust has managed to see its dividends grow over the year by 5.6 per cent. Trusts with the best protected dividends include Diverse Income Trust, whose holdings include Royal Dutch Shell and trading platform IG Group. The trust currently raised its dividend by more than 7 per cent between 2017 and 2018 and increased its revenues.

 Source: Beioley, K. (2018) 'UK dividends look unsustainable, investors warned', *Financial Times*, 13 April. © The Financial Times Limited 2018. All Rights Reserved.

Questions

1 What are the potential dangers associated with companies paying dividends that are unsustainable?

2 Are dividend cover and dividend yield useful ratios for investors deciding on how to invest their money?

These three factors will combine to influence what a company decides to pay out in dividends. An example of an individual company's dividend history is given in Table 10.2. Between 2001 and 2004, J Sainsbury plc increased its dividend per share as profitability improved. However, in 2005 profits crashed and the company had no choice but to slash its nominal dividend. In the subsequent three years profits have recovered and the company has managed to increase dividends in nominal terms while at the same time gradually reducing its payout ratio. The company has also managed to increase its dividend in real terms in consecutive years since 2006. However, reduced earnings led to a cut in nominal dividends in 2015 and subsequent years. Sainsbury now appear to be targeting a 50 per cent payout ratio, which has led to the fall in real dividends for the last four years.

Table 10.2 Dividend policy of J Sainsbury plc, 2001–2018

	2001	2002	2003	2004	2005	2006	2007	2008	2009	2010	2011	2012	2013	2014	2015	2016	2017	2018
EPS (p)	18.8	21.5	24.2	23.4	9.0	10.5	13.0	17.4	21.2	23.9	26.5	28.1	30.8	32.8	26.4	24.2	21.8	20.4
Nominal DPS (p)	14.3	14.8	15.6	15.7	7.8	8.0	9.75	12.0	13.2	14.2	15.1	16.1	16.7	17.3	13.2	12.1	10.2	10.2
Growth rate (%)	N/A	3.5	5.4	0.6	−50.3	2.6	21.9	23.1	10.0	7.6	6.3	6.6	3.7	3.6	−23.7	−8.3	−15.7	nil
Payout ratio (%)	76.1	68.8	64.5	67.1	86.7	76.2	75.0	69.0	62.3	59.4	57.0	57.0	54.0	53.0	50.0	50.0	46.8	50.0
Inflation (%)		1.5	3.1	3.0	2.9	3.3	3.8	5.0	−1.4	4.8	5.0	3.1	3.1	2.5	1.0	1.9	3.6	3.3
Real DPS (p)	14.3	14.6	14.9	14.6	7.0	7.0	8.2	9.6	10.7	11.0	11.1	11.5	11.6	11.7	8.9	8.0	6.5	6.3
Growth rate (%)		2.1%	2.1%	−2.0%	−52.1%	0.0%	17.1%	17.1%	11.5%	2.8%	0.9%	3.6%	0.9%	0.9%	−23.9%	−10.1%	−18.8%	−3.1%

Note: Inflation as measured by RPI is taken from July to July to reflect the final dividend date.

Source: J Sainsbury plc annual reports. Reproduced by kind permission of Sainsbury's Supermarkets Ltd.

10.7 ALTERNATIVES TO CASH DIVIDENDS

In addition to paying cash dividends, there are other ways in which companies can reward their shareholders.

10.7.1 Scrip dividends

Scrip dividends involve the offer of additional ordinary shares to equity investors, in proportion to their existing shareholding (e.g. 1 for every 20 shares held), as a partial or total alternative to a cash dividend. Usually, shareholders are given the choice of taking either the declared cash dividend or the scrip alternative, allowing them to choose the alternative that best suits their liquidity and tax position.

The major advantage with paying a scrip dividend is that it allows a company to keep the cash that would have been paid out in cash dividends. From a personal tax point of view, the scrip dividend received is treated as income, with tax deemed to have been paid at the basic rate of income tax. Scrip dividends will be unattractive to investors who are exempt from paying tax on dividends as they are not able to reclaim tax which is only 'deemed' to have been paid. A scrip dividend may sometimes be enhanced, which means that the value of the scrip dividend exceeds the value of the cash dividend alternative, making it a more attractive choice to shareholders. If the enhancement is more than 15 per cent of the cash alternative though, shareholders may be liable to pay additional tax. If used carefully, however, scrip dividends can provide generous tax savings for investors.

Another possible advantage associated with paying a scrip dividend is that it allows a company to decrease its gearing ratio slightly. It should also be noted that, if the capital market is efficient, the share price will not be depressed since the scrip dividend merely replaces a cash dividend which would have caused the price to fall anyway.

10.7.2 Share repurchases

Share repurchases have become an increasingly common way of returning value to ordinary shareholders in the UK, following their adoption by some leading companies in recent years. Such companies include BP Amoco, whose two 'buybacks' in 2000 amounted to £1,993m in total. More recently, Vodafone plc instigated an aggressive buyback programme in 2003 which had reached its target of £6.8bn of repurchases by mid-2012. An estimated £34bn of 'buybacks' occurred in the UK between 1995 and 2000, with £9bn in 2000 alone. In the year to January 2018, total UK share repurchases were £15bn, almost matching new share issuance over the same period, including the energy and financial services sectors. The boom in share buybacks in the UK is the subject of Vignette 10.3.

Share repurchases have been commonplace in the USA over a much longer period and continue to be popular. In 2014 shareholder returns exceeded $903bn, with $350bn (39 per cent) in dividends and a massive $553bn (61 per cent) in share repurchases. Companies such as Dell Inc and Apple Inc were heavily involved in repurchasing their own shares, with Apple launching a new buyback scheme for $100bn in May 2018.

Vignette 10.3

UK share buybacks accelerate as market lags behind

By Chloe Cornish

UK share buybacks are close to matching the amount of new equity issued for the first time in five years, but investors cautioned they are not yet at a level to help a stock market that has been a global laggard over the past year.

Repurchases have totalled almost £15bn in the 12 months to January 2018, according to research from Goldman Sachs, with energy and financial services industries leading the upturn. That compares with new equity issuance of £17bn, snapping the trend of the past four years in which the volume of buybacks has trailed.

Oil company BP says it has purchased $90m worth of shares this year, adding to $343m of buybacks in 2017 – its first in three years. Rival Royal Dutch Shell in November announced a $25bn share buyback scheme that would run until 2020.

Ben Lofthouse, a fund manager at Janus Henderson, said that some UK stocks are relatively cheap compared with global peers, with the pick-up in buybacks suggesting that some companies share that view. 'The UK is a pretty unloved equity market [at the moment]. In some areas – energy, financials, utilities – there's definitely a UK discount', he said.

The FTSE 100, London's blue-chip index, has notably lagged behind global share markets over the past 12 months. In local currency terms it has fallen 3 per cent, while the broader FTSE 350 has dropped 1.7 per cent. The S&P 500 has risen 17 per cent in the same period. Improving earnings and cash flows returning to oil and banking sectors are driving the buybacks trend, said Sharon Bell, a European equity strategist at Goldman Sachs. 'In some sense,

I think it's a sign of confidence. You certainly don't get vulnerable companies buying back shares'.

The more than doubling in the oil price since early 2016 has buoyed the energy sector after a couple of years of distress that accompanied a falling crude price. However, Andrew Milligan, head of global strategy at Aberdeen Standard Investments, cautioned that while buybacks could indicate confidence, they might also reflect a hesitancy to make significant investments. 'In a world of considerable uncertainty about future outlook . . . firms may decide that the horizon is more in favour of share buybacks than capital spending,' he said.

Within financial services, Lloyds Banking Group launched a £1bn share buyback programme in February. Aviva, the insurer, last week announced plans to return £500m to investors, which could include ordinary shares, but the company stirred controversy after raising the possibility of buying back preferred shares.

The volume of share buybacks by London-listed companies has been relatively muted since the financial crisis, and in sharp contrast to the US where corporate purchases, led by the technology and pharma sectors, have supported the bull market on Wall Street. US companies have bought back more than $3tn worth of shares since 2010.

In Europe, Allianz and Zurich, the Swiss insurer, have recently announced buybacks. 'I personally feel more European companies should probably be doing it because interest rates are so low,' said Mr Lofthouse. But while he predicted that buybacks were here to stay until interest rates move higher, the volume was not yet enough to 'drive markets significantly'.

 Source: Cornish, C. (2018) 'UK share buybacks accelerate as market lags behind', *Financial Times*, 16 March 2018. © The Financial Times Limited 2018. All Rights Reserved.

Questions

1 Why are share buybacks often concentrated in certain industrial sectors?

2 If companies are seen to be buying back their shares as they perceive them as being undervalued, what implication does this have for finance theory?

In the UK the Companies Act 1981 first opened the way for British companies to repurchase their own shares. The current legislation can be found in the Companies Act 2006. Before any share repurchase takes place however, a company must obtain approval from both its current shareholders and any warrant, option and convertible holders it may have, and the company is limited to repurchasing up to 15 per cent of its total share capital in any 12-month period.

The main benefit to shareholders of a share repurchase is that they receive surplus funds from the company which they can use more effectively. The main benefit for a company of a share repurchase is that it enhances the value of the remaining shares. In addition, since capital employed is reduced by repurchasing shares, return on capital employed (ROCE) will increase, as will earnings per share (EPS). While this must be balanced against an increase in gearing, it is argued that the increase in financial risk associated with a share repurchase is negligible and so, since the cost of equity is unaltered, the value of shares and the company will increase.

Another reason behind companies repurchasing their shares is if they consider the stock market to be undervaluing their company. This was the justification used for Vodafone's £1bn share buyback in the UK in 2008. Many commentators put the late 1990s boom in share repurchases down to the abolition of dividend tax credits in 1997 and the removal of advance corporation tax (ACT) in 1999. However, the more cynical among them believe that managers with EPS-based performance measures were using share repurchases as a way of increasing EPS and hence enhancing executive rewards.

There are three ways via which a company to repurchase its shares. The first two we consider are classified as 'off-market' as the shares are not repurchased on a recognised investment market. A *tender offer* is where all shareholders are invited to sell back their shares at a price set by the company. The main advantage with this method is that it allows all shareholders to participate in the repurchase. Secondly a company repurchases its shares *by arrangement* with individual shareholders. Often companies employ a broker as an agent to organise the repurchase of its shares from institutional shareholders who are clients of the broker. Hence, this method of repurchase is sometimes known as an *agency buyback.* The third method, a *stock market purchase,* is described as a 'market' purchase. This is more flexible than a tender offer as there is no one unique price at which the shares are to be repurchased and, in addition, less documentation is required.

As with scrip dividends, share repurchases have tax implications for both companies and investors. In the case of tender offers and repurchases by private arrangement, the capital amount (equivalent to the current market price of the shares) is taxed as a capital gain. Any payment in excess of the current market price of the share is treated as a net dividend payment and therefore carries a tax credit, which tax-exempt shareholders cannot reclaim from the UK tax authority. With stock market repurchases, the whole payment is treated as a capital gain and taxed accordingly. We can conclude that shareholders with differing tax situations will have different preferences for how a company should go about repurchasing its shares.

10.7.3 Special dividends

Companies occasionally return surplus funds to shareholders by making a **special dividend** payment, which is a cash payout far in excess of the dividend payment usually made by the company. If a company has funds surplus to its investment requirements, paying out these funds via a special dividend enables shareholders to reinvest them according to their preferences. A special dividend scheme was used by East Midlands Electricity plc in October 1994 to return £186.5m of surplus funds to its shareholders. In subsequent years, special dividends have become a less frequent occurrence, although there has been a recent upsurge in special dividend activity. The London Stock Exchange paid a special dividend worth £162m in 2004, and in 2005, De Vere plc announced a special dividend of £1.59 per share following the sale of the De Vere Belfry. More recently in May 2018 National Grid returned approximately £3.2bn to its shareholders via a special dividend of 84 pence per share, funded by the £4.0bn disposal of its UK gas distribution business.

Whether companies are best advised returning surplus funds to their shareholders via a special dividend or a share repurchase is the subject of Vignette 10.4.

Vignette 10.4

Companies face difficult calls on returning cash

By Alison Smith

What should we do with all this cash? Every company has faced harder questions than that. Yet even this enviable position can contain difficult decisions within the 'corporates hand out money to shareholders, everybody happy' narrative. Investors are generally pleased to see the increased payouts unveiled by companies during the latest results season. In recent months, many shareholders have been making clear they think it is time for companies to distribute some of the cash that has been hoarded through uncertain times even as profits revived.

David Cumming, head of UK equities at Standard Life Investments, says: 'Sometimes you might hear a company say that it needs to hold on to the cash because it has a big deal in mind. As shareholders, our response would tend to be: "Until we see that acquisition, why don't you just have the right balance sheet?".' Even so, shareholders typically do not want payouts today to come at the expense of investment that will sustain business growth tomorrow.

Richard Pennycook, finance director of Wm Morrison, which last week announced a £1bn share buyback programme over two years, says the group's balance sheet review made clear that the food retailer could afford its forward investment programme, maintain its investment-grade balance sheet rating and still have cash to spare. Having consulted shareholders over the past six months, he says: 'They were certainly keen to get reassurance that we were making all the investment we wanted to make in the business'. Companies must also consider how to split the cash between an increase in ordinary dividends and special payouts.

Graham Secker of Morgan Stanley says big rises in ordinary dividends are a sign of management confidence that the group can sustain the earnings improvement. This can make companies wary of raising expectations, not just that a dividend policy will be progressive, but that the annual rate of increase will be maintained. 'Some companies I know have gone with 10–15 per cent dividend growth this year and, to my mind, that can create confusion,' says Martin Bride, finance director of Beazley, the insurance company that in February announced a 2.5p special dividend. 'Capital markets don't like surprises and, in an industry with profit volatility, you need to distinguish completely between what is sustainable and what is not,' he says.

'So widespread has been the move towards returning extra cash to investors that examples of three

Vignette 10.4 (continued)

different ways of doing so were on display last week: B share schemes, special dividends and buybacks (or equity retirement programmes).

Aggreko, the temporary power company, said it intended to return £150m to shareholders through a 'tax-efficient' B share scheme that allows the Salvesen family, which owns a stake of about 20 per cent, to take the return as a capital gain rather than income. Some other companies that considered this option dismissed it either as too expensive in terms of ongoing costs or irrelevant because it applies only to private shareholders and does not benefit institutional investors.

The other two methods tend to be more widely used. 'Traditionally in the UK, the general preference across the investor base has been for dividends over buybacks, but I think that is changing a bit,' says Mr Secker. A special dividend has the advantages of certainty and immediacy: the full amount can be paid out within a few weeks of its being announced. A buyback programme is flexible – the company can choose when and at what price to buy and can suspend the programme, as Anglo American did in February 2009, if conditions worsen. Buybacks also enhance some financial performance measures. 'If you buy in your shares, you do permanently improve some key measures, such

as earnings per share,' says Mr Bride. 'The thing with special dividends is that people take them, spend them and forget them.' Neither is the right answer in every circumstance and buybacks attract some opposition in principle. 'We are very against buybacks because they do not treat shareholders equally, which companies could do through, for example, extra dividends or B share schemes,' says Jim Stride, head of UK equities at Axa Investment Managers. 'We also think that one perverse and negative effect of a buyback is to attract further selling of the stock. As a buyback decreases the number of shares in a company, in due course index funds will sell down as well.'

Mr Cumming of SLI does not agree that buybacks are unfair. 'All a buyback does is create another buyer in the market. It would only be unfair if a particular holder is targeted.' Announcing an extra payout in any form can often give an immediate boost to a share price. But long-term rerating depends more on investors believing that the return of capital is part of a coherent plan. As Mr Cumming puts it: 'A buyback that looks like a one-off made under duress, but where a management team will still spend on acquisitions if they can get away with it, will have less of an impact than one that is about reaching an appropriate level of gearing.'

 Source: Smith, A. (2011) 'Companies face difficult calls on returning cash', *Financial Times*, 17 March.
© The Financial Times Limited 2011. All Rights Reserved.

Question

Do share buybacks or special dividends represent the best way to return a company's surplus cash to its investors?

10.7.4 Non-pecuniary benefits

Also referred to as shareholder perks, these can take the form of discounts on a company's goods and services and/or the offer of complimentary goods and services. Perks can be available to all shareholders, but normally a minimum number of shares must be held to qualify for the benefits. Next plc, for example, gives investors a 25 per cent discount voucher for use on most goods for investors with 100 or more shares. Meanwhile, shareholders with 500 or more shares in Marston's plc receive a 20 per cent discount on food and accommodation. The true value of shareholder perks is the focus of Vignette 10.5.

Vignette 10.5

Do shareholder perks add up for investors?

By Lucy Warwick-Ching

Twenty years ago, shareholder perks played a major part in persuading investors to buy shares. Discounts of thousands of pounds on new-build properties were commonplace for shareholders in house-builders, while generous shopping vouchers for retail share owners abounded.

Today's investors, however, often need to spend hundreds, if not thousands, of pounds to accumulate enough shares to qualify for perks attached to shares. The tough economic climate of the past few years has resulted in some companies focusing on other priorities such as dividend payments at the expense of their most generous shareholder offers.

'The 1990s marked the peak for these discount and reward schemes as many companies saw some mileage in trying to turn shareholders into customers,' says Gavin Oldham, chief executive at The Share Centre. 'Offering perks tends to lead to strong loyalty among customers who are also shareholders.'

Guy Ellison, head of UK equities at Investec Wealth & Investment, agrees. He says that when it comes to investing, familiarity breeds fondness. Recent research carried out by Investec Wealth & Investment found that people were more inclined to buy shares in well-known companies, with many individuals saying they would continue to hold these shares even if they performed poorly. Thirteen per cent of investors interviewed said they held on to shares for the shareholder perks.

Mr Ellison adds that companies use perks to encourage individuals to support them as consumers as well as shareholders – and that they can sometimes be a useful way for a business to offload unused stock or use up spare capacity on services.

One company that has caught investors' attention is Merlin Entertainments, the theme park operator, which operates sites including Legoland, Alton Towers, Chessington and Madame Tussauds. Its recent flotation included a flurry of perks for private investors such as discount entry to attractions.

'The discounts made Merlin look like an attractive option for investors who had young children or grandchildren,' says Tim May, chief executive of the Wealth Management Association (formerly Apcims). Investors with £1,000 worth of shares can get a 30 per cent discount on a family Merlin annual pass, priced at £356, although there is no guarantee the discount will be permanent.

Not surprisingly, perks are most common among companies selling 'lifestyle' goods and services, such as clothes, cars, restaurants and holidays. Sheridan Admans, investment research manager at The Share Centre, likes the perks offered by Marks and Spencer, Mulberry and BT, all of which he says have sound fundamentals and feature on The Share Centre buy list.

A £4.96 share in Marks and Spencer will earn you a booklet of vouchers giving a one-off discount of 10 per cent across a range of shopping, while a £5.62 share in Restaurant Group gets an investor a discount of 25 per cent at food outlets such as Chiquitos and Frankie & Benny's. For investors with 20 shares in Mulberry, the designer retailer, (costing around £2,500 at current prices) there is a 20 per cent discount on purchases up to £10,000 in any single year at certain named outlets.

Shareholders with just one share, costing around £10.10, in Young & Co's Brewery receive a 50 per cent discount off the price of its hotel rooms.

'Some investors think of perks as a 'return on their investment' in a similar way to dividends,' says Mark Till, head of personal investing at Fidelity. 'Depending on where you shop, these perks could help you get a higher 'effective' return on investment. For example, someone who is a frequent traveller could save themselves money each year by holding shares in Eurotunnel for the discount shuttle tickets. And the same for someone who buys a lot of their clothes from M&S and owns the company's shares.'

So how do the schemes work? In some cases, investors will be sent a book of vouchers with the annual report, outlining discounts up to a certain value for each year. In other cases, shareholders will be provided with a discount card giving a set reduction on purchases made from company outlets.

For deals such as holidays and travel, investors will need to book via the companies' shareholder hotline, while house-buyers purchasing a new home are asked to let the developer's sales negotiator know that they want to claim their discount.

Vignette 10.5 (continued)

Mr Oldham warns that certain companies will stipulate the minimum number of shares that must be held by a shareholder before any perks are distributed. In some cases the shares must also be held for a certain length of time before the shareholder is entitled to receive benefits. That can mean investors end up holding a large number of shares, possibly for a long period, to pick up a relatively small benefit.

For example, in order to receive a one-off 25 per cent discount voucher in clothes retailer Next, an investor needs to buy 500 shares – currently an outlay of £27,000.

The high entry levels for these perks highlight how disinterested some companies are in using their shareholder perk schemes to attract investors. 'The hurdles for receiving perks will only get higher – as share prices continue to rise – and it will be interesting to see which companies lower the barriers to entry for those discounts. Only then will we be able to see who is truly committed to offering their perks,' says Mr Ellison.

Time stipulations can also catch investors out. Some house-builders insist on a minimum 12-month period of share ownership before discounts become available. Or you may have to hold the share on a particular date before the time you try to use it.

Savings can be less significant than expected, too. Some companies such as Mulberry stipulate that discounts only apply to full-price items or standard rates, or that you cannot use them in conjunction with any other discount. But you may find you can do better by buying a limited-period special offer of some sort.

And while some investors view perks as a return on capital similar to dividends, most are advised to look beyond the discounts on offer. 'People have become more sophisticated in their investment requirements, and they are focusing on real returns in terms of capital and income,' says Mr Oldham.

Paul Taylor, managing director of McCarthy Taylor, supports this view, telling investors not to be swayed by the perks when deciding where to invest. 'Over the years many listed companies have offered shareholder perks, many quite attractive if you want a discount on cruise holidays, for example. We have always advised clients to ignore these when looking at buying investments.

'Like all inducements they have to be paid for out of profits and this must impact on dividends, even if only to a small extent. In addition, a company might be a good investment but you might not always want to book your cruises or hotel rooms with them. Best to keep your options open.'

Experts add that there is little sense in buying shares in a company that is inefficiently run or has failed to move with the times, just because you'll get a book of discount vouchers or a privilege card.

Mr Oldham also recommends weighing up the cost of buying a share, including dealing costs and stamp duty, against any potential perk. Investors should also confirm any perks are still on offer before buying shares as the benefits can change or be withdrawn completely.

 Source: Warwick-Ching, L. (2013) 'Do shareholder perks add up for investors?', *Financial Times*, 22 November. © The Financial Times Limited 2013. All Rights Reserved.

Questions

1 Should the shareholder perks associated with buying a company's shares be the main reason for investing in that company?

2 Does a company providing perks to its shareholders maximise their wealth?

10.8 EMPIRICAL EVIDENCE ON DIVIDEND POLICY

Dividend policy is an area of corporate finance that has been the subject of extensive empirical research. This is due in no small part both to the continuing debate on whether dividend payments are relevant in determining the share price of a company and to the readily available supply of data on corporate dividend payments.

Before Miller and Modigliani's 1961 paper, the generally held belief of both academics and the business community was that dividends were preferred by investors to capital gains because of their certainty. The implication of this belief is that companies could increase their share prices by generous dividend policies. Lintner (1956) surveyed the financial managers of 28 US companies and concluded that the dividend decision was seen as important, with dividend payments being determined independently from companies' investment decisions. He found that companies gradually changed dividend payments towards their desired payout ratio as earnings increased, reducing the need for subsequent dividend reductions should earnings decrease. A later study by Fama and Babiak (1968) of 201 US companies came to similar conclusions.

Gordon (1959) found that companies with high payout ratios also had high price/earnings ratios, implying that investors valued companies with high payout ratios more highly than companies with low payout ratios. However, this research has been discredited. First, price/earnings ratios and payout ratios tend to move together as earnings fluctuate, since both ratios have earnings per share as a denominator. Second, the relationship between price/earnings ratios and payout ratios may be explained *by the level of risk* of companies, rather than by shareholders preferring companies with high payout ratios. Companies with volatile earnings tend to have lower price/earnings ratios because of their higher risk; they usually pay out a lower proportion of earnings as dividends to reflect the volatility of their earnings.

After Miller and Modigliani's 1961 paper on dividend policy, a large amount of empirical research focused on dividends and their tax implications. Seminal work by Brennan (1970) in the USA put forward the proposition that the market price of a company's shares would change in order to give the same after-tax rate of return regardless of its dividend policy. For example, if a company were to distribute a higher level of earnings, thereby increasing the amount of tax paid by its shareholders, its share price would fall to reflect the increase in tax liability. The implication of Brennan's proposition was that companies could increase their share price by adopting lower levels of earnings distribution.

Black and Scholes (1974) tested Brennan's proposition by examining whether companies with high dividend yields gave greater before-tax returns to compensate investors for the undesirable tax implications of high dividend distribution. Their results were inconclusive and they failed to find any positive relationship between dividend yields and before-tax returns. In contrast, Litzenberger and Ramaswamy (1979) did find a statistically significant relationship between dividend yields and before-tax returns. Litzenberger and Ramaswamy's findings were later discredited by Miller and Scholes (1982), who repeated Litzenberger and Ramaswamy's analysis and concluded that the relationship between high dividend yields and high before-tax returns could be explained by dividend information effects rather than by dividend tax effects.

Elton and Gruber (1970) investigated the existence of tax clienteles by examining share price falls at the time when share prices went ex dividend. By looking at the magnitude of the share price fall they inferred the average marginal rate of income tax that a company's shareholders were paying. They concluded that high dividend shares were associated with lower marginal rates of income tax, hence supporting the proposition of the existence of a tax clientele. Subsequent investigations by Pettit (1977) in the USA and by Crossland et al. (1991) in the UK have given further support to the existence of a clientele effect.

Miller and Scholes (1978) showed that US shareholders could negate less preferential tax rates on dividends compared with capital gains by the appropriate use of tax planning, hence lending support to Miller and Modigliani's dividend irrelevance theory. However, Feenberg (1981) concluded that very few investors had taken advantage of the tax planning suggested by Miller and Scholes. This was, in some part, due to the transaction costs associated with such a course of action. More recently, Bond et al. (1996) examined the effects of the now defunct ACT system on dividend policy in the UK. They concluded that for companies with surplus (unrelieved) ACT, the higher tax cost of paying dividends exerted significant downward pressure on their dividends.

Research into the effect on share prices of the information content of dividends has been carried out by Pettit (1972), Watts (1973), Aharony and Swary (1980) and Kwan (1981). All of these studies, apart from that of Watts, concluded that dividend changes *do* convey new information to shareholders. Perhaps unsurprisingly Bozos et al. (2011) found that dividends have less informational content in times of economic stability than in times of economic recession. Ham et al. (2018) used an event window-based approach to show that market reaction to dividend change announcements reflects new information about future earnings.

More recently Booth and Zhou (2015) found that market power positively affects the dividend decision, both in terms of the probability of a dividend being paid and the amount of the dividend payment. Baker and Weigand (2015) in their comprehensive literature survey noted that US evidence indicated the importance of cash dividends had declined while share repurchases were playing an increasingly important role in providing returns to shareholders.

10.9 CONCLUSION

In recent years corporate dividend policy has become an important decision area in its own right. Among the many factors influencing the dividend policy of a company are the levels of personal and corporate taxation, the number of reinvestment opportunities available to the company relative to its distributable earnings, the company's liquidity position and the characteristics and composition of a company's shareholders. Broadly speaking, companies have the choice of three types of dividend policy: paying no dividend at all, paying out a fixed proportion of earnings, and paying a constant or slightly increasing dividend. In addition to cash dividends, companies can also use scrip dividends, share repurchases and non-pecuniary benefits as ways of rewarding shareholders.

The debate over whether dividend policy affects the value of a company is a continuing one. While Miller and Modigliani's argument for dividend irrelevance is logical within the restrictive assumptions they made, recent trends in corporate dividend policies lend more support to the relevance school. Given that over half of ordinary shares are owned by large institutional investors looking for a regular income stream, only a naïve financial manager would fail to appreciate that the dividend decision of his or her company might affect its share price.

■ ■ ■ KEY POINTS

1 A company's dividend decision has important implications for both its investment and its financing decisions.

2 Dividends in the UK are paid semi-annually on a gross basis. Investors get a £5,000 tax free allowance. Above that, basic rate taxpayers pay 7.5 per cent, higher-rate taxpayers 32.5 per cent and additional-rate taxpayers 38.1 per cent.

3 Interim dividends are generally smaller than final dividends because of cash-flow and financial planning considerations.

4 When a share passes from being cum dividend to ex dividend, its market price will fall by the value of the net dividend forgone to reflect a change in the intrinsic value of the share.

5 Legal constraints on the payment of dividends include the Companies Act 2006, which states that dividends must be paid out of 'accumulated net realised profits', and restrictive loan agreements or covenants.

6 Other restrictions on a company's dividend policy include its liquidity position, its interest payment obligations and the number of attractive investment opportunities available.

7 A dividend should be paid only if it increases shareholder wealth, i.e. if $d_1 + P_1 > P_0$.

8 Miller and Modigliani argued that dividend payments are irrelevant to valuing ordinary shares and that a company's value is maximised if it uses an optimum investment policy. A dividend might be a residual payment after all attractive investments have been accepted. Shareholders requiring dividends who did not receive them could make 'home-made' dividends by selling shares.

9 While the Miller and Modigliani model is academically sound, its underlying assumptions are not applicable to the real world.

10 Lintner and Gordon argued that investors preferred dividends to capital gains because of their certainty.

11 Dividend relevance to share valuation is further supported by the argument that dividends are seen by investors as signals of a company's future profitability.

12 The existence of tax at both a personal and corporate level further undermines Miller and Modigliani's dividend irrelevance theory.

13 Dividend policies that companies can choose from include paying no dividend, adopting a fixed payout ratio, and maintaining a constant or steadily increasing dividend in nominal or real terms.

14 In practice most companies try to keep dividends rising smoothly by accommodating temporary drops in earnings through a higher payout ratio and by increasing dividends only gradually in response to an increase in earnings.

15 Payout ratios vary from industry to industry and depend on the risk and level of required reinvestment associated with each industry.

16 Scrip dividends, where new shares are offered as an alternative to cash dividends, allow companies to retain money for reinvestment purposes.

17 Share repurchases (or buybacks) and special dividends are sometimes used by companies to return surplus cash to shareholders.

18 Empirical research on the importance of dividends is by no means clear-cut. While Miller and Modigliani's model has not been totally discredited, there is substantial evidence to support the existence of tax clienteles and to support the view that dividends are seen by investors as signalling new information about a company's future prospects.

SELF-TEST QUESTIONS

Answers to these questions can be found on pages 464–5.

1 Discuss the practical issues to be considered by a company when deciding on the size of its dividend payment.

2 Which of the following statements lends support to dividend irrelevance rather than to dividend relevance?

(a) Investors prefer the certainty of dividends to the uncertainty of capital gains.

(b) Companies build up a clientele of shareholders due to their dividend policy.

(c) Dividends are believed to signal information about the company.

(d) Taxes distort the desirability of dividends relative to capital gains.

(e) Shareholders can make their own dividends by selling some of their shares.

3 XYZ's has just announced a dividend of 20p per share and the cum dividend share price is £3.45 per share. If the current share price is fair and if shareholders require a rate of return of 15 per cent, what future dividend growth rate is expected by shareholders?

4 The ordinary share price of Chock-stock plc is £2.00 per share and the company has been paying a dividend of 30p per share for 10 years. The company plans to retain the next three years' dividends to invest in a new project. The project cash flows will begin in year 4 and the company will pay an increased constant dividend of 40p per share from that year onwards. What is the change in the share price if the company puts the plan into effect?

(a) minus 24.7p

(b) minus 14.2p

(c) plus 5.8p

(d) plus 0.2p

(e) plus 17.6p

5 Which of the following is the best course of action for a company that wants to retain funds while still rewarding its shareholders?

   (a) Paying a special dividend.

   (b) Announcing a share repurchase scheme.

   (c) Paying an increased ordinary dividend.

   (d) Offering shareholders a scrip dividend.

   (e) Announcing a share split.

6 Given the assumptions made by Miller and Modigliani's dividend irrelevance theory, do you consider their conclusions to be logical?

7 Discuss whether the assumptions made by Miller and Modigliani's dividend irrelevance theory fail to mirror the real world. If you agree that they fail to mirror the real world, does that invalidate the usefulness of their theory?

8 How do you consider the increased ownership of shares by institutional shareholders has affected the dividend policies of UK public limited companies?

9 Explain the following terms:

   (a) the residual theory of dividends;

   (b) the clientele effect;

   (c) the signalling properties of dividends;

   (d) the 'bird in the hand' argument.

QUESTIONS FOR REVIEW

1 Deciding how much earnings to retain and how much to return to ordinary shareholders as a dividend is a key financial management decision. Discuss some of the factors that should be considered by the senior managers of a listed company in deciding on the size of the annual dividend to pay to its shareholders.

2 (a) Stant has just announced an ordinary dividend per share of 20p. The past four years' dividends per share have been 13p, 14p, 17p and 18p (most recent dividend last) and shareholders require a return of 14 per cent. What is a fair price for Stant's shares?

   (b) Stant now decides to increase its debt level, thereby increasing the financial risk associated with its equity shares. Stant's shareholders consequently increase their required rate of return to 15.4 per cent. What is the new price for Stant's shares?

   (c) Outline any problems with using the dividend growth model as a way of valuing shares.

3 It has become increasingly common for companies to offer shareholders a choice between a cash dividend and a scrip dividend. Briefly consider the advantages of scrip dividends from the points of view of both the company and the shareholders.

4 (a) Critically discuss the extent to which the following factors affect dividend policy:

- the industry in which a company operates;
- the level of inflation;
- a company's past dividend policy.

(b) Identify and discuss the situations in which a company should pay:

- special dividends;
- zero dividends;
- scrip dividends.

5 Ropeonfire is currently deciding on the level and form of its next dividend. It is considering three options:

i.   a cash dividend payment of 20p per share;
ii. a 6 per cent scrip dividend;
iii. a repurchase of 15 per cent of ordinary shares at the current market price.

Extracts from the company's financial statements are given below:

	£m	£m
Operating profit		23.0
Taxation		7.3
Distributable earnings		15.7
Non-current assets		70
Current assets		
Trade receivables	22	
Inventory	21	
Cash	41	84
Total assets		154
Equity finance		
Ordinary shares (50p)	20	
Reserves	103	123
Current liabilities		31
Total liabilities		154

(a) If the current cum dividend share price is 420p, calculate the effect of each of the three options on the wealth of a shareholder owning 1,000 shares in Ropeonfire.

(b) Explain briefly how the company's decision will be influenced by the opportunity to invest £60m in a project with a positive net present value.

QUESTIONS FOR DISCUSSION

1 The ordinary shares of ZZZ are currently trading at 80p. The last dividend per share was 15p and its dividends have been constant for ten years. The company plans to finance a new investment project out of retained earnings and so for the next two years the dividend per share will fall to 10p. Benefits from the investment project will be gained from year 3 onwards and so ZZZ will pay a constant dividend of 18p per share in that and subsequent years. If shareholders have all this information, what would be a fair price for ZZZ shares?

2 (a) It is said that financial management is concerned with investment decisions, dividend decisions and financing decisions. Critically discuss why financial management theory has claimed that only investment decisions have any importance, and that decisions about financing and dividends depend upon a firm's optimal investment schedule.

(b) In the context of dividend policy, discuss the meaning of the following terms:
(i) asymmetric information;
(ii) scrip dividends;
(iii) shareholder perks.

(c) Discuss whether a policy of paying no dividends means that a company has no value.

3 BMT is a company that has been listed on the London Stock Exchange for many years. Institutional investors own approximately 45 per cent of the ordinary shares of the company. The recent financial performance of the company is shown below. Using the information provided, comment on the dividend policy of BMT and critically discuss whether this dividend policy is likely to be acceptable to its institutional investors.

Year	6	5	4	3	2	1
Turnover (£ million)	3.3	3.1	2.7	2.6	2.5	2.0
Earnings per share (pence)	34.2	33.0	29.2	28.6	27.6	25.4
Dividend per share (pence)	11.4	11.1	9.9	9.6	9.2	8.5
Annual inflation (%)	3.1	3.4	3.1	2.4	3.4	2.5

4 It is the start of Year 7 and the managers of Dilbert plc are thinking about a change in the company's dividend policy. Dilbert's earnings per share for Year 6 were 22.8p, and the finance director has said that he expects this to increase to 25p per share for Year 7. The increase in earnings per share is in line with market expectations of the company's performance. The pattern of recent dividends, which are paid at the end of each year, is as follows:

Year	6	5	4	3	2	1
Dividend per share (pence)	11.4	11.1	9.6	9.6	9.2	8.5

The managing director has proposed that 70 per cent of earnings in Year 7 and subsequent years should be retained for investment in new product development. It is expected that, if this proposal is accepted, the future dividend growth rate will be 8.75 per cent per year. Dilbert's cost of equity capital is estimated to be 12 per cent.

Calculate the share price of Dilbert in the following circumstances:

(a) The company decides not to change its current dividend policy.

(b) The company decides to change its dividend policy as proposed by the managing director and announces the change to the market.

References

Aharony, J. and Swary, I. (1980) 'Quarterly dividend and earnings announcements and stock holders' returns: an empirical analysis', *Journal of Finance,* vol. 35, March, pp. 1–12.

Baker, K. and Weigand, R. (2015) 'Corporate dividend policy revisited', *Managerial Finance,* vol. 41, issue 2, pp. 126–443.

Black, F. and Scholes, M. (1974) 'The effects of dividend yield and dividend policy on common stock prices and returns', *Journal of Financial Economics,* vol. 1, pp. 1–22.

Bond, S., Chennells, L. and Devereux, M. (1996) 'Company dividends and taxes in the UK', *Fiscal Studies,* vol. 16, pp. 1–18.

Booth, L. and Zhou, J. (2015) 'Market power and dividend policy', *Managerial Finance,* vol. 41, issue 2, pp. 145–63.

Bozos, K., Nikolopoulos, K. and Ramgandhi, G. (2011) 'Dividend signalling under economic adversity: evidence from the London Stock Exchange', *International Review of Financial Analysis,* vol. 20, pp. 1–18.

Brennan, M. (1970) 'Taxes, market valuation and corporate financial policy', *National Tax Journal,* vol. 23, pp. 417–27.

Crossland, M., Dempsey, M. and Mozier, P. (1991) 'The effect of cum and ex dividend changes on UK share prices', *Accounting and Business Research,* vol. 22, no. 85, pp. 47–50.

Elton, E. and Gruber, M. (1970) 'Marginal stockholder tax rates and the clientele effect', *Review of Economics and Statistics,* vol. 52, pp. 68–74.

Fama, E. and Babiak, H. (1968) 'Dividend policy: an empirical analysis', *Journal of the American Statistical Association,* vol. 63, pp. 1132–61.

Feenberg, D. (1981) 'Does the investment interest limitation explain the existence of dividends?', *Journal of Financial Economics,* vol. 9, no. 3, pp. 265–9.

Gordon, M. (1959) 'Dividends, earnings and stock prices', *Review of Economics and Statistics,* vol. 41, pp. 99–105.

Ham, C., Kaplan, Z. and Leary, M. (2018) 'Do dividends convey information about future earnings?', *Working paper,* April. Available at SSRN: *https://ssrn.com/abstract=3176055*

Kwan, C. (1981) 'Efficient market tests of the information content of dividend announcements: critique and extension', *Journal of Financial and Quantitative Analysis,* vol. 16, June, pp. 193–206.

Lintner, J. (1956) 'Distribution of incomes of corporations among dividends, retained earnings and taxes', *American Economic Review,* vol. 46, pp. 97–113.

Litzenberger, R. and Ramaswamy, K. (1979) 'The effect of personal taxes and dividends on common stock prices and returns', *Journal of Financial Economics,* vol. 7, June, pp. 163–95.

Miller, M. (1986) 'Behavioural rationality in finance: the case of dividends', *Journal of Business,* vol. 59, pp. 451–68.

Miller, M. and Modigliani, F. (1961) 'Dividend policy, growth and the valuation of shares', *Journal of Business,* vol. 34, pp. 411–33.

Miller, M. and Scholes, M. (1978) 'Dividends and taxes', *Journal of Financial Economics,* vol. 6, pp. 333–64.

Miller, M. and Scholes, M. (1982) 'Dividends and taxes: some empirical evidence', *Journal of Political Economy,* vol. 90, pp. 1118–41.

Pettit, R. (1972) 'Dividend announcements, security performance and capital market efficiency', *Journal of Finance,* vol. 27, pp. 993–1007.

Pettit, R. (1977) 'Taxes, transaction cost and clientele effects of dividends', *Journal of Financial Economics*, vol. 5, December, pp. 419–36.

Porterfield, J. (1965) *Investment Decisions and Capital Costs*, Englewood Cliffs, NJ: Prentice Hall.

Rozeff, M. (1986) 'How companies set their dividend payout ratios', reprinted in Stern, J. and Chew, D. (eds) (2003) *The Revolution in Corporate Finance*, 4th edn, Oxford: Basil Blackwell.

Watts, R. (1973) 'The information content of dividends', *Journal of Business*, vol. 46, pp. 191–211.

Recommended reading

This title has a comprehensive and very well-written chapter on dividend policy from a US perspective:

Damodaran, A. (2015) *Applied Corporate Finance*, 4th edn, New York: Wiley.

An extensive guide to all you need to know about dividend policy with an American spin:

Baker, H. (2009) *Dividends and Dividend Policy*, Hoboken, NJ: Wiley.

The following collect together interesting articles on dividend policy.

Managerial Finance (2015) *Special Issue: Dividends and Dividend Policy*, vol. 41, issue 2.

Stern, J. and Chew, D. (eds) (2003) *The Revolution in Corporate Finance*, 4th edn, Malden, MA: Blackwell.

Important and informative papers and articles recommended for further reading on dividend policy include:

Dittmar, A. (2008) 'Corporate cash policy and how to manage it with stock repurchases', *Applied Corporate Finance*, vol. 20, no. 3, pp. 22–34.

Pettit, A. (2001) 'Is share buyback right for your company?', *Harvard Business Review*, April, vol. 79, no. 40, pp. 141–7.

11 MERGERS AND TAKEOVERS

Learning objectives

After studying this chapter, you should have achieved the following learning objectives:

- a familiarity with the different types of merger and takeover;

- an understanding of the justifications and motives behind merger and takeover activity;

- the ability to value target companies using a range of valuation techniques and to decide on an appropriate valuation;

- an awareness of the ways in which mergers and takeovers can be financed;

- an understanding of the strategies and tactics employed in the takeover process by bidding and target companies;

- an understanding of why a company may choose to divest part of its operations and an awareness of the different routes to divestment available;

- an appreciation of the effects of merger and takeover activity on stakeholder groups.

■ ■ ■ INTRODUCTION

Mergers and takeovers play a vital role in corporate finance. For many companies, mergers and takeovers are a source of external growth when organic growth is not possible, whereas to other companies they represent a constant threat to their continuing independent existence.

Acquiring another company is a far more complex process than simply buying a machine or building a factory. First, valuing a target company and estimating the potential benefits of acquiring it are more difficult propositions than valuing a simple investment project. Second, the takeover process is often complicated by bids being resisted by the target company and hence acquisition may become a long and unpleasant contest. This contest often results in the bidder paying a price considerably higher than it had anticipated. Third, due to the size of many takeover deals, there are often serious financial implications for the acquiring company after it has paid for its acquisition. We must also recognise the amount of valuable senior management time absorbed by the takeover process.

The subject of mergers and takeovers is large and many books have been written on it. In this chapter, therefore, we cannot give the subject a detailed treatment, but you will obtain more than simply a general understanding of this fascinating area of corporate finance.

11.1 THE TERMINOLOGY OF MERGERS AND TAKEOVERS

Although the terms 'merger' and 'takeover' tend to be used synonymously, in practice there is a narrow distinction between them. A merger is a friendly reorganisation of assets into a new organisation, i.e. A and B merge to become C, a new company, with the agreement of both sets of shareholders. Mergers involve similar-sized companies, reducing the likelihood of one company dominating the other. A takeover is the acquisition of one company's ordinary share capital by another company, financed by a cash payment, an issue of securities (such as shares) or a combination of both. Here, the bidding company is usually larger than the target company. In practice, most acquisitions are takeovers rather than mergers since one of the two parties is dominant. Perhaps the closest thing to a true merger in recent years was the joining of Lattice and National Grid in October 2002 to form National Grid Transco.

Takeovers can be classified into three broad types:

- *Horizontal takeover*: the combination of two companies operating in the same industry and at a similar stage of production.
- *Vertical takeover*: the combination of two companies operating at different stages of production within the same industry. A vertical takeover can involve a move forward in the production process to secure a distribution outlet, or a move backward in the production process to secure the supply of raw materials.
- *Conglomerate takeover*: the combination of two companies operating in different areas of business.

Table 11.1 Major UK takeovers including total value of bid and classification

Date	Bidder	Target	Deal value (£m)	Classification of takeover
1988	BP	Britoil	2,323	Vertical backwards
1988	Nestlé	Rowntree	2,666	Horizontal
1995	Glaxo	Wellcome	9,150	Horizontal
1995	Hanson	Eastern Electric	2,400	Conglomerate
2000	Royal Bank of Scotland	National Westminster Bank	20,700	Horizontal
2000	Vodafone AirTouch	Mannesmann AG	101,246	Horizontal cross-border
2000	GlaxoWellcome	SmithKline Beecham	38,600	Horizontal
2002	National Grid	Lattice Group	8,400	Horizontal (merger)
2004	Morrisons	Safeway	2,900	Horizontal
2005	Telefónica SA	O$_2$	17,700	Horizontal cross-border
2007	Rio Tinto	Alcan Inc	18,542	Horizontal cross-border
2009	Kraft Foods Inc	Cadbury	11,500	Horizontal cross-border
2011	Hewlett-Packard Company (US)	Autonomy Corporation	7,091	Horizontal cross-border
2015	Aviva	Friends Life	5,600	Horizontal
2017	BAT	Reynolds	42,000	Horizontal cross-border
2018	Tesco	Booker Group	3,700	Horizontal
2018	Melrose	GKN	8,100	Horizontal

Examples of these different types of business combinations are shown in Table 11.1. Takeovers with an international dimension are called cross-border acquisitions.

11.2 JUSTIFICATIONS FOR ACQUISITIONS

Although companies may offer many justifications for takeovers, theoretically an acquisition is justified only if it increases the wealth of the acquiring company's shareholders. Similarly, a merger can be justified financially only if it increases the wealth of the shareholders of both companies. Justifications or motives for acquisitions are generally considered to be economic, financial or managerial in origin. These motives are now discussed.

11.2.1 Economic justifications

The economic justification for takeovers is that shareholder wealth will be increased by the transaction as the two companies are worth more combined than as separate companies. This can be shown algebraically as:

$$PV_{X+Y} > (PV_X + PV_Y)$$

Here, PV represents present value and X and Y are the two companies involved. Economic gains may be generated for the following reasons.

Operational synergy

Operational **synergy** occurs when the assets and/or operations of two companies complement each other, so that their combined output once merged is more than the sum of their separate outputs. For example, a company may have to buy in an expensive service which it cannot provide for itself. By acquiring a company which can supply this service it may be able to reduce its costs. The problem with this justification is that synergy is difficult to *quantify* before companies combine, and difficult to *achieve* once combination has occurred, since this achievement depends on a high degree of post-merger corporate integration.

Economies of scale

Economies of scale are like synergy benefits and occur because the scale of operations is larger after a takeover. Economies of scale are most likely to arise in horizontal acquisitions but may also arise in vertical acquisitions, in areas such as production, distribution, marketing, management and finance. An example of a production economy is where two companies, producing the same good from similar machines, produce their combined output from a single, larger, cheaper machine after merging. An example of a distribution economy is where two companies, distributing their products in small vans, distribute their combined output using a large lorry after merging. Another example of an economy of scale is where a company gains the ability to enjoy bulk-buying discounts following an acquisition because of the larger scale of its operations.

Managerial synergy

A company may be poorly run by its current managers, perhaps because they are pursuing their own objectives rather than those of the shareholders. The company's declining share price will attract potential bidders who believe they can manage the company more efficiently. Following a successful takeover bid, efficient personnel who can deliver a better level of performance will replace inefficient managers, or managerial expertise may be transferred from the acquiring company to the target company. Eliminating inefficient managers through a takeover has been called managerial synergy and may be more attractive to shareholders than voting them out of office (which is difficult to achieve in practice) or suffering a loss of wealth in a liquidation.

Entry to new markets

Companies may want to meet their strategic objectives by expanding into new geographical and business areas. Organic or internal growth may be deemed to be too slow or too costly and so acquisition may be chosen as a more efficient route to expansion. This is particularly true of the retail trade, where starting operations from scratch is both costly and time consuming. The costs involved will result from purchasing and fitting out premises, hiring and training personnel, and building up market share. Iceland plc's acquisition of Bejam in 1987 is an example of a company using acquisition to break into a new market; as a result, Iceland established a retail presence in the north of England. Building market share by competing with Bejam and other retailers in the area from a zero base would have been prohibitively expensive.

To provide critical mass

Smaller companies may experience a lack of credibility because of their size. In addition, owing to the increasing importance of research and development and brand investment, merging companies can pool resources to establish the critical mass required to provide sufficient cash flows to finance these requirements.

To provide growth

Once a company reaches the mature stage of its growth cycle it will find organic growth difficult. Acquisitions provide a quick solution for a company following a growth strategy that finds itself in this position.

Market power and market share

Horizontal acquisitions increase market share and hence increase a company's ability to earn *monopoly profits*, whereas vertical acquisitions increase a company's power in raw material or distribution markets. One problem for UK companies here is the risk of investigation by the Competition and Markets Authority, a risk which is highest in horizontal acquisitions. A referral can be expensive for a company and can potentially damage its reputation (see below).

There is no doubt about the general validity of these economic justifications for acquisition in terms of their ability to increase shareholder wealth. The potential for economic gains in specific cases is not guaranteed and if such potential exists, it is not certain that economic gains can be realised during the post-takeover integration process. (This issue is considered further in 'Empirical research on acquisitions', Section 11.9.)

11.2.2 Financial justifications

Acquisitions can be justified on the grounds of the financial benefits they bring to the shareholders of the companies involved. These are now considered in turn.

Financial synergy

Financial synergy is said to occur if a company's cost of capital decreases as a direct result of an acquisition. One way in which financial synergy can occur is through a conglomerate takeover, where the lack of correlation between the cash flows of the different companies will reduce cash-flow volatility. A reduction in cash-flow volatility represents a decrease in business risk and as a result the cost of capital of the company may decrease. Managers may therefore justify a conglomerate takeover by claiming it reduces the risk faced by shareholders.

This risk reduction cannot be justified from a shareholder wealth perspective since shareholders are assumed in theory to have eliminated unsystematic risk by holding a diversified portfolio of shares (see 'The concept of diversification', Section 8.2). Diversifying operations at the company level will therefore have little impact on the level of unsystematic risk faced by shareholders.

Financial synergy can also occur because of increased size following an acquisition, as a larger company can expect to have a lower interest rate on new debt. A larger company can also gain economies of scale in new finance issue costs (e.g. brokers' fees).

Target undervaluation

This justification for an acquisition suggests that some target companies may be bargain buys, in the sense that their shares are undervalued by the market. The implication here is that capital markets are not efficient, since the idea of companies being undervalued for more than a short period is not consistent with pricing efficiency. Whether a takeover can be justified on these grounds therefore depends on the view taken of capital market efficiency. While the evidence strongly supports market efficiency (see 'Capital market efficiency', Section 2.3), in practice companies are difficult to value with certainty, leaving scope for undervalued companies to exist.

Tax considerations

It may be beneficial for a tax-exhausted company to take over one that is not tax-exhausted, so it can bring forward the realisation of tax-allowable benefits. This may apply to companies with insufficient profits against which to set off capital allowances and interest. A tax inversion takeover is where one company buys a target company in a different country due to that country's less onerous tax policy. By shifting its headquarters to that country, the acquirer thus reduces its tax burden. US drugs company Pfizer tried to acquire the Irish-based Allergan for £100bn in 2016 for this very purpose but the deal was abandoned when US tax rules changed.

Increasing earnings per share

If a bidding company has a higher price/earnings ratio than its target company, it can increase its overall earnings proportionally more than it needs to increase its share capital if the takeover is financed by a share-for-share issue. Its post-acquisition earnings per share (EPS) will therefore be higher than its pre-acquisition EPS: its EPS has been boosted through acquisition. This boosting can be beneficial to the company as market analysts see EPS as a key ratio by and an increase in EPS can, potentially, lead to a share price rise.

The process whereby companies seek to increase their EPS through acquisitions is termed **boot-strapping**. This process cannot be used to justify an acquisition in shareholder wealth terms, however, since changes in EPS do not indicate whether an acquisition is wealth creating. There are many drawbacks associated with using EPS alone as a guide to company performance: it ignores both cash flow and risk, and that it is based on accounting profit, which is subject to both arbitrary accounting policies and possible manipulation by management. In fact, boot-strapping may be considered as merely an exercise in creative accounting.

Example	Boot-strapping

Big plc is to take over Little plc and plans to offer its shares in payment for Little's shares.

	Big plc	Little plc
Number of shares	200m	25m
Earnings	£20m	£5m
Earnings per share	10p	20p
Price/earnings ratio	25	5
Share price	£2.50	£1
Market value	£500m	£25m

If we assume that Big has to pay £25m (market value) to take over Little, Big must issue 10 million new shares. Details of the enlarged company are as follows:

$$\text{Number of shares} = (200 + 10) = 210\text{m}$$
$$\text{Earnings} = (20 + 5) = £25\text{m}$$
$$\text{EPS} = (25/210) = 11.9\text{p}$$

We can see that Big has manufactured an increase in its EPS. Big plc hopes that the market will apply its original price/earnings ratio of 25 to its higher post-takeover EPS. If this is the case, then Big's shares and hence its market value will increase:

EPS	11.9p
P/E ratio	25
Share price = 25 × 0.119 =	£2.97
Market value = 2.97 × 210m =	£623.7m

Whether in practice the market applies a P/E ratio of 25 will depend on its expectations of the performance of Little once it has been taken over by Big. If there is an expectation that Big will pull Little's performance up to its own level, the market may well apply a P/E ratio of 25 to Big's EPS. A more likely scenario, though, is for the market to apply some other P/E ratio to the earnings of the enlarged company. We must recognise, however, that in practice it is the market price of the share that determines the P/E ratio and not the other way round.

11.2.3 Managerial motives

Takeovers can also arise because of the agency problem that exists between shareholders and managers, whereby managers are more concerned with satisfying their own objectives than with increasing the wealth of shareholders. From this perspective, the motives behind some acquisitions may be to increase managers' pay and power. Managers may also believe that the larger their company, the less likely it is to be taken over by another company and hence the more secure will be their jobs. Takeovers on these grounds have no shareholder wealth justification as managers are likely to increase their own wealth at the expense of the shareholders.

11.2.4 The case against acquisition

We must consider arguments against growth by acquisition to offer a balanced view.

Possible investigation by the Competition and Markets Authority

An investigation by the Competition and Markets Authority (CMA) can be very damaging to both the image of a bidding company and to its pocket. A CMA investigation may delay the proposed takeover for a considerable time. Depending on the result of the investigation, the takeover may not even be allowed to proceed.

Paying too much for the target

With takeover premiums often ranging between 30 per cent and 50 per cent, acquisition is an expensive way of expanding. Bidding companies often overpay to acquire their targets and if a bid is contested the possibility of overpaying increases. Vodafone plc's £101bn take-over of the German telecom company Mannesmann in 2000 led to a £45.2bn goodwill write-off, arising from a 45 per cent premium on Mannesmann's fair value. More recently, in August 2017, US on-line retail giant Amazon.com made a $13.7 billion all-cash offer for Whole Foods Market Inc which represented a 27 per cent premium on the pre-announcement share price.

Are mergers and takeovers beneficial?

Research on post-merger performance (see 'Empirical research on acquisitions', Section 11.9) suggests that the expected benefits from synergy and scale economies rarely materialise and that, in general, the only beneficiaries from takeovers are target company shareholders and the bidding company's management.

The cost of financing a takeover

If a takeover bid is financed by a share-for-share offer, the bidding company will have to find money to pay dividends on the newly issued shares. There will also be changes in the bidding company's ownership structure. Conversely, if a takeover bid is financed by debt, the bidding company's gearing may increase to a level where it has difficulty meeting future interest payments. Arrangement and issue fees incurred by issuing securities to finance the takeover must also be considered.

Other difficulties

There are other difficulties that acquiring companies may face. Cultural problems are likely to exist, especially when the two companies are in different industries, or in different countries if the takeover is a cross-border one. Cross-border takeovers are also subject to exchange rate risk, from both a transaction and a translation perspective (see 'What is meant by exchange rate risk?', Section 12.1.3). Takeovers can involve complicated taxation and legal issues and may incur large advisory fees. In some cases, the quality of the assets purchased may turn out to be lower than initially expected. A classic example of this occurred after the purchase of the US Crocker Bank by Midland Bank plc in the early 1980s, when a large amount of the advances previously made by the Crocker Bank turned out to be bad debts rather than assets.

11.3 TRENDS IN TAKEOVER ACTIVITY

It is apparent from Table 11.2, showing the number of takeovers and the total outlay involved, that merger and takeover activity tends to occur in *waves*. Such waves, which have all been different in nature, occurred in 1972–3, the late 1970s, the end of the 1980s and the mid-1990s. This final wave was by far the largest in terms of total outlay.

The late 1980s saw high levels of takeover activity by conglomerate companies, that bought what they considered to be underpriced targets in a diverse range of industries, in many cases subjecting them to restructuring and break-up. In contrast, the most recent wave, beginning in the mid-1990s and peaking in 2000, involved horizontal acquisitions concentrated in specific industries such as electrical distribution, pharmaceuticals and financial services. Here, acquiring companies sought scale economies and synergy in areas such as research and development and marketing by acquiring businesses with similar

Table 11.2 The scale and method of financing takeover activity in the UK between 1970 and 2017

Year	Number acquired	Outlay (£m)	Cash (%)	Shares (%)	Debt and preference shares (%)
1970	793	1,122	22	53	25
1971	884	911	31	48	21
1972	1,210	2,532	19	58	23
1973	1,205	1,304	53	36	11
1974	504	508	69	22	9
1975	315	291	59	32	9
1976	353	448	71	27	2
1977	481	824	62	37	1
1978	567	1,140	57	41	2
1979	534	1,656	56	31	13
1980	469	1,475	52	45	3
1981	452	1,144	67	30	3
1982	463	2,206	58	32	10
1983	568	5,474	53	34	13
1984	447	2,343	44	54	2
1985	474	7,090	40	53	7
1986	842	15,370	26	57	17
1987	1,528	16,539	35	60	5
1988	1,499	22,839	70	22	8
1989	1,337	27,250	82	13	5
1990	779	8,329	77	18	5
1991	506	10,434	70	29	1
1992	432	5,941	63	36	1
1993	526	7,063	80	17	3
1994	674	8,269	64	34	2
1995	505	32,600	78	20	2
1996	584	30,457	63	36	1
1997	506	26,829	41	58	1
1998	635	29,525	53	45	2
1999	493	26,166	62	37	1
2000	587	106,916	37	62	1
2001	492	28,994	79	13	8
2002	430	25,236	69	27	4
2003	558	18,679	86	9	5
2004	741	31,408	63	33	4
2005	769	25,134	88	11	1
2006	779	28,511	91	8	1
2007	869	26,778	76	18	6
2008	558	36,469	94	5	1
2009	286	12,195	30	69	1
2010	325	12,605	85	12	3

Year	Number acquired	Outlay (£m)	Cash (%)	Shares (%)	Debt and preference shares (%)
2011	373	8,089	86	10	4
2012	266	3,413	82	10	8
2013	238	7,665	92	6	2
2014	189	8,032	65	35	0
2015	245	6,920	74	22	4
2016	428	24,688	43	55	2
2017	364	18,783	59	39	2

Source: Business Monitor and Financial Statistics, National Statistics. © Crown Copyright 2018. Reproduced by permission of the Office for National Statistics.

operations. Since 2000 the total value of deals declined sharply while the number of takeovers remained reasonably buoyant. The economic downturn of 2008, however, had a significant impact on the level of M&A activity undertaken by UK companies, both at home and abroad. Despite the global depression, M&A activity showed signs of recovery in early 2009, although this proved to be short-lived. Table 11.2 shows that the value of UK domestic deals plummeted after 2008 and remained at low levels up until 2014. However, the first half of 2018 saw M&A activity in the USA rise drastically, as indicated in Vignette 11.1.

Vignette 11.1

Global dealmaking reaches $2.5tn as US megadeals lift volumes

Worldwide deal volumes rise 65% from the same time a year ago

By James Fontanella-Khan and Arash Massoudi

Global dealmaking has reached $2.5tn in the first half of 2018, breaking the all-time high for the period and underscoring the intense nature of mergers and acquisition activity in spite of increasingly bitter geopolitical tensions. A wave of megadeals led by the US media and telecoms sector helped to lift worldwide deal volumes 65 per cent from the same time a year ago and the most, on a nominal basis, since Thomson Reuters began keeping data on M&A in 1980.

The record-breaking pace of dealmaking stands in contrast to a looming trade war sparked by US President Donald Trump against China and renewed fears of political instability in the Eurozone, particularly in Italy and Spain, that have shaken markets. Enriched by corporate tax cuts from the Trump administration and stronger economic growth, US corporate boardrooms have sought to strike deals that allow them to either consolidate their industries or compete against a tide of powerful digital disrupters.

'Technological disruption continues to be a big driver behind large M&A,' said Blair Effron, co-founder of advisory firm Centerview Partners. 'Big shifts in technology are forcing companies across all industries to be creative and forge more strategic combinations. Adding in economic tailwinds and a continuing strong financing environment makes the current robust M&A market unsurprising.'US cable group Comcast and media rival Disney are locked up in a $70bn bidding war to buy the majority of Rupert Murdoch's 21st Century Fox as well as a £22bn battle to acquire pan-European broadcaster Sky. The two companies believe both assets are crucial if traditional media groups are going to remain competitive against the likes of Amazon, Google and Netflix.

Vignette 11.1 (continued)

Other blockbuster deals in the first half include the acquisition of Irish drugmaker Shire by Japan's Takeda for $77bn and T-Mobile's $59bn merger with rival US telecom operator Sprint. 'The M&A market has continued to be extremely robust in the first half of 2018 and current indications point to that continuing into the second half of the year,' said Scott Barshay, partner at law firm Paul Weiss. 'That said, the spectre of trade wars and interest rate hikes and increasing concerns over equity valuations are major risks.'

Globally companies signed 79 deals above $5bn, surpassing the previous year-to-date record set in 2007, and a record 35 deals above $10bn, as large companies across all sectors being disrupted by technology felt the need to merge with old rivals to have enough scale to compete. 'Rising interest rates are not the major concern for corporates,' said Stephen Arcano, global co-head of the transactions practices at law firm Skadden. 'Most companies are primarily focused on how to increase earnings in an economic environment where organic growth may be improving, but not fast enough. Deals are often still the best solution to that problem.'

Deal activity was spread across all regions: in the US it returned to the highs experienced before the 2008 crisis, in Europe deal activity nearly doubled and in Asia dealmaking was up 29 per cent compared with a year earlier. Colm Donlon, head of mergers and acquisitions for Morgan Stanley in Europe, the Middle East and Africa, said a series of factors have converged to feed the record pace of activity, including a focus on consolidation in corporate Europe and a targeted return to dealmaking into the region by Chinese and Japanese companies. 'You've got almost a perfect storm for the M&A market. We've never been busier,' he said.

Big ticket acquisitions have increasingly become the norm. Deals above the $5bn mark account for more than half of the $2.4tn of transactions already struck this year, a record high level, including 35 deals worth at least 11 figures, writes Eric Platt in New York.

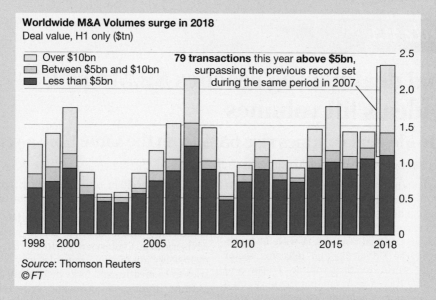

Worldwide M&A Volumes surge in 2018
Deal value, H1 only ($tn)

- Over $10bn
- Between $5bn and $10bn
- Less than $5bn

79 transactions this year **above $5bn**, surpassing the previous record set during the same period in 2007

Source: Thomson Reuters
©FT

Source: Fontanella-Khan, J. and Massoudi, A. (2018) 'Global dealmaking reaches $2.5tn as US megadeals lift volumes', *Financial Times*, 28 June.
© The Financial Times Limited 2018. All Rights Reserved.

Question

What are the main drivers behind, and characteristics of, the increased level of M&A activity in the USA in the first half of 2018?

Why do mergers and takeovers tend to occur in waves? No overriding consensus view has been reached, although reasons have been advanced. The combination of a booming stock exchange (enabling companies to use shares to finance acquisitions) and increasing corporate liquidity and profitability levels is often cited as a factor encouraging takeover activity. Against this, however, we should consider that one of the biggest booms in takeover activity followed the 1987 stock market crash. There are clearly factors that have had a positive effect on takeover financing. Deregulation in the capital markets, for example, making external sources of finance such as debt more available, in combination with low levels of corporate gearing in the early 1980s, certainly increased the capacity of companies to acquire debt financing for takeovers and to accommodate borrowings on their financial position statements. Possible causes of the recent surge of M&A activity in the USA are quantitative easing by the government, pushing down interest rates, and a wave of deals in the pharmaceutical sector. Globally, recent M&A activity has been driven by China's ever-increasing cross-border transactions, the increasing importance of private equity and an increasing volume of 'tech' deals.

11.4 TARGET COMPANY VALUATION

Valuing a potential target company is a key stage in the takeover process. The feasibility of the bidder's strategy will not become clear until the target's value has been established and compared with the expected cost of the acquisition. Unfortunately, valuing the target company is a complicated process, partly because of the wide range of valuation methods available. In this sense, business valuation is considered by some to be more of an art than a science.

There are two broad approaches to valuing a company. *Asset-based valuations* focus on the value of the company's assets. *Income-based valuations* consider the future earnings or cash flows expected to be obtained by gaining control of the target company. Owing to the existence of many different techniques within these two broad approaches, it is possible to come up with multiple valuations of a company. Indeed, two bidding companies can produce different valuations of the same target company because each has different plans for it. Each valuation method has its associated advantages and disadvantages and its usefulness will depend on the intentions of the acquirer towards its target. For example, does the acquirer want to break up its acquisition or does it want to integrate it into its own operations?

The different company valuation methods are now considered in turn and illustrated with the help of a numerical example.

11.4.1 Stock market valuation

Stock market value or market capitalisation is the number of issued ordinary shares of the target company multiplied by their market price. Whether stock market value is a fair value will depend on the efficiency of the stock market. It gives the bidding company a guide to the likely minimum *purchase price* of the target company. It does not give an estimate of how much the target company is *worth* to the bidder since it does not reflect the bidder's post-acquisition intentions. It is therefore a useful starting point for estimating the purchase price of the target company as it represents the minimum that target shareholders will

Example	Takeover (Commons and Hulse)

Commons plc has distributable earnings of £120m, a weighted average cost of capital of 7 per cent and a price/earnings ratio of 18.2 times. It is in the process of taking over Hulse plc, whose financial details are as follows:

Hulse plc: key financial data

Profit before interest and tax (PBIT)	£77.00m
Interest paid	£12.30m
Corporate tax	£19.41m
Distributable earnings	£45.29m
Current dividend per share	12p
Last 4 years' dividends (most recent last)	10.5p, 11p, 11.2p, 11.5p
Earnings per share (EPS)	18.4p
Price/earnings ratio	13.59 times
Market price of ordinary shares	£2.50
Equity beta	1.17
Replacement cost of non-current assets	£305m
Net realisable value of non-current assets	£270m

Hulse plc financial position statement information

	£m	£m
Non-current assets		290
Current assets		70
Total assets		360
Equity finance		
Ordinary shares (nominal value 50p)	123	
Reserves	19	142
Non-current liabilities		
6% bonds (redemption after 10 years)		175
Current liabilities		43
Total liabilities		360

Commons plc expects to maintain an annual increase in distributable earnings of 2 per cent due to anticipated synergy as a result of the takeover. The company will also be able to sell surplus non-current assets for £60m in two years' time. The current estimate of cash flows of Hulse plc is £38m, but these are expected to grow at an annual rate of 4 per cent in future years. The risk-free rate of return is 4.5 per cent and the equity risk premium is 5 per cent. Companies in the same sector as Hulse plc have an average price/earnings ratio of 15.5 times and a weighted average cost of capital of 9 per cent.

accept, but a substantial *premium* will need to be added as an incentive to persuade the shareholders to sell their shares.

It must be noted that a company's quoted share price does not reflect the value of all its shares. Since only a small proportion of them are traded at any one time, the quoted share price reflects only **marginal trading**. This reduces the reliance that can be placed on the stock market value and suggests the need to investigate the movement of the target company's share price over time. A further limitation of stock market value is that it has limited applicability if the ordinary shares of the target company are not frequently traded or if the shares of the target company are not listed on a stock exchange.

For Hulse plc:

$$\text{Number of ordinary shares} = \text{Book value/nominal value} = 123\text{m}/0.5 = 246\text{m}$$

Therefore:

$$\text{Stock market valuation} = 246\text{m} \times £2.50 = £615\text{m}$$

11.4.2 Asset-based valuation methods

There are three ways by which a company's assets are commonly valued.

Net asset value (book value basis)

The most straightforward net asset value is the book value of the net assets in the company's financial position statement. This can be defined as:

> Net asset value (book value) = Total assets − Current liabilities − Long-term debt

In our example, using Hulse's financial position statement values:

$$\text{NAV (book value)} = 360\text{m} - 43\text{m} - 175\text{m} = £142\text{m}$$

While this valuation method has the advantage that it uses historical values that are both factual and easily available, it has several disadvantages. For example, historical values do not reflect current asset valuations, while trade receivables and inventory figures may be unreliable. Furthermore, intangible assets such as goodwill, human capital and brands are ignored. Even at its most reliable, therefore, net asset value offers only a lower limit of target company value.

Net asset value (net realisable value basis)

Assets can be valued using their *net realisable value* (NRV) rather than their book value. NRV is the cash that could be gained by selling the target company's assets on the open market, then deducting liquidation costs and paying off all liabilities: it is often called *liquidation value*. In theory, the market value of a company should be higher than its NRV; if it is not, the company is by implication undervalued, perhaps due to stock market inefficiency, and a bidding company can make a risk-free gain by buying the company and liquidating it.

However, calculating the NRV of a target company is not easy. The book values of its assets are unlikely to be indicative of their market values as they are largely based on historical cost. The value of property in the financial position statement may underestimate its true value. The book value of inventory is likely to overestimate its realisable value if items need to be sold quickly or have become obsolete, even though accounting standards require that inventory is valued at the lower of cost and net realisable value. The assets of some companies are unique and resale values for such assets may be unavailable; the realisable values of such assets can only ever be estimates.

The NRV is not the most appropriate valuation method in most takeovers since very few acquisitions involve the total break-up of the target company. This method may be useful if the bidder plans to sell off part of the target and integrate the remainder into existing business operations. In our example, using the disposal value of Hulse's non-current assets:

$$NAV \text{ (net realisable value)} = 270m + 70m - 43m - 175m = £122m$$

Net asset value (replacement cost basis)

This valuation method seeks to find the cost of acquiring the separate assets of a target company on the open market. Replacement cost has an advantage over book value in that replacement cost estimates of asset values are more relevant than historical cost estimates. Unfortunately, replacement costs, like realisable values, do not take account of goodwill. The bidding company also has the difficulty of identifying the target company's separate assets and determining their replacement costs. Using the replacement costs of Hulse's non-current assets we have:

$$NAV \text{ (replacement cost value)} = 305m + 70m - 43m - 175m = £157m$$

Most bidding companies could find the book values of a target company's assets in its published accounts but will have difficulty in determining replacement costs and realisable values because they lack access to the necessary inside information.

11.4.3 Income-based valuation methods

Valuing a target company on an income basis is appropriate if the bidding company intends to continue the target company's business operations for the foreseeable future, as opposed to liquidating it or selling some of its assets (asset stripping) after acquisition.

Earnings yield valuation

This valuation is calculated by discounting a company's annual maintainable future earnings by a suitable required earnings yield or return on investment (ROI). *Annual maintainable expected earnings* can be estimated by, for example, taking an average of historical earnings, weighted or otherwise, and allowing for any expected future increase in earnings due to synergy or economies of scale. The *discount rate* applied to this earnings stream should reflect factors such as the size of the company and the industry in which it is operating. The valuation using this method is as follows:

$$\text{Earnings yield value} = \frac{\text{Annual maintainable expected earnings}}{\text{Required earnings yield}}$$

In our example, the required earnings yield is as follows:

$$\text{Required earnings yield} = \text{EPS/share price} = (18.4/250) \times 100 = 7.36\%$$

This is also the reciprocal of the P/E ratio:

$$(1/13.59) \times 100 = 7.36\%$$

We have only the current distributable earnings, but if we assume that they are equivalent to the annual maintainable expected earnings, we have:

$$\text{Earnings yield value} = £45.29\text{m}/0.0736 = £615\text{m}$$

Because of the way we calculated the required earnings yield, this is the same as the stock market value obtained earlier. However, if we factor in the expected future growth rate of earnings of 2 per cent into an adaptation of the dividend growth model we obtain a much higher value:

$$\text{Earnings yield value (with growth)} = £45.29\text{m} \; (1 - 0.02)/(0.0736 - 0.02) = £862\text{m}$$

An advantage of this valuation method is that it is forward-looking (it uses *expected* or future earnings) and it therefore encourages forecasting of future performance. A disadvantage is the uncertainty about the accuracy of the earnings figure, which may be subject to differing accounting policies and to different treatments of exceptional and extraordinary items compared to the bidding company.

Price/earnings ratio valuation

This valuation method involves multiplying the target company's future distributable earnings by an appropriate price/earnings ratio (P/E ratio) where:

$$\text{P/E ratio value} = \frac{\text{Market value of company}}{\text{Distributable earnings}}$$

A major factor in this valuation method is the P/E ratio used. Possible P/E ratios include the bidding company's P/E ratio, the target company's P/E ratio, a weighted average of these, or alternatively, an appropriate sector average P/E ratio. If the target company's P/E ratio is used, we obtain the following result for Hulse:

$$\text{P/E ratio value} = 13.59 \times £45.29\text{m} = £615\text{m}$$

This figure is like the earnings yield valuation since, as noted earlier, the P/E ratio is the reciprocal of the earnings yield. Alternatively, if the bidding company is sure that it can raise the target company's performance up to its own performance level, it is more appropriate to use its own P/E ratio. In our example, if Commons is convinced that it can improve Hulse's performance, then:

$$\text{P/E ratio value} = 18.2 \times £45.29m = £824m$$

If the future performances of neither bidding nor target company are expected to change, logic suggests that we apply a weighted average of the two companies' P/E ratios. If we weight the P/E ratios of Hulse and Commons by their current earnings, we obtain:

$$(13.59 \times (45.29/165.29)) + (18.2 \times (120/165.29)) = 16.93$$

$$\text{P/E ratio value} = 16.93 \times £45.29m = £767m$$

A third alternative is use a sector average P/E ratio on the assumption that the target company has similar characteristics to the average company in its sector. Here we have:

$$15.5 \times £45.29m = £702m$$

While this valuation method is straightforward in calculation terms, the values produced fluctuate widely according to the P/E ratio applied. In addition to the problems associated with using distributable earnings, therefore, there is the difficulty of estimating an appropriate post-acquisition P/E ratio to apply.

Dividend growth model

The value of a target company can be estimated by using the dividend growth model (see Section 10.4.3) to calculate the present value of future dividends accruing to its shares. Here:

$$P_0 = \frac{D_0(1 + g)}{(r - g)}$$

where: D_0 = current total dividend payment
g = expected annual growth rate of dividends
r = required rate of return of the company's shareholders

To apply this model to Hulse, we need a value for the annual dividend growth rate, g. The **geometric mean** growth rate of historical dividends can be used:

$$10.5 \times (1 + g)^4 = 12$$

Hence:

$$g = \sqrt[4]{12/10.5} - 1 = 3.39\%$$

The total dividend paid recently (D_0) is the dividend per share multiplied by the number of Hulse's shares:

$$£0.12 \times 246m \text{ shares} = £29.52m$$

We now require a value for the cost of equity, r. The cost of equity of Hulse plc must be used, rather than the cost of equity of the bidding company, since it is the target company shareholders who are being asked to give up their future dividends by selling their shares. The cost of equity of Hulse plc can be found using the CAPM and the data supplied earlier:

$$r = 4.5\% + [1.17 \times 5\%] = 10.35\%$$

Putting our calculated data into the dividend growth model we obtain:

$$\text{Company value} = \frac{£29.52m \times (1 + 0.0339)}{(0.1035 - 0.0339)} = £439m$$

The limitations of this model have already been discussed (see 'The dividend growth model', Section 10.4.3). The major drawback noted here is the sensitivity of the model to the value of g, the future dividend growth rate.

Discounted cash flow valuation

The maximum amount that Commons (Y) should be prepared in theory to pay for Hulse (X) is the difference between the present values of its pre- and post-acquisition cash flows:

$$PV_{X+Y} - PV_Y$$

This should be equal to the present value of the incremental cash flows that Commons (Y) gains by acquiring Hulse (X). Determining these present values requires estimating relevant cash flows and calculating an appropriate discount rate. While a discounted cash flow (DCF) valuation is preferred in theory, it has problems that must be overcome before any useful information is obtained from this valuation method. These include:

■ the difficulty of quantifying and incorporating into cash-flow forecasts any expected synergy or scale economy benefits, and deciding on their growth rates;
■ deciding on an appropriate period over which to forecast future cash flows and determining a terminal value for the company at the end of this period. Corporate forecasting often uses a five-year time horizon and so a five-year period may be most appropriate;
■ determining which discount rate should be used. The bidding company's cost of capital may be most appropriate, but the difficulties of calculating it must be overcome. The bidding company's WACC is not appropriate, however, if the target company's risk profile differs significantly from that of the bidder. In such a case, the CAPM can be used to determine a discount rate that takes account of the target company's systematic risk.

Referring to our example, we note that the cash flows accruing to Hulse are currently estimated at £38m and expected to grow at an annual rate of 4 per cent. Commons also expects to sell off surplus assets for £60m in two years' time. Using Commons' WACC as the discount rate, the present value of Hulse's post-acquisition cash flows is given by:

$$((£38m \times 1.04)/(0.07 - 0.04)) + (60/1.07^2) = £1,370m$$

This valuation, which uses an adaptation of the dividend growth model, assumes that growth in cash flows will occur only if the acquisition goes ahead. Given that Hulse is a smaller company than Commons, it could be argued that a discount rate reflecting the higher risk of Hulse relative to the risk of Commons should be used. We are told that companies in the same sector as Hulse have a WACC of 9 per cent, so if this is used as the discount rate, we have:

$$((\pounds38m \times 1.04)/(0.09 - 0.04)) + (60/1.09^2) = \pounds841m$$

11.4.4 Summary of valuation methods

We said earlier that some might see company valuation as more of an art than a science and that a wide range of valuation methods can be applied to a target company. The range of different methods has been illustrated by calculating values for Hulse plc in our example that range from £122m to £1,370m. The accuracy of these values depends on the reliability of the data used. The valuation method deemed most appropriate will depend on the information available to the bidding company and its intentions for the target company.

Here is a summary of the calculated values of Hulse plc:

	£m
Stock market valuation	615
NAV (book value basis)	142
NAV (net realisable value basis)	122
NAV (replacement cost basis)	157
Earnings yield valuation	615
Earnings yield valuation (with earnings growth)	862
P/E ratio valuation (using acquirer's P/E ratio)	824
P/E ratio valuation (using a weighted average P/E ratio)	767
P/E ratio valuation (using a sector average P/E ratio)	702
Dividend growth model valuation	439
DCF valuation (using acquirer's WACC)	1,370
DCF valuation (using sector average WACC)	841

11.5 THE FINANCING OF ACQUISITIONS

Owing to their size, takeovers have significant financial implications for the companies involved. These implications depend on the financing methods used for the takeover. Ultimately, when deciding on its financing method, the bidding company must recognise that the needs of both sets of shareholders involved must be satisfied if its bid is to be successful.

Table 11.2 shows that the ways in which takeovers have been financed have changed significantly over time. A large percentage of takeovers between 1985 and 1987 were financed through share-for-share offers, primarily due to a bullish stock market during this period. However, in the wake of the stock market crash of October 1987, cash offers proved much more popular than share-for-share offers. The late 1990s saw a gradual recovery in the popularity of share-for-share offers, but after 2000 volatile share prices on the London Stock Exchange and the recession towards the end of the decade pushed share-for-share offers back into relative obscurity. More recently, share-for-share offers made a slight come-back in 2014 and then overtook cash offers in terms of importance in 2016.

11.5.1 Cash offers

Here target company's shares are purchased by the bidding company for cash. A cash offer is attractive to target company's shareholders because the compensation they receive for selling their shares is certain. This is not the case with a share-for-share offer as the bidding company's share price is not constant, but is likely to change during the takeover. Cash offers allow target company shareholders to adjust their investment portfolios without incurring selling costs. These advantages must be balanced against the disadvantage that if target shareholders sell their shares to the bidding company at a higher price than they originally paid for them, they may be liable to pay capital gains tax on their disposals. Clearly, this will be unattractive to UK shareholders with large investment portfolios as they are more likely to have used up their annual UK capital gains allowance (see 'The clientele effect', Section 10.4.2). From the point of view of large institutional investors, cash offers are more attractive since pension funds and unit trusts are exempt from paying capital gains tax. The differing tax positions of small and large private and institutional investors help to explain why *mixed offers*, which involve cash and a share-for-share alternative, have grown in popularity. (These are considered in 'Mixed bids', Section 11.5.5.)

Cash offers can also offer advantages to the bidding company and its shareholders. First, they allow them to see exactly how much is being offered for the target company. Second, cash offers will not affect the number of ordinary shares the bidding company has in issue and so will neither alter its ownership structure nor lead to a dilution of its earnings per share.

The major issue surrounding cash issues is *where* the cash is raised from. In most cases, owing to the size of the transaction, the bidding company will not have sufficient cash to hand and it will need to raise cash from external sources. These may include borrowing from banks (often in the form of **mezzanine finance**) or an issue of bonds. Where large amounts of cash are borrowed to make a cash offer, the takeover is referred to as a **lever- aged takeover**. A problem for highly-geared bidding companies is that it may be difficult for them to find enough banks or other financial intermediaries prepared to offer the large amounts of debt they need.

Because of the undesirable side-effects of high gearing (see Section 9.8), many bidders that become highly geared from financing a takeover subsequently sell off parts of the acquired business to bring their gearing down to a more manageable level.

In the UK in 1988 there was a large increase in the number of cash-offer takeovers that were financed by debt (see Table 11.2). At the time, high levels of gearing were not seen as being problematic as interest rates were at a relatively low level. As the 1980s ended, however, interest rates increased rapidly and the gearing levels of these highly leveraged companies became a cause for concern. As a result, some companies that had borrowed heavily to finance acquisitions had to reduce their gearing, for example through rights issues, to repair their financial position statements.

There were also many leveraged takeovers in the USA during the 1980s. A relatively common occurrence was for small companies to borrow massive amounts of cash from banks or to issue unsecured, high-risk, high-return **junk bonds** to take over companies much larger than themselves. A classic high-profile example was the $31.1bn takeover of RJR Nabisco in 1988 by the small private company Kohlberg Kravis Roberts (KKR). KKR financed the transaction through borrowing and issuing junk bonds, and subsequently reduced its gearing by selling off part of RJR Nabisco.

11.5.2 Share-for-share offers

Here, target company shareholders are offered a fixed number of shares in the bidding company in exchange for the shares they hold in their own company. For target company shareholders, one advantage of a share-for-share offer is that they still have an equity interest in the company they originally invested in, even though it is now part of a larger concern. In addition, they do not incur the transaction costs of reinvesting any cash received, nor do they incur any capital gains tax liability arising from a share disposal (see Vignette 11.2).

A disadvantage to both the acquiring company and its shareholders is that equity payments tend to work out more expensive than cash offers. Because the value of the shares being offered will vary over time, the share-for-share offer must be on the generous side to prevent it becoming unattractive should the bidding company's share price fall during the offer period. There are also possible disadvantages arising from the bidding company increasing the number of its shares in circulation. The effect on the company's share price is unknown, although a fall in price is likely, which will be unpopular with shareholders. Issuing new shares will also lead to dilution of control. More subtly, the decrease in gearing resulting from issuing shares could move the bidding company away from its optimal capital structure and therefore increase its cost of capital. Equally, though, a share-for-share offer may move the bidding company *towards* its optimal cost of capital if it has too much debt finance.

Bidding companies can use share-for-share offers to engineer an increase in their earnings per share if the target company has a lower P/E ratio. This was rejected in 'Financial justifications' (Section 11.2.2) as an acceptable justification for acquisition since the increase in the bidding company's earnings per share may not involve any intrinsic or real increase in the wealth of its shareholders.

Vignette 11.2

Altria clouds SABMiller deal prospects

By Lindsay Whipp

Beer and cigarettes are not the healthiest combination, but for Altria, the maker of Marlboro, owning 27 per cent of brewer SABMiller has proven lucrative.

The stake has contributed 10–19 per cent of Altria's annual pre-tax profits over recent years, so the prospect of a bid for SAB by Anheuser-Busch InBev, its larger rival, has left investors watching keenly to see what Altria opts to do with its holding.

The size of the stake also means that the tobacco group could be an important influence over SAB's

discussions on whether to accept an offer, and how the deal should be structured. Most analysts say that the best outcome for Altria, the biggest tobacco company in the US, is to push for terms that allow it to keep a stake in an AB InBev-SABMiller combination.

Vivien Azer, an analyst at Cowen & Company, expects Altria to use its three board members to lobby for a 50-50 stock and cash deal that would allow it to maintain a 'meaningful' position in the merged company. One reason being that selling Altria's stake for cash would incur significant tax costs, analysts noted.

'They would have a tremendous tax bill if they were to sell,' says Michael Zbinovec, an analyst at Fitch, the rating agency. 'They have repeatedly said they are happy with earnings from the business.' Morningstar's Adam Fleck estimates that its stake in SAB could be worth roughly $24bn in a takeover, with the research company estimating a fair value for the brewer of £36 per share. Others suggest the price could be higher.

This is close to where SAB trades now, standing at £37.22 in morning trade on Wednesday. It is difficult to determine the company's undisturbed share price, however. It has rallied nearly 20 per cent since an approach was confirmed on September 16, but speculation about an offer was rife even before this, bolstering the stock.

Regardless, any final price would be far higher than the $6.2bn book value of the asset as recorded on Altria's balance sheet at the moment. And the tax rate on its gains would be 35 per cent, analysts say.

Altria, then Philip Morris, gained a 36 per cent share in SAB worth $3.4bn, after it sold Miller Brewing to SAB in 2002. This was gradually diluted to 27.3 per cent by 2009, according to its annual reports.

But tax is not the only reason that holding on to a stake would be in Altria's interest, according to analysts. SAB's substantial contribution to Altria's earnings provides a steady cash flow for the company as it seeks to bolster shareholder returns amid a secular decline in its core tobacco business.

It has also been a form of diversification for Altria, given that most of the group's profit still comes from cigarettes, despite expanding its 'smokeless' offerings and wine business. The group's geographic spread has also narrowed since it spun off Philip Morris International to focus on the US market.

By securing a stake in a combined AB InBev-SABMiller, Altria could share in the gains that analysts expect from a deal backed by 3G Capital, the cost-cutting Brazilian private equity group that owns 22.7 per cent of AB InBev.

Fitch's Mr Zbinovec also notes that AB InBev's dividend yield exceeds SAB's at 3.17 per cent and 2.07 per cent respectively, suggesting a continued stake could increase its dividend income.

Altria's long-term goal of earnings per share growth of 7–9 per cent 'seems to imply growing equity contributions from SABMiller', Morningstar's Mr Fleck points out.

'If management wants to continue to hit those targets without increasing equity contributions, it would need to boost pricing and likely accelerate volume declines in its tobacco products,' he says.

Altria's Marlboro brand, which accounts for almost all of its 'smokable' cigarette sales, has nearly 44 per cent of the US market – more than the next 10 brands combined. The segment, which also includes cigars, enjoys generous margins of 44 per cent. Its smokeless offerings, while a much smaller contributor to profit, are growing and have margins of 63 per cent. But with limited ability to advertise and regulation only likely to get stiffer, tobacco is a difficult industry.

Domestic competition is intensifying at a time of significant consolidation. Reynolds American recently completed its acquisition of Lorillard, with some brands from those two companies sold to Imperial Tobacco's US subsidiary, while Japan Tobacco this week announced it is to buy $5bn of assets from Reynolds.

More consolidation could come, though. There has been market speculation that Imperial itself could be a target either for BAT or Japan Tobacco.

One key focus for investors and analysts if Altria maintains an investment in brewing through an AB InBev-SAB deal, is how big its holding will be. At the moment, its 27.3 per cent stake and three board members gives it 'significant influence' in accounting terms, allowing it to use so-called equity method accounting and consolidate its share of SAB's profit on its income statement.

While letting its stake fall below 20 per cent could force it to change the way it accounts for its holding and only count dividends, there is no hard and

Vignette 11.2 (*continued*)

fast rule, analysts say, adding that it could prove in other ways that it continues to exert 'significant influence'. As the Marlboro Man said of his smokes back in 1954 'You get a lot to like'. For Altria, when it comes to maintaining a stake in a newly formed AB InBev-SAB, the same probably applies.

 Source: Whipp, L. (2015) 'Altria clouds SABMiller deal prospects', *Financial Times*, 30 September. © The Financial Times Limited 2015. All Rights Reserved.

Question

Why is Altria, which has a substantial shareholding in SABMiller, likely to prefer a share-for-share offer from AB InBev?

11.5.3 Vendor placings and vendor rights issues

With a *vendor placing*, the bidding company offers shares to target company shareholders, giving them the option to continue their shareholding. However, the bidding company simultaneously arranges for the new shares to be placed with institutional investors and for the cash to be paid to the target company's shareholders. A *vendor rights issue* works in a similar way, differing only in the final destination of the offered shares. Instead of being placed with institutional investors, the shares are offered to the acquiring company's shareholders. If they are accepted, the cash is then paid to the target company's shareholders. Any rights shares not taken up are placed with institutional investors.

11.5.4 Security packages

Paying target company shareholders with securities other than bidding company shares is rare. Table 11.2 shows that security packages containing bonds, convertible bonds or preference shares have played only a minor role in takeover financing since the mid-1980s, although they were a popular financing choice for companies before 1972. The popularity of debt security packages was severely damaged by the high levels of inflation (and corresponding high levels of interest) caused by the oil crises of the 1970s, since when they have been of minor importance.

11.5.5 Mixed bids

Mixed bids are share-for-share offers with a cash alternative. They have become increasingly popular as a means of financing takeovers in the UK for two reasons. First, they can be more acceptable to target company shareholders as they can select the method of payment that best suits their liquidity preferences and tax positions. Second, Rule 9 of the City Code on Takeovers and Mergers requires companies acquiring 30 per cent or more of a target company's shares to make a cash offer (or offer a cash alternative if a share-for-share payment is being used) at the highest price paid by the bidding company for the target company's shares over the previous 12-month period.

11.6 STRATEGIC AND TACTICAL ISSUES

When a company is seeking acquisitions, it is vital that it considers the strategy and tactics it is going to employ. It must satisfy itself that acquisition represents a more efficient alternative than organic growth or the independent purchase of required assets *before* it becomes involved in takeover activity. Once the company is satisfied on this count, the strategic process of acquiring a target company can be summarised as follows:

1 Identify suitable target companies.
2 Obtain as much information about the target companies as possible.
3 Using the information obtained, value each target company and decide on the maximum purchase price that should be paid for each alternative.
4 Decide which of the potential target companies is most appropriate.
5 Decide on the best way to finance the acquisition, taking account of which methods of payment are acceptable to both sets of shareholders.

Once an acquiring company has completed this process it must decide on the tactics it will use. Failing to use the right tactics can result in a bidding company paying over the odds or, in the worst-case scenario, failing to acquire its target altogether. Companies must also be aware of the rules and regulations governing mergers and takeovers.

Before we look in more detail at the regulatory environment governing mergers and takeovers, it is important to establish the significance, both legal and otherwise, attached to various levels of shareholding. A summary of levels of shareholding and their associated implications is given in Table 11.3.

The most significant level of shareholding from an acquisition perspective is holding 50 per cent of a company's voting rights. Once a bidding company has more than 50 per cent of its target company's ordinary shares, it has the power to dismiss and appoint directors and in effect has control of the target company's decision-making process.

11.6.1 Merger regulation and control

Broadly speaking, there are two types of regulation that govern merger and takeover activity. Legal controls, often referred to as *antitrust regulation*, consider from a public interest point of view whether mergers and takeovers should be allowed to proceed in the first place. In addition, *self-regulatory controls* focus on the regulation of the bid process itself.

Legal controls

The amended Enterprise Act of 2002 forms the cornerstone of UK antitrust legislation. Any takeover activity in the UK falling outside of EC Merger Regulation (ECMR) due to a lack of a 'Community Dimension' is the responsibility of the Competition and Markets Authority (CMA). The CMA was formed out of the abolition of the Office of Fair Trading (OFT) and the Competition Commission (CC) in 2014. Prior to 2014 the OFT carried out initial reviews of mergers and takeovers. If, after the review, there was deemed to be a 'relevant merger situation' that *might* lead to a substantial lessening of competition (SLC), the OFT referred the relevant transaction on to the CC for further investigation. The review and investigation

Table 11.3 The implications associated with different proportions of shareholding

Voting rights held (%)	Implications and legal obligations of shareholding level
90 and over	The company has a right to compulsorily purchase the remaining shares
75 and over	The acquiring company can change the Articles of Association of the company taken over and put it into liquidation
50 and over	The company can influence dividend policy and appoint directors
30 and over	Implies effective control with respect to public companies and hence requires the launch of a formal takeover bid
25 and over	Minority influence on dividend policy and management and an ability to block changes to the company's articles
20 and over	According to the Companies Act 1981, implies related company status
10 and over	Can prevent a complete takeover
1 and over	Taking a holding over 1% in a company requires formal notification

process is now under one organisation's jurisdiction, the rationale behind the change being to cut red tape and save costs. The CMA can review transactions where the target company UK turnover exceeds £70m or where the newly formed entity accounts for more than 25 per cent of the relevant market. Reviews occur through the CMA's own initiative or because the merging companies have completed a 'Merger Notice'. The CMA has 40 days to complete the initial stage of its review process (Phase 1). If there is a realistic prospect of a substantial lessening of competition the CMA is then duty-bound to launch an in-depth assessment (Phase 2). Resolution can come at Phase 1 if merging parties agree to undertake 'Undertakings in Lieu' (UILs). Likewise, after the Phase 2 findings are made public (typically before 24 weeks), if an SLC is believed to be present, the transaction may progress after the guarantee of UILs by the businesses concerned. Alternatively, the transaction may be blocked by the CMA.

Historically, only a small number of mergers and takeovers reviewed by the OFT were referred and an even smaller proportion were found by the CC to be against the public interest. During the first year of the new system (April 2014–April 2015), 82 transactions in total were reviewed (Phase 1). Of these, 63 were cleared, 3 were cleared subject to UILs by the parties concerned and 10 were found not to qualify, leaving 6 that were referred on to a Phase 2 investigation. For the most recent period (April 2017–April 2018), 62 transactions in total were reviewed (Phase 1). All were found to qualify with 41 being cleared, 12 cleared subject to UILs and 9 being referred. From October 2009 the OFT charged fees to mergers that qualified for referral regardless of whether one was made. The CMA has subsequently carried on this practice. The referral of the proposed merger of UK energy suppliers SSE and Npower is the subject of Vignette 11.3.

Looking to the future, there will be post-Brexit implications for UK antitrust legislation. Potentially there could be transactions that are investigated by both the CMA and the ECMR. The CMA is likely to need additional time and resources to investigate more transactions with a higher level of complexity. An interesting question is whether the two bodies will reach the same conclusion and remedy for jointly investigated notifications. Going forward, the key will be cooperation between the CMA and the ECMR, and agreement on potential remedies for jointly investigated transactions.

Vignette 11.3

Competition watchdog refers SSE and Npower merger for full probe
CMA concerned by possible impact of cutting 'big six' suppliers

By Sylvia Pfeifer

The UK competition watchdog has referred the proposed merger between household energy suppliers SSE and Npower for an in-depth investigation after the two companies failed to provide remedies to ease competition concerns.

The Competition and Markets Authority said the decision followed an initial investigation that found the deal could potentially lead to higher prices for some consumers. A decision on the merger will now be made by an independent panel supported by a case team of CMA staff. The deadline for the final report is 22 October [2018].

The watchdog said last month it was concerned the merger, which was announced last November, could impact competition. The companies had seven days – until midnight last Thursday – to offer undertakings to address these concerns.

The combination of the household supply business of London-listed SSE and Npower, owned by Germany's Innogy, would reduce Britain's 'big six'

energy suppliers to five and create a new company with just under 13m customer accounts. It would have a larger share of electricity supply than British Gas, the market leader, with a 24 per cent share compared with 22 per cent. Its market share for gas, however, would still be dwarfed by British Gas.

Concerns are likely to focus on the impact of the proposed deal on 'standard variable tariffs (SVTs)', the most common type of energy tariff. The government has promised to tackle 'rip off' energy bills and legislation is going through parliament to cap SVTs. SSE has the highest proportion of customers on SVTs among the 'big six' suppliers.

Npower owner Innogy is in turn controlled by Germany's RWE. The merged business would initially be part-owned by SSE shareholders with a minority share held by Innogy. Since the merger was announced in November, a separate deal has been agreed whereby RWE has agreed to sell Innogy to Eon, another German supplier which also has a UK retail business.

Source: Pfeifer, S. (2018) 'Competition watchdog refers SSE and Npower merger for full probe', *Financial Times*, 8 May. © The Financial Times Limited 2018. All Rights Reserved.

Question

What do you consider to be the main reasons behind the referral of the above proposed bid by the CMA?

Self-regulatory controls

In the UK the bid process falls under the non-statutory regulation of the Takeover Panel through its enforcement of the City Code on Takeovers and Mergers. The City Code, based on 6 general principles and 38 more specific rules, applies to all listed and unlisted public companies resident in the UK. Its aim is to ensure that target company shareholders are treated fairly and equally during the bidding process and it lays down a strict timetable which must be followed by all takeover bids. While the principles and rules of the City Code are not legally enforceable, non-compliance can result in public reprimands.

The City Code has been developed by other self-regulatory organisations, including the London Stock Exchange and the Bank of England, and a company must comply with it to be regarded as reputable in the UK financial system.

11.6.2 The bidding process

When a company launches a bid, it considers its tactics carefully and consults financial advisers such as merchant banks. Having decided on a maximum price that it is prepared to pay, the acquiring company aims to pay as far below this price as possible. The market price of the shares of the target company will act as a lower limit, on top of which the acquiring company can expect to pay a premium. Jensen (1993) found that, historically, the premiums paid in successful takeovers tended to be no less than 30 per cent and averaged approximately 50 per cent. Major determinants of the acquisition price finally paid include whether a bid is contested and whether the acquiring company uses the most appropriate tactics during the takeover.

The City Code, which must be followed during the bidding process, is designed to protect the interests of the various shareholders involved. It includes the following procedures:

- The acquiring company must notify its potential target two days after it has built up a 3 per cent holding of its shares. This reduces the possibility of **dawn raids**, where acquiring companies sneak up on their targets before they have organised their defences. Acquiring companies can circumvent this through *concert parties,* where a coalition of friendly companies each acquire just less than the notifiable 3 per cent level of shareholding.
- After an approach by a bidding company has been announced, it has an automatic deadline of 28 days in which to table a bid.
- Once 30 per cent of the target company's shares are held, the bidding company must make a cash offer to all remaining shareholders at a price no less than the highest price paid in the preceding 12-month period.
- The bidding company must then post the terms of its offer to the target company's shareholders 28 days after its announcement.
- When the bidding company makes the offer, it must first inform the target company board of the nature and terms of its offer. This information must then be passed on by the target company board to its shareholders.
- Once the offer has been received, the target company board will express their views on its acceptability. The bidding company may also be required by stock exchange rules to gain approval from its own shareholders with respect to the proposed bid. Once posted, offers are open for 21 days. This is extended by 14 days if any amendments are made to the initial offer.
- An offer becomes unconditional when the bidding company has obtained more than 50 per cent of target company shares. Once the offer is unconditional, existing shareholders have 14 days either to sell their shares or to become minority shareholders in the new company.

Vignette 11.4

Mylan readies its poison pill defences

By Arrash Massoudi

Israel's Teva faces an uphill battle in its $40bn takeover pursuit of rival generics drugmaker Mylan, thanks to recent corporate governance changes by the US-listed company designed to complicate an unsolicited approach.

Mylan, which moved its domicile to the Netherlands this year, finalised a powerful poison pill defence in early April that allows the issuance of preferred shares to a Dutch foundation in the event of a hostile bid. The move came as speculation of a possible Teva bid for Mylan was rife and just days before Mylan unveiled its own unsolicited $28.9bn offer for generics drugmaker Perrigo. Perrigo rejected Mylan's offer on Tuesday. Mylan has yet to respond since Teva unveiled its offer, though the company did pre-emptively dismiss the logic of a deal with Teva last week. Poison pill strategies differ depending on a company's legal jurisdiction and come in various forms.

Though listed and run out of the US, Mylan moved its domicile to the Netherlands through a $5.3bn deal last year to acquire parts of the generic drug business of Abbott Labs. The manoeuvre was intended to help Mylan escape US corporate tax rates. Dutch law is somewhat unique to the rest of Europe with respect to anti-takeover measures as it allows companies to adopt poison pill type struc-

tures. In most other European countries, the UK principle of a board remaining passive in a takeover situation applies. Thus, many boards in Europe cannot adopt poison pills as defensive measures.

Mylan has put in place a poison pill that is customary in the Netherlands, involving the formation of an independent foundation, which is known as a 'stichting'. Under the terms, the foundation can exercise a call option agreement set up between it and the company that would dilute the voting rights of the company's ordinary shareholders. The foundation has the right to exercise the option if it determines it is in the best interests of the company and if it allows the company's management to explore alternative scenarios.

Pieter Bouw, a former president of Dutch airline KLM, was named as the chairman of the foundation by Mylan. Mr Bouw was part of a foundation that intervened and prevented Carlos Slim's €7.2bn takeover attempt of Dutch telecoms company KPN.

One person familiar with the use of Dutch foundations as a takeover defence said that it is clear in Dutch case law that its use can only be temporary and it is not allowed to be used permanently to deter a bidder.

Source: Massoudi, A. (2015) 'Mylan readies its poison pill defences', *Financial Times*, 22 April.
© The Financial Times Limited 2015. All Rights Reserved.

Questions

1 How do poison pills make takeovers more difficult for bidding companies?
2 Why do many regulatory authorities seek to outlaw the use of poison pills?

■ Partial bids, where a company bids for a specific percentage of the target company's share capital, are allowed only in certain circumstances and require prior approval from the Takeover Panel. Permission is usually given only for partial bids of less than 30 per cent of the target company's overall equity.

11.6.3 Bid defences

When a company receives a bid for its shares, the managers must decide whether to contest the bid. If they decide to contest it, they should make this decision purely on the grounds that the offer is not in the best interests of their shareholders and not because they do not wish to lose their jobs. They must communicate their decision to contest the bid to their shareholders. It may be difficult for them to convince shareholders to reject the bid if it appears to be in the financial interests of shareholders to accept it. They may seek to convince shareholders that the acquiring company's share price is artificially inflated and will drop after the proposed takeover, or perhaps argue that their own shares are currently undervalued by the market. Bid defences can be conveniently grouped by whether they were deployed before or after a bid was received.

Pre-bid defences

The simplest and most constructive form of pre-bid defence is to make a company too expensive to take over in the first place. This constructive form of defence is consistent with the objective of shareholder wealth maximisation and can be achieved through the following means:

- *Improving operational efficiency*: rationalising production, cutting overheads and improving labour productivity can raise a company's EPS and share price, making a potential takeover both more expensive and less likely.
- *Examining asset portfolios and making necessary divestments*: managers can sell off non-core, low-growth business and concentrate on the markets in which they have relative strengths. Again, this should lead to higher profits, a higher EPS and a higher share price.
- *Ensuring good investor relations*: maintaining good relations with investors and analysts can make a takeover more difficult and more expensive. Companies should keep investors well informed about company strategy, policies and performance and also try to satisfy investors' risk–return preferences.

Less desirable types of pre-bid defences are those deployed with the sole purpose of making a company both difficult and expensive to take over. These *obstructive* defences are often at odds with shareholder wealth maximisation and include the following techniques:

- *Restructuring of equity*: a range of tactics are available here. For example, companies can repurchase their own shares to make it more difficult for bidders to build up a controlling position, or they can increase their gearing level to make themselves less attractive to bidders. More intriguingly, companies can plant **poison pills** within their capital structure, for example options giving rights to shareholders to buy future bonds or preference shares. If a bidder tries to take over the company before the rights must be exercised, it is obliged to buy up the securities, hence increasing the cost of the acquisition. Poison pills are prohibited by the Takeover Panel in the UK, while the European Union has led a lengthy and troubled campaign to outlaw them.
- *Management retrenchment devices*: the best known of these are **golden parachutes**, which give generous termination packages to incumbent senior managers and increase the cost of the takeover, as large amounts of money are paid to these managers. However, this form of takeover defence is becoming increasingly unpopular with institutional investors. The topic of golden parachutes and the wider issues they raise is the subject of Vignette 11.5.

■ *Strategic defence via cross-holdings*: this defence ensures that a significant proportion of equity is in friendly hands through companies arranging to take a mutual shareholding in each other to block potential takeover bids.

Vignette 11.5

Golden parachutes leave unhappy investors behind

Shareholders have reason to resent excessive rewards for failure

By Sarah Gordon

Who knows what temptations a golden parachute can open up? Reports suggest that senior executives at Mead Johnson, the US baby formula maker talking to Reckitt Benckiser about a $17bn takeover, could walk away with more than $30m if the deal goes through.

According to the Evening Standard, Mead introduced a 'golden parachute' pay scheme in 2014, which means six executives will receive a total of $31.7m if they are let go within two years of a takeover. Suggesting that this might distort Mead's attitude to a potential deal might be going too far but the prospect of being paid because you decide to leave a job may seem decidedly odd. Not, sadly, in the wider context of executive pay agreements, where Mead's example is anything but unusual.

Alberto Minali, chief financial officer of Generali, the Italian insurer being stalked by bank Intesa Sanpaolo, left last month with a pay-off of at least €5.8m. Most of the money was severance pay and €2.2m of 'gross notice value'. Half a million euros stops him working for Generali's main rivals for six months, which seems reasonable enough. But the remainder is open to question.

Mr Minali was a kind of super-CFO, with responsibility for strategy and operations. He seems to have been arguing with chief executive Philippe Donnet over the direction to take with Generali – and, most likely, over how to respond to predators. Disagreements at the top are both healthy and, if they cannot be resolved, ultimately a good reason for one of the parties to leave. But paying a departing CFO for simply having met his job description is difficult to justify.

Other Italian examples abound. Alessandro Profumo, the veteran Italian banker, probably set a record when he pocketed a €40m golden goodbye when he left Italy's UniCredit in 2010, prompted by shareholder discontent over its plunging share price. There are plenty of more recent examples, like Marco Patuano, who walked away with €7m from Telecom Italia, after a row with its controlling shareholder, Vincent Bolloré's Vivendi.

Getting rid of those impeding progress at the top may be worth a pay-off. But at Volkswagen, the most recent golden parachute suggests the opposite. Christine Hohmann-Dennhardt was taken on as head of compliance in January 2016 to tackle deep-rooted problems at the carmaker, which had cheated on emissions tests on millions of vehicles. Last month she left after just 13 months in the job, taking with her €10m-€15m. This included three years' of full pay despite leaving 23 months early. VW blamed 'differences in vision'. The carmaker's management and union certainly did not like much of what she proposed, such as hiring Louis Freeh, a former director of the US FBI, as an independent monitor.

The payment was linked to a 'transfer fee' that brought Ms Hohmann-Dennhardt from Daimler before her contract was up, although this would only account for up to half. But it is impossible not to relate the size of the payout to the scale of the problems Ms Hohmann-Dennhardt was trying to clean up.

It is also a worrying sign that institutional resistance to reform at VW is deep-seated. That the board thought such a payout the right thing to do, when VW investors have suffered a collapse in the share price as well as billions of dollars in fines for its transgressions, demonstrates that its tin ear remains firmly in place.

Vignette 11.5 (continued)

Most golden parachutes are a consequence of complicated pay packages and opaque long-term incentive plans, which departing executives must be bought out of. The complexity of senior managers' pay is difficult for shareholders to understand. Even remuneration committees often struggle. Companies rarely make public statements on compensation packages and, when reported, details are buried in the small print of annual reports. This lack of transparency does not just relate to pay-offs, but also obscures the link between pay and performance.

Reducing the complexity of these pay packages would have a number of good results, not least in forcing companies to justify pay-offs. Until that happens, shareholders should kick up a fuss about golden parachutes, not just those that appear to reward failure, but those that mark someone just doing their job. A fuss can have an effect, after all. Two years ago, the departing chief of Alcatel-Lucent, Michel Combes, had his golden parachute cut in half after pressure from politicians and the public.

 Source: Gordon, S. (2018) 'Golden parachutes leave unhappy investors behind', *Financial Times*, 8 February. © The Financial Times Limited 2018. All Rights Reserved.

Question

Can the use of golden parachutes as a pre-bid takeover defence be justified?

Post-bid defences

Post-bid defences are used by target companies to repel a bid once one has been made. Post-bid defences that are often used include the following:

■ *Rejection of the initial offer*: when a takeover bid is made, the bid is attacked to signal to the bidder that the target company will contest the takeover. In some cases, this may be enough to scare the bidder off.

■ *A pre-emptive circulation to shareholders*: target companies can appeal to their own shareholders, explaining why the bid is not in their favour from both a logic and a price perspective.

■ *Formulation of a defence document*: the board of the target company can prepare a formal document for circulating to its own shareholders which praises the company's performance and criticises the bidding company and its offer.

■ *Profit announcements and forecasts*: a target company can produce a report indicating that its future profits will be much better than those expected by the market. If these profit forecasts are accepted by the market, this acceptance will force up the market price and make the proposed takeover more expensive. A major problem here is that, if the company does not meet the increased forecasts, its share price is likely to fall, putting it at risk from another takeover bid and making this defence less likely to be successful if used again.

■ *Dividend increase announcements*: a company can announce an increased current dividend and an intention to pay increased future dividends. This expected rise in shareholder returns may dissuade them from selling their shares. Equally, they may ask why increased returns were not paid before the arrival of a takeover bid.

■ *Revaluation of assets*: before or after a bid is made a company can revalue certain assets on its financial position statement, such as land and buildings, or capitalise intangible assets such as brands and goodwill in its financial position statement, to make the company look stronger or more valuable. While this may lead to a bidder having to make an increased offer, it could be argued that, if capital markets are efficient, no new information is being offered to the market and the existing share price is a fair one.

■ *Searching for a* **white knight**: the target company can seek a more suitable company to take it over, although this tactic tends to be used only as a last resort. The City Code allows this tactic, but if the target company passes any information to the 'white knight' it must also be passed to the initial bidder. A variation of this technique is to issue new shares to a 'white knight' to dilute the bidding company's holdings. The defending company must get its shareholders' approval before it defends the takeover bid in this way, however.

■ *Pac-man defence*: this defence involves the target company making a counter-bid for the shares of the bidding company. This defence is difficult to organise and expensive to carry out, but it has been used on occasion in the USA.

■ *Acquisitions and divestments*: the target company can either buy new assets or companies that are incompatible with the bidder's business, or sell the 'crown jewels' or assets that the bidder is particularly interested in. This tactic is more common in the USA than in the UK since, in the UK, the City Code restricts asset sales once a takeover bid has been made.

11.7 DIVESTMENT

So far, we have considered transactions that expand the size of a company. In practice, many acquisitions are followed by a period of divestment or *asset stripping,* where the acquirer sells off parts of the acquired company seen as surplus to requirements. Recent decades have also witnessed prominent conglomerates dismantling themselves through divestments, such as the high-profile 1996 dissolution of Hanson plc. In addition, the 1980s and 1990s saw some companies divesting peripheral operations to focus on their core business to survive in an increasingly competitive commercial environment. Comment and Jarrell (1995) concluded that 'greater corporate focus through divesting activities is consistent with shareholder wealth maximization'. Table 11.4 shows examples of major divestments involving UK companies.

11.7.1 Reasons for divestment

Many arguments have been advanced to explain why companies divest parts of their business:

■ Divestment allows significant amounts of cash to be raised which can then be used to ease a company's liquidity situation or to reduce its level of gearing.

■ Divestment allows companies to concentrate on core activities, which they can then expand and use to generate benefits such as economies of scale.

■ Synergy may be generated by selling off part of the business as the divested assets may be worth more in the hands of management specialising in that line of business.

■ A company, on rare occasions, could be divesting its *crown jewels* to dissuade an unwanted predator company from taking it over.

Table 11.4 Major UK divestments including total value and classification

Date	Divestor	Divested	Value (£m)	Classification of divestment
1987	Asda	MFI	620	MBO (by MFI's management)
1997	British Gas	Centrica	2,900	Spin-off
2001	Kingfisher	Woolworth	424	Spin-off
2001	P&O	P&O Princess Cruise	2,000	Spin-off
2001	BT	Various properties	2,000	Sell-off
2004	Saga	N/A	1,350	MBO (by incumbent management)
2005	Rentokil	Style Conferences	325	Sell-off
2005	GUS	Burberry	1,150	Spin-off
2008	Akzo	Crown Paints	70	MBO (by private equity group)
2009	AIG	Hastings Direct	23	MBO
2009	Time Warner	AOL	2,500	Spin-off
2014	Permira and Apax	New Look	780	Sell-off
2016	Thomas Reuters Corporation	Intellectual property and sciences division	2,700	Sell-off

11.7.2 Divestment strategies

Different divestment strategies can have markedly different characteristics and implications for the parties involved.

Sell-off

A company can sell off part of its operations to a third party, usually for cash. A sell-off is most likely to occur in a multi-product company. A company may sell off a division or subsidiary that is peripheral to its main business to raise cash and ease any management control problems. Sometimes also referred to as a *trade sale,* this represents the quickest, easiest and lowest risk way for a company to dispose of its unwanted assets and in consequence it is also the most common type of divestment strategy. The decision on whether to sell a part of the business should ideally be based on net present value considerations (see 'The net present value method', Section 6.3). If selling off part of the business yields a positive NPV and hence adds to shareholder wealth, then the company should go through with the proposed divestment.

Spin-off

A spin-off is another name for a **demerger**. The formal definition is 'a pro rata distribution of subsidiary shares to the shareholders of the parent'. The structure of the parent company changes but, unlike a sell-off, the ownership of the assets remains with the parent and no cash is raised. Where, before, there was one company, now there are two or more companies, one with a majority shareholding in the other. The new company *may* have different management from the original company but will still be owned by the same set of shareholders. The benefits put forward to justify a spin-off are as follows:

- It results in a clearer management structure, which can lead to a more efficient use of the assets of the demerged company and of the assets remaining in the original company.
- It can facilitate future merger and takeover activity for the demerged company.
- It can enhance the overall value of the company as the demerged company's assets may not have been fully appreciated within the original company. The company may currently be valued at what is referred to as a *conglomerate discount,* where investors cannot see the wood for the trees. Once spun off, the assets stand alone and hence are more visible to the market. The tough economic conditions of 2008 led to proposed spin-offs being mooted and demergers rose to make up a record share of global merger and takeover activity by the summer of 2011. However, demerged companies face significant challenges in the first few years of operation.

Vignette 11.6 looks at Whitbread's 2018 announcement of its intention to spin off Costa Coffee in 2018.

Vignette 11.6

Whitbread bows to investor pressure to spin off Costa

Hedge funds have been calling for demerger of coffee chain from Premier Inn hotel business

By Jonathan Eley

Whitbread has said it will spin-off its Costa Coffee business after pressure from two hedge funds, but the process will take up to two years, frustrating some investors. Hedge funds Sachem Head and Elliott Advisors have been calling on the FTSE 100 company, which also owns the Premier Inn hotel chain, to separate Costa from the rest of the business.

Alison Brittain, Whitbread's chief executive, has previously declared herself open to the idea but maintained that both businesses need more investment first. After announcing the demerger on Wednesday, she said: 'We have always said you wouldn't sell your house at a time when you've got the roof off and you're doing all the rewiring – and that is what we are doing at the moment.' She added: 'What has changed is that we have announced it, because there has been so much noise in the system recently.'

She said a demerger, rather than a sale, 'represented the simplest and quickest way to achieve the most appropriate valuation for both businesses'. The two divisions are already separate legal entities and have their own senior leadership teams.

Investors welcomed the plan but said it should happen more rapidly. Elliott said it was pleased Whitbread had announced a demerger but added: 'In Elliott's view this should be achieved within six months.' Ed Meier, a manager at Old Mutual Global Investors, another shareholder, agreed that allowing 24 months for the process 'is longer than most would have anticipated'.

Other demergers over the past decade have completed in considerably less time: spin-offs of Indivior from Reckitt, Spirit Pub from Punch Taverns and C&W Worldwide from Cable & Wireless all took about 20 weeks from date of announcement to the start of

Vignette 11.6 (continued)

trading in the demerged company's shares. However, splitting TalkTalk from Carphone Warehouse took 49 weeks and demerging Dr Pepper Snapple from Cadbury Schweppes took more than a year.

Ms Brittain said splitting the Whitbread businesses would take a year, even without further investment or restructuring. As well as separating IT and other functions, Whitbread is the sponsor of a £3bn defined-benefit pension scheme. Given that this will be supported by a smaller earnings base in future, the company will have to reach agreement with the fund trustees, said independent pensions consultant John Ralfe. 'It will probably seek pre-clearance from the [UK] Pensions Regulator.' Whitbread shares fell slightly on the news.

'Some quick money probably followed Sachem and Elliott into the stock, and that money doesn't want to hang around for two years,' said Richard Clarke, analyst at Bernstein. 'It looks like management wants to stick to its own timetable here.' Greg Johnson, analyst at Shore Capital, estimated a fair value of about £46 a share for Whitbread, compared with a current share price of £41. He added that an uplift in excess of that would require either a 'significant reappraisal' of Costa or more aggressive use of debt or property sale-and-leasebacks in its hotel business.

Currently, about three-fifths of Premier Inns are owned rather than leased, and Ms Brittain said there were no plans to change this after the split. Costa is in the process of changing its UK store estate, putting Costa Express machines into convenience stores and investing in IT to enable

functions such as click-and-collect coffee ordering and variable pricing. Its previously heady growth rates have slowed recently, as consumers have turned more cautious.

Full-year results released alongside the demerger announcement showed same-store sales rising 1.2 per cent – an improvement on the growth rate after nine months of the fiscal year, but well below the 2 per cent reported in fiscal 2017 and 2.9 per cent in 2016.

Whitbread warned that 'the current UK consumer environment naturally means our near-term profit growth may be lower than in previous years'. Mr Clarke said Costa had been slow to expand into food and that its store estate was heavily exposed to places where footfall has declined. 'I suspect the outlets in airports, train stations and motorway service areas are doing better.'

Scott Ferguson, managing partner at Sachem Head, told a hedge fund conference in New York this week why he thought Costa would be better off as an independent business: 'When management no longer has a big brother to lean on, problems tend to be solved.'

Both Costa and Premier Inn, which accounts for three-quarters of Whitbread's earnings before interest, tax, depreciation and amortisation, are market leaders in the UK. They are now making initial forays outside their home market. Premier aims to have at least 31 hotels in Germany by 2021, while Costa is expanding in China. Ms Brittain said international expansion was needed as a basis for long-term growth.

 Source: Eley, J. (2018) 'Whitbread bows to investor pressure to spin off Costa', *Financial Times*, 25 April. © The Financial Times Limited 2018. All Rights Reserved.

Questions

1 Why has Whitbread decided to spin-off Costa rather than sell it off?

2 Why is the proposed divestment going to take so long?

Management buyout

A **management buyout (MBO)** is the purchase of part or all of a business from its parent company by the existing management of the business, for example the purchase of a subsidiary company from the parent by the subsidiary's management. Sometimes, however, there may be insufficient skills among subsidiary managers and the subsidiary may be sold to an external management team through a **management buy-in (MBI)**. MBOs are widespread phenomena and are considered in more detail in the next section.

11.7.3 Management buyouts

The motivation behind MBOs usually comes from the parent company's board of directors. The reasons behind their desire to sell the subsidiary are usually like those attributed to sell-offs. However, an MBO may be a preferred divestment strategy to a sell-off as the divesting company is more likely to get the cooperation of the subsidiary's management if it sells using an MBO. Additionally, if the subsidiary is loss-making, the current management may be more optimistic that they can turn the situation around than an outside buyer. Alternatively, the motivation may come from the managers of the subsidiary as they may be finding it difficult to obtain funds from the parent company and feel marginalised from the decision-making process in the group. Sometimes MBOs come about because of a seller's failure to find a suitable buyer via a sell-off. This was the situation Barclays plc found itself in when trying to dispose of one of its private equity businesses in June 2015 (see Vignette 11.7). MBOs face major challenges early in their lives and many do not survive. This was demonstrated by the fate of Zavvi, a 2007 MBO that saw the divestment of the Virgin Megastore retail chain from its parent company Virgin, only for it to fall into administration one year later.

The financing of MBOs

Third-party financing is crucial for most MBOs to proceed, as existing managers are unlikely to have sufficient funds at their disposal for the purchase. The management buyout team requires a well-thought-out business plan, incorporating future cash-flow projections, as a prerequisite to obtaining the external finance it needs. Without such a business plan, the MBO team is unlikely to win the confidence of funding institutions such as venture capitalists.

Vignette 11.7

Management to buy Barclays private equity arm after stalled sale

By Martin Arnold and Madison Marriage

Barclays has negotiated a management buyout of its private equity business specialising in energy and commodity investments, having struggled to find an acceptable buyer for the unit. The deal, which is expected to be announced in the coming weeks, leaves Barclays still looking to sell its roughly $1bn of investments in the private equity unit's portfolio, tying up capital for much longer than it wanted.

Barclays Natural Resources Investment will be bought by its managers, led by Mark Brown, chief executive, as it spins out from the bank in the coming months and seeks to raise a new fund from third-party investors.

The unit, which has 14 staff, was placed into Barclays' non-core unit as part of a restructuring of its investment bank announced a year ago, which included plans to exit the trading of physical commodities. The disposal is a response to new regulations, including the so-called Volcker rule in the US, that make it harder for banks to own and invest in captive private equity operations.

Barclays had hoped to sell the entire portfolio of BNRI along with its management team, which operate from three of the bank's offices in London, New York and Doha. However, it failed to reach a deal with any potential buyer. The planned management buyout, first reported by Sky News, will result in

Vignette 11.7 (continued)

BNRI changing its name to Global Natural Resource Investment and moving into new offices. It will continue to manage the 17 investments in its portfolio on behalf of the bank. But it will need to raise a new fund from third-party investors as Barclays will not put more money in. An earlier fundraising effort was postponed in 2012. Third-party investors have co-invested $1bn alongside the bank in earlier deals.

BNRI, founded in 2006, has invested $3bn in 28 companies, which include Chrysador, a North Sea oil explorer, Cupric Canyon, a US copper miner, and Mainstream Renewable Power, a wind and solar power developer. The bank has already spun off,

sold or shut down several other private equity activities, including Barclays Private Equity, which was renamed Equistone after being sold to its managers; and its infrastructure unit, which was sold to 3i. The restructuring of Barclays' investment bank is designed to reduce its risk-weighted assets by £90bn and to cut 7,000 jobs in an attempt to boost its faltering performance.

Tom King, the unit's chief executive, will on Thursday give a presentation to an off-site board meeting that will help John McFarlane, the group's new chairman, to determine if more restructuring is needed.

Source: Arnold, M. and Marriage, M. (2015) 'Management to buy Barclays private equity arm after stalled sale', *Financial Times*, 23 June.
© The Financial Times Limited 2015. All Rights Reserved.

MBOs are normally financed using a mixture of debt and equity, although there has been a trend towards *leveraged* MBOs (known as leveraged buyouts or LBOs) that use very high levels of debt, with in some cases as much as 90 per cent of the finance in debt form. How much debt is used in practice will depend on the amount of debt that can be supported by the MBO, given its line of business, perceived risk, existing level of gearing and quality of assets. Typically, the finance for an MBO will be drawn from the following sources:

- *Equity*: the small amounts of ordinary shares issued tend to be bought by the management team itself, except where venture capitalists buy large amounts of equity in the new company. The management team might be reluctant to use a large amount of equity finance, though, because of the loss of control it may bring. Venture capitalists normally look to hold on to their shares in the medium term, selling them off after about five years to realise their investment. Many MBOs therefore have flotation on, say, the Alternative Investment Market as a medium-term goal to provide an *exit route* for venture capitalists.
- *Debt finance*: this can be obtained from sources such as clearing, merchant and overseas banks, in addition to venture capitalists specialising in financing MBOs. Debt finance can take many forms, including term loans and bonds.
- *Mezzanine finance*: this is unsecured debt finance that, while having less risk than ordinary shares, is more risky than secured debt and so offers a return somewhere between the two.

In many cases, major suppliers of finance will require representation at board level because of the large stake they have in the business. While this allows them to have a say in the long-term strategic decisions of the board, they will have no significant interest in the operational aspects of the company.

The difficulties faced by MBOs

As mentioned earlier, suppliers of finance must be convinced that an MBO will be a success. They will therefore consider the quality and expertise of management, the reasons behind the sale of the assets, the prospects of the company and the stake the management team is taking in the venture. They will know that certain types of company and product are more suitable to MBOs than others, for instance those with good cash flows and stable technology.

MBOs will clearly face problems that managers will need to negotiate if their venture is to be successful. A major problem for MBOs when they sever links with their parent is how to provide, internally, services previously provided by the parent. For example, MBOs may have to develop their own financial management and financial accounting systems since their managers, while knowledgeable in the operational areas of their business, may not have the required knowledge and experience in these important financial areas. Other problems are likely to include the following:

- determining a fair price for the MBO: the sale price will be higher than the liquidation value of the division's assets but the final price will be determined by negotiation;
- the complicated tax and legal considerations surrounding the MBO;
- maintaining relationships with previous customers and suppliers;
- generating reinvestment funds if refurbishment or replacement of assets is required;
- maintaining the pension rights of both managers and employees;
- engineering changes in work practices to turn company performance around.

Despite their problems, MBOs play an important role in corporate restructuring strategy. Predictably, the level of MBO activity is influenced by prevailing economic conditions. For example, 2007 saw a record level of MBO activity, with 671 deals totalling £45.9bn being completed in the UK. This shrank in 2008 to 549 deals totalling £19.1bn due to the credit crunch accompanying the global recession in that year. However, with the global economy showing signs of recovery, the UK saw over 100 buyouts worth £10.5bn in the first half of 2015. Despite the uncertainty surrounding Brexit, 2017 saw 181 deals worth £23bn.

11.8 PRIVATE EQUITY

Private equity investors have increasingly become big players in the mergers and acquisitions market in recent years. At the peak of their importance between 2003 and 2004, private equity funds were behind nearly a third of all UK mergers and acquisitions. Private equity investment funds (or financial sponsors) are pooled funds, usually in limited liability partnership form. They are managed by private equity firms which, acting as a general partner, coordinate the raising of private equity funds from a variety of investors, including institutional investors and high net worth individuals. The funds are then used, along with significant amounts of debt financing, to buy a majority stake in firms including **venture capital** investments and management buyouts. The target firm's board are then supplemented with managers from the private equity firm who help manage the company to maximise cash-flow generation with the aim of reselling it in three to five years' time and securing capital gains. Hence they differ from **hedge funds** who tend to invest over the short- to medium term and do not take direct control of the assets and business' they are investing in.

Private equity funds have made headlines due to some high-profile purchases of listed companies which have been taken off the stock market and privatised with the aim of refloating the companies on the stock market later. An example of such a transaction was the purchase of Debenhams in 2003 by a private consortium including CVC Capital Partners and Merrill Lynch Global Private Equity, followed by its refloating in 2006. A year later, in 2007, Alliance Boots plc was approached by New York-based private equity firm Kohlberg Kravis Roberts (KKR). Its £12.4bn offer, formulated in conjunction with Alliance Boots' then executive deputy chairman, Stefano Pessina, resulted in the first FTSE 100 company to be bought out by a private equity firm. KKR sold Alliance Boots to US group Walgreens in December 2014 and the two combined to form Walgreens Boots Alliance Inc.

Private equity funds continue to be major players in the M&A market. According to 2017 rankings, the largest private equity firm in the world was the US-based Blackstone Group with total assets of $34.4bn and assets under management of $434.1bn. As the size of deals continues to increase, private equity funds have looked to pool funds and team up in 'club' deals, which are the focus of Vignette 11.8.

Vignette 11.8

Private equity funds find strength in numbers
Club deals are back in fashion but not all investors are happy

By Javier Espinoza

Private equity groups are again teaming up to buy high-priced businesses in so-called club deals as global investors seek to share the mounting costs as well as the risk of acquiring assets at an uncertain part of the economic cycle in some regions. But while the strategy may make sense for investment managers, clients among the large institutions are becoming concerned. These private equity partnerships can increase exposure to a single deal through different managers, they say, and leave the private equity firms less able to influence the business directly if something goes wrong.

'[We make] majority control private equity investments in North America and Europe,' says Mark Redman, global head of private equity at the Ontario Municipal Employees' Retirement System (OMERS). 'Why specifically majority control? As an investor you need to retain the ability to make meaningful changes effectively, efficiently and quickly. If you invest as part of a club deal it can be significantly harder to do that.'

Club deals were popular during the frenetic years that preceded the financial crisis but fell out of favour when investors – stung by losses incurred in the crash – pushed back to minimise the risk when they were invested in more than one fund. Falling prices helped make one-fund deals more manageable. But some advantages have always been clear for the industry, and in particular at a point in time when prices are again at a level equalling the previous boom. Multiples paid for assets are on average as high as those in the lead up to the financial crisis, according to Preqin, the data provider.

This has led to a resurgence in recent years of deals involving two or more private equity groups. According to Preqin, deals made by two or more private equity firms grew from 247 in 2015 to 270 last year and there have been 160 so far this year.

'Some of the deals are much bigger now and the equity cheques to do this can't be too concentrated on one single transaction,' says Marco Compagnoni, a senior partner at Weil, Gotshal & Manges. 'People are happier working together,' adds Mr Compagnoni. 'You can diversify the deals you do and can do bigger deals.'

Executives point to the success of recent auctions, including the sale of Stada, the German maker of generic Viagra, which was acquired by Cinven and Bain Capital, two buyout funds. After a difficult takeover process, the consortium completed their

Vignette 11.8 (continued)

€4.1bn takeover over the summer, with the deal becoming Europe's largest buyout in four years. Earlier this year, Advent International and Bain Capital signed a deal to buy Concardis, a German payment processing firm, valuing the company at $700m.

Some auctions draw multi-fund consortiums, vying with each other in broad groups. GTCR, Charlesbank Capital Partners, Berkshire Partners and Stonepeak Infrastructure Partners teamed up to bid on a data business unit of CenturyLink, which was eventually sold to a group led by Medica Capital and BC Partners for about $2.8bn.

As private equity groups grow comfortable with club deals again, some are even predicting further bids from three or more groups in the next year. Any loosening of antitrust rules in the US – notwithstanding the specific difficulties experienced by AT&T and Time Warner – could lead to another round of mega deals.

'You had three or four groups partnering in the crisis,' said a London-based banker who has worked on multiple auctions advising private equity firms. 'I can see this going forward because of all the capital that has been raised and the need to deploy it.' Executives at buyout funds say that their chances in forthcoming high-profile, high-price auctions could be improved, even as they seek to spread their bets.

Sanofi, the French drugmaker, is seeking to sell its European generic drug business for about ⊠3bn, drawing interest from a consortium formed by Cinven and Bain Capital. A decision on the buyer is expected in the next few months. Akzo Nobel's specialty chemicals unit is also for sale, with a price expected at about ⊠9bn. Given its size, buyout funds KKR and CVC have teamed up to bid for the asset, people familiar with the move said. The company said it hoped to sell the unit by April next year. Rival consortiums have formed to bid for Unilever's spreads business.

Consortium building is not always easy, however. Private equity owners need to show a united front from the onset or they risk losing out on deals. 'If you look like a strange group of people that got together and cracks start to appear, a seller may decide the bidder is flaky', says Mr Compagnoni.

Club deals have also, in the past, drawn regulatory scrutiny, with accusations that groups have teamed up to bring down asset prices. In 2006, the US Department of Justice, concerned with bid rigging, launched an investigation of private equity firms in relation to their participation in consortiums. Carlyle, Blackstone, TPG collectively paid more than $300m to settled claims without admitting these were true.

Of greater immediate concern is that some club deals have recently gone sour, including the recent collapse of Toys R US, a 69-year old toy retailer owned by a consortium that included KKR and Bain Capital. When filing for bankruptcy, the company attributed its demise partly to 'expensive debt service' and 'unrelenting competition' from online and brick-and-mortar retailers. The collapse led to both private equity groups and Vornado Realty Trust to lose out on the $1.3bn of equity they sank into the retailer. However, the losses were offset by the more than $360m in fees. The investors had disagreed over the timing to sell off the toy seller, according to one person familiar with the situation. KKR and Bain Capital declined to comment.

In light of these risks, large institutional investors are speaking out against club deals, worried that co-owner structures make it less easy to influence a business strategy or the investment exit timetable. Private equity firms need to choose partners wisely and make sure there is alignment both when they buy and sell, say advisers. 'You have to choose your partners very well. Otherwise you can risk falling out in the future when it comes to strategic questions and growth plans,' says a veteran adviser to buyout funds. 'Groups can disagree on when to sell a business because of the different times at which they raise money from investors, for example. Interests need to be aligned.'

 Source: Espinoza, J. (2017) 'Private equity funds find strength in numbers', *Financial Times*, 28 November.
© The Financial Times Limited 2018. All Rights Reserved.

Questions

1 What are the reasons behind the increasing number of 'club' deals in recent times?
2 What are the advantages and disadvantages for private equity groups teaming up to make investments?

11.9 EMPIRICAL RESEARCH ON ACQUISITIONS

Many empirical investigations into the performance of acquisitions have considered the impact of acquisitions on the wealth of the various interest groups involved, although research has reduced over the last few years due to the world recession and the downturn in M&A activity. Between 1971 and 2001 no fewer than 130 such studies were carried out. It is difficult to establish whether acquisitions have been successful, however, as evaluating success or failure involves, in many cases, a series of subjective judgements. In theory, benefits such as economies of scale and synergy are available to companies involved in acquisition. Whether companies manage to crystallise these potential gains in practice is another matter and will depend heavily on post-merger planning and management. Grubb and Lamb (2000) had no such doubts about the benefits of acquisitions, stating that 'the sobering reality is that only about 20 per cent of all mergers really succeed. Most mergers typically erode shareholder wealth.'

There is also a large body of information and research on how companies can increase the chances of successful acquisitions, as well as studies of post-merger integration. De Noble et al. (1988) cite some lessons for merger success, including involving line managers in takeover activity, searching out any hidden costs that takeovers incur, management being aware of the existence of culture differences, and appreciating the vital link between corporate structure and strategy.

The best way to build up a picture of whether acquisitions are beneficial is to identify the stakeholder groups affected and then to consider the evidence regarding the impact of acquisitions on them.

11.9.1 The economy

The key question here is whether acquisitions produce a social gain for the economy as a whole. The answer to this question, in theory, is 'potentially, yes'. This is because the possibility for acquisitions to create an economy-wide gain does exist if acquisitions transfer assets from the control of inefficient managers to the control of efficient managers. Unfortunately, the motives for acquisitions often owe more to managerial self-interest than to more efficient use of assets.

The weight of empirical evidence suggests that acquisitions have at best a neutral effect and that there are no extreme efficiency gains. Cowling et al. (1980) used cost–benefit analysis to examine nine mergers that occurred between 1965 and 1970 in the UK to determine whether increased efficiency through scale economies outweighed welfare loss from increased industrial concentration. They concluded that no real efficiency gains were made and that in the UK, where most takeovers were of a horizontal nature, any such gains were neutralised by increased monopoly power. They did, however, identify benefits in one or two instances where superior management gained control. Subsequent research has echoed the findings of Cowling et al. that the effect of acquisitions on the economy is, by and large, neutral. Although the economic wealth to be shared out between parties may not increase, scope still exists for certain parties to benefit at the expense of others.

11.9.2 The shareholders of the companies involved

The impact of acquisitions can be assessed at a company level by examining their effect on the wealth of acquiring and target company shareholders. Two broad approaches can be used here.

The first method is to use accounting and financial data to compare the performance of companies pre- and post-acquisition. The results of such surveys, including those carried out by Singh (1971) in the UK between 1955 and 1960 and Kelly (1967) in the USA between 1946 and 1960, concluded that acquisitions have proved unprofitable from the acquiring company's viewpoint. It must be noted, however, that the results of such investigations rely heavily on the quality and reliability of the accounting data used.

The second and more commonly used method to quantify the benefits of mergers to the two shareholder groups is to examine pre- and post-bid share prices. Research in this area uses the capital asset pricing model (see Section 8.5) to calculate expected returns for both acquiring and target companies' shares before and after the announcement of a takeover bid. These are then compared with actual returns to allow the identification of any abnormal returns generated during the takeover period.

The results of empirical studies employing this methodology have concluded that *target company shareholders* tend to enjoy significant positive abnormal returns whereas *acquiring company shareholders* experience statistically insignificant negative or positive abnormal returns. Following on from this, many surveys conclude that, in most cases, the gain made by the target company's shareholders outweighed the loss made by the acquiring company. A study by Jensen and Ruback (1983) in the USA showed average abnormal returns to acquiring company shareholders of 4 per cent for successful bids, compared with a 1 per cent loss for failed bids. This contrasted heavily with shareholders of the target company, who on average experienced benefits of 30 per cent for successful bids and losses of 3 per cent for failed bids. In the UK, studies by Firth (1980) and Franks et al. (1988) found that acquiring companies experienced little or no abnormal gain during the takeover period. However, we must not lose sight of the *size* effect. Even if there is a significant improvement in the performance of the target company, the gain will always be less significant in percentage terms when it is spread over the larger share base of the acquiring company.

A likely explanation of the benefits accruing to target company shareholders is that they represent a **bid premium** which must be paid for target company shareholders to be persuaded to part with their shares. The observed lack of benefits to acquiring company shareholders at the time of takeover may be explained by the efficiency of capital markets, i.e. the market predicts takeovers long before they occur and consequently impounds the benefits of the takeover into the acquiring company's share price a number of months before its announcement. This explanation was supported by Franks et al. (1977), who found evidence that the market began to anticipate acquisitions at least three months before they were announced.

Some surveys have considered the abnormal returns of acquiring and target companies over periods starting well before takeovers were made. The results suggest that acquirers, on average, earned positive abnormal returns over these periods whereas their target companies experienced negative abnormal returns. This may give support to the idea that acquisitions facilitate the transfer of assets and resources from less efficient to more efficient management. Traditionally, bid premiums on average have been between 25 per cent and 35 per cent. In their 2017 M&A Report, Boston Consulting Group (BCG) reported average global bid premiums to be 33 per cent. Dimopoulos and Sacchetto (2014) studied a sample of US takeovers between 1988 and 2006 and found that, on average, companies were prepared to pay up to a maximum premium of 81 per cent. They also concluded that pre-emptive bidding reduced this premium while target resistance increased it.

While most empirical studies have tended to reach the same broad conclusion, some have reported more specific findings, which are summarised here:

■ Diversification destroys value whereas increasing focus on core activities conserves value. This conclusion was supported by, among others, Berger and Ofek (1995). Meanwhile, DeLong (2001) found this to be particularly true of takeovers involving banks.
■ Acquisitions aimed at building monopoly power were found by Eckbo (1992) not to enhance acquiring company performance.
■ Cosh et al. (2006) found that acquirers whose CEOs hold a larger proportion of equity shares make acquisitions that perform better in terms of operating performance and long-run returns compared with acquisitions where CEOs have less at stake.
■ Travlos (1987) found that paying for takeovers with shares was more expensive for acquirers than using cash.
■ Rau and Vermaelen (1998) and Sudarsanam and Mahate (2003) concluded that 'glamour-buying' acquiring companies were more likely to destroy wealth compared with acquirers who acquired underperforming target companies.

Concluding this section, empirical studies appear to agree that substantial benefits accrue to target company shareholders. There is less agreement over the benefits to acquiring company shareholders: some surveys found no gains, others found small but statistically insignificant gains and losses. Many surveys concluded that acquisitions are not wealth *creating*, but rather involve the *transfer* of wealth from acquiring company shareholders to target company shareholders.

11.9.3 Managers and employees of acquiring and target companies

It is generally agreed that acquiring company managers benefit from successful takeovers. This is due to the increased power and status of running a larger company, often linked to increased financial rewards. In addition, managers' jobs become more secure as it is more difficult for other companies to acquire the enlarged company. In contrast, target company managers lose out. In most cases they are dismissed, either because they are deemed inefficient or because they are surplus to the acquirer's requirements. The same is true of target company employees, as redundancies tend to follow most acquisitions. An obvious way to achieve scale economies is to streamline business operations by reducing the number of employees in duplicated functions and to close down unwanted parts of the acquired business.

11.9.4 Financial institutions

Financial institutions, predominantly investment banks, are involved in the M&A process as fee-making advisers to both acquiring and target companies. They help in many aspects, from advising on bid values and organising defence tactics, to arranging finance for acquisitions. Wall Street's JP Morgan Chase knocked Goldman Sachs off the top spot for the world's leading financial adviser on M&A in 2008, advising on 350 deals totalling $818bn in value. However, in 2014, Goldman Sachs were back on top, earning fees of just over $2bn (their closest rival Morgan Stanley's earned fees of $1.6bn) and remained there in 2017 with just over a fifth of the market share. Malcolm Glazer's £790m acquisition of Manchester United in 2005 generated advisory and bankers' fees of £22m. Defending takeover bids comes at a price too, as evidenced in the same year by Rentokil paying out £20m in bid defences to a variety of advisers.

11.9.5 Summary of research on acquisitions

The clear winners from acquisitions appear to be target company shareholders, who receive substantial premiums over and above pre-bid share prices. Other parties that benefit from acquisitions are investment banks, lawyers and accountants, who earn substantial fee income from offering advice, and acquiring company managers, who experience increased job security and remuneration. Evidence suggests that little or no benefit arises for acquiring company shareholders, especially when acquisitions are contested and the acquiring company pays over the odds for its target as a result. There appears to be no clear evidence of any general economic benefits of acquisitions; if individual acquisitions transfer assets to more efficient use, however, society will ultimately gain. The clear losers are target company managers and employees, who may well lose their jobs once their company has been acquired.

11.10 CONCLUSION

In this chapter we have given thorough consideration to acquisitions, an area that continues to maintain a high profile in modern corporate finance and has implications for corporate dividend, financing and investment policies. Many justifications have been offered for acquisitions, not all of which have been accepted as valid by academics. The existence of many company valuation methods illustrates the fact that determining a fair price for a target company is a very imprecise activity. The financing implications of takeovers are also far from straightforward and can have serious implications for a company's financial position statement. The methods most commonly used are share-for-share offers, cash offers and mixed bids.

Takeovers can take months to complete, especially if the target company considers the bid to be hostile and tries to repel it, and once completed, acquiring company shareholders rarely benefit from the acquisitions. This is not only because of the substantial bid premiums paid but also because acquiring companies fail to obtain the expected post-acquisition benefits. These benefits tend not to materialise due to the difficulties faced by the acquirer in successfully integrating the assets of the two companies. Parties that do tend to gain from acquisitions are acquiring company managers and target company shareholders.

On the opposite side of the takeover coin is divestment. If used sensibly, companies can use divestment to increase shareholders' wealth. Acquiring companies often follow acquisitions with a series of divestments as they sell off parts of the target company that do not figure in their long-term plans. There are three major divestment strategies: sell-offs, spin-offs and management buyouts. The choice of strategy depends very much on the individual circumstances involved.

■ ■ ■ KEY POINTS

1   Acquisitions have significant effects on companies' assets and financial structures.

2   Acquisitions tend to be far more common than mergers owing to the relative sizes of the companies involved.

3   Acquisitions can be classified as vertical, horizontal or conglomerate.

4   The motives put forward by companies to justify acquisitions can be economic, financial and managerial in nature.

5   Economies of scale and synergy are the economic benefits most frequently cited to justify acquisitions, especially those that are horizontal in nature.

6   When a company is considering an acquisition it is important for it to consider the associated costs and disadvantages as well as the benefits.

7   Acquisitions tend to come in waves, usually coinciding with booms in the economy and times of high corporate liquidity.

8   An accurate valuation of the target company is crucial to the success of an acquisition.

9   The two broad approaches to valuing a company are based either on the value of the assets of the company or on the income associated with owning those assets.

10 The most common ways for companies to finance acquisitions are by using share-for-share offers, cash offers or mixed offers.

11 It is important that companies consider the implications of their financing method on their shareholders' wealth, their level of gearing, their liquidity and their ownership structure.

12 Companies must understand the regulatory framework governing acquisitions.

13 Strategic and tactical aspects of acquisitions play an important part in determining whether bids are successful.

14 Target companies have many ways of defending themselves after an unwanted takeover bid has been received. A better strategy, though, is to use constructive pre-bid defences to dissuade potential acquirers from making a bid in the first place.

15 A company can increase the wealth of its shareholders through a well-thought-out divestment strategy.

16 Companies should dispose of underperforming and peripheral businesses through a spin-off, a sell-off or a management buyout.

17 An increasing number of mergers and acquisitions are financed by funding provided by private equity firms.

18 Empirical evidence suggests that acquisitions have a neutral effect on the economy, while benefiting target company shareholders and acquiring company managers.

SELF-TEST QUESTIONS

Answers to these questions can be found on pages 466–7.

1 Outline briefly the economic reasons used to justify acquisitions.

2 Outline briefly the financial reasons used to justify acquisitions.

3 Why might growth by acquisition not be in the best interests of a company?

4 Explain why acquisitions occur in waves.

5 Discuss the use of the price/earnings ratio and dividend growth methods of determining the value of a target company.

6 Explain why the DCF valuation method is preferred by academics and identify the practical difficulties in using this method.

7 Discuss briefly the advantages and disadvantages of financing a takeover by an issue of convertible bonds.

8 Describe briefly four defences that a company can use after it has received a takeover bid.

9 Explain why a company may wish to divest part of its operations.

10 Describe briefly some of the important contributing factors which explain why shareholders of acquiring companies rarely benefit from takeovers.

QUESTIONS FOR REVIEW

1 Explain the major justifications likely to be put forward to explain the following types of acquisitions:

(a) horizontal acquisitions;

(b) vertical backwards and forwards acquisitions;

(c) conglomerate acquisitions.

2 Restwell plc, a hotel and leisure company, is planning to take over a smaller private limited company, Staygood Ltd, and needs to place a value on the company. Restwell has gathered the following data:

Restwell	
Weighted average cost of capital	12%
Price/earnings ratio	12
Shareholders' cost of equity	15%
Staygood	
Current dividend payment	27p
Past five years' dividend payments	15p, 17p, 18p, 21p, 23p
Current EPS	37p
Number of ordinary shares in issue	5m

It is estimated that the cost of equity of Staygood is 20 per cent higher (in relative terms) than the cost of equity of Restwell, owing to the higher risk of Staygood's operations. Restwell estimates that cash flows at the end of the first year will be £2.5m and these will grow at an annual rate of 5 per cent. Restwell also expects to raise £5m in two years' time by selling off hotels of Staygood that are surplus to its needs.

Given the earlier information, estimate values for Staygood using the following valuation methods:

(a) price/earnings ratio valuation;

(b) dividend growth model;

(c) discounted cash flow valuation.

3 Carsley plc and Powell plc are planning to merge to form Stimac plc. It has been agreed that Powell's shareholders will accept three shares in Carsley for every share in Powell they hold. Other details are as follows:

	Carsley plc	Powell plc
Number of shares	40m	10m
Annual earnings	£10m	£5.8m
P/E ratio	8	10

Post-merger annual earnings of the enlarged company are expected to be 8 per cent higher than the sum of the earnings of each of the companies before the merger, due to scale economies and other benefits. The P/E ratio of Stimac plc is expected to be 9.

Determine the extent to which the shareholders of Powell will benefit from the proposed merger.

4 What are the major considerations that an acquiring company must consider when deciding how to finance a proposed takeover?

5 It is currently 1 January 20X4 and Lissom plc is looking to divest itself of one of its subsidiaries to focus on its core business activities. Financial information relevant to the divestment is given below. Lissom plc has been negotiating the disposal with the subsidiary's current management team.

Revenue and profit after tax of the subsidiary over the last four years:

Year ending December:	20X0	20X1	20X2	20X3
Revenue (£m)	40.0	41.6	42.8	43.7
Profit after tax (£m)	6.0	6.2	6.3	6.3

Other financial information:

Current liquidation value of subsidiary	£42m
Cost of capital of Lissom plc	14%
Long-term debt of subsidiary	£10m of 13% bonds repayable in 20X6

(a) Using the information provided, determine a purchase price for the subsidiary that could be acceptable to both Lissom plc and the management buyout team. All relevant supporting calculations must be shown.

(b) Discuss any financial aspects of the proposed buyout that you feel should be brought to the attention of the management buyout team.

(c) Discuss the stages that will theoretically be followed by the management buyout of the subsidiary of Lissom plc.

(d) Critically discuss the financing of management buyouts.

QUESTIONS FOR DISCUSSION

1 The board of Hanging Valley plc wishes to take over Rattling Creek Ltd. Financial data relating to the two companies is shown below.

	Hanging Valley plc	Rattling Creek Ltd
Profit before interest and tax	£420,000	£200,000
Ordinary share dividends	6.9p	14.0p
Corporate tax rate	35%	35%

Financial position statement extracts:

	Hanging Valley plc	Rattling Creek Ltd
Non-current assets	1,750,000	800,000
Current assets	800,000	500,000
Total assets	2,550,000	1,300,000
Equity		
Ordinary shares (£1)	1,500,000	500,000
Reserves	600,000	400,000
	2,100,000	900,000
10% bonds	N/A	200,000
Current liabilities	450,000	200,000
Total liabilities	2,550,000	1,300,000

Hanging Valley's earnings and dividends have been increasing at 15 per cent per year in recent times, while over the same period the earnings and dividends of Rattling Creek have remained static. The current market price of Hanging Valley's ordinary shares is £1.60. The board of Hanging Valley believes that Rattling Creek shareholders will accept a share-for-share offer of four shares in Hanging Valley for every five shares in Rattling Creek.

(a) Using three different valuation methods, determine the effect on the wealth of Hanging Valley plc's shareholders if Rattling Creek Ltd's shareholders accept the proposed share-for-share offer.

(b) Critically discuss the economic reasons why one company looks to take over another.

2 Two companies, Blur plc and Oasis plc, are considering a merger. Financial data for the two companies is given below:

	Blur	Oasis
Number of shares issued	3m	6m
Profit after tax	£1.8m	£0.5m
Price/earnings ratio	12.0	10.3

The two companies have estimated that, due to economies of scale, the newly merged company would generate cost savings of £200,000 per year.

(a) It is suggested initially that 100 per cent of Oasis's shares should be exchanged for shares in Blur at a rate of one share in Blur for every three shares in Oasis. What would be the expected reduction of EPS from the point of view of Blur's shareholders?

(b) An alternative is for Blur's shares to be valued at £7.20 and for the total share capital of Oasis to be valued at £10.5m for merger purposes. A percentage of Oasis's shares would be exchanged for shares in Blur, while the remaining shares of Oasis would be exchanged for 6.5 per cent bonds (issued at £100 nominal value) in the new company. Given that the corporate tax rate is 30 per cent, how much would have to be raised from the bond issue as part of the purchase consideration for there to be no dilution of EPS from Blur's existing shareholders' point of view?

3 The managing directors of Wrack plc are considering what value to place on Trollope plc, a company which they are planning to take over shortly. Wrack plc's share price is currently £4.21 and the company's earnings per share is 29p. Wrack's WACC is 12 per cent.

The board estimates that annual after-tax synergy benefits resulting from the takeover will be £5m, that Trollope's distributable earnings will grow at an annual rate of 2 per cent and that duplication will allow the sale of £25m of assets, net of corporate tax (currently standing at 30 per cent), in a year's time. Information referring to Trollope plc:

Financial position statement extracts

	£m
Non-current assets	296
Current assets	70
Total assets	366
Equity	
Ordinary shares (£1)	156
Reserves	75
	231
7% bonds	83
Current liabilities	52
Total liabilities	366

Statement of profit or loss extracts

	£m
Profit before interest and tax	76.0
Interest payments	8.3
Profit before tax	67.7
Taxation	20.3
Distributable earnings	47.4

Other information:

Current ex div share price	£2.25
Latest dividend per share payment	16p
Past four years' dividend payments	13p, 13.5p, 14p, 15p
Trollope's equity beta	1.15
Treasury bill yield	5%
Return of the market	12%

(a) Given the above information, calculate the value of Trollope plc using the following valuation methods:
  (i)   price/earnings ratio;
  (ii) dividend valuation method;
  (iii) discounted cash flow method.

(b) Discuss the problems associated with using the above valuation techniques. Which of the values would you recommend the board of Wrack to use?

(c) Critically discuss which factors will influence a company to finance a takeover by either a share-for-share offer or a cash offer financed by an issue of bonds.

4 Goldblade plc is about to launch a bid for Membrane plc. Both companies are in the light manufacturing industry. Goldblade plc is currently deciding how it will go about financing the takeover. You are provided with information on the two companies below:

Statements of profit or loss extracts

	Goldblade plc £m	Membrane plc £m
Profit before interest and tax	122	48
Interest payments	49	18
Profit before tax	73	30
Corporate tax (at 30%)	22	9
Profit after tax	51	21
Dividends	18	8
Retained profit	33	13

Financial position statements extracts

	Goldblade plc £m	Membrane plc £m
Non-current assets	508	228
Current assets		
Inventory	82	34
Trade receivables	66	30

	Goldblade plc £m	Membrane plc £m
Cash	59	25
Total assets	715	317
Equity finance		
Ordinary shares (50p)	80	46
Reserves	144	86
	224	132
Long-term bank loans	353	121
Current liabilities	138	64
Total liabilities	715	317
Current share price	£3.65	£2.03
Year low:	£3.12	£1.85
Year high:	£3.78	£2.47
Average industry gearing:	40%	

(debt divided by debt plus equity; equity at market value, debt at book value)

Goldblade expects that to secure a controlling share in Membrane it will have to offer a premium of 20 per cent on the current market price of Membrane's shares. Goldblade's long-run cost of borrowing is 10 per cent. The company is considering whether to finance the deal using a share-for-share offer or a cash offer.

(a) If the takeover is to be financed by a share-for-share offer, advise Goldblade plc on what form the offer should take and the number of shares it will issue.

(b) Using the information available, critically evaluate whether a cash offer or a share-for-share offer would be more appropriate for Goldblade plc.

5 Magnet plc is in the process of divesting part of its operations via a proposed management buyout (MBO). The buyout team is currently looking for venture capital to finance the MBO. They have agreed a price of £25m with Magnet and have proposed that the financing will involve their putting up £5m of their personal funds to purchase an equity stake in the business with the remaining funds (£20m) coming from the venture capitalist in the form of long-term unsecured mezzanine debt finance.

The venture capitalist has indicated that it will require an interest rate on its debt investment of 11 per cent given that its finance will be unsecured. The four members of the MBO team have indicated that they intend to draw an annual salary of £150,000 each. The MBO team has just presented the venture capitalist company with the following five-year cash-flow predictions (excluding directors' salaries), which they consider to be on the pessimistic side:

Year	1	2	3	4	5
Predicted sales	£6.78m	£6.82m	£7.23m	£7.51m	£8.02m
Cash outflows	£3.39m	£3.34m	£3.47m	£3.53m	£3.84m
Reinvestment			£1.5m		

The new entity will pay corporate tax at a rate of 20 per cent in the year that profits arise. The reinvestment of £1.5m in Year 3 will not qualify for capital allowances.

Using this information, critically evaluate whether the proposed MBO is viable from a cash-flow perspective in light of the two parties' financial requirements and the predicted sales and costs. Support your answer with appropriate calculations.

References

Berger, P. and Ofek, E. (1995) 'Diversification's effect on firm value', *Journal of Financial Economics,* vol. 37, pp. 39–65.

Boston Consulting Group (2017) *The 2017 M&A Report: The Technology Takeover,* September, Boston, MA: Boston Consulting Group.

Comment, R. and Jarrell, G. (1995) 'Corporate focus and stock returns', *Journal of Financial Economics,* vol. 37, pp. 67–87.

Cosh, A., Guest, P. and Hughes, A. (2006) 'Board share-ownership and takeover performance', *Journal of Business Finance and Accounting,* vol. 33, nos 3–4, pp. 459–510.

Cowling, K., Stoneman, P., Cubbin, J., Cable, J., Hall, G. and Dutton, P. (1980) *Mergers and Economic Performance,* Cambridge: Cambridge University Press.

DeLong, G. (2001) 'Stockholder gains from focusing versus diversifying bank mergers', *Journal of Financial Economics,* vol. 59, pp. 221–52.

De Noble, A., Gustafson, L. and Hergert, M. (1988) 'Planning for post-merger integration: eight lessons for merger success', *Long Range Planning,* vol. 2, no. 4, pp. 82–5.

Dimopoulos, T., and Sacchetto, S. (2014) 'Pre-emptive bidding, target resistance and takeover premiums', *Journal of Financial Economics,* vol. 114, no. 3, pp. 444–70.

Eckbo, B.E. (1992) 'Mergers and the value of antitrust deterrence', *Journal of Finance,* vol. 47, pp. 1005–29.

Firth, M. (1980) 'Takeovers, shareholders' returns and the theory of the firm', *Quarterly Journal of Economics,* vol. 94, no. 2, March, pp. 235–60.

Franks, J., Broyles, J. and Hecht, M. (1977) 'An industry study of the profitability of mergers in the United Kingdom', *Journal of Finance,* vol. 32, December, pp. 1513–25.

Franks, J., Harris, R. and Mayer, C. (1988) 'Means of payment in takeovers: results for the UK and US', in Avernick, M. (ed.) *Corporate Takeovers: Causes and Consequences,* Chicago Il: University of Chicago Press.

Grubb, M. and Lamb, R. (2000) *Capitalize on Merger Chaos,* New York: Free Press.

Jensen, M. (1993) 'The takeover controversy: analysis and evidence', in Chew, D. (ed.) *The New Corporate Finance: Where Theory Meets Practice,* New York: McGraw-Hill.

Jensen, M. and Ruback, R. (1983) 'The market for corporate control: the scientific evidence', *Journal of Financial Economics,* vol. 11, pp. 5–50.

Kelly, E. (1967) *The Profitability of Growth Through Mergers,* Pennsylvania, PA: Pennsylvania State University.

Rau, P. and Vermaelen, T. (1998) 'Glamour, value and the post-acquisition performance of acquiring firms', *Journal of Financial Economics,* vol. 49, no. 2, pp. 223–53.

Singh, A. (1971) *Takeovers: Their Relevance to the Stock Market and the Theory of the Firm,* Cambridge: Cambridge University Press.

Sudarsanam, S. and Mahate, A. (2003) 'Glamour acquirers, method of payment and post-acquisition performance: the UK evidence', *Journal of Business Finance and Accounting,* vol. 30, nos 1 and 2, pp. 299–341.

Travlos, N. (1987) 'Corporate takeover bids, method of payment, and bidding firms' stock returns', *Journal of Finance,* vol. 42, September, pp. 943–63.

Recommended reading

For a book totally dedicated to the topic of mergers and takeovers with a UK focus see:

Sudarsanam, S. (2010) *Creating Value from Mergers and Acquisitions,* 2nd edn, Harlow: FT Prentice-Hall.

For an up-to-date advanced book on mergers and takeovers with a US focus see:

Gaughan, P. (2018) *Mergers, Acquisitions and Corporate Restructurings,* 7th edn, Hoboken, NJ: John Wiley and Sons Inc.

For a book that takes you through the M&A process step-by-step see:

Moeller, S. and Brady, C. (2014) *Intelligent M&A: Navigating the Mergers and Acquisitions Minefield,* 2nd edn, Chichester, West Sussex: John Wiley and Sons Ltd.

For a book wholly focused on the valuation of companies see:

Koller, T., Goedhart, M. and Wessels, D. (2015) *Valuation: Measuring and Managing the Value of Companies,* 6th edn, Hoboken, NJ: John Wiley and Sons Inc.

The following book collects together a series of readable and interesting articles on mergers and takeovers and helps to bridge the gap between theory and practice:

Faulkner, D., Teerikangas, S. and Joseph, R. (eds) (2014) *The Handbook of Mergers and Acquisitions,* Oxford: Oxford University Press.

The following article gives an excellent summary and overview of the research done into the success of mergers and takeovers:

Bruner, R. (2002) 'Does M&A pay? A review of the evidence for the decision-maker', *Journal of Applied Finance,* vol. 12, pp. 48–68.

Important and informative papers and articles recommended for further reading include the following:

Benzie, R. (1989) 'Takeover activity in the 1980s', *Bank of England Quarterly Bulletin,* vol. 29, pp. 78–85.

Borstadt, L., Zwirlein, T. and Brickley, J. (1991) 'Defending against hostile takeovers: impact on shareholder wealth', *Managerial Finance,* vol. 17, no. 1, pp. 25–33.

Ravenscraft, D. (1991) 'Gains and losses from mergers: the evidence', *Managerial Finance,* vol. 17, no. 1, pp. 8–13.

Severiens, T. (1991) 'Creating value through mergers and acquisitions: some motivations', *Managerial Finance,* vol. 17, no. 1, pp. 3–7.

Sudarsanam, P.S. (1991) 'Defensive strategies of target firms in UK contested takeovers', *Managerial Finance,* vol. 17, no. 6, pp. 47–56.

Useful websites giving information on UK antitrust legislation and UK bid regulation, respectively, are: *http://www.gov.uk/cma* and *http://www.thetakeoverpanel.org.uk*

The website for the Mergers and Acquisitions Research Centre (MARC) at Cass Business School, London, provides a useful hub for up-to-date M&A news and research: *http://www.cass.city.ac.uk/research-and-faculty/centres/marc*

12 RISK MANAGEMENT

Learning objectives

After studying this chapter, you should have achieved the following learning objectives:

- an understanding of the theoretical and practical issues relating to interest rate and exchange rate risk;
- an understanding of the internal and external methods of managing interest rate and exchange rate risk;
- the ability to select and evaluate appropriate risk management techniques according to the nature of the risk being faced;
- an appreciation of the benefits and costs of risk management techniques;
- an understanding of the significance of political risk to a company.

■ ■ ■ INTRODUCTION

Exchange rate and interest rate risk management are of key importance to companies that operate internationally or that use debt finance. Many currencies float freely against each other and exchange rates can be volatile as a result. The need for hedging interest rate risk arises from the size and complexity of company borrowing.

In this chapter we consider the different types of exchange rate and interest rate risk that companies face. We also consider the techniques available to control and manage such risk, including the increasingly complex derivatives available for external hedging of interest and exchange rate exposures. At the end of the chapter we consider the issue of political risk and how companies investing internationally can manage this type of risk.

12.1 INTEREST AND EXCHANGE RATE RISK

Companies are increasingly aware of the potential benefits of managing or hedging their interest and exchange rate risk exposures. The recent global financial crisis and uncertainty surrounding Brexit have further focused the minds of corporate treasurers on the issue of risk management. The importance of hedging to companies depends largely on the magnitude of the potential losses that may result from unfavourable movements in interest and exchange rates. With interest rate exposures, the magnitude of such losses depends on the volatility of interest rates, the level of companies' gearing and the proportion of floating rate corporate debt. Short-term interest rate yields were relatively volatile during the 1970s and 1980s, as shown in Figure 12.1, and the need for companies to manage their interest rate exposures consequentially increased. Figure 12.1 also shows that interest rates peaked in 1989 and 1990, declined in the period to 1993 and stabilised in the period 1993–2008 at between 4 and 7 per cent. One could be forgiven for dismissing the importance of

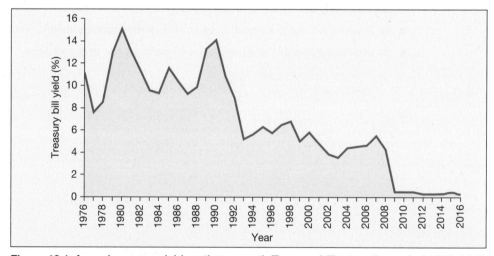

Figure 12.1 Annual average yield on three-month Treasury bills over the period 1976–2016
Source: Bank of England. © Crown Copyright 2017. Reproduced by permission of the Bank of England.

interest rate risk to companies, given the move to low interest rates that prevailed from 2008, which saw three-month sterling London Interbank Offered Rates (LIBOR) eventually settle below 0.5 per cent (with a negative real rate of interest). But to twist an old saying, whatever goes down must go up! A very significant development in UK interest rates is the phasing-out of LIBOR by the Financial Conduct Authority (FCA) by the end of 2021. This is in response to the rate-fixing scandal that came to light in 2012 and showed LIBOR to be both unsustainable and unreliable. The implications of this are the focus of Vignette 12.1.

Vignette 12.1

Alternatives to Libor begin to make an impact

Large institutions have already issued bonds linked to new benchmarks such as Sofr and Sonia

By Joe Rennison

It was during the US financial industry's sleepy summer months, when traders were heading to their vacation homes, that a seismic shift in global financial markets started to be felt.

After years of consultation between industry groups and regulators, plans to develop an alternative benchmark interest rate to the now disgraced London Interbank Offered Rate, or Libor, were swinging into motion.

In July, US government mortgage agency Fannie Mae issued $6bn of bonds linked to a new interest rate called the Secured Overnight Financing Rate (Sofr). The World Bank followed in August with a $1bn issuance and Credit Suisse became the first commercial bank to issue debt tied to Sofr. "The recent issuance has really spurred the market into action," says Mark Cabana, an interest rate analyst at Bank of America Merrill Lynch. "It lit a fire under the seat of those market participants that were not yet able to transact in Sofr to get their systems up to speed. If we continue to see Sofr issuance grow, that will only further advance efforts to move away from Libor." George Richardson, director of capital markets for the World Bank, puts it more bluntly: "The switch to Sofr is going to happen."

Different regions across the globe are following suit, developing their own new reference rates. In the UK, Lloyds Banking Group sold $750m of debt pegged to the reformed interest rate benchmark Sonia, weeks after the European Investment Bank pioneered its use to sell a $1bn bond.

Recommended Benchmark reform Banker warns of Herculean task to escape Libor's tentacles "It gives a sense of the potential," says Chris Conetta, head of US rates cash trading at Barclays.

Libor was disgraced after a rigging scandal that has seen bankers across the industry jailed and fined. Part of the problem stemmed from the lack of actual transactions tied to the interest rate. Despite underpinning the interest payments on trillions of dollars worth of loans, derivatives and other securities, the interest rate itself has been largely a gauge of big banks' borrowing costs curated from banks' own estimates of what it would cost them to borrow cash, rather than real transactions.

The Sofr rate is a broad measure of the cost of borrowing cash overnight secured against Treasury securities, based on real transactions.

Even as Libor-linked transaction volumes have continued to decline, the benchmark remains interwoven with the fabric of capital markets and the way institutions borrow and lend money. In the US alone, Libor underpins $200tn worth of financial contracts — predominantly derivatives, according to the Alternative Reference Rates Committee, an industry group set up by the Federal Reserve to explore alternative reference rates in the US.

It is so pervasive that after the World Bank issued its Sofr-linked swap, it used a derivative to in effect change the interest it paid back to Libor. "It goes to the core of the problem," said Subadra Rajappa, head of US interest rate strategy at Société Générale. "The DNA of the financial system has to ultimately switch over to Sofr."

Vignette **12.1** (continued)

Despite such views among many in the industry, obstacles remain. It is not yet clear how long Libor will be around. UK regulators have said they will not compel banks to keep submitting to Libor after 2021. If enough banks continue after that date, there will be less urgency to move to Sofr. Instead, they can simply let existing Libor-linked contracts mature before replacing them with contracts linked to Sofr.

But if Libor vanishes more quickly then another question arises: what happens to contracts that reference a defunct interest rate? Industry groups are working on "fallback language" to introduce a way for a current Libor contract to reference a new rate if Libor stops being published.

In advance of these details being finalised, it is hard for institutions to determine whether it is economically optimal to begin using Sofr now or whether it is more beneficial to wait. "I don't think many people feel overly compelled to change away from Libor just yet," says Mr Cabana. "Once these issues get resolved they will be in a better position to make that decision."

But optimism remains. Investor appetite for the recent bonds tied to new interest rates was strong. Barclays, which became the second bank to issue debt tied to Sofr, having also underwritten the Fannie Mae deal, initially planned to issue up to $100m of debt but ended up selling $525m because of investor demand, according to people familiar with the transaction.

New derivatives contracts have also seen a rapid uptake, with further developments expected before the end of the year. Trading activity begets more trading activity, with more bonds requiring more use of derivatives, and more derivatives volume making it easier to sell bonds, says Ms Rajappa.

Mr Conetta also expects Sofr to grow. "Based on the investor demand that we have seen for the transactions we have participated in and the number of conversations that have occurred as a result of these transactions, I would anticipate there is a very robust pipeline of issuance that should be expected going forward," he says.

 Source: Rennison, J. (2018) 'Alternatives to Libor begin to make an impact', *Financial Times*, 1 October.
© The Financial Times Limited 2018. All Rights Reserved.

Questions

1 Why is LIBOR being phased out by the Financial Conduct Authority (FCA)?

2 What are the implications of the demise of LIBOR for companies when trying to manage interest rate risk?

Exchange rate risk has increased greatly since the early 1970s, when the collapse of the Bretton Woods exchange rate system led the major currencies to float against each other. This is illustrated clearly by Figure 12.2, which shows the volatility of sterling–dollar exchange rates over the period 1962–2018. Furthermore, continuing growth of world trade means that virtually all companies are now involved in some transactions denominated in a foreign currency. The UK plays a major role in foreign exchange activity, accounting for 36.9 per cent of the global market in 2016 (compared with 19.5 per cent for the USA). According to the Bank for International Settlements (2016) the daily turnover for the year to April 2016 was $5.07tn, with $1.65tn in spot transactions and $3.42tn in forward and derivative-based transactions. Increasing exchange rate risk and growing world trade mean that foreign exchange risk management has become increasingly important to companies. Adverse exchange rate movements that are not hedged can wipe out profits on foreign currency deals or cause a company financial

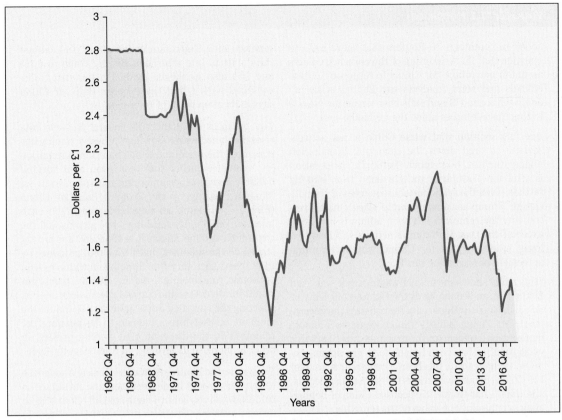

Figure 12.2 Quarterly average sterling–dollar exchange rate over the period 1962–2018

Source: Bank of England. © Crown Copyright 2018. Reproduced by permission of the Bank of England.

Vignette 12.2

Trade dispute teeters on verge of currency war as Trump weighs in

US president accuses China of manipulating renminbi to gain trade advantage

By Gabriel Wildau

After suffering its worst month ever in June, China's currency has continued its descent. The renminbi hit its lowest point for a year against the dollar on Friday, and overall has lost more than 5 per cent against the greenback since the start of last month.

The question being asked – in the Oval Office and beyond – is whether the currency's slide is an effort by Beijing to open up a second front in Donald Trump's trade battle with China and transform it into a currency war.

On Friday, the same day that the US president reiterated his threat to impose tariffs on all of China's $500bn imports to his country, Mr Trump took to Twitter to criticise 'China, the EU and others [for] manipulating their currencies and interest rates lower'. Steven Mnuchin, US Treasury secretary,

➡

added in comments to Reuters that there was 'no question that the weakening of the currency creates an unfair advantage' for China. In response Chinese officials and some analysts say Beijing is simply doing what the US and IMF have urged for years – letting market forces guide the exchange rate.

But they caution that while China is not actively seeking to drag down the renminbi, Washington underestimates how much Beijing's co-operation is vital for preventing the currency from sinking further, given the economic consequences of the policies Mr Trump has already put in place. One big reason why the renminbi has been falling is investors' expectations that Mr Trump's actions will lead to a lower trade surplus for China, whether through agreement or escalating tariffs.

'This really shows the folly of waging trade war,' said Zhang Bin, an economist at the Chinese Academy of Social Sciences, a think-tank that advises the government. Mr Zhang added: 'China wants to promote market-based reform [of the exchange rate]. Isn't this what America has been hoping for?' The dollar–renminbi exchange rate has been a contentious issue in US–China economic relations for more than a decade, and the US has frequently accused China of deliberately suppressing the value of the renminbi.

After Beijing ended the renminbi's strict peg to the dollar in 2005, the currency appreciated by 37 per cent against the greenback before hitting an all-time high of 6.03 in early 2014. The IMF declared in 2015 that the renminbi was 'no longer undervalued' and other issues such as disputes over technology, investment barriers and tariffs have become more prominent sources of Washington-Beijing tension.

But the currency's weakness still touches a raw nerve in the US – as has become clear after its

renewed slide. The renminbi fell 0.3 per cent against the dollar in late afternoon Beijing trade to 6.788 and has also weakened against a broader, trade-weighted basket that the People's Bank of China says is its main point of reference.

The prospect of further US Federal Reserve rate rises combined with a slowing Chinese economy has pressured the renminbi, which had shown remarkable resilience earlier this year, even as a surging dollar battered other emerging market currencies. Monetary easing by the People's Bank of China (PBoC) – including an unprecedented $72bn cash injection on Monday morning – has also fuelled the renminbi's decline. Meanwhile, the PBoC has mostly stayed on the sidelines, apart from oral guidance by PBoC party secretary Guo Shuqing, in which he said economic fundamentals did not justify persistent renminbi weakness and warned speculators against shorting the currency. Some analysts say that at the moment market forces happen to be pushing the renminbi in the direction that Beijing prefers, in order to increase its leverage in trade negotiations.

They note the contrast between Beijing's response to the recent bout of depreciation and its stance in 2015-16, when the central bank sold off about $1tn in foreign exchange reserves to protect the renminbi and punish speculators.

'The big story in China's exchange rate policy is how little they've intervened,' said David Loevinger, former senior co-ordinator for China affairs at the US Treasury and managing director of emerging markets sovereign research at TCW Group in Los Angeles. 'I think PBoC is most pleased that they don't have to repeat the mistakes of 2015 when they were forced to blow hundreds of billions of reserves propping up the [renminbi].'

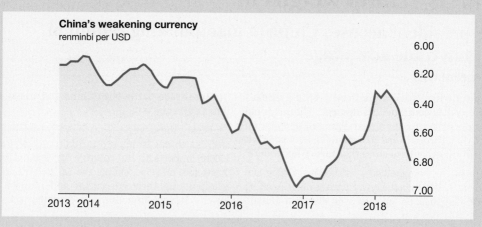

China's weakening currency
renminbi per USD

Vignette **12.2** (continued)

Such commentators caution that Chinese officials are unlikely to actively encourage weakness, since doing so would risk sparking another de-stabilising bout of capital flight. While Beijing has tightened capital controls since 2016, reducing the risk of uncontrolled outflows, a shift in market sentiment would still put the PBoC in an unpleasant position. Foreign exchange reserves are now at $3.1tn, down from nearly $4tn at their peak in 2014. That leaves the central bank with less ammunition to defend the currency than in 2015–16, given the desire to hold reserves above $3tn.

The little PBoC market intervention that has taken place in recent weeks has been aimed at preventing renminbi depreciation from spiralling into panic selling. 'The PBoC has been seeking to temper depreciation rather than encourage declines,' Capital Economics wrote in a note.

Source: Wildau, G. (2018) 'Trade dispute teeters on verge of currency war as Trump weighs in', *Financial Times*, 23 July. © The Financial Times Limited 2018. All Rights Reserved.

Questions

1 Why has the value of the Renminbi fallen against the dollar over the first half of 2018?

2 What are the implications for China and the US of this exchange rate movement?

distress. The increased visibility of foreign exchange gains and losses has also been cited as a reason for the increasing importance of exchange rate risk management (Demirag and Goddard 1994). The issue of changes in the exchange rate between the US dollar and the Chinese yuan and their implications are considered in Vignette 12.2.

One of the easiest ways to understand interest and exchange rate management is to see them as a form of insurance, whereby companies insure themselves against adverse exchange movements and interest rate movements in the same way that individuals insure themselves against personal injury or loss of personal possessions.

12.1.1 Interest rate risk

The form of interest rate risk most commonly faced by a company is that associated with having a high proportion of floating rate debt. One consequence of interest rate volatility in this case is that forecasting and planning future cash flows becomes more difficult. More seriously, a company with a high proportion of floating rate debt will be afraid of interest rates increasing sharply, as significantly higher interest payments will have an adverse effect on cash flow and will increase *financial risk*. In extreme cases, a sharp increase in interest rates may increase the likelihood of bankruptcy (financial risk and bankruptcy risk are discussed in Chapter 9).

A company with a high proportion of fixed rate debt will also face interest rate risk. Here the concern is that interest rates may *fall* sharply in the future. The commitment to fixed interest payments will lead to loss of competitive advantage compared with companies whose debt is primarily at floating rates. Such competitors will pay less interest, increasing the profitability of existing operations, and they will experience a fall in their cost of capital due to decreasing financial risk, increasing the number of attractive projects open to them in the future.

Interest rate risk is not faced solely by companies with debt liabilities but also by companies with debt investments. For example, a company with surplus cash invested on the money markets at a floating interest rate faces the risk of interest rates falling, while a company that has purchased fixed interest rate bonds faces the risk of interest rates rising.

In reality, interest rate risk may not be quite as obvious as in the examples considered so far. **Basis risk** and **gap exposure** represent more subtle types of interest rate risk exposure that companies may encounter.

Basis risk

A company may have assets and liabilities of similar sizes, both with floating interest rates, and so will both receive and pay interest. At first sight it may not appear to have any interest rate risk exposure. However, if the two floating rates are not determined using the same basis (e.g. one is linked to LIBOR, but the other is not), it is unlikely that they will move perfectly in line with each other: as one rate increases, the other rate might change by a different amount.

Gap exposure

Even more subtle is the situation where a company has assets and liabilities which are matched in terms of size, and where the floating interest rates on each are determined on the same basis, for example, by reference to LIBOR. It is still possible for interest rate risk to exist as the rates on loans may be revised on a three-monthly basis, whereas the rates on assets may be revised on a six-monthly basis.

12.1.2 Spot and forward rates

Before we consider the different types of exchange rate risk we need to discuss *exchange rates* themselves. In practice, many exchange rates exist, not only the buy and sell rates between different currencies, but also for the same currency over different time horizons. The different rates can be illustrated by considering the exchange rate between sterling and the dollar:

$ spot rate	1.7368–1.7372
One-month $ forward rate	1.7445–1.7455
Three-month $ forward rate	1.7580–1.7597

The *spot rate* refers to the rate of exchange if buying or selling the currency immediately. The higher of the two spot rates (1.7372) is the *buy rate* (the dollars you have to give up to receive one pound), whereas the lower spot rate (1.7368) is the *sell rate* (the dollars you receive for giving up one pound). The difference between the two spot rates is called the *spread*. The spread for frequently traded major currencies is often *very* narrow.

The rates below the spot rate are called *forward rates* and these allow the fixing of buy and sell rates for settlement and delivery at a specific date in the future. The forward rates are in fact a consensus estimate of the future spot rate, and their accuracy depends on how efficiently the foreign exchange market forecasts future spot rates.

Forward rates can be at either a *premium* or a *discount* to the current spot rate. In our example, the one- and three-month rates are higher than the spot rate. Because the future value of the dollar is expected to be less, the forward rates are at a discount to the current spot rate. We can therefore see that the foreign exchange market is expecting an *appreciation* of the pound against the dollar (i.e. the market expects that you will be able to buy more dollars for each pound in the future).

12.1.3 What is meant by exchange rate risk?

Exchange rate risk can be divided into **transaction risk**, **translation risk** and **economic risk**.

Transaction risk

Companies may expect either to pay or to receive amounts of foreign currency in the future due to either importing or exporting raw materials, goods or services. *Transaction risk* is the risk that the amount of domestic currency either paid or received in these foreign currency transactions may change due to movements in the exchange rate. An example of transaction risk is given below.

Example	Transaction risk

A UK company sells a car to a German customer for €22,000 and gives three months' credit, with payment to be received in euros. At the current spot rate of €1.124/£ the company expects to receive 22,000/1.124 = £19,573. If the German customer takes three months' credit and in this period the exchange rate moves to €1.208/£, the UK company will receive only £18,212 when it exchanges euros into sterling. This is 7 per cent less than the current sterling value.

Companies expecting to *receive* foreign currency in the future will therefore be concerned about the possibility of the domestic currency *appreciating* against the foreign currency, while companies expecting to *pay* foreign currency in the future are concerned about the possibility of the domestic currency *depreciating* against the foreign currency.

Translation risk

When consolidating financial statements, the foreign-currency denominated values of the assets and liabilities of foreign subsidiaries in the financial position statement need to be translated into the domestic currency. The foreign currency–denominated statement of profit or loss will also need to be translated and consolidated. *Translation risk* refers to the possibility that the parent company may experience a loss or a gain due to exchange rate movements on translating foreign assets, liabilities and profits into the domestic currency. Additionally, financial statement consolidation may lead to companies being in breach of loan covenants (e.g. a maximum gearing ratio). While translation losses or gains only appear on paper and do not represent *actual* cash flows, they may affect perceptions and opinions of investors and financial institutions regarding a company's financial health. However, as Buckley (2003) points out, translation risk is simply a function of the accounting treatment of foreign assets and liabilities on consolidation and does not give any indication of the real effect of currency fluctuations on the value of a company. An example of transaction risk is given below.

Example	Translation risk

Translation risk can be illustrated by considering a UK company that buys a hotel in the USA for $1.5m and finances the purchase with sterling debt. At the prevailing exchange rate of $1.737/£, the sterling value of the debt is £863,558. A year later, the hotel is still valued at $1.5m but the exchange rate now stands at $1.796/£. The sterling value of the debt used to finance the hotel will be the same (£863,558), but the value of the hotel, translated into sterling for consolidation purposes, has fallen to £835,189.

Economic risk

Economic risk refers to the risk of long-term exchange rate movements undermining the international competitiveness of a company or reducing the present value of its future cash flows. Economic risk is a more general type of exchange rate risk than transaction and translation risk. While companies can avoid transaction risk and translation risk by avoiding foreign currency transactions and not engaging in foreign operations, economic risk is almost impossible to avoid. It is also difficult to hedge against due to its ongoing nature.

Example	Economic risk

Consider a company, based solely in the UK, which buys its raw material and sells its finished goods in the domestic market. While not facing any transaction risk or translation risk, it faces domestic competition from a US company. If the pound appreciates against the dollar, reducing the sterling cost of the US company's dollar-denominated imports, the UK company will lose its competitive edge.

Now that we have examined the range of interest rate and exchange rate risks to which companies can be exposed, we can consider the methods companies use to manage these risks.

12.2 INTERNAL RISK MANAGEMENT

Internal risk management refers to hedging either interest rate or exchange rate risk by the way in which a company structures its assets and liabilities. Internal risk management is cheaper than external hedging since using external hedging methods incurs a range of costs and arrangement fees, as we shall see later. Unfortunately, there are several factors which limit the amount of risk that can be hedged internally.

12.2.1 Internal management of interest rate risk

There are two general methods of internal hedging that can be used to manage interest rate exposure within a company's financial position statement.

Smoothing

Smoothing is where a company maintains a balance between its fixed rate and floating rate borrowing. If interest rates *rise*, the disadvantage of the relatively expensive floating rate loan will be offset by the advantage of the less expensive fixed rate loan. If interest rates *fall*, the disadvantage of the relatively expensive fixed rate loan will be offset by the advantage of the less expensive floating rate loan. One drawback of this hedging method is that it reduces the *comparative advantage* a company may gain by using fixed rate debt in preference to floating rate debt or vice versa (for discussion of comparative advantage, see 'Interest rate swaps', Section 12.6.1). In addition, a company may incur two lots of transaction and arrangement costs.

Matching

This hedging method involves the internal matching of assets and liabilities with a common interest rate. Consider a company with two subsidiaries. One subsidiary may be investing in the money market at LIBOR, while the other is borrowing through the same money market at LIBOR. If LIBOR rises, one subsidiary's borrowing cost increases while the other's returns increase: the interest rates on the assets and liabilities are matched. One problem with this method is that it may be difficult for commercial and industrial companies to match the magnitudes and characteristics of their assets and liabilities as many companies, while paying interest on their financial liabilities, receive little interest income from their financial assets. Matching is most widely used by financial institutions such as banks, which receive large amounts of income from interest paid on advances.

12.2.2 Internal management of exchange rate risk

There are some techniques that can be used to hedge exchange rate risk internally. It is easier to internally hedge transaction and translation risk than economic risk, owing to the difficulty of quantifying economic risk and the long period over which economic risk exposure occurs.

Matching

Matching can be used to reduce the levels of translation or transaction risk a company faces. For example, to reduce *translation risk*, a company buying foreign currency–denominated assets could borrow funds denominated in the same foreign currency, matching if possible the term of the debt to the expected economic life of the asset. As the exchange rate varies, the translated values of the asset and the liability increase and decrease in parallel. To reduce *transaction risk*, a company selling dollar-denominated goods in the USA, for example, could import raw materials through a supplier that invoices in dollars.

Netting

In this internal hedging technique, companies net off their foreign currency transactions and then hedge any remaining exchange rate risk. The technique is used by multinationals with foreign subsidiaries and by large organisations with decentralised financial transactions.

Consider a UK company with a French subsidiary. The UK company expects to pay $5m to a supplier in three months' time, while the French subsidiary expects to receive $7m from a customer in three months' time. If this information is centralised at a group level, the net exposure of $2m to be received in three months' time ($7m–$5m) can be identified and hedged externally. This will be cheaper than the UK company and its French subsidiary independently hedging their respective currency exposures of $5m and $7m.

Leading and lagging

This technique involves settling foreign currency accounts either at the start (leading) or after the end (lagging) of the allowed credit period. The choice of whether to lead or lag depends on the company's expectations of future exchange rate movements. For example, a UK-based company paying for goods in dollars that expects the pound to appreciate against the dollar will lag its payment. While *leading* or *lagging* payments is not strictly a hedging technique, it can be used by companies facing transaction risk on foreign currency–denominated foreign trade payables.

Invoicing in the domestic currency

A company exporting goods could invoice its customers in its domestic currency rather than in the currency of the company to which it is exporting. The transaction risk is then transferred to the foreign customer. The drawback of this method is that it may deter potential customers as they are likely to transfer their orders to companies invoicing in their own currency.

12.3 EXTERNAL RISK MANAGEMENT

Having recognised that companies are limited in the amount of risk they can hedge using internal methods, we now consider the many types of external hedging available to them. Two of the longest-standing external methods of hedging interest rate and exchange rate risk are *forward contracts* and *money market hedges* (borrowing and lending in the money markets). Companies can also choose from a wide variety of *derivative* instruments, including **futures contracts**, **swaps** and options. Derivatives can also be divided according to whether they are standardised *traded* derivatives or bank-created **over-the-counter** derivatives.

12.3.1 Hedging using forward contracts

There are two types of forward contract. *Forward rate agreements* (FRAs) enable companies to fix in advance for a given period either a future borrowing rate or a future deposit rate, based on a nominal principal amount. While the contracts themselves are binding, the company taking out the FRA does not need to take out a loan with the provider of the FRA. *Forward exchange contracts* (FECs) enable companies to fix in advance the future exchange rate on an agreed quantity of foreign currency for delivery or purchase on an agreed future date. Forward contracts are generally set up via banks and are non-negotiable, legally binding contracts.

An advantage of forward contracts is that they can be tailor-made with respect to maturity and size to meet company requirements. In this respect they differ from their traded equivalent, *financial futures contracts.* Forward contracts cannot be traded as they are not standardised. While there is an initial arrangement fee, forward contracts do not require the payment of *margin*, as with financial futures, and they do not require the payment of a *premium*, as with **traded options**. Cash flows occur only on the execution date of the contract. While a company gains protection from any adverse interest rate or exchange rate movements, the binding nature of a forward contract means that it loses any potential benefit from favourable movements in exchange rates and interest rates.

Example	Forward rate agreements

A company wants to borrow £5.6m in three months' time for a period of six months. The current interest rate is 6 per cent and the company, fearing that in three months' time the interest rate may have increased, decides to hedge using a forward rate agreement (FRA). The bank guarantees the company a rate of 6.5 per cent on a notional £5.6m for six months starting in three months' time (known as a 3 v 9 FRA). If interest rates have *increased* after three months to say 7.5 per cent, the company will pay 7.5 per cent interest on its £5.6m loan, which is 1 per cent more than the rate agreed in the FRA. The bank will make a compensating payment of £28,000 (1 per cent × £5.6m × 6/12) to the company, covering the higher cost of its borrowing. If interest rates have decreased after three months to say 5 per cent (1.5 per cent below the agreed rate), the company will have to make a £42,000 payment (1.5 per cent × £5.6m × 6/12) to the bank.

12.3.2 Hedging using the money markets and eurocurrency markets

Companies can also hedge interest and exchange rate risk by using the money markets and the eurocurrency markets. These types of transaction are also referred to as **cash market hedges**.

Consider a company that wants to borrow £1m in three months' time for six months but fears that interest rates will rise. The company can borrow £1m now on the money markets for nine months and deposit this on the money markets for three months. If interest rates rise in the three months before the loan is needed, the company will pay more on the loan but will benefit by receiving a higher rate of interest on the money market deposit.

Hedging exchange rate risk using the eurocurrency markets is more complex and involves setting up the opposite foreign currency transaction to the one being hedged. It is best illustrated with a numerical example.

Example	Money market hedge

A company expects to receive $180,000 in three months' time and wants to lock into the current exchange rate of $1.65/£. It fears that the pound will appreciate against the dollar. To set up a money market hedge, the company sets up a dollar debt by borrowing dollars now. It converts the dollars to sterling at the current spot rate and deposits the sterling proceeds on the sterling money market. When the dollar loan matures, it is paid off by the future dollar receipt. If the *annual* dollar borrowing rate is 7 per cent, the three-month dollar borrowing rate is 1.75 per cent, i.e. 7% × 3/12: if Z is the amount of dollars to be borrowed now, then:

$$Z \times 1.0175 = \$180,000$$

and so:

$$Z = \$180,000/1.0175 = \$176,904$$

The sterling value of these dollars at the current spot rate is:

$$Z = \$180,000/1.0175 = \$176,904$$

If the *annual* sterling deposit rate is 6 per cent, the three-month sterling deposit rate is 1.5 per cent and the value of these dollars in three months' time will be:

$$£107,215 \times 1.015 = £108,823$$

The three-month sterling value of the money market hedge can be compared with the sterling receipt from a forward exchange contract in order to determine which hedging method is the most financially beneficial. The financial benefit of different hedging methods must always be compared from the same point in time.

12.4 FUTURES CONTRACTS

A futures contract can be defined as an agreement to buy or sell a standard quantity of a specified financial instrument or foreign currency at a specified future date at a price agreed between two parties. Financial futures resemble *traded options* (Section 12.5.2) in that both are standardised contracts, but financial futures are a binding contract locking buyer and seller into an agreed rate and an agreed amount: the buyer must complete the contract. When a company takes out a futures contract it has to place an *initial margin*, representing between 1 and 3 per cent of the contract value, with the futures exchange clearing house. On £500,000 three-month sterling interest rate contracts, this could be a margin of £1,500 per contract. As the interest or exchange rate specified in the futures contract changes daily, money is either credited to or debited from the company's margin account, depending on whether the rate change is favourable or adverse respectively. The cash-flow movements of a margin account are referred to as accounts being *marked to market*. If initial margin drops below a specified safety level, *variation margin* will be called for by the clearing house to top up the account.

Financial futures were first traded in the USA on the Chicago Mercantile Exchange (CME) in 1972. In 2007 the 'Merc' acquired the Chicago Board of Trade and formed CME Group, the world's largest derivatives exchange. In the UK, the London International Financial Futures Exchange (LIFFE) was set up in 1982 to trade futures contracts. LIFFE merged with the London Traded Options Market (LTOM) in 1992 to form a unified UK derivative securities market. LIFFE was bought by Euronext in 2002 and renamed Euronext LIFFE, before merging with the NYSE in 2007 to become NYSE Euronext. In 2013 NYSE Euronext was acquired by the US-based Intercontinental Exchange group who then spun off Euronext via an IPO in 2014, retaining LIFFE under its new name of ICE Futures Europe.

The mechanics of hedging interest rate and exchange rate risk using financial futures are illustrated below.

12.4.1 Using futures contracts to hedge interest rate risk

When hedging interest rate risk, companies must *buy* futures contracts if they want to guard against a *fall* in interest rates and *sell* futures contracts to guard against a *rise* in interest rates. Interest rate futures contracts run in three-month cycles (March, June, September and December). The two most useful contracts for hedging sterling interest rate risk are the three-month LIBOR sterling short-term interest rate contracts (STIRs) and long gilt contracts. The former have a nominal value of £500,000 while the latter are based on contract sizes of £100,000. Futures are priced in nominal terms by subtracting the value of the specified interest rate from 100 (e.g. a futures contract price of 93 corresponds to an interest rate of 7 per cent). Profits or losses made on a futures contract are determined by reference to changes in this nominal price. Contract price changes are given in **ticks**, a tick being equal to a movement of one basis point or 0.01 per cent of the contract price. In value terms on a three-month £500,000 short sterling contract, a movement of one tick is worth £12.50 (i.e. £500,000 × 0.0001 × 3/12).

Example	**Using interest rate futures**

A company plans to borrow £500,000 in three months' time for a period of three months, but expects the future interest rate to be higher than the current interest rate of 10 per cent. To hedge its position, it therefore *sells* one £500,000 interest rate contract at 90 (i.e. 100 − 10).

Suppose that, after three months, the interest rate has gone up by 3 per cent and the contract price has moved by the same amount. The seller of the contract now *buys* a contract at 87 (i.e. 100 − 13), thereby *closing out* his position. The contract price movement in terms of ticks is 3/0.01 = 300 ticks.

Profit made by selling and buying futures = 300 × £12.50 = £3,750

The profit compensates the company for the higher cost of borrowing £500,000 in three months' time, which is £3,750 (500,000 × 0.03 × 1/4). Because the contract price movement exactly matched the interest rate change, the company has exactly offset its higher borrowing cost and hence constructed a perfect hedge for its interest rate risk.

The example above makes the unrealistic assumption that changes in interest rates exactly match changes in futures prices. In practice this is unlikely to be the case as the futures market, like any other financial market, is subject to pricing inefficiencies. Futures contracts therefore suffer from what is known as *basis risk.* Take, for example, a three-month LIBOR futures contract with three months to maturity. The current futures contract price is 93.46 and three-month LIBOR stands at 6 per cent. Here we would expect the futures contract to be priced at 94.00. The difference between 94.00 and 93.46 represents the basis risk – in this case 0.54 per cent or 54 basis points. This basis risk will taper away over the next three months (at a rate of 18 basis points a month if we assume a linear decline) until it has disappeared as the contract matures. Clearly this will affect the hedge efficiency. Returning to the earlier example, assume now that the futures contract price was actually priced at 89.54 rather than 90. If interest rates rose by 3 per cent the futures contract price will have dropped to 87. Here the investor will have made a gain of 254 ticks $(89.54 - 87)$, giving a value of £3,175 (12.50×254). This is against a loss of £3,750 in the cash market, giving a *hedge efficiency* of $(3,175/3,750) \times 100 = 85$ per cent. Basis risk can work in the reverse direction, making hedge efficiency greater than 100 per cent.

12.4.2 Using futures contracts to hedge exchange rate risk

Sterling-denominated **currency futures** contracts were discontinued by LIFFE in 1990 due to a lack of demand. However, the takeover of LIFFE by Euronext saw the introduction of €/US$ currency futures on their Amsterdam exchange. While the Singapore Exchange (SGX) has also followed suit in discontinuing sterling-denominated currency futures contracts, they are still available on the CME.

Example | **Using US currency futures**

It is 1 January and a UK company expects to receive $300,000 in three months' time. Being concerned about the pound strengthening against the dollar, it decides to use CME-traded currency futures to hedge its transaction risk.

Current spot rate	$1.54–$1.55
Sterling futures price (1 April)	$1.535
Standard size of futures contracts	£62,500

The first thing to establish is whether the company should buy or sell futures contracts. Given that holding a futures contract (often referred to as *taking a* **long position**) allows future delivery of a *foreign* currency, and that in this case *sterling* is the foreign currency, the company should *buy* US sterling futures. This allows the company to take delivery of sterling in return for the dollars it expects to receive. The futures price quoted is the amount of US dollars needed to buy one unit of the foreign currency. Translating the expected dollar receipt into sterling at the exchange rate implicit in the currency future, we have:

$$\$300,000/1.535 = £195,440$$

Number of contracts required $= 195,440/62,500 = 3.13$

The company therefore buys three contracts, allowing it to take delivery of £187,500 (62,500 × 3) in return for a payment of $287,813 (187,500 × 1.535). Given that the company is to receive $300,000, it will have to sell the $12,187 surplus, either now via a forward exchange contract or in the future at the spot rate in three months' time. We can see that the company has locked into a particular exchange rate ($1.535/£) and knows how much sterling it will receive from its future dollar receipts, except (perhaps) for the $12,187 surplus. In this example the company has *under-hedged* by using three contracts when it needed 3.13 contracts for a perfect hedge.

12.4.3 Advantages and disadvantages of using futures to hedge risk

An informed decision on hedging with financial futures will consider the advantages and disadvantages of this risk management method. One advantage of futures is that, unlike options, there is no up-front premium to pay, although money must be put into the margin account. Another advantage is that, unlike forward contracts, futures are tradeable and can be bought and sold on a secondary market. This gives *pricing transparency* as prices are set by the futures market rather than by a financial institution. Finally, as contracts are daily marked to market, favourable interest rate and exchange rate movements are immediately credited to a company's margin account.

Arguably the biggest drawback associated with futures is that, unlike options, they do not allow a company to take advantage of favourable movements in interest and exchange rates. A further problem is that, because contracts are standardised, it is difficult to find a perfect hedge with respect to the principal to be hedged and its maturity. This is illustrated in our earlier example, where four currency futures would over-hedge the exposure and three currency futures would under-hedge it. Considering cost, while there are no premiums to be paid with futures contracts, the initial margin must still be found. *Variation margin* may also be required as interest or exchange rates move adversely. Finally, we noted that *basis risk* may exist if changes in exchange and interest rates are not perfectly correlated with changes in the futures contract prices, which in turn affects the hedge efficiency of the futures contracts.

12.5 OPTIONS

Currency and interest rate options give their holders the right, *but not the obligation*, to borrow or lend at a specific interest rate, or to buy or sell foreign currency at a specific exchange rate. This flexibility allows option holders to take advantage of favourable interest rate and exchange rate movements. A price is paid for this flexibility, however, in the form of an *option premium*. This is a non-refundable fee paid when the option is acquired. There are two kinds of options which companies use to hedge their exposures: over-the-counter options and traded options.

12.5.1 Over-the-counter options

Over-the-counter (OTC) options can be bought from financial institutions such as banks and are tailor-made to meet company requirements. OTC options, which can be divided into **caps**, **floors** and **collars**, specify a principal amount, a period over which the option runs and a particular currency or interest rate.

With an *interest rate cap*, if the specified interest rate goes above a predetermined level the financial institution pays the excess, thereby guaranteeing or *capping* the interest rate to be paid by the company. Alternatively, a UK company wanting to convert an amount of dollars into sterling in the future can buy an *exchange rate cap*. The company will be guaranteed an exchange rate, say $1.5/£. If the exchange rate increases to say $1.67/£, the company can use the cap and exchange at the more favourable rate of $1.5/£ with the bank from which it purchased the cap.

With an *interest rate floor*, if a specified interest rate falls below a certain rate, the financial institution pays the company the difference. Interest rate floors allow companies receiving floating rate interest income to guarantee a minimum level of receipts. Similarly, an *exchange rate floor* guarantees a minimum rate of exchange, should the pound depreciate against the specified currency, to a UK company wanting to buy foreign currency in the future.

A *collar* is the combination of a floor and a cap and it is used by a company wanting to keep an interest rate or exchange rate between an upper and lower limit. Using a collar is cheaper for companies compared with using caps or floors on their own. Take, for example, a company with floating rate income that takes out a collar to keep the interest rate between 3 per cent and 5 per cent. It is paying a premium to buy a floor of 3 per cent from the bank and at the same time it receives a premium for selling the bank a cap of 5 per cent. A collar will also work out cheaper than a floor since any beneficial interest rate changes over and above 5 per cent are paid to the bank. Conversely, a collar for a company wanting to keep its borrowing rate between an upper and lower limit combines buying a cap with selling a floor.

12.5.2 Traded options

Traded options are like over-the-counter options except that they are standardised with respect to the principal amount and the maturity date specified by the contract. The standardised nature of these contracts allows them to be bought and sold on a secondary market. The world's oldest options market is the Chicago Board Options Exchange (CBOE). It trades share, interest and currency options and is now part of the CME Group. In the UK, currency, equity and interest rate options trade on the ICE Futures Europe in London.

Traded options mature in three-month cycles (March, June, September and December) and the standard size of a three-month sterling interest rate option on ICE Futures Europe, for instance, is £500,000. Traded options are of two kinds: *put* options carry the right to *sell* currency or to *lend* at a fixed rate; whereas *call* options carry the right to *buy* currency or to *borrow* at a fixed rate. Puts and calls can be further divided into **American options**, which are exercisable up to and on their expiry date, and *European options*, which are exercisable only on their expiry date.

12.5.3 Using traded options to hedge interest rate risk

Interest rate option contracts traded on the ICE Futures Europe use futures contracts as the **underlying** asset, rather than cash market transactions, because futures positions can be

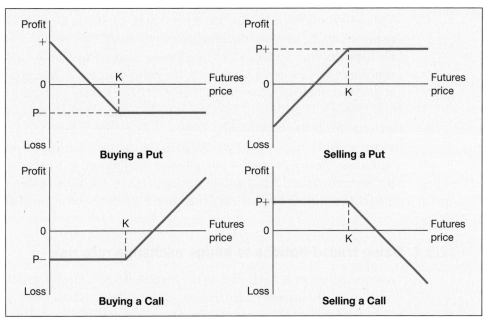

Figure 12.3 Diagrams showing the pay-offs associated with buying and selling interest rate options that use futures as the underlying asset

closed out by buying or selling contracts whereas cash market transactions require delivery. The diagrams in Figure 12.3 show the profit or loss associated with buying or selling put and call interest rate options, where K is the **strike price** at which futures can be bought or sold and P is the premium paid if the option is bought or the premium received if the option is sold.

Figure 12.3 shows that when selling or *writing* call and put options, the downside risk (i.e. the risk of loss) is unlimited. For this reason, only buying puts and calls is recommended for hedging commercial transactions (other than collars), as this limits the company downside risk to losing the option premium paid initially.

Example — Using interest rate options

It is 15 December and a company wants to borrow £2m, for a period of three months, in three months' time. The three-month LIBOR rate stands at 6 per cent and the company wants to guard against an interest rate increase. To give the company the option to borrow at an effective rate of 6 per cent, it buys four 15 March LIBOR sterling put option contracts of £500,000 each, with a strike price of 94. The price the company pays for these option contracts is 0.17 per contract, i.e. a cost of 17 ticks per option contract. Given that ticks have a value of £12.50, this represents a cost per contract of £212.50 (17 × £12.50). The cost of four option contracts to the company is therefore £850.

If interest rates have increased to 8 per cent by 15 March, the company exercises its option contracts, allowing it to sell futures contracts at 94. The futures price, assuming no basis risk (see Section 12.4.1), will have dropped to 92 (i.e. 100 − 8), so the company makes a 2 per cent gain on its futures transactions by buying at 92 and selling at 94. This represents a gain of 200 ticks at £12.50 each per contract, giving a gain on four contracts of 200 × £12.50 × 4 = £10,000. This exactly balances the 2 per cent increase in its borrowing cost, which is 2 per cent × £2m × 1/4 = £10,000. In exchange for an option premium of £850, the company has guaranteed a maximum borrowing rate of 6 per cent. If interest rates had dropped to 5 per cent on 15 March, the company would let its option contracts expire and would borrow at the lower market rate of 5 per cent. Its loss would be limited to the premium of £850 paid.

12.5.4 Using traded options to hedge exchange rate risk

Currency options were first traded on the Philadelphia Stock Exchange in 1982. They were introduced on the London Traded Options Market in 1985, but discontinued in 1990 owing to a lack of popularity. The most important currency options are those of the CME, closely followed by those of the Philadelphia Stock Exchange and the International Securities Exchange (ISE).

As with OTC options, traded options can be combined to create collars and so decrease the costs of hedging with options. The combinations of put and call options required to create various interest rate and currency collars are shown in Table 12.1.

Example   Using exchange rate options

It is 19 December and a UK company is expecting to receive $1m in three months' time in payment for exports. The company wants to guard against the pound appreciating against the dollar, which currently stands at $1.65/£. As sterling currency options are not available on ICE Futures Europe, the company will have to use US currency options. It decides to use CME sterling currency options, which have futures contracts as the underlying asset. These come in contract sizes of £62,500 and require physical delivery of the currency. From the US perspective, sterling is the foreign currency and so the company will buy call options. By buying sterling currency call options, the company obtains the right, but not the obligation, to sell dollars and buy sterling at an exchange rate of $1.65 to the pound. To find how many contracts are needed, the future dollar receipt is converted to pounds at the option strike price, giving £606,061 (i.e. $1m/$1.65), and then divided by the standard contract size, giving the number of contracts needed as 9.7 (i.e. £606,061/£62,500). It is impossible to get a perfect hedge here owing to the standard size of the contracts. The company must either under-hedge by buying nine contracts or over-hedge by buying ten contracts. Any shortfalls or excess amounts of dollars can be dealt with via forward exchange contracts or currency market transactions when the options are exercised. Assume that the company decides to buy 10 contracts.

If March sterling currency call options with a $1.65 strike price are currently trading at a premium of 7 cents (per pound of contract), the total cost of 10 contracts will be:

$$62,500 \times 10 \times 0.07 = \$43,750$$

By buying March sterling currency call options with a $1.65 strike price the company will, in the worst case, exchange its dollars at a rate of $1.72 to the pound (i.e. $1.65 plus the 7 cents premium). If, in three months' time, the spot rate is below $1.65/£, the company will allow the option to expire and exchange its dollars in the **spot market**.

Conversely, if the company had imported goods and therefore needed to buy dollars in three months' time, it would buy US sterling currency put options, giving it the option to sell sterling and receive dollars at a predetermined rate.

Table 12.1 The combinations of put and call options required to create interest and currency collars

Using ICE Futures Europe interest rate options on interest futures	
Borrower's collar: to keep interest rate between an upper and lower limit	Buy a put option and sell a call option
Lender's collar: to keep interest rate between an upper and lower limit	Buy a call option and sell a put option
Using US sterling currency options	
Exporter's collar: to keep exchange rate between an upper and lower limit	Buy a call option and sell a put option
Importer's collar: to keep exchange rate between an upper and lower limit	Buy a put option and sell a call option

12.5.5 Factors affecting the price of traded options

Determining option premiums is a complex process owing to the large number of factors influencing the price of traded options. These factors are as follows.

Strike price

The higher the strike price specified in an interest rate option contract, the lower the price of a call option and the higher the price of the corresponding put option. A put option to lend at 10 per cent, for example, will cost more than a put option to lend at 8 per cent. Similarly, a put option to sell the dollar at a rate of $1.5/£ will cost less than a put option to sell the dollar at a rate of $1.3/£.

Changes in interest and exchange rates

Rising interest rates will increase the value of interest rate call options but decrease the value of interest rate put options. A call option to borrow at 12 per cent, for example, will become more valuable if interest rates rise from, say, 11 per cent to 13 per cent.

Similarly, a US sterling put option to sell sterling at $1.5/£ will increase in value if the pound depreciates against the dollar.

Volatility of interest rates and exchange rates

Both call and put options will have a higher value if interest rates and exchange rates are volatile, as greater volatility means a greater potential gain for the option holder and a greater potential loss for the option writer; a higher premium is therefore charged.

Time to expiry of the option

The longer the time an option has before its expiry date, the more valuable it will be, as it can be used by a company to hedge unfavourable movements in exchange or interest rates for a longer period of time. Like a warrant, the value of an option can be split into two parts:

Intrinsic value + Time value = Total value

The *intrinsic value* of an option represents the value of the option if it is exercised immediately. If the current exchange rate between the dollar and the pound is $1.5/£, then a US sterling currency put option with a strike price of $1.7/£ will have intrinsic value, whereas a similar option with a strike price of $1.3/£ will not. The first option is *in the money* while the second option is *out of the money*.

If an option is out of the money and thus has no intrinsic value, it may still possess *time value*. Take the put option with a strike price of $1.3/£. This option has no intrinsic value but, if it has three months before expiry, there is time for the exchange rate to fall from its current rate of $1.5/£ to below the option's $1.3/£ strike price. Time value, therefore, is proportionate to the time left before the option expires and is at a maximum when a contract starts and at a minimum (i.e. zero) when the contract expires.

12.5.6 Advantages and disadvantages of hedging with options

While not the cheapest method of hedging owing to the premiums payable on them, options have the great advantage of offering the holder the opportunity to benefit from favourable movements in exchange and interest rates.

There are two situations where using options to hedge risk are likely to be beneficial. The first situation is where a company expects to undertake a transaction but is not certain that it will occur. For example, it may plan to borrow money in the future or it may be tendering for a foreign contract. If the transaction does not occur, the company can either let the option expire or, as options are traded, sell it on to another party if it has any value. The second situation is where a company expects interest or exchange rates to move in a certain direction, but also believes there is a chance that they might move in the opposite direction. By using options, the company can take advantage of any favourable movements in rates should they arise.

In addition to the disadvantage of their cost, using options makes it difficult to create a hedge that perfectly matches both the duration and size of a company's exposure. As with futures, this problem is due to the standardised nature of traded option contracts. Using over-the-counter options may be a better choice than traded options for hedging large non-standard exposures.

12.6 SWAPS

The **currency swaps** market was developed in the early 1980s to facilitate access to international capital markets by multinational companies. In these markets, companies raise funds in *vehicle currencies* (in which they can borrow relatively cheaply but which are not the currency in which the debt is required) and swap into the desired currency at a lower rate than if they borrowed the funds directly. The development of interest rate swaps followed closely on the heels of currency swaps and the market in interest rate swaps is now larger in terms of both size and importance. Interest rate swaps now represent the largest component of the global OTC derivatives market and by May 2018 the notional amounts outstanding on interest rate swaps stood at $437tn.

Swaps are used extensively by companies and banks to capitalise on their comparative advantages in the different debt markets and to hedge their interest and exchange rate exposures. The counterparties (companies) in a swap deal are normally brought together by a dealer (usually a bank) acting as an intermediary. Where a swap partner is not immediately available, the bank can **warehouse** the swap by acting as a temporary swap partner until a suitable counterparty is found. By acting as swap brokers, banks benefit from the arrangement fees they receive from the counterparties.

A major advantage of swaps over other derivatives such as traded options, forward rate agreements and financial futures is that they can be used to lock into interest and exchange rates for much longer periods, and do not require frequent monitoring and reviewing. However, their 'off exchange' status is gradually changing as trading moves onto exchanges to comply with new derivatives rules. This change is the subject of Vignette 12.3.

Vignette 12.3

Clearing houses see record volume as new rules boost activity

LCH and other clearers benefit as banks and investors reduce derivative risks

By Philip Stafford

Clearing houses are experiencing record activity as banks and investors comply with new derivative rules and push their over-the-counter fixed income and foreign exchange swaps towards centralised venues that bolster risk management for the industry.

LCH, the world's largest swaps clearer, said it had enjoyed a record March and first three months of the year processing notional amounts of interest rates, inflation and non-deliverable forex forwards. Small rivals, such as Germany's Eurex Clearing, have also reported strong growth over

Vignette 12.3 (continued)

the same period amid signs the vast off-exchange market is being remade by post-financial crisis reforms.

The boost in activity underlines the industry's expectation that a March 1 milestone in derivatives regulation will fundamentally change the behaviour of hundreds of asset managers, corporations, credit institutions and pension funds who use the OTC market to hedge their liabilities. At the beginning of last month, global rules required investors to post more margin or collateral to backstop private swap deals. Historically, the industry has supplied minimal margin, meaning there were few protected funds to cover losses if one of the parties defaulted.

The new regulations were expected to raise overall costs for the market, which had been blamed by policymakers for exacerbating the financial crisis. Authorities backed down from a hardline introduction as hundreds of asset managers were unprepared, and instead demanded 'good faith' efforts to comply. That has coincided with increasing business at clearing houses, which manage the credit risk to the rest of the market if one side defaults.

'The vague terms of the regulators' statements may have given a push to central clearing in the short term,' said Edmund Parker, global head of derivatives at law firm Mayer Brown in London. 'Whether that is a long-term trend is more difficult to

ascertain, and will come down to cost and quality of hedging arrangements.'

LCH processed $244tn of newly transacted gross notional in interest rate swaps in the three months to March 31, a rise of 45 per on the same period in 2016 and was boosted by investors like asset managers and institutional investors clearing swaps. More than $100tn of that total was cleared in March alone, a year-on-year rise of 72 per cent, it added. It also cleared a notional $2.4tn in foreign exchange, from more than 330,000 trades.

Inflation swaps, used by asset managers and pension funds looking to hedge against rising inflation and interest rates, benefited from rising expectations the US will raise rates this year. LCH cleared a record $858bn in notional value in the first quarter. Germany's Eurex Clearing has also seen a 30 per cent increase in the volume it processes and now has notional outstanding of €1.2tn.

A push to central clearing is having other effects on the over-the-counter markets. 'The data tells us that so far, more clearing means more [trading] volumes,' said Chris Barnes, an analyst at Clarus Financial Technology, a UK data provider, in a blog last week. Separately, KfW, the German development bank, said on Wednesday that it would voluntarily clear its euro-denominated interest rate swaps via Eurex.

Source: Stafford, P. (2017) 'Clearing houses see record volume as new rules boost activity', *Financial Times*, 5 April. © The Financial Times Limited 2018. All Rights Reserved.

Questions

1 Why is there regulatory pressure for swap market trades to be centrally cleared?

2 What are the advantages and disadvantages to counterparties if swap transactions are centrally cleared?

12.6.1 Interest rate swaps

Winstone (2000) offers a definition of an interest rate swap as an exchange between two parties of interest obligations or receipts in the same currency on an agreed amount of notional principal for an agreed period. Interest rate swaps can be used to hedge against adverse interest rate movements or to achieve a chosen blend of fixed and floating rate debt. Companies may become involved in swap agreements because their borrowing or lending requirements do not coincide with their comparative advantages with respect to fixed and floating rate borrowing or lending. The most common type of interest rate swap is a *plain vanilla swap*, where fixed interest payments based on a notional principal are swapped with floating interest payments based on the same notional principal. The swap agreement will include the following details:

- the start and end dates of the swap;
- the notional principal on which the swap is based (amount and currency);
- which party is paying floating interest and receiving fixed interest in return, and vice versa;
- the level of the fixed rate and the basis of the floating rate (e.g. one-, three- or six-month LIBOR) upon which the agreement is based.

| Example | **Plain vanilla interest rate swap** |

Consider two companies, A and B. The interest rates at which they can borrow are shown in the first part of Figure 12.4.

Company A, with a better credit rating, can borrow at a lower fixed and a lower floating rate than Company B. We refer to A as having an *absolute advantage* over B. However, B has a *comparative advantage* over A with floating rate borrowing, as its floating rate is proportionately less expensive than its fixed rate when compared with A's rates. If, for example, LIBOR stands at 5 per cent, then B's floating rate is 4 per cent more expensive than A's floating rate (i.e. 0.2 per cent/5 per cent). This compares with B's fixed rate being 10 per cent more expensive (i.e. 1 per cent/10 per cent) than A's. Conversely, A has a comparative advantage in fixed rate borrowing.

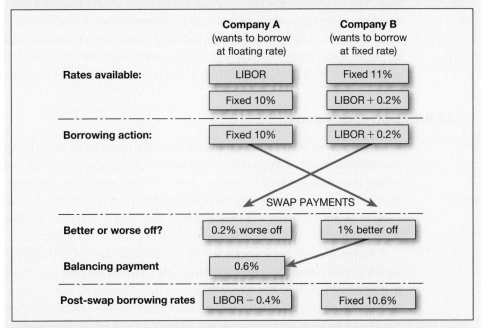

Figure 12.4 An example of a plain vanilla interest rate swap between two companies, A and B

The prerequisite for a swap agreement to proceed is for both companies to be able to benefit from it. For this to be the case, the companies must want to raise funds by borrowing at the rate in which they do not possess a comparative advantage. In our example, this means that A must want to borrow at a floating rate and B must want to borrow at a fixed rate.

If A raises a fixed rate loan at 10 per cent and B raises a floating-rate loan at LIBOR plus 0.2 per cent, and they swap interest payments, then B is 1 per cent better off while A is 0.2 per cent worse off. If B makes a payment of 0.2 per cent to A, then A is neither better nor worse off, whereas B is still 0.8 per cent better off. If the benefits of the swap agreement are to be split evenly between the two parties, then B will have to make a further payment of 0.4 per cent to A. The post-swap borrowing rates are shown in Figure 12.4, where A ends up with a floating rate of LIBOR minus 0.4 per cent and B with a fixed rate of 10.6 per cent.

In practice, as swaps are arranged through bank intermediation, the bank's arrangement fee will decrease the benefit that companies derive from the transaction. In our example, if the arranging bank took a fee of 0.2 per cent, equally divided between the two parties, the post-swap rates would become LIBOR minus 0.3 per cent for Company A and 10.7 per cent for Company B. Furthermore, companies will not swap interest payments but make a balancing payment from one company to another, representing the difference between the fixed and the floating rate. These balancing payments will vary as the floating rate varies.

So far we have considered only plain vanilla swaps. More complex swap agreements exist. The most common type of swap after a plain vanilla swap is a *basis* swap in which two floating rate payments determined on different bases are exchanged. An example of a basis swap would be a bank that swaps its base-rate-determined interest income (from the advances it has made) for, say, LIBOR-determined income. This allows the company to match its LIBOR-related cost of raising funds with a LIBOR-determined income stream.

12.6.2 Currency swaps

A currency swap is a formal agreement between two parties to exchange principal and interest payments in different currencies over a stated period. Currency swaps enable companies to acquire funds in a foreign currency, while avoiding any exchange rate risk (transaction risk) on the principal or servicing payments. A company can also use a currency swap to acquire funds in a specific currency at a more favourable rate than if it borrowed the funds itself.

A currency swap begins with the exchange of an agreed principal amount at a par exchange rate (usually the prevailing spot rate), followed by the exchange of interest payments over the life of the swap. When the swap matures, the principal amount is re-exchanged at the par exchange rate agreed earlier. An alternative to the initial exchange of principal is for both counterparties to make the appropriate spot market transactions, then to exchange interest payments over the duration of the swap and re-exchange the principal on maturity.

The information included in currency swap contracts is similar to the information included in an interest rate swap agreement. In addition, though, it will specify which currency is to be paid, which currency is to be received and the exchange rate to be used as the par rate.

Implicit within currency swaps is an interest rate swap. The simplest form of currency swap is a *fixed to fixed* agreement, where the interest payments to be exchanged on the two currencies are both fixed. If the swap involves exchanging fixed and floating interest rates it is then called a *fixed to floating* or *currency coupon* swap.

An example of how currency swaps can be used to hedge exchange rate risk is explained in the following example.

Example	**Fixed to floating currency swap**

A UK airline is buying a new aeroplane. Payment will be in US dollars, so the airline will finance its purchase with a fixed interest dollar loan from a US bank (stage 1 in Figure 12.5). As the airline's income is predominantly in sterling, it has approached another bank to arrange a currency swap. Within this swap will be a par exchange rate which is used to convert dollar cash flows into pounds. It will be used to convert the dollar loan into a sterling principal on which to base the sterling LIBOR payments the

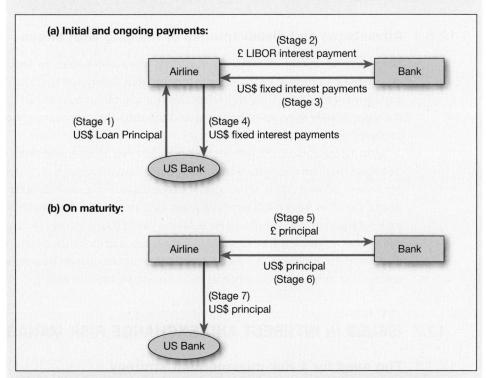

Figure 12.5 Example of a currency swap indicating (a) the initial and ongoing payments, and (b) the payments made on the swap's maturity. The chronological order of payments is indicated by the stages in brackets

airline will make to the bank (stage 2), in return for the bank paying to the airline the dollar interest payments on the airline's dollar loan (stage 3). These dollar interest payments will then be paid to the US bank by the airline (stage 4). When the swap matures the airline will pay the sterling principal to the bank (stage 5) and in return will receive a dollar payment (stage 6) with which to pay off its maturing dollar loan (stage 7). Looking at the swap as a whole, we can see that the airline has paid off a sterling loan principal and sterling LIBOR-determined interest payments, hence avoiding exchange rate risk.

12.6.3 Swaptions

As the name suggests, **swaptions** are a combination of a swap and an option. They give the holder the option to become involved in a swap, i.e. they are a derivative of a derivative. They are like traded and over-the-counter options but are less flexible as, once the option to swap is exercised, the company is locked into a specified exchange or interest rate and can no longer benefit from subsequent favourable movements in rates. Swaptions represent a cheaper way to hedge risk as the premiums paid on them tend to be lower than the premiums charged for options.

12.6.4 Advantages and disadvantages of hedging with swaps

The major advantage of swaps is that they allow companies to hedge interest and exchange rate exposures for relatively long periods compared to other derivatives. The arrangement fees are usually much less than the premiums paid on options, while swaps are more flexible in terms of principal and duration than standardised derivatives such as traded options and futures.

Swap agreements are not without their risks, however. Once entered into, a swap prevents a company from benefiting from favourable movements in exchange and interest rates, unless of course it defaults on the agreement. If a counterparty to a swap defaults on interest payments, the other party is still legally required to make the servicing payments as it originally took out the loan. This risk of interest default is called counterparty risk. Since the company will not be hedged, it will be exposed to interest rate and exchange rate risk while a replacement swap party is found. It is therefore advisable that companies entering into swap agreements do so only with counterparties of an acceptable credit standing.

12.7 ISSUES IN INTEREST AND EXCHANGE RISK MANAGEMENT

12.7.1 The need for a risk management strategy

Hedging interest rate and exchange rate risk is a complicated and dynamic process. Hedging strategies and the techniques and instruments used will vary from company to company, depending on the markets the companies operate in, their attitudes towards risk and their awareness and understanding of the techniques available. When formulating hedging strategies, it is important for companies to clarify their objectives, identify and quantify their likely exposures and select appropriate hedging techniques. The consequences for senior company management of not getting their hedging strategies right can be very serious, as Vignette 12.4 illustrates.

Vignette 12.4

JPMorgan loss exposes derivatives dangers

By Michael Mackenzie, Nicole Bullock and Telis Demos

As JPMorgan reels from a complicated hedging strategy, one that misfired to the tune of at least $2.3bn in losses, derivatives-market participants worried about new rules on trading fear it will be harder to argue for more lenient treatment. The loss is also a reminder of the dangers of seeking bigger profits by minimising the cost of hedging. While credit derivatives were created to allow lenders to offset the threat of a default by a borrower, the product has been associated with a number of blow-ups in recent years.

These include the effect on many Wall Street trading books in 2005 when US carmakers lost their investment-grade rating. Then came AIG's huge losses from writing credit insurance on mortgage bonds to major banks in 2008, which precipitated a bailout from the Federal Reserve. Also at that time, Deutsche Bank lost more than $1bn from credit derivative trading as the financial crisis intensified.

'It is an indictment of risk management,' says Ed Grebeck, chief executive of Tempus Advisors, a global debt management strategy group. 'What has happened in the last several years is that every time everybody says everything is OK, another one of these situations happens. And there are more coming.'

While the specific details of JPMorgan's strategy are unclear, traders say the bank created a large portfolio of swaps over underlying holdings of bonds that involved selling protection on one credit index, the so-called CDX North American investment-grade index series 9, while purchasing insurance on other contracts. Income from writing insurance on one index helps pay for buying insurance on other indices.

Such positioning reflects how much of Wall Street's hedging activity is actually based on assumptions about the future changes in the relationship between different indices and their constituents. As such, it relies heavily on models that look to economise the costs of hedging and allow profits to run.

'All financial institutions are only profitable if they take risk, if you hedge away all risk, there is no return,' says Andrew Lo, professor at MIT. Trading in the credit default swaps market is conducted on a bilateral basis between two counterparties. This means the market still operates in the dark, with trades privately negotiated between two parties and with no public record of transactions for each day. Within this opaque world, banks and investors that amass large positions can become vulnerable to a so-called 'squeeze'.

That is the situation JPMorgan found itself in as hedge funds sensed strains in the bank's management of its huge positions and began to trade aggressively against the bank. 'Trading in size in a bilaterally negotiated world can put you in the worst position you can be in: the trade going against you and the Street knows,' says Christian Martin, a former swaps trader at Merrill Lynch and co-founder of TeraExchange, a nascent electronic CDS market platform.

Major dealers dislike the idea of trading derivatives on an exchange type platform, as it stands to substantially reduce their profit margins. But a public record of real-time transactions would mean a more transparent market that is less prone to being dominated by a single player.

While JPMorgan's losses to date are a fraction of its balance sheet and it is believed the trades were centrally cleared, satisfying one key area of derivatives reform, there is nevertheless much at stake for the industry and swaps trading. Wall Street has resisted efforts to reform the trading of derivatives since

Vignette **12.4** *(continued)*

the signing of the Dodd Frank Act in 2010. The industry has warned tough rules for derivatives trading could harm liquidity and impair the ability of banks to hedge loan and bond risk, ultimately raising the cost of financing for a swath of companies.

Over the past year, moreover, CDS trade volumes have fallen by a fifth as the market has reduced risk and banks grapple with the prospect of higher capital charges. The credit derivatives index in which JPMorgan is believed to have amassed a large

position initially moved higher on the news of its losing position, an indication that the losses could be higher than the bank reported (though the bank is thought to have moved to neutralise its positions). Therein resides a risk for the wider market. JPMorgan 'is a major player in credit derivatives and by no means the worst managed or the most aggressive in risk taking,' says Satyajit Das, a derivatives trader turned consultant. 'If it curtails its activities then the loss of liquidity may affect other players and result in unrelated losses.'

Source: Mackenzie, M., Bullock, N. and Demos, T. (2012) 'JPMorgan loss exposes derivatives dangers', *Financial Times*, 15 May.
© The Financial Times Limited 2012. All Rights Reserved.

Questions

1 How did JPMorgan manage to lose so much money when trying to hedge its exposure?

2 What are the implications for the derivatives market of 'blow-ups' like these?

The objectives of hedging policy

Companies must clearly define the objectives of their hedging policy. Is the objective to secure a certain interest income or interest cost? Is the objective to minimise foreign currency expense, or to maximise or fix the domestic value of foreign currency income? An important determining factor here is whether a company's treasury department is designated as a *cost centre* or a *profit centre*. Within a cost centre, hedging will be seen solely as a means of reducing risk and providing a service to the rest of the company. If the treasury department is seen as a profit centre, however, there will be pressure to use derivatives in a more speculative manner. The consequences of speculating with derivatives can be disastrous, however.

Cornell and Shapiro (1988) argue that since exchange rate risk affects all aspects of a company's operations, exposure management should not be left solely in the hands of financial managers, but rather should be integrated into the company's general management. On this view, exchange rate expectations should inform production, marketing and other operational decisions so that hedging is an anticipatory strategy.

Identifying and quantifying the risk exposure

Companies must identify and quantify their interest and exchange rate risk exposures before they can implement an appropriate hedging strategy. They will have to decide whether to hedge exposures selectively or on a continuous basis. This choice will depend on a company's attitude to risk as well as its expectations on future interest rate and exchange rate changes. For example, a company may choose to hedge its interest rate exposure selectively only if it expects interest rates to change significantly.

Time horizon of hedging policy

It is important for companies to consider the time horizon they take when hedging exposures. While some companies hedge exposures up to and beyond 12 months, others take a shorter-term view.

Selection of hedging method

The final component of a company's hedging strategy is the selection of hedging methods appropriate to the nature of its exposure. A sensible strategy is to hedge as much interest and exchange rate risk as possible using internal hedging methods. Any remaining exposure can then be hedged using appropriate external methods. A number of factors restrict a company's ability to hedge internally, however, increasing the need to use external methods (see 'Internal risk management', Section 12.2). While there is a wide range of external instruments to choose from, the choice of derivative will depend heavily upon the relative importance to the company of the costs and benefits of the available derivatives. Some of the considerations are as follows:

- For exposures of non-standard size and duration, tailor-made derivatives (swaps, FRAs, OTC options) represent more appropriate hedging tools than traded options and futures.
- Options, while costing more, are appropriate when a company is not completely certain of making a transaction or when it is not completely certain about the direction in which interest or exchange rates will move.
- Bank-created products may be more appropriate for smaller companies as their treasury functions probably lack the experience and knowledge needed to use more complex traded derivatives.

12.7.2 The pros of risk management

There is an ongoing debate at both an academic and a practical level about the desirability of hedging by companies. Common sense tells us that a company should hedge an exposure if, and only if, the costs of executing the hedge are outweighed by the expected benefits. The actions of financial managers would seem to support the importance and benefits of hedging, given the enormous growth in the use of exchange and interest rate management instruments in recent years. It has been known for some time that large UK companies, including Tate & Lyle and Cadbury-Schweppes, have found benefits in adopting such instruments. The potential benefits which may arise from hedging exposures include the following:

Maintaining competitiveness

Adverse changes in interest and exchange rates may reduce the competitive position of a company compared with companies with lower levels of gearing or smaller exchange rate exposures, or compared with companies that have taken the precaution of hedging against rate changes.

Reducing bankruptcy risk

Adverse movements in interest and exchange rates may undermine the continued operation of a company. An example is that of a highly geared company with a large proportion of floating rate debt being forced into bankruptcy due to an increase in interest rates. Chen and King (2014) looked at the impact of hedging on companies' cost of debt based on a large sample of US firms from 1994 to 2009 and found that hedging reduced the cost of debt through lessening bankruptcy risk, reducing agency costs, and the lowering information asymmetry.

Restructuring capital obligations

Interest rate hedging methods can be used to restructure a company's capital profile by altering the nature of its interest obligations, thereby avoiding repaying existing debt or issuing new securities. Considerable savings can consequently be made in call fees and issue costs. At the same time, a wider range of financial sources becomes available to the company.

Reducing the volatility of corporate cash flows

Acting to reduce cash-flow volatility may increase the market rating or credit rating of a company and facilitate the process of forward planning.

Enhancing debt capacity

If interest rate hedging methods are being used to manage interest rate exposure, companies may be able to increase gearing levels or enhance their debt capacities. Academic research in the USA by Graham and Daniel (2002) substantiated this as a real benefit for companies that hedge. This view was supported by Belghitar et al. (2008) via their UK research that concluded both foreign currency and (to a greater extent) interest rate hedging created shareholder value via enhanced debt capacity.

Tax benefits of hedging

Research in the USA by Graham and Smith (1999) suggests that hedging increases the value of the company if it faces a convex tax function. In this case, income volatility leads to low tax payments in some periods and higher tax payments in others, causing the average tax burden to exceed the average tax the company would have had to pay on an equivalent stable stream of income. Research by Graham and Daniel (2002), however, discredited these findings.

Research by Geyer-Klingeberg et al. (2018) used meta-analysis to aggregate and analyse the empirical evidence of 132 previously published studies on the determinants of hedging. They concluded that 'hedging' companies were characterised by larger firms with high dividend payouts and lower levels of liquidity.

12.7.3 The cons of risk management

The benefits of hedging must be balanced against the problems of hedging, some of which may dissuade companies from engaging in exposure management.

The complicated nature of hedging instruments

A combination of unfamiliarity with the range of hedging methods available and a belief by potential users that such methods are complex may result in treasurers choosing not to hedge exchange and interest rate exposures.

The costs associated with derivatives

Companies may be dissuaded from using derivatives by the various fees, premiums, margin requirements and transaction costs associated with them.

The risks associated with using external hedging instruments

The perceived risk associated with using hedging instruments can sometimes dissuade potential users. In February 1995, in a now legendary disaster, Barings Bank went into receivership after making losses of over £860m on Nikkei index futures deals on SIMEX in Singapore and the Osaka derivatives exchange in Japan. The losses were accumulated by trader Nick Leeson, who was responsible for both the trading and back-office records of his deals, so there was no effective system of monitoring and checking his trading in derivatives.

In 1998, US hedge fund Long Term Capital Management (LTCM) was near to collapse with close on $1,400bn of derivatives on its financial position statement despite having investors' funds of only $3bn. LTCM had been using the steep gearing effect of derivatives to speculate on the pricing of various financial instruments. Derivatives were again cast in an unfavourable light in 2001 by the collapse of US energy giant Enron. While Enron's involvement in the USA's unregulated OTC derivatives market was not the reason for its failure, its questionable operations in the OTC market highlight the dangers of unregulated derivatives trading.

More recently, in January 2008 rogue trader Jérôme Kerviel at French bank Société Générale lost an estimated €4.9bn through the misuse of futures contracts. Worse was to come later in the year, however, when an AIG subsidiary lost a reported $18bn due to an overexposure in the much-criticised credit default swaps (CDS) market. The US Federal Reserve Bank swiftly announced the creation of an $85bn secured credit facility, resulting in, at the time, the largest government bailout of a private company in US history.

With an ever-expanding list of derivative disasters, it is no wonder that US investor and businessman Warren Buffett famously described derivatives bought for speculative purposes as 'financial weapons of mass destruction'.

The complicated financial reporting and tax treatments of derivatives

Traditionally, the accounting and tax treatment of derivatives has tended to lag behind the pace of their development owing to the dynamic nature of derivative markets. In the past the major problem regarding the accounting treatment of derivatives was knowing what information to disclose and how to disclose it. This led to companies reporting only superficial information and general strategies rather than disclosing detailed information. Accounting for derivatives has become increasingly complicated when the International Accounting Standards Board (IASB) adopting the rule-based approach of FAS 133, the US's Financial Accounting Standards Board's far-reaching accounting standard on derivatives and hedging, combining it with its own standard IAS 39 and IFRS9. Companies must now show any fair value changes in derivative prices in their income statements unless derivatives meet strict criteria on hedge effectiveness.

As far as the tax treatment of derivatives is concerned, companies should seek specialist advice before engaging in the derivatives market. This represents a further cost and may cause companies to be reluctant to use derivatives. As a guide, if a financial instrument is treated as a derivative for accounting purposes, the UK tax authorities will treat it as a derivative for tax purposes.

Diversification by shareholders may be superior to hedging

An alternative to hedging by individual companies is for shareholders to diversify away interest and exchange rate risk themselves by holding a diversified portfolio of shares, hence saving the costs associated with hedging at a corporate level. If shareholders hold diversified portfolios, some commentators argue that hedging by individual companies is motivated purely by management's desire to safeguard their jobs rather than a desire to enhance shareholder wealth.

The question of whether exchange rate risk should be hedged is the subject of Vignette 12.5.

Vignette 12.5

Hedging exchange rate risk: a tempting option

By Dan McCrum

Slicing and dicing of risk was one of the ways the financial system got itself into trouble, but the principle is sound: some investors would like to pick and choose the dangers they want exposure to, and cut out the rest. So when it comes to investing overseas, there is the tempting option of hedging out any gyrations in exchange rates, but it is one with a cost and the question remains as to whether in the long term it makes sense. In theory, the starting point for investing is that additional risks should be compensated by a satisfying increase in the level of return.

'With foreign currency the big difference is that a risk is not rewarded,' says Michael Shilling, chief executive of currency manager Pareto. 'With foreign currency there is no expectation of a return because there is no investment in wealth producing assets.' So if currency investing is a zero sum game – meaning one person's gain is another's loss – it makes sense not to play and instead hedge the risk away. Indeed, predicting currency movements is a thankless task, one which routinely defeats the best efforts of professionals.

A paper by Momtchil Pojarliev, director of currency trader Hathersage, and NYU Stern academic Richard M. Levich looked at returns for managed currency funds between 1990 and 2006. Over the

period the sector produced steady returns of about 25 basis points per month, but the majority of that performance could be attributed to just four factors or 'styles' of investing: trend following (by far the most important), carry trades, value and volatility. Less than a quarter of managers produced statistically significant excess returns, or 'alpha'.

Practicalities can also favour hedging. While some academics may argue that over time currency movements even out, it provides little comfort when sitting on the wrong side of a three-year trend in a pair of currencies. For funds such as corporate pension plans that have to mark to market asset values, assuming the trade will come good eventually is not an option.

'If you take a 10-year view it does matter where you start,' says Mr Shilling. 'You can always find a 10-year period where you come back to where you started, but there are a lot more 10-year periods where you do not.' For an institutional investor, the direct costs of hedging are also very low, with tight spreads and an expense as low as one or two basis points. A static investment can be passively hedged for currency risk by entering into forward contracts. When they mature there will be a cash settlement, and that cash flow will offset the change in value of the underlying asset. That hedge can then be rolled forward at regular intervals, and each one compensates for any movement in the exchange rate. The wrinkle is transaction cost.

The further into the future a hedge is agreed, the more expensive it becomes, but every time a hedge matures it generates cash flows that either require investing, or, if the hedge has incurred a loss, assets must be sold to meet the payment. For a growing fund with regular inflows of cash this just forms part of the regular investing activities. But that ongoing management and cash churn does impose a cost.

There is also a body of academic work that challenges the idea of a 'free lunch' from currency hedging. Real returns are naturally hedged by purchasing power parity, the tendency for prices of goods to equalise over time, so there is an argument that hedging increases portfolio volatility for investors with a time horizon of several years. Or more intuitively, for some investors currency exposure can be an intentional part of portfolio construction to

protect against inflation. Many UK savers, for instance, traditionally invested abroad as a hedge against a weak currency and an inflationary economy. Furthermore, correlation between equity markets and currencies can also mean that hedging is imperfect.

To hedge a diversified portfolio properly might mean calculating the correlation between, say the Canadian market and the US dollar versus the euro, and adjusting accordingly. But then the process becomes more complicated and, by extension, more expensive. So, perhaps surprisingly, there is no clear answer. As movements in bond prices tend to be highly unrelated to currency movements, the argument to hedge appears strongest for bond investors, who typically want to avoid equity-like risks and volatility. Money managers are increasingly offering hedged bond products to retail customers wanting the returns but not the risk of foreign markets. Investors can take the slice of risk they like, and disregard the rest.

 Source: McCrum, D. (2011) 'Hedging exchange rate risk: a tempting option', *Financial Times*, 1 April.
© The Financial Times Limited 2011. All Rights Reserved.

Questions

1 Is hedging exchange rate risk difficult from a practical point of view?

2 Do companies need to hedge exchange rate risk from a theoretical perspective?

12.7.4 Managing the use of derivatives

Despite the drawbacks just considered, there can be little doubt that, if used properly, derivatives can and do bring real benefits to the user company. In the cases cited where companies have made huge losses through the trading of derivatives, the problems were not so much with the derivatives themselves, but rather with the way that they were used (or misused). Some of these financial disasters have involved unauthorised trading (e.g. the Barings Bank collapse), raising the possibility that many companies may not have appropriate controls or monitoring procedures in place to regulate their derivatives dealings. The lesson for such companies is that they cannot ignore the need for well-defined risk management policies, referring specifically to:

■ the types of derivative instrument that can be used;

■ limits on the volume and principal amount of derivative transactions allowed;

■ the need to calculate regularly the market value of the company's derivative positions;

■ systems and procedures to prevent unauthorised dealings.

It is also sensible for companies to forbid using derivatives for speculative purposes. Once such policies are implemented, a company's derivatives transactions should be both more visible and more easily understood.

It might be argued that corporate treasurers are effectively in a 'no win' situation when it comes to risk management. Deciding not to hedge a specific exposure and doing nothing can be construed as speculation if an unfavourable movement in rates occurs. However, if the treasurer hedges the exposure and locks into a specific rate, and the market subsequently moves in a favourable direction, it might be considered bad judgement. This dilemma is perfectly illustrated in Vignette 12.6.

Vignette 12.6

MetLife to review hedging strategy after $2.1bn loss

Insurer reports its worst quarterly result in a decade because of derivatives losses

By Alistair Gray

MetLife posted its biggest quarterly loss in at least a decade after shifts in financial markets fuelled by Donald Trump's election victory triggered a $3.2bn hit to its derivatives portfolio. Steven Kandarian, chairman and chief executive, said the biggest US insurer by assets was reviewing protection it had taken out against low interest rates after the company appeared to be taken off guard by rising bond yields.

MetLife bought hedges to soften the impact of low rates, which hurt insurers by reducing the income they can generate from investments. Mr Kandarian has long positioned MetLife for persistently low rates. '"Lower for longer" is not going away anytime soon,' he said in the summer. But with yields on 10-year government bonds having risen markedly after Mr Trump's election victory in November, MetLife's hedges against low interest rates have become less valuable.

The company late on Wednesday reported a $2.1bn net loss for the three months to December 31, compared to $785m profit during the same period in 2015. The quarterly loss was the biggest in at least 10 years, according to data tracked by Bloomberg. MetLife recorded $3.2bn in net derivative losses in the fourth quarter, which it said reflected changes in interest rates, foreign currencies and equity markets. The company's operating earnings – which exclude the impact of the derivatives losses – rose 3 per cent to $1.4bn.

The loss at MetLife was triggered because generally accepted accounting principles – GAAP, the standard US framework for financial accounting – require insurers to mark the value of their derivatives to market. Mr Kandarian sought to reassure the market that MetLife would benefit from rising interest rates. Rising bond yields benefit insurers by reducing the value of their liabilities. However, the accounting rules do not allow insurers to mark their liabilities to market. This means the costs of rising rates show up in GAAP net income while the benefits of falling liabilities do not.

'Despite this accounting-related volatility [in the fourth quarter], rising interest rates remain favourable for MetLife over the longer term,' Mr Kandarian told analysts. Mr Kandarian said the company may modify its hedging strategy. 'We're examining various options,' he added.

Some analysts questioned whether the $3.2bn hit to MetLife's derivatives portfolio had an impact on the company's underlying business. They noted several other life insurers, which also reported their results this week, had not posted heavy

Vignette **12.6** (continued)

losses. Sean Dargan, analyst at Wells Fargo Securities, said the hedges against low interest rates had benefited MetLife over the years. However, he added: 'There are a lot of investors who now want MetLife to unwind these hedges.' Shares in MetLife were down 4.3 per cent on Thursday lunchtime in New York, giving the company a market capitalisation of $57.2bn.

Source: Gray, A. (2017) 'MetLife to review hedging strategy after $2.1bn loss', *Financial Times*, 2 February. © The Financial Times Limited 2018. All Rights Reserved.

Question

Could MetLife be considered to have made a mistake with their hedging policy given these reported record losses?

12.8 POLITICAL RISK

While most companies must consider the effects of interest rate risk and exchange rate risk, only multinational companies making direct foreign investments need consider political risk. Goddard (1990) defines political risk as 'the possibility of a multinational company being significantly affected by political events in a host country or a change in the political relationships between a host country and one or more other countries'. These may be favourable, such as granting investment incentives to encourage inward investment, or unfavourable, such as expropriation or seizure of assets.

Political risk management involves two stages: first, the assessment of political risk and its potential consequences; and second, the development and implementation of policies to minimise political risk.

12.8.1 Assessment of political risk

Demirag and Goddard (1994) point out that, since there is no consensus definition of political risk or political risk events, the development of a reliable method for measuring and analysing political risk is not easy. Two approaches to measuring political risk are commonly cited: *macro-assessment* and *micro-assessment.* Macro-assessment seeks to assess political risk on a country basis, without considering factors which are business-specific, whereas micro-assessment looks at political risk from the perspective of the investing company's business.

Macro-assessment of political risk can produce risk indices giving an indication of the level of political risk in each country. These indices focus on political stability and look at a range of political and social factors: relative power of political factions; extent of division by language, race or religion; social conditions; internal conflict; bureaucratic infrastructure, and so on. Rankings of countries by political risk indices and political risk maps of the world are produced regularly by *Marsh*, *Euromoney* and *AON*, or are available by subscription.

Individual companies that are considering investing in a specific country can use a number of different methods to assess its political risk from both a micro- and a macro-assessment perspective, including the following:

- *Checklist approach*: this involves making a judgement on all the factors that are thought to contribute to political risk and weighting them to produce a political risk index.
- *Delphi technique*: this calls for collecting expert opinions, perhaps using a question-naire, and weighting or aggregating them. Euromoney's analysis combines this tech-nique with a checklist approach.
- *Quantitative analysis*: quantitative analysis techniques such as sensitivity analysis or discriminant analysis can be used to identify the key factors influencing the level of political risk of a country.
- *Inspection visits*: Also known as the *grand tour*, this involves company staff visiting the country under consideration on a fact-finding visit.

Goddard (1990) found that UK multinationals typically used a subjective rather than a systematic approach to political risk analysis, with little use made of external advisers. A more recent approach to macro-assessment of political risk calculates a country's implied volatility (i.e. the volatility of the value of a country's economy) as a measure of its risk and this technique has shown itself to be a useful one (Clark 2002). Macro-assessment of political risk must be complemented by assessing the impact of political risk on a specific company – micro-assessment – since one company may be affected favourably by a risk factor which affects another company adversely. Import tariffs, for example, could adversely affect an importer but favourably affect a host country manufacturer.

12.8.2 Policies to manage political risk

The simplest way to manage political risk is to choose not to invest in those countries which are perceived as having too high a level of political risk. However, this ignores the fact that the returns from such an investment might more than compensate for the risk incurred.

Insuring against political risk

It is possible to insure against political risk through private companies such as Lloyd's of London and Allianz SE subsidiary Euler Hermes, but most insurance of this kind is through government departments or agencies. The government agency responsible for political risk insurance in the UK for trades over six months is the UK Export Finance department.

Negotiating agreements

Political risk can be addressed by negotiating concession agreements with host govern-ments, setting out the rules and restrictions under which the investing company may con-duct business. The weakness of such agreements is that they may be renegotiated or repudiated by the same or subsequent governments, although this is much less likely to occur with developed nations.

Financing and operating policies

It is possible to reduce political risk exposure by appropriate structuring of company operations. *Operating policies* suggest locating different stages of production in different countries; controlling the means by which finished goods are exported; concentrating key services such as research and development, marketing and treasury outside the host country; and avoiding becoming dependent on the output of any particular manufacturing facility.

Political risk exposure can also be reduced by choosing appropriate *financing policies*. As noted earlier, expropriation of assets is less likely if investment is financed locally as much as possible and if international banks and government agencies are involved in financing arrangements. Another financial strategy that could be employed is securing unconditional guarantees from the host government.

12.9 CONCLUSION

The area of exchange rate and interest rate risk management has grown rapidly in importance over the past 30 or so years and treasurers find themselves spending increasing amounts of time engaged in hedging company risk exposures. This elevation in importance has been mainly due to the increased volatility of interest and exchange rates and to the rapid growth in the risk management tools and techniques available.

Risk can be managed by using internal and external techniques. Internal techniques allow companies to hedge risk within their own financial position statement by the way in which they structure their assets and liabilities. Alternatively, companies can use one or more of the many external techniques available, such as swaps, options, futures and forwards. While these derivative instruments give more scope and flexibility to companies to manage their risk, their associated costs and their complicated nature must be considered.

There have been some huge losses reported by companies in recent years due to the misuse of derivatives. This should not detract, however, from the very real benefits that can be derived from hedging, whether by internal or external methods, provided that hedging techniques are used in an appropriate manner.

Growing levels of globalisation and foreign direct investment in the world economy mean that an increasing number of companies need to be aware of the impact that political risk can have on their foreign activities. This requires companies to be able to identify, quantify and manage their political risk exposures.

■ ■ ■ KEY POINTS

1 Interest and exchange rate risk management now plays an increasingly important role within corporate finance, owing to recent instability of interest and exchange rates.

2 Interest rate risk is faced by companies regardless of whether they lend or borrow at fixed or floating rates of interest.

3 Exchange rate risk can be classified into transaction, translation and economic risk: transaction risk and translation risk are faced only by companies with some form of foreign operations, whiles all companies face economic risk.

4 Interest and exchange rate risk can be hedged internally by how companies structure their assets and liabilities, but the degree to which companies can hedge their exposures internally is often limited.

5 External derivatives can be either traded derivatives or over-the-counter (OTC) derivatives.

6 Before the advent of derivatives, external hedging took the form of forward contracts and money market hedges. These techniques remain a popular way of hedging risk.

7 Financial futures are standardised agreements to buy or sell an underlying financial asset. They are traded on exchanges such as ICE Futures Europe and allow companies to lock into specified interest or exchange rates for set periods.

8 Options give the holder, on payment of a premium, the right but not the obligation to pay or receive interest, or to sell or buy currency, at a predetermined rate. Traded options are standardised with respect to maturity and principal, whereas OTC options are tailor-made.

9 Interest rate swaps are agreements to exchange interest payments based on a specified principal. They allow companies to hedge interest rate risk over long periods and to raise funds at more favourable rates than if they raised funds directly. Currency swaps are like interest rate swaps, but also involve exchange of principal. They allow companies to hedge translation and transaction risk, and to raise currency more cheaply than if they were to borrow it directly.

10 For companies to hedge effectively, it is important that they have a risk management strategy which specifies hedging objectives, identifies and quantifies exposures and selects appropriate hedging methods.

11 Advantages of using derivatives include greater certainty with respect to interest rates and currency transactions. Disadvantages include the complicated nature and expense of such instruments.

12 Recent derivatives disasters have come from derivatives misuse rather than from problems with derivatives themselves. If companies have well-defined guidelines to control the use of derivatives, and the required expertise and knowledge to monitor them, then they should benefit from their use.

13 Political risk is concerned with the effect on a company's value of political events in the host country. It can be managed by assessing political risk and its consequences, and by developing policies to minimise it.

14 Companies can assess political risk by using the checklist approach, the Delphi technique, quantitative analysis and inspection visits. Many companies use a subjective approach.

15 Political risk can be managed through insurance, negotiation of agreements, and financing and operating policies.

SELF-TEST QUESTIONS

Answers to these questions can be found on pages 467–9.

1 In the following cases, state which type of exchange rate risk the company is facing and whether this risk is beneficial or harmful in nature.

   (a) A power-generating company imports coal from Germany, paying for the coal in euros. The company expects the pound to weaken against the euro over the next few months.

   (b) A UK toy company supplies only the domestic market. Its only major competitor in this market is a US toy company. The pound is expected to weaken against the dollar over the next year.

   (c) A UK company has bought a factory in France, financing the purchase with sterling borrowing. Over the next year the pound is expected to appreciate against the euro.

2 Recommend internal hedging methods that a company can use to reduce translation risk and transaction risk.

3 What are the major differences between OTC options and traded options?

4 A company is going to borrow £6m in three months' time for a period of six months. It is afraid that interest rates will rise between now and the time that the loan is taken out. It intends to hedge the risk using futures contracts. Given that the contract size of three-month interest futures is £500,000, what kind of futures hedge should it create?

5 Identify the factors that influence a company's decision to hedge interest rate risk.

6 Which factors determine whether a company, having decided to hedge its interest rate exposure, uses internal hedging methods or external instruments? If it decides to use external instruments, what factors will determine which instruments will be used?

7 Which of the following will *not* help a company to hedge successfully against an *increase* in interest rates?

   (a) Selling interest rate futures contracts.

   (b) Swapping floating rate interest for fixed interest rate payments.

   (c) Buying a bank-created floor.

   (d) Splitting borrowing between fixed and floating rate interest loans.

   (e) Buying a put option on futures contracts.

8 What are the drawbacks of hedging exchange rate risk by using a swap agreement?

9 Given the following list of US sterling currency options (all with three months to run) and the fact that the current spot rate is $1.55/£, which option do you expect to have the highest market value?

   (a) Put option, strike price $1.55.

   (b) Call option, strike price $1.66.

   (c) Put option, strike price $1.42.

   (d) Call option, strike price $1.55.

   (e) Put option, strike price $1.71.

10 Explain how political risk may be assessed by a company considering foreign direct investment and identify the policies and strategies that it could use to mitigate the risk.

QUESTIONS FOR REVIEW

1 Discuss the factors that may persuade a company to hedge an interest rate exposure by using OTC options rather than financial futures contracts.

2 It is 1 January and Carrycan plc must make a payment of $364,897 in six months' time. The company plans to hedge its transaction exposure and has collected the following information.

> *Exchange rates:*
> $/£ spot rate   1.5617–1.5773
> Six-month $/£ forward rate   1.5455–1.5609

> *Money market rates:*

	Borrow	Deposit
US dollars	6%	4.5%
Sterling	7%	5.5%

> *Foreign currency option prices* (cents per £ for contract size £12,500):

Exercise price	Call option (June)	Put option (June)
$1.70	3.7	9.6

Calculate which of the following hedges is most attractive to Carrycan plc:

(a) forward market (i.e. a forward exchange contract);

(b) cash market (i.e. a money market hedge);

(c) currency options.

3 Discuss the factors that influence the price of traded options.

4 Two companies with the borrowing rates below are considering a swap agreement.

	Floating rate	Fixed rate
Company A	LIBOR	12%
Company B	LIBOR + 0.3%	13.5%

Company A needs a floating rate loan of £5m and Company B a fixed rate loan of £5m.

(a) Which company has a comparative advantage in floating rate debt and which company has a comparative advantage in fixed rate debt?

(b) At what rate will Company A be able to obtain floating rate debt and Company B be able to obtain fixed rate debt, if the two companies agree a swap and the benefits of the swap are split equally between them? Ignore bank charges.

5 Discuss the problem of political risk in the context of foreign direct investment, and the difficulties that political risk make cause for companies.

QUESTIONS FOR DISCUSSION

1   Goran plc is a UK company with export and import trade with the USA. The following transactions, in the currency specified, are due within the next six months:

Purchases of goods, cash payment due in three months   £116,000
Sale of finished goods, cash receipt due in three months $197,000
Purchase of goods, cash payment due in six months $447,000

Data relating to exchange rates and interest rates are as follows:

Exchange rates:	$/£	
Spot	1.7106 – 1.7140	
Three months forward	1.7024 – 1.7063	
Six months forward	1.6967 – 1.7006	

Interest rates	Borrow	Deposit
Sterling	12.5%	9.5%
Dollars	9.0%	6.0%

(a) Discuss four techniques that Goran might use to hedge against the foreign exchange risk involved in foreign trade.

(b) Calculate the net sterling receipts/payments that Goran might expect for both its three-month and six-month transactions if the company hedges foreign exchange risk using (i) the forward market and (ii) the money market.

2   Give a detailed explanation of how interest rate risk can be hedged using options and swaps. What are the advantages and disadvantages of these hedging methods?

3   Explain how a company can use financial futures to hedge its interest rate risks and identify any advantages and disadvantages that arise from their use.

4   The monthly cash budget of HYK Communications plc shows that the company will need £18 million in two months' time for a period of four months. Financial markets have been volatile recently and the finance director fears that short-term interest rates could either rise by as much as 150 basis points, or fall by 50 basis points. LIBOR is currently 6.5 per cent and HYK can borrow at LIBOR + 0.75 per cent.

The finance director wants to pay no more than 7.50 per cent, including option premium costs, but excluding the effect of margin requirements and commissions.

ICE Futures Europe £500,000 three-month futures prices: The value of one tick is £12.50

December	93.40
March	93.10
June	92.75

ICE Futures Europe £500,000 three-month options prices (premiums in annual per cent)

Exercise price	Calls			Puts		
	December	March	June	December	March	June
92.50	0.33	0.88	1.04	–	–	0.08
93.00	0.16	0.52	0.76	–	0.20	0.34
93.50	0.10	0.24	0.42	0.18	0.60	1.93
94.00	–	0.05	0.18	0.36	1.35	1.92

Assume it is now 1 December and that exchange-traded futures and options contracts expire at the end of the month. Ignore margin requirements and default risk.

Required:

Estimate the results of undertaking EACH of an interest rate futures hedge and an interest rate options hedge on the ICE Futures Europe exchange, if LIBOR:

(i) increases by 150 basis points;

(ii) decreases by 50 basis points.

Discuss how successful the hedges would have been, stating clearly any assumptions made.

References

Bank for International Settlements (2016) *Triennial Central Bank Survey of Foreign Exchange and Derivatives Market Activity in 2016*, Basel: BIS.

Belghitar, Y., Clark, E. and Judge, A. (2008) 'The value effects of foreign currency and interest rate hedging: the UK evidence', *International Journal of Business*, vol. 13, no. 1.

Buckley, A. (2003) *Multinational Finance*, 5th edn, Harlow: FT Prentice Hall.

Chen, J. and King, T. (2014) 'Corporate hedging and the cost of debt', *Journal of Corporate Finance*, December, vol. 29, pp. 221–45.

Clark, E. (2002) 'Measuring country risk as implied volatility', *Wilmott Magazine*, September, pp. 64–7.

Cornell, B. and Shapiro, A. (1988) 'Managing foreign exchange risks', in Chew, D. (ed.) *New Developments in International Finance*, Malden, MA: Blackwell.

Demirag, I. and Goddard, S. (1994) *Financial Management for International Business*, London: McGraw-Hill.

Geyer-Klingeberg, J., Hang, M., Rathgeber, A., Stöck, S. and Walter, M. (2018) 'What do we really know about corporate hedging? A meta-analytical study', *Business Research*, vol. 11, February, Issue 1, pp. 1–31.

Goddard, S. (1990) 'Political risk in international capital budgeting', *Managerial Finance*, vol. 16, no. 2, pp. 7–12.

Graham, J. and Daniel, A.R. (2002) 'Do firms hedge in response to tax incentives?', *Journal of Finance*, vol. 57, pp. 815–39.

Graham, J. and Smith, C. (1999) 'Tax incentives to hedge', *Journal of Finance*, vol. 54, no. 6, pp. 2241–62.

Winstone, D. (2000) *Financial Derivatives: Hedging with Futures, Forwards, Options and Swaps*, Andover: Thomson Learning.

Recommended reading

For a book that gives a clear and easily understandable account of the use of derivatives and the markets on which they trade from a UK perspective, see:

Taylor, F. (2011) *Mastering Derivatives Markets*, 4th edn, London: FT Prentice Hall.

For a book with a US perspective on risk management and derivatives, see:

Kolb, R. and Overdahl, J. (2009) *Financial Derivatives: Tools and Techniques for Modern Risk Management and Pricing*, 4th edn, Hoboken, NJ: John Wiley & Sons.

For a book which gives a good overview of international finance including useful chapters on foreign exchange, hedging and derivatives, see:

Buckley, A. (2012) *International Finance*, Harlow: FT Prentice Hall.

Important and informative books, papers and articles recommended for further reading include the following:

Baird, S. (2004) 'What do rising interest rates mean for treasurers?', *www.gtnews.com*, November.

Black, F. and Scholes, M. (1973) 'The pricing of options and corporate liabilities', *Journal of Political Economy*, vol. 18, pp. 637–59.

Cooper, S. and Weston S. (1995) 'The pricing of over-the-counter options', *Bank of England Quarterly Bulletin*, Q4, pp. 375–81.

Dhanani, A., Fifield, S., Helliar, S. and Stevenson, L. (2007) 'Why UK companies hedge interest rate risk', *Studies in Economics and Finance*, vol. 24, pp. 72–90.

Hull, J. (2017) *Options, Futures and Other Derivatives*, 9th edn, Harlow: Pearson Education.

Hutton, A. and Kent, E. (2016) 'The foreign exchange and over-the-counter interest rate derivatives market in the United Kingdom', *Bank of England Quarterly Bulletin*, Q4, pp. 224–37.

Useful websites of derivatives exchanges from around the world include:

http://www.cboe.com: Chicago Board Options Exchange

http://www.cmegroup.com: CME Group

http://www.euronext.com: Euronext

http://www.eurexchange.com: Eurex, European Derivative Exchange

http://www.theice.com/futures-europe: ICE Futures Europe

http://www.sgx.com: Singapore Exchange

Chapter 1

1 *See* Sections 1.1.1 and 1.1.2.

2 (a) $500 \times (1 + 0.12)^5 = £881$

   (b) $500/(1 + 0.12)^5 = £284$

   (c) $500/0.12 = £4,167$

   (d) $500 \times 3.605 = £1,803$

3 The financial manager's job normally falls under the control of the financial director. He oversees the financial controller, who deals with the accounting side, and the corporate treasurer, who carries out financial management tasks. These tasks will include:

   – investment decisions, capital budgeting and investment appraisal;

   – financing decisions, including raising debt and equity finance;

   – managing working capital, including cash, trade receivables and inventory;

   – dividend policy formulation;

   – interest rate and foreign currency management.

4 Examples could include the following:

   – insufficient finance or expensive finance, leading to rejection of investment projects;

   – high dividends, restricting retained earnings and increasing the need for external finance;

   – many attractive projects, financed by increased retained earnings, decreasing dividends.

5 (a) *Profit maximisation*: the problem with this as the main goal of the financial manager is that profit figures can be manipulated, they have no time dimension if profits are maximised year after year and also they do not take risk into account.

   (b) *Sales maximisation*: as the main goal of the financial manager this is even further off the mark than profit maximisation. Market share may be an initial goal in obtaining a market foothold. Sales maximisation, taken to the extreme, can lead via overtrading to bankruptcy.

   (c) *Maximisation of benefit to employees and the local community*: this is also off the mark as the main goal of the financial manager. If taken to the extreme, it could lead to cash-flow problems. While it is important to keep both employees and the local community happy, this is not the main goal.

   (d) *Maximisation of shareholder wealth*: this is the correct goal, since as owners their wealth should be maximised.

6 How does a financial manager maximise shareholder wealth? Shareholders derive wealth from share ownership through capital gains and dividend payments. The financial manager, then, should maximise the present value of these. If capital markets are efficient, the current market price of a share should be the net present value of all future benefits accruing to the share. Current market share price, then, can be used as a proxy for shareholder wealth. To maximise shareholder wealth, a financial manager should accept all projects with positive net present values, as this will maximise the market share price.

7   The agency problem arises because of a divorce of ownership and control. Within a public limited company (plc), there are a number of examples of the agency problem, the most important being that existing between shareholders (principal) and managers (agent). The problem exists because of divergent goals and asymmetry of information. Managers act to maximise their own wealth rather than the shareholders' wealth. There are various ways to reduce the agency problem:

- do nothing, if the costs of divergent behaviour are low;
- monitor agents, if contracting or divergent behaviour costs are high;
- use a reward/punishment contract, if monitoring and divergent behaviour costs are high.

As regards the shareholders/managers agency problem, monitoring costs and divergent behaviour costs are high so shareholders can use contracts to reward managers for good performance and could give managers shares in the company they manage, making them shareholders themselves.

8   The correct answer is (d), because including covenants in bond deeds is relevant to providers of debt finance as a way of encouraging optimal behaviour by shareholders. It does not therefore lead to a reduction in the agency problem experienced by shareholders.

9   Some possible managerial goals are given in Section 1.5.1.

10   The size of the agency problem reflects the relative power of shareholders with respect to managers. Since, in the UK, institutional investors now have significant holdings in UK public limited companies, they can bring significant pressure to bear on company managers as a way of encouraging goal congruence. As in the USA, shareholder groups are growing as a way of enhancing and focusing this pressure. It can be argued that, for institutional investors in UK companies, the agency problem is being slowly attenuated. For smaller investors, however, this may not be the case.

Chapter 2

1   This topic is discussed in Section 2.1.3. The main factors influencing the split between internal and external finance are as follows:

- the level of finance required;
- the cash flow from existing operations;
- the opportunity cost of retained earnings;
- the costs associated with raising external finance;
- the availability of external sources of finance;
- dividend policy.

2   The relevance of the efficient market hypothesis for financial management is that, if the hypothesis holds true, the company's 'real' financial position will be reflected in the share price. If the company makes a 'good' financial decision, this will be reflected in an increase in the share price. Similarly, a 'bad' financial decision will cause the share price to fall. In order to maximise shareholder wealth, the financial manager need only concentrate on maximising

the NPV of investment projects, and need not consider matters such as the way in which the future position of the company will be reflected in the company's financial statements. The financial manager, then, may use rational decision rules and have confidence that the market will rapidly reflect the effects of those decisions in the company's share price.

3 The incorrect statement is (b) since, if capital markets are strong form efficient, then nobody, not even people with insider information, will be able to make abnormal returns.

4 These terms are discussed in Section 2.3.1.

5 It is hard to test for strong form efficiency directly, i.e. by studying the market's *use* of information, because it can always be objected that investors with access to inside information can make abnormal gains. Tests for strong form efficiency are therefore *indirect,* examining the performance of *users* of information who may have access to inside information or who have special training for share dealing, such as fund managers.

6 Anomalies in share price behaviour are discussed in Section 2.3.6. You could discuss calendar effects, size anomalies and value effects.

7 Financial performance measures and financial ratios mean little in isolation. To assess financial performance, we need to compare ratios with benchmarks such as:
- target performance measures set by managers;
- sector or industry norms;
- performance measures and ratios of similar companies;
- performance measures and ratios of the same company from previous years.

All such comparisons should be made with caution due to the problems in analysing financial performance arising from differing accounting policies and creative accounting.

8 The answer to this question is given in Section 2.4.2 and following sections. You should be able to define *all* the ratios. If you cannot, study these sections further until you can. Compare your calculations to the illustrative calculations given.

9 The problems that may be encountered in using ratio analysis to assess the health and performance of companies include:
- all ratios are imperfect and imprecise and should be treated as guidelines;
- ratios are only as reliable as the accounting figures they are based on;
- no two companies are identical, so inter-company comparisons need care;
- ratios mean little in isolation and need other information to explain them;
- ratio analysis tends to be performed on historical data and so may not be an accurate guide to either current position or future activity.

10 Economic value added (EVA) is the difference between adjusted operating profit after tax and a cost of capital charge on the adjusted value of invested capital. It can help managers to increase shareholder wealth by directing their attention to the drivers that create value for shareholders, such as increasing net operating profit after tax, investing in projects with a return greater than the company's cost of capital or reducing the cost of capital or the value of invested capital.

Chapter 3

1 It is important to match the financing with the life of assets. We can analyse assets into non-current assets, permanent current assets and fluctuating current assets. Permanent current assets, being 'core' current assets which are needed to support normal levels of sales, should be financed from a long-term source. The working capital policy chosen should take account of the relative risk of long- and short-term finance to the company and the need to balance liquidity against profitability. An aggressive financing policy will use short-term funds to finance fluctuating current assets as well as to finance part of the permanent current assets. A conservative financing policy will use long-term funds to finance permanent current assets as well as to finance part of the fluctuating current assets. An aggressive financing policy will be more profitable, but riskier.

2 The cash conversion cycle is the sum of the inventory conversion period (inventory days) and the trade receivables conversion period (trade receivables days), less the trade payables deferral period (trade payables days). Investment in working capital must be financed and the longer the cash conversion cycle, the more capital is tied up and the higher the cost. A company could reduce the working capital tied up by optimising the components of the cash conversion cycle. So, for example, shortening the inventory conversion period could reduce the working capital requirement and increase profitability.

3 The solution to this question is given in Section 3.2.2.

4 Overtrading arises when a company seeks to do too much too quickly, without sufficient long-term capital to support its operations. While a company which is overtrading may well be profitable, it is likely to meet difficulties with liquidity and may be unable to meet its financial obligations to trade payables and others as they fall due. Strategies that could be considered by management wishing to address the problem of overtrading include: introduction of new capital, possibly from shareholders; better control and management of working capital and a reduction in business activity in order to consolidate the company's position and build up capital through retained earnings.

5 Cash-flow problems can arise from:
  – making losses, since continuing losses will lead to cash-flow problems;
  – inflation, since historical profit may be insufficient to replace assets;
  – growth, since this calls for investment in non-current assets and working capital;
  – seasonal business, due to imbalances in cash flow;
  – significant one-off items of expenditure, such as repayment of debt capital.

Cash-flow problems can be eased in several ways. Examples include postponing capital expenditure (e.g. extending vehicle replacement life), accelerating cash inflows (e.g. offering cash discounts, chasing up slow payers), shelving investment plans, selling off non-core assets and reducing cash outflows. Economies could be found in normal operations as well.

6 There are three reasons why a company may choose to have reserves of cash. Companies need to have a cash reserve to balance short-term cash inflows and outflows: this is the transactions motive for holding cash. The precautionary motive for holding cash refers to the fact that a company may choose to have cash reserves to meet unexpected demands. Companies may also build up cash reserves to take advantage of investment opportunities that may occur: this is the speculative motive for holding cash.

7   Short-term cash surpluses should be invested on a short-term basis without risk of capital loss. In selecting investment methods, the finance director should consider: the size of the surplus; how easy it is to get back the cash invested; the maturity, risk and yield of different investments and any penalties for early liquidation. Short-term instruments which could be discussed include term deposits, sterling certificates of deposit, Treasury bills, sterling commercial paper and gilts.

8   The risk of bad debts could be minimised if the creditworthiness of new customers is assessed and reviewed on a regular basis. Relevant information should be obtained from a variety of sources, including bank references, trade references, published information, such as accounts and the financial media, and credit reference agencies. In addition, the credit analysis system should adopt a cost-effective approach so that the extent of the credit assessment should reflect the size of the order, the likelihood of subsequent business and the amount of credit requested.

9   Proposed changes to credit policy should be evaluated in terms of the additional costs and benefits that will result from their being undertaken. For example, the cost of introducing cash discounts can be compared with the benefit of faster settlement of accounts in terms of reduced interest charges, and possibly the additional business that may result. The change should be undertaken only if the marginal benefits arising from the new policy exceed its marginal costs.

10 Factors offer a range of services in sales administration and collecting cash due from trade receivables, including administration of sales invoicing and accounting, collecting cash due, chasing up late payers, advancing cash against the security of trade receivables due and offering protection against non-payment via non-recourse factoring. Invoice discounting, however, involves the sale of selected invoices to another company. Its main value lies in the improvement in cash flow that it offers.

Chapter 4

1   In corporate finance, a key concept is the relationship between risk and return. The higher the risk associated with a given investment, the higher will be the return required in exchange for investing in it. Bonds are debt finance paying a fixed annual return and are secured on assets of the company. They therefore have a much lower risk than ordinary equity, which is unsecured and which has no right to receive a dividend. If a company fails, the ordinary shareholders may receive nothing at all. In exchange for this higher risk, ordinary shareholders will require a higher return.

2   Some of the important rights, which are available to shareholders in their position as owners of a company, are mentioned in Section 4.1.1.

3   A company may obtain such a quotation through a public offer, a placing or an introduction, as discussed in Section 4.2.2.

4   The advantages and disadvantages to be considered by an unquoted company considering seeking a stock exchange listing include the following.

   Advantages of obtaining a quotation:

   — opens up new avenues for the company to raise finance;

   — increases the marketability of the company's shares;

   — raises the profile of the company;

– the company may obtain a better credit rating;

– the company can use its shares to fund future takeover activity.

Disadvantages of obtaining a quotation:

– the costs of flotation must be met;

– the cost of compliance with listing regulations;

– the company may be open to a hostile takeover bid;

– dilution of control will result from wider share ownership;

– the company may have to satisfy increased shareholder expectations.

5 Pre-emptive rights mean that the company has an obligation to offer any new issue of shares to the existing shareholders before making a public offer. The importance to shareholders of pre-emptive rights is that it prevents significant changes in the structure of ownership and control of the company since the shares are offered to existing shareholders (although not necessarily taken up) in proportion to their existing holdings.

6 The advantage to a company of a rights issue is that, depending on market conditions, it may be a cheaper method of raising equity finance than a public offer. This is partly because the issue costs of a rights issue are lower than in the case of a public offer. A disadvantage is that, if insufficient funds are raised from the rights issue, the company must take further steps to secure the finance that it needs. This will be a more expensive and lengthy process than would be the case with a single placing of shares.

7 Rights issue price $= £2.50 \times 0.8 = £2.00$

Theoretical ex-rights price $= ((4 \times 2.50) + 2.00)/5 = £2.40$

Value of rights per existing share $= (2.40 - 2.00)/4 = 0.1$, i.e. 10p per share

The correct answer is therefore (a).

8 The correct answer is (d), a scrip issue, also known as a bonus issue. If you are unsure about this, see Section 4.4.

9 Preference shares do not enjoy great popularity as a source of finance because they are less tax efficient than debt. They are also riskier than debt since there is no right to receive a preference dividend, although cumulative preference shares will preserve the right to receive unpaid dividends.

10 You should have chosen (c), that a cumulative preference share carries forward the right to receive unpaid preference dividends. The right to be converted into ordinary shares at a future date (a) is carried by convertible preference shares, and the right to receive a share of residual profits (b) is carried by participating preference shares. All three types of preference share entitle their holders to a fixed dividend rate (d). Voting rights at the company's AGM (e) may be attached to preference shares, but it is very unlikely.

Chapter 5

1 The answer to this question can be found at the start of Section 5.1.

2 (a) A covenant places limitations on the actions of managers in order to safeguard the investment made by providers of debt finance.

(b) Refinancing involves replacing existing finance with new finance. This may occur at redemption, if existing debt is replaced by a new issue of debt, or as part of a restructuring of a company's capital structure in line with financial plans.

(c) A redemption window is a period during which bonds can be redeemed.

3 (a) Deep discount bonds are bonds issued at a large discount to nominal value, which will be redeemed at or above nominal value on maturity. They may be attractive to companies which need a low servicing cost during the life of the bond and which will be able to meet the high cost of redemption at maturity. Investors might be attracted to the large capital gain on offer, which will have tax advantages for some.

(b) Zero coupon bonds are bonds issued at a large discount to nominal value which pay no interest. The investor obtains a capital gain from the difference between the issue price and the redemption value, which is usually nominal value. Attractions for companies are similar to those for deep discount bonds.

(c) A warrant is a right to buy new shares at a future date at a fixed, predetermined price. Warrants are usually issued as part of a package with unsecured loan notes to make them more attractive. They are detachable from the loan notes and can be sold and bought separately. Investors may find them attractive because they offer potentially high gains compared with investing in the underlying shares.

(d) Convertible bonds are bonds which can be converted into ordinary shares at the option of the holder. The interest rate on convertibles is therefore lower, since the holder has the option to participate in the growth of the company, unlike the holder of ordinary bonds.

4 The answer to this question can be found by referring to Section 5.3.1.

5 The conversion premium is the premium per share on converting a convertible bond into equity. The rights premium is the premium per share of a convertible security over an equivalent bond with a similar coupon, reflecting the option to convert carried by the convertible security. The relationship between conversion premium, rights premium and market value of a convertible bond can be illustrated by a diagram (*see* Figure 5.2).

6 The company will consider the length of time remaining to maturity: the general level of interest rates and the term structure of interest rates; the rate of return on other securities, especially ordinary equity; expectations of likely movements in interest rates and inflation rates and the required return of investors in debentures.

7 *Advantages:*

- convertibles may be attractive to some investors;
- interest rates on convertibles are usually lower than on straight bonds;
- interest charges on bonds are tax allowable;
- bonds increase gearing but might decrease the cost of capital;
- convertible bonds can be self-liquidating;
- conversion will not harm the capital structure and may even help it.

Disadvantages:

- there may be covenants attached to convertible bonds;
- issuing bonds decreases debt capacity;

    — dilution of EPS may occur on conversion;

    — conversion may cause dilution of control of existing shareholders.

8 As the price of the underlying share changes, there is a larger proportionate movement in the price of the warrant than in the price of the underlying share. In consequence, it is possible to make a greater proportionate gain (or loss) by investing in warrants than by investing in the underlying share. This is called the gearing effect of warrants.

9 Current ex-interest market value = $(9 \times 2.487) + (100 \times 0.751) = £97.48$
If the bonds had been irredeemable, ex-interest market value = $£9/0.1 = £90$

10 A discussion of the attractions of leasing as a source of finance can be found by referring to Sections 5.8.2 and 5.8.3.

Chapter 6

1 The payback method cannot be recommended as the main method used by a company to assess potential investment projects because it has serious disadvantages, including:

    — payback ignores the time value of money;

    — payback ignores the timing of cash flows within the payback period;

    — payback ignores post-payback cash flows;

    — the choice of payback period is arbitrary;

    — payback does not measure profitability.

2 *Project A*

Average annual accounting profit = $(13,000 - 10,000)/4 = £750$

Average annual investment = $10,000/2 = £5,000$

Return on capital employed = $(750 \times 100)/5,000 = 15\%$

Project B

Average annual accounting profit = $(30,000 - 15,000)/5 = £3,000$

Average annual investment = $15,000/2 = £7,500$

Return on capital employed = $(3,000 \times 100)/7,500 = 40\%$

Project C

Average annual accounting profit = $(24,000 - 20,000)/4 = £1,000$

Average annual investment = $20,000/2 = £10,000$

Return on capital employed = $(1,000 \times 100)/10,000 = 10\%$

Project	ROCE (%)	Ranking
A	15	2
B	40	1
C	10	3

If the target ROCE is 12 per cent, projects A and B will be accepted.

3 The shortcomings of return on capital employed (ROCE) as an investment appraisal method are: it ignores the time value of money; it ignores the timing of cash flows; it uses accounting profits rather than cash flows and it does not take account of the size of the initial investment. However, ROCE gives an answer as a percentage return, which is a familiar measure of return, and is a simple method to apply. It can be used to compare mutually exclusive projects and can also indicate whether a project is a 'good' one compared to a target ROCE. For these reasons, it is used quite widely in industry.

4 *Project A*

Year	Cash flow (£)	12% discount factor	Present value (£)
0	(10,000)	1.000	(10,000)
1	5,000	0.893	4,465
2	5,000	0.797	3,985
3	2,000	0.712	1,424
4	1,000	0.636	636
		Net present value	510

Project B

Year	Cash flow (£)	12% discount factor	Present value (£)
0	(15,000)	1.000	(15,000)
1	5,000	0.893	4,465
2	5,000	0.797	3,985
3	5,000	0.712	3,560
4	10,000	0.636	6,360
5	5,000	0.567	2,835
		Net present value	6,205

Project C

Year	Cash flow (£)	12% discount factor	Present value (£)
0	(20,000)	1.000	(20,000)
1	10,000	0.893	8,930
2	10,000	0.797	7,970
3	4,000	0.712	2,848
4	2,000	0.636	1,272
		Net present value	1,020

Summary

Project	NPV (£)	Ranking
A	510	3
B	6,205	1
C	1,020	2

Since all three projects have a positive NPV, they are all acceptable.

5 The advantages of the net present value method of investment appraisal are that it:
- takes account of the time value of money;
- takes account of the amount and timing of cash flows;
- uses cash flows rather than accounting profit;
- takes account of all relevant cash flows over the life of the project;
- can take account of both conventional and non-conventional cash flows;
- can take account of changes in discount rate during the life of the project;
- gives an absolute rather than a relative measure of the desirability of the project;
- can be used to compare all investment projects.

6 If an investment project has positive and negative cash flows in successive periods (non-conventional cash flows), it may have more than one internal rate of return. This may result in incorrect decisions being taken if the IRR decision rule is applied. The NPV method has no difficulty in accommodating non-conventional cash flows.

7 There is no conflict between the NPV and IRR methods when they are applied to a single investment project with conventional cash flows. In other situations, such as comparing mutually exclusive projects, the two methods may give conflicting results. In all cases where this conflict occurs, the project with the highest NPV should be chosen. This can be proven by examining the incremental cash flows of the projects concerned. The reason for the conflict between the two methods can also be viewed graphically.

8 The answer to this question is contained in Section 6.4.

9 If a company is restricted in the capital available for investment, it will not be able to undertake all projects with a positive NPV and is in a capital rationing situation. Capital rationing may be either soft (owing to internal factors) or hard (owing to external factors). Soft capital rationing may arise if management adopts a policy of stable growth, is reluctant to issue new equity or wishes to avoid raising new debt capital. It may also arise if management wants to encourage competition for funds. Hard capital rationing may arise because the capital markets are depressed or because investors consider the company to be too risky.

10 If projects are divisible and independent, they can be ranked by using the profitability index or cost–benefit ratio. If projects are not divisible, then combinations of projects must be examined to find the investment schedule giving the highest NPV.

Chapter 7

1 The cash flows that are relevant to an investment appraisal calculation are those which will arise or change by undertaking the investment project. Direct costs incurred, such as purchased raw materials, are relevant, as are changes in existing cash flows (incremental cash flows), such as additional fixed costs. The opportunity cost of labour and raw materials, which have alternative uses, may be a relevant cost. Tax liabilities are also relevant.

2 The real cost of capital can be found by deflating the nominal (or money terms) cost of capital. Nominal project cash flows can be obtained by inflating estimated cash flows to take account of inflation which is specific to particular costs and revenues. Real project cash flows can be obtained by deflating nominal project cash flows to take account of general inflation.

The NPV of the project can then be found either by discounting nominal cash flows by the nominal cost of capital (the nominal or money terms approach) or by discounting real cash flows by the real cost of capital (the real terms approach). The NPV will have the same value whichever method is used.

3   Evaluating investment projects is made more difficult by the existence of inflation. While it may be possible to forecast general inflation into the near future, it is much harder to forecast specific inflation rates for individual costs and revenues. If specific inflation forecasts can be obtained and used, it is likely that the evaluation of an investment project will be more accurate than if account were taken only of general inflation. The incremental benefit of this increased accuracy would need to be weighed against the cost of obtaining and processing the necessary data, however. Failure to take account of inflation at all might lead to unrealistic estimates of the value of an investment project.

4   The answer to this question can be found in the discussion at the start of Section 7.4 on the relationship between risk and the variability of returns.

5   Sensitivity analysis examines how responsive the project's NPV is to changes in the variables from which it has been calculated. There are two methods: in the first, variables are changed by a set amount and the NPV is recalculated; in the second, the amounts by which individual variables would have to change to make the project's NPV become zero are determined. In both methods, only one variable is changed at a time. Both methods give an indication of the key variables within the project. These variables may merit further investigation and indicate where management should focus attention in to ensure the success of the project. However, sensitivity analysis gives no indication of whether changes in key variables are likely to occur or are even possible, and so it is not a method of assessing risk.

6   The reasons why payback is commonly used to deal with risk in investment projects are that it is a useful test for companies concerned about short-term liquidity; it focuses attention on the short term, which is more certain and hence less risky than the long term; and it guards against unforeseen changes in economic circumstances.

7   The answer to this question can be found by referring to Section 7.4.4.

8   The answer to this question can be found by referring to Section 7.4.6.

9   The answer to this question can be found by referring to Section 7.5.1.

10   The answer to this question can be found by referring to Section 7.6.

Chapter 8

1   Risk may be divided into systematic risk and unsystematic risk. Systematic risk refers to the extent to which a company's cash flows are affected by factors not specific to the company. It is determined by the sensitivity of the cash flows to the general level of economic activity and by its operating gearing.

Unsystematic risk refers to the extent to which a firm's cash flows are affected by company-specific factors, such as the quality of its managers, the level of its advertising, the effectiveness of its R&D and the skill of its labour.

By careful choice of the investments in a portfolio, unsystematic risk can be diversified away. Systematic risk, however, cannot be diversified away, since it is experienced by all companies. The risk of a well-diversified portfolio will be similar to the systematic risk of the market as a whole.

2 Investments may not perform as expected. In a well-diversified portfolio, investments that perform well will tend to balance those that do not, and only systematic risk will remain. The systematic risk of the portfolio will be the same as the average systematic risk of the market as a whole. If an investor wants to avoid risk altogether, he or she must invest in risk-free securities.

A company's managers may feel that shareholders' interests will be best served by spreading risk through diversification. A shareholder with a well-diversified portfolio, however, will already have eliminated unsystematic risk. For such shareholders, diversification at the company level is of no value.

For a shareholder who does not hold a well-diversified portfolio, and who has not eliminated unsystematic risk, such diversification may be of some value.

3 If the set of all possible portfolios that can be formulated from a large number of given securities is considered, there are a large number of portfolios which are the most desirable to a rational investor. These are the portfolios that offer the highest return for a given level of risk, or the lowest risk for a given level of expected return. Such portfolios are known as efficient portfolios and lie along the efficient frontier of the set of all possible portfolios in a graph of portfolio returns against portfolio risk. However, it is not possible to say which portfolio an individual investor would prefer as this would depend solely on his or her attitude to risk and return.

The efficient portfolio which is best suited to the risk–return characteristics of a particular individual investor is an optimal portfolio for that investor. It represents a tangency point of the individual investor's utility or indifference curve on the efficient frontier.

4 Risk-free assets are important to portfolio theory as they allow the market portfolio, the optimum combination of risky investments, to be identified. If a line is pivoted clockwise about the risk-free rate of return until it touches the efficient frontier, the point of tangency represents the market portfolio. The line linking the risk-free rate of return and the market portfolio is known as the capital market line. Subsequently, investors can distribute their funds between the risk-free assets and the market portfolio and move along this line. This allows investors to attain higher levels of utility compared with the situation where no risk-free assets are available and investors are limited to investing along the efficient frontier. Hence, the identification of risk-free assets is of vital importance to portfolio theory.

5 The risk-free rate is approximated in practice by using the yield on government securities such as Treasury bills. As for the capital market line, it will not be a straight line in practice because investors, while being able to lend at the risk-free rate, cannot borrow at the risk-free rate. Therefore, the CML will kink downwards to the right-hand side of the market portfolio.

6 The limitations of portfolio theory as an aid to investment are:
   - it assumes that investors can borrow at the risk-free rate is unrealistic;
   - transaction costs deter investors from making changes to portfolios;
   - the composition of the market portfolio is difficult to determine;
   - should not the market portfolio include all securities in all capital markets?
   - securities are not divisible in practice;

– how can we determine the expected risks and returns of securities?

– how do investors make choices from the wide variety of possibilities?

– how can investors determine their own utility function?

7 The answer to this question can be found by referring to Section 8.5.

8 The answer to this question can be found by referring to Section 8.6.1.

9 The answer to this question can be found by referring to Section 8.6.2.

10 $R_m = 10$ per cent, $R_f = 4$ per cent, $Cov_{ls,m} = 7.5$, $\sigma_m^2 = 4.5$

$\beta_{ls} = Cov_{ls,m}/\sigma_m^2 = 7.5/4.5 = 1.67$

$R_{ls} = R_f + \beta_{ls}(R_m - R_f) = 4 + (1.67 \times (10 - 4)) = 14\%$

The required rate of return on Lime Spider's shares is therefore 14 per cent.

Chapter 9

1 Market value of equity, $E = 500,000 \times 1.50 = £750,000$

Market value of debt, $D = $ nil

Cost of equity capital, $K_e = $ dividend/market value of share $= 100 \times 27/150 = 18\%$

Since there is no debt capital, WACC $= K_e = 18\%$

2 $K_d = 100 \times 8/92 = 8.7\%$

$K_d(\text{after tax}) = 8.7 \times (1 - 0.3) = 6.1\%$

3 $E = 1,000,000 \times 0.49 = £490,000$

$D = 100,000 \times 82/100 = £82,000$

$E + D = 82,000 + 490,000 = £572,000$

$K_e = 100 \times 6/49 = 12.24\%$

$K_d \text{ (before tax)} = $ Interest/market value $= 100 \times 8/82 = 9.76\%$

$$\text{WACC} = ((K_e \times E) + (K_d(1 - t) \times D))/(E + D)$$

$$= ((12.24 \times 490,000) + (9.76 \times 0.7 \times 85,000))/572,000$$

$$= 11.46\%$$

4 There are certain conditions that must be met for it to be appropriate to use a historical WACC to appraise new projects, as follows:

■ The new project must have a similar level of business risk to the average business risk of a company's existing projects.

■ The amount of finance needed for the new project must be small relative to the amount of finance already raised.

■ The company must be intending to finance the new project by using a similar financing mix to its historical financing mix.

5   The asset beta is the weighted average of the betas of equity and debt. Assuming the beta of debt is zero, the asset beta will always be lower than the equity beta (unless the company is all-equity financed) because the market value of debt is not zero.

6   Currently, $\beta_e = 1.30$, $D = 0.25$, $E = 0.75$

$$\text{Hence: } \beta_a = \beta_e \times (E/(E - D(1 - C_T)))$$
$$= 1.30 \times 0.75/(0.75 - (0.25 \times 0.7))$$
$$= 0.975/0.9125 = 1.0541$$

If, now, $D = 0.33$ and $E = 0.67$ then:

$$\beta_e = \beta_a \times (1 + (D(1 - t)/E)) = 1.0541 \times 1.345 = 1.42$$

The new equity beta is therefore 1.42.

7   The following difficulties may be encountered by analysts:
   ■ How can they determine an appropriate value of beta?
   ■ With reference to which market should it be calculated?
   ■ What value of the market premium should be used?
   ■ Which risk-free rate should be selected?
   ■ If the company's share price changes, should the cost of capital be recalculated?

8   The main factors influencing the choice and mix of financing used in foreign direct investment are gearing, taxation, political risk and currency risk. The financing decision should aim to minimise the cost of capital and thereby maximise the value of the firm.

9   Here we are assuming that the world of Miller and Modigliani's first paper exists. The two companies should therefore have identical WACCs. Because York is all-equity financed, its WACC is the same as its cost of equity finance, i.e. 16 per cent. It follows that Johnson must have a WACC equal to 16 per cent.

Therefore: $(1/3 \times 10\%) + (2/3 \times K_e) = 16\%$

Hence: $K_e = 19\%$

10 The traditional theory of capital structure proposes that an optimal capital exists, and so under this theory a company can increase its total value by the sensible use of gearing. The traditional theory argues that:
   ■ K_e rises with increased gearing due to the increasing financial and bankruptcy risk;
   ■ K_d rises only at high gearing levels when bankruptcy risk increases;
   ■ replacing more expensive equity finance with less expensive debt finance decreases the company's WACC, up to a point;
   ■ once an optimum level of gearing is reached, K_e increases by a rate which more than offsets the effect of using cheaper debt, and so the WACC increases.

Chapter 10

1   The answer to this question can be found by referring to Section 10.1.

2   The correct answer is (e). The argument that shareholders could manufacture their own dividends by selling off part of their shareholding was used by Miller and Modigliani in 1961 to

argue that the dividend policy of a company was irrelevant. All the other points can be used to support a case for dividends having an effect on the value of the shares of a company.

3 First, convert the cum dividend share price to ex-dividend: $P_0 = 3.45 - 0.20 = £3.25$
Using the dividend growth model:

$$£3.25 = (0.20 \times (1 + g)/(0.15 - g))$$

Rearranging:

$$g = 0.2875/3.45 = 8.33\%$$

4 Calculating the cost of equity:

$$K_e = D_0/P_0 = 30/200 = 15\%$$

Future value in year 3 of dividend of 40p per year paid in perpetuity $= 40/0.15 = 266.7$p
Discounting back to the current time: $P_0 = 266.67/(1.15)^3 = 175.3$p
The share price has fallen by $200 - 175.3 = 24.7$p
Option (a) is therefore the correct answer.

5 Option (d) is the correct response. If a company wants to retain funds, it can offer shareholders a scrip dividend (share dividend) as an alternative to a cash dividend.

6,7 Here the discussion should focus on the fact that Miller and Modigliani's assumptions are simplifications of the real world. These assumptions, while not mirroring the real world, do not totally invalidate the model. Given these assumptions, the conclusions made by the model are perfectly logical. The nature of some of the assumptions only weakens the conclusions of the model, without actually invalidating it.

8 An increase in institutional share ownership has concentrated control of UK companies. This fact, coupled with the fact that institutional investors require a regular dividend stream from their investments, has led the institutional investors to become involved in trying to influence the dividend policy of companies.

9 (a) *Residual theory of dividends*: if the capital investment needs of the company are fully met and there are funds left over, these could be paid out as dividends. While corporate profits are cyclical, capital investment plans involve long-term commitment, so it follows that dividends may be used to take up the slack.

(b) *Clientele effect*: this term refers to the fact that companies can attract particular types of shareholder due to their dividend decisions. Companies can establish a track record for paying a certain level of dividend and shareholders recognise this. Because of their shareholders' preferences, companies find it difficult to change their dividend policies suddenly.

(c) *Signalling properties of dividends*: with asymmetry of information, dividends can act as signals from the company's managers to shareholders and the financial markets. With some exceptions, empirical studies show that dividends convey some new information to the market.

(d) *The 'bird in the hand' argument*: this arises from the existence of uncertainty. If the future were certain and there were no transaction costs, potential dividends retained by a company for investment purposes would lead to share price increases reflecting increases in wealth. With uncertainty, however, risk-averse investors are not indifferent to the division of earnings into dividends and capital gains in the share price.

Chapter 11

1   The economic reasons for taking over another company relate to the belief that the deal will increase shareholder wealth. This wealth increase can arise from several sources, as follows:

  - synergy, whereby the value of the combined entity exceeds its parts;
  - economies of scale, e.g. in distribution and production;
  - elimination of inefficient management;
  - direct entry into new markets instead of starting from scratch;
  - to provide critical mass;
  - to provide growth;
  - to provide market share.

2   The financial reasons used to justify acquisitions will include:

  - financial synergy, i.e. a decrease in the cost of capital;
  - acquisition of an undervalued target (unlikely if markets are efficient);
  - benefit from relative tax considerations;
  - increase in EPS or boot-strapping (not accepted as a justification).

3   Arguments against using acquisitions and mergers as a way of achieving growth include:

  - investigation of the bid by the Competition and Markets Authority, leading to delay and potentially refusal;
  - the bid might be contested and result in an unpleasant battle;
  - the only beneficiaries from mergers and acquisitions are target company shareholders;
  - financing an acquisition is expensive;
  - it is difficult to achieve post-merger integration.

4   There is no consensus view on why mergers and acquisitions come in waves, but some contributory factors have been identified:

  - a bull market can encourage the use of shares to finance acquisitions;
  - increasing liquidity and profitability can encourage companies to find acquisition targets;
  - deregulation of financial markets has made access to finance easier;
  - low levels of gearing allow companies to use debt to finance acquisitions.

5   Using P/E ratios to value companies is a rough rule of thumb and must be used with caution. EPS is an accounting figure that can be subject to manipulation and creative accounting. In addition, earnings will vary over time and not stay at their current level, so the EPS figure may need to be normalised to reflect this. Problems with using the P/E ratio method include the difficulty of selecting an appropriate P/E ratio to apply, and the fact that the ratio combines a current value (share price) with an historical value (EPS).

The accuracy of the dividend growth model relies heavily on forecast future dividend payments and the calculated shareholders' required rate of return. Both figures are difficult to estimate with any accuracy. There are also difficulties in using the model in this context because it considers the dividends flow to individual investors, rather than the company's ability to generate cash flows.

6 The DCF valuation method is preferred by academics because it is directly related to the objective of shareholder wealth maximisation. Practical difficulties with this method include:

— estimating future cash flows;

— the choice of an appropriate discount rate;

— the selection of an appropriate period over which to evaluate;

— how to forecast accurately any economies of scale and synergies;

— taking account of the risk of the target company;

— estimating the future cost of capital.

The appropriate discount rate to use with expected cash flows could be the acquiring company's cost of capital or a discount rate reflecting the systematic risk of the target company.

7 The answer to this question can be found in Section 11.5.4.

8 Possible post-bid defences that you could have described include:

— formulating a defence document;

— announcing forecasts of increased profits;

— announcing an increase in dividends;

— looking for a 'white knight';

— getting rid of the 'crown jewels'.

9 The answer to this question can be found in Section 11.7.1.

10 Possible contributory factors explaining why the shareholders of acquiring companies rarely benefit from takeovers include the following:

— if the bid is contested, the acquisition can cost the company more than it originally intended to pay, reducing its shareholders' wealth;

— predicted economies of scale and synergy may fail to materialise;

— the acquiring company's managers may lack knowledge and expertise in the business they have acquired;

— the quality of the acquired assets may turn out to be lower than expected;

— cultural problems may be experienced between acquirer and target;

— if the takeover is for cash, the acquiring company may be drained of liquidity and face a high level of gearing. This restricts its ability to accept attractive projects.

Chapter 12

1 (a) Here the company is facing transaction exposure. If the pound weakens against the euro, the sterling cost of the company's coal imports will increase. Therefore, the risk here is harmful in nature.

(b) The type of exchange rate risk being faced here is economic risk. The UK toy company is facing beneficial risk here because a weakening of the pound against the dollar will make the US company's imports less attractive to domestic customers.

(c) Here the UK company faces translation risk. The risk is harmful in nature because, as the pound appreciates against the euro, the translated sterling value of the factory will decrease, increasing the value of the company's liabilities relative to its assets.

2   Translation risk is best managed by using matching. For example, if purchasing an asset in a foreign country, a company should raise the funds for the purchase in the foreign currency so both the asset and liability are in the same currency.

   There are a number of ways to hedge transaction risk internally. Matching, for example, could mean paying for imports in the same currency that a company invoices its exports in. Alternatively, a company could invoice customers in the domestic currency and find a supplier which does the same. The problem with this method, though, is that the company may lose foreign sales and also restrict the potential suppliers it can purchase from. Companies can also manage transaction risk by leading and lagging payments according to their expectations of exchange rate movements.

3   The major difference between OTC options and traded options is that the latter come in the form of contracts standardised with respect to amount and duration, whereas the former are non-standard and negotiable with respect to amount and duration. Traded options are available from ICE Futures Europe whereas OTC options are provided by banks. One of the consequences of traded options being standardised is that they can be sold on to other parties. OTC options can be tailor-made to match the characteristics of the exposure a company wants to hedge.

4   If we sell futures contracts and interest rates increase, we close out our position in the future by buying futures contracts at a lower price, thereby making a gain. We therefore need to sell futures contracts to offset the increased cost of borrowing. How many contracts should we sell? Our transaction is equal to 12 contracts, but we are borrowing for a six-month period, so we need to sell 24 contracts to fully hedge our exposure.

5   Interest rate risk is concerned with the sensitivity of profit and operating cash flows to changes in interest rates. A company will need to analyse how its profits and cash flows are likely to change in response to forecast changes in interest rates, and take a decision as to whether action is necessary. Factors which could influence the decision to hedge interest rate risk include:

   − the expected volatility of interest rates;
   − the sensitivity of profits and cash flows to interest rate changes;
   − the balance between fixed and floating rate debt in a company's capital structure;
   − the financial plans of the company.

6   A company can use internal measures such as matching if it has cash inflows and outflows that can be matched in respect of timing and amount. If it wishes to transfer risk to a third party, however, it will need to use external hedging instruments. The following factors will determine which external hedging instruments will be used:

   − whether the company wishes to profit from favourable rate movements or wants to lock into a particular interest rate;
   − the view the company takes on future interest rate movements and volatility;
   − the timing, nature and duration of the interest rate exposure;
   − the extent to which the company wishes to hedge its interest rate exposure;

      – the knowledge and experience of the company's treasury staff;

      – the relative costs associated with the different derivatives.

7   The correct answer is (c). A bank-created floor is sought only if a company wants to guard against interest rates going down. The rest of the responses will all successfully hedge against interest rate increases.

8   The drawbacks include the following points:

      – A company may have difficulty finding a counterparty with equal but opposite requirements to itself (although warehousing reduces this problem significantly).

      – Once engaged in a swap agreement it is not possible to benefit from favourable movements in the exchange rate.

      – The swap partner must be vetted so as to reduce the possibility of counterparty default.

9   Put options allow the holder to sell the pound at a fixed rate. If a put has a strike price lower than $1.55 it is out of the money, i.e. option (c). Put option (a) is at the money while (e) is in the money. Call options allow the holder to buy the pound at a fixed rate. If a call has a strike price higher than $1.55 it is out of the money, i.e. option (b). Call option (d) is at the money. Hence, the most valuable option is (e), the $1.71 put option, as it is the only option in the money. The holder of this option can sell sterling at a much more favourable rate than the current spot rate.

10 A company can assess political risk using one of several techniques. It could look at the country's political risk index and compare it with that of other countries. It could use the Delphi technique, statistical analysis or a checklist approach or visit the country concerned. If it seeks to assess political risk in a systematic way, the results of the assessment are more likely to be useful.

    Apart from doing nothing, one way to mitigate political risk is insurance, either through a private firm or through a government agency such as the UK Export Finance department. A second option is negotiating a concession agreement with the host government, as long as it can be trusted to keep such an agreement. A third option is using financing and operating policies, which reduce the political risk faced in a particular country. An example of such a financing policy is using a significant amount of local debt. An example of such an operating policy is locating different stages of production in different countries to make expropriation less likely.

accounting rate of return (ARR): the average annual accounting profit of an investment relative to the required capital outlay. Also known as return on capital employed.

accounts payable: *see* trade payables.

accounts receivable: *see* trade receivables.

acid test ratio: *see* quick ratio.

acquisition: the purchase of one company by another, also called a takeover.

agency: the theoretical relationship existing between the owners of a company (principals) and the managers (agents) employed by the owners to run the company on their behalf.

agency costs: the costs arising from an agency relationship.

Alternative Investment Market (AIM): the London Stock Exchange's junior market where smaller, growing companies can list their shares.

American option: an option that can be exercised at any time up to, and on, its expiry date.

amortised loan: a loan where interest and principal are paid off through regular, equal payments.

annuity: a regular payment of a fixed amount of money over a fixed period.

arbitrage: the simultaneous buying and selling of assets or securities (e.g. shares) in different markets in order to yield a risk-free gain.

arbitrage pricing theory: a multi-factor model used to calculate the return on a security that does not depend solely on systematic risk.

arithmetic mean: the average of a population of data calculated by dividing the sum of the observations by the number of observations.

asset beta: the sensitivity to systematic factors of the cash flows accruing to a set of productive assets; the beta reflecting systematic business risk.

asymmetry of information: the situation where one party (e.g. management) is in an advantageous position compared to another party (e.g. shareholders) due to its access to, or possession of, privileged information.

auction market preferred stock (AMPS): a form of preference share where the dividend yield is periodically adjusted by a process of auction.

authorised share capital: the book value (nominal value) of shares that a company is allowed to issue according to its articles of association.

balloon repayments: loan repayments occurring towards the end or maturity of the loan period.

base rate: interest rate from which commercial banks' deposit and lending rates are calculated.

basis risk: the risk that a specific percentage movement in the cash market will not be matched by an equal and opposite movement in the futures market when hedging interest and exchange rate risk.

bear market: a market in which share prices are being driven down by the selling activities of pessimistic investors.

beta: a measure of the sensitivity of a security's returns to systematic risk.

bid–offer spread: the difference between the bid (or sale) price and the offer (or buy) price. This can refer to shares, interest rates and currencies.

bid premium: the additional amount an acquirer has to offer over and above the pre-bid share price in order for a takeover bid to be successful.

bid price: the price that a market maker or dealer will pay to buy financial assets.

BIMBO: the combination of a management buy-in and a management buyout.

bond: medium- or long-term debt security, in bearer form, that commits the issuer to a specific repayment date and to interest payments at a fixed or variable rate.

bonus issue: also known as a scrip issue, this is an issue of new shares to existing shareholders, in proportion to their existing holdings, without any cash being paid by the shareholders.

book value: the value given to an asset or liability in the financial statements of a company.

boot-strapping: the practice whereby a company with a high price/earnings ratio can engineer an increase in its earnings per share by buying a company with a lower price/earnings ratio.

buffer inventory: inventory held to guard against the possibility of running out of raw materials or finished goods.

bull market: a market in which share prices are being driven up by the buying activities of optimistic investors.

business risk: the variability of a company's distributable profit, given its business operations.

call option: an option that allows the holder to buy an asset at a predetermined price.

called-up share capital: the nominal value of the ordinary shares that a company has issued.

cap: an agreement that fixes a maximum rate of interest at which a party can borrow.

capital allowance: a tax allowance given against the purchase of certain non-current assets.

capital gain: the difference between the original purchase price of a security and its current market price.

capital gearing: the proportion of a company's total capital that is in the form of debt.

capital market line: the linear risk/return trade-off for investors spreading their money between the market portfolio and risk-free assets.

capital markets: financial markets where long-term securities are bought and sold.

capital rationing: the situation when a company has to limit the number of projects it invests in due to insufficient funds being available to invest in all desirable projects.

cash conversion cycle: the time period between a company paying cash for its costs of production and receiving cash from the sale of its goods.

cash market hedge: where a company hedges a risk exposure by making an equal and opposite cash market transaction.

certificate of deposit: a tradeable security issued by banks to investors who deposit a given amount of money for a specified period.

Chartism: the practice of studying past share price movements in order to make gains through the buying and selling of shares.

clientele effect: the theory that suggests that investors are attracted to companies that satisfy their requirements, for example, as regards dividends.

collar: an agreement that keeps either a borrowing or a lending rate between specified upper and lower limits.

commercial paper: short-term money market instruments companies can issue to raise finance.

compound interest: interest which is calculated both on the initial amount invested and on the accumulated interest from earlier periods.

concert party: a group of investors acting together under the control of one party to purchase shares in a company.

conglomerate merger: the merger of two companies operating in unrelated businesses.

consumer price index (CPI): the weighted average of the prices of a basket of goods which is taken as a guide to general inflation.

conversion premium: the amount by which the market price of a convertible bond exceeds the current market value of the shares into which it may be converted.

convertible bonds: bonds that can, at some specified date(s), be converted at the option of the holder into a predetermined number of ordinary shares.

convertible preference shares: preference shares that can, at some specified date(s), be converted at the option of the holder into a predetermined number of ordinary shares.

corporate bond: a long-term debt security issued by a company, paying periodic interest with repayment of the principal on maturity.

corporate governance: the way in which companies are controlled and directed by their stakeholders, and by statutory and non-statutory regulation.

correlation coefficient: a relative measure of the degree to which the returns of two investments move in the same direction as each other.

cost of capital: the rate of return required by investors supplying funds to a company and hence the minimum rate of return required on prospective projects.

cost of debt: the rate of return required by the suppliers of debt finance.

cost of equity: the rate of return required by the suppliers of equity finance.

counterparty risk: the risk that a counterparty (for example to a SWAP contract) fails to live up to its contractual obligations.

country risk: the risk of adverse effects on a multinational company's net cash flows due to political and economic factors associated with the country in which a foreign direct investment is located.

coupon rate: the rate of interest paid by a bond relative to its par or nominal value.

covenants: clauses included in bond deeds designed to place restrictions on a company's future actions in order to protect existing creditors' interests.

creative accounting: the practice of manipulating company accounts in order to make a company's performance appear more favourable than it actually is.

credit rating: an assessment of the creditworthiness of a company's debt securities based on its borrowing and repayment history, as well as the availability of assets.

creditor hierarchy: the pecking order in which a company's creditors are paid should it go into liquidation.

cum dividend price: the market price of a share whose purchase gives the right to receive a recently declared dividend.

cum rights price: the market value of a share if the current rights have yet to expire.

currency futures: derivative instruments that allow companies to lock in to current exchange rates with respect to the future purchase or sale of currencies.

currency swaps: *see* swaps.

current assets: short-term assets in the financial position statement that are expected to be used within a one-year time period.

current ratio: the ratio of a company's current assets to its current liabilities.

dawn raid: where an acquiring company instructs one or more brokers to purchase as many available shares as possible in a target company as soon as the market opens. The aim is to enable the acquiring company to build a significant position before the target company is aware of the takeover attempt.

debentures: fixed interest redeemable bonds that are normally secured on the non-current assets of the issuing company.

deep discount bonds: bonds that are issued at a significant discount to their par or nominal value and pay less interest than bonds issued at par.

default risk: the risk that a borrower will not fulfil its commitments with respect to paying interest or repaying the principal amount.

defensive shares: shares that have an equity beta of less than one.

demerger: the separation of a company's operations into two or more separate corporate entities.

derivatives: financial securities whose values are based on the values of other securities or assets such as bonds, shares, commodities and currencies.

discount rate: the rate applied to cash flows so as to change future values into present values.

disintermediation: the process whereby companies raise finance and lend through financial markets directly, rather than through financial institutions.

distributable profit: profit after tax and preference dividends, i.e. profit that can be distributed as dividends to ordinary shareholders.

diversifiable risk: risk that can be avoided by spreading funds over a portfolio of investments.

dividend cover: an accounting ratio comparing distributable profit to the annual dividend payment on ordinary shares; a measure of how safe a dividend is.

dividend payout ratio: the percentage of distributable earnings paid out as dividends.

dividend reinvestment plan (DRIP): an offer by companies that allows investors to reinvest their cash dividends by buying additional shares on the dividend payment date.

dividend yield: an accounting ratio where dividend per share is divided by share price.

drop lock bonds: floating-rate bonds that have a minimum interest rate.

earnings per share: distributable profit (earnings) divided by the number of shares in issue.

earnings yield: an accounting ratio where earnings per share is divided by share price.

earn-out: an agreement where the amount paid by an acquiring company for the target company depends on the future performance of its acquisition.

EBITDA: earnings before interest, tax, depreciation and amortisation.

economic exposure: *see* economic risk.

economic order quantity (EOQ): the amount of inventory to order on a regular basis so as to minimise the combined costs of ordering and holding inventory.

economic profit: the amount earned by a company over a given period, after deducting operating expenses and a charge representing the company's opportunity cost of capital.

economic risk: the risk of long-term exchange rate movements undermining the international competitiveness of a company and decreasing its economic value.

economic valued added (EVA): a measure of a company's financial performance developed by Stern Stewart and based on the residual wealth calculated by subtracting the cost of capital from operating profit adjusted for taxes on a cash basis.

economies of scale: a decrease in the average cost per unit arising from an increase in the number of goods produced by a given economic resource, e.g. a factory.

efficient frontier: the set of optimum portfolios when investing in risky securities.

employee share ownership plans (ESOPs): schemes designed to encourage the ownership of company shares by its employees.

enhanced scrip dividends: a scrip dividend worth significantly more than the cash dividend alternative.

envelope curve: the set of portfolios available to investors when investing in risky assets.

equity risk premium: the difference between the return on the market and the risk-free rate of return in the capital asset pricing model.

equity sweetener: warrants attached to bonds in order to make them more attractive to investors.

Eurobonds: long-term debt securities denominated in a currency outside of the control of the country of their origin.

Eurocurrency: currency held outside of its home market.

Euronotes: the short-term equivalent of Eurobonds, normally issued with maturities of up to six months.

exchange rate risk: the risk of adverse movements in exchange rates leading to companies experiencing actual losses, or losses in their financial position statement.

exercise price: the price at which an option holder can buy or sell the specified financial asset.

face value: *see* nominal value.

factoring: the managing of a company's trade receivables by a specialist company, with finance advanced against invoices raised.

financial engineering: the combining or splitting of different financial instruments to create new or synthetic securities.

financial gearing: the relationship between a company's debt and equity finance, usually expressed as a percentage and calculated by dividing the value of debt by the value of equity.

financial risk: the variability of a company's distributable profit arising from the need to pay interest on debt finance.

fixed assets: *see* non-current assets.

fixed charge security: bonds secured against a specific non-current asset.

floating charge security: bonds secured against a pool of company assets.

floor: an agreement that fixes a minimum rate of interest at which a party can borrow.

fluctuating current assets: current assets which vary with normal business activity, such as seasonal variations.

foreign bond: a bond issued in a domestic market by a foreign company, but in the domestic market's currency.

forward rate agreements (FRA): contracts that allow companies to fix, in advance, future borrowing and lending rates, based on a nominal principal over a given period.

free cash flow: a company's cash flow after the subtraction of all obligatory payments, i.e. interest, taxation and replacement investment.

free riders: parties who enjoy the benefits of corrected management behaviour without contributing to the associated costs.

fundamental analysis: the use of financial information to determine the 'fundamental value' of a share and so to profit from shares incorrectly priced by the market.

futures contract: an agreement to buy or sell a standard quantity of a specific financial instrument or foreign currency at a future date and price agreed between two parties.

gap exposure: the interest rate risk arising when a company has assets and liabilities whose interest rates, though based on similar underlying floating rates, are revised at differing frequencies.

geometric mean: the mean of a set of n positive numbers expressed as the nth root of their product, i.e. the compound rate of return.

gilt-edged government securities (gilts): long-term bonds issued by the government.

goal congruence: the situation where agents and principals have identical objectives.

golden parachutes: generous redundancy terms for directors of a company, used to deter bidding companies from dismissing them after a takeover.

hedge fund: an investment vehicle used by corporate institutions, high net worth individuals and private partnerships that is permitted by regulators to undertake a wider range of investment and trading activities, including using derivatives, short-selling and managing investments, that use significant levels of borrowing.

hedging: the mitigation of risk exposure by undertaking equal and opposite transactions.

horizontal merger: the combining of two companies operating in the same industry and at a similar stage of production.

hybrid finance: a financial security exhibiting the characteristics of both debt and equity.

income gearing: the proportion of the profit before interest and tax that is needed to meet the interest claims of debt holders. The reciprocal of income gearing is interest cover.

indifference curves: a series of curves that join up points of equal utility for an individual investor; also known as utility curves.

initial public offering (IPO): issuing shares for the first time in order to obtain a stock market listing.

insider dealing: using inside information to buy and sell securities in order to obtain abnormal returns.

institutional investors: large financial intermediaries, such as insurance companies and pension funds, which invest large amounts of money in company shares.

interbank market: a money market that facilitates banks' short-term borrowing and lending.

interest cover: the number of times a company's interest payments can be covered by its profits before interest and tax.

interest rate risk: the risk of a company's profits being adversely affected by interest rate changes.

internal funds: *see* retained earnings.

international bonds: bonds issued by a borrower in a foreign country, including foreign bonds and Eurobonds.

irredeemable bonds: bonds that have no redemption date and hence pay interest in perpetuity.

junior debt: *see* subordinate debt.

junk bonds: unsecured corporate bonds which pay high interest rates to compensate investors for their high default risk.

just-in-time: an inventory management system where materials and work-in-progress are delivered just before they are required, and finished goods are produced just before being sent to customers.

lagging: delaying foreign currency payments in order to benefit from favourable exchange rate movements.

lead time: the delay between placing an order and its delivery.

lessee: a company that leases an asset from its owner.

lessor: the owner of an asset who leases it to another party.

leveraged takeover: a takeover whose cost is predominantly financed by debt.

loan note: an alternative name for a corporate bond that is widely used in accounting.

London Interbank Offered Rate (LIBOR): key interbank money market interest rate.

long position: the position taken when an investor purchases and holds a security.

management buy-in (MBI): the purchase of an existing business by a team of outside managers who plan to manage the business themselves.

management buyout (MBO): the purchase of an existing business by a group of managers from within that business.

mandatory offer: a bid for all remaining shares that is required by the Takeover Panel when an investing company passes a certain level of shareholding.

marginal trading: where the share price of a company is determined by trading in only a small proportion of its issued share capital.

market capitalisation: the market price per share multiplied by the total number of shares issued by a company.

market portfolio: the optimal portfolio of risky assets to combine with investment in risk-free assets in portfolio theory.

market risk: *see* systematic risk.

matching: an internal hedging technique where liabilities and assets are matched in order to mitigate exposure.

merchant bank: a bank specialising in wholesale transactions rather than retail transactions.

merger: the coming together of two equal organisations to form one unified entity.

mezzanine finance: debt finance, often used to finance takeovers, that has risk and return characteristics somewhere between those of secured debt and equity.

money markets: markets for the borrowing and lending of short-term funds.

negative covenants: *see* covenants.

netting: the offsetting of amounts owed between companies in a group in order to minimise intercompany indebtedness and exchange rate risk.

nominal return: the money rate of return on an asset or investment, which includes inflation.

nominal value: the face value of a financial asset or a cash flow in money terms.

non-current assets: company assets, such as buildings and machinery, which give benefit to the company over a number of years and which are not being processed or bought and sold.

non-executive directors (NEDs): directors brought in from outside a company to sit on its board and oversee its operations, but who are not involved in its day-to-day operations.

non-pecuniary benefits: benefits other than those in the form of cash.

non-recourse factoring: a factoring agreement where the factor, not the company, bears the risk of bad debts.

off-balance-sheet financing: using financing, that does not have to appear on the financial position statement.

Official List: the list of companies registered on the London Stock Exchange.

operating gearing: the proportion of a company's fixed costs relative to its total costs.

opportunity cost: the benefit foregone by not using an asset in its next best use.

option: an agreement giving the holder the right, but not the obligation, to buy or sell a specified amount of a commodity or financial instrument over a specific time period and at a specified price.

ordinary shares: shares that represent the ownership of a limited company.

over the counter: this term refers to derivatives that are tailor-made by banks to suit the requirements of their customers.

overtrading: the situation where a company experiences liquidity problems due to its trading beyond the capital resources available to it.

par value: *see* nominal value.

payables: *see* accounts payable.

payout ratio: the ratio of dividend per share to earnings per share, or the ratio of total dividend to distributable profit.

peppercorn rent: the reduced rent paid by a lessee following the primary lease period of a lease.

permanent current assets: current assets which are maintained at a core level over time, such as buffer inventory.

perpetuity: the payment of equal cash flows at regular intervals for an indefinite period of time.

poison pill: a financial transaction, such as a share issue, which is triggered when one company makes a bid for another, hence making the takeover more expensive.

political risk: the risk that the political actions of a country will adversely affect the value of a company's operations.

pre-emptive right: the legal right of existing shareholders of a company to first refusal on any new shares that the company may issue.

preference shares: shares giving the right to receive dividends before any dividends can be paid to ordinary shareholders.

present value: the value of a future cash flow in current terms, once the future value has been discounted by an appropriate discount rate.

primary markets: markets where securities are issued for the first time.

profitability index: the ratio of a project's net present value to its initial investment, or the ratio of the present value of its future cash flows to its initial investment.

put option: a contract that gives the right, but not the obligation, to buy a good, security or currency at a fixed price at a future date.

quick ratio: the ratio of current assets less inventory to current liabilities.

random walk hypothesis: the suggestion that share prices on a stock market appear to move in a random manner, rather than in a predictable way.

real cost of capital: a company's cost of capital which makes no allowance for the effects of inflation, or the deflated nominal cost of capital.

real option: an alternative or choice that becomes possible as a result of taking a business investment opportunity.

receivables: *see* trade receivables.

recourse: if trade receivables are sold to a factor, the factor can return to the vendor for payment in the event of the debtor failing to pay.

redemption yield: the return required by an investor over the life of a bond, taking into account both interest and capital repayment.

refinancing: replacing one kind of financing with one or more different forms of finance with different characteristics, such as replacing fixed rate long-term debt with floating rate long-term debt, or with equity.

reinvestment rate: the rate at which cash flows generated from a project can be reinvested.

replacement cost: the cost of replacing an asset with one of similar age and condition.

retained earnings: cash retained by a company for re-investment purposes.

rights issue: an issue of shares to existing shareholders, pro rata to their existing shareholdings, in exchange for cash.

risk averse: a term used to describe investors who are not keen to take risk, regardless of the potential returns.

risk-free rate of return: the yield earned on securities which are considered to be free from risk, such as short-dated government securities.

risk premium: the return in excess of the risk-free rate that is required by an investor before accepting a high-risk investment.

running yield: also called interest yield or flat yield, this is calculated by dividing the interest rate of a security by its current market price.

scrip dividend: an offer of new shares in a company to existing shareholders as an alternative to a cash dividend.

scrip issue: *see* bonus issue.

secondary markets: markets where securities are traded once issued.

securitisation: the process whereby companies, instead of raising finance by borrowing from financial institutions, convert assets into securities for sale in the marketplace.

security market line: the linear relationship between systematic risk and return in the capital asset pricing model.

senior debt: debt that has a primary claim on an issuer's assets compared to subordinate debt, should the issuer default on its obligations.

sensitivity analysis: the technique of analysing how changes in an individual project variable affect a project's overall net present value.

share option schemes: schemes that offer share options to employees or directors of a company in order to provide an incentive.

share split: the issuing of a number of new shares of lower nominal value in return for each existing share held by investors (also known as a stock split).

sinking fund: an amount of money put aside annually for use in redeeming bonds on maturity.

special dividends: a large cash dividend that is not expected to be repeated in the near future.

specific risk: *see* unsystematic risk.

spot market: a market for immediate transactions, for example, in buying currency.

spread: the difference between the buying (offer) price and the selling (bid) price of a financial security.

stakeholder: any party that has a share or interest in a business.

sterling commercial paper: commercial paper denominated in UK pounds rather than in another currency, such as dollars.

Sterling Overnight Index Average (SONIA): a benchmark interest rate expected to replace LIBOR.

stock: in the UK, stock is another term for a bond, but in the USA it is taken to mean a share.

stock split: another term for a share split.

strike price: the price at which an option holder can purchase or sell a specified financial asset.

subordinate debt: debt that has a secondary or lesser claim on an issuer's assets compared to senior debt, should the issuer default on its obligations.

sunk costs: costs that have already been incurred and therefore cannot be retrieved.

swaps: an agreement between two parties to exchange interest payments based on an agreed principal.

swaptions: derivatives that give the holder the option to engage in a swap agreement.

synergy: creating wealth by combining complementary assets.

systematic risk: also known as market risk, this represents the relative effect on the returns of an individual security of changes in the market as a whole.

tax-allowable depreciation: *see* capital allowances.

tax exhaustion: the position where a company's profits are insufficient to take advantage of the capital allowances or tax-allowable depreciation available to it.

tax shield: the benefit of shielding profits from corporate tax, calculated as the present value of the future tax savings arising from debt finance.

technical analysis: using past share price data and statistical analysis to predict future share prices.

tender offer: a public offer to purchase securities.

terminal value: the value of an asset at the end of a specified period of time, for example, the maturity value of a bond or the value of an asset on disposal.

tick: the smallest movement in the price of futures contracts, standardised as 0.01 per cent of the contract size.

time value of money: the concept that £1 received in the future is not equivalent to £1 received today, due to factors such as risk and opportunity cost.

total shareholder return: the total return earned on a share over a given time period, calculated by dividing the sum of the dividend per share and the capital gain by the initial share price.

traded option: a standardised agreement giving the holder the right, but not the obligation, to buy or sell a specified amount of a commodity or financial instrument over a specific period and at a specified price.

trade payables: money owed by a company to suppliers of goods and services.

trade receivables: money owed to a company by the customers to whom it has supplied goods and services.

transaction risk: the risk that exchange rate movements will change the value of a short-term foreign currency transaction.

transfer price: the price at which goods and services are transferred between subsidiaries in a group of companies.

translation risk: the exchange rate risk associated with consolidating financial statements containing assets and liabilities denominated in currencies other than that of the home country (also known as accounting risk).

Treasury bills: short-dated debt securities issued by governments.

uncertainty: where there is more than one possible outcome to a course of action and the probability of any one outcome is not known.

unconventional cash flows: also called non-conventional cash flows, these are a series of cash flows that involve more than one change in sign.

undercapitalisation: *see* overtrading.

underlying: the asset which a derivative security is based upon.

underwriting: the process whereby companies issuing securities arrange for financial institutions to buy up any unsold securities, for example, in a rights issue.

unique risk: *see* unsystematic risk.

unsystematic risk: the risk that is specific to a company and hence can be diversified away by investing in a portfolio of assets.

upside risk: the possibility of a favourable outcome due to the movement of a financial variable.

utility curves: *see* indifference curves.

vanilla: a term often used to describe the simplest form of a bond or derivative, e.g. a vanilla swap.

venture capital: risk capital supplied by specialist organisations to smaller companies that would otherwise struggle to raise capital due to their high risk.

vertical merger: the combination of two companies operating at different stages of production within the same industry.

warehouse: where a financial institution such as a bank acts as an intermediary for a swap, even though a suitable counterparty has not yet been found.

warrants: tradeable share options issued by companies, usually attached to an issue of bonds.

weighted average cost of capital (WACC): the average rate of return required by all sources of finance used by a company: it can be used as a discount rate in investment appraisal and is a key factor to consider in decisions about new finance.

white knight: a favourable takeover partner which may be sought by a company receiving an unwanted takeover bid.

withholding tax: a tax levied by a foreign country on profits remitted to the home country.

working capital: the difference between a company's current assets and current liabilities.

work-in-progress (WIP): partly completed products which need additional processing before becoming finished goods.

writing down allowance: *see* capital allowances.

yield to maturity: *see* redemption yield.

zero coupon bonds: bonds issued at a substantial discount to nominal value and which do not pay interest.

zero sum game: a situation where for one party to gain by a certain amount, another party must lose by the same amount.

PRESENT VALUE TABLES

Table of present value factors

Present values of $1/(1 + r)^n$

Discount rates (r)										
Periods (n)	1%	2%	3%	4%	5%	6%	7%	8%	9%	10%
1	0.990	0.980	0.971	0.962	0.952	0.943	0.935	0.926	0.917	0.909
2	0.980	0.961	0.943	0.925	0.907	0.890	0.873	0.857	0.842	0.826
3	0.971	0.942	0.915	0.889	0.864	0.840	0.816	0.794	0.772	0.751
4	0.961	0.924	0.888	0.855	0.823	0.792	0.763	0.735	0.708	0.683
5	0.951	0.906	0.863	0.822	0.784	0.747	0.713	0.681	0.650	0.621
6	0.942	0.888	0.837	0.790	0.746	0.705	0.666	0.630	0.596	0.564
7	0.933	0.871	0.813	0.760	0.711	0.665	0.623	0.583	0.547	0.513
8	0.923	0.853	0.789	0.731	0.677	0.627	0.582	0.540	0.502	0.467
9	0.914	0.837	0.766	0.703	0.645	0.592	0.544	0.500	0.460	0.424
10	0.905	0.820	0.744	0.676	0.614	0.558	0.508	0.463	0.422	0.386
11	0.896	0.804	0.722	0.650	0.585	0.527	0.475	0.429	0.388	0.350
12	0.887	0.788	0.701	0.625	0.557	0.497	0.444	0.397	0.356	0.319
13	0.879	0.773	0.681	0.601	0.530	0.469	0.415	0.368	0.326	0.290
14	0.870	0.758	0.661	0.577	0.505	0.442	0.388	0.340	0.299	0.263
15	0.861	0.743	0.642	0.555	0.481	0.417	0.362	0.315	0.275	0.239
16	0.853	0.728	0.623	0.534	0.458	0.394	0.339	0.292	0.252	0.218
17	0.844	0.714	0.605	0.513	0.436	0.371	0.317	0.270	0.231	0.198
18	0.836	0.700	0.587	0.494	0.416	0.350	0.296	0.250	0.212	0.180
19	0.828	0.686	0.570	0.475	0.396	0.331	0.277	0.232	0.194	0.164
20	0.820	0.673	0.554	0.456	0.377	0.312	0.258	0.215	0.178	0.149

Discount rates (r)										
Periods (n)	11%	12%	13%	14%	15%	16%	17%	18%	19%	20%
1	0.901	0.893	0.885	0.877	0.870	0.862	0.855	0.847	0.840	0.833
2	0.812	0.797	0.783	0.769	0.756	0.743	0.731	0.718	0.706	0.694
3	0.731	0.712	0.693	0.675	0.658	0.641	0.624	0.609	0.593	0.579
4	0.659	0.636	0.613	0.592	0.572	0.552	0.534	0.516	0.499	0.482
5	0.593	0.567	0.543	0.519	0.497	0.476	0.456	0.437	0.419	0.402
6	0.535	0.507	0.480	0.456	0.432	0.410	0.390	0.370	0.352	0.335
7	0.482	0.452	0.425	0.400	0.376	0.354	0.333	0.314	0.296	0.279
8	0.434	0.404	0.376	0.351	0.327	0.305	0.285	0.266	0.249	0.233
9	0.391	0.361	0.333	0.308	0.284	0.263	0.243	0.225	0.209	0.194
10	0.352	0.322	0.295	0.270	0.247	0.227	0.208	0.191	0.176	0.162
11	0.317	0.287	0.261	0.237	0.215	0.195	0.178	0.162	0.148	0.135
12	0.286	0.257	0.231	0.208	0.187	0.168	0.152	0.137	0.124	0.112
13	0.258	0.229	0.204	0.182	0.163	0.145	0.130	0.116	0.104	0.093
14	0.232	0.205	0.181	0.160	0.141	0.125	0.111	0.099	0.088	0.078
15	0.209	0.183	0.160	0.140	0.123	0.108	0.095	0.084	0.074	0.065
16	0.188	0.163	0.141	0.123	0.107	0.093	0.081	0.071	0.062	0.054
17	0.167	0.146	0.125	0.108	0.093	0.080	0.069	0.060	0.052	0.045
18	0.153	0.130	0.111	0.095	0.081	0.069	0.059	0.051	0.044	0.038
19	0.138	0.116	0.098	0.083	0.070	0.060	0.051	0.043	0.037	0.031
20	0.124	0.104	0.087	0.073	0.061	0.051	0.043	0.037	0.031	0.026

Table of cumulative present value factors

Present values of $[1 - (1 + r)^{-n}]/r$

	Discount rates (r)									
Periods (n)	1%	2%	3%	4%	5%	6%	7%	8%	9%	10%
1	0.990	0.980	0.971	0.962	0.952	0.943	0.935	0.926	0.917	0.909
2	1.970	1.942	1.913	1.886	1.859	1.833	1.808	1.783	1.759	1.736
3	2.941	2.884	2.829	2.775	2.723	2.673	2.624	2.577	2.531	2.487
4	3.902	3.808	3.717	3.630	3.546	3.465	3.387	3.312	3.240	3.170
5	4.853	4.713	4.580	4.452	4.329	4.212	4.100	3.993	3.890	3.791
6	5.795	5.601	5.417	5.242	5.076	4.917	4.767	4.623	4.486	4.355
7	6.728	6.472	6.230	6.002	5.786	5.582	5.389	5.206	5.033	4.868
8	7.652	7.325	7.020	6.733	6.463	6.210	5.971	5.747	5.535	5.335
9	8.566	8.162	7.786	7.435	7.108	6.802	6.515	6.247	5.995	5.759
10	9.471	8.983	8.530	8.111	7.722	7.360	7.024	6.710	6.418	6.145
11	10.368	9.787	9.253	8.760	8.306	7.887	7.499	7.139	6.805	6.495
12	11.255	10.575	9.954	9.385	8.863	8.384	7.943	7.536	7.161	6.814
13	12.134	11.348	10.635	9.986	9.394	8.853	8.358	7.904	7.487	7.103
14	13.004	12.106	11.296	10.563	9.899	9.295	8.745	8.244	7.786	7.367
15	13.865	12.849	11.938	11.118	10.380	9.712	9.108	8.559	8.061	7.606
16	14.718	13.578	12.561	11.652	10.838	10.106	9.447	8.851	8.313	7.824
17	15.562	14.292	13.166	12.166	11.274	10.477	9.763	9.122	8.544	8.022
18	16.398	14.992	13.754	12.659	11.690	10.828	10.059	9.372	8.756	8.201
19	17.226	15.678	14.324	13.134	12.085	11.158	10.336	9.604	8.950	8.365
20	18.046	16.351	14.877	13.590	12.462	11.470	10.594	9.818	9.129	8.514

	Discount rates (r)									
Periods (n)	11%	12%	13%	14%	15%	16%	17%	18%	19%	20%
1	0.901	0.893	0.885	0.877	0.870	0.862	0.855	0.847	0.840	0.833
2	1.713	1.690	1.668	1.647	1.626	1.605	1.585	1.566	1.547	1.528
3	2.444	2.402	2.361	2.322	2.283	2.246	2.210	2.174	2.140	2.106
4	3.102	3.037	2.974	2.914	2.855	2.798	2.743	2.690	2.639	2.589
5	3.696	3.605	3.517	3.433	3.352	3.274	3.199	3.127	3.058	2.991
6	4.231	4.111	3.998	3.889	3.784	3.685	3.589	3.498	3.410	3.326
7	4.712	4.564	4.423	4.288	4.160	4.039	3.922	3.812	3.706	3.605
8	5.146	4.968	4.799	4.639	4.487	4.344	4.207	4.078	3.954	3.837
9	5.537	5.328	5.132	4.946	4.772	4.607	4.451	4.303	4.163	4.031
10	5.889	5.650	5.426	5.216	5.019	4.833	4.659	4.494	4.339	4.192
11	6.207	5.938	5.687	5.453	5.234	5.029	4.836	4.656	4.486	4.327
12	6.492	6.194	5.918	5.660	5.421	5.197	4.988	4.793	4.611	4.439
13	6.750	6.424	6.122	5.842	5.583	5.342	5.118	4.910	4.715	4.533
14	6.982	6.628	6.302	6.002	5.724	5.468	5.229	5.008	4.802	4.611
15	7.191	6.811	6.462	6.142	5.847	5.575	5.324	5.092	4.876	4.675
16	7.379	6.974	6.604	6.265	5.954	5.668	5.405	5.162	4.938	4.730
17	7.549	7.120	6.729	6.373	6.047	5.749	5.475	5.222	4.990	4.775
18	7.702	7.250	6.840	6.467	6.128	5.818	5.534	5.273	5.033	4.812
19	7.839	7.366	6.938	6.550	6.198	5.877	5.584	5.316	5.070	4.843
20	7.963	7.469	7.025	6.623	6.259	5.929	5.628	5.353	5.101	4.870

INDEX

Page numbers in bold refer to entries in the Glossary